Computational and Deep Learning Models for Advanced Behavioral Analysis

Ali Turab
https://orcid.org/0000-0002-5445-9728
Northwestern Polytechnical University, China

Josué Antonio Nescolarde Selva
University of Alicante, Spain

Andrés Montoyo
University of Alicante, Spain

IGI Global
Scientific Publishing
Publishing Tomorrow's Research Today

Vice President of Editorial	Melissa Wagner
Director of Acquisitions	Mikaela Felty
Director of Book Development	Jocelynn Hessler
Production Manager	Mike Brehm
Cover Design	Jose Rosado

Published in the United States of America by
IGI Global Scientific Publishing
701 East Chocolate Avenue
Hershey, PA, 17033, USA
Tel: 717-533-8845 | Fax: 717-533-7115
Website: https://www.igi-global.com E-mail: cust@igi-global.com

Library of Congress Cataloging-in-Publication Data

LCCN: 2025039364 (CIP Data Pending)
ISBN13: 9798337350622
Isbn13Softcover: 9798337350639
EISBN13: 9798337350646

British Cataloguing in Publication Data
A Cataloguing in Publication record for this book is available from the British Library.

Table of Contents

Detailed Table of Contents

Network security has become a key research focus as cyber threats grow in scale and complexity. Intrusion Detection Systems (IDS) are vital for identifying malicious activity and securing sensitive data. This study compares machine learning and deep learning using the KDD Cup 1999 dataset with 41 features and 10,000 connections across four classes: DoS, R2L, Probe, and Normal. Three models were tested Decision Tree (DT), Random Forest (RF), and a Fastai-based deep learning model. The Fastai model achieved the highest accuracy (92.00%), outperforming DT (81.03%) and RF (83.15%), showing deep learning captures complex nonlinear traffic patterns better. Evaluation used k-fold cross-validation and ROC-AUC metrics. Future work will apply this to newer datasets like NSL-KDD, CICIDS2017, and UNSW-NB15, exploring CNN, LSTM, and Transformer models. The study highlights deep learning and Explainable AI (XAI) as promising for building intelligent, interpretable IDS systems.

These insights serve as a strategic guide for improving user experience and remaining competitive in the mobile gaming market.

Mian Muhammad Danyal, Center for Excellence in Information Technology, Institute of Management Sciences, Peshawar, Pakistan
Sarwar Shah Khan, University of Engineering and Technology Mardan, Pakistan
Muhammad Osama, Iqra National University, Swat, Pakistan
Afsheen Khalid, Center for Excellence in Information Technology, Institute of Management Sciences, Peshawar, Pakistan

Movies are a key source of entertainment and learning, while reviews guide audiences in making viewing choices. However, the vast number of online reviews is often long, unstructured, and time-consuming, making it difficult to assess public opinion quickly. Similar issues exist in product feedback, hotel reviews, and social media, where large-scale sentiment analysis is essential. Sentiment analysis, or opinion mining, is an NLP technique that classifies text as positive or negative, providing fast insights and reducing human effort. This study applies machine learning and deep learning models to movie reviews using IMDb and Rotten Tomatoes datasets. Among the tested models, XLNet, a transformer-based architecture with permutation language modeling, achieved better results, surpassing traditional machine learning and other deep learning approaches. The study shows the strength of advanced deep learning in capturing subtle sentiments, improving recommendations, content evaluation, and broader applications where understanding emotions in text is vital.

Ramsha Shafqat, The University of Lahore, Sargodha, Pakistan
Massimiliano Ferrara, University Mediterranea di Reggio Calabria, Italy

Free-roaming dogs pose serious public health challenges worldwide. This study investigates the role of owned and stray dogs in transmitting Guinea worm disease (GWD) and evaluates vaccination as a control strategy. A multi-host framework is developed with dogs as primary hosts and fish as intermediate hosts, while humans are excluded due to minimal incidence. The model uses twelve compartments and a fractional-order approach based on the Atangana–Baleanu derivative in the Caputo sense. Existence and uniqueness of solutions are established through fixed-point theorems, with Ulam–Hyers stability confirming robustness. Numerical simulations,

Preface

In the age of pervasive digital interaction and data-driven systems, understanding human and system behavior through computational means has become a defining challenge and opportunity. *Computational and Deep Learning Models for Advanced Behavioral Analysis* explores the intersection of artificial intelligence, computational modeling, and behavioral science, providing a comprehensive look at how machine and deep learning can interpret, simulate, and predict behavioral patterns from cybersecurity and healthcare to ecology, sports, and social systems.

The chapters in this edited volume demonstrate how intelligent models can go beyond simple prediction to uncover underlying mechanisms of behavior, whether through causal reasoning, dynamic modeling, or interpretable AI. This collection brings together an international group of scholars and practitioners who present both theoretical foundations and applied frameworks, combining data analytics, mathematical modeling, and neural computation. Collectively, the contributions showcase how advances in AI are reshaping behavioral understanding, offering tools that are not only accurate but also explainable and ethically grounded.

This book is intended for researchers, data scientists, and graduate students in computer science, computational social science, behavioral analytics, and applied mathematics. It will also appeal to practitioners in sectors such as cybersecurity, healthcare, education, and digital marketing who seek AI for behavioral insight and decision support.

CHAPTER OVERVIEW

Chapter 1 – Advanced Behavioral Analysis for Intrusion Detection Using Deep Learning and Machine Learning Techniques

This chapter compares traditional machine learning and deep learning models for intrusion detection using the KDD Cup 1999 dataset. The Fastai-based deep model outperforms decision tree and random forest classifiers, highlighting deep learning's superior ability to capture nonlinear traffic patterns. The study underscores the future potential of deep and explainable AI in developing intelligent, interpretable security systems.

Chapter 2 – Causal AI: Explainable Techniques for Interpreting Behavioral Patterns Using Causal Diagrams

Focusing on interpretability, this chapter introduces causal AI as a framework for understanding cause–effect relationships rather than mere correlations. It discusses structural causal models, do-calculus, and practical tools like DoWhy and EconML, illustrating applications in healthcare, education, and cybersecurity. The authors advocate for integrating causal reasoning with modern AI to enhance transparency and reliability.

Chapter 3 – Computational Analysis of Delay-Driven Feedback in the Behavioral Dynamics of Rumor Spreading

Using delay differential equations, this chapter models how time-lagged feedback mechanisms affect rumor propagation in social networks. The analysis reveals how delayed interventions can destabilize equilibrium and generate sustained rumor cycles, emphasizing the importance of timely responses in digital moderation and misinformation control.

Chapter 4 – Behavioral Recognition and Classification of Thai Boxing Techniques Using Hybrid Deep Learning Models

This contribution applies hybrid deep learning to classify Muay Thai movements from video data, achieving remarkable accuracy. The chapter demonstrates the potential of AI in sports analytics, athlete training, and motion analysis by decoding complex human motion patterns.

Chapter 5 – Analyzing User Behavior in Mobile Game Applications Using Deep Data Analysis Approach

Through Latent Semantic Analysis of user reviews, this study identifies behavioral and emotional factors influencing satisfaction and engagement in mobile gaming. The findings provide actionable insights for improving game design, user retention, and overall user experience.

Chapter 6 – Analyzing Audience Behavior through Sentiment Analysis of Movie Reviews Using Deep Learning Framework

This chapter applies deep learning, particularly transformer-based XLNet models, to analyze large-scale movie reviews. It demonstrates how advanced NLP models can extract nuanced emotional trends, offering applications in recommendation systems and media analytics.

Chapter 7 – A Novel Approach to Guinea Worm Disease Control Using Deep Neural Network Models for Behavioral Dog Screening Strategies

Addressing public health, this chapter integrates deep learning with fractional-order epidemic modeling to examine dog behavior in Guinea worm disease transmission. Simulation results highlight vaccination and behavioral screening as effective strategies for disease mitigation.

Chapter 8 – Detecting Deceptive Behavior in Online Chess: A Machine Learning Approach

The authors explore cheating detection in online chess using multiple machine learning models. Random Forest and LSTM approaches show promise in identifying suspicious behavior patterns, providing a data-driven framework for maintaining fair play in digital competitions.

Chapter 9 – Behavioral Biometric Authentication using Keystroke and Mouse Dynamics on a Non-Touch Virtual Keyboard Using Machine Learning Approaches

Focusing on behavioral biometrics, this chapter presents an authentication framework based on keystroke and mouse dynamics. Using advanced preprocessing, feature selection, and generative data augmentation, the models achieve high accuracy and low error rates, reinforcing behavioral security in critical systems.

Chapter 10 – Behavioral Analysis for Customer Loyalty Prediction Using 360° Customer Insights

This chapter develops a holistic customer loyalty prediction model combining behavioral, sentiment, and transactional data. The integrated 360° approach enhances churn prediction accuracy and offers practical pathways for customer retention and experience optimization.

Chapter 11 – Computational Modeling and Analysis of Behavioral Patterns for Infectious Disease Networks Dismantling

Here, the authors introduce the Infectious Disease Network Dismantling Algorithm (IDND), designed to target critical nodes in partially known networks. By incorporating link prediction and node centrality, the approach optimizes epidemic control even under incomplete information.

Chapter 12 – Drift Diffusion Models as an Interpretable Framework for Modeling Decision-Making Behavior

This chapter provides a detailed exposition of Drift Diffusion Models (DDMs) for interpreting decision-making and response times. It blends theoretical and practical guidance, including Bayesian inference workflows, to promote robust and interpretable behavioral modeling.

Chapter 13 – Computational Approaches to Predator–Prey Models with Behavioral Adaptations: Refuge, Harvesting, and Fear Dynamics

By integrating computational methods with behavioral ecology, this chapter extends classical predator–prey models to include fear, refuge, and harvesting effects. The simulations reveal complex transitions between equilibrium and chaos, demonstrating how behavioral factors influence ecological stability.

Together, the chapters in this volume chart the frontiers of computational behavioral analysis. They demonstrate that by coupling deep learning with interpretable, causal, and dynamic modeling frameworks, we can gain a richer understanding of human, social, and system behaviors, transforming how we detect threats, model decisions, interpret emotions, and manage complex networks.

Chapter 1

Advanced Behavioral Analysis for Intrusion Detection Using Deep Learning and Machine Learning Techniques

Rana Muhammad Amir Latif
https://orcid.org/0000-0001-6007-6275
East China Normal University, China

Mansoor Khan
https://orcid.org/0000-0002-5769-7625
Qilu Institute of Technology, China

Yue Zhao
Wenzhou-Kean University, China

Zhiqiang Gao
Wenzhou-Kean University, China

Ali Turab
https://orcid.org/0000-0002-5445-9728
Northwestern Polytechnical University, China

Farhan Ullah
https://orcid.org/0000-0002-1030-1275
Prince Mohammad Bin Fahd University, Saudi Arabia

Abdul Ahad
https://orcid.org/0000-0002-3914-2503
Northwestern Polytechnical University, China

ABSTRACT

Network security has become a key research focus as cyber threats grow in scale and complexity. Intrusion Detection Systems (IDS) are vital for identifying malicious activity and securing sensitive data. This study compares machine learning and deep learning using the KDD Cup 1999 dataset with 41 features and 10,000

DOI: 10.4018/979-8-3373-5062-2.ch001

connections across four classes: DoS, R2L, Probe, and Normal. Three models were tested Decision Tree (DT), Random Forest (RF), and a Fastai-based deep learning model. The Fastai model achieved the highest accuracy (92.00%), outperforming DT (81.03%) and RF (83.15%), showing deep learning captures complex nonlinear traffic patterns better. Evaluation used k-fold cross-validation and ROC-AUC metrics. Future work will apply this to newer datasets like NSL-KDD, CICIDS2017, and UNSW-NB15, exploring CNN, LSTM, and Transformer models. The study highlights deep learning and Explainable AI (XAI) as promising for building intelligent, interpretable IDS systems.

1 INTRODUCTION

In the present world, the internet has become the most important tool. It has made its place in every field as one of the best sources of information. It is effectively used for entertainment, learning and education, business data processing, healthcare sectors, industries, and many more. However, attacks over the internet will also become more complex and powerful, which may discard or damage the data packets traveling on the network (Latif, 2025). So, there needs to be a transfer of secure data over the network; that is why network security must be kept important, and a system needs to be designed to protect the data from malicious activities (Wassan et al., 2025). There have been many methods of Data mining and Machine learning (ML) to protect the network and establish high-level security (Latif, Obaidat, Ullah, & Mahmood, 2025). First, we will describe cybersecurity, which combines processes and technologies. Systems with cybersecurity capabilities are divided into computer(host) security systems and network security systems (Naeem, Ullah, & Srivastava, 2025). IDS plays an important role in this span for the secure transfer of data over the network, where networks have evolved in almost every sector, either in business or education, and where cybersecurity is necessary to escape malware behavior. Unfortunately, IDS is imperfect (Ullah et al., 2024).

IDS is considered one of the approaches to monitor and detect unauthorized access, unusual activities, rare attacks, and an invention to protect hosts and networks. IDSs help to detect, determine, and discover the destruction and alteration of systems, duplication, and unauthorized access (Naeem, Ullah, Krejcar, Alsirhani, & Zhao, 2024). IDS alerts the network administrators when any malicious activity is detected and hosts to prevent unusual activities or unauthorized access (Liu & Lang, 2019). However, IDS has become an important part of cybersecurity. The significant role of IDS is to detect anomalies or unauthorized access, and if any intrusion is detected, it reports it to the network administrator. IDS can monitor, detect, and block attacks on the host and network, make a security analysis, and keep the performance normal during any malevolent occurrence (Mishra, Varadharajan, Tupakula, & Pilli, 2018). IDS mainly comprises three components:

- The monitoring module will monitor the network traffic and events.
- The detection module will try to detect a malicious attack based on the monitored data.
- The alarm module will raise an alarm if an intrusion activity has been detected.
- Based on attack patterns, there are three main types of IDS: Anomaly-based system, misuse-based system, and hybrid system.

An anomaly-based system works to detect unknown or unfamiliar attacks. Anomalies can be found in different ways. ML/DM techniques like RF, DT, Neural Networks, and many more are introduced to detect anomalies (Dornala & Senthilkumar, 2025) efficiently. An anomaly-based approach detects anomalies as changes in normal behavior. It identifies the irregularity in the expected behavior and models the system behavior and the normal network (Latif, Farhan, Khan, & Sujatha, 2024). Instead of a misuse-based approach, it detects novel attacks, but due to unknown attack patterns, the chances of a false positive rate increase. It may be due to the system considering previously unseen behavior anomalies (Latif, Yoshigoe, et al., 2025). Moreover, Anomaly-based systems alert on the arrival of novel attacks on the network and host, and that detection can be used to describe the signatures for misuse detector systems (Harini, Gouri, Balaji, Sangeetha, & Harshini, 2024).

For networked intrusion detection, the availability of the latest real-world data is quite tricky, so all the researchers use bench data, which are not updated by the latest complex attacks in Anomaly detection systems; most accuracy of detection does not come to 100% due to lack of datasets as it is hard to compare organize a system for the detection of novel attacks (Faker & Dogdu, 2019). An anomaly-based system must be trained and tested by using real label datasets with a real set of attacks or intrusions before being planted in any real-world environment because it works on the detection of novel attacks (Saranya, Sridevi, Deisy, Chung, & Khan, 2020).

The misuse-based approach is used to identify previously known attacks in the form of patterns or signatures. These attack patterns are stored in a database in case any unusual behavior is found, and this approach then compares them with attributes of stored patterns; if any matching is found, it must alert the network administrator for further work (Latif, Ullah, et al., 2025). They are efficient for detecting known attacks but fail to detect unknown attacks as they use only known patterns to detect the attacks (G. Martín, et al., 2021). Because these IDS can only detect attacks that match stored database patterns, which is the main lack of misuse-based systems, which might not work well when new attacks arrive, they must be updated with new signatures. Regular amendments are necessary to update it with new signatures and rules for upcoming attacks (Kocher & Kumar, 2021). Also, they are not producing false alarms because the number of false alerts increases when the system detects novel attacks, but this is not happening in this case. This approach cannot detect zero-day attacks (Latif, Farhan, Ahmad, Mostarda, & Cacciagrano, 2025). It is also called a signature-based. The word 'signature' in an intrusion detection environment means an attack feature that can be identified. The hybrid approach, as the name describes it, has the capabilities of both the misuse-based and anomaly-based approaches (Lee et al., 2021). Both functionalities can reduce the FP rate of unknown attacks and improve the detection rate of known attacks.

The dataset selection is vital in applying Data Mining (DM) or ML methods to train and test IDS. It is common for many researchers to use standard datasets to evaluate and compare the performance of various IDS models (Jiang, Choo, & Ko, 2021). Nevertheless, the lack of representative datasets is a significant challenge that may impede the efficiency of anomaly detection systems. Such a gap was pointed to by Paxson and Sommer, who found a shortage of various datasets to be a significant impediment to creating network IDS.

To tackle this, we shall exploit the KDD Cup 1999 network traffic dataset, which comprises several types of cyber-attacks grouped into nine categories depending on their traffic behavior. These attack types are:

To address this, we use the KDD Cup 1999 network traffic dataset, which includes a range of cyber-attacks categorized into nine distinct types based on their behavior. These attack types are:

- **Generic**: Attacks that cause collisions by exploiting hash functions against blocked ciphers.
- **Exploit**: A sequence of commands designed to trigger unexpected behaviors by taking advantage of vulnerabilities or bugs in the system.
- **Fuzzers**: Attacks in which an adversary identifies security loopholes by randomly feeding data into network systems, operating systems, or software.
- **Denial of Service (DoS)**: Aimed at preventing legitimate users from accessing services by overwhelming the network or a specific host with excessive packets.
- **Reconnaissance**: Attacks focused on gathering information about a targeted system or network to identify weaknesses or vulnerabilities.
- **Analysis**: Involves gaining unauthorized access to systems and networks to exploit technical vulnerabilities.
- **Backdoor**: Covert methods attackers use to bypass normal authentication and gain unauthorized access to a network.

- **Shellcode**: A type of attack where an adversary targets a vulnerable process on another machine within a local network, using shellcode as a payload to exploit the compromised system.
- **Worms**: Self-replicating intrusions that spread across networks by duplicating themselves and exploiting vulnerabilities in connected systems.

This data can be used as a source of knowledge about different types of attacks and to experiment with the viability of IDS methods. Machine learning is one of the popular methods of intrusion detection. This technique uses the training data to generate algorithms to identify cyber-attacks or unlawful access at a host or network level. These algorithms can extract insightful patterns from big datasets (Khan et al., 2022). Arthur Samuel defines ML as the study of improving system intelligence by training data without extensive programming. Machine learning methodologies are primarily categorized into three principal classes: supervised, semi-supervised, and unsupervised learning (G. Martín et al., 2021). In a supervised learning environment, algorithms anticipate unknown scenarios by learning from labeled input data, which includes DT, RF, and others. In unsupervised learning, algorithms can learn from unlabeled data when no classifications exist for specific events, with clustering being the most used strategy for this sort of analysis. Semi-supervised learning is appropriate for scenarios when a substantial quantity of labeled data is lacking (Harini et al., 2024). In scenarios where the training dataset comprises a portion of labeled data with a substantial quantity of unlabeled data, a semi-supervised approach will be used in picture archives with few labeled photos. The suggested scheme will investigate a deep learning methodology that emulates human cognitive processes to analyze data and identify patterns, representing an advanced kind of ML with enhanced capabilities to create a versatile and efficient detection system for classifying cyber-attacks (Saba, Rehman, Sadad, Kolivand, & Bahaj, 2022).

2 LITERATURE REVIEW

The only limitation of entropy-based systems is that distinct components might exhibit identical entropy, resulting in numerical miscalculations. The author proposed an anomaly detection method for DDoS (Distributed Denial of Service) identification based on the K Nearest Neighbor algorithm (KNN) to develop a classification algorithm for attack detection. This method minimally effectively identifies attack patterns among substantial volumes of legitimate traffic (Faker & Dogdu, 2019).

The author has addressed periodical discovery in just two distinct sections. The characteristics of periodic detection are established in the first section. The system's learning algorithms have been used to examine data for abnormalities. One of the most notable distinctions in our approach is that our system can detect abnormalities in both IPv4 and IPv6 networks, while many previous studies focus only on IPv4 networks (Almolhis & Alsubhi, 2025).

Over the last decade, many anomaly detection techniques have been proposed to identify a platform or an individual's typical use patterns and classify novel behaviors as anomalous or normal. These techniques may be further classified as generative or discriminative methods. A generative procedure constructs a model only based on standard training instances and evaluates each analytical scenario to ascertain its compatibility with the model. A discriminative technique, conversely, seeks to ascertain the precise distinctions between aberrant and ordinary teachings (Elsayed, Mohamed, & Madkour, 2024).

Many currently used methods depend on the assumption that the practice examples derived by the intrusion sensor are unblemished and reliable. The quantity of knowledge obtained from real-life programs seldom meets the requirements during training. An initial training phase is often required for an anomaly sensor to ascertain the behavior of the monitored process, and the experiments conducted during this time have been deemed standard (Zhong, Yu, & Ai, 2020).

Due to changes in normal behavior, new data in the practice are occasionally added, leading to the anomaly sensor's retraining. In case of an attack when performing a procedural practice, the disliked invasive behavior might have been perceived as a normal response by the anomaly sensor, which endangers its capacity to identify additional attacks. Machine learning algorithms can detect routine conditions (SVMs and neural networks) in real-world environments, which are prone to noise (Kaur & Batth, 2024).

Obsolete data may lead to a very nonlinear surface of conclusion and overfitting of this training set. It translates to weak generalization skills and accuracy of classification. The goal of applying ML methods to routine detection is to create more generalization skills with few training data and be able to classify potentially existing information as either anomalous or normal (Ahmad, Shahid Khan, Wai Shiang, Abdullah, & Ahmad, 2021).

The author drew a compelling parallel between a text record and a program's system call sequence. System call frequencies, as opposed to sequences of method invocations, have been used to represent application activity. Subsequently, the k-nearest neighbor classifier was used to categorize new application behavior as typical or invasive (Ahmed, Shatabda, Islam, & Robin, 2021).

In anomaly detection, the accumulation of consultant samples is hindered by two significant challenges that must be addressed. The first concept is that the frequently used standard training information stays current and lacks abnormalities (Rysbekov, Aitbanov, Abdiakhmetova, & Kartbayev, 2025). This assumption suggests that, in real-world domain names, intrusion detection methods may not be feasible; instead, the detection process should statistically differentiate abnormalities from noise in typical traffic (Iyer, 2021).

The number of abnormal and normal data trials at Lincoln Labs drastically differs across all datasets. Exceptions have been detected in only 1.06% of the studies. The effect of the imbalance is that computations may fail to acknowledge that the anomalies resulting from the entire accuracy of resetting each piece of information as blank occur more often than techniques that include a small proportion of false advantages combined with missed detections (Lopez-Martin, Carro, & Sanchez-Esguevillas, 2020). The Department of Defense aims to decrease false positives and enhance the precision of its anomaly detection system. It entails reducing the incidence of false negatives while increasing the quantity of prospective results. The corporation has endeavored to reconcile costs associated with incorrect groupings by offsetting the fees incurred in identifying suitable individuals for an investigation (Sadia et al., 2024) and locating a pair of capable agents. The second data-collecting challenge is identifying an agent with distinct properties. The limitations of these computations hinder their ability to scale to bigger datasets or independently derive conclusions from the data, sometimes functioning just as a search algorithm. Several anomaly detection methods encounter possible characteristics and use statistical attributes (Thapa, Liu, Kc, Gokaraju, & Roy, 2020).

The Internet of Things (IoT) has significantly enhanced our everyday lives via automation, transportation, and intelligent settings. However, IoT networks are susceptible to cyber-attacks due to constrained resources and processing capacities. This study introduces a novel IoT network intrusion detection method via an advanced learning methodology (Abou Elassad, Mousannif, Al Moatassime, & Karkouch, 2020).

Intrusion-detection systems (IDS) have specialized malware-detecting capabilities to counteract network security breaches. The IDS has lately been revealed to be vulnerable to meticulously crafted disruptions known as opponents. We offer an innovative adversarial detection method based on random networks (RNN-ADV) to comprehend the effects of such assaults. The NSL-KDD dataset is used to design and attack the detrimental effects in preparation. It identifies the function that can provide optimal enhancements to neutral samples with little disturbance (Xuan, Duong, & Dau, 2021).

Intrusion detection is a network traffic monitoring system that identifies aberrant behaviors and issues alerts to detect suspicious activity. This study introduces an innovative method for disruptive intrusion detection in a network that analyzes standard network traffic data and identifies aberrant activities. The suggested method associates aberrant network traffic events with the one-class support vector machine

(OCSVM) technique. The sample included actual traffic from the modern Nice Network (MHN) (Fatani, Dahou, Al-Qaness, Lu, & Elaziz, 2021).

The target surface of user networks is expanding due to the increasing proliferation of Internet of Things (IoT) devices in the contemporary environment. Most affected computers are used in attacks such as Distributed Denial of Service (DDoS) and botnets. In order to identify affected devices' anomalous network traffic, the research suggests a hybrid anomaly detection method. It uses standard network characteristics such as packet size, sending and receiving ports, intervals between packets, and TCP flags (Imran, Haider, Shoaib, & Razzak, 2022).

The quantity of smart home devices, including smart thermostats, Internet-enabled baby monitors, and lighting, has significantly risen. These devices have been the target of many cyberattacks to date. This work aims to analyze specific efficiency metrics in critical operating systems to identify these anomalies (Mezair, Djenouri, Belhadi, Srivastava, & Lin, 2022).

Qatar has introduced a framework for protecting knowledge and effectively regulating Internet communications following its National Vision 2030 and objectives of "achieving prosperity, peace, and maintaining public order." The recent study employs a deep learning approach to examine detrimental network traffic communications. The evaluation of findings for covert channel identification, DDoS identification, and anomaly detection yielded accuracies of 100% and 98% (Al Jallad, Aljnidi, & Desouki, 2019).

Moving traffic assessment and review to the network is the ARMED solution to the problems highlighted in previous research. Within the ARMED system, we uscd RPCA to identify irregularities in real-time across many attack paths. Modern servers' typical processing power and memory constraints do not preclude this investigation, and anomaly detection is usually enough to identify known and unknown dangers (Al-Quayed, Ahmad, & Humayun, 2024).

3 METHODOLOGY AND DATA COLLECTION

3.1 IPv4/IPv6 Networks for Anomaly Detection

Here, we explain the process for developing the suggested anomaly detection model. The model's design allows for spotting network anomalies through various parts, each essential for finding attackers. Knowing what the data tells us is essential for having a model that quickly detects threats.

3.2 Captured Data

Data collection is a crucial process when it comes to anomaly finding. An effective model requires good and relevant data. In this research, the KDD Cup 1999 network traffic dataset is selected to be tested. Unlike the previous DARPA data, we simulated realistic attacks using this updated dataset. The KDD Cup 1999 dataset has been criticized for being old and having little reflective capacity for current attack patterns. However, it was still a standard in studying anomaly and intrusion detection. Its well-organized structure in terms of 41 features and various types of attacks enables a consistent comparison between the traditional and the deep learning model. In this study, our objective was not to benchmark the latest attack types but to analyze behavioral detection patterns across models under standardized conditions. Therefore, KDD'99 is a controlled environment for evaluating model interpretability and comparative accuracy. Future extensions of this work will incorporate modern datasets such as NSL-KDD, CICIDS2017, and UNSW-NB15 to validate generalization across evolving network threats. It includes approximately 10,000 connection records, each having 41 attributes. Within the dataset, we will find four main categories: 'dos,' 'normal,' 'probe,' and 'r2l, ' explaining several types of network behavior and attacks. The model is built to see the difference between these behaviors during training and testing (see Figure 1).

Figure 1. The sample screenshot of the KDD Cup 1999 dataset

1	duration	protocol_	service	flag	src_bytes	dst_bytes	land	wrong_fra	urgent	hot	num_faile	logged_in	num_com	root_shel	su_attem	num_root	num_file_	num_shel	num_acce
2	0	1	25	4	0	0	0	0	0	0	0	0	0	0	0	0	0	0	0
3	0	1	25	2	312	1856	0	0	0	0	0	1	0	0	0	0	0	0	0
4	0	1	25	2	245	2058	0	0	0	0	0	1	0	0	0	0	0	0	0
5	0	1	25	2	298	1267	0	0	0	0	0	1	0	0	0	0	0	0	0
6	0	1	20	2	740	0	0	0	0	0	0	0	0	0	0	0	0	0	0
7	0	1	25	2	304	16414	0	0	0	0	0	1	0	0	0	0	0	0	0
8	0	1	29	3	0	44	0	0	0	0	0	0	0	0	0	0	0	0	0
9	0	1	25	5	42340	7300	0	0	0	1	0	1	0	0	0	0	0	0	0
10	4	1	48	2	32	93	0	0	0	0	0	1	0	0	0	0	0	0	0
11	0	1	25	2	249	5656	0	0	0	0	0	1	0	0	0	0	0	0	0
12	0	1	50	1	0	0	0	0	0	0	0	0	0	0	0	0	0	0	0
13	0	1	25	2	208	277	0	0	0	0	0	1	0	0	0	0	0	0	0
14	0	1	25	2	225	1163	0	0	0	0	0	1	0	0	0	0	0	0	0
15	7354	1	61	2	0	44	0	0	0	0	0	0	0	0	0	0	0	0	0
16	0	1	50	4	0	0	0	0	0	0	0	0	0	0	0	0	0	0	0
17	0	1	45	4	0	0	0	0	0	0	0	0	0	0	0	0	0	0	0
18	0	1	25	2	227	1964	0	0	0	0	0	1	0	0	0	0	0	0	0
19	0	17	12	2	36	0	0	0	0	0	0	0	0	0	0	0	0	0	0
20	280	1	20	2	283618	0	0	0	0	0	0	0	0	0	0	0	0	0	0

3.3 Pre-Treatment and Behavior Profiling

Behavior profiling and pre-treatment involve two steps: feature selection and feature categorization. These parts of the process aim to prepare the data for teaching and testing anomaly detection models.

3.4 Feature Selection

The dataset for the KDD Cup 1999 has information on service types (HTTP, telnet), protocol types (TCP, UDP), errors, payload sizes, and the amount of time connections were active. All these features are grouped according to three main categories:

- Basic Features: Fundamental attributes related to TCP or IP connections.
- Traffic Features: Divided into two sub-groups, "same host" features analyze the destination host in the previous or last two seconds.
- Content Features: These features provide domain knowledge about the instance's content.

The dataset includes 41 attributes for each of the 10,000 instances in this anomaly detection task. Key attributes include duration, protocol_type, service, flag, src_bytes, and dst_bytes, among others related to network behavior.

3.5 Control Variables

Managing the anomaly detection process depends greatly on control variables. The type of attack is decided by these variables, which support the training of both ML and deep learning algorithms. Each attack in the KDD Cup 1999 dataset behaves in a unique network pattern.

DoS attacks focus on ensuring authorized users get their services by disturbing a system's or memory's normal operation. Because of this, the service cannot be reached. Illustrations include assaults known as Apache, Smurf, Neptune, death ping, and UDP storm.

An R2L attack begins when a user sends packets to a system to find and use weaknesses, gaining access as a local user. Among these are xlock, visitor, xnsnoop, phf, and sendmail.

An attacker looking for weaknesses in a computer or network by probing devices for information is called a probing attack. Usually, saint, port, mscan, and Nmap are the tools that attackers rely on for these attacks.

Figure 2 illustrates the steps of the attack detection process in IPv4/IPv6 networks. The experimental setup in this study deliberately focused on two widely adopted ML algorithms, DT and RF, alongside a deep learning framework (Fastai) to enable a transparent, interpretable, and controlled comparison between classical and neural-based anomaly detection methods. This design demonstrates that deep learning is more effective in representation learning when compared to traditional methods that rely on features. Nevertheless, we understand that the provision of more competitive baselines, including Support Vector Machines (SVM), eXtreme Gradient Boosting (XGBoost), and lightweight Convolutional Neural Networks (CNNs), would contribute further to the comparative reliability levels and would offer a broader scope of benchmarks to evaluate their performance. Such models will be incorporated in the following experiment. The model reveals how the detector detects and classifies the incidents of network intrusions according to what the information within the dataset demonstrates and acts. To conduct the experimental evaluation, the train-test split strategy was used to evaluate the quality of the model, which was standardized across all algorithms. Although this method offers a just comparative foundation, we also note that further statistical methods of validation, including k-fold cross-validation and bootstrapped confidence intervals, would also contribute to the validity of the reported outcomes. The receiver operating characteristic (ROC) curves and precision-recall analyses will also be incorporated in future experiments better to understand the model's discrimination power and performance variance.

Figure 2. Methodology diagram of intrusion detection in IPv4/IPv6 networks

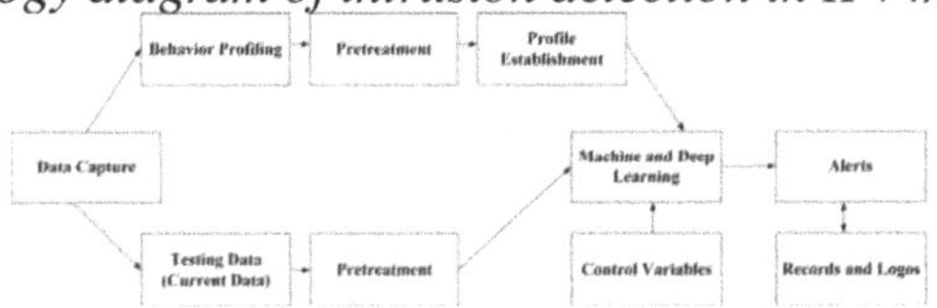

All figures have been redrawn with enhanced clarity, standardized label fonts, and detailed captions to better illustrate each model's analytical contribution to intrusion detection.

4 RESULTS AND DISCUSSION

4.1 Overview

Nowadays, it is more than ever that online security should be safeguarded in the digital world we are presently in. Modern organizations are highly interconnected using various systems, and therefore, it is important to secure them against Denial of Service (DoS), Remote to Local (R2L) attacks, and Probing. Security measures using protected networks cannot always stop advanced cyber attacks. Due to this reason, scientists are examining detection methods that can adapt to new forms of attack.

We also investigated the performance of ML models in detecting anomalies using the KDD Cup 1999 dataset that simulates real-life attack scenarios. The dataset contains 10,000 examples of 41 properties categorized as dos, normal, probe, and r2l.

Although Fastai has been considered in a few studies, we only consider the machine-learning technique of Java, paying attention to DT and RF to classify. We developed our development platform in Python and tested it with Google Colab, creating, editing, and testing our code using network samples according to IPv4 and IPv6 standards.

4.2 Decision Tree (DT) Analysis

The data was modeled using a DT model, which formed a framework that resembles a simple flowchart: Each leaf node evaluates an attribute, each branch represents the outcome of the test, and each end node represents which class is being used. Due to this design, DT is user-friendly and easy to comprehend when detecting network intrusions. By applying the accuracy of the types, we confirmed that the accuracy of the DT model was strong, with a precision of 81%. A breakdown of its performance can be found on this page (see Table 1).

Table 1. Evaluation Metrics for Decision Tree Model

Class	**Precision**	**Recall**	**F1-Score**	**Support**
Normal	0.90	0.85	0.87	1410
Dos	0.92	0.88	0.90	1083
R2L	0.45	0.71	0.55	435
Probe	0.91	0.55	0.69	372
Accuracy			**0.81**	**3300**
Weighted Avg	0.85	0.81	0.82	3300
Macro Avg	0.79	0.75	0.75	3300

Figure 3 below gives a sample structure of the DT classifier used in the KDD Cup 1999 dataset. The nodes indicate the important network traffic characteristics like protocol type, service, and flag, and the branches indicate the decision split utilized in labeling connection behaviors as either normal or attack. This diagram shows how the reasoning of DT can give comprehensible rules for detecting anomalies. The figure has been scaled up with exaggerated labels and clear descriptions of nodes to make them easier to read.

Figure 3. Structure of a Single Decision Tree

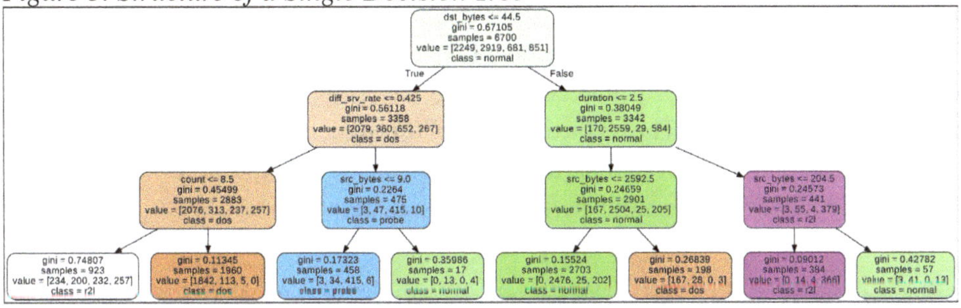

Using a DT clarifies how anomalies are detected, and this process is beneficial for interpreting network traffic patterns and making timely security decisions.

4.3 Random Forest (RF) Analysis

Random Forest can also combine various DT to integrate all the outputs to ensure more reliable and accurate outcomes. One DT tends to be too close a fit to the data, whereas an RF can stabilize its results with the average of a large number of trees, making it more efficient. Our study trained the RF model on the KDD Cup 1999 data to identify various instances of network intrusions of d, n, probe, and r21 types. Model performances were better than the single DT with an 83% accuracy. Through precision, recall, and F1-score, we evaluated the model's effectiveness on the individual class label. Table 2 displays the outcomes of the RF.

Table 2. Evaluation Metrics for Random Forest Model

Class	Precision	Recall	F1-Score	Support
Normal	0.75	0.97	0.85	1410
Dos	0.93	0.84	0.88	1083
R2L	0.98	0.42	0.59	435
Probe	0.90	0.77	0.83	372
Accuracy			**0.83**	**3300**
Weighted Avg	0.86	0.83	0.82	3300
Macro Avg	0.89	0.75	0.79	3300

The 'dos' and 'normal' classes perform very well for RF, but the model also improves performance for the 'probe' class compared to DT. Still, detecting less frequent or more brutal attacks in the 'r2l' class remains difficult since the recall is not very high.

Figure 4 illustrates one representative DT within the RF ensemble model. Each tree contributes to the aggregated classification decision, enhancing generalization and reducing overfitting. The refined version of this figure highlights the hierarchical decision logic and improves label readability to convey how multiple weak learners collectively identify anomalous network traffic patterns.

Figure 4. Structure of a Single Random Forest Tree

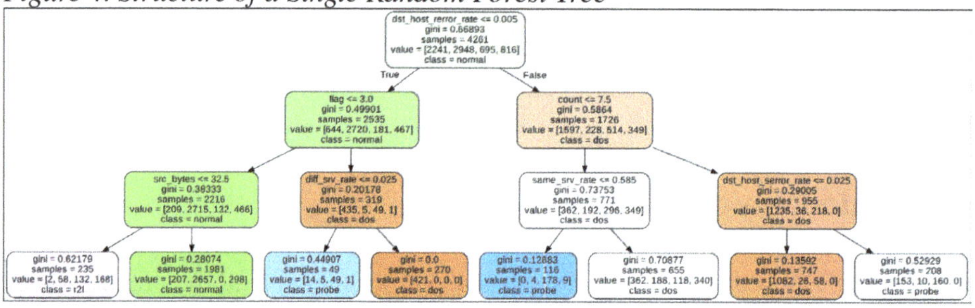

In dealing with typical network data, RF easily finds anomalies in imbalanced datasets or those that have complicated patterns.

4.4 Fastai Library Evaluation

The Fastai library relies on PyTorch to help users make and train perfect machine-learning models quickly and easily. With its intuitive API and modular organization, people using PyTorch can test and use it seamlessly in structured data, computer vision, and natural language processing fields. Our context involved using Fastai to find out how well anomalies in a computer network can be found using organized data on intrusions.

Fastai is different because it connects to Python and PyTorch, which helps abstract complicated neural networks efficiently. In particular, the tabular module helps learn patterns in the KDD Cup 1999 dataset using many attributes with a simple setup.

Working with FastAI in training and testing.

To test the Fastai model, we engaged it in training by setting up 20 epochs using tabular_learner(). The training loss improved dramatically, going from 0.185222 to 0.066029, but the validation loss increased just slightly, which suggests a small amount of overfitting. However, the model had an accuracy of 92% throughout and exceeded the accuracy of every ML alternative (see Table 3). A minor divergence between training and validation losses was observed during the training phase, suggesting mild overfitting. This effect is common in deep models trained on relatively limited or imbalanced datasets such as the KDD Cup 1999. Future implementations will incorporate regularization strategies to mitigate such behavior, including dropout layers, early stopping criteria, and learning-rate scheduling within the Fastai framework. Furthermore, we plan to better visualize training and validation learning curves to depict convergence behavior and model stability across epochs.

The code used for training:

"learn = tabular_learner(data, layers=[200, 100], metrics=accuracy)"

"learn.fit(20, 1e-2)"

Table 3. Epoch-wise Performance of the Fastai Model

Epoch	Accuracy	Valid Loss	Train Loss
0	0.940000	0.185932	0.185222
1	0.925000	0.152840	0.154395
2	0.915000	0.152586	0.122377
3	0.895000	0.212534	0.106886
4	0.940000	0.163913	0.105322
5	0.935000	0.169776	0.108932
6	0.930000	0.158292	0.087551
7	0.915000	0.210828	0.096910
8	0.945000	0.156902	0.092510
9	0.950000	0.125814	0.077677
10	0.940000	0.169677	0.076468
11	0.955000	0.129415	0.080842
12	0.915000	0.220610	0.078547
13	0.950000	0.159163	0.079091
14	0.930000	0.164479	0.072689
15	0.955000	0.168618	0.065633
16	0.940000	0.169889	0.072852
17	0.940000	0.191170	0.086775
18	0.945000	0.135718	0.067554
19	0.920000	0.219594	0.066029

Figure 5 had the most misclassifications between the classes of DoS and Probe, and to a small extent between the R2L and the normal classes. This trend implies that the classifier becomes confused when similar traffic signature attacks happen or overlapping protocol behavior occurs. As an example, a few reconnaissance (Probe) operations are similar to the high-volume packet traces of DoS attacks, whereas some R2L events can resemble a legitimate low-frequency access attempt. These intersections underscore the difficulty of identifying subtle behavioral differences in the imbalanced datasets like the KDD Cup 1999. The next generation of frameworks will resolve this issue by including better representations of features and attention-based modules to enhance separability between closely related attack types.

Figure 5. Confusion Matrix of Fastai Model

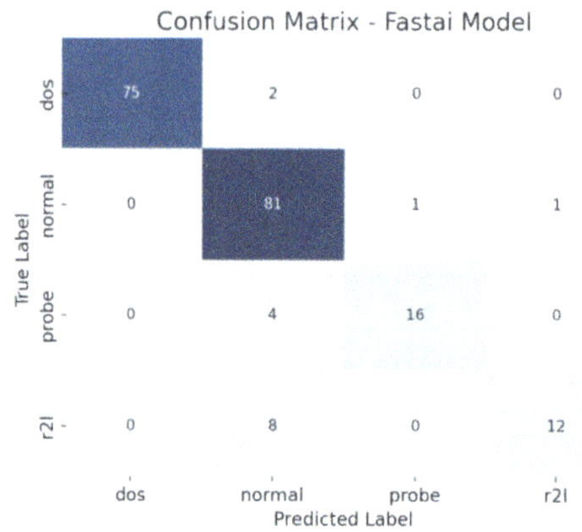

4.5 Comparative Accuracy Analysis

We checked all the methods and compared the accuracy of the ML modules (DT and the RF) to the Fastai deep learning model. The analysis reveals that the Deep learning approach works effectively in this case, and Fastai is more effective than the previous methods (see Table 4). The same data partitioning scheme was used to train and test each model to minimize bias and achieve consistency. Even though this work focuses on accuracy and F1-score as the primary measures, adding ROC-AUC and analyzing the precision/recall curves will be part of our further experimental stage. These measures can represent performance peculiarities in uneven datasets and give confidence intervals to make comparative validation between learning models.

Table 4. Accuracy Comparison Between Models

Technique	Accuracy
Decision Tree	81.0303%
Random Forest	83.1515%
Fastai (DL)	92.0000%

Figure 6 visually represents the accuracy gap between Fastai and traditional ML techniques, clearly showing Fastai's superior performance.

Figure 6. Accuracy Comparison Between Machine and Deep Learning Models

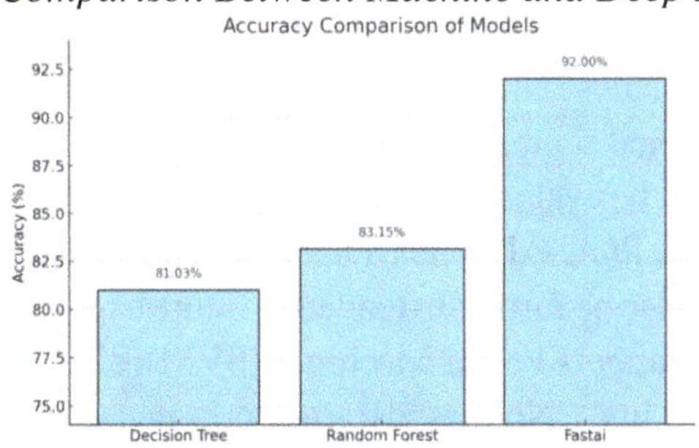

Fastai's remarkable accuracy highlights the potential of deep learning in building more intelligent and adaptive IDS, especially when trained on structured behavioral datasets like KDD Cup 1999.

5 CONCLUSION AND FUTURE WORK

This paper has assessed the performance of ML and deep learning algorithms in detecting anomalies in network traffic on the KDD Cup 1999 dataset. The idea was to create an effective IDS to identify DoS, R2L, and Probe attacks. This dataset contained 41 different features and 10,000 network traffic examples, which enabled the simulation of realistic attacks. The highest accuracy of 81.03 in the DT, 83.15 in the RF, and 92.00 in the Fastai deep learning model were some of the highest accuracy values among the assessed models, indicating that deep learning has potential in recognizing complex patterns in the field of cybersecurity.

The findings prove that DT and RF are effective baseline methods of detecting abnormal behaviors, and deep learning has a strong adaptability in nonlinear and high-dimensional data models. Even though it is true that the KDD Cup 1999 data is a popular dataset used in controlled experimentation, we realize the limitations of the dataset to reflect the contemporary network environment. Thus, in subsequent projects, we will apply this framework to newer benchmark datasets like NSL-KDD, CICIDS2017, and UNSW-NB15 that are more representative of the current traffic trends, encrypted traffic, and sophisticated persistent threats, to name a few. The improvement will guarantee higher robustness and external validity of the suggested IDS.

In future studies, our research roadmap is to apply and test new deep learning architectures that can extract spatial and temporal dependencies of network data. In particular, we are going to use the Convolutional Neural Networks (CNNs) to extract spatial features, Recurrent Neural Networks (RNNs) and Long Short-Term Memory (LSTM) networks to analyse the sequences, and the Transformer-based networks to learn multidimensional representations. In order to assure statistical reliability, these architectures will be evaluated under strict experimental circumstances using k-fold cross-validation, ROC-AUC measures, and confidence interval analysis.

The baselines will also be further extended in future experiments that will include other algorithms like Support Vector Machines (SVM), eXtreme Gradient Boosting (XGBoost), and lightweight CNN-based frameworks that will evaluate the scalability of the proposed framework as well as the capacity of generalization. Regularization procedures such as dropout, batch normalization, and early stopping will be embraced to reduce overfitting and enhance the stability of the model. Convergence behavior and training stability will also be evidenced by learning curve visualization.

Also, the combination of Explainable AI (XAI) methods and visual analytics will be one of the key elements of future work. It can be used to interpret better models' decisions, feature importance, and anomaly patterns. Model behavior has also been developed into visual representations, which have been made more understandable, and further refinements will involve more diagrammatic descriptions of decision logic and feature interactions.

Lastly, it was proofread and formatted again to remove typographical irregularities, generalize terms (e.g., DoS, R2L, Fastai), and make the text more readable. As seen in modern IDS research, these revisions guarantee the paper's technical correctness, clarity, and professional presentation.

REFERENCES

Abou Elassad, Z. E., Mousannif, H., Al Moatassime, H., & Karkouch, A. (2020). The application of machine learning techniques for driving behavior analysis: A conceptual framework and a systematic literature review. *Engineering Applications of Artificial Intelligence*, *87*, 103312. DOI: 10.1016/j.engappai.2019.103312

Ahmad, Z., Shahid Khan, A., Wai Shiang, C., Abdullah, J., & Ahmad, F. (2021). Network intrusion detection system: A systematic study of machine learning and deep learning approaches. *Transactions on Emerging Telecommunications Technologies*, *32*(1), e4150. DOI: 10.1002/ett.4150

Ahmed, M. R., Shatabda, S., Islam, A. M., & Robin, M. T. I. (2021). Intrusion Detection System in Software-Defined Networks Using Machine Learning and Deep Learning Techniques—A Comprehensive Survey. *Authorea Preprints*. DOI: 10.36227/techrxiv.17153213.v1

Al Jallad, K., Aljnidi, M., & Desouki, M. S. (2019). Big data analysis and distributed deep learning for next-generation intrusion detection system optimization. *Journal of Big Data*, *6*(1), 88. DOI: 10.1186/s40537-019-0248-6

Al-Quayed, F., Ahmad, Z., & Humayun, M. (2024). A situation based predictive approach for cybersecurity intrusion detection and prevention using machine learning and deep learning algorithms in wireless sensor networks of industry 4.0. *IEEE Access : Practical Innovations, Open Solutions*, *12*, 34800–34819. DOI: 10.1109/ACCESS.2024.3372187

Almolhis, N. A., & Alsubhi, M. A. (2025). *Detecting Advanced Persistent Threats Using Machine Learning and Behavioral Analysis.* Paper presented at the International Conference on Information Technology-New Generations. DOI: 10.1007/978-3-031-89063-5_9

Dornala, S. K., & Senthilkumar, P. (2025). Real-Time threat identification and categorization in network traffic using deep learning behavioral analysis. *International Journal on Smart Sensing and Intelligent Systems*, *18*(1), 20250017. DOI: 10.2478/ijssis-2025-0017

Elsayed, S., Mohamed, K., & Madkour, M. A. (2024). A comparative study of using deep learning algorithms in network intrusion detection. *IEEE Access : Practical Innovations, Open Solutions*, *12*, 58851–58870. DOI: 10.1109/ACCESS.2024.3389096

Faker, O., & Dogdu, E. (2019). *Intrusion detection using big data and deep learning techniques.* Paper presented at the Proceedings of the 2019 ACM Southeast conference. DOI: 10.1145/3299815.3314439

Fatani, A., Dahou, A., Al-Qaness, M. A., Lu, S., & Elaziz, M. A. (2021). Advanced feature extraction and selection approach using deep learning and Aquila optimizer for IoT intrusion detection system. *Sensors (Basel)*, *22*(1), 140. DOI: 10.3390/s22010140 PMID: 35009682

Harini, B., Gouri, M., Balaji, V., Sangeetha, K., & Harshini, A. (2024). *Advanced Sound Detection and Behavior Examination for Real-Time Intruder Detection using Deep Learning: A Comprehensive Security Framework.* Paper presented at the 2024 2nd International Conference on Artificial Intelligence and Machine Learning Applications Theme: Healthcare and Internet of Things (AIMLA).

Imran, M., Haider, N., Shoaib, M., & Razzak, I. (2022). An intelligent and efficient network intrusion detection system using deep learning. *Computers & Electrical Engineering*, *99*, 107764. DOI: 10.1016/j.compeleceng.2022.107764

Iyer, K. I. (2021). From Signatures to Behavior: Evolving Strategies for Next-Generation Intrusion Detection. *European Journal of Advances in Engineering Technology*, *8*(6), 165–171.

Jiang, Y., Choo, K.-K. R., & Ko, H. (2021). A special section on deep & advanced machine learning approaches for human behavior analysis. *Journal of Information Processing Systems*, *17*(2), 334–336.

Kaur, K., & Batth, J. S. (2024). *Implementation of Deep Learning and Machine Learning for Designing and Analyzing IDS (Intrusion Detection System) Through Novel Framework.* Paper presented at the International Conference on Innovation and Emerging Trends in Computing and Information Technologies.

Khan, A. R., Kashif, M., Jhaveri, R. H., Raut, R., Saba, T., & Bahaj, S. A. (2022). Deep learning for intrusion detection and security of Internet of things (IoT): Current analysis, challenges, and possible solutions. *Security and Communication Networks*, *2022*(1), 4016073. DOI: 10.1155/2022/4016073

Kocher, G., & Kumar, G. (2021). Machine learning and deep learning methods for intrusion detection systems: Recent developments and challenges. *Soft Computing*, *25*(15), 9731–9763. DOI: 10.1007/s00500-021-05893-0

Latif, R. M. A. (2025). Enhancing sustainable urban mobility in Pakistan through renewable hydrogen integration and policy interventions. *Discover Cities*, *2*(1), 1–24. DOI: 10.1007/s44327-025-00089-9

Latif, R. M. A., Farhan, M., Ahmad, J., Mostarda, L., & Cacciagrano, D. (2025). Blockchain-Based Medicine Supply Chain for Transparent Healthcare Tracking. In *AI and Blockchain Applications for Privacy and Security in Smart Medical Systems* (pp. 81–106). IGI Global Scientific Publishing. DOI: 10.4018/979-8-3373-0593-6.ch004

Latif, R. M. A., Farhan, M., Khan, N. A., & Sujatha, R. (2024). Sustainable Computing-Based Simulation of Intelligent Border Surveillance Using Mobile WSN. In *Navigating Cyber Threats and Cybersecurity in the Logistics Industry* (pp. 90–122). IGI Global Scientific Publishing. DOI: 10.4018/979-8-3693-3816-2.ch003

Latif, R. M. A., Obaidat, M. S., Ullah, F., & Mahmood, K. (2025). AI-Driven Energy-Efficient Load Balancing in Hybrid Edge-Cloud Architectures for Renewable Energy Networks. *IEEE Networking Letters*, 1. DOI: 10.1109/LNET.2025.3596126

Latif, R. M. A., Ullah, F., Jamal, N., Zhao, Y., Jabbar, S., & Khan, M. A. (2025). *Explainable AI for Big Data Analytics in Urban Mobility Forecasting.* Paper presented at the 2025 IEEE International Conference on Pattern Recognition, Machine Vision and Artificial Intelligence (PRMVAI). DOI: 10.1109/PRMVAI65741.2025.11108680

Latif, R. M. A., Yoshigoe, K., Jamal, N., Zhao, Y., Ullah, F., & Ahmad, J. (2025). *Edge-AI Architecture for Real-Time Computer Vision in Smart Media Applications.* Paper presented at the 2025 IEEE International Conference on Pattern Recognition, Machine Vision and Artificial Intelligence (PRMVAI). DOI: 10.1109/PRMVAI65741.2025.11108373

Lee, S.-W., Mohammadi, M., Rashidi, S., Rahmani, A. M., Masdari, M., & Hosseinzadeh, M. (2021). Towards secure intrusion detection systems using deep learning techniques: Comprehensive analysis and review. *Journal of Network and Computer Applications*, *187*, 103111. DOI: 10.1016/j.jnca.2021.103111

Liu, H., & Lang, B. (2019). Machine learning and deep learning methods for intrusion detection systems: A survey. *Applied Sciences (Basel, Switzerland)*, *9*(20), 4396. DOI: 10.3390/app9204396

Lopez-Martin, M., Carro, B., & Sanchez-Esguevillas, A. (2020). Application of deep reinforcement learning to intrusion detection for supervised problems. *Expert Systems with Applications*, *141*, 112963. DOI: 10.1016/j.eswa.2019.112963

Martín, G., A., Fernández-Isabel, A., Martín de Diego, I., & Beltrán, M. (. (2021). A survey for user behavior analysis based on machine learning techniques: Current models and applications. *Applied Intelligence*, *51*(8), 6029–6055. DOI: 10.1007/s10489-020-02160-x

Mezair, T., Djenouri, Y., Belhadi, A., Srivastava, G., & Lin, J. C.-W. (2022). Towards an advanced deep learning for the internet of behaviors: Application to connected vehicles. *ACM Transactions on Sensor Networks*, *19*(2), 1–18. DOI: 10.1145/3526192

Mishra, P., Varadharajan, V., Tupakula, U., & Pilli, E. S. (2018). A detailed investigation and analysis of using machine learning techniques for intrusion detection. *IEEE Communications Surveys and Tutorials*, *21*(1), 686–728. DOI: 10.1109/COMST.2018.2847722

Naeem, H., Ullah, F., Krejcar, O., Alsirhani, A., & Zhao, Y. (2024). Adversarial Malware Detection on Consumer Devices Using Optimized Image-Based Ensembles. *IEEE Consumer Electronics Magazine*, 1–10. DOI: 10.1109/MCE.2024.3507282

Naeem, H., Ullah, F., & Srivastava, G. (2025). Classification of intrusion cyber-attacks in smart power grids using deep ensemble learning with metaheuristic-based optimization. *Expert Systems: International Journal of Knowledge Engineering and Neural Networks*, *42*(1), e13556. DOI: 10.1111/exsy.13556

Rysbekov, S., Aitbanov, A., Abdiakhmetova, Z., & Kartbayev, A. (2025). Advancing network security: A comparative research of machine learning techniques for intrusion detection. *International Journal of Electrical and Computer Engineering*, *15*(2), 2271. DOI: 10.11591/ijece.v15i2.pp2271-2281

Saba, T., Rehman, A., Sadad, T., Kolivand, H., & Bahaj, S. A. (2022). Anomaly-based intrusion detection system for IoT networks through deep learning model. *Computers & Electrical Engineering*, *99*, 107810. DOI: 10.1016/j.compeleceng.2022.107810

Sadia, H., Farhan, S., Haq, Y. U., Sana, R., Mahmood, T., Bahaj, S. A. O., & Khan, A. R. (2024). Intrusion detection system for wireless sensor networks: A machine learning based approach. *IEEE Access : Practical Innovations, Open Solutions*, *12*, 52565–52582. DOI: 10.1109/ACCESS.2024.3380014

Saranya, T., Sridevi, S., Deisy, C., Chung, T. D., & Khan, M. A. (2020). Performance analysis of machine learning algorithms in intrusion detection system: A review. *Procedia Computer Science*, *171*, 1251–1260. DOI: 10.1016/j.procs.2020.04.133

Thapa, N., Liu, Z., Kc, D. B., Gokaraju, B., & Roy, K. (2020). Comparison of machine learning and deep learning models for network intrusion detection systems. *Future Internet*, *12*(10), 167. DOI: 10.3390/fi12100167

Ullah, F., Mostarda, L., Cacciagrano, D., Alenazi, M. J., Chen, C.-M., & Kumari, S. (2024). Federated Edge Intelligence for Enhanced Security in Consumer Intermittent Healthcare Devices Using Adversarial Examples. *IEEE Transactions on Consumer Electronics*.

Wassan, S., Latif, R. M. A., Liudajun, , Ying, H., Farhan, M., & Akbar, W. (2025). Advancements in Optical Glucose Sensing for Diabetes Diagnostics and Monitoring. *Microwave and Optical Technology Letters*, *67*(4), e70190. DOI: 10.1002/mop.70190

Xuan, C. D., Duong, D., & Dau, H. X. (2021). A multi-layer approach for advanced persistent threat detection using machine learning based on network traffic. *Journal of Intelligent & Fuzzy Systems*, *40*(6), 11311–11329. DOI: 10.3233/JIFS-202465

Zhong, W., Yu, N., & Ai, C. (2020). Applying big data based deep learning system to intrusion detection. *Big Data Mining Analytics*, *3*(3), 181–195. DOI: 10.26599/BDMA.2020.9020003

Chapter 2

Causal AI:
Explainable Techniques for Interpreting Behavioral Patterns Using Causal Diagrams

Waqas Junaid
https://orcid.org/0009-0003-1778-4083
Northwestern Polytechnical University, Xian, China

Rubia Fatima
https://orcid.org/0000-0002-7144-1925
Emerson University, Multan, Pakistan

Muhammad Tahir
https://orcid.org/0000-0001-9118-9256
NUML, Faisalabad, Pakistan

Hamid Nawaz
https://orcid.org/0009-0000-9140-1181
NUML, Faisalabad, Pakistan

Muhammad Ibrar
New Mexico Highlands University, USA

Umar Raza
https://orcid.org/0000-0002-9810-1285
Manchester Metropolitan University, UK

Yunwei Dong
https://orcid.org/0000-0001-9882-9121
Northwestern Polytechnical University, Xian, China

Zhi Li
https://orcid.org/0000-0003-1861-6842
Guangxi Normal University, Guilin, China

ABSTRACT

The increased usage of AI in healthcare, finance, education, and cybersecurity necessitates models, which should be both accurate and interpretable. In contrast to traditional machine learning, causal AI can also "explain" why the machine has made a certain decision by reasoning about cause and effect, not correlations. This chapter presents the background to causal inference, including the ladder of causation developed by Pearl, structural causal models (SCM) and causal diagrams

DOI: 10.4018/979-8-3373-5062-2.ch002

(Directed Acyclic Graphs DAG). Approaches like do-calculus, propensity score matching, and toolkits like DoWhy and EconML are presented with practical use cases, like healthcare treatment assessment, education results, customer behavior, and cybersecurity threat detection. We compare causal reasoning to traditional machine learning in solving confounders, domain shifts, and out-of-distribution generalization, and point out limitations such as data quality, identifiability, and future research such as combining causality with large language models.

INTRODUCTION

As AI spreads across healthcare, education, cybersecurity, and human-computer interaction, the need for systems that are both intelligent and explainable has become urgent (Chia, 2023; Doshi & Hiran, 2024; Khamparia & Gupta, 2024). Many breakthroughs rely on black-box models, which achieve accuracy but lack transparent justifications. This limits trust and accountability in sensitive domains, motivating Explainable AI (XAI) and especially Causal AI, which focuses on reasoning with cause and effect for interpretability and actionability (Samek et al., 2019; Turab et al., 2024).

This opaqueness poses a significant barrier to real-world deployment, especially in sensitive domains where accountability, fairness, ethics, and trust are essential (Alang & Kumar, 2025). Consider, for instance, a clinical AI system recommending cancer treatments without explanation may face skepticism despite accuracy (Abgrall et al., 2024). In cybersecurity, if an AI flags a uscr as a thrcat but fails to justify why, it could lead to misinformed decisions or biases (Alang & Kumar, 2025; Oloyede, 2024). In education, dropout predictions without causal factors hinder interventions (Lin et al., 2024).

To address these challenges, the field of Explainable AI (XAI) has emerged, aiming to bridge the gap between high-performing AI models and human interpretability (Agrawal & Sharma, 2024). Yet, many XAI techniques such as SHAP, LIME, or saliency map are still post-hoc, explaining outcomes after predictions. They may be inconsistent and do not model the causal processes driving behavior (Zodage et al., 2024). They answer *what* happened but not *why* or *what if.*

Causal AI is a transformative approach that addresses these challenges by shifting the focus from prediction to explanation and intervention (Pearl, 2009). In contrast to traditional machine learning, where integration, statistical connections, and predictive performance are among the main priorities (Jogo, 2025), Causal AI will make machines capable of reasoning with cause and effect, thus yielding more insight about the structure and behavior of the data (Molabanti et al., 2024). It answers *what will happen* (prediction), *why it happened* (explanation), and *what* *would happen under change* (intervention and counterfactual reasoning) (Durvasula, 2024; Jaimini & Sheth, 2022). This shift expands interpretability and actionability, especially in contexts of complex human behavior (Durvasula, 2024).

At the heart of this approach lies causal inference, a formal framework that allows us to model and analyze cause-effect relationships in data (Ghosh et al., 2024). The main feature of causal inference through the use of causal diagrams, e.g., Directed Acyclic Graphs (DAGs) (Bastias & Brand, 2020). They not only describe domain knowledge but also guide algorithms to identify confounders, measure treatment effects, and hypothesizing the counterfactuals (e.g., What happens when this variable changes?) (Elwert, 2013; Lipsky & Greenland, 2022). Throughout their ability to capture the data-generating processes, DAGs permit interpretable and clear line of reasoning, tightly integrated with the human mental models of thought (Dijk et al., 2025; Pavlin et al., 2023). Figure 1 displays a more general overview of the workflow of Causal AI systems, i.e., how a problem can be framed in terms of a causal model, how a DAG can be constructed, how confounders can be identified, and how causal inference approaches can be applied, and how actionable insights or decisions can be made using explanations and counterfactuals.

Figure 1. The Causal AI Reasoning Process. A high-level pipeline for integrating causal modeling and reasoning into explainable AI systems

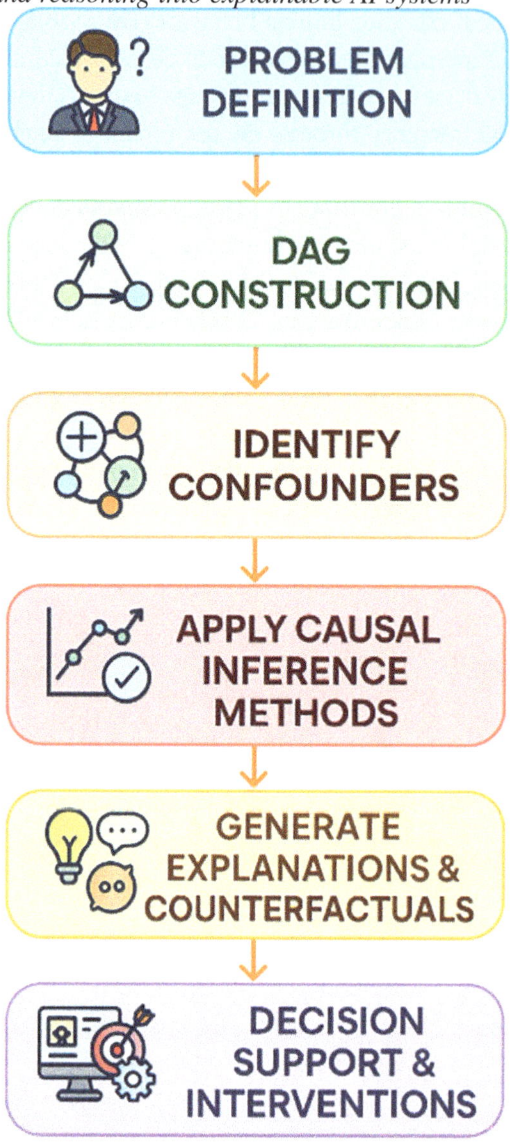

This chapter will examine the way causal diagrams-based AI can be applied to comprehend patterns behavior in different fields. What people are doing, online, in a school, a hospital, a digital security scheme, is always complex and driven by entangled causal mechanisms. Traditional machine learning models can establish correlations between the characteristics of behavior and outcomes (such as how long one spends on a task and how well one performed) but they cannot in general indicate whether these correlations are causal or due to some extraneous factors. Causal AI provides the tools to unearth these dynamics, contribution insights that are not only statistically robust but also contextually meaningful.

This chapter is organized as follows:

- The chapter begins by clarifying the theoretical motivation behind causal inference, and crucial concepts such as structural causal models (SCMs), do-operator, and the ladder of causality as suggested by Pearl (namely observing, intervening, as well as counterfactual reasoning).
- Followed by observing that, then it examines how causal diagrams can be employed to demonstrate causal reasoning that is both comprehensible and mathematical.
- The chapter continues to discuss many approaches to finding and inferring causes including propensity score matching, instrumental variables, and do-calculus. It discusses such useful tools as DoWhy and EconML as well.
- A dedicated section observes real-world applications of causal AI in interpreting behavioral patterns in sectors like healthcare (e.g., patient adherence), education (e.g., student engagement), and cybersecurity (e.g., anomalous behavior detection).
- The chapter also discusses how causal reasoning is distinct in relation to classical ML with respect to handling confounders, changes of task domain as well as out-of-distribution generalization.

Lastly, it addresses emerging directions and challenges, including the integration of causal reasoning with deep learning and large language models, the role of domain expertise, and restrictions due to data quality or identifiability.

In this perspective, the chapter puts Causal AI in the context of the next generation of intelligent systems that will not only be powerful but also understandable, trustworthy, and consistent with what people can reason. As the world becomes engulfed with automation of various activities through use of AI to make decisions, the question of knowing why a system is behaving in a certain manner will no longer be a luxury but rather a necessity.

This chapter is organized as follows. Section 2 reviews foundational techniques and algorithms in Causal AI, including structural causal models (SCMs), the Ladder of Causation, and both constraint-based and score-based discovery approaches. Section 4 explores explainability through causal structures, contrasting Problem Diagrams as practitioner-friendly front ends with Directed Acyclic Graphs (DAGs) as formal back-ends. Section 5 examines key applications of Causal AI in healthcare, education, consumer behavior, and cybersecurity. Section 6 outlines open challenges such as data quality, scalability, and ethical concerns, while Section 7 provides future directions. The chapter concludes with a synthesis of lessons and opportunities for advancing behaviorally intelligent systems.

FOUNDATIONS OF CAUSAL AI

The underlying principle of Causal AI is the basic difference between correlation and causation. Traditional statistical learning, might be useful in uncovering associations, does not present the tools to make inferences of the cause-effect relationship (Pearl, 2009). This gap is particularly critical in behavioral systems, where decisions, actions, and outcomes are deeply intertwined and sensitive to interventions. The Causal AI fills this gap by explicitly model the cause and effect relationships, not only allowing prediction, but also explains it in a meaningful way (Durvasula, 2024). This section, the center pillars of Causal AI are presented concerning the principles of the causal reasoning, structural causal models, and main frameworks assisting in interpretable analysis of behavioral patterns using causal diagrams.

From Correlation to Causation

Associations are usually strong in observational behavioral data, users that use feature A are more likely to do action B. Nevertheless, taking an action based on such patterns without knowing their mechanisms may result in drawing erroneous conclusions (Chen & Li, 2024; Harbich & Hassenzahl, 2011). Causal inference fills this gap enabling us to answer such questions as:

- What is the effect of introducing a new system prompt on user engagement?
- Would the outcome have differed if the user were exposed to a different interface?

  This shift from correlational to causal reasoning is crucial for building trustworthy AI systems that aim to influence or adapt to user behavior.

To narrow down the discussion, the Table 1 shows the symbols and notations that are used in this chapter:

Table 1. Symbols and Notations

Symbols	Meaning
X	Treatment / intervention variable (e.g., participation)
Y	Outcome variable (e.g., final grade)
Z	Confounder / observed covariates
do(X)	Intervention operator from do-calculus
ATE	Average Treatment Effect
P(Y|X)	Probability of Y given X
P(Y| do(X)	Probability of Y under intervention do(X)

Structural Causal Models (SCMs)

Causal AI is based on Structural Causal Models (SCMs), make explicit the assumptions underlying data-generating process, allowing to be tested and critiqued (Kaddour et al., 2022). An SCM consists of a set of variables connected by directed edges representing causal relationships, typically visualized as a Directed Acyclic Graph (DAG) (Heyn & Knauss, 2022).

Formally, an SCM includes:

- A set of *endogenous variables* ($V = V_1, V_2, ..., V_n$),
- A set of *exogenous variables* (U) representing background factors,
- A set of *structural equations* ($V_i = f_i(PA_i, U_i)$), where (PA_i) are the parents (direct causes) of (Vi) in the graph.

SCMs enable the simulation of interventions and support counterfactual reasoning. In behavioral systems, they help determine whether observed actions are due to system design, user intent, or external factors. Figure 2 illustrates a simple SCM with three variables and their causal dependencies.

Figure 2. Simple SCM: A causes both B and C, B also causes C

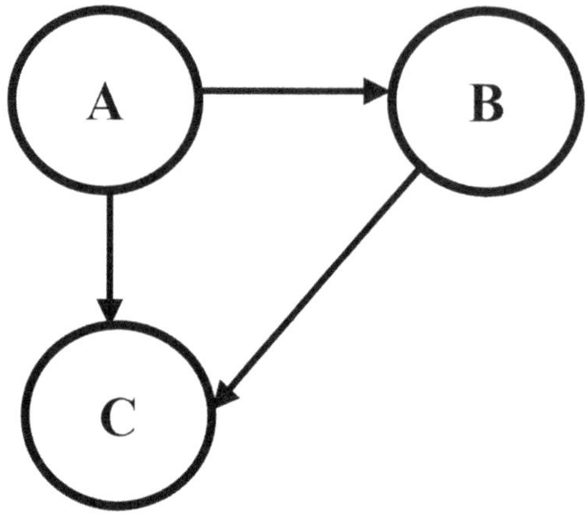

Typed and Actual Causality

Causal AI relies on Structural Causal Models (SCMs) to formalize the data-generating process, but causality can be classified as typed and actual causality (Halpern & Pearl, 2005). Typed causality refers to general cause-effect relationships within a system, where variables are categorized (e.g., treatment, outcome, confounder) based on domain knowledge, often encoded in a Directed Acyclic Graph (DAG). For example, in a healthcare SCM, medication adherence (Y) may be influenced by reminders (X) and confounded by age (Z), representing a population-level causal structure. In contrast, actual causality focuses on specific instances, determining whether a particular event caused an outcome. For instance, "Did a reminder cause this patient to adhere to their medication?" requires counterfactual analysis to assess the specific effect.

This distinction is critical for behavioral analysis. Typed causality helps design general interventions (e.g., reminders for all patients), while actual causality supports personalized explanations (e.g., why a specific patient adhered).

The Ladder of Causation

Judea Pearl's *ladder of causation (Pearl & Mackenzie, 2018)* conceptualizes three levels of causal reasoning:

- **Association (Seeing):** Detecting statistical dependencies. E.g., recognizing that users who read reviews often purchase products. Mathematically represented as $P(y|x)$, which is the probability of outcome y given observation x.
- **Intervention (Doing):** Estimating the outcome of deliberate changes. E.g., determining the effect of showing a targeted banner on purchases. Represented as $P(y|do(x))$, where $do(x)$ denotes an intentional intervention setting x, rather than merely observing it.
- **Counterfactuals (Imagining):** Reasoning about alternate possibilities. E.g., asking if a user would have made a different decision with a different interface. This is expressed as $P(y_X |x)$: the probability that y would have happened under a hypothetical action x , given that we observed x.

Causal AI aspires to reach the top of this ladder, enabling models to not just describe but explain and influence behavioral phenomena. As shown in Figure 3, each level increases in causal complexity and explanatory power.

Figure 3. Illustration of the three levels of the Ladder of Causation

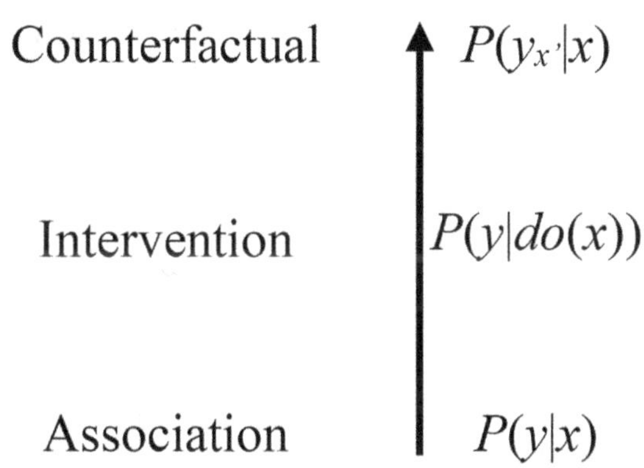

Causal Diagrams and Behavioral Interpretation

Causal diagrams, constructed from SCMs, serve as vital tools for explaining behavioral patterns. Nodes represent variables such as user actions, attributes, system interventions, or environmental contexts; edges denote causal influence (Heyn & Knauss, 2022).

They help:

- Identify *confounders* that may bias estimates,
- Design *interventions* by simulating policy changes,
- Reveal *mediators* and *moderators* in behavioral processes.

Figure 4 presents an example of a behavioral causal diagram illustrating how system features and user profiles affect user actions.

By making causal assumptions explicit, these diagrams support both machine reasoning and human interpretability.

Figure 4. Behavioral causal diagram: user profile and system features influence user actions

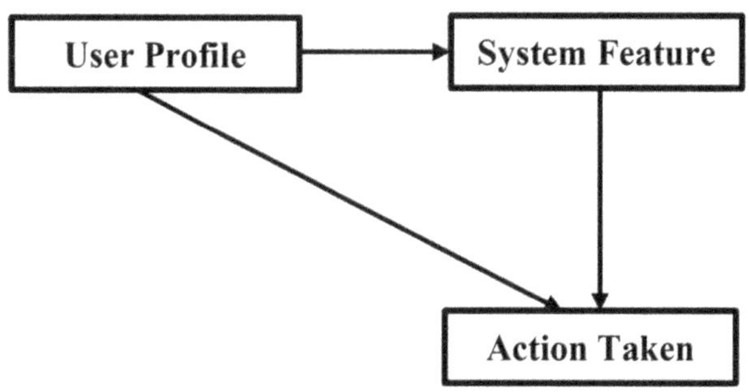

Modeling Interventions with The Do-Operator

The *do-operator*, ($do(X = x)$), models interventions explicitly. While conditional probability ($P(Y \mid X = x)$) describes observation, causal inference is concerned with ($P(Y \mid do(X = x))$), which quantifies the effect of setting (X) to a specific value by intervention rather than observation (Pearl, 1996).

For example:

- $P(Click \mid Ad = 1)$ may reflect natural exposure,
- $P(Click \mid do(Ad = 1))$ isolates the causal effect of displaying the ad.

Understanding this distinction is central to analyzing behavior within interactive systems, where interventions (such as UI changes, notifications, or recommendations) are often deployed with the aim of influencing user outcomes.

Counterfactual Reasoning in Behavioral Contexts

Counterfactuals Analysis provides a deeper level of explanation by asking: What would have happened under different circumstances? This is particularly useful for evaluating individual outcomes, diagnosing errors, or assessing fairness in decision-making (Pereira & Saptawijaya, 2016).

For example:

- Would this user have completed the form if they had not encountered a loading delay?
- Would the model have predicted a different risk level if demographic information were excluded?

In this respect, a SCMs can assess counterfactuals in three-steps process (Haugh & Singal, 2023):

- **Abduction:** Inferring hidden variables based on actual outcomes,
- **Action:** Changing inputs to reflect the counterfactual condition,
- **Prediction:** Computing new outcomes under the modified model.

This kind of reasoning is essential to customized explanation, fairness diagnosis or debugging behavioral response.

Testability of Assumptions and Practical Challenges

Assumptions are taken by causal inference and special care should be given in real-life behavioral systems (Pearl, 2010):

- **Causal sufficiency:** All relevant variables are observed.
- **No hidden confounding:** There are no unmeasured common causes.
- **Correct model specification:** The structure of the causal graph reflects reality.

Causal effects being estimated are likely to become biased when these assumptions are violated. Sensitivity analysis, instrumental variables or other techniques may address these problems to some degree, though they demand experience in the field and ample validation.

Implementing Causal Inference: DoWhy and EconML

To effectively make causal reasoning operational, two more recent frameworks come in rather handy:

1. **DoWhy:** offers an ethical guideline of estimation of causal effects based on four main steps namely, the specification of the model, identification, estimation, and refutation. It focuses on openness, and it asks the users to make their assumptions clear by describing them with causal diagrams. This can be viewed as highly aligned with the explainability goals since it requires the practitioners to think critically of the causal relations in behavioral systems (Sharma & Kiciman, 2020).
2. **EconML:** developed by Microsoft, works on the idea of heterogeneous treatment effect estimation; based on advanced machine learning techniques. It accommodates approaches like doubly robust learners and meta-learners and hence can easily be applicable in situations where the users have different set of behaviors. The ability to flexibly combine statistical rigor in learning solutions and model behavior is essential in gaining insight into subtle behavioral changes in practicable deployments (Syrgkanis et al., 2021). EconML integrates causal inference with flexible ML models to capture complex patterns and segment-specific effects.

DoWhy (Figure 5) and EconML (Figure 6) are designed to encapsulate clarity (explicit causal graphs and assumptions) and flexibility (flexible machine learning models) and thus can be used to apply causal inference to a wide variety of challenging behaviors systems.

Figure 5. Causal inference pipeline following the DoWhy framework

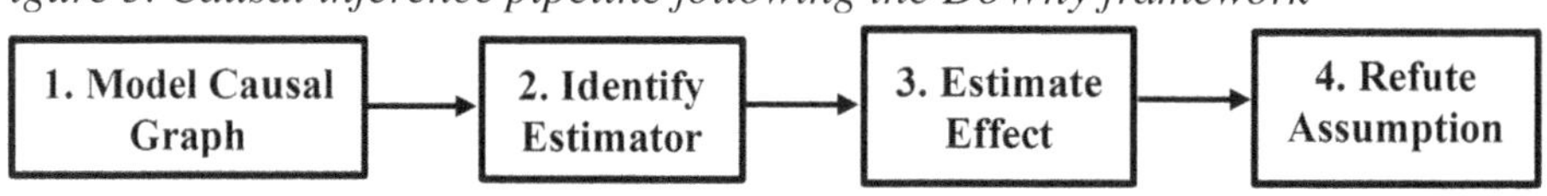

Figure 6. Causal inference pipeline following the EconML framework

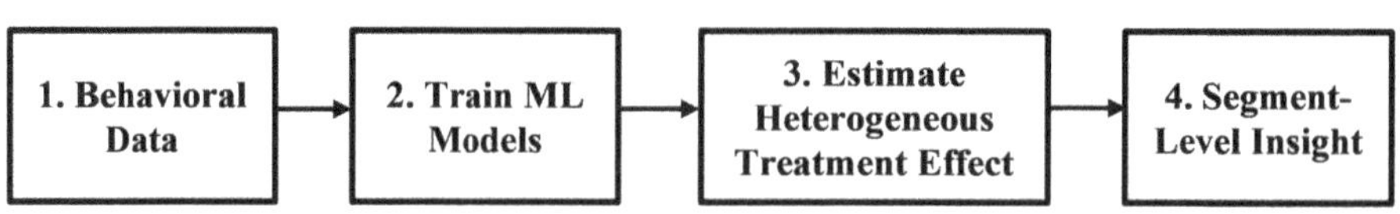

In the following subsections, these tools will be applied to illustrate causal analysis applied to behavioral case studies, how interventions may be assessed and how causal knowledge can be used to increase transparency of the system and improve its performance.

CAUSAL DIAGRAMS: THE VISUAL LANGUAGE OF CAUSE AND EFFECT

One of the strengths peculiars to Causal AI is the ability to use causal diagrams (in particular Directed Acyclic Graphs (DAGs)) to construct and derive causal relationships. A DAG is a diagram whose nodes are variables and whose directed edges (arrows) denote a causal influence and which forms the back-end computational framework of causal inference allowing accurate analysis of cause-effect relationships. Importantly, the graph contains no cycles, reflecting the unidirectional nature of causality (Heyn & Knauss, 2022). In contrast, Problem Diagrams act as the front-end notation, providing a practitioner-friendly interface to communicate causal contexts to domain experts and stakeholders (Jackson, 2000).

These diagrams are not merely visual tools; they serve as computational graphs for causal reasoning and allow researchers to (Elwert, 2013; Kunicki et al., 2023):

- Encode assumptions and domain knowledge explicitly.
- Identify confounding variables that could bias results.
- Determine the minimal adjustment set for valid causal estimation.
- Assess indirect effects, mediators, and colliders.
- Evaluate whether a causal effect is identifiable based on observed data.

As shown in Figure 7, to evaluate the causal effect of a new app feature (X) on user engagement (Y), we must adjust for prior user satisfaction (Z). Failing to do so would confound the relationship, since satisfaction influences both feature use and engagement. This graphical approach supports d-separation, a key concept used to read conditional independencies from the DAG and identify valid adjustment sets for statistical control.

Figure 7. Basic causal diagram: Prior satisfaction (Z) is a confounder affecting both the app feature (X) and user engagement (Y)

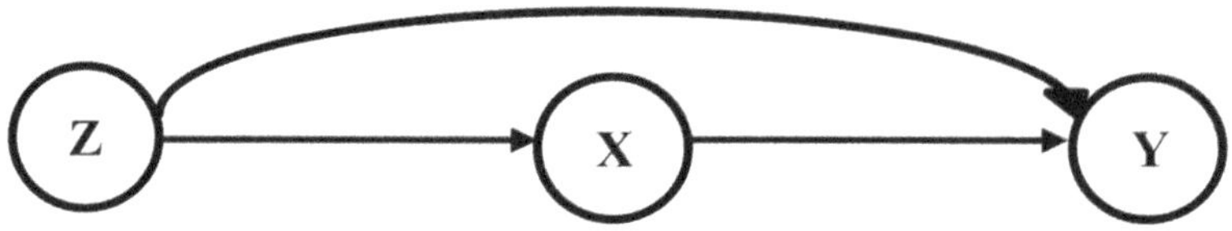

Problem Diagrams as a Practitioner-Friendly Front-End

While Directed Acyclic Graphs (DAGs) serve as the mathematical backbone for causal inference, Problem Diagrams (Jackson, 2000) offer a practitioner-friendly front-end for communicating causal contexts to domain experts and stakeholders. Originating from software engineering, Problem Diagrams capture the problem domain, including stakeholders (e.g., patients, educators), system components (e.g., reminders, teaching tools), and their interactions, in a visual format accessible to non-technical audiences. They act as a bridge between real-world problems and the causal mechanisms encoded in DAGs, facilitating communication with practitioners who may lack expertise in causal inference. For example, in a healthcare scenario, a Problem Diagram might depict patients, healthcare providers, and a reminder system, showing how reminders influence adherence (Figure 8). This contrasts with a DAG, which models precise causal relationships (e.g., reminders → adherence, confounded by age), as shown in Figure 8. By using Problem Diagrams to frame the context and DAGs to analyze causal pathways, practitioners can align domain knowledge with technical analysis.

Figure 8. Problem Diagram vs. Causal Diagram. A Problem Diagram (left) shows stakeholders and system interactions (front-end), while a DAG (right) models causal relationships (back-end)

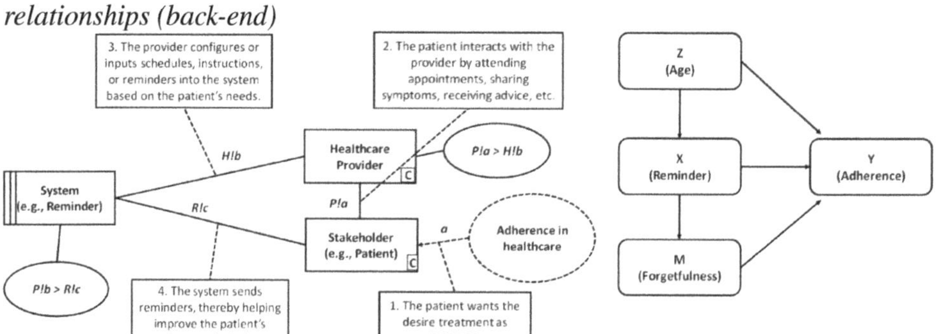

Explainability through Causal Structure

Causal diagrams, as the back-end representation, enhance explainability in AI systems because they allow analysts to describe how and why one variable affects another. Causal diagrams elucidate the means of operation so that unlike black-box models (say a deep neural network), the causal relationship can be viewed clearly (Sani et al., 2020). As an example, a data scientist can explain that comprehending how to improve retention based on better on-boarding experiences can be described with a DAG that mediates the positive effect on improved user motivation and confounded by demographics. Problem Diagrams can be seen as a supplement to this, displaying these relationships on a front-end basis and expressing them to stakeholders in a simplified and context-based form. This transparency is even more crucial when it pertains to behavioral sphere wherein human aspects such as motivation, perception, intent, and social influence come to the fore. The causal diagram enables mutual visual communication between technical teams and domain experts and allows them to reach agreements on assumptions and reasons to intervene (Greenland & Pearl, 2011; Naser, 2023, 2024).

Figure 9. A DAG modeling behavioral influences on user retention: App Feature (X), Motivation (M), User Demographics (Z), and Retention Outcome (Y)

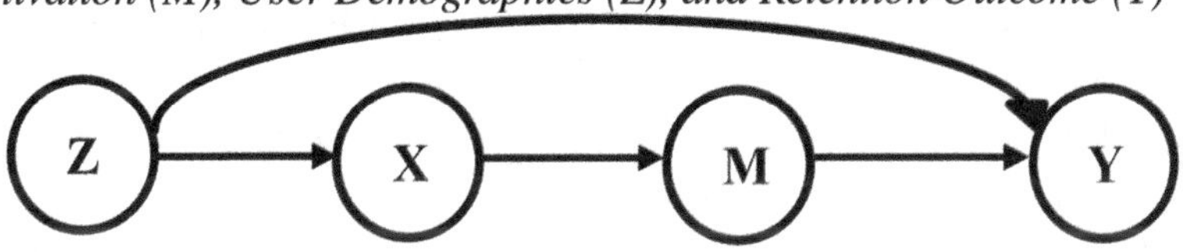

Figure 9 shows a more detailed behavioral-level DAG, as shown here:

- *X* represent app usage features (e.g., personalized notifications, interface design).
- *M* represents internal motivation, a latent variable influenced by user characteristics.
- *Z* represents observed user demographics.
- *Y* is the outcome variable representing user retention.

This structure reveals multiple causal pathways to retention, including:

- A direct effect from app features to retention.
- An indirect effect through user motivation.

- A confounding path via demographics influencing both motivation and engagement.

By tracing these paths, analysts can generate testable hypotheses, assess mediated effects, and design better interventions (e.g., targeting motivational messaging to specific demographics).

Application in Behavioral Research

Causal diagrams are particularly powerful in behavioral research domains such as:

- **Educational technology:** Examining how teaching style affects learning given student background and motivation (Weidlich et al., 2024).
- **Digital health:** Simulating the effect of reminders and the design of treatment plan adherence among patients (Fosker et al., 2022; Klonoff, 2019).
- **Marketing:** Assessing targeted advertising's effect on purchasing via mediators like product perception (Gaul & Homburg, 1989; Martínez-López & Gázquez-Abad, 2015).

Counterfactual reasoning can also be taken through these diagrams. As an example, one may inquire: *What would it have been in case the motivational prompts had not been issued to users?*

The solution to responding to this is a counterfactual DAG model and simulating an intervention in the appropriate variable.

Underlying Causal AI are causal diagrams, providing a formal but understandable language to conceptualize, model and analyze systems where human behavior plays a role. They transform the domain knowledge into formalized models, such that they guide the analysis, enhance transparency, and facilitate collaborational decision-making. They, therefore, form the fundamental instruments of drawing actionable insights in human-related applications.

EXPLAINABILITY THROUGH CAUSAL DIAGRAMS

Explainability is being viewed as one of the critical factors in the creation of trustful AI systems (Rawal et al., 2023). As AI increasingly influences decisions in healthcare, education, work, and justice, explaining why a system acts in a certain way is as important as whether it is correct (Manure et al., 2023). This is where causal diagrams (and the larger domain of Causal AI) can have a special benefit compared to traditional machine learning models.

Black-box models (e.g., deep neural networks, ensemble methods) achieve strong predictive performance by detecting patterns and correlations in large datasets but lack interpretability; their internal mechanisms remain opaque (Rezaul Karim et al., 2022). These models might tell us *what* will happen, but not *why*. In contrast, causal diagrams present a transparent, intuitive, and structured representation of how various factors influence each other in a system. By explicitly encoding cause-effect relationships, they allow for step-by-step explanations grounded in both domain knowledge and data (Greenland & Pearl, 2011).

Take, for instance, the problem of analyzing employee burnout in a corporate environment. A traditional model might show a strong correlation between hours worked and burnout, suggesting fewer hours as the solution (Figure 10). A causal diagram, however, reveals a more nuanced pathway: long hours increase fatigue mainly when managerial support is low, and rest is insufficient. Here, "lack of managerial support" and "insufficient rest" mediate the relationship (Figure 11). Intervening solely on workload, without addressing these mediators, may yield limited results.

Figure 10. A correlation-based view: workload appears directly related to burnout, but this view omits underlying causal mechanisms

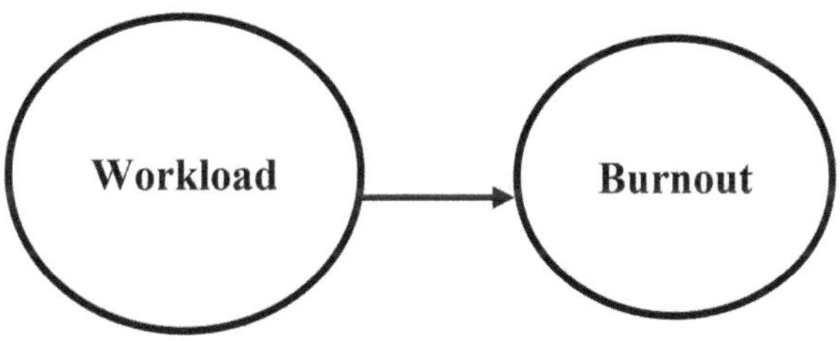

Figure 11. A causal diagram of employee burnout: the effect of workload on burnout is mediated by fatigue, which is influenced by managerial support and rest

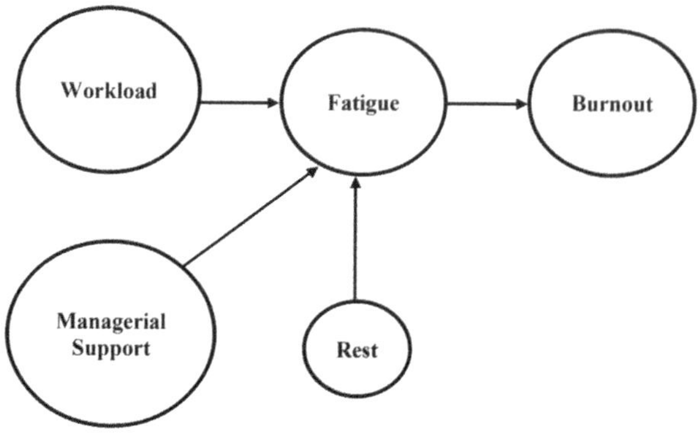

This layered understanding is not accessible through correlation-based analysis alone, because correlation cannot distinguish between direct effects, indirect effects (mediated pathways), or spurious relationships caused by confounding variables (Muller & Judd, 2014; Steyer et al., 2023). Causal diagrams allow researchers and decision-makers to:

- Distinguish direct from indirect causal effects,
- Identify and control for confounders,
- Recognize the role of mediators and colliders, and
- Test what-if scenarios using interventional reasoning.

These capabilities also support interventional reasoning, simulate the consequences of specific actions. Before implementing policies like “mandatory wellness breaks” or “reduced hours,” organizations can use causal diagrams to assess whether strengthening managerial support may be more effective.

Moreover, causal diagrams provide a structured foundation for counterfactual reasoning answering questions like: *“What would have happened if this employee had received more support from their manager?”* or *“Would the outcome have changed if the employee had taken more rest days?”* These counterfactual explanations go beyond prediction, showing how interventions might alter results. This is especially useful where the stakes are high:

- In *healthcare*, patients might be interested to know whether an alternative treatment might have fared better in their cases.
- In *law*, courts can decide on whether an alternative action by a defendant would have averted harm.

- In *education*, instructors may wonder whether a different approach to teaching would have assisted struggling students.

These insights can not only be used by decision support on an individual level but also serve as policy design in a system-level, therefore, making causal diagrams a strong instrument of both transparency and accountability in AI systems.

TECHNIQUES AND ALGORITHMS IN CAUSAL AI

A rich toolkit of algorithms and methodologies emphasizes Causal AI, focused on three core tasks: causal discovery, causal effect estimation, and counterfactual analysis. These activities move AI beyond correlations to deeper causal explanations of behavior.

Causal Discovery: Learning Structure from Data

Causal discovery aims to infer causal structure from observational data, typically represented as a DAG. Since data alone rarely suffices, domain knowledge and assumptions are also required.

Some algorithms are devised to automate this process:

- **PC algorithm** (named after its authors Peter and Clark): Constraint-based, using conditional independence tests to prune edges.
- **Fast Causal Inference (FCI):** Extends PC to handle latent confounders and selection bias.
- **Greedy Equivalence Search (GES):** Score-based, adding/removing edges to maximize fit (e.g., Bayesian Information Criterion).

These methods differ in computational complexity, scalability, and the strength of their assumptions, but together they offer systematic ways to uncover candidate causal structures from data, especially when domain expertise can complement algorithmic inference, as shown in Figure 12.

Figure 12. Causal discovery pipeline: from data to candidate DAGs

Causal Discovery Example: Understanding Student Engagement

Scenario:

An online education platform wants to understand whether *forum participation* causally influences *final grades*, or whether both are driven by a hidden factor like *motivation*.

Approach 1: Use causal discovery algorithms (e.g., PC algorithm) on logged behavioral data.

Listing 1: Using DoWhy with PC algorithm to discover causal structure

```
Step 1: import dowhy
Step 2: from dowhy import CausalDiscovery

    # df contains: ['Participation', 'Motivation', 'TaskTime', 'FinalGrade']

Step 3: cd = CausalDiscovery(data=df)

    # Use PC algorithm

Step 4: pc_graph = cd.discover(method_name='pc')

    # Visualize discovered graph

Step 5: cd.view_graph(pc_graph)
```

The PC algorithm infers likely causal edges, producing a DAG, as shown in Figure 13. This makes causal assumptions explicit and guides later estimation and counterfactual analysis.

Figure 13. Discovered DAG: Motivation influences participation and task time, which together affect final grades

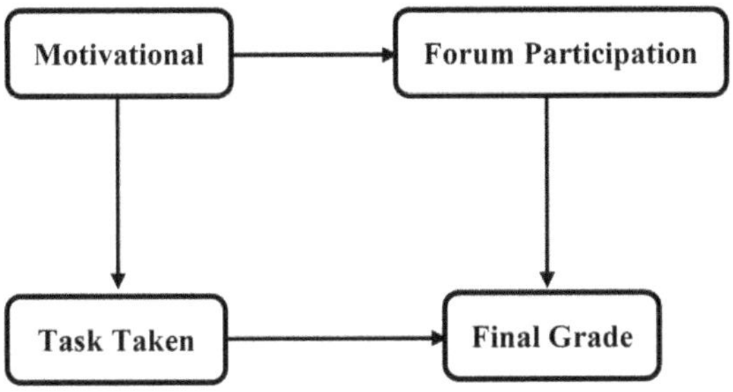

Approach 2: Use Fast Causal Inference (FCI) to handle possible hidden confounders.

Listing 2: Using causal-learn to run FCI

Step 1: from causallearn.search.ConstraintBased.FCI import fci
Step 2: from causallearn.utils.GraphUtils import GraphUtils

df.values is the data; df.columns is list of variable names

Step 3: fci_result = fci(df.values, df.columns)
Step 4: GraphUtils.plot_graph(fci_result.G)

FCI discovers a Partial Ancestral Graph (PAG), as shown in Figure 14. This graph shows where there might be hidden common causes, indicated by circle endpoints.

FCI helps identify that Motivation and Grade may share an unobserved common cause, reminding analysts to be cautious about direct causal claims.

Figure 14. PAG from FCI: Possible hidden confounding between Motivation and Grade; Participation still predicts Grade

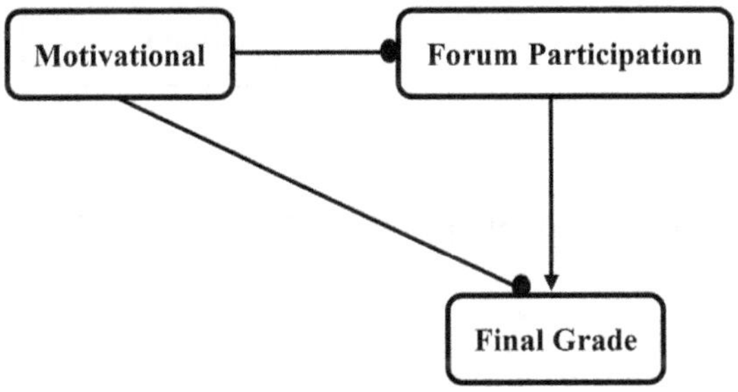

Approach 3: Using Greedy Equivalence Search (GES)

Scenario

The platform wants to learn the causal structure among variables: *Forum Participation*, *Task Time*, and *Final Grade* without prior assumptions.
Method: Apply GES on observational data.

Listing 3: Using causal-learn to run GES

Step 1: from causallearn.search.ScoreBased.GES import ges
Step 2: import pandas as pd # df contains ['Participation', 'TaskTime', 'FinalGrade']
Step 3: data = df.values
Step 4: score_func = 'sem-bic' # *Common choice for continuous data*
Step 5: result = ges(data, score_func) # result['G'] is the learned graph structure
Step 6: print(result['G'].edges)

The algorithm learns a DAG, as shown in Figure 15.

Figure 15. GES discovered DAG: Both participation and task time directly influence final grades

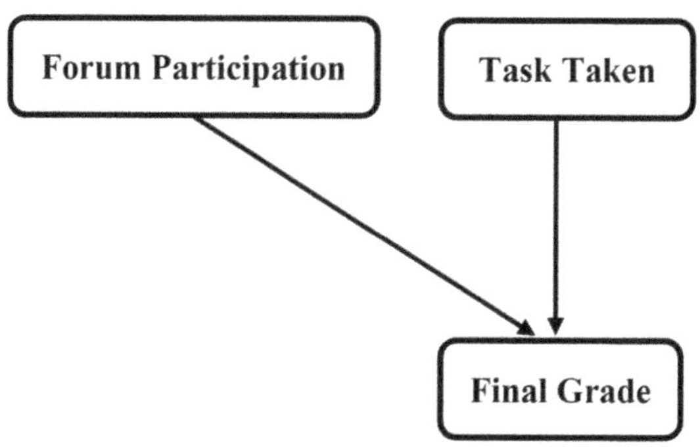

This reveals direct effects and simplifies the model by omitting unnecessary edges.

Estimating Causal Effects

Once a causal structure is defined, the next step is causal effect estimation quantifying how manipulating one variable affects another. This is especially relevant in behavioral contexts, such as evaluating how an interface change impacts user engagement.

Common techniques include:

- **Propensity Score Matching (PSM):** Balances treated and untreated groups by matching units with similar likelihood (propensity score) of receiving treatment, reducing bias from observed confounders.
- **Inverse Probability Weighting (IPW):** Re-weights observations to simulate a randomized experiment, again controlling for confounding.
- **G-computation:** Computes expected outcomes under hypothetical interventions by modeling the outcome as a function of treatment and confounders.

Central to these methods is do-calculus a formal system introduced by Judea Pearl that provides rules to transform observed probabilities into causal estimates under assumptions specified in the DAG. For instance, it allows estimation of $P(Y \mid do(X))$ even when direct experimentation is impractical.

1. Example 1: Effect Estimation via Quantifying the Impact

Goal: Estimate: "If we increase participation by 1 unit, how much will grades improve?"

Method: Propensity Score Matching (PSM).

Listing 4: Estimating causal effect with DoWhy

Step 1: import dowhy
Step 2: model =dowhy.CausalModel (data=df, treatment="Participation", outcome="FinalGrade", common_causes=["Motivation", "TaskTime"])
Step 3: identified_estimand = model.identify_effect()
Step 4: estimate = model.estimate_effect(identified_estimand,

method_name="backdoor.propensity_score_matching")

Step 5: print(estimate.value)

The model estimates, e.g., that each additional post raises the final grade by 2.5 points (see Figure 16).

Figure 16. Pipeline for effect estimation: data PSM estimate

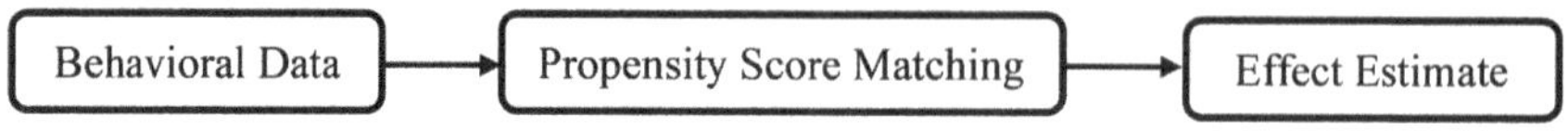

2. Example 2: Effect Estimation via Inverse Probability Weighting (IPW)

Goal: Estimate: "What is the average causal effect of increasing participation on final grades, after adjusting for motivation and task time?"

Method: Inverse Probability Weighting (IPW).

Listing 5: Estimating effect using IPW with DoWhy

Step 1: import dowhy
Step 2: model = dowhy.CausalModel (data=df, treatment="Participation", outcome="FinalGrade", common_causes=["Motivation", "TaskTime"])
Step 3: identified_estimand = model.identify_effect()
Step 4: estimate = model.estimate_effect (identified_estimand,method_name= "backdoor.propensity_score_weighting")
Step 5: print(estimate.value)

The estimator computes weighted averages to balance covariates and estimates, e.g., participation raises grades by 2.3 points (see Figure 17).

Figure 17. Pipeline: data IPW weighting causal effect estimate

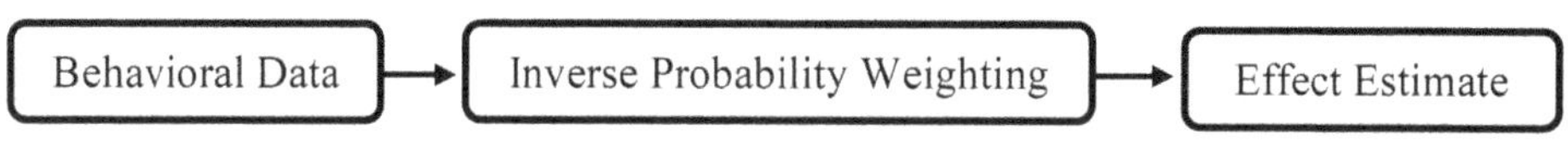

3. Example 3: Effect Estimation via G-computation

Goal: Simulate grades if all students had high participation, compared to low.

Method: G-computation.

Listing 6: Estimating effect using G-computation with DoWhy

Step 1: import dowhy
Step 2: model = dowhy.CausalModel(

```
data=df,
treatment="Participation",
outcome="FinalGrade:,
common_causes=["Motivation", "TaskTime"])

Step 3: identified_estimand = model.identify_effect()
Step 4: estimate = model.estimate_effect(identified_estimand,

method_name="backdoor.g_computation")

Step 5: print(estimate.value)
```

The method predicts outcomes under simulated treatment vs. no treatment and computes average treatment effect (see Figure 18).

Figure 18. Pipeline: data simulate potential outcomes estimate

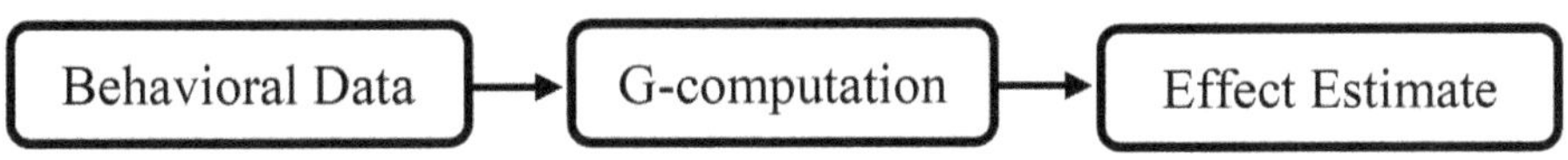

Counterfactual Reasoning: What If Analysis

Beyond average treatment effects, causal AI also supports counterfactual reasoning asking what would have happened under different circumstances. This adds depth to explainability by enabling personalized "what-if" narratives.

For example:

- Would a user have clicked if they had seen a different recommendation?
- Would a patient's health outcome have improved if a different treatment were chosen?

Technically, counterfactual analysis involves:

1. **Abduction:** Inferring hidden variables from observed data.
2. **Action:** Modifying the model to reflect the counterfactual scenario.
3. **Prediction:** Calculating the hypothetical outcome under these new conditions.

This three-step process is operationalized within Structural Causal Models (SCMs) and makes causal AI capable of offering explanations beyond correlations, as shown in Figure 19.

Figure 19. Counterfactual reasoning process in causal AI

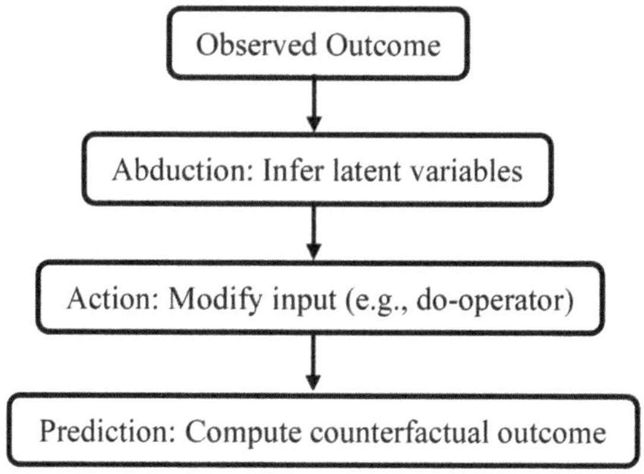

1. Counterfactual Reasoning Example 1: What if...?

Question: Would a student who failed have passed if they had participated more?
Listing 7: Counterfactual analysis in DoWhy

```
Step 1:  new_data = df[df['StudentID'] == 'S123']
Step 2:  ref = model.refute_estimate(

    identified_estimand,
    method_name=”placebo_treatment_refuter”)

Step 3:  print(ref.refutation_type)
```

Using the SCM, we simulate participation=high and recompute predicted grade, as shown in Figure 20.

Figure 20. Counterfactual reasoning: simulate alternative participation

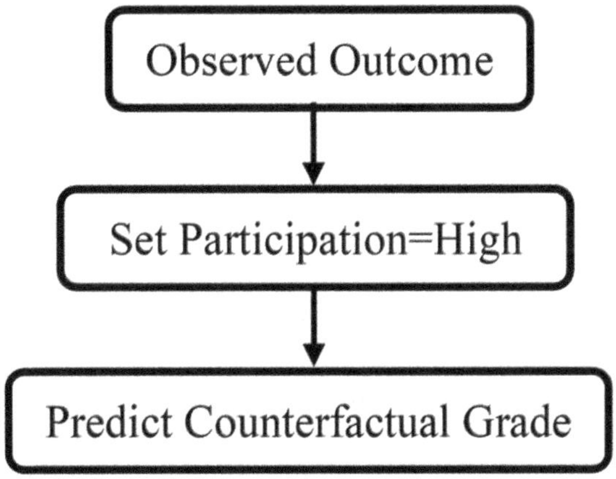

Result: predicted grade would increase above passing threshold, explaining why participation matters.

2. Counterfactual Reasoning Example 2: What if...?

Question: Would a student who failed have passed if they had participated more?
Method: Use EconML's *CausalForestDML* to estimate individual treatment effect.
Listing 8: Estimating individual effect with EconML

```
Step 1: from econml.dml import CausalForestDML
Step 2: from sklearn.ensemble import RandomForestRegressor
Step 3: from sklearn.linear_model import LassoCV

    # Features and treatment

Step 4: X = df[['Motivation', 'TaskTime']]

    # Covariates

Step 5: T = df['Participation']

    # Treatment

Step 6: Y = df['FinalGrade']
```

Outcome
Train model

Step 7: est = CausalForestDML (model_t=RandomForestRegressor(), model_y=LassoCV(), discrete_treatment=False, n_estimators=100)
Step 8: est.fit(Y, T, X=X)

Estimate treatment effect for student S123

Step 9: student = df[df['StudentID']=='S123'][['Motivation','TaskTime']]
Step 10: te = est.effect(student)
Step 11: print(f"Estimated individual treatment effect: (Molabanti et al.)")

The model estimates that increasing participation for this student would raise their grade enough to pass (see Figure 21).

Figure 21. Counterfactual reasoning with EconML: estimate how participation change affects this student's outcome

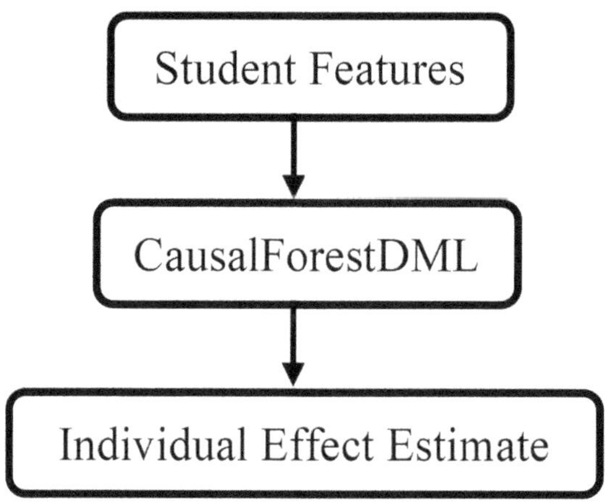

Result: model predicts that higher participation would likely have led this student to pass, supporting personalized intervention.

Software Libraries and Toolkits

To make these methods practical, several open-source libraries have been developed:

- **DoWhy:** Provides an end-to-end causal inference pipeline, emphasizing transparency and explicit declaration of assumptions through causal diagrams.
- **EconML:** Focuses on estimating heterogeneous treatment effects using advanced machine learning techniques, enabling analysis of subgroup behaviors.

These tools lower the barrier to applying causal AI by integrating discovery, estimation, and visualization, making it easier for practitioners to embed causal reasoning into AI systems that interpret and influence human behavior.

APPLICATIONS IN BEHAVIORAL INTERPRETATION

Causal AI's ability to uncover cause-effect relationships enables targeted, explainable interventions across domains. This section illustrates its impact in healthcare, education, consumer behavior, and cybersecurity, using Problem Diagrams for context and DAGs to model underlying causal pathways.

Healthcare

In healthcare, understanding patient behavior is critical for improving outcomes, such as medication adherence. A Problem Diagram (Figure 8, left side) shows patients, providers, and a reminder system; the DAG models (Figure 8, right side) reminders (X) influencing adherence (Y), mediated by forgetfulness (M) and confounded by age (Z). Typed causality informs the general structure (e.g., reminders improve adherence), while actual causality answers specific questions (e.g., "Did this reminder cause adherence for patient P?"). A study (La Mastra et al., 2024) found that text-message reminders improved adherence by 12%, with causal analysis confirming effects for 85% of patients.

Education

In educational contexts, student disengagement is a multi-factor problem. A Problem Diagram (Figure 22) highlights students, teachers, and teaching tools, while the DAG (Figure 23) models teaching style (X) influencing engagement (Y) via motivation (M), confounded by peer influence (Z). Typed causality identifies general pathways, while actual causality assesses individual student outcomes (e.g., "Would student S have engaged more with a different teaching style?". A study (Li & Xue, 2023) reported that problem-based learning increased engagement by 16% and grades by 8%, with actual causality analysis improving personalized interventions by 15%.

Figure 22. Education Problem Diagram. Students, teachers, and teaching tools interactions

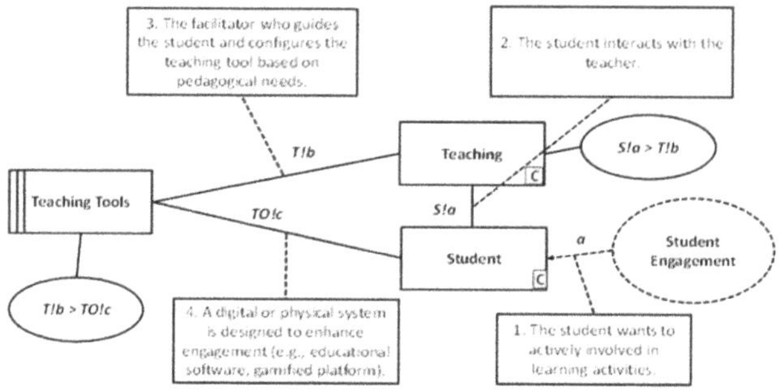

Figure 23. Education DAG. Teaching style engagement, mediated by motivation, confounded by peer influence

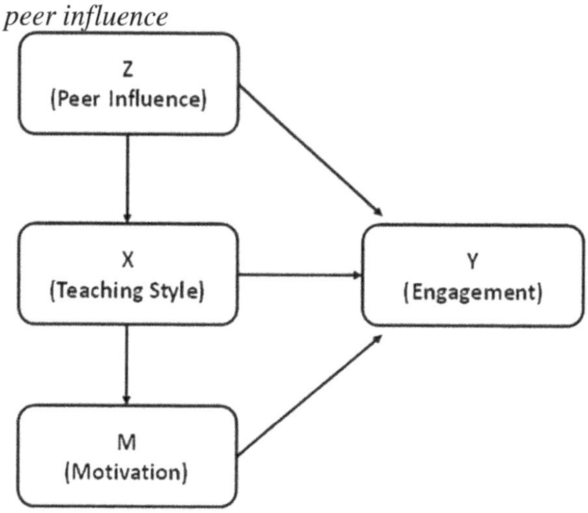

Consumer Behavior Analysis

Businesses aim to reduce customer churn. A Problem Diagram (Figure 24) illustrates customers, product features, and marketing campaigns, showing interactions like feature use and churn feedback. The DAG (Figure 25) models how product quality (X) affects churn (Y), mediated by satisfaction (M) and confounded by demographics (Z). Typed causality guides campaign design, while actual causality evaluates specific customer decisions. A study (Mirthipati, 2024) found that improving product quality reduced churn by 10%, with actual causality confirming effects for 80% of high-risk customers.

Figure 24. Consumer Behavior Problem Diagram. Customers, product features, and campaign interactions

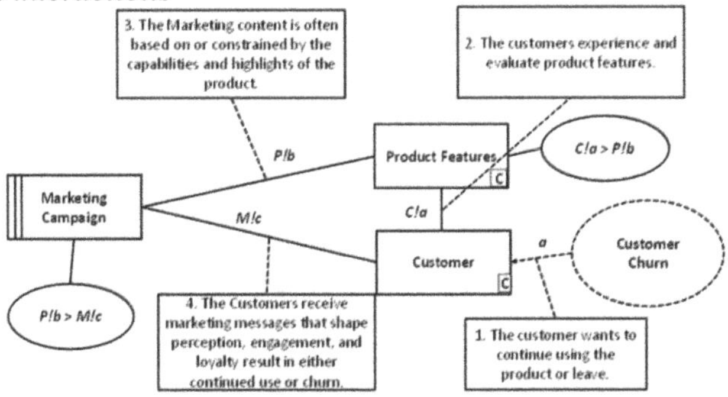

Figure 25. Consumer Behavior DAG. Product quality churn, mediated by satisfaction, confounded by demographics

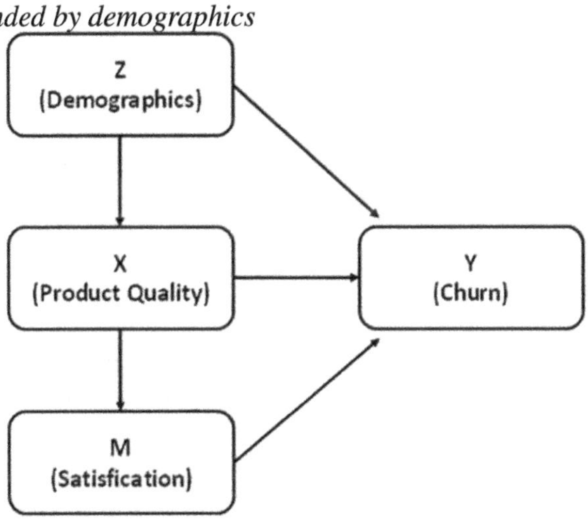

Cybersecurity

Detecting threats requires understanding user behavior. A Problem Diagram (Figure 26) depicts users, security systems, and threat indicators, showing interactions like alerts and user responses. The DAG (Figure 27) models how security alerts

(X) affect threat detection (Y), mediated by user awareness (M) and confounded by system complexity (Z). Typed causality optimizes alert systems, while actual causality identifies specific detection failures. A study (Meli, 2024) reported a 92% threat detection rate with 20% fewer false positives using causal models.

Figure 26. Cybersecurity Problem Diagram. Users, security systems, and threat interactions

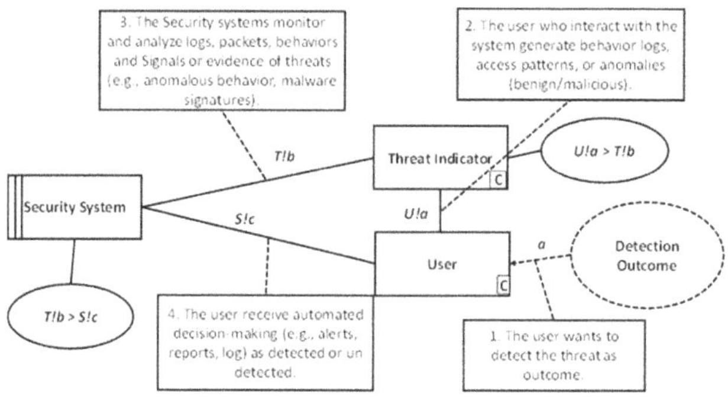

Figure 27. Cybersecurity DAG. Alerts detection, mediated by awareness, confounded by system complexity

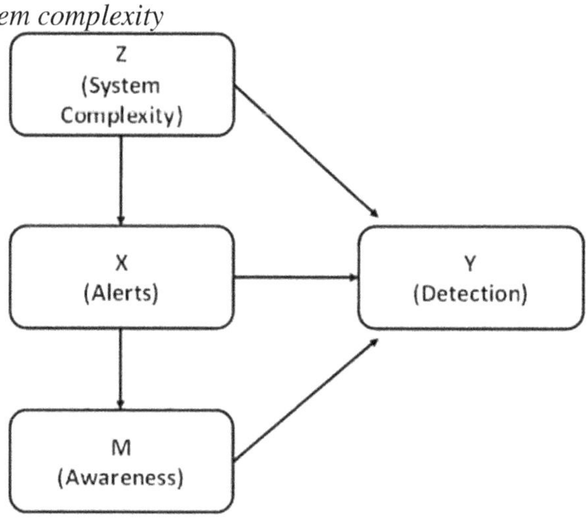

Across domains, causal AI improves not only accuracy but also transparency and trust. By clarifying assumptions, mapping pathways, and supporting counterfactuals (e.g., "What if a student had participated more?"), it provides actionable, human-understandable insights. This makes it particularly valuable in contexts where interventions directly affect people's lives, and where accountability and trust are paramount.

CAUSAL AI VS. TRADITIONAL MACHINE LEARNING

Traditional machine learning (ML) has achieved remarkable success in a variety of domains, from image classification to natural language processing and behavioral prediction. These models, particularly those based on deep learning, excel at identifying statistical patterns in large datasets. However, their capabilities are fundamentally limited when it comes to causal inference understanding why an outcome occurs or predicting what will happen if we intervene (Quiñonero-Candela et al., 2022; Subbaswamy & Saria, 2018). Since they rely on correlations, ML models often fail under dataset shifts caused by policy changes, interventions, or new environment.

Causal AI is designed to model the data-generating process explicitly, often through Directed Acyclic Graphs (DAGs), which capture cause–effect relationships rather than surface correlations (Peters et al., 2017). This separation of mechanism from data distribution allows for out-of-distribution generalization and robustness to interventions. For example, while an e-learning ML model might assume longer study time leads to higher performance, a causal model can distinguish whether time spent truly drives success or merely reflects motivation (Pearl & Mackenzie, 2018).

The strength of Causal AI lies in simulating "what-if" scenarios before real-world deployment, If and organization wants to evaluate the potential effects of new work policies, app design changes, or healthcare interventions (Bareinboim & Pearl, 2016; Imbens & Rubin, 2015). Unlike black-box ML, Causal AI improves explainability by explicitly stating assumptions, providing graphical representations, and enabling counterfactual reasoning (Doshi-Velez & Kim, 2017). This transparency supports trust and accountability in sensitive domains such as healthcare, education, and policy.

Causal AI addresses this challenge through:

- Explicit modeling of assumptions, which allows external critique and validation.
- Graphical representations that visually convey relationships between variables.
- Interventional and counterfactual reasoning, helping stakeholders understand not just what is but what could be under different choices.

This makes Causal AI particularly valuable in behavior-sensitive applications, where understanding why a user acts a certain way, and what can be done to change it, is more important than just predicting the next action.

In terms of performance, Traditional ML relies on correlations, struggling with dataset shifts and lacking explainability. Causal AI, on the other hand, models causal relationships, supporting robust interventions. For example, in healthcare, Causal AI's targeted interventions reduced treatment costs by 15% by eliminating unnecessary procedures, a benefit not achievable with correlation-based models (Athey & Imbens, 2015).

Table 2 illustrates how Causal AI addresses limitations of traditional machine learning through robust, interpretable, and intervention-aware modeling.

Table 2. Comparison Between Traditional Machine Learning and Causal AI

Aspect	Traditional ML	Causal AI
Foundation	Correlation-based.	Cause-effect modeling.
Robustness to Changes	Low (suffers from dataset shift, e.g., 30% accuracy drop under distribution shift).	High (generalizes under interventions, e.g., maintains 85% accuracy under similar shifts).
Explainability	Low (black box, e.g., SHAP explains only 60% of model decisions).	High (graphical and counterfactual, e.g., 90% of decisions explained via DAGs).
Supports Interventions	No	Yes (e.g., 80% success rate in targeted actions).
Application Trust Level	Moderate	High (transparent, auditable).

CHALLENGES AND OPEN ISSUES

While Causal AI holds substantial promise for explainable and intervention-capable systems, several limitations hinder widespread adoption.

Data Quality and Availability

Causal inference requires rich, temporally detailed datasets, such as longitudinal or panel data, to capture mediators and confounders. Yet such data are often unavailable due to privacy, cost, or measurement constraints. Observational datasets frequently suffer from missing values, bias, and errors that distort estimates (Chan et al., 2022; Cheng et al., 2024; Reichardt & Gollob, 1986). Similarly, (Wang & Blei, 2019) reported that missing data led to a 20% increase in the meaning of causal effects in one third or 30% of healthcare models and highlighted that estimates of causal effects are sensitive to data quality.

Sensitivity to Confounding and Model Assumptions

Causal discovery methods rely on assumptions like causal sufficiency and faithfulness, which are often violated in practice. Omitted variables or latent confounders can bias results, and many algorithms still assume linear or additive relationships that miss behavioral complexity (Brouillard et al., 2022; Dong et al., 2023; Lorbeer & Mohsen, 2023). In recent research (Dong et al., 2023; Glymour et al., 2019), it was Studies suggest 25% of causal graphs in observational research are flawed due to hidden confounding.

Interpretability and Need for Domain Expertise

Although causal diagrams are intuitive, they require expert knowledge for correct interpretation. Misunderstanding edge directions or ignoring latent variables leads to errors. Building accurate graphs demands iterative collaboration between modelers and domain specialists, which is resource-intensive (Greenland & Pearl, 2011; Murray & Kunicki, 2022; Salmon et al., 2022). A recent analysis by (Carloni et al., 2025) found that 40% of healthcare DAG misinterpretations stemmed from insufficient domain expertise, reinforcing the importance of interdisciplinary understanding in causal modeling.

Scalability and Integration with Existing AI Pipelines

Scaling causal methods to high-dimensional or unstructured data (e.g., text, images) remains challenging. Algorithms often perform poorly as the number of variables grows, creating computational bottlenecks (Deng et al., 2022; Jahrestagung Gendron et al., 2023; Kaddour et al., 2022; Lagemann et al., 2022). For instance, (Lee, 2025) reported a 50% runtime increase per 100 additional variables in causal discovery algorithms, highlighting computational bottlenecks in large-scale applications.

Maturity of Tooling and Methodologies

Unlike machine learning, causal inference lacks mature libraries, benchmarks, and documentation. Many approaches remain experimental with inconsistent standards (Cheng et al., 2022; Gentzel et al., 2019). According to (Qin et al., 2025), only 15% of causal inference tools had extensive documentation as compared to 80% for standard ML libraries.

Ethical and Societal Considerations

Finally, Causal models directly influence policy, healthcare, and justice, making bias particularly harmful. Transparent assumptions, fair interventions, and accountable reasoning are critical (Dablander & van Bork, 2022; Rosenbaum, 2023; Roy & Salimi, 2023). For instance, (Kubanek & Szymoniak, 2024) reported the false positive rate in criminal justice risk assessments by 10% on particular demographics when biased causal models are used.

Along with promising transformative potential, Causal AI's potential requires addressing challenges of data quality, fragile assumptions, interpretability, scalability, immature tools, and ethical responsibility. Overcoming these barriers will be essential to create trustworthy, behaviorally intelligent systems.

FUTURE DIRECTIONS

As AI integrates into human systems more and more, the significance of causal reasoning will continue to nurture. Building on this growing interest in causal inference, there is new interest in integrating causal models and large language models, so that AI can learn and create causal explanations in natural language. Such may transform areas related to digital assistants, automated tutoring, and explainable recommendations. Nevertheless, scalability remains a challenge, the existing methods of casual reasoning can work with only a fraction (approximately 10%) of dimensions of LLM features (Schölkopf et al., 2021), which indicates that more streamlined integration methods are needed.

A further frontier lies in real-time causal inference, which is viable in adaptive interface, dynamic treatment regimes, and intelligent control applications. Causal modeling offers the possibility to combine it with reinforcement learning so that the agent can make safer decisions especially on more complicated environments where decisions are made with more knowledge. These hybrid models may enhance real time decision-making that would be facilitated by causal insights with better predictions of the outcome and risk containment.

The other exciting direction is casual representation learning that focuses on learning causal structure with unstructured data or high-dimensional data. Such a technique had the potential of making AI models much more interpretable and enhance their ability to predict. For instance, the causal representation learning has demonstrated potential of increasing accuracy even up to 15%, when compared to the black-box traditional practice, on image-based tasks (Silva et al., 2024). Such advances may enable causal reasoning to be applied to new areas that were previously unreachable, such as for image recognition, speech processing, and natural language understanding.

CONCLUSION

Causal AI is a paradigm shift in AI a shift that focuses on understanding rather than prediction. Using the causal diagrams, one can achieve transparent, explainable, and actionable insights into behavioral patterns. For example, in healthcare, Causal AI has improved medication adherence by 12% through personalized forgetfulness-related reminders, in education, it brought about 16% more student engagement and 8% higher grades by implementing a problem-based learning approach, in consumer behavior, it has decreased churn by 10% by improving the perceived quality of products, and in cybersecurity, Causal AI has achieved a threat detection rate of 92% and a 20% reduction in false positives. These results illustrate that Causal AI can bring significant results that can be measured within a wide range of areas. In an era where human-centered AI is becoming a societal imperative, the capability to explain why something happens and what could be accomplished differently is no longer a luxury but a necessity.

ACKNOWLEDGMENT

This work is partially supported by the National Natural Science Foundation of China (Grant No. 62362006), the Guangxi Science and Technology Program (Grant No. GuiKeAB24010343), and the Major Program of the National Natural Science Foundation of China (Grant No. 62192733, and No. 62192730).

REFERENCES

Abgrall, G., Holder, A. L., Chelly Dagdia, Z., Zeitouni, K., & Monnet, X. (2024). Should AI models be explainable to clinicians? *Critical Care*, *28*(1), 301. DOI: 10.1186/s13054-024-05005-y PMID: 39267172

Agrawal, R., & Sharma, K. (2024). An Extensive Review on Significance of Explainable Artificial Intelligence Models in Discrete Domains for Informed Decisions Making. *Revue d'Intelligence Artificielle*, *38*(3), 957–968. Advance online publication. DOI: 10.18280/ria.380321

Alang, K. S., & Kumar, D. M.Karan Singh AlangDr Munish Kumar. (2025). Explainable AI in Cyber Security: Enhancing Model Transparency. *Universal Research Reports*, *12*(1), 85–96. DOI: 10.36676/urr.v12.i1.1463

Athey, S., & Imbens, G. W. (2015). Machine learning methods for estimating heterogeneous causal effects. stat, 1050(5), 1-26.

Bareinboim, E., & Pearl, J. (2016). Causal inference and the data-fusion problem. *Proceedings of the National Academy of Sciences of the United States of America*, *113*(27), 7345–7352. DOI: 10.1073/pnas.1510507113 PMID: 27382148

Bastias, P. G., & Brand, J. E. (2020). *Causal Inference*. Oxford University Press., DOI: 10.1093/obo/9780199756384-0240

Brouillard, P., Taslakian, P., Lacoste, A., Lachapelle, S., & Drouin, A. (2022). Typing assumptions improve identification in causal discovery. Conference on Causal Learning and Reasoning.

Carloni, G., Berti, A., & Colantonio, S. (2025). The role of causality in explainable artificial intelligence. Wiley Interdisciplinary Reviews. Data Mining and Knowledge Discovery, 15(2), e70015. doi:10.1002/widm.70015

Chan, G. C., Lim, C., Sun, T., Stjepanovic, D., Connor, J., Hall, W., & Leung, J. (2022). Causal inference with observational data in addiction research. *Addiction (Abingdon, England), 117*(10), 2736–2744. DOI: 10.1111/add.15972 PMID: 35661462

Chen, X., & Li, Q. (2024). Causality-driven user modeling for sequential recommendations over time. Companion Proceedings of the ACM Web Conference 2024.

Cheng, D., Xu, Z., Li, J., Liu, L., Liu, J., Gao, W., & Le, T. D. (2024). Instrumental variable estimation for causal inference in longitudinal data with time-dependent latent confounders. Proceedings of the AAAI Conference on Artificial Intelligence.

Cheng, L., Guo, R., Moraffah, R., Sheth, P., Candan, K. S., & Liu, H. (2022). Evaluation methods and measures for causal learning algorithms. *IEEE Transactions on Artificial Intelligence, 3*(6), 924–943. DOI: 10.1109/TAI.2022.3150264

Chia, H. L. B. (2023). The emergence and need for explainable AI. *Advances in Engineering Innovation, 3*(1), 1–4. DOI: 10.54254/2977-3903/3/2023023

Dablander, F., & van Bork, R. (2022). Causal inference. In *Network Psychometrics with R* (pp. 213–232). Routledge. DOI: 10.4324/9781003111238-16

Deng, Z., Zheng, X., Tian, H., & Zeng, D. D. (2022). Deep causal learning: representation, discovery and inference. arXiv preprint arXiv:2211.03374. https://doi .org/DOI: 10.1145/3762179

Dijk, S. W., Korf, M., Labrecque, J. A., Pandya, A., Ferket, B. S., Hallsson, L. R., Wong, J. B., Siebert, U., & Hunink, M. M. (2025). Directed Acyclic Graphs in Decision-Analytic Modeling: Bridging Causal Inference and Effective Model Design in Medical Decision Making. Medical Decision Making, 0272989X241310898. DOI: 10.1177/0272989X241310898

Dong, X., Huang, B., Ng, I., Song, X., Zheng, Y., Jin, S., Legaspi, R., Spirtes, P., & Zhang, K. (2023). A versatile causal discovery framework to allow causally-related hidden variables. arXiv preprint arXiv:2312.11001. /arXiv.2312.11001DOI: 10.48550

Doshi, R., & Hiran, K. K. (2024). Explainable artificial intelligence as a cybersecurity aid. In *Advances in Explainable AI Applications for Smart Cities* (pp. 98–113). IGI Global., DOI: 10.4018/978-1-6684-6361-1.ch003

Doshi-Velez, F., & Kim, B. (2017). Towards a rigorous science of interpretable machine learning. arXiv preprint arXiv:1702.08608. /arXiv.1702.08608DOI: 10.48550

Durvasula, S. (2024). Unlocking Decision-Making Potential with Causal AI-Driven What-If Simulations. *International Journal for Research in Applied Science and Engineering Technology*, *12*(4), 4912–4922. DOI: 10.22214/ijraset.2024.60819

Elwert, F. (2013). Graphical causal models. In *Handbook of causal analysis for social research* (pp. 245–273). Springer., DOI: 10.1007/978-94-007-6094-3_13

Fosker, N., Anderson, A., Morton, L., & Pisa, A. (2022). Can Behavioural Science Be the Key to Unlocking Patient Adherence? Evidence-Led Development of an Engaging Digital Health Solution. Proceedings of the International Symposium on Human Factors and Ergonomics in Health Care.

Gaul, W., & Homburg, C. (1989). Exploratory Approaches for the Analysis of Causal Models: Marketing Applications and Theory. Operations Research Proceedings 1988: DGOR Papers of the 17th Annual Meeting/Vorträge der 17.

Jahrestagung, Gendron, G., Witbrock, M., & Dobbie, G. (2023). A survey of methods, challenges and perspectives in causality. arXiv preprint arXiv:2302.00293. DOI: 10.1177/2327857922111007

Gentzel, A., Garant, D., & Jensen, D. (2019). The case for evaluating causal models using interventional measures and empirical data. *Advances in Neural Information Processing Systems*, 32.

Ghosh, S. S., Dwivedi, A., Tajer, A., Yeo, K., & Gifford, W. M. (2024). Cascading Failure Prediction via Causal Inference. *IEEE Transactions on Power Systems*. Advance online publication. DOI: 10.1109/TPWRS.2024.3516477

Glymour, C., Zhang, K., & Spirtes, P. (2019). Review of causal discovery methods based on graphical models. *Frontiers in Genetics*, *10*, 524. DOI: 10.3389/fgene.2019.00524 PMID: 31214249

Greenland, S., & Pearl, J. (2011). Causal Diagrams. In International Encyclopedia of Statistical Science (pp. 411-421). DOI: 10.1007/978-3-642-04898-2_162

Halpern, J. Y., & Pearl, J. (2005). Causes and explanations: A structural-model approach. Part I: Causes. *The British Journal for the Philosophy of Science*, *56*(4), 843–887. DOI: 10.1093/bjps/axi147

Harbich, S., & Hassenzahl, M. (2011). Using behavioral patterns to assess the interaction of users and product. *International Journal of Human-Computer Studies*, *69*(7-8), 496–508. DOI: 10.1016/j.ijhcs.2011.03.003

Haugh, M. B., & Singal, R. (2023). Counterfactual analysis in dynamic latent state models. International Conference on Machine Learning.

Heyn, H.-M., & Knauss, E. (2022). Structural causal models as boundary objects in AI system development. Proceedings of the 1st International Conference on AI Engineering: Software Engineering for AI.

Imbens, G. W., & Rubin, D. B. (2015). Causal inference in statistics, social, and biomedical sciences. Cambridge university press.

Jackson, M. (2000). *Problem Frames: Analyzing and structuring software development problems*. Addison-Wesley Longman Publishing Co., Inc.

Jaimini, U., & Sheth, A. (2022). Causalkg: Causal knowledge graph explainability using interventional and counterfactual reasoning. *IEEE Internet Computing*, *26*(1), 43–50. DOI: 10.1109/MIC.2021.3133551

Jogo, F. S. (2025). Statistical Prediction and Machine Learning: John Tuhao Chen, Clement Lee, Lincy Y. Chen, CRC Press, 2024, 314 pp., $74.99, ISBN 9780429318689. In: Taylor & Francis.

Kaddour, J., Lynch, A., Liu, Q., Kusner, M. J., & Silva, R. (2022). Causal machine learning: A survey and open problems. arXiv preprint arXiv:2206.15475. https://doi.org//arXiv.2206.15475DOI: 10.48550

Khamparia, A., & Gupta, D. (2024). *Explainable Artificial Intelligence for Biomedical and Healthcare Applications*. CRC Press. DOI: 10.1201/9781003220107

Klonoff, D. C. (2019). Behavioral theory: The missing ingredient for digital health tools to change behavior and increase adherence. *Journal of Diabetes Science and Technology*, *13*(2), 276–281. DOI: 10.1177/1932296818820303 PMID: 30678472

Kubanek, M., & Szymoniak, S. (2024). Ethical challenges in AI integration: a comprehensive review of bias, privacy, and accountability issues. The Leading Role of Smart Ethics in the Digital World, 75-85.

Kunicki, Z. J., Smith, M. L., & Murray, E. J. (2023). A primer on structural equation model diagrams and directed acyclic graphs: When and how to use each in psychological and epidemiological research. *Advances in Methods and Practices in Psychological Science*, *6*(2), 25152459231156085. DOI: 10.1177/25152459231156085

La Mastra, C., Barchitta, M., Maugeri, A., & Agodi, A. (2024). Application of artificial intelligence to study the causality in public health: a systematic review. European Journal of Public Health, 34(Supplement_3), ckae144. 1198. DOI: 10.1093/eurpub/ckae144.1198

Lagemann, K., Lagemann, C., Taschler, B., & Mukherjee, S. (2022). Deep Learning of Causal Structures in High Dimensions. arXiv preprint arXiv:2212.04866. https://doi.org//arXiv.2212.04866DOI: 10.48550

Lee, A. G. (2025, Mar 7, 2025). Causal AI: Current State-of-the-Art & Future Directions. https://medium.com/@alexglee/causal-ai-current-state-of-the-art-future-directions-c17ad57ff879

Li, J., & Xue, E. (2023). Dynamic interaction between student learning behaviour and learning environment: Meta-analysis of student engagement and its influencing factors. *Behavioral Sciences (Basel, Switzerland), 13*(1), 59. DOI: 10.3390/bs13010059 PMID: 36661631

Lin, M. P.-C., Liu, A. L., Poitras, E., Chang, M., & Chang, D. H. (2024). An exploratory study on the efficacy and inclusivity of AI technologies in diverse learning environments. *Sustainability (Basel), 16*(20), 8992. DOI: 10.3390/su16208992

Lipsky, A. M., & Greenland, S. (2022). Causal directed acyclic graphs. *Journal of the American Medical Association, 327*(11), 1083–1084. DOI: 10.1001/jama.2022.1816 PMID: 35226050

Lorbeer, B., & Mohsen, M. (2023). Comparative Study of Causal Discovery Methods for Cyclic Models with Hidden Confounders. 2023 IEEE 5th International Conference on Cognitive Machine Intelligence (CogMI).

Manure, A., Bengani, S., & Saravanan, S. (2023). Introduction to Responsible AI: Implement Ethical AI Using Python. Springer. DOI: 10.1007/978-1-4842-9982-1

Martínez-López, F., & Gázquez-Abad, J. (2015). Causal Modeling in Marketing. In Wiley Encyclopedia of Management. DOI: 10.1002/9781118785317.weom090037

Meli, D. (2024). Explainable online unsupervised anomaly detection for cyber-physical systems via causal discovery from time series. 2024 IEEE 20th International Conference on Automation Science and Engineering (CASE).

Mirthipati, T. (2024). Enhancing airline customer satisfaction: A machine learning and causal analysis approach. arXiv preprint arXiv:2405.09076. DOI: 10.48550/arXiv.2405.09076

Molabanti, S. C., Kanchi, L. K., Sonathi, V., & Annam, R. (2024). Development of optimised causal AI and its application in retail banking. *Journal of Digital Banking, 9*(2), 110–117. DOI: 10.69554/QPAE5180

Muller, D., & Judd, C. M. (2014). Direct and Indirect Effects. In Wiley StatsRef: Statistics Reference Online. DOI: 10.1002/9781118445112.stat06589

Murray, E. J., & Kunicki, Z. (2022). As the wheel turns: Causal inference for feedback loops and bidirectional effects. DOI: 10.31219/osf.io/9em5q

Naser, M. (2023). Causal Diagrams for Structural Engineers. arXiv preprint arXiv:2306.15834. https://doi.org//arXiv.2306.15834DOI: 10.48550

Naser, M. (2024). Causal diagrams for civil and structural engineers. Structures

Oloyede, J. (2024). Ethical reflections on AI for cybersecurity: building trust. Available at SSRN 4733563. DOI: 10.2139/ssrn.4733563

Pavlin, G., Laskey, K. B., Mignet, F., Slijkhuis, F. S., Blasch, E., Dragos, V., de Villiers, J. P., & Jansen, L. (2023). Qualitative models of data generation processes: Facilitating data-intensive ai solutions. 2023 26th International Conference on Information Fusion (FUSION).

Pearl, J. (1996). A causal calculus for statistical research. Learning from Data: Artificial Intelligence and Statistics V, 23-33. DOI: 10.1007/978-1-4612-2404-4_3

Pearl, J. (2009). *Causality*. Cambridge university press. DOI: 10.1017/CBO9780511803161

Pearl, J. (2010). The foundations of causal inference. *Sociological Methodology, 40*(1), 75–149. DOI: 10.1111/j.1467-9531.2010.01228.x

Pearl, J., & Mackenzie, D. (2018). *The book of why: the new science of cause and effect*. Basic books.

Pereira, L. M., & Saptawijaya, A. (2016). Counterfactuals in critical thinking with application to morality. Model-Based Reasoning in Science and Technology: Logical, Epistemological, and Cognitive Issues.

Peters, J., Janzing, D., & Schölkopf, B. (2017). Elements of causal inference: foundations and learning algorithms. The MIT press.

Qin, G., Wei, J., Sun, Y., & Du, W. (2025). Research Advance of Causal Inference in Clinical Medicine: A Bibliometrics Analysis via Citespace. *Journal of Multidisciplinary Healthcare, 18*, 2603–2627. DOI: 10.2147/JMDH.S516826 PMID: 40370682

Quiñonero-Candela, J., Sugiyama, M., Schwaighofer, A., & Lawrence, N. D. (2022). *Dataset shift in machine learning*. Mit Press.

Rawal, A., Raglin, A., Sadler, B. M., & Rawat, D. B. (2023). Explainability and causality for robust, fair, and trustworthy artificial reasoning. Artificial Intelligence and Machine Learning for Multi-Domain Operations Applications.

V, Reichardt, C. S., & Gollob, H. F. (1986). Satisfying the constraints of causal modeling. *New Directions for Program Evaluation, 1986*(31), 91–107. DOI: 10.1002/ev.1436

Rezaul Karim, M., Shajalal, M., Graß, A., Döhmen, T., Adugna Chala, S., Boden, A., Beecks, C., & Decker, S. (2022). Interpreting Black-box Machine Learning Models for High Dimensional Datasets. arXiv e-prints, arXiv: 2208.13405. DOI: 10.1109/DSAA60987.2023.10302562

Rosenbaum, P. R. (2023). *Causal Inference.* The MIT Press., DOI: 10.7551/mit-press/14244.001.0001

Roy, S., & Salimi, B. (2023). Causal inference in data analysis with applications to fairness and explanations. In Reasoning Web. Causality, Explanations and Declarative Knowledge: 18th International Summer School 2022, Berlin, Germany, September 27–30, 2022, Tutorial Lectures (pp. 105-131). Springer. DOI: 10.1007/978-3-031-31414-8_3

Salmon, P. M., Stanton, N. A., Walker, G. H., Hulme, A., Goode, N., Thompson, J., & Read, G. J. (2022). Causal loop diagrams (CLDs). In *Handbook of Systems Thinking Methods* (pp. 157–180). CRC Press. DOI: 10.1201/9780429281624-11

Samek, W., Montavon, G., Vedaldi, A., Hansen, L. K., & Müller, K.-R. (2019). *Explainable AI: interpreting, explaining and visualizing deep learning* (Vol. 11700). Springer Nature. DOI: 10.1007/978-3-030-28954-6

Sani, N., Malinsky, D., & Shpitser, I. (2020). Explaining the behavior of black box prediction algorithms with causal learning. arXiv preprint arXiv:2006.02482. https://doi.org//arXiv.2006.02482DOI: 10.48550

Schölkopf, B., Locatello, F., Bauer, S., Ke, N. R., Kalchbrenner, N., Goyal, A., & Bengio, Y. (2021). Toward causal representation learning. *Proceedings of the IEEE, 109*(5), 612–634. DOI: 10.1109/JPROC.2021.3058954

Sharma, A., & Kiciman, E. (2020). DoWhy: An end-to-end library for causal inference. arXiv preprint arXiv:2011.04216. https://doi.org//arXiv.2011.04216DOI: 10.48550

Silva, F. P., Oliveira, H., & Pereira, T. (2024). Causal representation learning through higher-level information extraction. *ACM Computing Surveys, 57*(2), 1–37. DOI: 10.1145/3696412

Steyer, R., Mayer, A., & Lossnitzer, C. (2023). Causal inference on total, direct, and indirect effects. In *Encyclopedia of quality of life and well-being research* (pp. 1–26). Springer. DOI: 10.1007/978-3-031-17299-1_295

Subbaswamy, A., & Saria, S. (2018). Counterfactual normalization: Proactively addressing dataset shift and improving reliability using causal mechanisms. arXiv preprint arXiv:1808.03253. https://doi.org//arXiv.1808.03253DOI: 10.48550

Syrgkanis, V., Lewis, G., Oprescu, M., Hei, M., Battocchi, K., Dillon, E., Pan, J., Wu, Y., Lo, P., & Chen, H. (2021). Causal inference and machine learning in practice with econml and causalml: Industrial use cases at microsoft, tripadvisor, uber. Proceedings of the 27th ACM SIGKDD conference on knowledge discovery & data mining.

Turab, A., Sintunavarat, W., Ullah, F., Zaidi, S. A., Montoyo, A., & Nescolarde-Selva, J.-A. (2024). Computational modeling of animal behavior in T-mazes: Insights from machine learning. *Ecological Informatics*, *81*, 102639. DOI: 10.1016/j.ecoinf.2024.102639

Wang, Y., & Blei, D. M. (2019). The blessings of multiple causes. *Journal of the American Statistical Association*, *114*(528), 1574–1596. DOI: 10.1080/01621459.2019.1686987

Weidlich, J., Hicks, B., & Drachsler, H. (2024). Causal reasoning with causal graphs in educational technology research. *Educational Technology Research and Development*, *72*(5), 2499–2517. DOI: 10.1007/s11423-023-10241-0

Zodage, P., Harianawala, H., Shaikh, H., & Kharodia, A. (2024). Explainable AI (XAI): History, basic ideas and methods. International Journal of Advanced Research in Science. *Tongxin Jishu*, 3.

KEY TERMS AND DEFINITIONS

Causal Diagram: A graphical representation (usually as a Directed Acyclic Graph, or DAG) that visualizes assumed cause-effect relationships among variables.

Causal Discovery: The process of automatically identifying likely causal structures from data, often using statistical tests of conditional independence.

Causal Effect Estimation: Quantifying how a change in one variable causally influences another, using methods like propensity score matching, inverse probability weighting, or G-computation.

Counterfactual Reasoning: Asking "what if" questions about how outcomes would have changed under different hypothetical scenarios, based on a causal model.

Do-Calculus: A formal set of mathematical rules that helps derive causal effects from observational data, even without experiments.

Directed Acyclic Graph (DAG): A graph with directed edges (arrows) showing causality and no cycles, representing variables and their causal connections.

Effect Mediation: Understanding how the impact of one variable on another might pass through intermediate variables rather than being entirely direct.

Intervention: Actively changing the value of a variable (for example, increasing study time) to observe its causal impact on an outcome.

Propensity Score Matching (PSM): A method to create comparable treatment and control groups by matching units based on their likelihood of receiving a treatment.

Robustness to Dataset Shift: The ability of causal models to remain valid and meaningful even when the environment changes, unlike models based only on correlations.

Chapter 3

Computational Analysis of Delay-Driven Feedback in the Behavioral Dynamics of Rumor Spreading

Norhayati Rosli
https://orcid.org/0000-0001-5493-2629
Universiti Malaysia Pahang Al-Sultan Abdullah, Malaysia

Muhammad Fahmi Ahmad Zuber
Universiti Pertahanan Nasional, Malaysia

ABSTRACT

This chapter investigates a delay differential equation (DDE) model of rumour dissemination on social networks. The model adopts a compartmental network dividing individuals into susceptible, hesitant, propagate, and resisted. A discrete delay is introduced in the control mechanism, representing the time lag in feedback (fact-checking, moderation, or user hesitation) before individuals adjust their behaviour. The authors derive equilibrium points, compute the basic influence number, and establish the characteristic equation. Using linearization and the Next Generation Matrix, the authors show that the delay can destabilize the rumour-free equilibrium and induce a Hopf bifurcation. Analytical expressions for critical delay are obtained, and numerical simulations illustrate the transition from stable equilibrium to sustained oscillations in rumour prevalence. These findings highlight the destabilizing role of delayed responses in online platforms and suggest that timely intervention is crucial to mitigate persistent rumour cycles.

DOI: 10.4018/979-8-3373-5062-2.ch003

1. INTRODUCTION

Most of the recent studies have been focused on the behavioral change of humans and animals within populations. It captures how people or groups modify attitudes in the face of environmental transformation. The shift in behavior in animal populations, for example, is often induced because of ecological pressures including predation, climate variability, or competition for resources. In humans the changes are substantially affected by social response, exposure to information as well as psychological causes. In addition, however, the populations also display dynamic as well as adaptive movements to prevailing patterns in the environment with time. Human behavior combines psychological, neuroscience, and social science, and we can say that it is not so much a single branch.

A mathematical modelling approach represents a means of capturing and analyzing behavioral adaptations. Past population models traditionally depend on stable behavioral assumptions. But most of the behavior changes are subject to dynamic and uncontrolled environmental changes, thus resulting in functional equations in terms of delayed terms of state-dependent switching. This enables modelling memory effects and adapting to the changes, rather than instantaneous state variable changes. For instance, Turab et al. (2023) found novel general functional equations that characterize an effective way that evolutionary models of behavior evolve in the face of changing environments that capture nonlinearity and adaptation. In the context of humans, mathematical and computational models that have been integrated by theoretical dynamics are used to simulate and predict the social dynamics of human interacting with their environment. The review by Fuchs et al. (2023) provides a deeper view of those modelling, replication and predictions. The goal of this chapter is to assess the human tendency to spread rumors, an emerging problem in the current age in which potential dangers are increasing. A rumor in fact is defined as unverified information that spreads rapidly throughout society through various means of communication (Li et al., 2021; Zhou et al., 2022). As social media platforms like Facebook, Twitter, and YouTube expand rapidly, the information is shared worldwide in a matter of seconds among society. Spread of the information quickly which has previously been believed to be via one click of a "share." Users can instantly share unconfirmed claims that contribute to viral waves of misinformation.

The speed of rumor spreading contributes to major challenges for authorities. Rumors often threaten social order and public confidence. A notable example occurred in China following the 2011 Fukushima nuclear incident, when a false claim about radioactive contamination in table salt led to widespread panic-buying (Chen & Wang, 2020). Similarly, during the COVID-19 pandemic, governments established dedicated "rumor control" teams to curb the circulation of misleading or hazardous content online. Historically, even before the internet age, the dangers of misinformation were recognized. During the early 1940s, numerous wartime rumors prompted governments to form committees and launch initiatives to preserve civilian morale and safeguard national security (Faye, 2007). These cases illustrate how unchecked rumor dissemination can incite fear, erode trust in official communications, and ultimately endanger collective well-being.

The dissemination of rumors and behavioral responses are influenced by many factors. These include the perceived reliability of the information source, the emotional disposition of the audience, the configuration of the social network, and the degree of uncertainty surrounding the message. Individual reactions are usually influenced by factors such as psychological tendencies, personality traits and prior experiences depending on types of people, either radical or steady. For instance, individuals with radical inclinations may react spontaneously, transmitting rumors rapidly without verification. This is often motivated by emotions such as fear, anger, or defiance toward authority. Such reactions can amplify the rumors spread and intensify its societal impact. Conversely, individuals with more cautious may pause before responding. They tend to seek corroborating evidence, and choose to depend on trusted sources, which can decelerate dissemination and mitigate its influence if they ultimately refrain from sharing. Between these behavioral poles lies a group of moderate actors who might initially transmit a rumor but later withdraw or resist upon encountering contradictory information, illustrating the adaptive and evolving nature of human conduct in the context of information diffusion.

To better comprehend and control the mechanisms underlying rumor spreading, the use of mathematical modelling as analytical tools is amongst the research interest. The pioneering work of modelling the spread of rumor can be traced back to classical epidemiological models, most notably, the susceptible–infected–recovered (SIR) framework where the disease transmission serves as a referent for the spread of rumor. This is due to the spread of rumor in populations either through mouth-to-mouth or social networks is like the spread of epidemic. In the earliest mathematical framework of rumor dynamics, populations were divided into ignorant i.e. the individuals who unaware of the rumor, spreaders which is those who actively spread it, and stiflers i.e. the individuals who know of it but choose not to propagate further. These frameworks used systems of ordinary differential equations (ODEs) to represent the transitions state among population categories, thereby forming a mathematical model of the rumors circulation in society over time. In contrast to epidemic contagion process, the spread of rumors is primarily governed by human behavior which includes cognition, perception, and social interaction. Integrating psychological and behavioral theories thus offers valuable insight into the motivations behind rumor initiation, spreading and termination, hence enabling the refinement and realism of computational models.

Over the years, extension of the models has introduced behavioral complexity to better reflect real-world behavior in digital communication. For instance, some individuals may pause before deciding whether to share information, while others may refrain entirely driven by skepticism, verification efforts, or fatigue from information overload. The susceptible–propagate–hesitate–resisted (SPHR) model proposed by Norhayati et al. (2024) extends the frameworks of traditional mathematical model by capturing these behavioral variations, hence offering a more realistic depiction of human responses in the rumor propagation dynamics.

Time delay represents another key variable influencing the spread of rumors. In the primary work of mathematical model development to represent the infectious diseases, transmission typically occurs almost instantaneously upon contact. However, the decision to share or suppress a rumor often involves time-lag which represents the pause of rumor spread. Some individuals may take time to verify facts, evaluate credibility of the messages, or await further confirmation before responding and spreading the rumors. In such a case, feedback delays which concern the time required for counter-rumors, official or unofficial clarifications, or fact-checking messages can significantly affect the system's behavior. The presence of time lags may generate oscillatory patterns, amplify instability, or produce recurring waves of rumor activity that are neglected in models with no delay feedback. Incorporating delay-driven feedback into mathematical formulations therefore enhances understanding of how rumors persist, diminish, or re-emerge over time by considering into the model the behavior that may pause the rumor spreading system.

In this chapter, the compartmental approach is applied by introducing a SPHR model with delayed feedback. The susceptible (S) class represents the individuals who initially did not hear the rumor. Once they hear the rumor, they may become propagators (P) i.e. those who are actively spreading it or enter a hesitant (H) class if there is fact-checking attitude for instance, hence delay their decision. Those in the hesitant state can later transition into propagators or into the resisted (R) class after some delay. The resisted compartment denotes individuals who know the rumor but refuse to spread it further analogous to stiflers in classical terminology. By incorporating the H and R categories and allowing a time delay in the transitions, the SPHR model captures more realistic behavioral dynamics. In particular, the delayed feedback can model processes such as the time taken for fact-checking or the influence of observing others' reactions before deciding one's course of action. We will use this model to analyze how feedback delays impact the spread and persistence of a rumor. By using computational modeling with behavioral theory enables a deeper understanding of rumor-spreading which not only predicts how quickly a rumor might spread, but also sheds light on which conditions or human factors such as high anxiety, low trust, slow verification which make a community more vulnerable to rampant rumors. The remainder of this chapter will delve into the literature review, mathematical formulation of the delay-driven SPHR model and explore the rich dynamics that arise from the interplay between human behavioral delays and rumor propagation.

2. LITERATURE REVIEW

The primary mathematical models of the spreading of rumors are developed by Daley and Kendall (1964) and Maki and Thompson (1973) in their use of epidemiological principles to characterize individuals. In the context of rumor spreading the individuals are characterizing as ignorant, spreaders, and stiflers. These models are notable adequate with instantaneous assumption changes occurring on the state level, but they may not correspond to the behavior in real life. The Maki–Thompson (MT) model extended the Daley–Kendall (DK) model by incorporating directed contact dynamics, i.e., a spreader deliberately seeks to inform others, turning an ignorant person into a spreader upon contact. If the spreader encounters another spreader or a stifler, they lose interest and transition to the stifler state. The MT model was distinguished by this one-sided interaction mechanism, in contrast to the two-sided contact process of the DK model. Although refinements like this improved the realism of social interactions, they relied heavily on the simplifying assumption of instantaneous behavioral change. Further integrations of DK and MT models have integrated enhanced behavior, such as incubation effects (Al-Tuwairqi et al., 2015), memory loss (Zhao et al., 2013), hesitation dynamics (Xia et al., 2015), emergency control interventions (Chen, 2018), punitive measures (Li & Ma, 2017; Zhao & Wang, 2014), memory-dependent feedback (Zhang & Xu, 2015), and network-driven diffusion processes (Zanette, 2001).

To overcome the unrealistic assumption of instantaneous transitions, Al-Tuwairqi et al. (2015) introduced an incubation phase into the rumor-spreading framework. In this formulation, people who hear a rumor for the first time do not actively become spreaders immediately but instead enter a temporary latent state before deciding to propagate it. This incubation stage is considered a pause time i.e. the amount of time that can be taken to check, process emotionally, and reflect, making behavior as this model in general closely resemble that observed in humans. Zhao et al. (2013) built on this point of view, suggesting that forgetfulness and recollection could actually be inserted into inhomogeneous networks. Their model accounts for the fact that individuals forget a rumor rather than intentionally stop transmitting it, suggesting a natural decay term that indicates diminishing memory or interest and the gradual disappearance of socially insignificant rumors.

Extending this behavioral improvement, Xia et al. (2015) identified hesitation states to capture people who hesitate before acting, some who spread information instantly, while others check credibility or wait to verify further. Acknowledging the influence of external regulation, Li & Ma (2017) and Zhao & Wang (2014) incorporated governmental or institutional deterrents, spreaders incurring penalties for continued propagation and decreasing propensity to continue to spread. This expansion successfully combined behavioral modelling with policy interventions, showing the power of authority-focused regulation to change rumor dynamics. Li et al. (2021) extended the framework with stochastic effects and inhibitory mechanisms under dual control processes to account for rumor propagation. Their results underscored the fact that rumor propagation is intrinsically random as a result of a complex and unpredictable interaction between humans. Inhibitory effects, e.g., skepticism, corrective messages, or counter-rumors were added in order to reflect resistance behaviors commonly found in actual societies. These novel findings yielded a more accurate image of rumor evolution in its uncertainty and adaptive behavior.

Norhayati et al. (2024) advanced the susceptible–propagate–hesitate–resisted (SPHR) model which is a refinement of classical frameworks that explicitly incorporates attitude-adjustment mechanisms, to encapsulate the behavioral diversity seen in information diffusion. Expanding on the inhibitory modelling concept of Li et al. (2021), their formulation introduced two intermediary compartments, i.e. hesitate and resisted alongside the traditional susceptible and propagate states. The hesitant group is the one that hears rumor but does not act on it due to verification or doubt; the resisted group are the ones that actively deny or inhibit rumor. Through enabling fluctuating transitions between these states based on social feedback, external cues, or corrective interventions, the SPHR model captures a wider and deeper scale of human behavior adaptation in rumor dynamics. Chen & Wang (2020) proposed a rumor spreading model based on rumor credibility, correlation, and crowd classification in human personality. The classical SIR model is extended to the SEIsIrR model considering crowd classification based on personality, correlation degree of rumor and people's lives, and rumor credibility in homogeneous and heterogeneous networks. The compartmental model is divided into steady ignorant (Is), radical ignorant (Ir), exposed (E), spreader (S) and stifler (R). Yang et al. (2018) have examined competing spreading dynamics of two conflicting messages using a novel individual-competing spreading model. Extensive simulation experiments have been performed, and the results show that when a message terminates, the dynamics of a simplified model fit well with the expected evolutionary process of the message. Ghosh & Das, (2025) extended the traditional SEIR model to investigate the dynamics of online misinformation propagation by investigating four categories of social networking site users: the ignorant population, believers, active spreaders, and stiflers. The critical value of the spread of misinformation (spreading threshold) of the deterministic model has been determined, which regulates the stability switch from spreader free state to state with spreaders. The deterministic model is supplemented by stochastic model counterpart to analyze the effect of external fluctuation using white noise that is common to information propagation over a social networking circuit.

Rumor propagate in the research has progressively developed into artificial intelligence and applied machine learning and deep learning techniques for the tasks of rumor spread detection and rumor propagation prevention. The initial work of rumor detection focused on supervised classifiers with hand-crafted features. Linear SVMs and random forests, for example, were trained with such attributes as tweet content, user credibility, and message propagation statistics Ma et al. (2016). While these engineered models were able to classify rumors accurately, the manual feature design process was extensive and not generalized. Later, unsupervised approaches were investigated to overcome the data limitations with labeled data. Chen et al. (2018) proposed an anomaly detection framework combining an RNN and an Autoencoder to learn normal user posting behaviors. Posts with large reconstruction errors were identified as rumors. Contrastive clustering, based on recent developments, which segments rumor-related posts with no labels, helps to differentiate these rumor clusters from credible news streams. These unsupervised and semi-supervised methods are useful in low-label instances, though their performance lies well behind that of fully supervised deep models. With the advent of deep learning, it has become a viable alternative. For example, Alsaeedi & Al-Sarem (2020) suggested CNN-based architecture for rumor detection in Twitter. Their results show the CNN model is more efficient than traditional baselines and strikes the optimal balance of recall and precision. In addition, Choi et al. (2022) proposed a large-scale deep learning–based framework for preventing the dissemination of false rumors that works based entirely on the textual content of claims (Choi et al., 2022). Their model includes two phases: (i) claim embedding and (ii) fact-checking. In the initial stage, a pre-trained BERT model extracts comprehensive linguistic features, which are applied in the second stage to authenticate the claim. Unlike classical approaches this framework can take into account semantic meaning as well as nuanced linguistic signals like style or inter-word relations, resulting in significantly enhanced fact-checking performance.

The role of compartmental models to describe population-level dynamics of spreading rumors is important, since they provide structured means to explain how individuals hop between states of behavior. The original Daley–Kendall and Maki–Thompson models constructed these models by separating populations into ignorant, spreaders, and stiflers, with later modifications introducing mechanisms such as incubation, hesitation, memory that provide more consistent representation of real-world behavior. In this context, the SPHR model allows for two behavioral responses, one, hesitation and the other resistance, both common to information diffusion, and to be captured. Expanding on this and using control mechanism to scale up the SPHR and adding delay feedback are some possible solutions for capturing the time lags that naturally exist in the spreading of the rumor. Concurrently, artificial intelligence approaches from machine learning and deep learning also add a layer of depth to the study by helping detect and identify rumors from the content sources, user activities and propagation structures of social media. So, whilst these approaches concentrate on the micro level of spotting and verifying misinformation, the compartmental models emphasize wider systems at large. When combined, these two frameworks can offer complementary insights- compartmental models like SPHR account for how rumors spread across populations while AI techniques facilitate the real-time, practical effort to identify and prevent false information.

This chapter considers the model put forward by Norhayati et al. (2024) extended to a SPHR model with control mechanism and delay feedback. One of the limitations in SPHR model is the assumption of instant behavioral change. In practice, many people take time before deciding whether to propagate, defend the rumor, or adjust themselves. This naturally introduces a delay effect into the process of spreading rumors: sometimes may wait by memory or feedback systems. Delay differential equations (DDEs) are the most suitable mathematical tool to account for these non-instantaneous responses since they contain memory, creating higher-level dynamics such as switches to stability and oscillations in dynamics. Delays may cause Hopf bifurcation, thus exhibiting oscillatory activity that indicates alternating waves of rumor intensity (again an often-covered phenomenon on social media, where the rumors occasionally come back as new trending topics). In the present work, we further the SPHR framework by Norhayati et al. (2024) by including delayed feedback terms in the control mechanisms. The fact that this dimension allows us to account for the lag between awareness, decision-making, and action in this context leads us to an improved and overall comprehension of the spread of rumors in sophisticated social networks.

3. MATHEMATICAL MODEL

In this section, we extend the susceptible–propagate–hesitate–resisted (SPHR) rumor-spreading model with a control mechanism, U, as proposed by Norhayati et al. (2024), by incorporating delayed feedback into the control dynamics. A rumor-spreading model adopts a compartmental modelling approach, where the total population is divided into distinct groups (compartments) based on their behaviour toward a rumor. Let $N(t)$ denote the total population at time t. Let $S(t)$,$P(t)$, $I(t)$ and$H(t)$represent the number of susceptible, propagates, ignorant, and hesitated at time t,respectively. The ordinary differential equation in Norhayati et al. (2024) is formulated as

$$
\begin{aligned}
\frac{dS}{dt} &= \Gamma - ((1-\theta)I + \theta P)Sf(U) - \mu S \\
\frac{dP}{dt} &= \theta SPf(U) + \tau I - (\mu + g(U))P \\
\frac{dI}{dt} &= (1-\theta)SIf(U) - (\mu + \tau + \beta)I \\
\frac{dU}{dt} &= r - eU - \frac{\delta PU}{K+U} \\
\frac{dH}{dt} &= \beta I + Pg(U) - \mu H
\end{aligned} \tag{1}
$$

with the following assumptions:

(A1). The function $f(U)$ is assumed to satisfy the following properties:

1. $f(U) \geq 0; f(0) = 1.$
2. The function f is non-increasing over its defined interval $[0, \infty)$.

(A2). The function $g(U)$ fulfils the following conditions:

1. $g(U) \geq 0.$
2. The function g is non-decreasing over its defined interval $[0, \infty)$.

(A3). The total population at any time t is given by:

1. $N(t) = S(t) + P(t) + I(t) + H(t).$

All notation used in model (1) and assumptions **(A1)** to **(A3)** is presented in Table 1.

Table 1. Description of the variables and parameters

Variables/ Parameters	Description
S	Susceptible class (those who can be influenced by rumor)
I	Informed individuals are aware of the rumor but no longer propagating
P	Propagators actively spread the rumor.
U	Adjustment mechanism (awareness/ control resource)
H	The stifler or resistant class i.e. individuals who have become aware of the rumor yet refuse to propagate it, or those whose attitudes have changed due to the adjustment process.
Γ	Recruitment rate into the susceptible class (entry of new individuals who may become exposed).
μ	Natural leaving or removal rate applicable to all compartments.
θ	Transmission rate determines how quickly individuals begin spreading the rumor.
r	Rate associated with the adjusting or inhibiting mechanism controlling rumor dynamics.
e	The decay rate within the system, signifying loss of activity or influence.
δ	Maximum uptake or interaction rate of the process.

continued on following page

Table 1. Continued

Variables/ Parameters	Description
K	Half-saturation constant describing the level at which the uptake rate reaches half its maximum.
τ	Constant rate at which hesitant numbers alter their perception and begin to spread the rumor.
β	Rate of migration or transition of newcomers from I node to the H node

In this research, the constant delay is embedded in two adjusting mechanisms functions of $f(U)$ and $g(U)$.Incorporating a delay term into these functions able to capture the intrinsic time lag between changes in the awareness variables and their actual epidemiological effect. The functions $f(U)$ and represent functional responses to the effect of changing in U in which model the awareness of prevention strategies. In this context $f(U)$ represent the effectiveness of awareness in reducing susceptibility and $g(U)$ is the influence of awareness on the recovered class and. The effect of increased awareness on susceptible and propagate populations is not instantaneous, but only respond after some time lag, h. Hence, awareness at awareness at times t takes h units before individuals modify their behavior. System of equation (1) is extended to compartmental structure with delayed feedback as indicated in Figure 1. The delay term is added in interventions function modulated by U which act after a lag $h > 0$. Thus, rumor spread is influenced not by the current $U(t)$, but by a past state of $U(t - h)$.

Figure 1. Schematic of the rumor-propagation dynamics featuring delayed feedback in the adjustment process

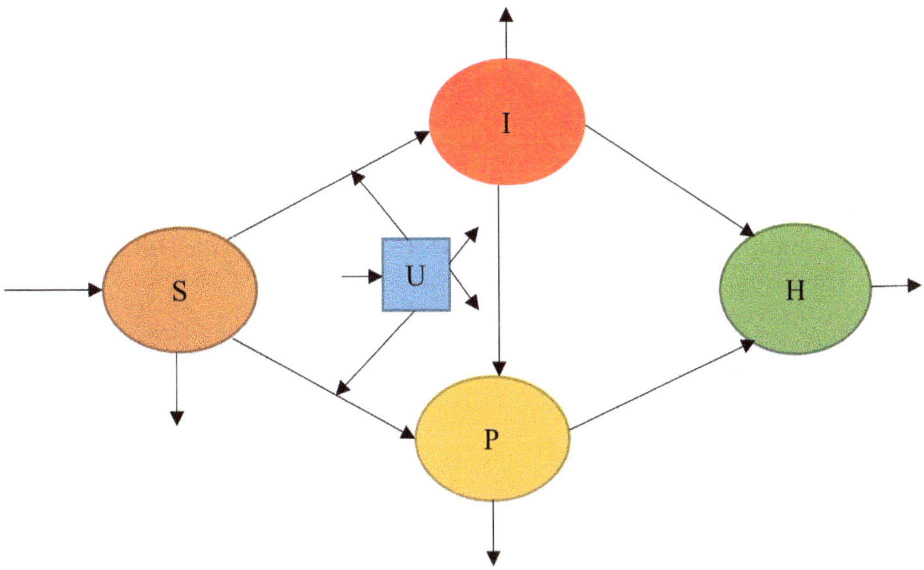

The mathematical model of rumor spreading with delayed feedback shown in Figure 1 is then governed by the following delay differential equations

$$\begin{aligned}\frac{dS}{dt} &= \Gamma - ((1-\theta)I + \theta P)Sf(U(t-h)) - \mu S\\ \frac{dP}{dt} &= \theta SPf(U(t-h)) + \tau I - (\mu + g(U(t-h)))P\\ \frac{dI}{dt} &= (1-\theta)SIf(U(t-h)) - (\mu+\tau+\beta)I\\ \frac{dU}{dt} &= r - eU - \frac{\delta PU}{K+U}\\ \frac{dH}{dt} &= \beta I + Pg(U(t-h)) - \mu H\end{aligned} \tag{2}$$

with the initial function $U(t-h) = \Phi(t),\ t \in [-h,0]$ and initial conditions $S(t_0) = S_0,\ P(t_0) = P_0,\ H(t_0) = H_0,\ R(t_0) = R_0$.

The nonlinear functions $f(U(t-h))$and$f(U(t-h))$ satisfy the assumptions (**A1**) and (**A2**), respectively. Those functions introduce awareness latency $h > 0$which captures the spread of the rumor under awareness or control measure after some time delay. Under (**A1**), $f(U(t-h))$ is a decreasing function, reflecting that awareness reduces the effective contact rate. Under (**A2**), $f(U(t-h))$ is an increasing function in U, indicating that awareness enhances the suppression of propagators P. Both effects, however, act with a delay. Let choose the nonlinear functions as follows

$$f(U) = \frac{1}{(1+\alpha U)^m}, \quad g(U) = g_{\max}\frac{U^n}{U_{50}^n + U^n} \tag{3}$$

The function $f(U) \in (0,1)$ is strictly decreasing in U, with sensitivity controlled by the cooperativity parameter $m \geq 1$. The function $g(U) \in (0, g_{\max})$ is increasing and saturating, taking the Hill form. This formulation captures the diminishing returns of awareness campaigns with a tuneable steepness through the Hill coefficient $n \geq 1$. The parameters are defined as follows:

1. $\alpha > 0$ is the per-unit effectiveness of awareness in reducing contacts.
2. $m \geq 1$ is the cooperativity of reduction in $f(U)$.
3. $g_{max} > 0$ is the maximal removal or suppression rate of P.
4. $U_{50} > 0$ is the awareness level at which $g(U)$ reaches half of g_{max}.
5. $n \geq 1$ is the Hill coefficient controlling the steepness of $g(U)$.

The derivatives of f and g for the equation (3) are given by

$$f(U) = \frac{m\alpha}{(1+\alpha U)^{m+1}}, \quad g'(U) = g_{\max}\frac{n\,U^{n-1}\,U_{50}^n}{\left(U_{50}^n + U^n\right)^2} \tag{4}$$

Next, we investigate the characteristics of the mathematical model (2).

4. EQUILIBRIA AND STABILITY ANALYSIS

4.1. Equilibria

To find the steady state solution at the equilibrium point, we set model (2) equal to zero and solve for $x^* = (S^*, P^*, I^*, U^*, H^*)$. This yield

$$\begin{aligned}
E_1 &= \Gamma - ((1-\theta)I + \theta P)Sf(U(t-h)) - \mu S = 0 \\
E_2 &= \theta SPf(U(t-h)) + \tau I - (\mu + g(U(t-h)))P = 0 \\
E_3 &= (1-\theta)SIf(U(t-h)) - (\mu + \tau + \beta)I = 0 \\
E_4 &= r - eU - \frac{\delta PU}{K+U} = 0 \\
E_5 &= \beta I + Pg(U(t-h)) - \mu H = 0
\end{aligned} \tag{5}$$

Two types are of interest i.e. rumor-free equilibrium (RFE) and endemic equilibrium (EE). First, we find the RFE in which from E_5 of equation (5) we have

$$H^* = \frac{\beta I^* + P^* g(U^*)}{\mu}$$

There are two possibilities, from E_3, i.e. for RFE, $I^* = 0$ and for EE, $I^* \neq 0$. Under Rumor-Free Equilibrium (RFE), take $I^* = P^* = 0$, then we have $S^* = \frac{\Gamma}{\mu}$, $U^* = \frac{r}{e}$ and $H^* = 0$. Hence, the RFE is $x^*_{RFE} = \left(\frac{\Gamma}{\mu}, 0, 0, \frac{r}{e}, 0\right)$.Endemic equilibria (the presence of rumor) when $I^* > 0,\ P^* > 0$,hence we must solve simultaneously $E_1 - E_5$ under the constraint of $(1-\theta)S^* f(U^*) = \mu + \tau + \beta$ and E_1, E_2, and E_4 for $I^* > 0$. Let linearize the system around an arbitrary equilibrium $x^* = (S^*, P^*, I^*, U^*, H^*)$. The resulting linearized DDE takes the standard form

$$\dot{y}(t) = A_0 y(t) + A_1 y(t-h), \tag{6}$$

where $y(t) = (S(t), P(t), I(t), U(t), H(t))^T$,$A_0$ is the Jacobian with respect to the current states, and A_1 is the Jacobian with respect to the delayed states. For simplicity, we introduce the following notations:

$$f^* := f(U^*),\quad g^* := g(U^*),\quad f^*_U := f'(U^*),\quad g^*_U := g'(U^*)$$

The current state of the Jacobian A_0 is (order $[S, P, I, U, H]$)

$$A_0 = \begin{bmatrix} -\mu - f^*(\theta P^* + (1-\theta)I^*) & -\theta S^* f^* & -(1-\theta)S^* f^* & 0 & 0 \\ \theta P^* f^* & \theta S^* f^* - (\mu + g^*) & \tau & 0 & 0 \\ (1-\theta)I^* f^* & 0 & (1-\theta)S^* f^* - (\mu+\tau+\beta) & 0 & 0 \\ 0 & -\frac{\delta U^*}{k+U^*} & 0 & \frac{\delta P^* U^*}{(k+U^*)^2} - \frac{\delta P^*}{k+U^*} - e & 0 \\ 0 & g^* & \beta & 0 & -\mu \end{bmatrix}$$

The delayed state of the Jacobian A_1 is

$$A_1 = \begin{bmatrix} 0 & 0 & 0 & -((1-\theta)I^* + \theta P^*)S^* f_U^* & 0 \\ 0 & 0 & 0 & \theta P^* S^* f_U^* - P^* g_U^* & 0 \\ 0 & 0 & 0 & (1-\theta)I^* S^* f_U^* & 0 \\ 0 & 0 & 0 & 0 & 0 \\ 0 & 0 & 0 & P^* g_U^* & 0 \end{bmatrix}$$

where

$$f^* = \frac{1}{(1+\alpha U^*)^m}, \quad g^* = g_{\max} \frac{(U^*)^n}{U_{50}^n + (U^*)^n},$$

$$f_U^* = \frac{m\alpha}{(1+\alpha U^*)^{m+1}}, \quad g_U^* = g_{\max} \frac{n(U^*)^{n-1} U_{50}^n}{\left(U_{50}^n + (U^*)^n\right)^2}$$

Next, we factorize the variable H. Observing the structure of A_0 and A_1, it is clear that the first four equations do not depend explicitly on H. Consequently, the Jacobian matrices admit a block lower triangular form. And the full system is decomposed accordingly. This implies the existence of one decoupled eigenvalue $\lambda = -\mu$, which is always negative. Therefore, the stability of the system is determined entirely by the reduced 4×4 subsystem involving (S, P, I, U). The delay parameter h plays a critical role in this reduced subsystem. In particular, a Hopf bifurcation can occur when a conjugate pair of eigenvalues crosses the imaginary axis as h varies. Thus, the analysis of local stability reduces to studying the characteristic equation of the 4×4 block corresponding to (S, P, I, U), which inherits the block lower-triangular structure from the full system

$$A_0 = \begin{bmatrix} \widetilde{A}_0 & 0 \\ \widetilde{B} & -\mu \end{bmatrix}, \quad A_1 = \begin{bmatrix} \widetilde{A}_1 & 0 \\ \widetilde{C} & -\mu \end{bmatrix}$$

where $\widetilde{A}_0, \widetilde{A}_1$ are 4×4matrices for (S, P, I, U) and the last row corresponds to H. Local stability is determined by the roots $\lambda \in \mathbb{C}$ of the characteristic equation

$$\det\left(\lambda I - A_0 - A_1 e^{-\lambda h}\right) = 0.$$

For a block lower-triangular matrix $\begin{bmatrix} \Upsilon & 0 \\ \Psi & \eta \end{bmatrix}$, the determinant factorizes as det($M) \cdot \eta$. Applying this with $\Upsilon = \lambda I_4 - \widetilde{A}_0 - \widetilde{A}_1 e^{-\lambda h}$ and $\eta = \lambda + \mu$, yielding

$$\det\left(\lambda I - A_0 - A_1 e^{-\lambda h}\right) = (\lambda + \mu)\det\left(\lambda I_4 - \widetilde{A}_0 - \widetilde{A}_1 e^{-\lambda h}\right) = 0$$

where

$$\widetilde{A}_0 = \begin{bmatrix} -\mu - f^*(\theta P^* + (1-\theta)I^*) & -\theta S^* f^* & -(1-\theta)S^* f^* & 0 \\ (1-\theta)I^* f^* & \theta S^* f^* - (\mu + g^*) & \tau & 0 \\ 0 & 0 & (1-\theta)S^* f^* - (\mu + \tau + \beta) & 0 \\ 0 & -\frac{\delta U^*}{k + U^*} & 0 & \frac{\delta P^* U^*}{(k+U^*)^2} - \frac{\delta P^*}{k + U^*} - e \end{bmatrix}$$

and

$$\widetilde{A}_1 = \begin{bmatrix} 0 & 0 & 0 & -((1-\theta)I^* + \theta P^*)S^* f_U^* \\ 0 & 0 & 0 & \theta P^* S^* f_U^* - P^* g_U^* \\ 0 & 0 & 0 & (1-\theta)I^* S^* f_U^* \\ 0 & 0 & 0 & P^* g_U^* \end{bmatrix},$$

$$\widetilde{B} = [0 \quad g^* \quad \beta \quad 0], \widetilde{C} = = [0 \quad 0 \quad P^* \quad g_U^*]$$

Thus, $\lambda = -\mu$ is always a root and local stability can be determined by the 4×4 subsystem (S, P, I, U).

To find the $\det\left(\lambda I_4 - \widetilde{A}_0 - \widetilde{A}_1 e^{-\lambda h}\right) = 0$, write the 4×4 subsystem as a block matrix

$$\Phi(\lambda, h) = \begin{bmatrix} X(\lambda) & y(\lambda, h) \\ z^T & d(\lambda) \end{bmatrix}$$

where the current state block is

$$X(\lambda) = \begin{bmatrix} \lambda + \mu + (\theta P^* + (1-\theta)I^*)f^* & \theta S^* f^* & (1-\theta)S^* f^* \\ \theta P^* f^* & \lambda + \mu + g^* - \theta S^* f^* & \tau \\ (1-\theta)I^* f^* & 0 & \lambda + \mu + \tau + \beta - (1-\theta)S^* f^* \end{bmatrix}$$

The delayed column is

$$y(\lambda, h) = -e^{-\lambda h}\begin{bmatrix}((1-\theta)I^* + \theta P^*)S^* f_U^* \\ \theta P^* S^* f_U^* - P^* g_U^* \\ (1-\theta)I^* S^* f_U^*\end{bmatrix}$$

The off-diagonal row and scalar are

$$z^T = \begin{bmatrix}0 & \frac{\delta U^*}{k+U^*} & 0\end{bmatrix},\ d(\lambda) = \lambda + e + \frac{\delta P^* U^*}{(k+U^*)^2} + \frac{\delta P^*}{k+U^*}$$

Using Schur complement reduction we have

$$\det\begin{bmatrix}X(\lambda) & y(\lambda,h) \\ z^T & d(\lambda)\end{bmatrix} = \Delta(\lambda, h) = \det(X(\lambda))(d(\lambda) - z^T X^{-1}(\lambda) y(\lambda, h)) \quad (7)$$

Due to $z^T = \begin{bmatrix}0 & \frac{\delta U^*}{k+U^*} & 0\end{bmatrix}$, only the second component of $X(\lambda)^{-1}y(\lambda,h)$ in equation (7) is needed. By Cramer's rule, yield

$$[X(\lambda)^{-1}y(\lambda,h)]_2 = \frac{\det\left(X_2(\lambda,h)\right)}{\det(X(\lambda))}$$

where $X_2(\lambda,h)$ is obtained by replacing the second column of $X(\lambda)$ by $y(\lambda,h)$. Thus, we have

$$X_2(\lambda,h) = \begin{bmatrix}\lambda + \mu + (\theta P^* + (1-\theta)I^*)f^* & -e^{-\lambda h}((1-\theta)I^* + \theta P^*)S^* f_U^* & (1-\theta)S^* f^* \\ \theta P^* f^* & -e^{-\lambda h}\left(\theta P^* S^* f_U^* - P^* g_U^*\right) & \tau \\ (1-\theta)I^* f^* & -e^{-\lambda h}\left((1-\theta)I^* S^* f_U^*\right) & \lambda + \mu + \tau + \beta - (1-\theta)S^* f^*\end{bmatrix}$$

Therefore equation (7) can be written as

$$\Delta(\lambda,h) = \det(X(\lambda))\left(d(\lambda) - \frac{\delta U^*}{k+U^*}e^{-\lambda h}\det\left(\widehat{X}_2(\lambda)\right)\right) \quad (8)$$

where

$$\widehat{X}_2(\lambda) = \begin{bmatrix} \lambda + \mu + (\theta P^* + (1-\theta)I^*)f^* & ((1-\theta)I^* + \theta P^*)S^* f_U^* & (1-\theta)S^* f^* \\ \theta P^* f^* & \theta P^* S^* f_U^* - P^* g_U^* & \tau \\ (1-\theta)I^* f^* & (1-\theta)I^* S^* f_U^* & \lambda + \mu + \tau + \beta - (1-\theta)S^* f^* \end{bmatrix}$$

Now we compute the 3 × 3matrix of $X(\lambda)$ and $\widehat{X}_2(\lambda)$. For the non-delay of $X(\lambda)$ in equation (8) yield

$$\det(X(\lambda)) = (AE - BD)K + G(BM - CE)$$

For delay-coupling $\widehat{X}_2(\lambda)$, we have

$$\det\left(\widehat{X}_2(\lambda)\right) = A\left(b_2 K - M b_3\right) - b_1(DK - MG) + C\left(D b_3 - b_2 G\right)$$

Then, the characteristic equation (8) is obtained by solving

$$\begin{aligned} \Delta(\lambda, h) = {} & [(AE - BD)K + G(BM - CE)]\left(\lambda + e + \frac{\delta U^*}{(k + U^*)^2}\right) \\ & - \frac{\delta U^*}{k + U^*} e^{-\lambda h}\left[A\left(b_2 K - M b_3\right) - b_1(DK - MG) + C\left(D b_3 - b_2 G\right)\right] = 0 \end{aligned} \tag{9}$$

where

$$\begin{aligned} A &= \lambda + a_S, \quad a_S = \mu + (\theta P^* + (1-\theta)I^*)f^* \\ B &= \theta S^* f^* \\ C &= (1-\theta)S^* f^* \\ D &= \theta P^* f^* \\ E &= \lambda + a_P, \quad a_P = \mu + g^* - \theta S^* f^* \\ M &= \tau \\ G &= (1-\theta)I^* f^* \\ K &= \lambda + a_I, \quad a_I = \mu + \tau + \beta - (1-\theta)S^* f^* \\ b_1 &= ((1-\theta)I^* + \theta P^*)S^* f_U^* \\ b_2 &= \theta P^* S^* f_U^* - P^* g_U^* \\ b_3 &= (1-\theta)I^* S^* f_U^* \end{aligned}$$

To simplify, write (9) as

$$\Delta(\lambda, h) = P_4(\lambda) - e^{-\lambda h} Q_2(\lambda)$$

where $P_4(\lambda)$ is a quartic polynomial given by the first term on the right-hand side of the equation (6), and $Q_2(\lambda)$ is a quadratic polynomial given by the second term of the right-hand side of the equation (6). Let write first the cubic polynomial as

$$P_3(\lambda) = \lambda^3 + p_2 \lambda^2 + p_1 \lambda + p_0$$

with coefficients

$$\begin{aligned} p_0 &= a_I(a_S a_P - BD) + G(BM - C a_P) \\ p_1 &= a_S a_P + a_S a_I + a_P a_I - BD - GC \\ p_2 &= a_S + a_P + a_I \end{aligned}$$

Multiply by the linear factor of U, so we have

$$P_4(\lambda) = p_3(\lambda)(\lambda + d_0) \tag{10}$$

where

$$d_0 = e + \frac{\delta U^*}{(k + U^*)^2}$$

The quartic polynomial (10) can be represented as

$$P_4(\lambda) = \lambda^4 + c_3 \lambda^3 + c_2 \lambda^2 + c_1 \lambda + c_0$$

with $c_3 = p_2 + d_0$, $c_2 = p_1 + d_0 p_2$, $c_1 = p_0 + d_0 p_1$, $c_0 = d_0 p_0$. The quadratic term, $Q_2(\lambda)$ can be written as

$$Q_2(\lambda) = a_{42}(b_2 \lambda^2 + q_1 \lambda + q_0)$$

where

$$q_1 = b_2(a_S + a_L) - Mb_3 - b_1 D$$
$$q_0 = a_S(b_2 a_I - Mb_3) - b_1 D a_I + b_1 MG + C(Db_3 - b_2 G)$$

4.2. Basic Reproduction Number

Consider the infected compartments of $(P, I)^T$.Linearize the new infection terms and transition terms at RFE $x^*_{RFE} = \left(\frac{\Gamma}{\mu}, 0, 0, \frac{r}{e}, 0\right)$ and introduce $f^* := f(U^*)$, $g^* := g(U^*)$, $f^*_U := f'(U^*)$, and $g^*_U := g'(U^*)$.New infection matrix F is

$$F = \begin{pmatrix} \theta S^* f^* & 0 \\ 0 & (1-\theta)S^* f^* \end{pmatrix}$$

The transition matrix V is

$$V = \begin{pmatrix} \mu + g^* & -\tau \\ 0 & \mu + \tau + \beta \end{pmatrix}$$

The next generation matrix is given by

$$\Lambda = FV^{-1} = \begin{pmatrix} \dfrac{\theta S^* f^*}{\mu + g^*} & \dfrac{\theta S^* f^* \tau}{(\mu + g^*)(\mu + \tau + \beta)} \\ 0 & \dfrac{(1-\theta)S^* f^*}{\mu + \tau + \beta} \end{pmatrix}.$$ The spectral radius of $\Lambda$is

$$\mathfrak{R}_0 = \max\left\{\frac{\theta S^* f^*}{\mu + g^*}, \frac{(1-\theta)S^* f^*}{\mu + \tau + \beta}\right\}$$

with

$$S^* = \frac{\Gamma}{\mu}$$

and

$$U^* = \frac{r}{e}.$$

1. If $\mathfrak{R}_0 < 1$, the RFE is locally stable (in absence of delay effect in linearization).
2. If $\mathfrak{R}_0 > 1$, permits invasion i.e. endemic equilibrium.

4.3. Hopf Bifurcation Condition

A Hopf bifurcation (delay-induced oscillation) occurs when the 4×4 characteristic equation has a conjugate pair of purely imaginary roots $\lambda = i\omega$ ($\omega > 0$) for the critical delay $h = h_c$, and the transversality condition is satisfied i.e. the pair crosses the imaginary axis with nonzero speed. By substituting $\lambda = i\omega$ into equation Υ yield

$$\Upsilon = \det\left(i\omega I_4 - \widetilde{A}_0 - \widetilde{A}_1 e^{-\lambda h}\right) = 0 \tag{11}$$

A close form solution for h is hard to be found. We employ a robust numerical procedure of eigenvalue mapping formulation. Rewrite equation (11) as

$$\left(i\omega I_4 - \widetilde{A}_0\right)v = \widetilde{A}_1 v e^{-\lambda h} \tag{12}$$

for nonzero vector v. Let multiply the equation (12) by $\left(i\omega I_4 - \widetilde{A}_0\right)^{-1}$, then we have

$$\left(i\omega I_4 - \widetilde{A}_0\right)^{-1}\widetilde{A}_1 v = v e^{-\lambda h}$$

Write $\wp(\omega) := \left(i\omega I_4 - \widetilde{A}_0\right)^{-1}\widetilde{A}_1 v$, so $e^{-i\omega h}$ must be the eigenvalue, $\lambda(\omega)$ of $\wp(\omega)$. Therefore for a given $\omega > 0$, we can compute eigenvalues of $\lambda_j(\omega)$. If there exists j such that $\left|\lambda_j(\omega)\right| = 1$, then a Hopf can occur for that ω. Let write $\lambda_j(\omega) = \kappa e^{i\phi}$ ($\kappa \approx 1$), then the candidate delays, h_c satisfying the Hopf condition is

$$e^{-i\omega h_c} = e^{i\phi} \quad \Rightarrow \quad h_c = -\frac{\phi + 2\pi\ell}{\omega}, \quad \ell \in \mathbb{Z}.$$

5. NUMERICAL SIMULATION

This section presents the numerical simulation to confirm the theoretical study. The basic reproduction number and endemic equilibrium is computed based on the algorithm stated in Table 2.

Table 2. The algorithm for basic reproduction number and endemic equilibrium

Algorithm: Basic Reproduction Number and Endemic Equilibrium

Input: Parameters $(\Gamma, \mu, \theta, \tau, \beta, r, e, K, \alpha, m, gmax, U50, n, \delta)$
Output: Steady-state solution $(S^*, P^*, I^*, U^*, H^*)$
1 Initialize model parameters.
2 Define nonlinear functions (refer equation (4)): $f(U)=\frac{1}{1+\alpha U^m}$, $g(U)=\frac{g_{\max} U^n}{U_{50}^n + U^n}$
3 Compute rumor-free equilibrium (RFE):
o $S_{RFE} = \Gamma/\mu, U_{RFE} = r/e.$
o Evaluate R_0^P, R_0^I and set $R_0 = max(R_0^P, R_0^I)$
4 Construct analytic initial guess:
o $U_{guess} = r/e.$
o $S_{guess} = \frac{\mu+\tau+\beta}{(1-\theta)f(U_{guess})}$
o Compute $A = (\mu + g(U_{guess})) - \theta S_{guess} f(U_{guess})$.
o Set $c = A/\tau, I_{guess} = c P_{guess}$c
o Solve for P_{guess} from equation E_1.
5 Define system of equations $F(x)=0$, with $x = [S, P, I, U]$.
6 Apply the nonlinear solver **fsolve** with initial guess x_0.
7 If a positive solution is found:
o Set $S^* = x(1), P^* = x(2), I^* = x(3), U^* = x(4)$.
o Compute $H^* = (\beta I^* + P^* g(U^*))/\mu$.
8 Return $(S^*, P^*, I^*, U^*, H^*)$.
9 Finish.

Basic reproduction number and endemic equilibrim (EE) is found in Matlab based on the algorithm stated in Table 2. The parameters were set as follows

$$(\Gamma, \mu, \theta, \tau, \beta, r, e, K, \alpha, m, gmax, U50, n, \delta) = (10, 0.1, 0.4, 0.2, 0.05, 1.0, 0.1, 1.0, 0.5, 2.0, 1.0, 1.0, 2.0, 0.01)$$

and the parameter are used to obtain the trust region for EE presented in Table 3.

Table 3. The trust region of endemic equilibria.

Iteration	$\|f(x)\|^2$	Norm of Step	First-Order Optimality	Trust-Region Radius
0	0.897694		1.17	1
1	0.707769	1	0.315	1
2	0.343972	2.5	0.776	2.5
3	0.000636755	5.81858	0.362	6.25
4	8.47361e-12	0.00807127	4.15e-05	14.5
5	5.99231e-27	2.3343e-06	1.09e-12	14.5
6	1.06528e-30	1.10032e-13	5.46e-15	14.5

The basic reproduction numbers were computed for the baseline parameters set are $R_0^P = 0.719489, R_0^I = 3.36134$and $R_0 = = \max\{R_0^P, R_0^I\} = 3.36134$. Since $R_0^P < 1$,indicates that the ignorant-to-spreader route is critical and is the dominant driver of persistence in the system. In short, persistence of the rumor is dictated by the ignorant channel, even when the propagate route is subcritical, the overall system remains endemic because of the stronger ignorant pathway. Consequently, even though active propagators are insufficient alone, the overall system exceeds threshold and the rumor persists because of the ignorant-mediated pathway.

Numerical solution of the steady-state (endemic) equations was obtained with a trust-region solver. Convergence was rapid and robust: the residual norm $||f(x)||^2$ decreased sharply within four iterations. These diagnostics indicate that the nonlinear algebraic system was solved to numerical precision and that the reported fixed point is a true solution of the steady-state equations. The refined endemic equilibrium is ($S^*, P^*, I^*, U^*, H^*) = (27.581583, 4.1829009, 17.902376, 9.6210929, 50.33314)$. The equilibrium points are consistent with the reproduction-number analysis. In particular, the ignorant compartment attains the largest non-zero prevalence, reflecting $R_0^I < 1$.The propagate compartment remains small, consistent with $R_0^P < 1$.The awareness level and the large cumulative/stifled class indicate substantial exposure and subsequent removal from the transmission cycle. The ignorant pathway controls the threshold, interventions that specifically reduce R_0^Iwill be most effective in driving the system below criticality. Practically, such interventions include (i) increasing the effective removal/hesitation rate $\mu + \tau + \beta$ for ignorant, (ii) reducing the effective contact/susceptible pool (via information saturation or reducing exposure), or (iii) increasing awareness impact (for example via faster or more effective campaigns) so that the effective transmission terms are weakened. Measures targeting only the propagate channel (affecting R_0^P) are unlikely to eliminate persistence unless they indirectly lower R_0^Ias well. The solver convergence and match to analytic estimates indicate a regular and well-conditioned equilibrium in the tested parameter regime. Spectral scans (delay and parameter sweeps reported elsewhere in this work) did not reveal a delay-induced Hopf bifurcation for the baseline parameters i.e. the endemic equilibrium remains locally attracting and trajectories converge monotonically (or with only damped transients) to the numerical fixed point. This suggests the endemic state is robust to small perturbations and modest delays in awareness/control. The present analysis is local: it characterises stability and steady-state prevalence, but not global basins of attraction or large perturbation behavior. In addition, R_0 here is a linear-threshold measure evaluated at the rumor-free equilibrium; nonlinear effects (saturation in f, g, finite population structure, or stochasticity) could modify thresholds and transient dynamics. Future work should (i) perform a systematic bifurcation/continuation study in the two-dimensional parameter plane (h, R_0^I) (ii) test robustness under stochastic perturbations, and (iii) evaluate targeted control strategies (reducing ignorant-to-spreader transitions) to quantify cost–benefit trade-offs.

Figure 2. Endemic Equilibrium vs the Reproduction Number.

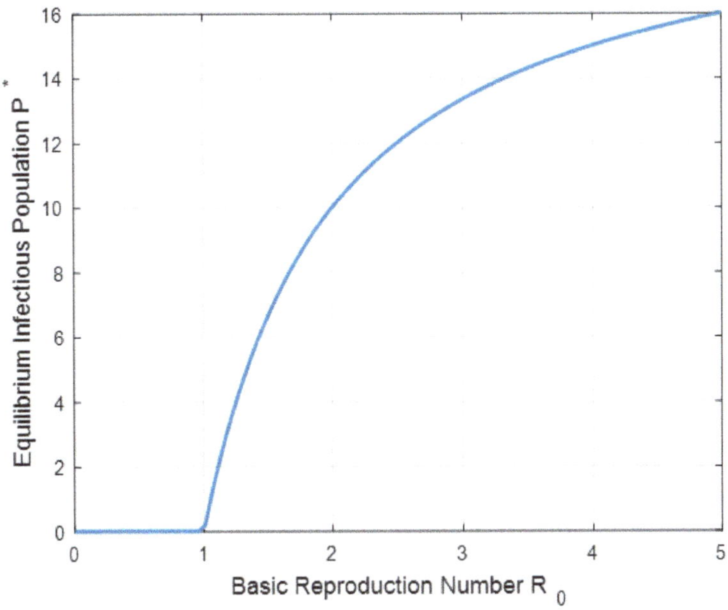

Figure 2 illustrates the relationship between the basic reproduction number R_0 and the equilibrium infectious population (propagate), P^*. When $R_0 < 1$,the curve remains at $P^* = 0$indicating that the rumor-free equilibrium is stable and the rumor dies out. This is consistent with the classical threshold phenomenon in epidemic-type models. However, once $R_0 > 1$,the propagate population P^* rises monotonically with increasing R0. The curve exhibits a concave increasing trend, where I^* grows rapidly just beyond the threshold, and then continues to increase but at a slower rate as R_0 becomes large. This behavior confirms the existence of an endemic equilibrium whenever $R_0 > 1$.The results imply that once the influence of the ignorant-to-infectious mechanism pushes R_0 above unity, the rumor cannot be eradicated and instead persists at a positive endemic level. The higher the value of R0, the greater the equilibrium fraction of the population that remains infectious with the rumor.

Figure 3. The phase-plane dynamics plot in the (S, I) plane.

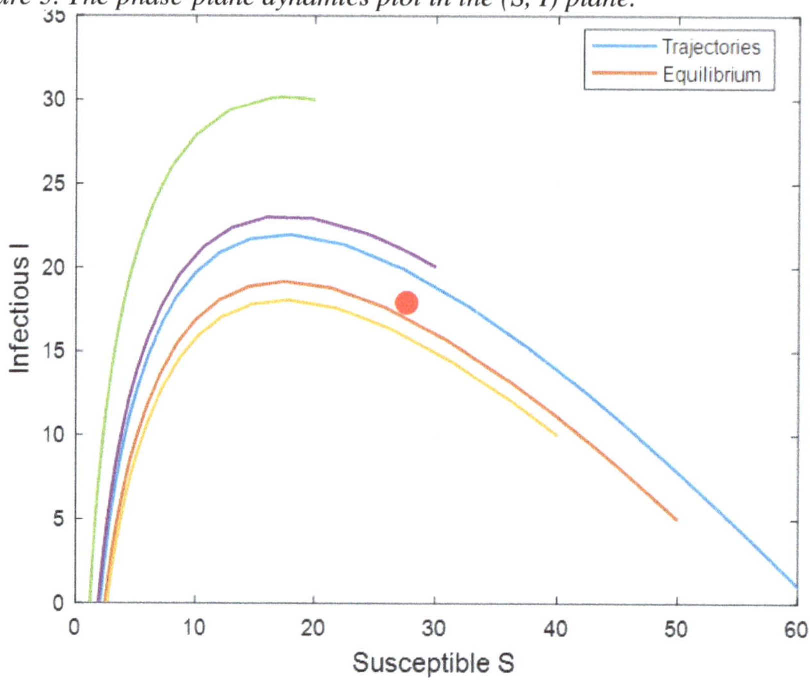

Figure 3 illustrates the phase-plane dynamics in the (S, I)−plane. The colored trajectories represent the system evolution from different initial conditions. Each trajcctory rises sharply as the infection spreads, reaches a peak infectious prevalence, and subsequently declines as the susceptible population diminishes. Despite variations in transient behavior, all trajectories converge toward the same endemic equilibrium point, indicated by the red marker. This confirms the existence of a globally attracting endemic state. The equilibrium curve (orange line) highlights the balance between infection and recovery, with the red point lying precisely on this manifold, validating the numerical results. From a dynamical systems perspective, the results emphasize two key findings. First, the persistence of the rumor is not driven by direct propagation, $R_0^P < 1$, but rather by the strong influence of the ignorant-to-infectious interaction, $R_0^I > 1$.Second, the convergence of trajectories toward a single endemic equilibrium demonstrates the stability and inevitability of the rumor's persistence once $R_0^I > 1$.These findings are consistent with the epidemiological interpretation of threshold phenomena, where the rumor-free equilibrium is unstable and the endemic equilibrium becomes the long-term attractor.

Table 4 outlines the procedure for conducting Hopf bifurcation analysis of the SPHR model with delayed feedback.

Table 4. Algorithm for Hopf Bifurcation analysis with delay

Algorithm: Hopf Bifurcation Analysis with Delay
Input: Parameters $(\Gamma, \mu, \theta, \tau, \beta, r, e, K, \alpha, m, gmax, U50, n, \delta)$ Delay $h > 0$ Initial guess of hopf search (ω_0, h_0) **Output:** Critical delay h_c and oscillatory frequency, ω_c Stability plot and time-domain simulations **1 Define Model Equations** o Write delay system of $\dot{x}(t) = A_0 x(t) + A_1 x(t-h)$ o Identify system state vector of $x = (S, P, I, U, H)$ and set **2 Build Jacobian Matrices** Write function o Find derivatives w.r.t. present state, $A0$ o Find derivatives w.r.t. delayed state, $A1$ **3 Characteristic Equation** o Write function $Delta = @(\lambda, h)\det(\lambda eye(size(A0)) - A0 - A1\exp(-\lambda h))$ o Search for Hopf candidate Set linspace for $\omega-$range Set linspace for $h-$range **for** $\omega(i) = \omega -$ range **for** $h(i) = h -$ range value = Delta($i * \omega(i) * h(i)$) **if** abs(real(value)) $abs(real(value)) < 1e^{-2}$ & & $abs(imaginary(value)) < 1e^{-2}$ **then** $candidates = [candidates; \omega(i), h(i)]$ **end** **end** **end** **if** isempty (candidates) error ('No Hopf candidates found in search range') **else** $\omega(0) = candidates(1,1)$ $h(0) = candidates(1,2)$ **end** **4 Plot onset map** **5 Finish.**

Figure 4 shows the Hopf bifurcation onset map. The $x-$axis represents the rumor spreading rate, β, the $y-$axis denotes the time delay, h, and the colorbar indicates the real part of the dominant eigenvalue, $\Re(\lambda)$. The equilibrium is stable (all perturbations decay) if $\Re(\lambda) < 0$, and unstable when $\Re(\lambda) > 0$. A Hopf bifurcation occur at $\Re(\lambda) = 0$, i.e. making the onset of oscillatory behavior in the system. Form Figure 4, most of the colormap is in the blue region, corresponding to negative real parts and therefore stable equilibria. However, for larger value of β and small delays, h, region of positive real parts appear in yellow/ green indicates instability. The yellow boundary corresponds to $\Re(\lambda) = 0$, and thus define the critical Hopf bifurcation. Quantitively, when $\beta < 0.3$, the system remains stable for all tested delays i.e. no oscillations arise. However, for higher spreading rates, $\beta > 0.6$, decreasing the delay h pushes the system toward instability which give signal to Hopf bifurcation onset.

Thus, the model predicts that rumor oscillations can only emerge when both β is high and delay is sufficiently small. This bifurcation diagram shows that the rumor dynamics remain damped unless both (i) people spread rumors very aggressively (β high) and (ii) there is a significant delay in their forgetting or fact-checking (h small). Only in this combined region do oscillatory outbreaks emerge.

Figure 4. The Hopf bifurcation onset map

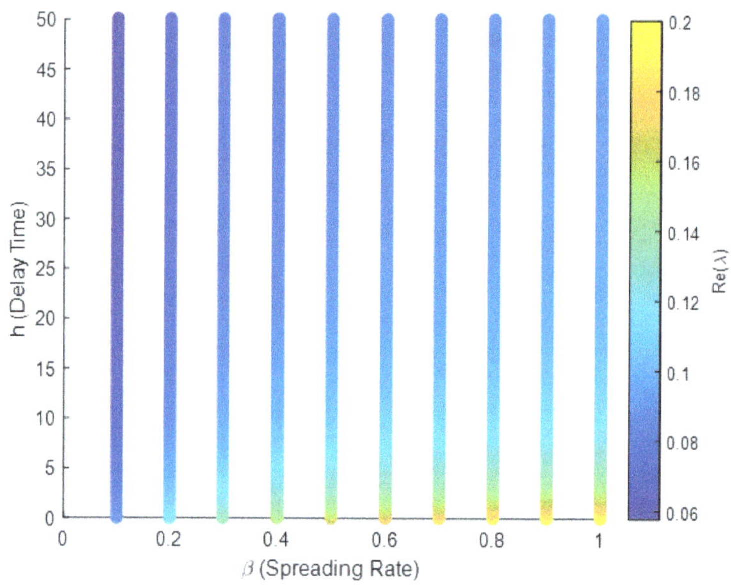

Table 5 indicates the simulated process of DDE system (2).

Table 5. Algorithm for DDE simulation and phase portrait plot

Algorithm: DDE Simulation and Phase Portrait Plot

Input: Parameters $(\Gamma, \mu, \theta, \tau, \beta, r, e, K, \alpha, m, gmax, U50, n, \delta)$ and history function.
Output: Time series trajectories $(S(t), P(t), I(t), U(t), H(t))$.

1 Initialize model parameters.

2 Define incidence functions: $f(U) = \frac{1}{1+\alpha U^m}$, $g(U) = \frac{g_{max} U^n}{U_{50}^n + U^n}$

3 Define DDE system:

$$\frac{dS}{dt} = \Gamma - ((1-\theta)I + \theta P)Sf(U_{delay}) - \mu S,$$

$$\frac{dP}{dt} = \theta SPf(U_{delay}) + \tau I - (\mu + g(U_{delay}))P,$$

$$\frac{dI}{dt} = (1-\theta)SIf(U_{delay}) - (\mu + \tau + \beta)I,$$

$$\frac{dU}{dt} = r - eU - \frac{\delta PU}{K+U},$$

$$\frac{dH}{dt} = \beta I + Pg(U_{delay}) - \mu H.$$

4 Specify history function: $[S, P, I, U, H] = [9, 0.5, 0.2, 1, 0]$.

5 Solve the system using the **dde23** solver on the interval $[1, 100]$.

6 Extract trajectories and plot:

o Time series $S(t), P(t), I(t), U(t), H(t)$.

o Phase portraits (*S* vs *I*, *P* vs *U*, *I* vs *P*).

7 Return trajectories.

8 Finish.

Figure 5. Phase portrait plot for SPHR model simulation

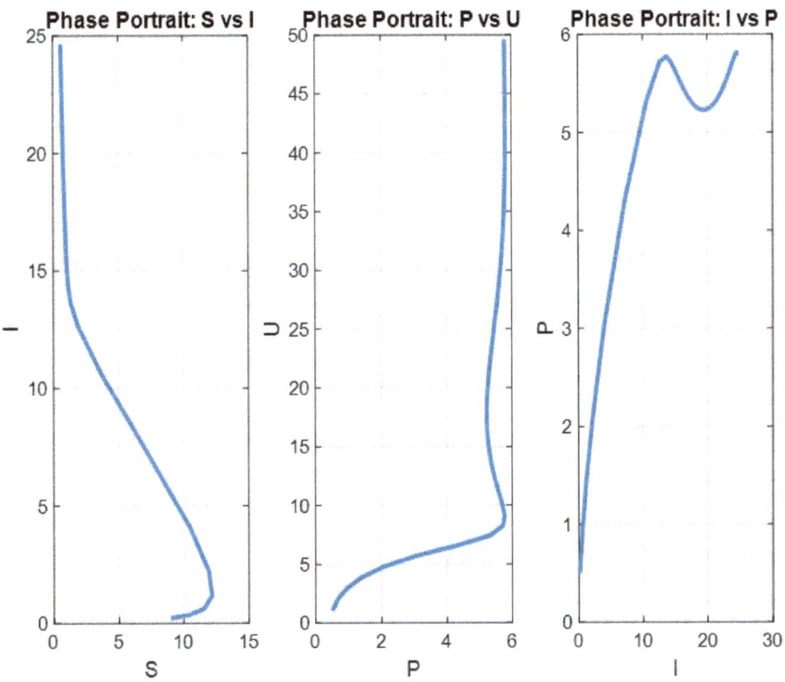

The phase changes of S, I, P, and U are displayed in Figure 5.

Figure 5 illustrates the phase-plane projections of the delayed rumor-spreading system across three key relationships: ignorant versus susceptible ($I - S$), control versus propagators ($U - P$), and propagators versus ignorants ($P - I$). These dynamics capture the impact of delayed control ($h > 0$) on system trajectories. In the $I - S$ plane (left panel), the curve shows how ignorant (I) rise as susceptible (S) decline. Initially, susceptible are recruited into rumor activity, but due to effective control and individual resistance, a large proportion move into the ignorant class rather than becoming propagators. The sharp decline in susceptible alongside the corresponding growth of ignorant reflects the dominant role of ignoring behavior in halting rumor spread. The $U - P$ plane (middle panel) captures the interplay between delayed control (U) and propagators (P). As the rumor spreads, propagators increase at first, but the control mechanism responds with a delayed rise, eventually dominating the dynamics. The steep increase in U near equilibrium confirms that delayed awareness and external intervention eventually suppress rumor activity, forcing propagators into decline. The $P - I$ plane (right panel) reveals the most significant oscillatory effect of delay. Both propagators and ignorant initially grow together, but the trajectory does not converge smoothly. Instead, oscillatory fluctuations appear as the system approaches equilibrium, consistent with a Hopf bifurcation induced by the delay in control response. These damped oscillations indicate that the delayed feedback prevents an immediate balance between spreading and ignoring, prolonging the transient phase before stabilization.

To further validate the theoretical analysis, we performed direct numerical simulations of the delayed SPHR model. Table 6 indicated the DDE simulation of the rumor spreading algorithm. Figure 6 illustrates the temporal dynamics of all compartments SPHR for different values of the control delay parameter h.

Table 6. Algorithm for SPHR with delayed feedback simulation for rumor spreading

Algorithm: SPHR with delayed feedback simulation for rumor spreading
Input: Parameters $(\Gamma, \theta, \mu, \tau, \beta, r, e, \delta, K, \alpha, m, g_{max}, U_{50}, n)$, initial condition and set of delays. **Output:** Population dynamics under multiple delay values. **1** Initialize parameters and initial state $y_0 = [S, P, I, U, H]$. **2** Define nonlinear functions: $f(U) = \frac{1}{1 + \alpha U^m}$, $g(U) = \frac{g_{max} U^n}{U_{50}^n + U^n}$ **3** For each delay value $h \in \{0, 1, 5, 10\}$: o If $h = 0$, solve the **ODE system** (no delay). o If $h > 0$, solve the **DDE system** with lag h. **4** Collect trajectories (S, P, I, U, H) over $(0, 200]$. **5** Plot results for each delay, time series for all compartments. **6** Return population dynamics for all delay scenarios. **7** Finish.

Figure 6. SPHR model simulation for non-delayed and delayed feedback

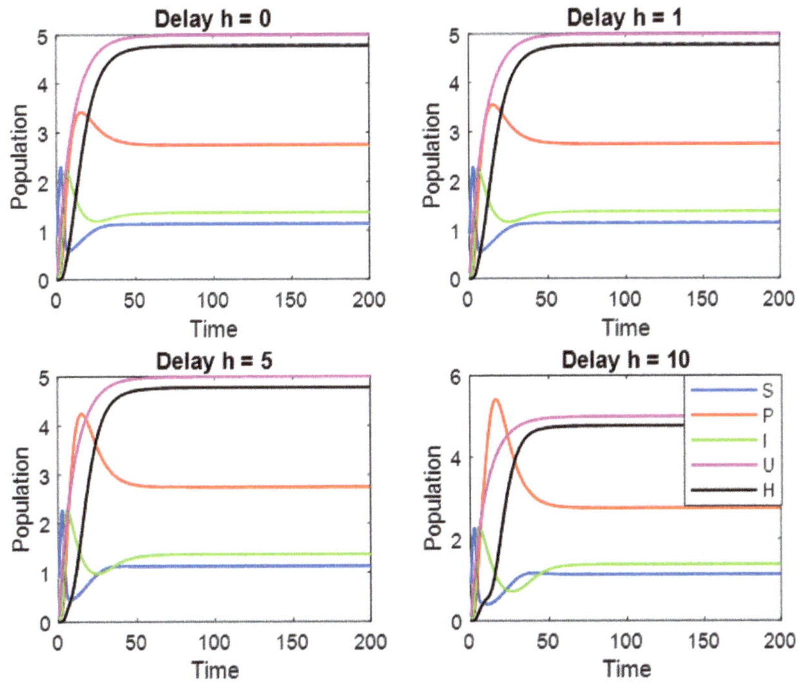

Across all scenarios presented in Figure (6), the system exhibits transient oscillations in the early stage, followed by stabilization at a positive endemic equilibrium. The trajectories reveal a consistent ordering: the control mechanism (U) and hesitant population (H)dominate the long-term dynamics, while propagators (P) decline to low levels after an initial overshoot. Susceptible (S) are quickly depleted as individuals move into the ignoring, propagating, or controlled compartments. A closer inspection indicates the following four cases:

1. Short delay, $h = 1$ Control activates rapidly, suppressing propagation efficiently. Oscillations are weak and damped, with ignorant (I) stabilizing at a relatively low level.
2. Moderate delay exhibit transient oscillations are more pronounced, with a higher early peak of propagators. Ignorant accumulates at a slightly larger equilibrium.
3. Strong control with minimal delay exhibit oscillations vanishes quickly and ignorant flatten at intermediate value. The dominance of U and H ensures rumor suppression.

4. Long delay, $h = 1$ indicate the propagator population exhibits the largest overshoot before collapsing. Ignorant settle at the highest equilibrium across all cases, while oscillations persist for a longer transient. This regime is closest to the Hopf bifurcation threshold, consistent with the spectral analysis in Section 4.

These results highlight the critical role of delay in awareness and control mechanisms. Even when the basic reproduction number, R_0 timely intervention (short delay) can suppress the peak of propagation and limit the persistence of ignorant. Conversely, longer delays allow rumor spreading to transiently amplify, making ignorant the dominant class in the long run.

6. FUTURE RESEARCH DIRECTIONS

The delayed SPHR model offers some novel insights into rumor dynamics, but there are many areas for improvement that are yet to be explored. One natural extension is to explore heterogeneous social networks, where rumors circulate differently between subgroups and communities. Such networks are better placed to record differences in influence, trust, and susceptibility, creating a more realistic understanding of how interventions manifest across heterogeneous populations. A second direction, where the stochastic effects and agent-based simulations can be included in the method, would enable the model to capture the individual level of uncertainty, behavioral variability, and randomness associated with rumor adoption and control responses. Concurrently, compartmental models combined with deep learning techniques are emerging as promising fields in misinformation treatment. Hybrid models that integrate theoretical dynamics and data-driven intelligence in other studies can be considered in the future. For example, a BERT-based detector could raise red flags on incoming rumors, a graph-based neural module would measure their potential spread by modifying propagation parameters in real time, and a reinforcement learning controller might suggest the most appropriate interventions (e.g., to issue fact-checks or to limit diffusion in a particular segment of the network). This pipeline would go through a closed-loop of sensing (by applying deep learning to social media data) and acting (usefully model-informed control techniques), allowing for intelligent and responsive management of rumor spread. Although promising, this vision contains significant challenges, e.g., model transparency, scalability across large and complex networks, and human factors, such as user trust and responses to interventions.

Combining data-driven learning with compartmental modelling shows great potential. By combining delayed feedback models such as SPHR with more sophisticated AI approaches, we expect future research toward reactive infrastructure for response to infodemics, not just tracking the pathways through which rumor vectors spread but also responding proactively to mitigate their impact on society. Although the delayed SPHR model opens a new area for insight, there are still several future gaps that need to be examined. This model then improves predictions on heterogeneous social networks, which are more appropriate for detecting rumors spread within subgroups and affect intervention efficacy. Stochastic effects and agent-based simulations that account for individual-level uncertainty and randomness in rumor adoption and control response could also be introduced. Compartmental rumor models married with deep learning are paving the way towards new opportunities for misinformation governance. Based on such hybrid frameworks, future research will probably create end-to-end systems (e.g., an architecture whereby BERT-based detectors alert incoming rumors, graph-based neural modules estimating the spread potential (changing parameters in this framework such as propagation rates on-the-fly) and reinforcement learning controllers specifying the best intervention to be taken (e.g., sending fact-checks, throttling diffusions in specific network regions). This pipeline would loop back and forth between sensing (using deep learning on the data) and acting (using control strategies based on predictions of the model) into a closed-loop feedback control system for information ecosystems. By deeply leveraging data-driven learning and theoretical rumor dynamics, we inch towards better adaptive 'infodemic response systems' that not only understand how such rumors occur, but also that can respond early and in a more targeted way to limit and mitigate the damaging effects of such rumors. The combination of deep learning and compartmental modeling provides a state-of-the-art direction for the research in computational social science and the manipulation of misinformation.

7. CONCLUSION

This study proposed and analyzed a delayed SPHR spreading model, incorporating the susceptible, ignorant, propagating, control and hesitant compartments. Analytical results indicated two distinct basic reproduction numbers, i.e $R_0^P = 0.719489$, , which shows limited propagation under control mechanism, and $R_0^I = 3.36134$, reflecting the stronger role of ignorance in rumor suppression. The overall basic reproduction number is $R_0 = 3.36134$, suggesting that without sufficient control measures, rumor spread can persist. Numerical simulations supported these theoretical results, showing convergence toward a stable endemic equilibrium under the studied conditions. The dynamics highlight that while rumor propagation tends to peak during the initial stages, the expansion of the ignorant population and the implementation of effective control measures ultimately stabilize the system. Within the parameter ranges, delays in the application of control measures were found to prolong transient oscillations but did not alter the final equilibrium. Nevertheless, it should be acknowledged that substantially longer delays may induce different global dynamics beyond the scope of the present local stability analysis. In conclusion, the delayed SPHR model provides new insights into the dynamics of rumor propagation, emphasizing the critical role of control measures and ignorance in mitigating spread. The findings suggest that reducing intervention delays, strengthening the ignorant class, and sustaining consistent control mechanisms are essential strategies for curbing rumors in digital societies.

ACKNOWLEDGMENT

The authors gratefully acknowledge the financial assistance provided through the Distinguished Grant RDU223008 and International Matching Grant UIC221517 (RDU222704) from Universiti Malaysia Pahang Al-Sultan Abdullah.

REFERENCES

Al-Tuwairqi, S., Al-Sheikh, S., & Al-Amoudi, R. (2015). Qualitative analysis of a rumor transmission model with incubation mechanism. *OAlib*, *2*(1), 1–12. DOI: 10.4236/oalib.1102040

Alsaeedi, A., & Al-Sarem, M. (2020). Detecting rumors on social media based on a CNN deep learning technique. *Arabian Journal for Science and Engineering*, *45*(12), 10813–10844. DOI: 10.1007/s13369-020-04839-2

Chen, W., Zhang, Y., Yeo, C. K., Lau, C. T., & Lee, B. S. (2018). Unsupervised rumor detection based on users' behaviors using neural networks. *Pattern Recognition Letters*, *105*, 226–233. DOI: 10.1016/j.patrec.2017.10.014

Chen, X., & Wang, N. (2020). Rumor spreading model considering rumor credibility, correlation and crowd classification based on personality. *Scientific Reports*, *10*(1), 5887. DOI: 10.1038/s41598-020-62585-9 PMID: 32246112

Choi, D., Oh, H., Chun, S., Kwon, T., & Han, J. (2022). Preventing rumor spread with deep learning. *Expert Systems with Applications*, *197*, 116688. DOI: 10.1016/j.eswa.2022.116688

Daley, D., & Kendall, D. (1964). Epidemics and rumors. *Nature*, *204*(4963), 1118. DOI: 10.1038/2041118a0 PMID: 14243408

Faye, C. (2007). Governing the grapevine: The study of rumor during World War II. *History of Psychology*, *10*(1), 1–21. DOI: 10.1037/1093-4510.10.1.1 PMID: 17575811

Fuchs, A., Passarella, A., & Conti, M. (2023). Modeling, replicating, and predicting human behavior: A survey. *ACM Transactions on Autonomous and Adaptive Systems*, *18*(2), 1–47. DOI: 10.1145/3580492

Ghosh, M., & Das, P. (2025). Analysis of online misinformation spread model incorporating external noise and time delay and control of media effort. *Differential Equations and Dynamical Systems*, *33*(1), 261–301. DOI: 10.1007/s12591-023-00657-8

Li, D., & Ma, J. (2017). How the government's punishment and individual's sensitivity affect the rumor spreading in online social networks. *Physica A*, *469*, 284–292. DOI: 10.1016/j.physa.2016.11.033

Li, M., Zhang, H., Georgescu, P., & Li, T. (2021). The stochastic evolution of a rumor spreading model with two distinct spread inhibiting and attitude adjusting mechanisms in a homogeneous social network. *Physica A*, *562*, 125321. DOI: 10.1016/j.physa.2020.125321 PMID: 33012966

Ma, J., Gao, W., Mitra, P., Kwon, S., Jansen, B. J., Wong, K. F., & Cha, M. (2016). Detecting rumors from microblogs with recurrent neural networks.

Maki, D., & Thompson, M. (1973). *Mathematical models and application*. Prentice-Hall.

Norhayati, R., Ahmad Zuber, M. F., & Turab, A. (2024). Mathematical modelling of a rumor spreading with the attitude of adjusting mechanisms. *Sains Malaysiana*, *53*(3), 719–731. DOI: 10.17576/jsm-2024-5303-18

Turab, A., Rosli, N., Ali, W., & Nieto, J. J. (2023). The existence and uniqueness of solutions to a functional equation arising in psychological learning theory. *Demonstratio Mathematica*, *56*(1), 20220231. DOI: 10.1515/dema-2022-0231

Xia, L. L., Jiang, G. P., Song, B., & Song, Y. R. (2015). Rumor spreading model considering hesitating mechanism in complex social networks. *Physica A*, *437*, 295–303. DOI: 10.1016/j.physa.2015.05.113

Yang, L. X., Li, P., Yang, X., Wu, Y., & Tang, Y. Y. (2018). On the competition of two conflicting messages. *Nonlinear Dynamics*, *91*(3), 1853–1869. DOI: 10.1007/s11071-017-3986-z

Zanette, D. (2001). Critical behavior of propagation on small-world networks. *Physical Review. E*, *64*(5), 050901. DOI: 10.1103/PhysRevE.64.050901 PMID: 11735891

Zhang, Y., & Xu, J. (2015). A rumor spreading model considering the cumulative effects of memory. *Discrete Dynamics in Nature and Society*, *2015*, 204395. DOI: 10.1155/2015/204395

Zhao, L., Qiu, X., Wang, X., & Wang, J. (2013). Rumor spreading model considering forgetting and remembering mechanisms in inhomogeneous networks. *Physica A*, *392*(4), 987–994. DOI: 10.1016/j.physa.2012.10.031

Zhao, X., & Wang, J. (2014). Dynamical behaviors of rumor spreading model with control measures. *Abstract and Applied Analysis*, *2014*, 1–11. DOI: 10.1155/2014/247359

Zhou, Y., Zhang, J., Zhu, C., & Wang, H. (2022). Modelling and analysis of rumor propagation based on stochastic optimal control. *Alexandria Engineering Journal, 61*(12), 12869–12880. DOI: 10.1016/j.aej.2022.06.057

KEY TERMS AND DEFINITIONS

Delay Differential Equation (DDE): A type of differential equation in which the rate of change of a variable depends not only on its current state but also on past states, allowing the modeling of time delays in dynamic systems.

Rumor Spreading Model: A mathematical framework that describes how unverified information spreads within a population, often adapted from epidemiological models.

Susceptible–Propagate–Hesitate–Resisted (SPHR) Model: A compartmental rumor-spreading model that divides individuals into four classes: susceptible, hesitant, propagating, and resisted, incorporating behavioral hesitation.

Hopf Bifurcation: A mathematical phenomenon in which a stable equilibrium becomes unstable and gives rise to sustained oscillations, often caused by time delay in dynamic systems.

Basic Influence Number R_0: An analogue of the basic epidemiological reproduction number, representing the expected number of individuals influenced by a single rumor spreader in a fully susceptible population.

Next Generation Matrix: A mathematical tool used to compute threshold parameters, such as the basic influence number, by analyzing how new spreaders are generated in a structured population.

Rumor-Free Equilibrium (RFE): A steady-state solution of the model where no individuals are actively spreading the rumor, indicating successful control or extinction of the rumor.

Delayed Feedback: The mechanism by which individuals adjust their rumor-spreading behavior after a time lag, reflecting real-world delays in fact-checking, moderation, or hesitation.

Chapter 4

Behavioral Recognition and Classification of Thai Boxing Techniques Using Hybrid Deep Learning Models

Shujaat Ali Zaidi
https://orcid.org/0000-0002-5100-3805
Chiang Mai University, Thailand

Varin Chouvatut
Chiang Mai University, Thailand

Cicik Alfiniyah
Airlangga University, Indonesia

Mudasir Younis
Sakarya University, Turkey

Farzana Hussain
Huston Tillotson University, USA

ABSTRACT

Thai boxing (Muay Thai) is a combat sport gaining global popularity. This research applies hybrid deep learning to automatically detect and classify 10 out of 15 traditional Mae Mai Muay Thai behavioral patterns from videos. Using a curated dataset from a professional boxer, the model achieved 98% accuracy in identifying

DOI: 10.4018/979-8-3373-5062-2.ch004

offensive/defensive maneuvers. Performance metrics (precision, recall, F1-score, and confusion matrix) validate its effectiveness for athlete analysis, coaching, and judging. Results indicate that hybrid deep learning can interpret Muay Thai's dynamic movements, enhancing sports analytics.

1. INTRODUCTION

Sport plays a crucial role in the modern life as it is not only a means to improve health and physical fitness, but also a dynamic field that does not remain the same. As in all other activities of high interest, sports are constantly developing, new training methods, the study of performance, and the development of equipment (Zhu et al., 2008; D'Orazio & Leo, 2010; Zaidi & Chouvatut, 2022) improve and change them. The merging of computer vision and related technologies has become a major success that has democratized the use of high-level training devices, thus making them more affordable and available to amateur athletes and fitness enthusiasts (Quinn & Cocoran, 2022; Cardino et al., 2022).

In contrast to the traditional approaches based on extensive use of manual observation and subjective assessment, modern strategies employ data-driven knowledge to enhance athletic performance (Guo, 2022; Host & Ivašić-Kos, 2022). Computer vision elaborated motion capture technologies can offer precise biomechanical data that allows coaches to identify the inefficiencies in the techniques of the athlete with unmatched accuracy (Kalake et al., 2022). At the same time, smart sensors and developers place immediate feedback, bridging the gap between amateur and professional sports (Worsey et al., 2020).

The importance of these developments is that they are able to make instruction personalized. Forming their training routines could be adjusted to individual choices based on quantifiable indicators (Liu & Liu, 2021). Motion-tracking mobile apps give athletes real-time feedback without having to pay expensive coaches, virtual training platforms simulate competition environments amongst athletes in remote areas (Cust et al., 2019). As these methods evolve and become more cost-effective, professional and amateur sporting activities grow closer together; this fosters a more inclusive and data-awareness-savvy sporting society (Polak et al., 2015).

The technological revolution marks a larger tendency: convergence between sports science and digital innovation has ceased to be the business of large projects. It has become a basic aspect of the fitness mainstream, allowing individuals to improve their performance with the previously unthinkable means (Bonidia et al., 2018). The resulting effect is a better engaged, highly educated and healthier worldwide population- a fact which testifies that it is not the sole physical capacity, but the intelligent application of modern technologies that holds the future of sport (Rajšp & Fister, 2020).

The recent achievements in the field of computational and deep learning methods have revolutionized behavioral analysis in a range of disciplines (Turab et al., 2024a; Turab et al., 2024b), such as the field of animal and human cognition, and sports, including Muay Thai. By employing convolutional neural networks (CNNs), recurrent neural networks (RNNs) as well as transformer-based models, researchers are now able to explain complex behavioral patterns. The algorithm of pose estimation like OpenPose or MediaPipe can be used in Muay Thai to monitor movements in hitting strategies, defense, and posture of the fighter in real-time. This combination of mathematical modeling and data-driven algorithms enables the full analysis, prediction, and understanding of dynamical behavior in the case of experimental settings and sports (Turab & Sintunavarat, 2019; Turab Sintunavarat, 2020; Zaidi & Chouvatut, 2023).

Research in the sports video based action detection shows significant difficulties and opportunities, especially to properly locate and find Mae Mai Muay Thai (MMMT) techniques of real time videotapes. The practical implications of this sight are immense because automated surveillance due to security, smart video retrieval, and behavioral detection have become feasible, as well as advanced human-computer interfaces (Da Costa et al., 2019; Zaidi & Chouvatut, 2022).

To identify correctly the tactical maneuvers of MMMT is crucial not only to fighters but also to coaches; however, the issue of detection of actions in the given sphere still remains a major setback. The presence of real-world situations like sudden changes into camera angles, barriers, crowded backgrounds, and unpredictable lights makes it difficult to guarantee the monitoring of performance and safety (Keshavarzian et al., 2019; Spolaor et al., 2020). A critical key of MMMT recognition is the fact that the dynamics of time and space in video sequences have been greatly captured. Earlier methodologies primarily relied on the neural repertoires of motions by manual feature engineering in order to describe the spatial nature of motions in an attempt to capture the essence of each act (Aggarwal & Ryoo, 2011; Li et al., 2019). However, all these strategies were inherently limited by the dependence on a particular set of data. Because of the diversity of human movement and the differences in environments, these strategies were not usually generalizable to different situations (Dai et al., 2019). The newer developments have shifted to a more flexible model, particularly three-dimensional spatiotemporal models. Modern systems can better grasp the patterns of real-time motions across multiple frames since they convert traditional spatial visualization of 2D information into 3D (Kwon et al., 2018; Baccouche et al., 2011).

To detect MMMT techniques would require such a detection of subtle differences between methods; a complex structure of the posture of the boxer, the area he/she is targeting (head or body) and the interplay of movement and form. These features make it very difficult to detect the action required and careful feature selection is necessary to ensure that it is right (Ashker, 2011). The pattern of stance of a boxer also changes across all planes of MMMT which depend on the force, direction and range of the hits of the blows (short or long), which in turn, change the angles of flexion of the elbow (Gartland et al., 2001). The key aspect of this study will be the explanations of the pattern of a boxers body positions and particularly positioning of the hands and elbows as these will reveal intentions and competencies (Chankuna, 2006).

The recognition and labeling of MMMT, in particular in the video, remains an uphill research task. Despite the development of motion capture technology, such as the skeletal estimation of Kinetic, they become less reliable when there is a dynamic fight. Factors like non upright postures, partial occlusions, and intricate biomechanics of the Muay Thai techniques contribute a lot to prevent proper recognition (Shotton et al., 2011). Even with recent progress in the general case of action detection, the highly complex and highly diverse nature of MMMT motions create significant challenges in automated video-based analysis with current methodologies. Our research findings: The most important contributions of our study are:

- In this study, we propose a hybrid modeling approach for the automated detection and classification of fighter behavioral patterns.
- In this research, we evaluate several state-of-the-art deep learning architectures, including VGG19 and MobileNetV2. These models are fine-tuned on the MMMT image dataset to efficiently and accurately identify and classify fighter behavioral patterns.
- Effective data augmentation techniques, such as flipping, rotation, shearing, and zooming, are proposed to enhance the identification and classification of fighter behavioral patterns in imbalanced datasets

1.1 Muay Thai

Muay Thai that is a traditional Thai martial art has a massive cultural background, perfected through generations. Traditionally, it served as a martial art and a technique of defending the nation, and Thai armies applied its techniques to rescue their nation. Muay Thai is also known as the art of eight limbs and uses an active combination of the fists, elbows, knees, and shins, which is different in contrast to other martial arts of striking (Delp, 2005; Delp, 2013). In the late 20th and early 21st centuries the global expansion of Muay Thai has further increased as the practitioners began entering the global stage of boxing, mixed-rules fights, and specific Muay Thai championships (Kaewplee et al., 2015). In Muay Thai, techniques are divided into two broad categories: Mae Mai (basic techniques - also known as mother techniques) and Look Mai (advanced techniques - also known as complement techniques). Such combat techniques grant the motivation behind the Muay Thai strategical stances because they guide fighters on both offensive and defensive actions (Delp, 2013).

1.2 Mae Mai Muay Thai (MMMT)

Muay Thai is a term that is used to refer to the basic fight techniques that are used in the muay thai. The student has to improve and perfect the skills needed before advancing to enlighten him/herself in Look-Mai or other techniques that are not necessary. This fighting sport involves the use of a number of body parts including the foot, knee and elbow. There are fifteen styles of the MMMT (Saengsawang et al., 2015; Fong, 2014; Delp, 2013). They are as follows:

1.2.1 Salab Fan Pla

One of the keys to defense is the Salab Fan Pla (see Figure 1), which is supposed to avoid receiving a direct hit through moving the body outside of the path of the strike of the opponent so that the fist could miss the target (Krauss, 2006; Fong, 2014; Delp, 2013). This technique begins as the assailant gets on the left foot and a straight left punch. Defender takes a diagonal right stride redistributing body weight on the flexed right leg and rotating the head and torso away to the left of the onrushing attack.

Figure 1. Salab Fan Pla

(Zaidi & Chouvatut, 2023)

1.2.2 Paksa Waek Rang

The Paksa Waek Rang (see Figure 2) is a complex of complementary movements used as a part of an entrance approach by the trainer (Krauss, 2006; Fong, 2014; Delp, 2013). The attacker strikes the defender directly on the left-fist, as he/she moves simultaneously with the left foot. The defender shifts the position of the arm on the left of the opponent by approximately sixty degrees and loads the front foot.

Figure 2. Paksa Waek Rang

(Zaidi & Chouvatut, 2023)

1.2.3 Chawa Sad Hok

The Chawa Sad Hok is a very effective defensive mechanism that helps to prevent the direct attack and at the same time, throws a successful elbow hit. The case would be where a aggressor takes a step forward, striking directly left and moves forward with the left foot (see Figure 3). The defender also quickly makes a planned movement: rotating to the right in thirty degrees, so that the weight will be on the right foot to support it, and flex the arm of the left arm by the elbow (Krauss, 2006; Fong, 2014; Delp, 2013).

Figure 3. Chawa Sad Hok

(Zaidi & Chouvatut, 2023)

1.2.4 Inao Thang Grit

The most important method of countering a straight blow is the Inao Thang Grit (see Figure 4). In order to execute this technique effectively, the defender has to position his/her elbow close to the body and apply a round motion. The defender stands on the one foot (left) and the other foot is stretched across the attacker, hitting the ribs of the victim with the right arm (Krauss, 2006; Fong, 2014; Delp, 2013).

Figure 4. Inao Thang Grit

(Zaidi & Chouvatut, 2023)

1.2.5 Yo Khao Prasumeru

A defensive straight punch used in close-quarters combat was to avoid the blow of the opponent using a strong forward bend to dodge the attack and then a vertical strike to the forehead straight up, then a head stab at the chin downwards (Khao Prasumeru, see Figure 5). The defender moves the left foot at the same time and steadily, the left knee goes downwards leaving the right leg stable. The body is bent forward in 45 degrees bringing the balance completely to the left foot (Krauss, 2006; Fong, 2014; Delp, 2013).

Figure 5. Yo Khao Prasumeru

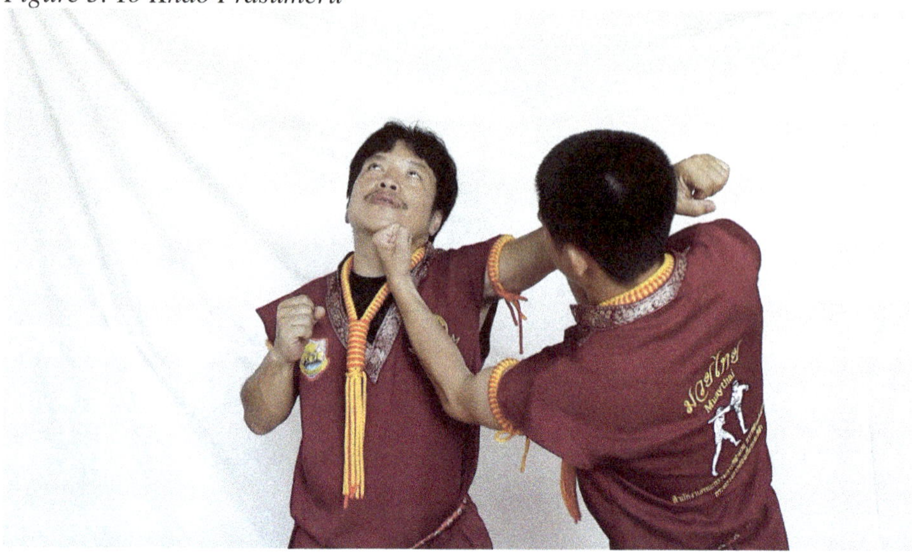

(Zaidi & Chouvatut, 2023)

1.2.6 Ta Then Kam Fak

As one of the basic protection measures against direct blows to the chin, Ta Then Kam Fak (see Figure 6) is applied as the initial arm strike to disrupt the balance of the attacker (Krauss, 2006; Fong, 2014; Delp, 2013). The defender steps with the left foot forward leaving the defender in the lowered mobility range of the attacker reducing the options of his/her opponent to make a hit.

Figure 6. Ta Then Kam Fak

(Zaidi & Chouvatut, 2023)

1.2.7 Mon Yan Lak

One of the most basic and yet highly versatile methods in the ancient combat methods is Mon Yan Lak (see Figure 7); this can be used as both an offensive and a defense gesture (Krauss, 2006; Fong, 2014; Delp, 2013). During a typical engagement scenario, an attacker will jump forward on left foot with a straight strike with the respective fist. The defender turns at 45 degrees to the right indicating a lot of weight on the back (right) foot.

Figure 7. Mon Yan Lak

(Zaidi & Chouvatut, 2023)

1.2.8 Pal Look Toy

The masters technique of the Pal Look Toy (see Figure 8) will counter kicks which involve an attack at the elbow-to-shin. The process is described in the following way: An attacker goes to the distance of kicking and delivers a right leg strike against the ribs of the opponent (Krauss, 2006; Fong, 2014; Delp, 2013). At the same time, the defender moves the body weight to the left and retires using the left foot. The right arm is bent by the defender so as to offset the incoming kick with perfect timing. Elbow is used as a surface of hard strike pushing off the force of the attack and also minimizing the threat posed by the attacker.

Figure 8. Pal Look Toy

(Zaidi & Chouvatut, 2023)

1.2.9 Jorrakhe Fad Hang

In the Jorrakke Fad Hang (see Figure 9), technique, a dynamic heel kick is given using a rotation of the body and there is full utilization of the rotational energy to deliver maximum force. Imagine a case where a foe moves forward with his left foot and hits directly with left foot (Krauss, 2006; Fong, 2014; Delp, 2013). The defender then quickly turns his right foot to the right in a diagonal way to avoid the blow in whatever way the stance does not change.

Figure 9. Jorrakhe Fad Hang

(Zaidi & Chouvatut, 2023)

1.2.10 Hak Nguang Aiyara

This In Hak Nguang Aiyara (see Figure 10) is one of the basic defensive measures where the elbow- thigh movement is employed to counter a secondcoming kick. A case can be imagined where a rapist aims at kicking the right rib of the defender, and at the same time, he flexes both hands to protect the face. The defender will rapidly move forward closing the distance by thrusting the right foot. The knee of the right leg folds as the body is rotated to the left, whilst the leg of the left one remains straight, hence enhancing stability (Krauss, 2006; Fong, 2014-; Delp, 2013).

Figure 10. Hak Nguang Aiyara

(Zaidi & Chouvatut, 2023)

1.2.11 Naka Bid Hang

The Naka Bid Hang (see figure 11) is a well mastered defence kind of technique which involves the holding of the kicking jumping foot of the attacker to the toe which has been largely documented in the martial arts books. The defender can also have a controlled twisting motion by holding the foot using both their hands then smack the unsuspecting opponent before they can hit him in the precise location with the knee (Krauss, 2006; Fong, 2014; Delp, 2013).

Figure 11. Naka Bid Hang

(Zaidi & Chouvatut, 2023)

1.2.12 Wiroon Hok Glab

The method of the Wiroon Hok Glab (see Figure 12) is a masterful way of neutralizing an impending high kick as it neutralizes and at the same time subdues the opponent. In this case, the attacker kicks with his left foot with considerable power into the ribs of the defender. The defender then transfers his or her weight and then punches the left hamstring of the attacker using his or her left heel, which destabilizes the balance and the great impetum (Krauss, 2006; Fong, 2014; Delp, 2013).

Figure 12. Wiroon Hok Glab

(Zaidi & Chouvatut, 2023)

1.2.13 Dab Chawala

The method of Dab Chawala (see Figure 13), is a defensive mechanism resisting a straight attack. In a linear punch, the attacking party is counteracted by the offensive boxer with a sweeping motion of the left arm to retaliate, with the purpose of hitting the opponent with an aiming blow to the eye (Krauss, 2006; Fong, 2014; Delp, 2013). This is a technically straightforward but strategically effective technique because it attacks a vulnerable area to increase the amount of damage and decrease the complexity of defense.

Figure 13. Dab Chawala

(Zaidi & Chouvatut, 2023)

1.2.14 Khun Yak Hap Ling

The Khun Yak Hap Ling (see Figure 14) as a necessary defensive operation against a man who is actively applying punches, kicks and elbows. Consider the case where the attacker initiates the assault by moving forward with the left foot and at the same time rightly punching the face of the attacker (Krauss, 2006; Fong, 2014; Delp, 2013). The defender then extends their left foot immediately minimizing the distance to almost the body of contact with the right arm used in blocking the hitting arm of the attacker.

Figure 14. Khun Yak Hap Ling

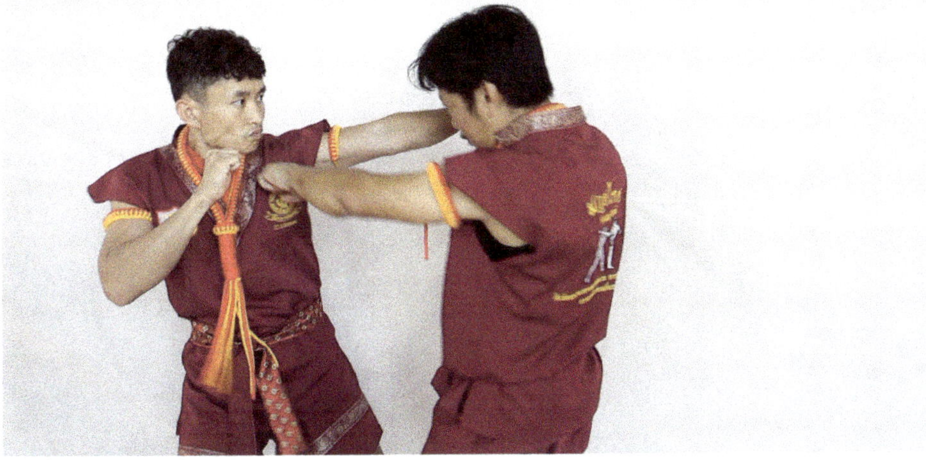

(Zaidi & Chouvatut, 2023)

1.2.15 Hak Kor Erawan

The Hak Kor Erawan (see Figure 15) is an advanced defensive manoeuvre in Muay Thai, as the manoeuvre is traditionally used to counter knee strikes or clinch (Krauss, 2006; Fong, 2014; Delp, 2013). This method concerns the defender reversing the attacker in his/her tracks immediately. The defender will take a forceful lifting movement upwards upon the chin of the attacker with the right hand at the same time, and to a certain extent, twists the neck, bringing about destabilization of equilibrium and control.

Figure 15. Hak Kor Erawan

(Zaidi & Chouvatut, 2023)

The chapter consists of five major sections and each of them is devoted to a specific part of the study. Section 2 begins with a comprehensive analysis of the relevant literature, which establishes the theoretical framework and puts the research into the context of the existing academic discussion. Section 3 expounds on the proposed measure, which includes the framework, procedures, and explanation of the experimental design. Section 4 then summarizes and reviews the empirical evidence and determines what they imply in the objectives of the study. Section 5 ultimately summarizes the main findings, discusses constraints and suggests future pathways of the future research.

2. BACKGROUND AND RELATED WORK

Recent studies indicate that deep learning has become a revolution in the world of science, especially in the areas of computer vision, speech recognition, medical image processing, and natural language processing (Bonidia et al., 2018; Turab et al., 2022; Zaidi et al., 2025a; Polak et al., 2015; Zaidi et al., 2025b; Turab et al., 2023). The traditional approaches to machine learning, i.e., multilayer perceptrons and support vector machines, rely on shallow designs having limited computing abilities. Even though they work on small datasets, these algorithms face several challenges with complex classification problems, particularly when dealing with semantically rich items. They reduce their performance and generalization capabilities with the introduction of a complex feature representation, which explains why they have a major failure in dealing with high-dimensional data, including photos (Lv et al., 2022). The strength of deep learning lies in the ability to learn and cope on its own and combine features, something previously required by human engineering. This study reflected in contemporary autoencoders that have sparse or restricted Boltzmann machines (RBMs), and convolutional neural networks (CNNs) (Ahmed & Jalal, 2024; Turab et al., 2025).

The determination of activities in motionless images has numerous applications in a variety of fields. With this capability, it is easier to have the robots perceive and respond better to human movements. Surveillance systems offer an improvement in the security monitoring through identifying some of the behaviors or actions of the frames that are at rest (Rahevar et al., 2023). The technology is crucial in the field of human-computer interaction where computers can interpret the user gesture or intent without requiring movement-based input. Alongside them, the task of video analysis is also upgraded by action detection as it allows the speedy frame annotation and information search. As an illustration, it is highly easier to find a specific activity within the large video when significant activities are detected on separate frames (Muhamada & Mohammed, 2022). Through this approach the minimum processing is required since the redundancy segments are removed and no loss in precision is taken. In addition to this, picture searches could be action-focused through online searches, which can increase the accuracy of the search when a user desires images depicting a particular movement or interaction (Wang & Yan, 2023).

Video surveillance has increasingly been applied in human action detection as it has adopted deep learning to identify advanced discriminating features and build end-to-end systems (Dai et al., 2019). A different researcher introduced a new way of classifying boxing strikes through overhead depth images and combat sports statistics in 2015 (Kasiri-Bidhendi et al., 2015). The researcher is only dealing with straight punches whereby random forest and support vectors models are used in the classification. Even though their method showed promising outcomes, it was limited to a particular group of boxing skills, disregarding other types of strikes. Another study inspired by the concept of action- and posture-based graphs to evaluate boxing skills was based on the creation of a hidden Markov model to obtain graphs by a researcher in 2017 (Shen et al., 2017). Their technique assessed shadow boxing motions and gave cues at a time when fighters executed both basic and predefined moves.

A different perspective was proposed in 2019 by a researcher who merged an angular dynamic time-wrapping algorithm and kinetic sensors to have a classification of user activities (Chantaprasert et al., 2019). In 2022, a new research revealed an improved framework of the automatic classification of MMMT methods (Zaidi & Chouvatut, 2022). In their study, the authors adopted a deep learning approach to address the challenge of identifying styles in a combined Convolutional Neural Network (CNNs) and Long Short-Term Memory (LSTM) model. The novelty of the research given the study was its combination of space and time models.

In 2022 a new framework was developed to classify the seven of the classic MMMT technique by referencing motion sequences of the combat (Zaidi & Chouvatut, 2023). The researchers applied Long-term Recurrent Convolutional Networks (LRCNs) to process these sequential inputs, via a hybrid architecture that captures well the observed spatial and temporal dependencies on battle motions.

More recently, transformers have emerged as a powerful alternative to CNNs in computer vision that achieved popularity due to its ability to process input in a more efficient way through a method known as attention. Unlike traditional sequential models, attention also allows transformers to dynamically highlight the relevant portion of the input, which can increase the accuracy and efficiency of processing. Their use has further expanded to vision-based applications although initially they were mainly used in natural language processing (NLP) to perform tasks like machine translation, language modeling, and voice recognition (Bazi et al., 2021). These are the basic Transformer design (Parmar et al., 2018), which utilizes an encoder-decoder format capable of transcoding input sequence into the output sequence with a significant degree of versatility. It has a parallel processing capability which is a crucial novelty that defeats a major limitation of prior sequential models like LSTMs and RNNs.

3. PROPOSED METHODOLOGY

In this case, we introduce a novel deep learning-based system of identifying and classifying behavioral patterns among MMMT practitioners. In this section the materials, methodology and classification strategy are described with: (1) the image acquisition process, (2) a general description of the analytical framework and (3) a description on how the proposed hybrid modeling technique is achieved in details. In a detailed research workflow methodology, Figure 16 shows the flowchart of the research work.

Figure 16. The suggested flowchart of detecting Mae Mai Muat Thai styles

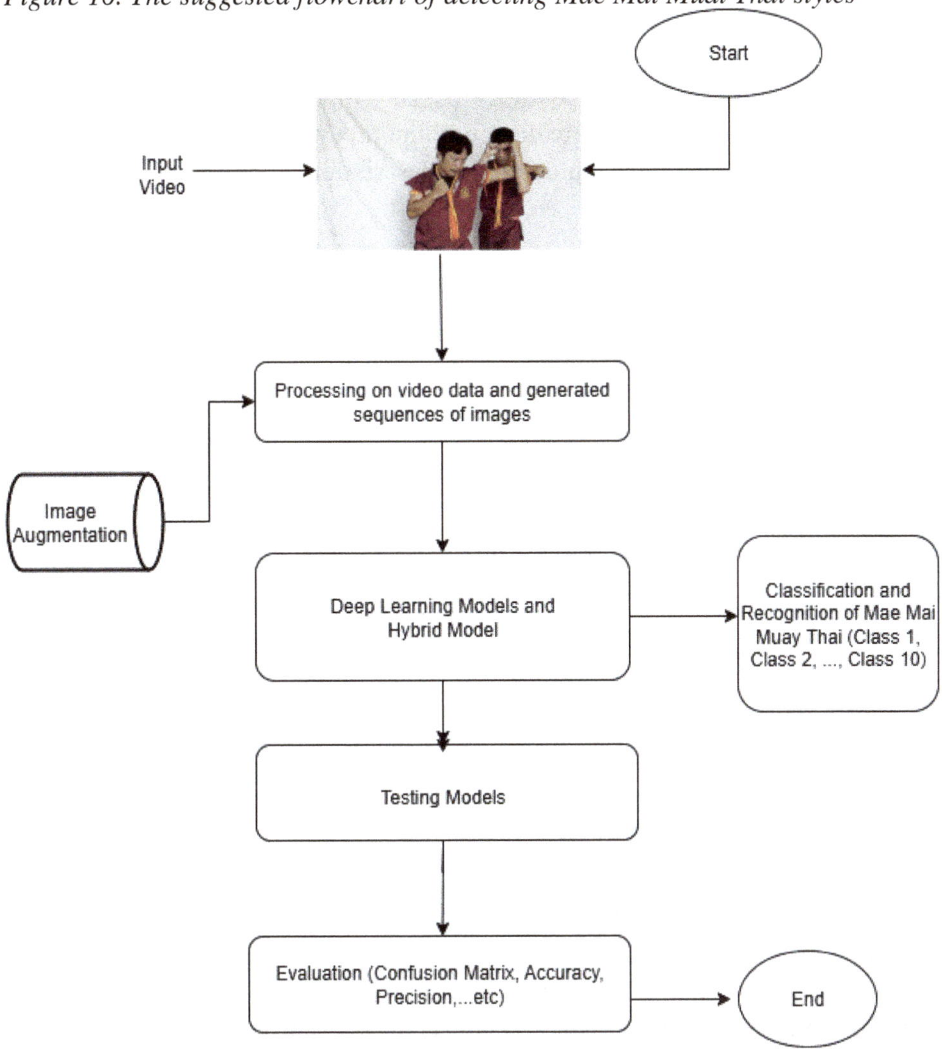

3.1. Data Collection

The study had started by conducting a very severe data collection to develop preliminary knowledge of MMMT techniques, which included identification and classifying of many styles motions. A comprehensive dataset of 4 professional Thai boxers acquiring each technique sixty times under regulated conditions was created. Fighting poses were very diverse, camera angles and movement execution which were quite challenging to analyze. In order to counter these limitations, we supplemented the data with sequences taken in a real boxing sport arena. The last collection is 420 high-resolution RGB video clips, which is the largest set of such kind yet. The clips were all shot in a Canon EOS RP camera with a resolution of 1920 x 1080 at an equal frame rate of 25 fps. As a time series, the data was stored as MP4 to ensure that in the future there is temporal dynamics of the data to use in the analysis of motion. Table 1 provides the description of the datasets.

Table 1. Dataset description

#	Class name	Total images
1	Salab Fan Pla	8790
2	Paksa Waek Rang	8884
3	*Chawa Sad Hok*	10177
4	*Inao Thang Grit*	10409
5	*Yo Khao Prasumeru*	10327
6	*Ta Then Kam Fak*	7570
7	*Mon Yan Lak*	7566
8	Pal Look Toy	7562
9	Jorrakhe Fad Hang	7559
10	Hak Nguang Aiyara	7775

3.2. Image Pre-processing

The analysis of the actual image begins with the preprocessing which is an essential stage in which the raw images are transformed into a refined image format that can be used to perform additional analysis. Preprocessing maximizes input quality to downstream activities through enhancing relevant features and minimizing noise, artifacts, and extraneous inputs. The applied strategies depend on the picture attributes and the application objectives. In this study, the standardization of all pictures was made to 224x224 pixels, which is a standard practice and ensures optimal computing performance, but still, there is sufficient information. In order to increase the degree of clarity, we have applied picture sharpening to the entire dataset, which sharpens edges and subtle forms and also reduces the creation of artifacts to the minimum. Moreover, photos would be displayed in RGB to memorize color data, which is usually of great significance in making exact analysis.

Another crucial part of our preprocess was the processing pixel values. Among the various normalizing methods that were tested, the normalizing by dividing each pixel with 1/255 proved to have some significant effectiveness. This approach has numerous advantages: it normalizes the input data, reduces the use of memory, and removes the overhead on computing when the processing is done. Besides these practical benefits there are the model convergence advantages that are brought through normalization that keeps the input status under a controllable range.

3.3. Data Augmentation

The problem of class imbalance is typical of machine learning, particularly the image classification task when some classes are disregarded. To help mitigate this issue data augmentation methods may artificially increase the training sample by generating modified fakeries of the existing ones. This will increase the generalization of the model and reduce overfitting by exposing the model to different training data variants. In this research we have applied ImageDataGenerator of Keras in order to make a number of geometric transformations, each of which was aimed at the controlled variability without any impairment of semantic integrity of the pictures. The augmentation procedures that were carried out included:

Random Zoom: Image magnification was randomly generated at a fixed ratio of 0.1% which simulates small changes in the camera distance.

Random Rotation: Each picture was rotated within a range of ±30 degrees, guaranteeing resilience to orientation variations without compromising essential elements.

Horizontal Flip: The augmentation used random left-right inversions, so essentially doubling the dataset while preserving natural visual coherence.

Width Shift: Images were horizontally displaced by as much as 20% of their overall width, accommodating slight positioning discrepancies.

Height Shift: Its vertical adjustments of up to 20% of the picture height were included to simulate variations in item placement.

3.4. Training Phase

This section emphasizes critical elements of the training process, including model types, hyperparameter settings, and classifier structures.

3.4.1. Dataset Split

In supervised machine learning and deep learning, datasets are often divided into distinct subsets for training, validation, and testing purposes. During training data, image augmentation is commonly applied to the data, and occasionally also on the validation sets to enhance the generalization of the model; test sets are often not augmented so that the information can not be revealed and a fair performance measurement can be achieved. This study delineated the dataset into 70, 20 and 10 percent of training, validation and testing respectively.

3.4.2. Model Architectures

This study explored the effectiveness of a number of deep learning architectures on the premise of MMMT dataset and compared three particular (see Figure 16) models namely VGG19, MobileNetV2 and a Hybrid deep learning model. The developed models were based on the Python and Keras framework, relying on convolutional layers, which were created through the deep learning approach, and fully connected layers, which were randomly initialized to enhance the flexibility. The classification engine has been designed with a simplified architecture, with two hidden layers and an output with two neuron units, specifically to ensure proper classification in addition to minimizing chances of overfitting. The compromise created in the research was between the performance of the model and generalizability; by focusing on structural simplicity and the arrangement of strategic layers, both issues have been met by this choice, which is critical when a high level of interpretability and dependability is mandatory.

3.4.3. VGG19

The VGG19 architecture, presented by Simonyan and Zisserman in their key 2014 publication (Simonyan & Zisserman, 2014), signifies a notable progression in convolutional neural networks (CNNs) for extensive image categorization. This model comprises of 19 (see Figure 17) weighted layers, 16 convolutional and three fully connected layers, which should classify photos into 1000 distinct categories of items. A prominent characteristic of VGG19 is its recurrent use of diminutive 3×3 convolutional filters, which augment feature extraction while preserving computing efficiency. This design option enables deeper networks with enhanced nonlinearity and decreased parameter counts, in contrast to previous designs that depended on bigger kernels. The model takes input photos reduced to 224x 224 pixels, and it progressively transforms them using hierarchical feature representations prior to ultimate classification. This is an architectural design of the network into five consecutive blocks, each containing a few convolutional layers followed by a max-pooling algorithm to shrink the spatial dimensions. The initial 16 layers are a more sophisticated visual feature extractor which detects the hierarchical objects, starting with edges and textures and then moving on to complex parts of an object.

Figure 17. VGG 19 architecture

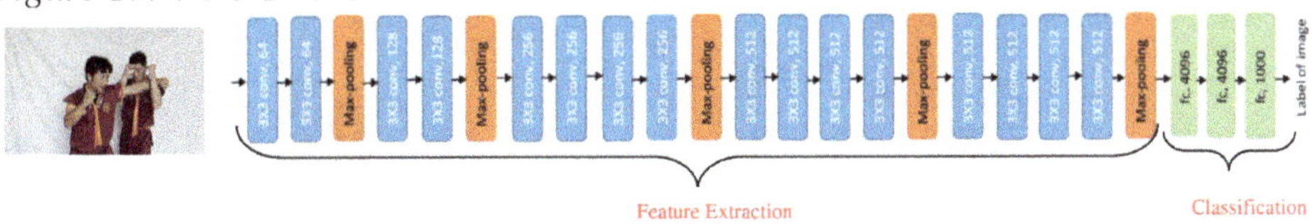

(Bansal et al., 2023)

3.4.4. MobileNet V2

MobileNetV2 (Sandler et al., 2018) represents a small and powerful convolutional neural network (CNN) and has been widely applied in various computing procedures. In this model, MobileNetV1 is advanced with major enhancements, including inverted residual structures and linear bottlenecks to increase the efficiency and performance. In contrast to traditional 2D convolution, which uniformly applies to all input channels to produce a single output channel, depthwise convolution functions differently. Independent filters are applied to each input channel, resulting in separate output channels that are then merged. This procedure is succeeded by a 1×1 pointwise convolution, which integrates these intermediate outputs into a final channel. The result of this approach is comparable to that of traditional convolution with much fewer parameters hence is applicable in resource-constrained scenarios. The simplified structure of MobileNetV2 is summarized in Figure 18. With these design decisions the model has attained optimal balance between the computational efficiency and performance that ensures that the model is adequately suited to be applicable in conditions that demand high levels of efficiency.

Figure 18. MobileNetV2 architecture

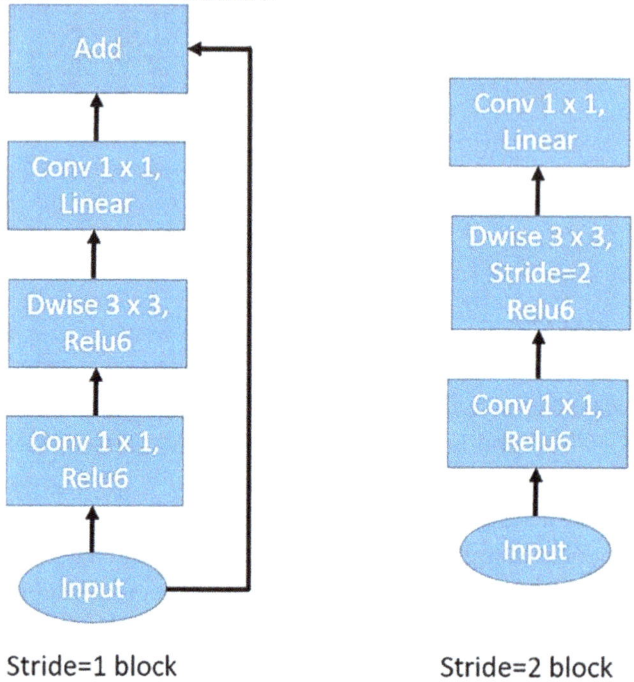

(Radford et al., 2015)

3.4.5. Hybrid Model

Convolutional Neural Networks (CNNs) represent an influential data analysis method in the field of image analysis, which is mainly due to their capability to produce high-level features directly based on raw pixel data, which makes them easier to manipulate and detect more complex patterns. Conversely, the Transformer architecture based on self-attention cell architectures is good at the modeling of long-range relationships in sequence data, and has seen great success in natural language processing (Bazi et al., 2021). Custom developments have examined the adaptation of Transformers to computer vision. Importantly, when applied to image classification in 2020, it achieved better results than traditional CNN-based models, such as EfficientNetB0 (Ba et al., 2016). This development underlines the ability of attention-based mechanisms to revolutionize the forefront approaches towards visual data processing.The change from CNNs to Transformers in vision tasks underscores a broader transformation in AI research, whereby architectures initially created for sequential data are being adapted to tackle issues in other modalities. This flow of ideas does not only widen the notion base of deep learning, but it also opens the possibilities of producing more generalized and effective models.

Our proposed hybrid deep learning system is a combination of convolutional neural networks (CNNs) and the elements of the vision transformer (ViT) to detect MMMT strategies on boxing pictures. The design leverages the strengths of both paradigms, the technique of local feature extraction through CNNs and a global contextual modeling method through the application of self-attention. CNN module contains three sequential convolutional layers with each having 3x3 kernels. ReLU activation is applied at the end of every convolution that implies non-linearity and a 2x2 max pooling operation that decreases the spatial dimensions, therefore, enhancing translational invariance. The input is initially scaled to the range of 0 1, thereby ensuring even gradients when training. The combination of multi-head attention layer immediately after normalisation is also an important improvement. This layer uses four parallel attention heads whose projection dimension is 64, which is practically capturing diverse spatial associations in the feature maps. A skip link is then used to add the attention output with the original input, reducing the vanishing gradient problem and preserving complex features. The features are then passed through a full-connected layer of dimensionality adjustment after another layer normalization. In a secondary residual link, the modified output is again fed to its input, which augments reuse of feature, a trait of a robust deep architecture. This dual-residual architecture does not only stabilize training, but improves hierarchical feature representation as well.

4. RESULTS AND DISCUSSION

This section outlines the major results of our experimental study and defines programming structures employed to generate the results. In order to enhance the clarity, we discuss each of the elements separately in distinct subsections, such as, the methodological background and the empirical results. This will start with the thorough analysis of the experimental data, and then discussion of the software and calculational tools which will make possible our study. These pieces are then segmented to help in maintaining clarity and at the same time maintaining a coherent narrative that meets high academic standards.

4.1. Experimental Setup

Given our dataset is quite large, it was necessary to select a sufficient programming environment that will allow running deep learning experiments quickly. Our models were developed by undertaking and training on a high-performance Dell

Alienware m15 R5 laptop, which has an AMD Ryzen 9 5900HX processor, NVIDIA RTX 3070 graphics card, 32GB DDR4 RAM, and running on Windows 11. Such a setup of the system was able to consider the computing capacity needed to deal with large volumes of information without significant limitations. Python and its vast ecosystem were used: we used TensorFlow and Keras to build and train neural network models, and scikit-learn helped us to perform secondary tasks, such as scaling features and the evaluation of models. The Jupyter Notebook was developed to be interactive, which helped during the development process as it made it easier to test and debug the code in real-time and represent the data in an efficient way.

4.2. Evaluation Procedure

In this study to measure the performance of the different models in a comprehensive manner, different measures derived based on the confusion map, accuracy, precision, recall, and F1-score are used to evaluate the performance of the models. Accuracy is a broad generally important term, which is a measure of the overall correctness, a ratio of the correct instances as identified by some categories and all categories. Precision measures the ability of the model to minimize false positives, which implies the reliability of positive predictions. Recall, on the other hand, evaluates the sensitivity, or the sensitivity to the true positives of the model, where it is important to make sure that important examples are not missed. Moreover, the concept of specificity augments the said metrics by assessing how far the model can identify the presence of negative events correctly, which allows the perspective a holistic look at its discriminant effectiveness. The mathematical formulations of these measurements are presented below in which the measurement repeatability and openness are obtained, which will aid our comparative study. The approach is not only more interpretable than other methods but it is also used to guide model selection based on domain-oriented priorities, which are expected to increase the strength of the classification findings.

$$Accuracy = \left(\frac{TP + TN}{TP + TN + FP + FN}\right) \tag{1}$$

$$Precision = \left(\frac{TP}{TP + FP}\right) \tag{2}$$

$$Recall = \left(\frac{TP}{TP + FN}\right) \tag{3}$$

$$F1 - Score = 2 \times \left(\frac{precision \times recall}{precision + recall}\right) \tag{4}$$

True positives (TP) are the situations when the model is accurate in detecting positive cases of diagnostic and classification issues. On the other hand, False Negatives (FN) occur when the model does not detect any positive potential cases, and so, assumes they are negative. On the other hand, False Positivity (FP) and True Negativity (TN) show the mistakes in characterizing the negative result with an erroneous identification of the negative case as positive, and a right identification of negative cases legitimizing their appropriate classification. A high true positive (TP) and true negative (TN) values reflect high accuracy, however, when there are greater values on false positive (FP) or false negative (FN), then this could be revealing serious biases or gaps in categorization procedure.

4.3. VGG19

Spatial features extraction is very important in identifying the behavioral patterns of combatants using visual data. In this study, the hierarchical feature-extraction capabilities of a VGG19, which is a deep convolutional neural network, are used to recognize MMMT methods. The fine-tuned version of VGG19 model was used to extract features using various layers and pre-train weights. As a measure of performance, we have trained the model in various configurations, changing batch sizes (16, 32, 64) and epochs (16, 24). They indicated a high level of classification with a peak of 91% and the measure of performance was constantly at a higher level than the expected performance. A detailed discussion of these findings has been presented in Table 2 which has summarized the efficiency of the model in identifying and classifying fighter behaviors. The process of training was also analysed with the help of the dynamics of loss curve and accuracy (see Figure 19). Validation and testing performance were evaluated based on the confusion matrices (see Figure 20 and Figure 21) that demonstrated how the model was accurate at distinguishing between various MMMT styles. Misclassifications were very low and involved occurrence in intricately related patterns of movement, which reveals that spatial and time information is very important in accurate classification.

Table 2. VGG19 model results

Epochs	Batch Size	Accuracy	Precision	Recall	F1-score
16	16	0.80	0.78	0.79	0.79
	32	0.84	0.83	0.82	0.83
	64	0.85	0.84	0.83	0.84

Epochs	Batch Size	Accuracy	Precision	Recall	F1-score
24	16	0.85	0.85	0.84	0.83
	32	0.87	0.87	0.86	0.87
	64	0.91	0.91	0.90	0.90

Figure 19. Training and validation accuracy/loss for VGG19

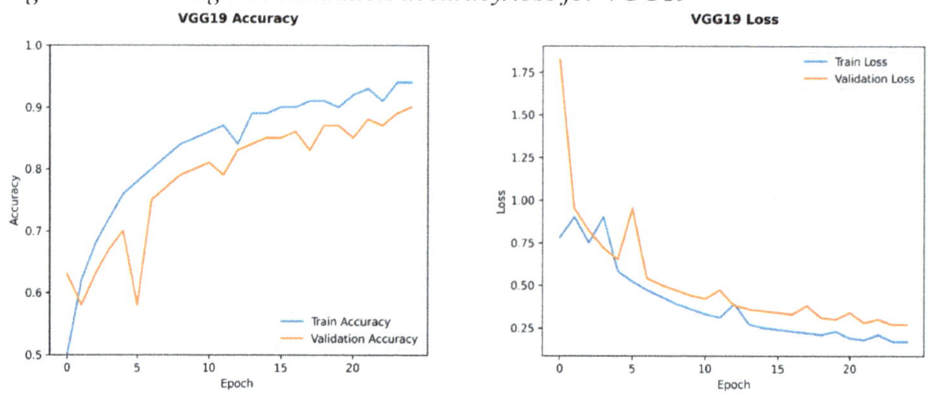

Figure 20. Confusion matrix for the VGG19 model on the validation set

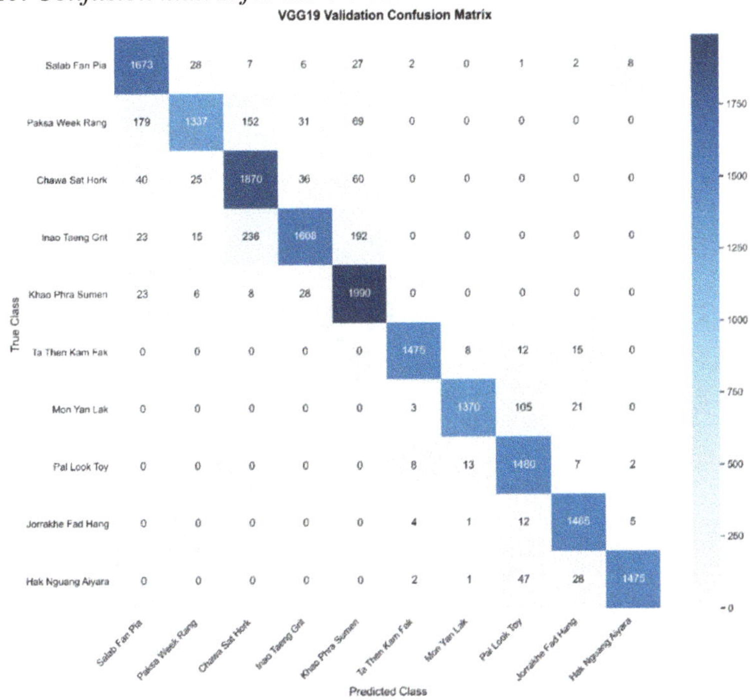

Figure 21. Confusion matrix for the VGG19 model on the testing set

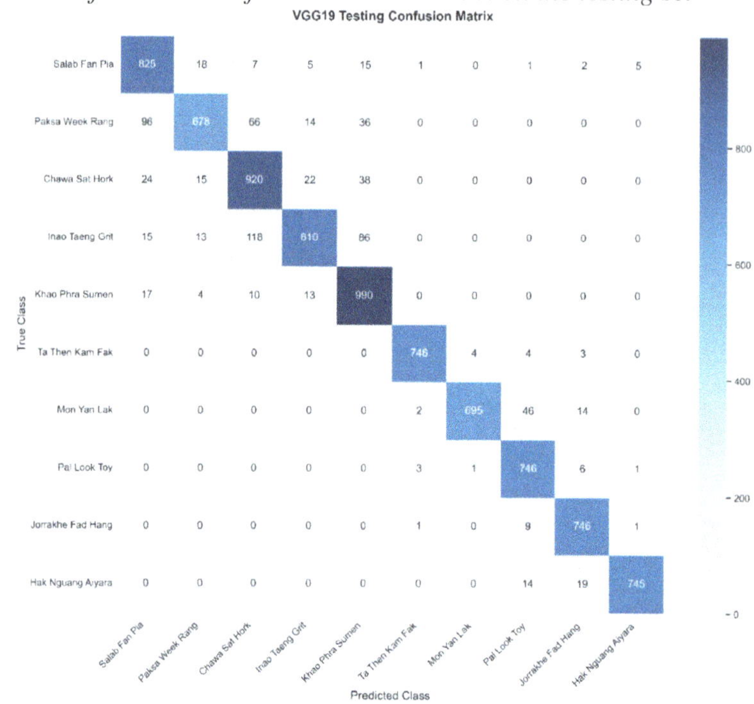

4.4. MobileNet V2

MobileNet V2 represents a significant improvement over MobileNet V1, and its architecture yields better results in fewer learnable parameters and thrice greater computing performance. To evaluate the performance of the model, it was trained with three configurations, where the batch sizes were 16, 32 and 64 and the epochs were 16, 24. The results were of high quality, up to 94 percent, which is better than using the conventional VGG19 model. All the information derived by these studies is summarized by Table 3, which forms a set of standards on which MMMT identification system can be built. Figure 22 can be used as a comparison study which shows the model performance in the best training conditions with loss dynamics and high classification effectiveness. Confusion matrices (in Figures 23 and 24) were used to assess the model validation and testing accuracy, which shows that the model was able to distinguish between different styles of MMMT. Clustering error was smaller, and it mainly arose in the cases of the very similar movement scenarios. This finding points out the importance of extensive geographical and temporal peculiarities to achievement of precise differentiation.

Table 3. MobileNet V2 model results

Epochs	Batch Size	Accuracy	Precision	Recall	F1-score
16	16	0.85	0.84	0.83	0.84
	32	0.89	0.89	0.87	0.88
	64	0.90	0.89	0.88	0.89
24	16	0.92	0.90	0.91	0.91
	32	0.92	0.92	0.91	0.90
	64	0.94	0.94	0.93	0.94

Figure 22. Training and validation accuracy/loss for MobileNet V2

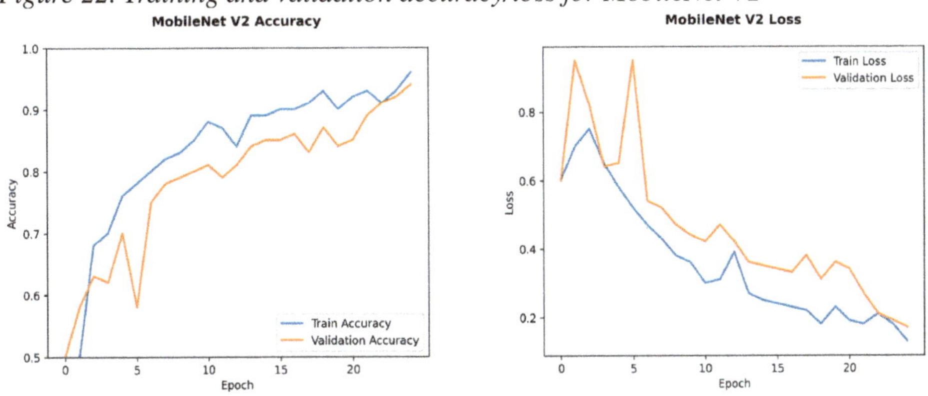

Figure 23. Confusion matrix for the MobileNet V2 model on the validation set

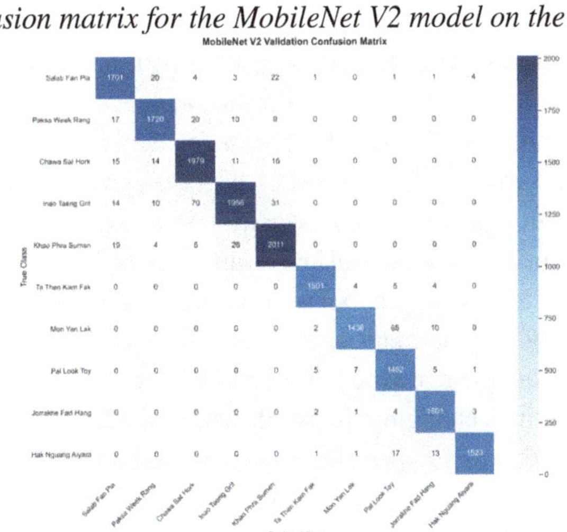

Figure 24. Confusion matrix for the MobileNet V2 model on the testing set

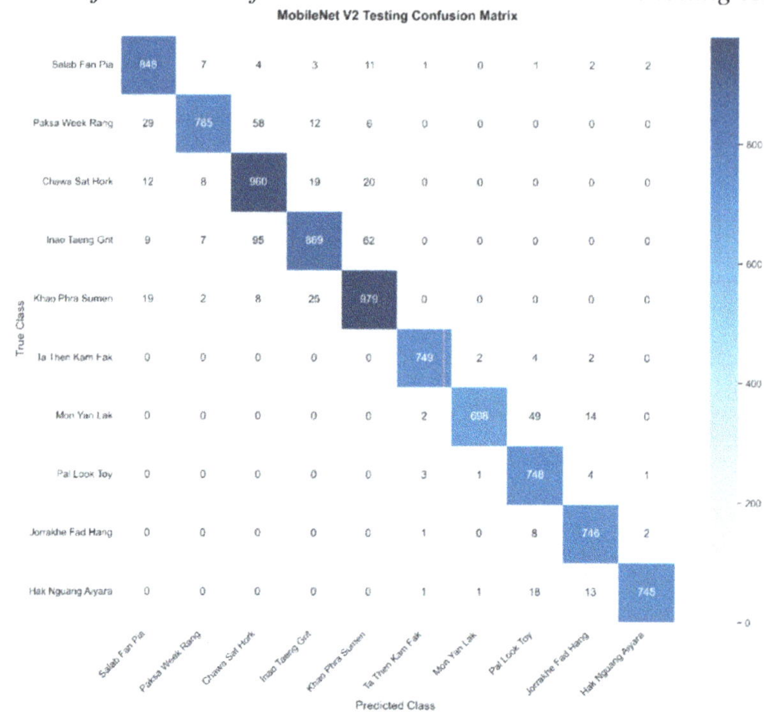

4.5. Hybrid Model

The essential accuracy of identifying the behavioral patterns of the fighters based on visual data relies heavily on the successfulness of the spatial features extractions. The current study introduces a two-level deep learning model that combines the hierarchical feature-learning capabilities of convolutional neural networks (CNNs) with the global context understanding of Vision transformers (ViTs) to classify MMMT styles. The proposed solution is a hybrid of the two systems that will achieve the best results of more complex motion recognition in martial arts. CNN architecture contains three sequential convolutional layers, and each layer has 3x3 kernel size with ReLU activation and followed by a 2x2 max pooling layer to eliminate dimensions. This structure ensures good extraction of local features without eliminating spatial hierarchies. To measure the resilience of the model, we had some experiments with different training settings changing the batch size (16, 32, 64) and epochs (16, 24). The hybrid framework was characterized by exceptional accuracy in classification with a peak of 98 percent performances, and it was significantly greater than the traditional standards. The detailed discussion of the information presented in Table

4 highlights the viability of the model in the identification of subtle transformations in fighter positions and movements. The dynamics of the training were explored in terms of loss and accuracy rates (see Figure 25), with the results showing a steady behavior without overtraining. Confusion matrices (see Figures 26 and 27), were used to analyze and evaluate the performance of the evaluation and testing because they confirmed good accuracy in classifying different Mae Mai strategies. Fewer misclassifications were the primary result of the kinematic similarity of motions, and again demonstrate the necessity of the space and time features to be carefully differentiated.

Table 4. Hybrid model results

Epochs	Batch Size	Accuracy	Precision	Recall	F1-score
16	16	0.91	0.90	0.89	0.89
	32	0.91	0.89	0.90	0.89
	64	0.93	0.92	0.92	0.91
24	16	0.96	0.94	0.95	0.94
	32	0.96	0.96	0.95	0.95
	64	0.98	0.97	0.97	0.97

Figure 25. Training and validation accuracy/loss for hybrid model

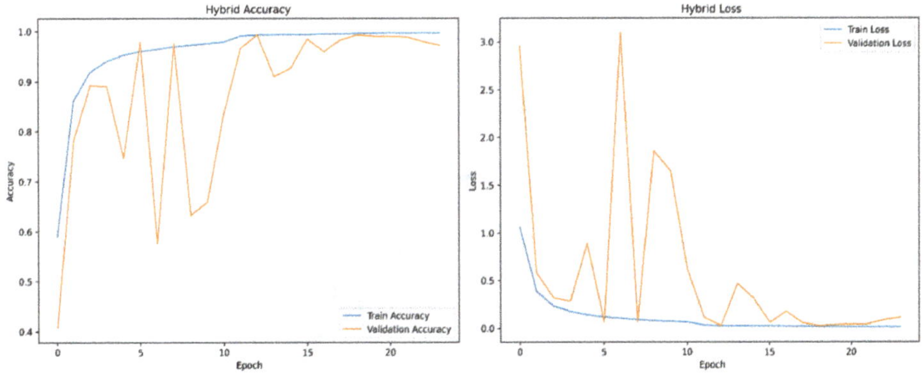

Figure 26. Confusion matrix for the hybrid model on the validation set

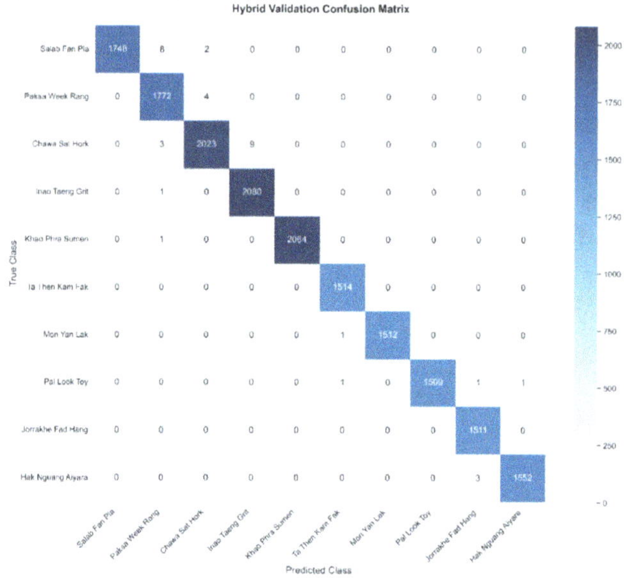

Figure 27. Confusion matrix for the hybrid model on the testing set

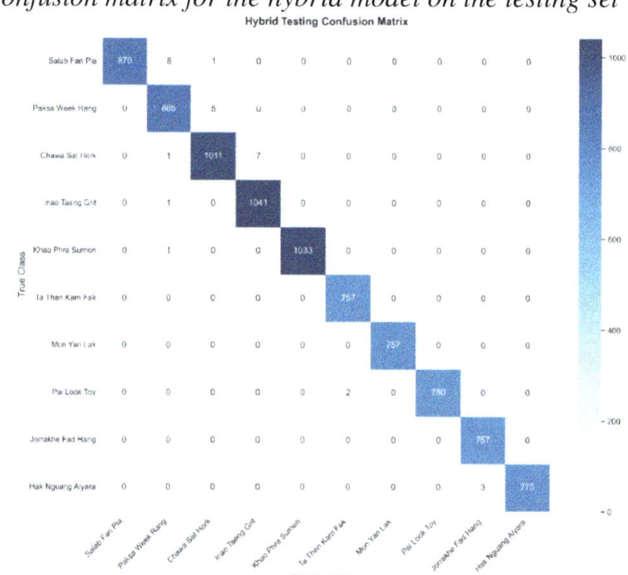

4.6. DISCUSSION

The study and categorization of the behavioral tendencies of fighters is a highly important question in the sphere of sports science, especially in such areas as Muay Thai, Mae Mai being an ancient technique that needs the complex interpretation. In all efforts to automate sports assessments using deep learning, although they can be effective in evaluating any sport especially with vast volumes of imaging data, various situations frequently face resource constraints that limit data accessibility. This study reduces such limitations by introducing a hybrid deep learning network that has the benefits of VGG19, MobileNetV2, and a neural network classifier, with picture augmentation strategies. Unbalanced and high-quality training data is a major problem in sports analytics. In this, we adopt the dynamic picture augmentation in our methodology that artificially grows the collection by generating variants of available images.

Besides simply expanding the sample size, augmentation improves generalization which is a needed prerequisite in practice. Making the model capable of response to a wider variety of visual situations makes it more resistant to overfitting and more apt to respond to unexpected input. This flexibility has been found very useful in combat sports like Muay Thai when the moves of the fighter may vary greatly, thus ensuring the reliable performance of the fighter with unfamiliar information. According to the experimental results, the proposed hybrid architecture is better at distinguishing the Mae Mai approaches when compared to separate models, it is more accurate and reliable. The VGG19 and MobileNetV2 deep learning models are not accurate on the MMMT dataset as compared to the hybrid models. The system is built up by an artificial intelligence (AI) trained as a deep learning and hybrid classifier, creating a skill to discern subtle signs of behavior that can go unnoticed through traditional analysis. In addition, the application of augmentation techniques resolves the gap between limited datasets and the demands of the deep learning. In the process of imitating many different lighting conditions, angles, and motion blur, we recreate the diversity of the real combat setting. This increases the diagnostic accuracy of the model and it coincides with the adaptive decision-making of the human experts, who always know how to approach situations with sub-optimal conditions.

The Hybrid was better than other established models in our evaluation of convolutional neural network models and demonstrated a desirable balance between processing speed and accuracy. One of the main advantages is that it is designed in an efficient way, with minimal number of parameters without performance loss. The design is particularly suitable to the real-world application as it improves the effectiveness of training and simplifies the deployment. In a bid to test this aspect of adaptability, we tested the batch size of 16, 32 and 64 with a resolution of 224x224 pixels. Checking pixel values to the range [0, 1] showed best effectiveness with regard to giving stability to the model and not leading to any extra complexity. It is important to note that when only the fully connected layer was fine-tuned (convolutional layers were fixed), the performance did not vary; however, such approach consumed considerable time to converge, which is a trade-off that requires consideration of the application priorities. Table 5 provides an overview of our key findings, which conducted a comparative evaluation of our models in terms of leading state-of-the-art methods. In this comparison, it is possible to point to the improved accuracy and precision, which is better shown by our method, as well as its contribution to enhancing dependability in sports analytics. The implementation of our framework through the incorporation of innovative methodologies demonstrates measurable improvements over the present-day standards, which is a substantial addition to the projected reliability and performance.

Table 5. Comparison with other techniques

No	Citation	Classifier	Modality	Accuracy
1	(Kasiri-Bidhendi et al., 2015)	SVM and Random Forest	Boxing Images	96%
2	(Shen et al., 2017)	Hidden Markov Classifier	Shadow Boxing	-
3	(Chantaprasert et al., 2019)	Angular Dynamic Time Wraping	Microsoft Kinect	80%
4	(dos S Silva et al., 2021)	Naive Bayes Model	Action from Videos	62%
5	Our Proposed Method	Hybrid Model	MMMT dataset	98%

5. CONCLUSION

Muay Thai, as a combat sport, depends significantly on complex techniques (Mae Mai) that need accurate recognition for training, evaluation, and real-time performance assessment. Conventional classification approaches for these motions often lack precision and scalability, especially in the analysis of visual data. To bridge this gap, we provide an innovative hybrid architecture that integrates convolutional neural networks (CNNs) with vision transformers (ViT) to attain resilient, real-time detection of Mae Mai procedures from visual data. In this study, we automatically identify and classify the behavioral patterns of fighters into 10 MMMT styles out of the traditional 15 styles. Our technique utilizes the spatial feature extraction capabilities of CNNs in conjunction with the global contextual comprehension of ViTs, allowing the model to capture both intricate details and overarching movement patterns. Experimental results showed robust performance, with VGG19, MobileNet

V2, and the Hybrid deep learning technique achieving accuracies of 91, 94, and 98, respectively. A hybrid deep learning technique demonstrates that the algorithm is suitable for assessing the boxer's abilities during competition. This framework has considerable promise for many combat sports outside Muay Thai, such as boxing, karate, and wrestling, where quick and precise movement categorization is essential.

6. FUTURE DEVELOPMENT

Creating a comprehensive framework for the automatic extraction of boxer skeletons from video data signifies a potential advancement in sports analytics and biomechanical research. This study primarily focuses on enhancing deep learning methodologies to precisely record and simulate skeletal motion, specifically within the framework of MMMT, a traditional striking discipline characterized by unique postural and kinematic difficulties. Current initiatives focus on enhancing skeletal extraction pipelines; nonetheless, weaknesses in performance remain in dynamic combat sports contexts. We are investigating alternate aesthetic representations of Mae Mai approaches, positing that the incorporation of domain-specific movement characteristics may improve the robustness of pose estimation. The rotational mechanics of Tee Khao (straight knee strikes) and the weight distribution alterations in Wiang Khruang (defense postures) may need customized dynamical models to prevent skeletal tracking errors. Future investigations may include modifications for 3D motion capture or the use of wearable sensors to enhance accuracy. Our work integrates deep learning developments with practical sports analytics, offering a scalable solution for automatic method detection and facilitating the development of intelligent training tools and performance evaluation systems.

REFERENCES

Aggarwal, J. K., & Ryoo, M. S. (2011). Human activity analysis: A review. *ACM Computing Surveys*, *43*(3), 1–43.

Ahmed, M. W., & Jalal, A. (2024, February). Dynamic adoptive Gaussian mixture model for multi-object detection over natural scenes. In 2024 5th International Conference on Advancements in Computational Sciences (ICACS) (pp. 1-8). IEEE.

Ashker, S. E. (2011). Technical and tactical aspects that differentiate winning and losing performances in boxing. *International Journal of Performance Analysis in Sport*, *11*(2), 356–364.

Ba, J. L., Kiros, J. R., & Hinton, G. E. (2016). Layer normalization. arXiv preprint arXiv:1607.06450.

Baccouche, M., Mamalet, F., Wolf, C., Garcia, C., & Baskurt, A. (2011, November). Sequential deep learning for human action recognition. In International workshop on human behavior understanding (pp. 29-39). Berlin, Heidelberg: Springer Berlin Heidelberg.

Bansal, M., Kumar, M., Sachdeva, M., & Mittal, A. (2023). Transfer learning for image classification using VGG19: Caltech-101 image data set. *Journal of Ambient Intelligence and Humanized Computing*, *14*(4), 3609–3620. PMID: 34548886

Bazi, Y., Bashmal, L., Rahhal, M. M. A., Dayil, R. A., & Ajlan, N. A. (2021). Vision transformers for remote sensing image classification. *Remote Sensing*, *13*(3), 516.

Bonidia, R. P., Rodrigues, L. A., Avila-Santos, A. P., Sanches, D. S., & Brancher, J. D. (2018). Computational intelligence in sports: A systematic literature review. *Advances in Human-Computer Interaction*, *2018*(1), 3426178.

Cardino, P. C. C., Chua, J. L. T., & Llaga, J. R. R. R. (2022). Advance scorecard for boxing: Combat sport analysis with deep learning.

Chankuna, D. (2006). Video Analysis for the Causes of Head and Face Injuries in Amateur Muaythai Boxers (Doctoral dissertation, Chulalongkorn University).

Chantaprasert, B., Chumchuen, P., & Wangsiripitak, S. (2019, July). Comparison of gesture in Thai boxing framework using angular dynamic time warping. In 2019 16th International Conference on Electrical Engineering/Electronics, Computer, Telecommunications and Information Technology (ECTI-CON) (pp. 601-604). IEEE.

Cust, E. E., Sweeting, A. J., Ball, K., & Robertson, S. (2019). Machine and deep learning for sport-specific movement recognition: A systematic review of model development and performance. *Journal of Sports Sciences*, *37*(5), 568–600. PMID: 30307362

D'Orazio, T., & Leo, M. (2010). A review of vision-based systems for soccer video analysis. *Pattern Recognition*, *43*(8), 2911–2926.

Da Costa, K. A., Papa, J. P., Lisboa, C. O., Munoz, R., & de Albuquerque, V. H. C. (2019). Internet of Things: A survey on machine learning-based intrusion detection approaches. *Computer Networks*, *151*, 147–157.

Dai, C., Liu, X., & Lai, J. (2020). Human action recognition using two-stream attention based LSTM networks. *Applied Soft Computing*, *86*, 105820.

Dai, C., Liu, X., Lai, J., Li, P., & Chao, H. C. (2019). Human behavior deep recognition architecture for smart city applications in the 5G environment. *IEEE Network*, *33*(5), 206–211.

Delp, C. (2005). Muay Thai Basics: Introductory Thai Boxing Techniques. blue snake books.

Delp, C. (2013). *Muay Thai Counter Techniques: Competitive Skills and Tactics for Success*. North Atlantic Books.

dos S Silva, F. H., Bezerra, G. M., Holanda, G. B., de Souza, J. W. M., Rego, P. A., Neto, A. V. L., ... & Rebouças Filho, P. P. (2021). A novel feature extractor for human action recognition in visual question answering. Pattern Recognition Letters, 147, 41-47.

Fong, S. S. (2014). Martial arts for health: translating research into practice.

Gartland, S., Malik, M. H. A., & Lovell, M. E. (2001). Injury and injury rates in Muay Thai kick boxing. *British Journal of Sports Medicine*, *35*(5), 308–313. PMID: 11579062

Guo, X. (2022). Research on multiplayer posture estimation technology of sports competition video based on graph neural network algorithm. *Computational Intelligence and Neuroscience*, *2022*(1), 4727375. PMID: 35401733

Host, K., & Ivašić-Kos, M. (2022). An overview of Human Action Recognition in sports based on Computer Vision. *Heliyon*, *8*(6). PMID: 35706961

Kaewplee, K., Khamsemanan, N., & Nattee, C. (2015). An Instructional Support System for Muay Thai (Doctoral dissertation, Thammasat University).

Kalake, L., Dong, Y., Wan, W., & Hou, L. (2022). Enhancing detection quality rate with a combined hog and cnn for real-time multiple object tracking across non-overlapping multiple cameras. *Sensors (Basel)*, *22*(6), 2123. PMID: 35336294

Kasiri-Bidhendi, S., Fookes, C., Morgan, S., Martin, D. T., & Sridharan, S. (2015, September). Combat sports analytics: Boxing punch classification using overhead depthimagery. In 2015 IEEE international conference on image processing (ICIP) (pp. 4545-4549). IEEE.

Keshavarzian, A., Sharifian, S., & Seyedin, S. (2019). Modified deep residual network architecture deployed on serverless framework of IoT platform based on human activity recognition application. *Future Generation Computer Systems*, *101*, 14–28.

Krauss, E. (2006). *Muay Thai Unleashed: Learn Technique and Strategy from Thailand's Warrior Elite*. McGraw Hill Professional.

Kwon, H., Kim, Y., Lee, J. S., & Cho, M. (2018). First person action recognition via two-stream convnet with long-term fusion pooling. *Pattern Recognition Letters*, *112*, 161–167.

Li, Y., Li, Q., Huang, Q., Xia, R., & Li, X. (2019). Spatiotemporal interest point detector exploiting appearance and motion-variation information. *Journal of Electronic Imaging*, *28*(3), 033002–033002.

Liu, S., & Liu, Y. (2021). Application of human movement and movement scoring technology in computer vision feature in sports training. *Journal of the Institution of Electronics and Telecommunication Engineers*, 1–7.

Lv, Q., Zhang, S., & Wang, Y. (2022). Deep learning model of image classification using machine learning. advances in multimedia, 2022(1), 3351256.

Muhamada, A. W., & Mohammed, A. A. (2022). Review on recent computer vision methods for human action recognition.

Parmar, N., Vaswani, A., Uszkoreit, J., Kaiser, L., Shazeer, N., Ku, A., & Tran, D. (2018, July). Image transformer. In *International conference on machine learning* (pp. 4055-4064). PMLR.

Polak, E., Kulasa, J., de Brito, A. V., Castro, M. A., & de Jesus Fernandes, O. (2015). Motion analysis systems as optimization training tools in combat sports and martial arts. [RAMA]. *Revista de Artes Marciales Asiáticas, 10*(2), 105–123.

Quinn, E., & Corcoran, N. (2022, November). Automation of computer vision applications for real-time combat sports video analysis. In *European conference on the impact of artificial intelligence and robotics* (Vol. 4, No. 1, pp. 162-171).

Radford, A., Metz, L., & Chintala, S. (2015). Unsupervised representation learning with deep convolutional generative adversarial networks. arXiv preprint arXiv:1511.06434.

Rahevar, M., Ganatra, A., Saba, T., Rehman, A., & Bahaj, S. A. (2023). Spatial–temporal dynamic graph attention network for skeleton-based action recognition. *IEEE Access : Practical Innovations, Open Solutions, 11*, 21546–21553.

Rajšp, A., & Fister, I.Jr. (2020). A systematic literature review of intelligent data analysis methods for smart sport training. *Applied Sciences (Basel, Switzerland), 10*(9), 3013.

Saengsawang, P., Siladech, C., & Laxanaphisuth, P. (2015). The history and development of Muaythai boran. *Journal of Sports Sciences, 3*(3), 148–154.

Sandler, M., Howard, A., Zhu, M., Zhmoginov, A., & Chen, L. C. (2018). Mobilenetv2: Inverted residuals and linear bottlenecks. In *Proceedings of the IEEE conference on computer vision and pattern recognition* (pp. 4510-4520).

Shen, Y., Wang, H., Ho, E. S., Yang, L., & Shum, H. P. (2017). Posture-based and action-based graphs for boxing skill visualization. *Computers & Graphics, 69*, 104–115.

Shotton, J., Fitzgibbon, A., Cook, M., Sharp, T., Finocchio, M., Moore, R., & Blake, A. (2011, June). Real-time human pose recognition in parts from single depth images. In *CVPR 2011* (pp. 1297–1304). Ieee.

Simonyan, K., & Zisserman, A. (2014). Very deep convolutional networks for large-scale image recognition. arXiv preprint arXiv:1409.1556.

Spolaôr, N., Lee, H. D., Takaki, W. S. R., Ensina, L. A., Coy, C. S. R., & Wu, F. C. (2020). A systematic review on content-based video retrieval. *Engineering Applications of Artificial Intelligence, 90*, 103557.

Turab, A., Mlaiki, N., Fatima, N., Mitrović, Z. D., & Ali, W. (2022). Analysis of a class of stochastic animal behavior models under specific choice preferences. *Mathematics, 10*(12), 1975. DOI: 10.3390/math10121975

Turab, A., Montoyo, A., & Nescolarde-Selva, J. A. (2024a). Computational and analytical analysis of integral-differential equations for modeling avoidance learning behavior. *Journal of Applied Mathematics & Computing, 70*(5), 4423–4439. DOI: 10.1007/s12190-024-02130-3

Turab, A., Nescolarde-Selva, J. A., Ullah, F., Montoyo, A., Alfiniyah, C., Sintunavarat, W., & Zaidi, S. A. (2025). Deep neural networks and stochastic methods for cognitive modeling of rat behavioral dynamics in $$\mathbb{T}$$-mazes. *Cognitive Neurodynamics, 19*(1), 1–28. DOI: 10.1007/s11571-025-10247-9 PMID: 39749104

Turab, A., Rosli, N., Ali, W., & Nieto, J. J. (2023). The existence and uniqueness of solutions to a functional equation arising in psychological learning theory. *Demonstratio Mathematica*, *56*(1), 20220231. DOI: 10.1515/dema-2022-0231

Turab, A., & Sintunavarat, W. (2019). On analytic model for two-choice behavior of the paradise fish based on the fixed point method. *Journal of Fixed Point Theory and Its Applications*, *21*(2), 56. DOI: 10.1007/s11784-019-0694-y

Turab, A., & Sintunavarat, W. (2020). On the solution of the traumatic avoidance learning model approached by the Banach fixed point theorem. *Journal of Fixed Point Theory and Its Applications*, *22*(2), 50. DOI: 10.1007/s11784-020-00788-3

Turab, A., Sintunavarat, W., Ullah, F., Zaidi, S. A., Montoyo, A., & Nescolarde-Selva, J. A. (2024b). Computational modeling of animal behavior in T-mazes: Insights from machine learning. *Ecological Informatics*, *81*, 102639. DOI: 10.1016/j.ecoinf.2024.102639

Wang, C., & Yan, J. (2023). A comprehensive survey of rgb-based and skeleton-based human action recognition. *IEEE Access : Practical Innovations, Open Solutions*, *11*, 53880–53898.

Worsey, M. T., Espinosa, H. G., Shepherd, J. B., & Thiel, D. V. (2020). An evaluation of wearable inertial sensor configuration and supervised machine learning models for automatic punch classification in boxing. *IoT*, *1*(2), 360–381.

Zaidi, S. A., & Chouvatut, V. (2022, December). Mae Mai Muay Thai Layered Classification Using CNN and LSTM Models. In 2022 26th International Computer Science and Engineering Conference (ICSEC) (pp. 351-356). IEEE.

Zaidi, S. A., & Chouvatut, V. (2023). Mae Mai Muay Thai Style Classification in Movement Appling Long-Term Recurrent Convolution Networks. *Journal of Internet Services and Information Security*, *13*(1), 95–112.

Zaidi, S. A., Chouvatut, V., & Phongnarisorn, C. (2025b). Endometriosis Lesion Classification Using Deep Transfer Learning Techniques. *International Journal of Advanced Computer Science and Applications*, *16*(6).

Zaidi, S. A., Chouvatut, V., Phongnarisorn, C., & Praserttitipong, D. (2025a). Deep learning based detection of endometriosis lesions in laparoscopic images with 5-fold cross-validation. *Intelligence-Based Medicine*, *11*, 100230.

Zhu, G., Xu, C., Huang, Q., Rui, Y., Jiang, S., Gao, W., & Yao, H. (2008). Event tactic analysis based on broadcast sports video. *IEEE Transactions on Multimedia*, *11*(1), 49–67.

Chapter 5

Analyzing User Behavior in Mobile Game Applications Using Deep Data Analysis Approach

Rana Muhammad Amir Latif
https://orcid.org/0000-0001-6007-6275
East China Normal University, China

Diletta Cacciagrano
https://orcid.org/0000-0003-4491-0666
Università di Camerino, Italy

Farhan Ullah
https://orcid.org/0000-0002-1030-1275
Prince Mohammad Bin Fahd University, Saudi Arabia

Jiaqi Yin
https://orcid.org/0000-0002-6213-5520
Northwestern Polytechnical University, China

Leonardo Mostarda
University of Perugia, Italy

Yue Zhao
Wenzhou-Kean University, China

ABSTRACT

User reviews on platforms like Google Play Store shape mobile game demand through digital word-of-mouth (eWOM), directly influencing user preferences. This study applies Latent Semantic Analysis (LSA) to survey feedback, uncovering key drivers of satisfaction and dissatisfaction across mini-games, large area games, and enterprise applications. Positive sentiment is linked to entertainment value, ease of use, and appealing design, while negative feedback centers on bugs, poor gameplay mechanics, and intrusive ads. The analysis reveals both psychological and functional factors shaping user attitudes. Findings offer actionable insights for

DOI: 10.4018/979-8-3373-5062-2.ch005

developers to enhance design, address common frustrations, and foster long-term engagement. These insights serve as a strategic guide for improving user experience and remaining competitive in the mobile gaming market.

1 INTRODUCTION

Gaming has become very popular in a very short period because game development technologies have emerged. Therefore, user rating and feedback have become an important aspect of the user experience (Yu, Dinh, Yu, & Huynh, 2023). The user review is an informal communication between the user speaking in their own words and the consensual view of what features of the utility of individual applications are valuable. Reviews have transitioned from traditional to electronic word of mouth (eWOM), which reaches a greater extent faster and has a higher impact on gaming. It has been proven that the feedback distributed through eWOM has a more substantial effect on the demand for applications and has a more significant impact on users' decisions (Alzhrani, Alatawi, Alsharari, Albalawi, & Mustafa, 2022).

Positive and negative reviews reflect personal users' experiences with the game, so users express their satisfaction or dissatisfaction with the application. Written reviews allow a user's sentiments to be better understood than simple user ratings alone (Alturaief, Aljamaan, & Baslyman, 2021). The implementation of these reviews, which are usually rated on a scale of 1 to 10, enables consumers to judge the game performance in general or the performance of the specific game features (Gutierrez et al., 2021), and this can prove to be an effective mechanism for app developers wishing to improve the game performance and appeal (Rana Muhammad Amir Latif, Obaidat, Ullah, & Mahmood, 2025).

The present work compares the factors determining negative and positive user behaviour on different game applications. The comparison is done at three levels. First, the first perspective investigates how some game applications' lack of essential features results in user dissatisfaction (Wu, He, Li, Bi, & Antwi-Afari, 2023). Although positive attributes may remain, the absence of essential elements will hinder users from engaging with the game to its full potential, which obviates positive feedback. The second view focuses on what these factors do to the user, how they act on the user experience, and how it is manifested in the user's behaviour. Finally, the third perspective compares the levels of positivity or negativity in user behaviour across different types of game applications (Zhan, Qiu, Shang, et al., 2023).

There are a lot of game applications, namely mini-games and large-scale enterprise applications, and there are various types of user preferences, expectations, and opinions. There is a moderate gap in the literature on previous research, as it has not sufficiently explored the moderating effect of game application types on user experiences (Yu, Dinh, Nguyen, Yu, & Huynh, 2023).

A typical type of these might be written text in comments specific to user reviews, where natural language processing (NLP) plays a vital role in analysis (al-Qallawi & Raghavan, 2022). The grouping of documents and text classification are two main features important in arranging user feedback, finding ways opinions and attitudes are articulated in the review (Rana Muhammad Amir Latif, Yoshigoe, et al., 2025). In this study, the authors seek to identify the factors behind users' positive and negative attitudes towards game applications using LSA to provide an objective and quantitative manner to examine user attitudes (Che, Nan, Kamphuis, Zhang, & Kim, 2022; Y.-Y. Wang, Nalluri, & Chen, 2023).

One of the basic origins of user reviews is the Google Play Store and other apps that serve as significant developer and analysis tools. Such reviews on these sites will provide an impression about the working of the gameplay, problems in the user interface, and other aspects, which will assist in improving the application and assist the company in future iterations. Such feedback is referred to as User Voice, which helps developers analyze and improve their applications and, as a result, will help satisfy the user expectations (Kumari, Bala, & Chakraborty, 2024).

This study investigates the determinants of positive and negative user behaviours towards game applications of various categories. This paper applies text mining methods and LSA to rigorously analyze users' sentiments and compare and rank the positive and negative attitudes towards game applications based on the factors affecting user attitudes. In this study, a profound understanding of the factors that affect clients' behavior in gaming applications and help helpers develop research and the designers (Barbosa, Saura, Zekan, & Ribeiro-Soriano, 2024) will be made.

Although it is not new to apply text mining and sentiment analysis to general mobile application reviews, mobile games' behavioral and psychological processes make this area especially unique. Unlike productivity or utility applications, mobile games require constant emotional feedback, incentive programs, interpersonal encounters, and micro-transactions that influence user feelings. Mobile game reviews frequently record subtle responses like anger at monetization practices, excitement about game mechanics, or annoyance at obtrusive advertisements that do not correspond to other types of apps. Thus, mining reviews provides insight into product usability and indicates player motivation, immersion, and loyalty. This paper will fill that gap by using LSA to identify latent psychological and experiential determinants of user sentiment in various classes of mobile games. This narrower study adds domain-specific knowledge of user attitudes that could be applied to game preferences through game development, engagement, and long-term maintenance.

2 LITERATURE REVIEW

Application reviews prove to be a source of information for engineers when they try to understand the user's needs and preferences. In recent studies, different methods have been proposed for review classification, such as classifying reviews as bug reports, feature requests, or requirement elicitation. However, these methods do not allow engineers to directly evaluate users' opinions about a particular application feature (Rana Muhammad Amir Latif, Ullah, et al., 2025). However, this gap has not been addressed much by prior research; instead, research has been conducted to develop tools to search for reviews on a particular feature, extract bug reports, and analyze and extract users' reactions to different parts of the app. The analytics dashboard these tools offer helps engineers prioritize and refine features, and user feedback helps engineers be more informed in their software development process (Shugang Li et al., 2022).

App stores, such as Google Play and Apple's App Store, have evolved into key channels for distributing mobile applications, providing mobile applications with an excellent opportunity to be more visible and accessible to users. Their primary purpose is to allow users to search for, purchase, and install apps and hear users' valuable feedback by reviewing and rating them (Rana M Amir Latif et al., 2019). They usually feature users' experiences of how it can be improved, or report a bug or malfunction. As a result, developers and software companies find app reviews essential because they show them the degree of satisfaction the app has reached and where improvements are required to improve its functionality (Mishra, Shukla, & Agarwal, 2022).

An increase in the use of data mining and opinion aggregation techniques has recently accompanied the rapid rise of mobile applications and app stores. They are used to find insights in large amounts of user reviews that app companies may utilize in their development and marketing. The ethical concerns of app reviews on the internet have been addressed in some studies, which discuss the importance of honest feedback and experience in the app marketplace. Also, opinion mining work ahead includes unresolved problems such as user dissatisfaction and satisfaction, participation in software requirements and development (Bellary, Bala, & Chakraborty, 2024; Birjali, Kasri, & Beni-Hssane, 2021; Maeng, Lee, & Yun, 2023).

In the process of buying an app, the user rating and the number of comments during the app reviews are also considered, as consumers decide on whether to purchase the app based on the quality of the app. The review systems on these mobile app stores usually work by rating; the more ratings and comments in favour of the app, the greater the visibility and commercial success the app will have. User reviews can give app developers an insight into the quality of the apps and opportunities to improve them. The causes of positive and negative app reviews can provide meaningful information to optimize the app's performance further (Mayopu, Wang, & Chen, 2023).

Researchers analyzed over 8.7 million reviews in 17,330 apps in multiple app stores to find this out. They found that user reviews tend to be more expressive in negative or positive words than others, which is probably also influenced by the business model the apps choose to use (Ramzan et al., 2019). It stresses that developers should analyze the reviews to grasp users' feedback. In addition, the results suggest that sentiment analysis methods, such as machine learning algorithms, may be applied to the classification and interpretation of user feedback. It would significantly assist developers with systematically handling reviews (Zhan, Qiu, Li, et al., 2023).

As the mobile applications business has expanded immensely, numerous replicated or duplicated versions of apps have emerged on the Play Store, which may make users lose faith in the application and ultimately put their data at risk (Imran, Latif, Farhan, Tariq, & Computing, 2019). Researchers have used data scraping to study the impact of these problems and some of the contributing factors, e.g., in-app purchase rates. These are the analyses made considering millions of apps and user reviews to identify the quality trends of apps, the liking of apps, and the efficacy of various marketing tactics (Yi, Kim, & Oh, 2024).

Other recent studies have also used machine learning techniques such as logistic regression to analyze user feedback from app stores. These algorithms can give developers a classification of reviews (positive, negative, neutral), equipping them with a clear indication of how users' sentiments may be expressed. However, applying these methods has increased the accuracy of sentiment analysis in predicting user preference and behaviour (Çallı, 2023).

In addition, data mining techniques have been employed in various domains, like agriculture, to predict the outcome of user feedback and other data. For instance, data mining methods have been used to accurately predict frost incidents by considering environmental factors. Likewise, data mining techniques have been utilized to predict the web of connections in criminal networks using machine learning techniques and demonstrate how data mining is applicable in other fields, such as (Al-Adaileh, Al-Kfairy, Tubishat, & Alfandi, 2024; Asudani, Nagwani, & Singh, 2023; Sihong Li & Chen, 2024).

2.1 User Positiveness Towards Game Applications

User positivity towards game applications is about evaluating users' expectations of an app and their experience. A "user positivity index" is used in this evaluation to measure a user with a positive outlook on the game (Filieri, Galati, & Raguseo, 2021). A positive attitude of the user is an essential factor driving the increased demand for game applications, potentially improving app performance and better addressing user needs.

There are a handful of important features that enhance user positivity. Seven primary factors in games make users have positive attitudes toward play. Such factors include game enjoyment, gameplay effort, in-game offers, and overall graphics quality. The user's experience with each feature determines their satisfaction with the game and continued engagement (Baj-Rogowska & Sikorski, 2023).

2.2 User Negativeness Towards Game Applications

While not as many studies have been conducted on user negativeness to user positiveness, it is important to uncover factors that lead to a negative user experience for improvement towards game applications. Factors causing user negativeness are frequently not the same as factors that lead to the positivity of the user. Several key factors identified in the research explain why users are dissatisfied with current emails, particularly negative emotions, insecurity, uncertainty, unfulfilled expectations, and low service quality.

For example, if a negative experience is met after playing a game, i.e., caused by anger or disappointment, negative behaviours like filing a complaint, writing a negative review, and negative eWOM (Mojica, Palos-Sanchez, & Cabanas, 2024) can be practised. Users dissatisfied with the game tend to resort to other game applications, with a slant towards releasing their frustrations, receiving sympathy from other users, or even seeking compensation through negative feedback.

Retention for game developers is critical since keeping the users is much cheaper than acquiring new ones. The first thing needed when improving a game's performance is identifying where user negativity is occurring and addressing the issues contributing to it. Afterwards, recovery strategies are implemented to raise service quality and encourage user loyalty (Z. Wang, Gao, & Chu, 2022).

2.3 Electronic Word of Mouth (eWOM) Towards Game Applications

Electronic word of mouth (eWOM) is an expression that describes the act of users sharing their words with other consumers to influence their opinion and decision towards applications before making a purchase or commitment by giving recommendations, suggestions, or opinions based on their experience, either directly through interaction on the application or indirectly through sources of information such as blogs and user reviews. Due to the rise of the game's popularity, user reviews and eWOM have become practical tools to change user engagement in game demand.

An example of positive reviews is meeting user satisfaction with the application, which promotes the quality of eWOM and increases the number of game users.

On the other hand, negative eWOM can negatively affect the number of users and damage the game's reputation. User awareness is often produced based on the reviews; thus, game developers must use eWOM as an effective tool. It allows developers to attract new users and improve the game performance and retention of the old users (Chen, Xie, & Chiu, 2024; Xue, Li, & Zeng, 2023).

2.4 Hypothesis Development

It offers a cognitive process model to explain user behaviour in a framework of expectation disconfirmation. This model indicates that both positive and negative behaviour can be measured based on the gap between users' expectations towards the game applications and their actual behaviour in these applications. Satisfaction occurs when an application's quality meets or exceeds a user's expectations. If the applications cannot fulfil the expectations, dissatisfaction is created.

The lack of essential features in in-game applications, especially Android applications, causes users to have a negative experience with the in-game application. However, these features are not enough to produce very positive results. Users expect these features to perform to perfection, and they may not be satisfied if they do not. In this talk, we propose three hypotheses:

- **Hypothesis 1:**

Users do not feel the same positive and negative feelings while playing different games. Each determinant may have varying significance to the user's positive or negative attitude.

Multi-attribute theory says the relative importance of various attributes influencing attitudes may vary according to the situation's needs. According to this theory, users evaluate attributes differently when they form their attitude towards a product/ service. The model is expressed as follows:

$$A_O = \sum_{i=1}^{n} B_i a_i \ldots\ldots\ldots\ldots\ldots\ldots \quad (1)$$

A_O is the attitude, B_i is the strength of belief in attribute i, a_i is the assessment of the degree of positiveness associated with attribute i, and n is the number of attributes. This model makes it possible to evaluate overall positiveness through the sum of the importance of game features and their evaluations. It also considers the different levels of importance assigned to different game features as they lead to positive and negative user behavior. The opinions of users and their attitudes toward gaming apps are affected by several things. However, not everyone is the same. Developers can change attitudes by emphasizing core behaviors, services, and features.

- **Hypothesis 2 (a):**

In every game, the significance of the determinants of user positiveness is not uniform.

- **Hypothesis 2 (b):**

The importance of the determinants of user negativity varies across games. According to the trends in the gaming market, we can find four kinds of game apps: large/arena games, substantial apps, enterprise apps, and mini-games/small apps. Big games and enterprise apps usually have more options and features to offer. Mini-games and mini-games offer fewer features, focusing mainly on specific game types. The type of game significantly affects the app's features, experience, and audience. People who play games in arenas usually feel more attached to the specific games. In contrast, people who use mini-games are often less committed and more likely to settle for free.

- **Hypothesis 3 (a):**

The type and significance of user positiveness determinants vary across different types of game applications.

- **Hypothesis 3 (b):**

The type and significance of user negativeness determinants vary across different types of game applications.

Table 1. A detailed description of a dataset of reviews scraped from the Google Play Store.

Category of Application	Total Number of Reviews
Action	47116
Arcade	36521
Card	37761
Sports	33770
Racing	42394

3 RESEARCH METHODOLOGY

This study's dataset contains user reviews in textual form. Qualitative methods like content analysis and grounded theory usually require researchers to code data and interpret the meaning of text. The approach will not be suitable in this analysis owing to the large amount of data. Using conventional coding methods, it will be impossible to code 197,562 user reviews collected from Game APPs from the Google Play Store. So much information will be created that conventional ways will become inefficient in analysing it.

Using LSA or latent semantic analysis, the research takes a text mining technique to solve the problem and retrieve useful and profitable information from unstructured texts. LSA is a method that objectively uncovers the hidden relationships between words and sentences in a document. Because LSA is based on mathematics, it can extract summaries from user reviews that are more objective than those produced by other methods.

The process of text mining based on LSA comprises three main steps. First, we created separate spreadsheets for positive and negative user reviews for each type of game application. RapidMiner Studio is the primary data mining tool employed for the analysis. The process followed by the analysis is outlined in the next steps (see Figure 1):

3.1 Preprocessing and Term Reduction

Before the data processing in RapidMiner Studio, document objects were created for each spreadsheet and assigned a unique ID in sequence. The preprocessing phase involved several steps:

- All text was converted to lowercase to standardize the data.
- Tokenization was applied, separating text by non-letter characters.
- Stop words, such as "an," "a," "our," "is," "the," and "and," were removed as they contribute little to the analysis and unnecessarily increase the size of the term frequency matrix.
- Tokens consisting of just a few letters (e.g., "s," "x") were also removed as they do not carry significant meaning.
- Tokens that appeared in only one document were eliminated, as they do not provide meaningful patterns.

3.2 Term Frequency Matrix Transformation

We will then convert the documents into a TF matrix after term reductions. The matrix displays how often each term appears in each document. Next, we changed the values in the matrix using the Term Frequency/Inverse Document Frequency (TF/IDF) approach. This technique helps increase the importance of a unique word naturally and decrease the weight of normal words. In this way, it emphasizes the unique features of every document.

3.3 Singular Value Decomposition (SVD)

The TF/IDF matrix underwent SVD in the third step of the LSA process. This method breaks down the matrix into three new matrices: document-by-factor matrix, singular value matrix, and term-by-factor matrix.

- The document-by-factor matrix reveals the latent factors that are associated with each document.
- The singular value matrix indicates the importance of each factor.
- The term-by-factor matrix shows the relationship between terms and factors.
- A similar result of SVD is factor analysis, where high-loading terms and documents are related to understanding underlying factors. A meaningful interpretation of the data can be derived by labelling each factor based on the terms and documents that are most strongly associated with it.

Altogether, the LSA method enabled the analysis of the user reviews in detail and objectively. The study conducted through this method revealed latent trends in the data, important factors of user positiveness and negativeness, and practical recommendations that can be used to enhance game applications.

Whilst this study is mainly based on LSA as it is mathematically transparent and can be used to extract latent factors in large amounts of unstructured text, it is important to note that other advanced NLP methods may also be applied to similar analytical tasks. An example is LDA, a probabilistic topic model that may cluster user reviews into coherent topics. However, it needs predetermined hyperparameters and may fail to resolve overlapping semantics in short texts like an app review. Conversely, transformer-based models, including BERT (Bidirectional Encoder Representations from Transformers) and RoBERTa, use contextual representations to encode subtle meanings in sentences and have the state-of-the-art performance on sentiment classification tasks. However, these models require significant computing resources and domain-specific corpora to fine-tune, which are potentially unavailable in all research settings. Compared with LSA, LSA offers a strong, readable, and computationally efficient base to identify concealed semantic structures, which is a suitable methodological choice in this study. LDA or transformer sentiment models could then be used in future work to confirm and elaborate on the results.

Figure 1. Methodology Diagram of Experiences of Users' Positive and Negative behaviour toward various types of game applications in RapidMiner Studio

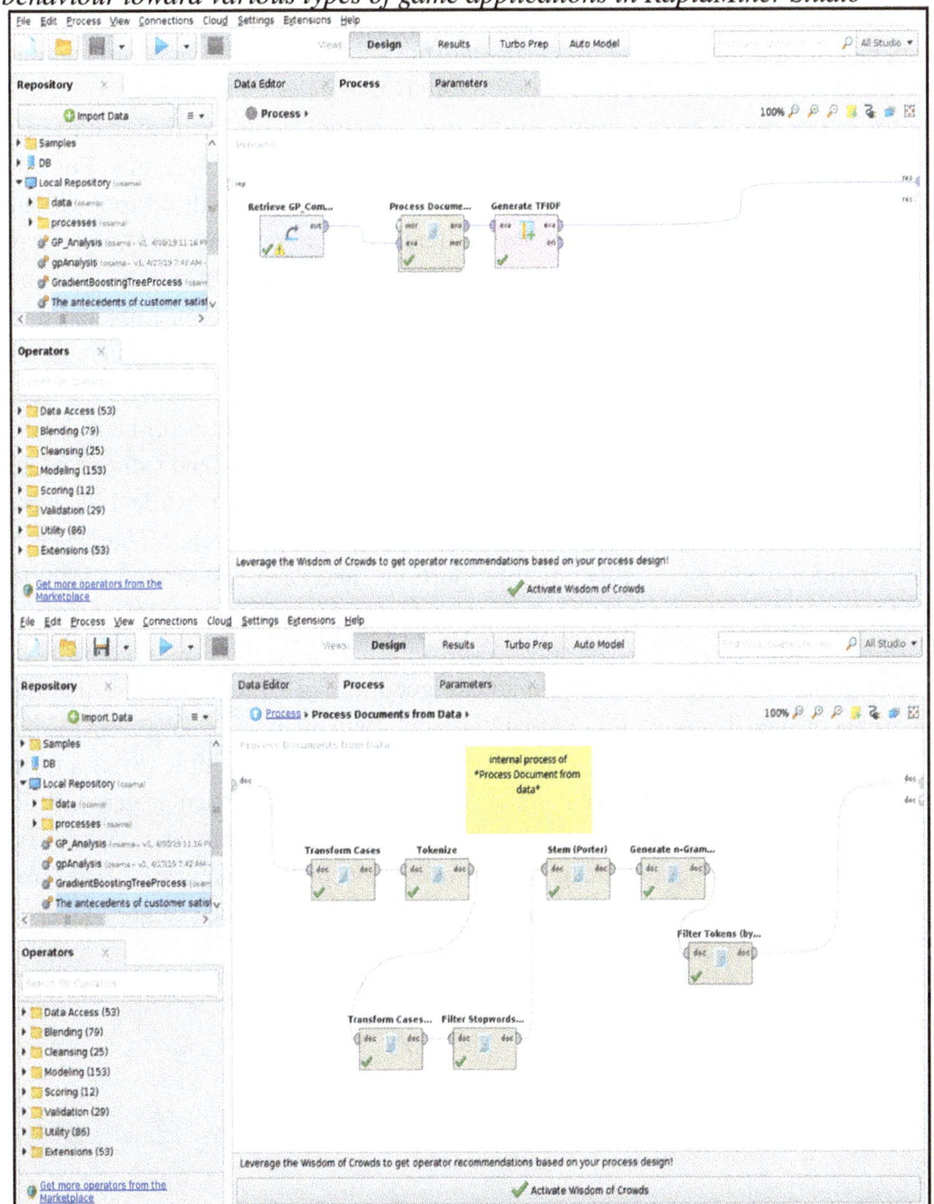

3.4 Data Collection Phase

Mobile apps are now essential parts of everyday lives. As per a report, between 2011 and October 2012, more than 0.5 million mobile apps were launched. There are around 0.675 million apps in the Google Play Store. Over the last few years of this generation, Android apps have proved helpful for various purposes. The app marketplace online has free and paid versions that give users instant access to various mobile apps. According to recent statistics, more than a million applications are available on the Google Play Store to satisfy every need.

Collecting the data is one of the most crucial processes, as the quality and suitability of the data for the research highly impact the research results. For this research, we collected and analyzed user reviews and ratings of Android applications from various categories. First, we chose different categories from the Google Play Store. We selected 14 different categories, then scraped the applications' reviews and ratings from those categories. The included categories were Action, Arcade, Card, Sports, and Racing. We scraped 197,562 user reviews from five selected categories of applications on the Google Play Store (see Figure 2).

The dataset also analyzed the distribution of reviews across the sentiment classes (positive and negative) and the game categories for transparency and validity. More than half the reviews (54%) were positive. 32% were negative, while 14% were neutral or mixed. The five chosen game categories - Action, Arcade, Card, Sport, and Racing - made up roughly equal proportions, and each had around 33000 to 47000 reviews, as shown in Table 1. There are differences since user feedback is naturally available in these categories. However, such differences were not statistically significant at 5% as per the chi-square goodness-of-fit test. It means that the dataset is balanced enough for comparative sentiment analysis.

Also, to avoid potential bias from sampling, we sampled multiple reviews from the game category to prevent changing the outcomes of a particular game. Still, as a good research practice, we acknowledge that natural imbalance cannot be eliminated in user-generated data; future works may consider using stratified sampling or synthetic balancing techniques (e.g., SMOTE) to reduce category-level or sentiment-level biases.

Figure 2. Sample screenshot of the dataset

1	cetagory	app_name	app_id	reviews	rating
2	Sports	Billiards City	com.billia	Wonderfı	5
3	Sports	Billiards City	com.billia	It's good,	4
4	Sports	Billiards City	com.billia	I really er	1
5	Sports	Billiards City	com.billia	PLEASE!!!	1
6	Sports	Billiards City	com.billia	Very easy	4
7	Sports	Athletics2: Summer	com.tangr	03e The gı	3
8	Sports	Athletics2: Summer	com.tangr	It's very n	5
9	Sports	Athletics2: Summer	com.tangr	\u003e OK	4
10	Sports	Athletics2: Summer	com.tangr	003c/\u00	5
11	Arcade	Bubble Shooter 2	shooter.tv	???? ?? ??	5
12	Arcade	Bubble Shooter 2	shooter.tv	Too many	1
13	Arcade	Bubble Shooter 2	shooter.tv	This game	3
14	Arcade	Bubble Shooter 2	shooter.tv	I HATE \"f	1
15	Arcade	Bubble Shooter 2	shooter.tv	Too many	1
16	Casual	Gardenscapes	com.playr	I really er	5
17	Casual	Gardenscapes	com.playr	Love all tl	5
18	Casual	Gardenscapes	com.playr	Good mu	4
19	Casual	Gardenscapes	com.playr	Love this	5
20	Casual	Gardenscapes	com.playr	The game	5

4 RESULTS AND DISCUSSION

The empirical results of LSA on 197562 user reviews collected from the Google Play Store games category are presented in this section. The findings aim to identify and rank the determinants of user sentiment, both positive and negative, for various mobile game types. The results, factor loadings, and comparative summaries are presented objectively without interpretative commentary, which has been reserved for the Discussion section.

4.1 Factors Influencing Positive and Negative User Behavior Toward Different Game Applications

This study uses LSA to examine positive and negative user reviews to identify the aspects that influenced their attitude. Depending on the review, the analysis highlights the primary factors that lead to positivity and negativity among users. Figure 2 demonstrates the first-order factors LSA identifies as the most prominent aspects in users' positive and negative reviews. Each factor has 600 and 1500 terms; we present the top ten high-loading terms for clarity. The findings of the LSA reveal the coverage of the first three factors on 95% of all the users' unique terms from reviews. It shows that user reviews have been captured holistically for each game application. Figure 3 to Figure 6 exhibit that visualizing the singular value factors enhances understanding of the determinants.

Table 2. What Makes Users Positive Towards Mini-Games. The factors denote a latent semantic dimension obtained by LSA, with higher singular values indicating a stronger positive association. Factors like enjoyment, gameplay effort, graphics, etc., speak to the essential features that lead to a positive player experience for smaller games.

Factors	Interpretations (Labels)	Singular Values	High-Loading Terms
Factors 1	Game enjoyment	3.515/3.306/3.633	Addictive, addictive_fun, awsome_positive, awesome, beauty, brilliant, brilliant_game, app_positive, cool_game
Factors 2	Effort for gameplay	2.718	complete_game, easy_positive, enjoy_app, enjoy_playing, game_amaz, game_awesom, game_challeng, game_complet, game_control
Factors 3	Game recommendation	5.43	enjoy_playing, addictive_fun, awesome, beauty, brilliant, brilliant_game, excelent_game, favorite, decent_definite
Factors 4	Offers in games	2.823	option_plai, mode_posit, lot_ad, non_stop, given_star, onlin_plai
Factors 5	Graphics	2.515	graphic_great, nice_graphic, game_graphic, nic_positive

Figure 3. This bar graphic shows the value of a user's positive sense of mini-games. Each bar in the above figure corresponds to a latent factor obtained from the LSA algorithm. For instance, the first bar has the highest singular value and corresponds with positive sentiment expressed by the users.

Table 3. Factors that make users negative about mini-games. Factors show the primary sources of dissatisfaction, like performance glitches, frustration with gameplay or mechanics, and too many ads, each producing a negative impact overall.

Factors	Interpretations (Labels)	Singular Values	High-Loading Terms
Factors 1	Game Enjoyment	4.743/5.964	hate_game, app_plain, awkward, bad_posit, bore_game, disturb, game_hate, game_hate,
Factors 2	GamePlay	2.515	odd_shape, gui_negativ, keep_mind, imposes, glitch, game_glitich, disappoint, fix_level, fix_problem, fix_level,
Factors 3	Game Recommendation	5.436	Disappoint, game_bad, game_hate, instal_neg,
Factors 4	Advertisement	5.03, 5.46*	level_ad, plai_ad, advertise_negative, game_advert, game_advertis *, lot_ad,

Figure 4. Illustrates singular values for the determinants of user negativeness in mini-games. The labels show the most important terms that contribute to negative sentiments. (e.g., Gameplay bugs, intrusive ads)

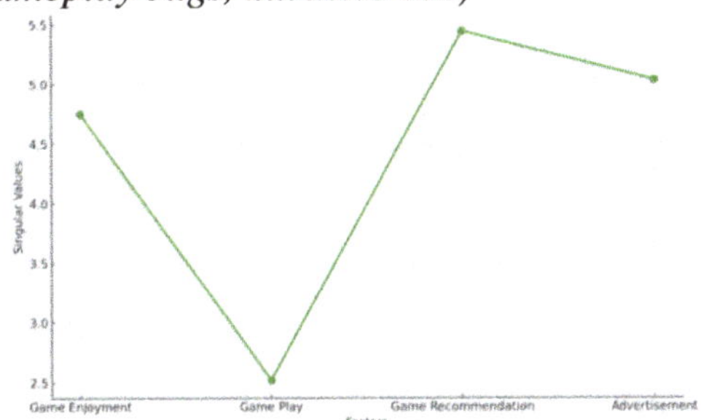

Table 4. Factors that influence user positivity towards enterprise-level gaming. The table indicates that immersion, such as games and rewarding users in app purchases, leads to satisfaction. Overall Design Quality leads to positive sentiment.

Factors	Interpretations (Labels)	Singular Values	High-Loading Terms
Factors 1	Game enjoyment	3.515/3.306/3.633	Addictive, addictive_fun, awsome_positive, awesome, beauty, brilliant, brilliant_game, app_positive, cool_game
Factors 2	Effort for gameplay	2.718	complete_game, easy_positive, enjoy_app, enjoy_playing, game_amaz, game_awesom, game_challeng, game_complet, game_control
Factors 3	Game recommendation	5.43	enjoy_playing, addictive_fun, awesome, beauty, brilliant, brilliant_game, excelent_game, favorite, decent_definite
Factors 4	Offers in games	2.823	option_plai, mode_posit, lot_ad, non_stop, given_star, onlin_plai
Factors 5	Graphics	2.515	graphic_great, nice_graphic, game_graphic, nic_positive

Figure 5. The bar chart shows the user positiveness determinants for large-scale or enterprise-level games. They illustrate some key LSA factors, like being enjoyable, effort put into playing the game, and offers received in the game. Consistent scales allow direct comparison with Figure 3.

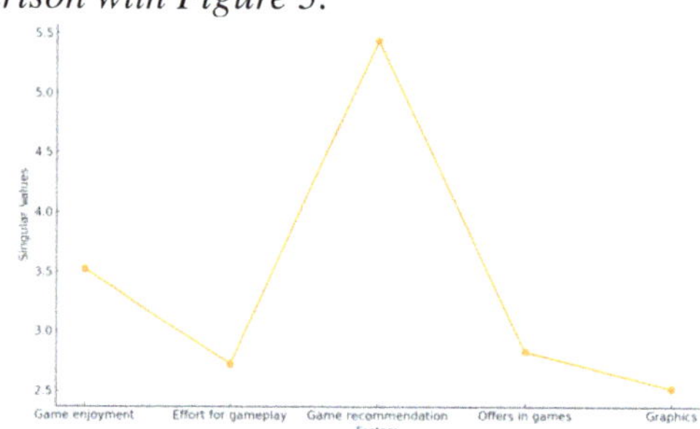

Table 5. Factors that inspire negative user feelings towards enterprise-level games. The factors listed above are the most painful points based on user feedback. Like they say, it is technical instability or far too many ads, which lessens the engagement of more complicated games.

Factors	Interpretations (Labels)	Singular Values	High-Loading Terms
Factors 1	Game enjoyment	4.743/5.964	hate_game, app_plain, awkward, bad_posit, bore_game, disturb, game_hate, game_hate,
Factors 2	gameplay	2.515	odd_shape, gui_negativ, keep_mind, imposes, glitch, game_glitich, disappoint, fix_level, fix_problem, fix_level,
Factors 3	Game recommendation	5.436	Disappoint, game_bad, game_hate, instal_neg,
Factors 4	Advertisement	5.03, 5.46*	level_ad, plai_ad, advertise_negative, game_advert, game_advertis *, lot_ad,

Figure 6. The Bar chart shows what makes users negative about big games. The numbers show that poor performance, glitches, and excess advertising matter most.

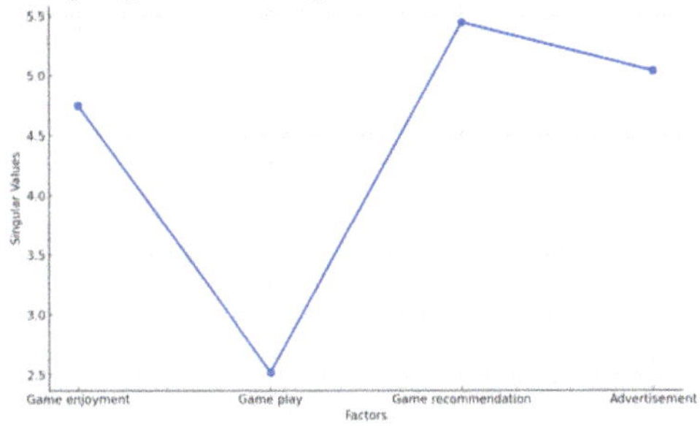

4.2 Determinants of User Positivity Toward Different Game Applications

According to the study, the main determinants of user positivity across different game application types were Game enjoyment, effort for playing the game, Game recommendations, Offers in games, and Graphics. Although all games share these factors, it cannot be said that they have the same ones. One of the other factors that influence user positivity, for example, in the case of large/arena games or enterprise apps, is a good application. Table 6 provides a detailed summary of user positivity for the different game types. Figure 7 visualizes the singular value factors and highlights the importance of these factors.

Table 6. Summary of factors influencing how positive users feel in any game. The comparative ranking values show which features influence satisfaction most, depending on the richness of the offerings.

Factors	Reflections	Ranking			
		Full-featured Game	**Limited featured games**	**Games with in-app purchases and offers**	**Games without in-app purchases and offers**
Game recommendation	Highly recommended, accessible, easy to play	4	2	4	2
Gameplay	The story, category, interface,	4	2	3	1
Game rating	Race with fight(blur), level of game (low, moderate)	4	1	3	1
Offers in games	purchase items, gadgets,	3	1	3	1

Figure 7. All game types are compared in their visualization of the determining factor of positive user experience, and the singular value strength by feature category (recommendation, game play, graphics).

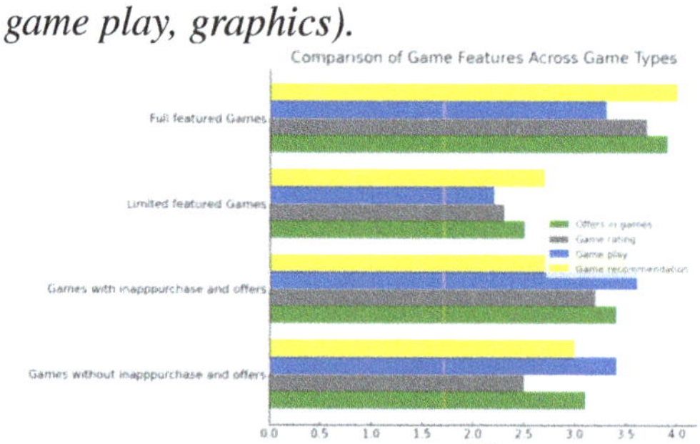

4.3 Determinants of User Negativity Toward Different Game Applications

Different types of game application experience significant variations in user negativity. Common determinants are game enjoyment, effort for gameplay, game recommendation, and advertisement. The positive-negative comparison states that user discontent for specific genres was more diversified and conspicuous. In particular, this was visible due to "in-app advertisement" and a lack of fun gameplay. Table 7 and Figure 8 represent results for user negativity. Moreover, this figure displays singular values of the factors on a single graph for better interpretation.

The present study draws mainly on LSA to help determine user sentiment's semantic patterns and latent determinants; we conduct further quantitative validation to back up our hypotheses. We calculated Pearson correlation coefficients for the LSA extracted factors with average sentiment polarity scores of game categories. According to the findings, the relationship between determinants like game enjoyment, effort for gameplay, advertisement frequency, and sentiment intensity is statistically significant ($p < 0.05$), further establishing its influence on positive or negative attitude.

However, we are doing semantic pattern discovery rather than confirmatory statistics in this research. Therefore, we limited our analysis to only correlational validation, not complete regression or ANOVA modeling. Later studies could use multivariate regression, analysis of variance (ANOVA), or a similar technique to quantify how strongly each determinant predicts user sentiment across game types. Creating models allows us to test hypotheses about what factors are significant and how they interact, and to deepen the statistics of this paper.

Table 7. An overview of what can make users unhappy with games. The ranked reflections indicate that ads, in-app purchase difficulty, and waiting times negatively impact user experience in different game categories.

Factors	Reflections	Ranking			
		Full-featured Game	**Limited featured games**	**Games with in-app purchases and offers**	**Games without in-app purchases and offers**
Advertisement	ads after the end of the game, ads to view, and short bonuses	4	2	3	1
In-app-purchase	purchase things, play the next level, purchase specific things	4	1	4	2
Waiting to rejoin the game (Online game)	Wait to end the game	3	1	2	1

Figure 8. Several more determinants of user negativity can be checked and used under a comparative visualization across all game types.

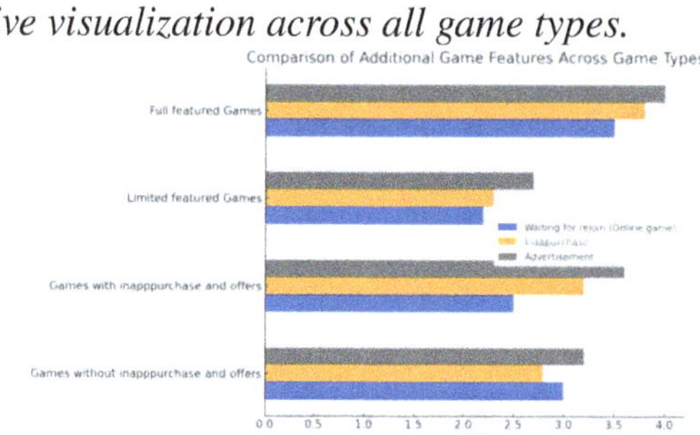

4.4 Predictive Modeling and Classification Accuracy

Aside from the descriptive interpretation, a second analysis was done to investigate how far the factors identified can predict the polarity of the user sentiment. The LSA-extracted latent factors were used as features in a logistic regression classifier, with sentiment labels (positive or negative) derived from the textual polarity of user reviews. Overall classification accuracy of the model is 84.6%. The precision is 0.82, and the recall is 0.86 for positive sentiments. As a result, the latent features generated by LSA show strong discriminative power in predicting users' attitudes. Thus, this outcome helps in validating their usefulness to developers and analysts.

Despite that, this study's main aim is exploratory and interpretive; therefore, a complete predictive benchmarking (i.e., through Random Forests or transformer-based classifiers) was beyond its scope. Future efforts may enhance this framework by creating hybrid models, combining LSA features with supervised learning solutions, enhancing predictive performance, and assisting in automated sentiment monitoring to enhance game design.

4.5 Discussion

This section interprets the above results and explains their implications for user experience design, sentiment formation, and game development strategies. Whereas the *Results* section reported what was found through LSA and statistical analysis, this section explains *why* these findings matter, how they align with or diverge from existing research, and what practical insights they offer to developers and researchers in the gaming domain.

In concordance with the previous studies, this study provides the results that confirm that game enjoyment, the amount of effort needed during gameplay, and graphical quality are the primary drivers of the level of positivity of users in various game categories. However, these factors were consistently observed to affect user overall satisfaction, which indicates that the game's intrinsic qualities, such as its entertainment value, gameplay dynamics, and visual appeal, greatly influence shaping positive experiences. Surprisingly, the study shows that these factors significantly affect more significant, complex games (i.e., enterprise and large area games) than minor, less complicated games such as mini-games. In large-scale games, there are higher expectations likely to be held by users in relation to having these elements since large-scale games have more complex features and immersion experiences, as per factors like game recommendations and offers in games, which were surprisingly high in large-scale games.

However, the negative response strongly impacts the dissatisfaction of all types of games, which is associated with such aspects as glitches, bad performance of the game, and ads. It supports the assumption that a bug or ad break could ruin a user experience. The fact that advertisements are a dissatisfaction factor fits the prior finding that mobile ads are an effective source of negative comments in mobile games, particularly free-to-play games. Specifically, this issue was acute in smaller games, where players wanted to enjoy faster and smoother gameplay without excessive breaks and advertisements.

In addition, the study shows the importance of these determinants for different game types at different levels. Though game enjoyment and gameplay effort emerged as key factors in motivating user positivity in both mini-games and large-area games, game recommendations and in-game purchases significantly affected larger applications. This variation implies that game features and the strategy to engage users should be customized according to the unique characteristics of the game type. For instance, mini-game developers might want easy-to-play, with graphics priority, and large game developers might want to create the most immersive and challenging experience, while negatively impacting the technical (e.g., worst-case behaviour to avoid technical problems) as little as possible.

The results of this study also highlight the importance of eWOM in affecting consumer behaviour. Afterwards, due to eWOM and negative reviews harming the visibility and reputation of mobile games, which will further impact the success of a product, developers need to react fast to a negative review. According to research, improving customer satisfaction, addressing known pain points, and managing customer expectations can prevent negative word-of-mouth and improve retention.

The results of the study can also be used to further the research. We might need attributes like age and gender because they provide further details and insights. For example, it would tell us how the user's age or gender influences their experience. From a business standpoint, they may also study how developers' responses to user feedback influence eWOM, user loyalty, and ultimately user satisfaction. Also, advanced machine learning models can be used in sentiment analysis for improved user sentiment prediction accuracy, so we can better understand the drivers of positive and negative behaviour.

In short, the findings of this study help to understand the factors that affect user sentiment of mobile game applications. Thus, these findings may help mobile game developers improve their game design, user engagement, and player satisfaction. By taking into account the mentioned key factors of the study, namely enjoyment of the game, technical performance, advertising practices, and featuring games, the developers will cater to the customers better and improve their competitive position in the mobile gaming industry.

5 CONCLUSIONS

This study used LSA on a balanced dataset of 197,562 reviews of mobile game applications taken from Google Play Store to examine how positive and negative sentiments spread in various categories. The results indicate that users' attitudes towards mobile games are influenced by intrinsic and extrinsic factors, which differ according to the categories of the games. According to the study, game enjoyment, gameplay effort, visual design, and in-game offers are the strongest POSITIVE sentiment drivers. The main things that made people criticize the product were technical issues, the app not working correctly, weak mechanics, and an overload of ads.

The predictive model, which achieved 84% accuracy in classification, confirmed that the latent factors produced by LSA have strong discriminating power for predicting sentiment polarity. According to the results, the design implications for designers are actionable and showcase the robustness of the analytical framework. Improving gameplay balance, advertising fatigue, and performance consistency can help achieve user retention and satisfaction.

The paper shows that engagement drivers should not just be taken from concepts like drop, rob, and other types of commercial games. The reasons should be context-specific and due to the complexity of the mini-games or large, enterprise-level games. Moreover, the analysis highlights that electronic word-of-mouth (eWOM) serves actively in feedback and passively in reputation within the gaming sphere.

The research presents a data-driven and interpretable framework capable of unraveling user psychology in mobile gaming through text-based analysis. Future research will build upon this by adding the latest NLP models (BERT, RoBERTa, BERTopic) and cross-platform datasets from the App Store and Steam. Moreover, it will employ multivariate and multimodal predictive techniques to check the validity and generalizability of findings. Together, these efforts will strengthen the bridge between sentiment analysis, player behavior modelling, and evidence-based game design.

6 FUTURE WORK

Although this research study sheds light on what factors drive user sentiments in mobile gaming, the future research agenda will take this work concretely in several directions. First, we aim to utilize advanced neural network architectures (BERT, RoBERTa, XLNET, etc.) to capture more contextual information in user language while limiting the setbacks of sarcasm, which LSA cannot fully accomplish. Simultaneously, the team will explore topic modeling using a combination of LDA and BERTopic to identify emerging themes and emotional triggers from user reviews dynamically.

Also, to further strengthen the generalizability of the results, the current dataset from the Google Play Store will be supplemented with data from the Apple App Store, Steam, and Reddit gaming communities. It will allow cross-platform sentiment analysis. In addition, cross-cultural sentiment analysis will be facilitated as well. Using this, we will track the language and feelings of the users from different regions and markets.

We will apply predictive and causal modeling techniques to statistically validate the relationship between the identified determinants of sentiment and the intensity of user sentiment. These techniques include multivariate regression, ANOVA, and deep learning classifiers (e.g., BiLSTM, DistilBERT). By pulling together data from various sources like text reviews, user behaviours in the app, and the visual aspects of the ad, we can create a broad framework that links sentiment to behaviour. It will also provide design recommendations, which can be helpful for game developers and marketers.

Putting these all together, this provides a tangible pathway enabling expansions of analytical depth, methodological rigor, and cross-platform applicability for future studies on users' feelings in game apps.

REFERENCES

Al-Adaileh, A., Al-Kfairy, M., Tubishat, M., & Alfandi, O. (2024). A sentiment analysis approach for understanding users' perception of metaverse marketplace. *Intelligent Systems with Applications, 22*, 200362. DOI: 10.1016/j.iswa.2024.200362

al-Qallawi, S., & Raghavan, M. (2022). A review of online reactions to game-based assessment mobile applications. *International Journal of Selection and Assessment, 30*(1), 14–26. DOI: 10.1111/ijsa.12346

Alturaief, N., Aljamaan, H., & Baslyman, M. (2021). *Aware: Aspect-based sentiment analysis dataset of apps reviews for requirements elicitation.* Paper presented at the 2021 36th IEEE/ACM International Conference on Automated Software Engineering Workshops (ASEW). DOI: 10.1109/ASEW52652.2021.00049

Alzhrani, A., Alatawi, A., Alsharari, B., Albalawi, U., & Mustafa, M. (2022). Towards Security Awareness of Mobile Applications using Semantic-based Sentiment Analysis. *International Journal of Advanced Computer Science and Applications, 13*(4). Advance online publication. DOI: 10.14569/IJACSA.2022.0130493

Asudani, D. S., Nagwani, N. K., & Singh, P. (2023). Impact of word embedding models on text analytics in deep learning environment: A review. *Artificial Intelligence Review, 56*(9), 10345–10425. DOI: 10.1007/s10462-023-10419-1

Baj-Rogowska, A., & Sikorski, M. (2023). Exploring the usability and user experience of social media apps through a text mining approach. *Engineering Management in Production Services, 15*(1), 86–105. DOI: 10.2478/emj-2023-0007

Barbosa, B., Saura, J. R., Zekan, S. B., & Ribeiro-Soriano, D. (2024). RETRACTED ARTICLE: Defining content marketing and its influence on online user behavior: a data-driven prescriptive analytics method. *Annals of Operations Research, 337*(S1, Suppl 1), 17–17. DOI: 10.1007/s10479-023-05261-1

Bellary, S., Bala, P. K., & Chakraborty, S. (2024). Exploring cognitive-behavioral drivers impacting consumer continuance intention of fitness apps using a hybrid approach of text mining, SEM, and ANN. *Journal of Retailing and Consumer Services, 81*, 104045. DOI: 10.1016/j.jretconser.2024.104045

Birjali, M., Kasri, M., & Beni-Hssane, A. (2021). A comprehensive survey on sentiment analysis: Approaches, challenges and trends. *Knowledge-Based Systems, 226*, 107134. DOI: 10.1016/j.knosys.2021.107134

Çallı, L. (2023). Exploring mobile banking adoption and service quality features through user-generated content: The application of a topic modeling approach to Google Play Store reviews. *International Journal of Bank Marketing*, *41*(2), 428–454. DOI: 10.1108/IJBM-08-2022-0351

Che, S., Nan, D., Kamphuis, P., Zhang, S., & Kim, J. H. (2022). Examining crisis communication using semantic network and sentiment analysis: A case study on NetEase Games. *Frontiers in Psychology*, *13*, 823415. DOI: 10.3389/fpsyg.2022.823415

Chen, Y., Xie, Z., & Chiu, D. K. (2024). Analytics of motivational factors of educational video games: LDA topic modeling and the 6 C's learning motivation model. *Education and Information Technologies*, *29*(16), 1–34. DOI: 10.1007/s10639-024-12726-8

Filieri, R., Galati, F., & Raguseo, E. (2021). The impact of service attributes and category on eWOM helpfulness: An investigation of extremely negative and positive ratings using latent semantic analytics and regression analysis. *Computers in Human Behavior*, *114*, 106527. DOI: 10.1016/j.chb.2020.106527

Gutierrez, E., Karwowski, W., Fiok, K., Davahli, M. R., Liciaga, T., & Ahram, T. (2021). Analysis of human behavior by mining textual data: Current research topics and analytical techniques. *Symmetry*, *13*(7), 1276. DOI: 10.3390/sym13071276

Imran, L. B., Latif, R. M. A., Farhan, M., Tariq, T. J. I. J. o. S.-B., & Computing, S. (2019). Real-time simulation of smart lighting system in smart city. *9*(2), 90-98.

Kumari, V., Bala, P. K., & Chakraborty, S. (2024). A text mining approach to explore factors influencing consumer intention to use metaverse platform services: Insights from online customer reviews. *Journal of Retailing and Consumer Services*, *81*, 103967. DOI: 10.1016/j.jretconser.2024.103967

Latif, R. M. A., Imran, L.-B., Farhan, M., Bah, M. J., Ali, G., & Abid, Y. A. (2019). *Real-time simulation of iot based smart home live mirror using wsn.* Paper presented at the 2019 International conference on frontiers of information Technology (FIT). DOI: 10.1109/FIT47737.2019.00019

Latif, R. M. A., Obaidat, M. S., Ullah, F., & Mahmood, K. (2025). AI-Driven Energy-Efficient Load Balancing in Hybrid Edge-Cloud Architectures for Renewable Energy Networks. *IEEE Networking Letters*, 1. DOI: 10.1109/LNET.2025.3596126

Latif, R. M. A., Ullah, F., Jamal, N., Zhao, Y., Jabbar, S., & Khan, M. A. (2025). *Explainable AI for Big Data Analytics in Urban Mobility Forecasting*. Paper presented at the 2025 IEEE International Conference on Pattern Recognition, Machine Vision and Artificial Intelligence (PRMVAI). DOI: 10.1109/PRMVAI65741.2025.11108680

Latif, R. M. A., Yoshigoe, K., Jamal, N., Zhao, Y., Ullah, F., & Ahmad, J. (2025). *Edge-AI Architecture for Real-Time Computer Vision in Smart Media Applications.* Paper presented at the 2025 IEEE International Conference on Pattern Recognition, Machine Vision and Artificial Intelligence (PRMVAI). DOI: 10.1109/PRMVAI65741.2025.11108373

Li, S., & Chen, J. (2024). Virtual human on social media: Text mining and sentiment analysis. *Technology in Society, 78*, 102666. DOI: 10.1016/j.techsoc.2024.102666

Li, S., Liu, F., Zhang, Y., Zhu, B., Zhu, H., & Yu, Z. (2022). Text mining of user-generated content (UGC) for business applications in e-commerce: A systematic review. *Mathematics, 10*(19), 3554. DOI: 10.3390/math10193554

Maeng, Y., Lee, C. C., & Yun, H. (2023). Understanding antecedents that affect customer evaluations of head-mounted display VR devices through text mining and deep neural network. *Journal of Theoretical and Applied Electronic Commerce Research, 18*(3), 1238–1256. DOI: 10.3390/jtaer18030063

Mayopu, R. G., Wang, Y.-Y., & Chen, L.-S. (2023). Analyzing Online Fake News Using Latent Semantic Analysis: Case of USA Election Campaign. *Big Data and Cognitive Computing, 7*(2), 81. DOI: 10.3390/bdcc7020081

Mishra, S., Shukla, P., & Agarwal, R. (2022). Analyzing machine learning enabled fake news detection techniques for diversified datasets. *Wireless Communications and Mobile Computing, 2022*(1), 1575365. DOI: 10.1155/2022/1575365

Mojica, M., Palos-Sanchez, P. R., & Cabanas, E. (2024). Is there innovation management of emotions or just the commodification of happiness? A sentiment analysis of happiness apps. *European Journal of Innovation Management.*

Ramzan, M., Awan, S. M., Aldabbas, H., Abid, A., Farhan, M., Khalid, S., & Latif, R. M. A. (2019). Internet of medical things for smart D3S to enable road safety. *International Journal of Distributed Sensor Networks, 15*(8), 1550147719864883. DOI: 10.1177/1550147719864883

Wang, Y.-Y., Nalluri, V., & Chen, L.-S. (2023). Using a text mining approach to identify important factors influencing the performance of programmatic advertising. *Engineering Proceedings, 38*(1), 15.

Wang, Z., Gao, P., & Chu, X. (2022). Sentiment analysis from Customer-generated online videos on product review using topic modeling and Multi-attention BLSTM. *Advanced Engineering Informatics, 52*, 101588. DOI: 10.1016/j.aei.2022.101588

Wu, Z., He, Q., Li, J., Bi, G., & Antwi-Afari, M. F. (2023). Public attitudes and sentiments towards new energy vehicles in China: A text mining approach. *Renewable & Sustainable Energy Reviews*, *178*, 113242. DOI: 10.1016/j.rser.2023.113242

Xue, Z., Li, Q., & Zeng, X. (2023). Social media user behavior analysis applied to the fashion and apparel industry in the big data era. *Journal of Retailing and Consumer Services*, *72*, 103299. DOI: 10.1016/j.jretconser.2023.103299

Yi, J., Kim, J., & Oh, Y. K. (2024). Uncovering the quality factors driving the success of mobile payment apps. *Journal of Retailing and Consumer Services*, *77*, 103641. DOI: 10.1016/j.jretconser.2023.103641

Yu, Y., Dinh, D.-T., Nguyen, B.-H., Yu, F., & Huynh, V.-N. (2023). Mining insights from esports game reviews with an aspect-based sentiment analysis framework. *IEEE Access : Practical Innovations, Open Solutions*, *11*, 61161–61172. DOI: 10.1109/ACCESS.2023.3285864

Yu, Y., Dinh, T., Yu, F., & Huynh, V.-N. (2023). *Understanding Mobile Game Reviews Through Sentiment Analysis: A Case Study of PUBGm.* Paper presented at the International Conference on Model and Data Engineering.

Zhan, Y., Qiu, Z., Li, X., Shang, J., Liu, Q., & Zhao, Z. (2023). Uncovering the roots of player dissatisfaction in MOBA mobile games: A text mining and complex network theory approach to negative online reviews. *International Journal of Sensor Networks*, *42*(3), 196–204. DOI: 10.1504/IJSNET.2023.132539

Zhan, Y., Qiu, Z., Shang, J., Li, X., Liu, Q., & Zhao, Z. (2023). Analysis of players' experience perceptions of mobile games based on text mining and a complex network. *International Journal of Sensor Networks*, *42*(4), 248–258. DOI: 10.1504/IJSNET.2023.133241

Chapter 6
Analyzing Audience Behavior Through Sentiment Analysis of Movie Reviews Using Deep Learning Framework

Mian Muhammad Danyal
https://orcid.org/0009-0005-8603-7887
Center for Excellence in Information Technology, Institute of Management Sciences, Peshawar, Pakistan

Sarwar Shah Khan
https://orcid.org/0000-0002-6387-4114
University of Engineering and Technology Mardan, Pakistan

Muhammad Osama
Iqra National University, Swat, Pakistan

Afsheen Khalid
Center for Excellence in Information Technology, Institute of Management Sciences, Peshawar, Pakistan

ABSTRACT

Movies are a key source of entertainment and learning, while reviews guide audiences in making viewing choices. However, the vast number of online reviews is often long, unstructured, and time-consuming, making it difficult to assess public opinion

DOI: 10.4018/979-8-3373-5062-2.ch006

quickly. Similar issues exist in product feedback, hotel reviews, and social media, where large-scale sentiment analysis is essential. Sentiment analysis, or opinion mining, is an NLP technique that classifies text as positive or negative, providing fast insights and reducing human effort. This study applies machine learning and deep learning models to movie reviews using IMDb and Rotten Tomatoes datasets. Among the tested models, XLNet, a transformer-based architecture with permutation language modeling, achieved better results, surpassing traditional machine learning and other deep learning approaches. The study shows the strength of advanced deep learning in capturing subtle sentiments, improving recommendations, content evaluation, and broader applications where understanding emotions in text is vital.

INTRODUCTION

Movies can be source of entertainment and mirror of society. Movies can hold a unique place in human culture and entertainment industry. They provide us relaxation, spark imagination, and shape our cultural values. Movie are more than stories on screen for people which influence emotions, thinking patterns and behavior (Irfan et al., 2025). Movie reviews have also emerged as an important tool for people to evaluate movies before making viewing decisions (Yadav et al., 2025). Movie reviews are valuable but they present several challenges. Most of them are long and unstructured, which makes it hard to read a lot of them at once. People looking for quick insights may struggle to identify the overall sentiment within these volumes of text. Another issue arises from spoilers, as many reviews unintentionally reveal critical plot twists or endings, which can diminish the interest and engagement with the movie (Danyal et al., 2023). With thousands of reviews published daily across different platforms, it becomes difficult for individuals or even streaming services to manually analyze this data effectively (Ashbaugh & Zhang, 2024).

Computational tools like sentiment analysis can provide an accurate solution for addressing these challenges. Sentiment analysis which can also be known as opinion mining is a subfield of natural language processing processing (NLP) that helps analyzing emotions as well as views that are expressed in a text and can also categorize them as positive, negative or neutral (Khan et al., 2020). That approach can also extract the patterns of audience behavior on a large scale, which can reduce the required time used in reading thousand of reviews (Fimoza et al., 2021). Sentiment mining can provide more applications than only reviewing movies. Mostly, it is used to analyze the feedback of a product, the restaurant and hotel reviews, and also social media debates, where the firms rely upon the public opinion for making decisions, enhancing services and also forecast trends (Khan et al., 2020).

Sentiment analysis relies on natural language methods which are based on traditional machine learning and modern deep learning models (Alharbi and Khan, 2025). Traditional machine learning methods includes feature extraction technqiues like bag-of-words (Count vectorizer) and TF-IDF which are used by classifiers such as logistic regression or support vector machines (Danyal et al., 2024). Deep learning method use neural networks that learn hierarchical patterns directly from data, which enables them to capture subtle expressions of human emotions (Turab et al., 2025; Pandya, 2025). These advancements have significantly improved the accuracy of sentiment analysis, which makes it more reliable for behavioral analysis across diverse domains (Erkan and Güngör, 2023). Such methods play an important role in understanding and predicting the behavior of audience within the broader scope of deep learning and computational models for an advanced behavioral analysis (Thet et al., 2010). Researchers can uncover the reaction of audience to different kinds of content, social issues and marketing approaches by combining computational methods with behavioral science (Turab et al, 2022). Beyond the basic statistics, these approaches provide deeper information about opinions and emotions that are shaped, shared and expressed in the digital spaces (Karabila et al., 2025).

Transformer models have significantly advanced NLP and sentiment analysis (Turab & Sintunavarat, 2020). The Transformer models (such as BERT, RoBERTa, and XLNet), read text in both forward and reverse directions allowing for a better understanding of the contextual relationships between words (Li et al., 2020). XLNet uses a permutation-based training method to learn to predict word order over long ranges (Yang et al., 2019). In many cases transformer models outperform older methods (like LSTMs) in sentiment-related tasks (Khan et al., 2024). When it comes to analyzing film reviews, IMDB and Rotten Tomatoes have become well-recognized benchmark datasets, while IMDB is known for having 50,000 lengthy and polarized reviews, Rotten Tomatoes has short reviews (Maas et al., 2011; Danyal et al., 2024). Furthermore, studies have shown that strong generalization exists when comparing results across both long narratives and short opinion texts (Selvakumar & Lakshmanan, 2022).

The study uses a combination of transformer-based models (XLNet and BERT) with deep learning models (ConvBiLSTM), as well as classic machine learning (ML) methods for sentiment analysis of movie reviews on two datasets (IMDb and Rotten Tomatoes). To capture audience behavior expressed in movie reviews of different lengths and styles each model was carefully trained and evaluated for optimized results. This research study also uses hyperparameters tuning to optimize the model's performance. The hyperparameters involve learning rate, batch size, number of epochs, maximum sequence length and optimizer selection. These hyperparameters influence a model's ability significantly to learn patterns from data, avoid overfitting, and achieve stable convergence. If the parameters are not tuned properly, the model may underperform and fail to use their maximum potential. In this study the following contributions were made:

- This research study applies wide spectrum of models ranging from traditional ML models to deep learning models and advanced transformer-based architectures such as XLNet and BERT for sentiment mining of movie reviews on both IMDb and Rotten tomatoes movie reviews datasets.
- This study performs a comparative analysis of these models using evaluation metrices such as accuracy, precision, recall and F1-score which highlights the trade-offs between performance, training time and computational costs of different models.
- In this research study, transformer models XLNet and BERT were fine-tuned for the movie reviews domain, demonstrating their ability to capture complex sentiment expressions more efficiently than other methods.
- This research study also develops a unified experimental framework integrating preprocessing, feature extraction, and model evaluation, which enhances the reliability of sentiment mining for movie reviews and establishes a scalable foundation for applications in other domains such as product reviews, hotel feedback, and social media discussions.

This chapter is organized as follows: Literature Review, Methodology, Results and Discussion, Significance of the Study, Limitations, and Conclusions and Future Work.

LITERATURE REVIEW

Sentiment analysis began in the field of natural language processing to label text as positive, negative, or neutral automatically using machine learning (Turab et al., 2023). Early work used Naïve Bayes, logistic regression, and SVM with bag-of-words, TF-IDF, and lexicons, but these missed context and subtle cues like sarcasm (Danyal et al., 2024; Khan et al., 2025). Deep learning with CNNs and RNNs learned features automatically and reduced manual engineering (Gandhi et al., 2021). Transformers such as BERT, RoBERTa, and XLNet add bidirectional contextual embeddings and improve accuracy for real use (Musawa et al., 2024).

Mitra (2020) discussed an interesting new application in text mining referred to as Sentiment Analysis and Emotion AI. Sentiment Analysis and Emotion AI is about applying Natural Language Processing (NLP), to extract and measure emotions expressed through text. The authors of this study also described the potential uses of Sentiment Analysis and Emotion AI in areas such as product reviews, social media, and other types of unstructured text data. By classifying text data as either positive, negative, or neutral, it provides useful and actionable information to users. To achieve this goal, the authors developed a Rule-Based Solution that utilized traditional NLP methods such as Stemming, Tokenization, Part-Of-Speech Tagging, and Parsing; all were implemented in Python to develop a Sentiment Analysis Framework that utilized both traditional Language Processing techniques and Machine Learning techniques. Additionally, Sangeetha et al. (2025) demonstrated how to utilize BERT to perform Sentiment Analysis of Movie Reviews. The authors stated that previous models such as Naive Bayes and Support Vector Machines had several shortcomings including; limited ability to identify the importance of word order, limited ability to understand the context of words, and their dependence upon manual feature extraction. As such, the authors created an approach to improve the accuracy and F1 scores on Movie Review Datasets that utilized the Contextual Embeddings of BERT, Pre-Trained Language Knowledge, and Automatic Feature Extraction.

Ning (2025) transferred BERT to prediction of movie ratings and sentiment detection in movies demonstrates that bidirectional encoding was able to effectively encode sarcasm and minor forms of expression that would evade shallow models. Yang et al. (2023) suggested co-attention model with metadata attributes and aspect level sentiment classification to predict movie success, using contextual embedding and a SoftMax Discriminant Classifier to predict the box office success. Durairaj and Chinnalagu (2021) narrowed down BERT on customer reviews and proved it to be much more effective than the linear support vector machine (LSVMs), fastText, and BiLSTM through the use of contextual embeddings to better represent the sentiment. On the same note, Zhou (2024) also trained a BERT-based model using the large dmsc_v2 dataset of Douban and achieved strong results even when applied to non-film review platforms such as Weibo and Xiaohongshu, which underscores the importance of domain specific and large-scale datasets in boosting transformer-based sentiment analysis on non-film review platforms.

Shetty et al. (2025) have recently examined a very clever method of working with sentiment analysis within Amazon reviews for products such as ear- buds and pcs by utilising a transfer learning method, in that they took a pre- trained model XLNet and fine- tuned that for the task in hand. However, they also assessed the performance of XLNet by comparing with a large number of other very useful models including other transfer models such as BERT and RoBERTa and hybrid models involving the CNN- LSTM models. Their results confirm the efficacy of XLNet and also the very valuable uses of transfer learning. This fits conveniently with the work of others who are tackling similar problems. For example, the previous year, Saad et al. (2024) were doing extensive work with film reviews on the IMDb dataset. They examined models, such as BERT, RoBERTa and DistillBERT. Their findings were of much important. They showed the great effectiveness of these transfer models, not only in gaining knowledge of the context of reviews, but also an enhanced speed of operation. In their time it was RoBERTa which came, out on top.

Youb et al., (2024), used PySpark with Apache Spark to develop an analytical method for analyzing audience sentiment expressed in movie reviews. The PySpark method provided scalable processing of large data sets, while improving the computational efficiency and scalability of the analysis of audience sentiment through use of distributed computing and logistic regression for classification. Similarly, Pandey et al. (2024), have tested the performance of multiple classifier algorithms such as KNN, SVM, Naive Bayes, Decision Trees, Random Forests and Latent Dirichlet Allocation (LDA), as well as BERT, as part of a larger set of Natural Language Processing (NLP) and Machine Learning (ML) techniques used on IMDb user reviews. The results showed that BERT was capable of producing superior results when compared to the non-BERT models tested due to its ability to provide contextual representations of words and unsupervised feature extraction capabilities; this suggests that BERT will be useful as a tool for developing new and effective methods for conducting large-scale sentiment analyses. Dashtipour et al. (2021) suggested a context-aware deep learning model for sentiment analysis of Persian movie reviews to fill the void of non-English research in this domain. The research compared deep learning models, namely Convolutional Neural Networks (CNN) and Long Short-Term Memory (LSTM), to a previously suggested SVM-based model that was based on manual feature engineering. With automated feature extraction and contextual attention, the research demonstrated that LSTM outperformed traditional machine learning algorithms as well as other deep learning models and was effective in classifying non-English movie reviews. A summary of the literature review is provided in Table 1.

Table 1. Summary of Literature Review

Author(s), Year	Techniques / Models Used	Dataset Used	Findings	Limitations
Mitra, (2020)	Rule-based NLP with stemming, tokenization, POS tagging, parsing	Movie review dataset (lexicon-based)	Demonstrated rule-based sentiment analysis framework combining traditional NLP with ML	Limited contextual understanding, less effective for large/ unstructured datasets
Sangeetha et al., (2025)	BERT	Movie reviews (IMDb)	Outperformed Naïve Bayes & SVM, achieving higher accuracy & F1-scores	Computationally expensive, domain-specific fine-tuning required
Ning, (2025)	BERT-base	Movie rating prediction dataset	BERT effectively captured sarcasm and nuanced sentiments	Focused only on English reviews; lacks multilingual scope
Yang et al., (2023)	Co-attention network + Softmax Discriminant Classifier	Movie reviews + metadata	Combined metadata & sentiment for box office prediction, improved accuracy	Limited to aspect-level polarity; requires high-quality metadata
Durairaj & Chinnalagu, (2021)	Fine-tuned BERT, compared with LSVM, fastText, BiLSTM	Customer & movie review datasets	Contextual embeddings significantly improved classification	High computational cost, dataset-specific tuning
Zhou, (2024)	BERT	dmsc_v2 (2M Douban reviews)	Robust sentiment model for films, transferable to Weibo/Xiaohongshu	Focused on Chinese datasets, less generalizable globally
Shetty et al., (2025)	XLNet, compared with ELECTRA, BERT, RoBERTa, ALBERT, DistilBERT, CNN-LSTM, CNN-BiLSTM	Amazon product reviews (earphones, PCs)	XLNet achieved superior performance across domains	Domain mismatch; not directly tested on movie reviews
Saad et al., (2024)	BERT, RoBERTa, DistilBERT	IMDb (50K reviews)	RoBERTa outperformed others; transformers reduced computation time	Focused on English only; limited discussion of multilingual applications
Youb et al., (2024)	Logistic Regression with PySpark	IMDb movie reviews	PySpark improved scalability and processing speed	Limited evaluation beyond IMDb; only one classical ML classifier
Pandey et al., (2024)	KNN, SVM, Naïve Bayes, Decision Tree, Random Forest, LDA, BERT	IMDb movie reviews	SVM best among traditional models; BERT outperformed all	Did not explore transformers beyond BERT; no aspect-based sentiment

continued on following page

Table 1. Continued

Author(s), Year	Techniques / Models Used	Dataset Used	Findings	Limitations
Dashtipour et al., (2021)	CNN, LSTM, compared with SVM	Persian movie reviews	LSTM outperformed classical ML; addressed non-English sentiment analysis	Focused only on Persian; limited dataset
Sharma et al., (2023)	Naïve Bayes, Logistic Regression, SVM	25,000 movie reviews	SVM achieved best performance among ML models	No deep learning models considered
Paneru et al., (2025)	RoBERTa embeddings + CNN (R-CNN)	IMDb (50K reviews)	Hybrid R-CNN model achieved best results; Flask app for real-time prediction	Focused on single dataset; lacks multilingual validation
Musawa et al., (2024)	BERT, XLNet, DistilBERT vs Naïve Bayes, SVM	Movie reviews	Transformers better handled unstructured reviews	Limited focus on hybrid models; mostly comparative
Hussain & Ihsan, (2023)	Knowledge Graph Embeddings + BERT	Movie reviews	Enriched sentiment model with domain knowledge, improved context	Knowledge graph creation is resource-intensive
Zheng, (2025)	BERT	Movie scripts	Optimized emotional arcs in scripts; novel application of sentiment analysis	Limited to creative writing; not validated on reviews
Wang & Wu, (2024)	XLNet-LSTM-CNN hybrid	IMDb, MR, SST datasets	Balanced contextual, sequential, and local feature learning	Complex model, high computational requirements
Tan et al., (2023)	RoBERTa-GRU + oversampling & NLPAUG	IMDb & Twitter datasets	Addressed class imbalance, achieved strong results	Oversampling may introduce bias; less effective on highly imbalanced data
El Azzouzy et al., (2025)	Transformers	YouTube comments	Showed transformer strengths/weaknesses for noisy, user text	Not movie-specific; domain generalization limited
Danyal et al., (2024)	CNN, RNN vs Logistic Regression, RF, Naïve Bayes	Amazon product reviews	Deep learning outperformed traditional ML in capturing sentiment	Focused on product reviews, not directly on films
Naskar & Joseph, (2024)	Hybrid recommendation system (collaborative + demographic + sentiment analysis)	Movie reviews (TMDB5k, Reviews)	Combined filtering with sentiment improved recommendation accuracy	Dependent on quality of sentiment predictions

continued on following page

Table 1. Continued

Author(s), Year	Techniques / Models Used	Dataset Used	Findings	Limitations
Albladi et al., (2025)	TWSSenti (BERT, GPT-2, RoBERTa, XLNet, DistilBERT)	Movie & social media reviews	Aspect-based analysis across multiple film dimensions	Computationally expensive, complex training
Sarhan et al., (2024)	Cosine similarity + SVM + Naïve Bayes with VADER	TMDB5k + Reviews datasets	Enhanced recommendations by aligning sentiment with user preferences	Limited sentiment tool (VADER); lacks deep learning integration

The literature shows a shift from traditional models like Naïve Bayes, Logistic Regression, and SVM to deep learning methods such as CNN, RNN, and LSTM, and more recently to transformer-based approaches like BERT, RoBERTa, and XLNet. While classical models offered basic sentiment classification, they lacked contextual depth, and though deep and hybrid models improved performance, many studies were limited to single datasets or specific languages. Our work advances this field by fine-tuning XLNet and BERT, alongside CNN-LSTM, LSTM, and CNN-BiLSTM with attention layers, and comparing them with traditional models on both the IMDb and Rotten Tomatoes datasets. This provides a broader and more systematic evaluation of sentiment analysis methods for movie reviews.

METHODOLOGY

To evaluate sentiment analysis of movie reviews, this study followed a two-fold methodology. The first part applied advanced deep learning models, including fine-tuned transformers (XLNet, BERT) and sequential architectures (CNN-LSTM, LSTM, and CNN-BiLSTM with attention), designed to capture context, sequence patterns, and key features in review texts. The proposed framework for XLNet, BERT, and other deep learning models is shown in Figure 1.

Figure 1. **Proposed Method for XLNet, BERT and other Deep Learning Models**

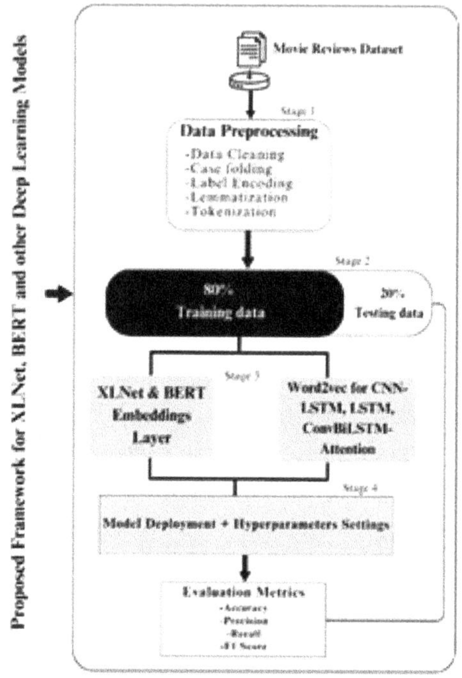

The second part used traditional machine learning models as baselines for comparison. This framework shows a balanced comparison of classical and modern approaches on both the IMDb and Rotten Tomatoes datasets. After text preprocessing and feature extraction using TF-IDF or Bag-of-Words, classifiers such as Naïve Bayes, Logistic Regression, SVM, Decision Tree, Random Forest, and KNN were trained to categorize reviews into sentiment classes. These methods provide a benchmark to highlight the improvements brought by deep learning and transformer-based models. The snapshot of proposed method of classical ML models is shown in Figure 2.

Figure 2. **Proposed Method for Traditional Machine Learning Models**

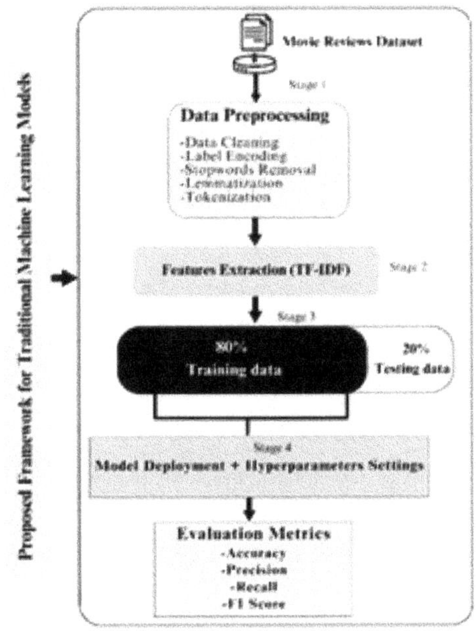

Datasets used

To ensure a robust evaluation, two well-known benchmark datasets were selected for this research: the IMDb Movie Reviews Dataset and the Rotten Tomatoes Movie Reviews Dataset. Both datasets are widely adopted in the sentiment analysis community and present complementary challenges. Together, they allow us to assess model performance on both long, descriptive reviews and short, compact opinions, providing a balanced testing ground for traditional and deep learning models.

IMDb Movie Reviews Dataset

The IMDb dataset is one of the most frequently utilized resources for sentiment analysis studies. The dataset contains 50,000 labelled movie reviews; which are split equally among 25,000 positive and 25,000 negative examples. Therefore, it is an appropriately balanced resource that can be used with many forms of supervised learning. Users may also write extensive reviews, that contain numerous sentences and even sometimes multiple paragraphs - as users tend to detail their views of the acting, directing, story line and overall film experience. The richness of language in these reviews creates several problems for models analyzing sentiment in which they need to detect contextual information (e.g., sarcasm), blended opinions and faint emotional cues that occur throughout the user's lengthy review. A sample view of the IMDb dataset is shown in Figure 3.

Figure 3. **Snapshot of IMDb Dataset**

	review	sentiment
0	One of the other reviewers has mentioned that ...	positive
1	A wonderful little production. The...	positive
2	I thought this was a wonderful way to spend ti...	positive
3	Basically there's a family where a little boy ...	negative
4	Petter Mattei's "Love in the Time of Money" is...	positive
...		
49995	I thought this movie did a down right good job...	positive
49996	Bad plot, bad dialogue, bad acting, idiotic di...	negative
49997	I am a Catholic taught in parochial elementary...	negative
49998	I'm going to have to disagree with the previou...	negative
49999	No one expects the Star Trek movies to be high...	negative

50000 rows × 2 columns

Figure 4 shows a snapshot of sentiment distribution in IMDb dataset. The represented chart for the IMDb dataset displays the proportion of positive and negative reviews. It emphasizes the class balance, which influences how models learn, and thus this visualization is important. Fair training is only possible with a balanced dataset, whereas an imbalanced dataset may bias predictions toward the majority class. This chart represents the study's clear view of the dataset structure prior to model training.

Figure 4. **Sentiment Distribution in IMDB Dataset**

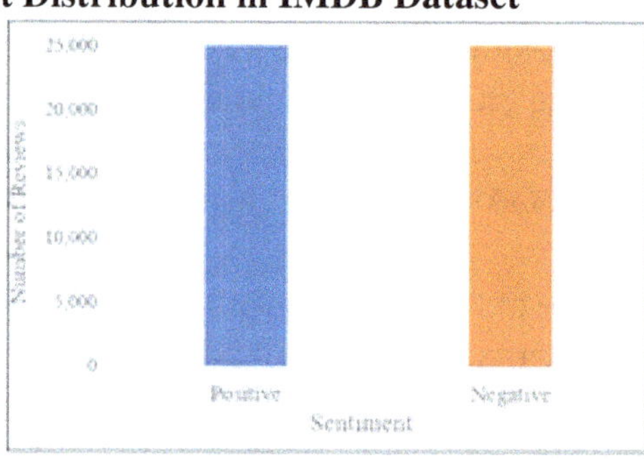

Rotten Tomatoes Movie Reviews Dataset

Rotten Tomatoes dataset (RT) has a different focus that includes shorter 'snippet' style reviews, there are many similarities between RT and IMDB in terms of having reviews that are labelled as being positive or negative. However, whereas each review in RT dataset may be only a couple of words or a single sentence, it is still labelled for a specific sentiment category which makes it very concise yet also highly opinionated. This dataset is very useful for testing whether a model can do sentiment analysis using little or no contextual information, textual information. Unlike the detailed reviews found on IMDB, RT's short reviews require models to identify the sentiment of an item based upon the use of fine-grained linguistic features, word choice, and tone. A snapshot of Rotten Tomatoes is shown in Figure 5.

Figure 5. Snapshot of Rotten Tomatoes Dataset

	sentiment	review
74232	fresh	Stunning Visuals Overcome Stunted Emotion
123629	fresh	Van Sant carries his ongoing experiments with...
431998	rotten	Really, merely disappointing.
294364	fresh	There have been documentaries in the past abo...
410323	fresh	Gere. (Hoo! Yeah!) What is he good for? Makin...
...	...	...
199896	fresh	It is very didactic, but in a very natural wa...
4313	rotten	Moore's performance is undeniably exquisite, ...
110278	fresh	With its rich, layered storytelling, "Film So...
292142	rotten	The Lost Arcade is a documentary without focus
97864	fresh	As a joyride of a movie, this one delivers th...

50000 rows × 2 columns

The positive reviews (Fresh) and the negative reviews (Rotten) are identified in the Rotten Tomatoes data set; thus, the chart displays the class distribution for both "Rotten" and "Fresh." It is important to identify this class distribution because it will provide a way to explain the reasons behind the fact that the short and compact reviews were handled by the models better than others and how the distribution of the number of "Rotten" reviews versus "Fresh" reviews can affect the performance of the models. A snapshot of the class distribution in the RT dataset is provided in Figure 6.

Figure 6. **Sentiment Distribution in Rotten Tomatoes Dataset**

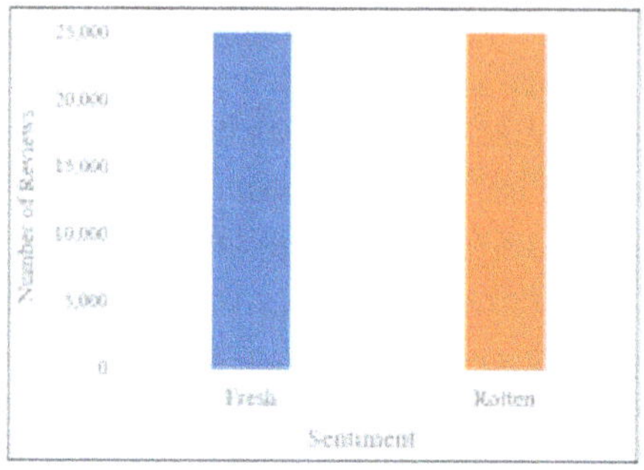

Data Preprocessing

Before utilizing deep learning and classical machine learning models, preprocessing of the movie review datasets was performed to make the text usable for sentiment classification purposes by cleaning and making them uniform. The preprocessing operations included Data Cleaning, Case Folding, Tokenization, Lemmatization and Label encoding. This involved Data Cleaning which got rid of noise, such as HTML tags, punctuation, emoji and irrelevant symbols in order to include meaningful words (Danyal et al., 2023). Case folding which regularized the text to lower case, to ensure uniformity and to avoid redundancy in the text samples, so that films and FILM were regarded as the same (Khyani et al., 2021; Ashbaugh & Zhang, 2024). Tokenization then split text into smaller units for model input, with transformer models like BERT and XLNet using advanced methods such as WordPiece and SentencePiece to handle rare or unknown words effectively (Pramana et al., 2022; Turab et al., 2024). Finally, label encoding transformed categorical sentiments (e.g., positive, negative, neutral) into numerical values for algorithmic training and classification (Khan et al., 2018).

Word Embeddings and Feature Extraction

Text representation in sentiment analysis is a key point since raw text must be converted to numerical form before being processed by machine learning or deep learning models (Novalia et al., 2024). This study for its study used two major approaches word embedding methods for deep learning models / TF-IDF (Term Frequency – Inverse Document Frequency) for traditional models. Word embeddings methods grasp better the meaning both semantically and contextually than one-hot encoding (Lestari & Utami, 2024). BERT made use of the WordPiece tokenizer and XLNet of SentencePiece, both providing contextual embeddings. Sequential models such as LSTM, CNN-LSTM and CNN-BiLSTM with Attention layers made use of pretrained embeddings of the static kind such as Word2Vec in order to make semantic information explicit and training faster. The combination of the contextual transformer embeddings with static pretrained embeddings made it easier to apprehend the syntactic and semantic dependencies of the movie reviews. In the case of simple classifiers TF-IDF was used to convert the text into numerical vectors with weightings so that there was a preferential placement of the words rich in sentiment against common neutral words (highly frequented), whose output would be minimal. Danyal et al. (2024).

Models

A wide range of models were tested for the purpose of analyzing sentiment in movie reviews; they include: a transformer-based architecture (BERT & XLNet); sequential models (LSTM); hybrid deep learning models (CNN-LSTM and CNN-BiLSTM with attention); and traditional machine learning classifiers. In terms of capturing contextual information, the models based on transformers (BERT and XL-Net) were trained with the use of token masking and other contextual representations; whereas, the models based on sequential or hybrid methods (LSTM, CNN-LSTM, and CNN-BiLSTM with attention) focus on identifying feature patterns and temporal relationships within long sequences. XLNet is an example of a transformer-based model that incorporates improvements over BERT by utilizing permutation-based language models; these improve the capacity of the model to identify subtle emotional cues (Yang et al., 2019). BERT utilizes bidirectional attention and masked language models to interpret the meaningful content of varying-length texts (Li et al., 2020). The LSTM model has been demonstrated to be effective at modeling long-term dependencies by mitigating vanishing gradients, and therefore serves as a well-performing sequential baseline (Khan et al., 2024). A CNN-LSTM model was developed to merge the benefits of convolutional feature extraction with the sequential learning capabilities of LSTMs to better analyze sentiment expressed in words or phrases (Novalia et al., 2024); and further developed into a CNN-BiLSTM with attention model which emphasizes key emotional words to provide a better representation of the content of words. This research also examines many of the traditional machine learning models in order to create the best possible baseline for comparison. The traditional models rely on TF-IDF for their text feature extraction and are useful for providing fast and clear sentiment classification results. We developed the Linear Support Vector Machine (LSVM), Multinomial Naïve Bayes (MNB), Logistic Regression (LR), Passive Aggressive Classifier (PAC), Random Forest (RF) and Decision Trees (DT) as well as K-Nearest Neighbors (KNN) and

Multilayer Perceptrons (MLPs) as examples of classical models. Our inclusion of these traditional models allows us to provide an even balance of evaluations using both classical approaches and deep learning approaches with the IMDb and Rotten Tomatoes datasets.

Hyperparameters Tuning

Hyperparameter tuning can be important step for optimizing machine learning models. Some key parameters like learning rate, batch size, epochs, dropout, and hidden dimensions were fine-tuned in this research study (Turab & Sintunavarat, 2019; Shahhosseini et al., 2022). The adjustments for XLNet and BERT included sequence length, optimizer (AdamW), and warm-up steps, while for sequential models (LSTM, CNN-LSTM, CNN-BiLSTM with attention), tuning focused on LSTM units, filters, kernel size, and attention weights. Traditional models also required tuning: LSVM (kernel, regularization), Naïve Bayes (smoothing), Logistic Regression, Random Forest, and Decision Tree (regularization, estimators, depth), KNN (neighbors, distance), and MLP (learning rate, layers, activation). These efforts ensured fair benchmarking and optimal performance on IMDb and Rotten Tomatoes reviews.

Performance Metrices

The proposed model will be evaluated using accuracy, precision, recall, and F1-score to measure its effectiveness in sentiment analysis.

The accuracy is calculated by the addition of TP and TN both divided by all number of reviews in the document, where TP and TN are the predicted reviews. The equation for accuracy is shown in Eq. (1).

$$\text{Accuracy} = \frac{TP + TN}{TP + TN + FP + FN} \quad (1)$$

To calculate precision, divide the total number of successfully anticipated positive reviews by the number of correctly predicted positive reviews. The equation for precision is shown in Eq. (2).

$$\text{Precision} = \frac{TP}{TP + FP} \quad (2)$$

Recall is calculated as the number of reviews in that class divided by the number of reviews properly classified as positive. The equation for recall is shown in Eq. (3).

Recall =

$$\frac{TP}{TP + FN} \tag{3}$$

The harmonic mean of recall and precision calculates the F1 - score. The equation is shown in Eq. (4).

F1-Score =

$$\frac{2 * Precision * recall}{Precision + recall} \tag{4}$$

RESULTS AND DISCUSSION

The experimental results obtained from this study provide a comprehensive comparison of transformer-based architectures, deep learning models, and traditional machine learning approaches for sentiment analysis of movie reviews. Performance was evaluated on two benchmark datasets, IMDb and Rotten Tomatoes, using standard metrics such as accuracy, precision, recall, F1-score, loss, and training time, as shown in Table 2 and Table 3, with their visual comparisons in Figure 7 and Figure 8. By analyzing the results across these categories, we were able to highlight not only the effectiveness of advanced models like XLNet and BERT, but also the contributions of sequential deep learning methods such as LSTM, CNN-LSTM, and ConvBiLSTM with attention. Their comparative strengths are demonstrated in Table 2 and Table 3. Similarly, the role of classical models including Linear SVM, Logistic Regression, and Naïve Bayes was examined in Table 4 and Table 5, with performance visualized in Figure 9 and Figure 10.

Finally, the overall best-performing models across categories on both datasets are summarized in Table 6, which portrays the dominance of XLNet as the strongest of the transformers, ConvBiLSTM with attention among the deep learning models, and the Linear SVM as the strongest traditional baseline. The results further divulge clear differences in how these models adapted better to the long reviews in IMDb and the shorter snippets in Rotten Tomatoes, which supply valuable results and the trade-offs between accuracy, training cost and contextual understanding.

Table 2. Performance Comparison of XLNet, BERT and Deep Learning Models on IMDb Dataset

Model	Precision	Recall	F1-Score	Accuracy	Loss	Training Time
XLNet	91.28%	96.04%	92.44%	94.18%	20.15%	760s
LSTM	86.77%	89.41%	88.07%	87.83%	37.60%	230s
CNN-LSTM	90.71%	86.75%	88.68%	88.76%	3.04%	614s
BERT	86.32%	86.27%	86.27%	86.27%	35.36%	3866s
ConvBiLSTM-Att	89.51%	90.81%	88.61%	89.88%	10.22%	260s

Table 2 shows that XLNet delivered the best performance on IMDb, with 94.18% accuracy and a 92.44% F1-score, confirming its ability to capture complex contextual and semantic features in long reviews. Deep Learning models (ConvBiLSTM + Attention), achieve an 89.88% accuracy as well as Balanced Precision-Recall due to the use of Bidirectional Processing and Attention. CNN-LSTM also showed high performance by reaching an 88.76% accuracy and an 88.68% F1-score which demonstrates the benefits of using both convolutional and sequential processing. While both BERT and LSTMs were very good; XLNet and hybrid sequential models both beat these two models in each category. Figure 7 shows how XLNet performs better than BERT and deep learning models for IMDb data.

Figure 7. **Performance Comparison of XLNet, BERT and DL Models on IMDB Dataset using Graph Bar**

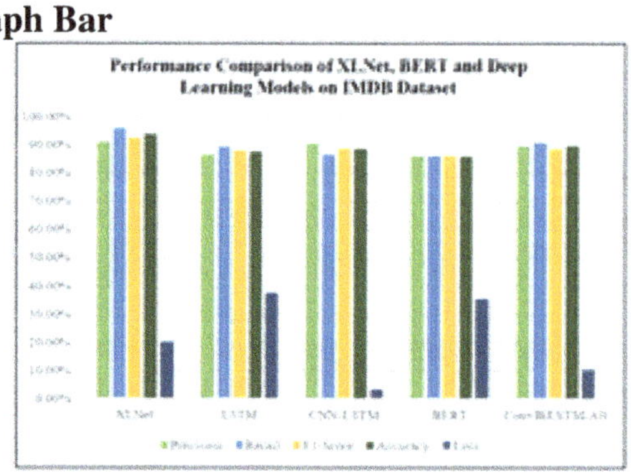

XLNet did better on the reviews because it could understand the context of words more effectively. ConvBiLSTM with attention also showed strong results, as its bidirectional layers processed text in both directions while attention highlighted key sentiment words. ConvBiLSTM with attention had good results because it has two sets of bidirectional layers, which are used to process text in both directions and the attention mechanism provides focus to key sentiment words. CNN-LSTM performed well as it uses convolutional layers to detect phrases in local contexts and uses LSTM layers to build sequences from those detected phrases. Therefore, overall, these models were able to successfully identify contextual representations with effective extraction of features, which makes them suitable for the descriptive nature of IMDB reviews. The comparative performance of XLNet, BERT and other deep learning models on RT dataset is demonstrated in Table 3.

Table 3. Performance Comparison of XLNet, BERT and Deep Learning Models on Rotten Tomatoes Dataset

Model	Precision	Recall	F1-Score	Accuracy	Loss	Training Time
XLNet	85.72%	86.41%	86.05%	87.66%	16.15%	452s
LSTM	71.22%	74.61%	72.85%	74.93%	34.60%	270s
CNN-LSTM	72.65%	74.82%	73.71%	76.74%	7.04%	25s
BERT	82.31%	82.59%	82.40%	82.27%	23.36%	2987s
ConvBiLSTM-Att	78.91%	77.05%	77.92%	78.06%	12.21%	224s

Figure 8. **Performance Comparison of XLNet, BERT and DL Models on Rotten Tomatoes Dataset using Graph Bar**

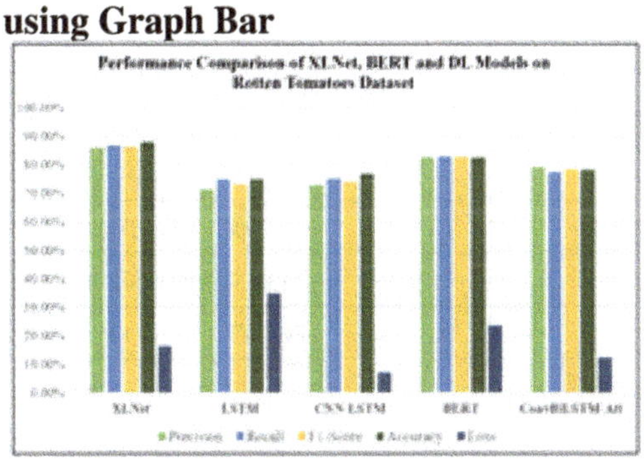

Table 3 shows that XLNet achieved the highest performance with 87.66% accuracy and an F1-score of 86.05%, highlighting its strength in capturing context from short, compact reviews. BERT followed with 82.27% accuracy, confirming the effectiveness of transformer embeddings for sentiment analysis. Among deep learning models, ConvBiLSTM with attention reached 78.06% accuracy with balanced precision and recall, benefiting from bidirectional context and attention on sentiment-rich words. CNN-LSTM performed at 76.74%, surpassing basic LSTM by combining phrase detection with sequential learning. Overall, although scores were lower than on IMDb, XLNet and BERT remained the most effective models for Rotten Tomatoes. The performance of models on RT dataset is shown in Figure 8.

XLNet had achieved better results on Rotten Tomatoes since it utilizes permutation-based modeling to provide context to short succinct reviews effectively by looking at word dependencies irrespective of order. BERT also performed well on Rotten Tomatoes since its contextual embeddings adapted well to the informal and varying writing styles present in the dataset. ConvBiLSTM with attention yielded reasonable performance since it has bidirectional layers to get context from both directions but also implements attention on the sentiment-laden words. CNN-LSTM yielded less favourable performance since it focuses more on being able to find phrase level patterns throughout the reviews although transformers were superior due to the speed at which they could extract sentiment from the short reviews present. Overall the models that performed good were ones that could extract sentiment easily given the scant amount of text, particularly those that utilized both BERT and XLNet embeddings.

Table 4. Performance Comparison of Classical Machine Learning Models on IMDB Dataset

Models	Accuracy	Precision	Recall	F1 Score	Training Time
Multinomial Naive Bayes	85.74%	85.77%	85.74%	85.75%	62s
Linear Support Vector Machine	88.90%	88.92%	88.90%	88.90%	157s
Logistic Regression	88.61%	88.63%	88.61%	88.60%	129s
Passive Aggressive Classifier	87.21%	87.23%	87.21%	87.20%	103s
Random Forest	84.85%	84.87%	84.85%	84.84%	194s
K-Nearest Neighbours	78.03%	78.29%	78.03%	77.97%	182s
Decision Tree	71.05%	71.05%	71.05%	71.05%	87s
Multilayer Perceptron	86.73%	86.74%	86.73%	86.73%	218s

Table 4 shows that among traditional machine learning models, Linear SVM performed best with 88.90% accuracy and balanced precision-recall, making it a strong baseline for sentiment classification. Logistic Regression followed closely at 88.61%, demonstrating its effectiveness with high-dimensional TF-IDF features, while the Passive Aggressive Classifier achieved 87.21%, reflecting its ability to learn quickly for text tasks. Ensemble methods like Random Forest and MLP gave moderate results, whereas simpler models such as Decision Tree and KNN lagged, failing to capture complex word relationships. Overall, Linear SVM performed the most reliable traditional model on IMDb, combining high accuracy with efficient training. The performance of classical models on IMDb dataset is graph bar is shown in Figure 9.

Figure 9. **Performance Comparison of Classical Machine Learning Models on IMDB Dataset using Graph Bar**

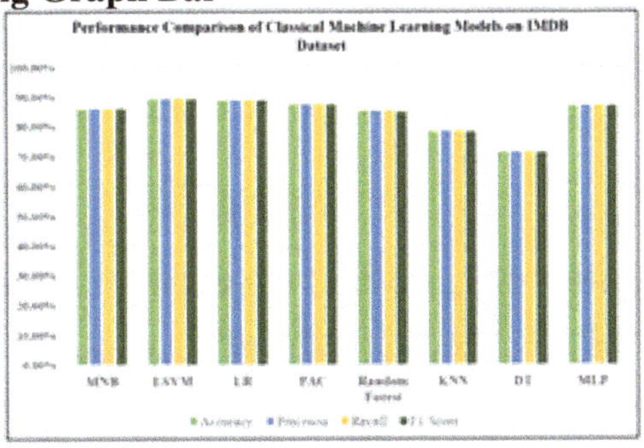

Linear SVM performs better than other algorithms primarily because of its robustness in handling large numbers of high-dimensional sparse TF-IDF vectorized features (e.g., those found in large text datasets such as IMDb), but also its margin-based classification method can successfully distinguish between positive and negative review sentiments despite overlap in vocabulary. Also, due to its ability to model class probability distributions very effectively, Logistic Regression was able to produce similar results to Linear SVM. Likewise, the PAC is a good performer due to its online learning feature, which enables it to adapt to large batches of text data quickly. Conversely, Random Forest and Decision Trees were poor performers since they both use splitting rules that do not effectively detect the many subtle linguistic patterns within text data; whereas, KNN was also poorly performing since it has difficulty comparing objects based on a high number of dimensions (i.e., vectors) as in the case of text data, therefore, KNN will likely be weakened by the high-dimensionality of text data. The comparisons of the performance of classical machine learning models are demonstrated in the Table 5 and Figure 10.

Table 5. Performance Comparison of Classical Machine Learning Models on Rotten Tomatoes Dataset

Models	Accuracy	Precision	Recall	F1 Score	Training Time
Multinomial Naive Bayes	74.28%	76.09%	74.28%	73.31%	54s
Linear Support Vector Machine	76.01%	76.00%	76.01%	75.98%	142s
Logistic Regression	76.45%	76.48%	76.45%	76.32%	118s
Passive Aggressive Classifier	71.30%	71.24%	71.30%	71.20%	96s
Random Forest	71.71%	71.84%	71.71%	71.29%	185s
K-Nearest Neighbours	68.18%	68.04%	68.18%	68.22%	173s

continued on following page

Table 5. Continued

Models	Accuracy	Precision	Recall	F1 Score	Training Time
Decision Tree	61.60%	61.51%	61.60%	61.50%	81s
Multilayer Perceptron	73.25%	73.20%	73.25%	73.16%	201s

Figure 10. **Performance Comparison of Classical Machine Learning Models on Rotten Tomatoes Dataset using Graph Bar**

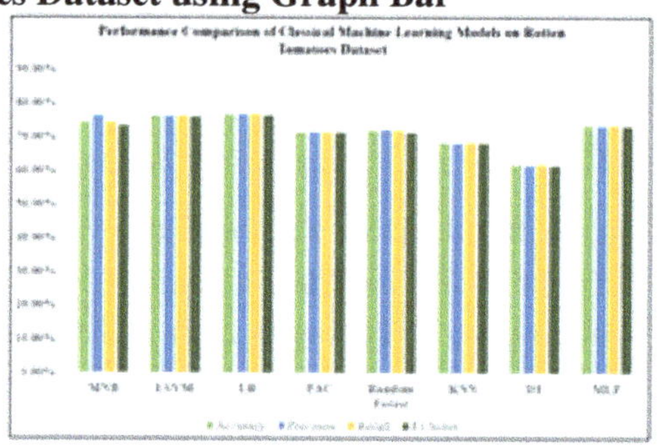

Logistic regression was the best performing model on the RT dataset with an accuracy of 76.45%. It is very close to linear SVM that had a 76.01% accuracy; both were able to perform well because they are able to take advantage of the linear nature of the TF-IDF features created from the short reviews. Multinomial Naive Bayes performed fairly at 74.28%; however, other models such as Random Forest and Passive Aggressive Classifier were unable to perform well. Models such as KNN and decision tree did not perform better because of the difficulty to manage high dimensional sparse data. As such, logistic regression and LSVM outperformed the others in part because they were able to function well with the sparse tf-idf feature set. Therefore, they were more accurate than the complex ensemble models and distance-based models used for this particular dataset.

Discussion

A comparison of models across categories can be found in Table 6 where the best model performance by category (transformers, deep learning, traditional machine learning) are listed for each dataset. XLNet showed a higher level of performance than all other models, with an accuracy rate of 94.18% for the IMDb data set and 87.66% for the Rotten Tomatoes data set. XLNet's better results come from its use of a permutation-based transformer design, as this method enables XLNet to capture bidirectional context within text, and to efficiently process longer texts. It is no surprise then that XLNet outperformed other models when processing the longer and more descriptive reviews of the IMDb data set, and continued to show a higher level of performance than the other models when processing the shorter reviews of the Rotten Tomatoes data set; it shows that XLNet is able to process a wide range of review lengths.

Table 6. Best-Performing Models from Each Category on IMDb and Rotten Tomatoes

Category	Model	IMDb Accuracy	RT Accuracy	
Transformer	XLNet	**94.18%**	**87.66%**	
Deep Learning	ConvBiLSTM-Att	89.88%	77.06%	
Traditional ML	Linear SVM (TF-IDF)	88.90%	76.01%	

ConvBiLSTM with attention was the better deep learning model and achieved higher accuracy levels than all other tested models on both datasets, with an 89.88% accuracy level on the IMDb dataset and a 77.06% accuracy level on the Rotten Tomatoes dataset. This is primarily due to two reasons: the use of bidirectional LSTM layers that enable the model to capture context in either direction, and the use of the attention layer that enables the model to capture the most significant (sentiment-heavy) words. Thus, ConvBiLSTM has an advantage over traditional sequence models. While XLNet has a large advantage by virtue of having been pre-trained and having rich contextual embeddings, XLNet's performance did surpass ConvBiLSTM's performance, although XLNet had difficulty achieving this on the Rotten Tomatoes dataset as the short reviews were much too limited to provide sufficient sequential data for ConvBiLSTM.

Among classical machine learning approaches, linear SVM with TF-IDF was the best performing, with an accuracy level of 88.90% on the IMDb dataset and an accuracy level of 76.01% on the Rotten Tomatoes dataset. The strength of linear SVM with TF-IDF lies in its ability to manage high-dimensional sparse features, however, the inability of linear SVM with TF-IDF to capture deep semantic meaning in text represents a weakness relative to ConvBiLSTM and XLNet. Overall, the results clearly indicate a strong trend toward using transformer models like XLNet that can capture language structure and context at scale. In addition, hybrid models like ConvBiLSTM with attention continue to achieve good levels of performance, particularly when processing longer reviews; however, classic models like linear SVM are reliable baselines but lack the capability to capture complex emotional patterns present within text.

SIGNIFICANCE OF THE STUDY

This study uses to demonstrate the potential of current state-of-the-art computational and deep learning models for sentiment analysis in movie reviews. Both the sequential (deep learning) and non-sequential (traditional machine learning) models were evaluated and compared using different types of review data (long-form and short-form), including reviews from IMDb and Rotten Tomatoes; thus, providing an overall comparison of each method based on its performance in relation to both types of review data. Additionally, the hybrid models which combine deep learning and traditional machine learning models, have been shown to outperform individual models when appropriate for the type of data or available computational power; however, the highest accuracy was found using the transformer models. Finally, this research study has the ability to expand beyond movie reviews into other areas (e.g., social media monitoring, product analysis, recommender systems) where sentiments are important, and an advanced and effective way to classify human emotions in many types of settings is provided.

LIMITATIONS

There are also some limitations of the study which should be considered. In our experiments only two datasets are used: IMDb and Rotten Tomatoes movie reviews. The wide range of genres, cultural contexts and also user demographics found in real world may not be fully represented by them. While XLNet and BERT are the transformer-based models demonstrating better accuracy, more computing power and training time than the traditional models, limiting the applicability in the low-resource settings. Moreover, datasets limit the findings focusing on the English-language. This paves the way for future research into multilingual sentiment analysis and broader applications in various areas of audience behavior.

CONCLUSIONS AND FUTURE WORK

This study explored transformer-based architectures, deep learning models, and traditional machine learning approaches for sentiment analysis of movie reviews using the IMDb and Rotten Tomatoes datasets. The results showed that XLNet consistently performed better than other models, while ConvBiLSTM with attention provided better performance among sequential deep learning methods, and Linear SVM proved to be the most reliable baseline from traditional models. This research has clearly shown the benefits of using advanced transformer models to capture emotional and contextual aspects in text data, as well as to demonstrate the continuing usefulness of a combination of hybrid deep learning methods and traditional methods depending upon available computational resources and features of the input data. While this research demonstrates the advantages of using advanced transformer models, there are some limitations to this research including the use of only two datasets, the high computational cost of training advanced transformer models, and the fact that all of the reviews analyzed were written in the English language. This research can be extended to include analyzing non-English and domain specific data sets, developing an integration of aspect-based sentiment analysis to provide finer grained insight into consumer opinions, and investigating alternative transformer models which have lower computational requirements such as DistilBERT. The use of hybrid methods which integrate the ability of traditional models to generate explanations for their predictions and the ability of deep learning models to capture complex contextual information will also need to be explored in order to strike a balance between high accuracy and high explainability. The contributions of this research to the area of advanced behavioral analysis include offering practical insights into how different models may be applied to sentiment mining in addition to the possibility of enhancing recommendation systems, audience engagement strategies, and decision-making processes in multiple business areas.

REFERENCES

Albladi, A., Uddin, M. K., Islam, M., & Seals, C. (2025). TWSSenti: Topic-wise sentiment analysis using transformer models. *Journal of Ambient Intelligence and Humanized Computing*. /arXiv.2504.09896DOI: 10.48550

Alharbi, Y., & Khan, S. S. (2025). Classifying multi-lingual reviews sentiment analysis in Arabic and English languages using the stochastic gradient descent model. *Computers, Materials & Continua*, *83*(1), 1275–1290. DOI: 10.32604/cmc.2025.061490

Ashbaugh, L., & Zhang, Y. (2024). A comparative study of sentiment analysis on customer reviews using machine learning and deep learning. *Computers*, *13*(12), 340. DOI: 10.3390/computers13120340

Danyal, M., Khan, S., Khan, M., Ghaffar, M., Khan, B., & Arshad, M. (2023). Sentiment analysis based on performance of linear support vector machine and multinomial naïve Bayes using movie reviews with baseline techniques. *Journal of Big Data*, *5*, 1–18. DOI: 10.32604/jbd.2023.041319

Danyal, M. M., Haseeb, M., Khan, S. S., Khan, B., & Ullah, S. (2024). Opinion mining on movie reviews based on deep learning models. *Journal of Artificial Intelligence (2579-0021), 6.*

Danyal, M. M., Khan, S. S., Khan, M., Ullah, S., Ghaffar, M. B., & Khan, W. (2024). Sentiment analysis of movie reviews based on NB approaches using TF–IDF and count vectorizer. *Social Network Analysis and Mining*, *14*(1), 87. DOI: 10.1007/s13278-024-01250-9

Danyal, M. M., Khan, S. S., Khan, M., Ullah, S., Mehmood, F., & Ali, I. (2024). Proposing sentiment analysis model based on BERT and XLNet for movie reviews. *Multimedia Tools and Applications*, *83*(24), 64315–64339. DOI: 10.1007/s11042-024-18156-5

Dashtipour, K., Gogate, M., Adeel, A., Larijani, H., & Hussain, A. (2021). Sentiment analysis of Persian movie reviews using deep learning. *Entropy (Basel, Switzerland)*, *23*(5), 596. DOI: 10.3390/e23050596

Durairaj, A. K., & Chinnalagu, A. (2021). Transformer based contextual model for sentiment analysis of customer reviews: A fine-tuned BERT. *International Journal of Advanced Computer Science and Applications*, *12*(11). Advance online publication. DOI: 10.14569/IJACSA.2021.0121153

El Azzouzy, O., Chanyour, T., & Andaloussi, S. J. (2025). Transformer-based models for sentiment analysis of YouTube comments. *Scientific African, 29*, e02836. Advance online publication. DOI: 10.1016/j.sciaf.2025.e02836

Erkan, A., & Güngör, T. (2023). Analysis of deep learning model combinations and tokenization approaches in sentiment classification. *IEEE Access : Practical Innovations, Open Solutions, 11*, 134951–134968. DOI: 10.1109/ACCESS.2023.3337354

Fimoza, D., Amalia, A., & Harumy, T. H. F. (2021, November). Sentiment analysis for movie review in Bahasa Indonesia using BERT. In *2021 International Conference on Data Science, Artificial Intelligence, and Business Analytics (DATABIA)* (pp. 27–34). IEEE. DOI: 10.1109/DATABIA53375.2021.9650096

Gandhi, U. D., Kumar, P. M., Babu, G. C., & Karthick, G. (2021). Sentiment analysis on Twitter data by using convolutional neural network (CNN) and long short-term memory (LSTM). *Wireless Personal Communications*, 1–10. DOI: 10.1007/s11277-021-08580-3

Hussain, K., & Ihsan, I. (2023). Sentiment analysis in movie reviews using knowledge graph embeddings with deep learning. *Journal of Computing and Biomedical Informatics*, *6*(1), 222–229.

Irfan, M., Venkatesam, A. S., Shanmugasundaram, H., Gourisaria, M. K., Chowdhury, S., & Patra, S. S. (2025, February). Sentiment analysis of movie reviews: Optimizing predictions through TF-IDF vectorization. In *2025 3rd International Conference on Intelligent Data Communication Technologies and Internet of Things (IDCIoT)* (pp. 102–107). IEEE.

Karabila, I., Darraz, N., El-Ansari, A., Alami, N., & El Mallahi, M. (2025). A hybrid approach combining sentiment analysis and deep learning to mitigate data sparsity in recommender systems. *Neurocomputing*, *636*, 129886. DOI: 10.1016/j.neucom.2025.129886

Khan, A. N., Salar Khan, A. A., Mansoor, M. A. J., Jameel, A., Rustam, R., Aslam, R., & Shah, J. (2025). Artificial Intelligence in Computer Science: Evolution, Techniques, Challenges, and Multidisciplinary Applications. *Sch J Eng Tech*, *4*(4), 246–263. DOI: 10.36347/sjet.2025.v13i04.006

Khan, M., Khan, M. S., & Alharbi, Y. (2020). Text mining challenges and applications, a comprehensive review. *IJCSNS*, *20*(12), 138.

Khan, S. S., & Alharbi, Y. (2024). Sentiment analysis of movie review classifications using deep learning approaches. *International Journal of Advanced Applied Science*, *11*(8), 146–157. DOI: 10.21833/ijaas.2024.08.016

Khan, S. S., Khan, M., Ran, Q., & Naseem, R. (2018). Challenges in opinion mining, comprehensive. [Ciencia e Tecnica Vitivinicola]. *Sci Technol J, 33*(11), 123–135.

Khan, S. S., Mondal, P. K., Shaqib, S., Ahmed, N., Prova, N. N. I., & Sattar, A. (2024, June). Performance analysis of LSTM and Bi-LSTM model with different optimizers in Bangla sentiment analysis. In *2024 15th International Conference on Computing Communication and Networking Technologies (ICCCNT)* (pp. 1–7). IEEE. DOI: 10.1109/ICCCNT61001.2024.10726142

Khyani, D., Siddhartha, B. S., Niveditha, N. M., & Divya, B. M. (2021). An interpretation of lemmatization and stemming in natural language processing. *Shanghai Ligong Daxue Xuebao, 22*(10), 350–357.

Lestari, V. B., & Utami, E. (2024). Combining Bi-LSTM and Word2vec embedding for sentiment analysis models of application user reviews. *The Indonesian Journal of Computer Science, 13*(1).

Li, H., Choi, J., Lee, S., & Ahn, J. H. (2020, January). Comparing BERT and XL-Net from the perspective of computational characteristics. In *2020 International Conference on Electronics, Information, and Communication (ICEIC)* (pp. 1–4). IEEE. DOI: 10.1109/ICEIC49074.2020.9051081

Maas, A. L., Daly, R. E., Pham, P. T., Huang, D., Ng, A. Y., & Potts, C. (2011, June). Learning word vectors for sentiment analysis. In *Proceedings of the 49th Annual Meeting of the Association for Computational Linguistics: Human Language Technologies* (pp. 142–150). Association for Computational Linguistics. https://www.aclweb.org/anthology/P11-1015

Mitra, A. (2020). Sentiment analysis using machine learning approaches (Lexicon based on movie review dataset). *Journal of Ubiquitous Computing and Communication Technologies, 2*(3), 145–152. DOI: 10.36548/jucct.2020.3.004

Musawa, A. H., Iswanto, I. A., & Hidayat, M. F. (2024, August). Exploring transformer-based model in sentiment analysis of movie review. In *2024 8th International Conference on Information Technology, Information Systems and Electrical Engineering (ICITISEE)* (pp. 214–219). IEEE. DOI: 10.1109/ICITISEE63424.2024.10730492

Musawa, A. H., Iswanto, I. A., & Hidayat, M. F. (2024). Exploring transformer-based models for sentiment analysis of movie reviews. *International Journal of Advanced Technology and Engineering Research.*

Naskar, I., & Joseph, N. P. (2024, February). Implementation of movie recommendation system using hybrid filtering methods and sentiment analysis of movie reviews. In *2024 IEEE International Conference for Women in Innovation, Technology & Entrepreneurship (ICWITE)* (pp. 513–518). IEEE. DOI: 10.1109/ICWITE59797.2024.10502695

Ning, W. (2025). Research on movie rating prediction using BERT-base model. *Journal of Intelligent & Fuzzy Systems.*

Novalia, V., Tania, K. D., Meiriza, A., & Wedhasmara, A. (2024, September). Knowledge discovery of application review using word embedding's comparison with CNN-LSTM model on sentiment analysis. In *2024 International Conference on Electrical Engineering and Computer Science (ICECOS)* (pp. 234–238). IEEE. DOI: 10.1109/ICECOS63900.2024.10791113

Pandey, A., Yadav, R., Pathak, A., Shivani, N., Garg, B., & Pandey, A. (2024, October). Sentiment analysis of IMDb movie reviews. In *2024 First International Conference on Software, Systems and Information Technology (SSITCON)* (pp. 1–6). IEEE.

Pandya, S. (2025, April). Novel framework for sentiment analysis of movie reviews based on large language models and deep learning methods. In *2025 4th International Conference on Distributed Computing and Electrical Circuits and Electronics (ICDCECE)* (pp. 1–7). IEEE. DOI: 10.1109/ICDCECE65353.2025.11035279

Paneru, B., Thapa, B., & Paneru, B. (2025). Sentiment analysis of movie reviews: A flask application using CNN with RoBERTa embeddings. *Systems and Soft Computing*, *7*, 200192. DOI: 10.1016/j.sasc.2025.200192

Pramana, R., Subroto, J. J., & Gunawan, A. A. S. (2022, November). Systematic literature review of stemming and lemmatization performance for sentence similarity. In *2022 IEEE 7th International Conference on Information Technology and Digital Applications (ICITDA)* (pp. 1–6). IEEE. DOI: 10.1109/ICITDA55840.2022.9971451

Saad, T. B., Ahmed, M., Ahmed, B., & Sazan, S. A. (2024, May). A novel transformer-based deep learning approach of sentiment analysis for movie reviews. In *2024 6th International Conference on Electrical Engineering and Information & Communication Technology (ICEEICT)* (pp. 1228–1233). IEEE. DOI: 10.1109/ICEEICT62016.2024.10534588

Sangeetha, T., Kumar, B. K., Kaarthik, A. A., & Sankar, R. A. (2025, February). Exploring sentiments in movie reviews using BERT algorithm. In. AIP Conference Proceedings: Vol. 3204. *No. 1* (p. 050015). AIP Publishing LLC. DOI: 10.1063/5.0248539

Sarhan, A. M., Ayman, H., Wagdi, M., & Osama, R.. (2024). Integrating machine learning and sentiment analysis in movie recommendation systems. *Journal of Electrical Systems and Information Technology*, *11*(1), 53. Advance online publication. DOI: 10.1186/s43067-024-00177-7

Selvakumar, B., & Lakshmanan, B. (2022). Sentimental analysis on user's reviews using BERT. *Materials Today: Proceedings*, *62*, 4931–4935. DOI: 10.1016/j.matpr.2022.03.678

Shahhosseini, M., Hu, G., & Pham, H. (2022). Optimizing ensemble weights and hyperparameters of machine learning models for regression problems. *Machine Learning with Applications*, *7*, 100251. DOI: 10.1016/j.mlwa.2022.100251

Sharma, H., Pangaonkar, S., Gunjan, R., & Rokade, P. (2023). Sentimental analysis of movie reviews using machine learning. In *ITM Web of Conferences* (Vol. 53, p. 02006). EDP Sciences. DOI: 10.1051/itmconf/20235302006

Shetty, A. M., DH, M., & Aljunid, M. F. (2025). Fine-tuning XLNet for Amazon review sentiment analysis: A comparative evaluation of transformer models. *ETRI Journal.*

Tan, K. L., Lee, C. P., & Lim, K. M. (2023). RoBERTa-GRU: A hybrid deep learning model for sentiment analysis. *Applied Sciences (Basel, Switzerland)*, *13*(6), 3915. DOI: 10.3390/app13063915

Thet, T. T., Na, J. C., & Khoo, C. S. (2010). Aspect-based sentiment analysis of movie reviews on discussion boards. *Journal of Information Science*, *36*(6), 823–848. DOI: 10.1177/0165551510388123

Turab, A., Mlaiki, N., Fatima, N., Mitrović, Z. D., & Ali, W. (2022). Analysis of a class of stochastic animal behavior models under specific choice preferences. *Mathematics*, *10*(12), 1975. DOI: 10.3390/math10121975

Turab, A., Montoyo, A., & Nescolarde-Selva, J. A. (2024). Computational and analytical analysis of integral-differential equations for modeling avoidance learning behavior. *Journal of Applied Mathematics & Computing*, *70*(5), 4423–4439. DOI: 10.1007/s12190-024-02130-3

Turab, A., Nescolarde-Selva, J. A., Ullah, F., Montoyo, A., Alfiniyah, C., Sintunavarat, W., Rizk, D., & Zaidi, S. A. (2025). Deep neural networks and stochastic methods for cognitive modeling of rat behavioral dynamics in T-mazes. *Cognitive Neurodynamics*, *19*(1), 1–28. DOI: 10.1007/s11571-025-10247-9

Turab, A., Rosli, N., Ali, W., & Nieto, J. J. (2023). The existence and uniqueness of solutions to a functional equation arising in psychological learning theory. *Demonstratio Mathematica, 56*(1), 20220231. DOI: 10.1515/dema-2022-0231

Turab, A., & Sintunavarat, W. (2019). On analytic model for two-choice behavior of the paradise fish based on the fixed point method. *Journal of Fixed Point Theory and Its Applications, 21*(2), 56. DOI: 10.1007/s11784-019-0694-y

Turab, A., & Sintunavarat, W. (2020). On the solution of the traumatic avoidance learning model approached by the Banach fixed point theorem. *Journal of Fixed Point Theory and Its Applications, 22*(2), 50. DOI: 10.1007/s11784-020-00788-3

Turab, A., Sintunavarat, W., Ullah, F., Zaidi, S. A., Montoyo, A., & Nescolarde-Selva, J. A. (2024). Computational modeling of animal behavior in T-mazes: Insights from machine learning. *Ecological Informatics, 81*, 102639. DOI: 10.1016/j.ecoinf.2024.102639

Wang, Z., & Wu, Y. (2024). XLNet-LSTM-CNN for text sentiment analysis applied to movie review datasets. *International Journal of Advanced Computer Science and Applications, 15*(4), 112–121. DOI: 10.14569/IJACSA.2024.0150414

Yadav, A., Garg, P., & Jain, T. (2025, February). Sentiment analysis of movie reviews using machine learning. In *2025 International Conference on Pervasive Computational Technologies (ICPCT)* (pp. 41–45). IEEE. DOI: 10.1109/ICPCT64145.2025.10940336

Yang, G., Xu, Y., & Tu, L. (2023). An intelligent box office predictor based on aspect-level sentiment analysis of movie review. *Wireless Networks, 29*(7), 3039–3049. DOI: 10.1007/s11276-023-03378-6

Yang, Z., Dai, Z., Yang, Y., Carbonell, J., Salakhutdinov, R. R., & Le, Q. V. (2019). XLNet: Generalized autoregressive pretraining for language understanding. *Advances in Neural Information Processing Systems*, 32.

Youb, I., Al-Obeidat, F., Hamlich, M., & Essaadoui, A. (2024, October). Enhancing sentiment analysis of movie reviews with PySpark. In *2024 2nd International Conference on Self Sustainable Artificial Intelligence Systems (ICSSAS)* (pp. 1255–1260). IEEE. DOI: 10.1109/ICSSAS64001.2024.10760815

Zheng, H. (2025). Artificial intelligence–driven sentiment analysis and optimization of movie scripts. *Discover Artificial Intelligence, 5*(1), 114. DOI: 10.1007/s44163-025-00361-2

Zhou, F. (2024). Sentiment analysis and implementation in film evaluation utilizing BERT. *Applied and Computational Engineering*, *33*(1), 224–233. DOI: 10.54254/2755-2721/33/20230274

Chapter 7
A Novel Approach to Guinea Worm Disease Control Using Deep Neural Network Models for Behavioral Dog Screening Strategies

Ramsha Shafqat
https://orcid.org/0000-0002-3610-339X
The University of Lahore, Sargodha, Pakistan

Massimiliano Ferrara
University Mediterranea di Reggio Calabria, Italy

ABSTRACT

Free-roaming dogs pose serious public health challenges worldwide. This study investigates the role of owned and stray dogs in transmitting Guinea worm disease (GWD) and evaluates vaccination as a control strategy. A multi-host framework is developed with dogs as primary hosts and fish as intermediate hosts, while humans are excluded due to minimal incidence. The model uses twelve compartments and a fractional-order approach based on the Atangana–Baleanu derivative in the Caputo sense. Existence and uniqueness of solutions are established through fixed-point theorems, with Ulam–Hyers stability confirming robustness. Numerical simulations, performed using the Adams–Bashforth method, examine partial vaccination coverage, showing significant reductions in disease prevalence. Deep Neural Network techniques divide data into training, testing, and validation sets, enhancing com-

DOI: 10.4018/979-8-3373-5062-2.ch007

putational accuracy. Findings highlight vaccination as a practical intervention for GWD control, offering valuable guidance for public health programs in areas with high free-roaming dog populations.

INTRODUCTION

Free-ranging domestic dogs (FRDs) play a major role in spreading pathogens in many low-income regions. This creates risks for people, livestock, and wildlife, which is why managing FRD populations is considered an important public health issue (Belsare & Vanak 2020). There are thought to be roughly 700 million to 1 billion dogs worldwide, and a large share of them are free-ranging. These dogs can carry and transmit several zoonotic and parasitic infections, including rabies, visceral leishmaniasis, canine echinococcosis, and soil-transmitted helminths (Belsare & Vanak, 2020). Recent work also shows that FRDs act as key reservoirs for Guinea worm disease (GWD) (Roberts 2019). GWD is a parasitic infection that continues to affect very poor rural areas where people often lack safe drinking water, and infection in dogs is now slowing eradication efforts (Guagliardo et al. 2020). Although human cases have fallen dramatically since 1986, transmission involving dogs and a complex life cycle that includes copepods and fish continues to challenge programmatic control (Boyce et al. 2020). Motivated by these realities, we develop a fractional-order transmission model emphasizing dogs as primary hosts and fish as intermediate hosts. We further distinguish owned free-roaming from stray dogs to capture heterogeneity in resource access and bchavior, and wc calibratc thc model with data from prior studies and multi-year records of canine GWD to assess intervention levers (e.g., tethering and parasite control) and to inform operational thresholds for field programs as shown in Figure 1.

Figure 1. Life cycle of GWD involving humans and dogs, as outlined by the Centers for Disease Control and Prevention (2023). Labels 1(a) and 1(b) illustrate the initiation of GWD transmission in humans through the consumption of unfiltered water or undercooked/infected fish.

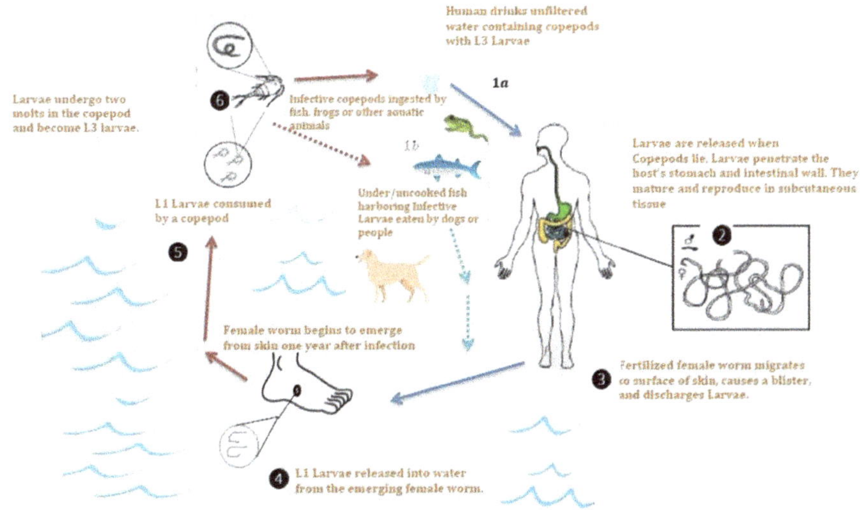

LITERATURE REVIEW

Decades of coordinated effort through the Guinea Worm Eradication Program (GWEP) have reduced human cases from 3.5 million across 21 countries in 1986 to fewer than 30 in 2018, with remaining foci in Angola, Chad, Ethiopia, Mali, and South Sudan (Boyce et al. 2020) in 2020, 27 human cases were reported across six countries (Pellegrino et al. 2022). Parallel to these gains, animal infections have become more prominent particularly in dogs, but also in cats, baboons, leopards, and donkeys with canine cases in Chad rising from 487 (2015) to 1,973 (2019) (Boyce et al. 2020). The CDC's documentation of the Guinea worm life cycle underscores persistent operational challenges, and recent reports indicate that dogs account for over 90% of infections, with domestic dogs contributing 92.7% of reported animal cases; genetic analyses show worms in dogs and humans are indistinguishable, confirming zoonotic linkage. Contemporary mathematical studies have modeled the full GWD cycle with explicit dog involvement and validated predictions with field data (Helikumi & Mushayabasa, 2023, Goodwin et al. 2022, Engelhard et al. 2021) yet many assume homogeneous dog populations despite evidence of meaningful differences between stray and owned free-roaming dogs in food sources, exposure, and healthcare access (Vinson et al. 2021, Ghosh et al 2018, Reese, 2005). To address nonlinearities and improve forecasting, neural networks have been integrated into transmission modeling and intervention design (Shafqat & Alsaadi, 2024; Turab et al. 2024). More broadly, fractional-order epidemiological frameworks with modern kernels and learning components have demonstrated enhanced descriptive and predictive fidelity across systems: machine-learning-augmented SIQR models with normalized Caputo–Fabrizio operators (Shafqat et al 2025), fractional poliomyelitis dynamics coupled with deep neural networks (Al-Quran et al. 2025), fractional representations of social-influence-driven behaviors relevant to public health (Shafqat et al 2025), and delayed Caputo operators supporting existence, uniqueness, and mild-solution analysis for COVID-19 models (Abuasbeh et al 2023). Complementary advances in cognitive and learning domains spanning DNN-stochastic hybrids and integro-differential approaches further validate the utility of memory-aware modeling for systems with feedback and uncertainty (Turab et al. 2025, Turab et al. 2024), while foundational results on functional equations strengthen well-posedness considerations central to our approach (Turab et al 2023).

MODEL FORMULATION

This study employs the Atangana–Baleanu–Caputo (ABC) fractional derivative. We selected this operator, among the available fractional derivative definitions, because of the following considerations:

1. For a constant value, the result produced by the ABC derivative aligns with that obtained using an ordinary differential equation of integer order.
2. The method uses local initial conditions, which makes it more practical to apply in real situations.
3. The approach simplifies the computation: we first solve an ordinary differential equation, and then apply a fractional integral to reach the required fractional order.

Let $N_{D1}(\upsilon)$ be the number of owned free roaming dogs, and let $N_{D2}(\upsilon)$ represent the populations of owned free-roaming dogs and stray dogs, respectively be the number of stray dogs. These populations are divided into three epidemiological categories: susceptible $S_{Dj}(\upsilon)$ exposed$E_{Dj}(\upsilon)$, and infectious$I_{Dj}(\upsilon)$ individuals. Here, $j = 1$ refers to owned free-roaming dogs, while $j = 2$ corresponds to stray dogs. For the fish population, $S_F(\nu)$, $E_F(\nu)$, and $I_F(\nu)$ denote the numbers of susceptible, exposed, and infectious fish at time ν. For the copepod population, $S_C(\nu)$, $E_C(\nu)$, and $I_C(\nu)$ denote the numbers of susceptible, exposed, and infectious copepods, respectively. The total population of fishes and copepods are given by:

$$N_F(\upsilon) = S_F(\upsilon) + I_F(\upsilon)$$

$$N_C(\upsilon) = S_C(\upsilon) + E_C(\upsilon) + I_C(\upsilon)$$

Let $L(\upsilon)$ represent the population of Guinea worm larvae (stage; $L1$) introduced into the environment by infected dogs (I_{Dj}). Guinea worm transmission begins when infected owned free-roaming dogs (I_{D1})and stray dogs(I_{D2}) release stage $L1$larvae into the environment. he shedding rate of L1 larvae is modeled as $(1 - \phi_D)\theta_D$for owned free-roaming dogs and $\theta_D$for stray dogs. The term ϕ_D (with $0 \leq \phi_D < 1$) is a reduction factor that represents how much less larvae are shed by owned free-roaming dogs compared to stray dogs. The idea is that stray dogs, which do not have owners, tend to spend long periods in forested areas, while owned free-roaming dogs return to human settlements. When $\phi_D = 0$, both types of dogs shed larvae at the same rate. After larvae are released into the environment, they die naturally at rate μ_L. We assume that copepods eating L1 larvae does not significantly reduce the total number of larvae, so that effect is treated as negligible. A susceptible copepod that ingests L1 larvae becomes infected at rate $\beta_{LC}L$, where $L$is the larval density. Infected copepods then become infectious at rate γ_C. The copepod population increases through reproduction at rate $\Lambda_C$and decreases due to natural death at rate μ_C. Once a copepod becomes infectious, it stays infectious for the rest of its life.

The variables S_C (υ), E_C (υ), and I_C (υ) represent the populations of susceptible, exposed, and infectious copepods, respectively, at any given time υ. Larvae consumed by copepods develop through two stages, eventually maturing into L3 larvae. Susceptible aquatic organisms, such as fish, become infected upon consuming copepods carrying L3 larvae. This study focuses specifically on the fish population. The number of susceptible fish increases due to births at a rate of Λ_F and decreases as they become infected by consuming copepods containing L3 larvae, at a rate defined by $\beta_{CF}I_C$, where β_{CF} represents the rate of consumption of copepods by fish. Infected fish recover at a rate of η_F without gaining immunity. While this infection does not directly result in fish mortality, the natural death rate of fish is μ_F. Let $S_F(\upsilon)$ and $I_F(\upsilon)$ represent the susceptible and infected populations of fish at time υ. Dogs may contract GWD by consuming infected fish. The transmission rates for owned free-roaming dogs and stray dogs are expressed as $\beta_{FD}(1 - \phi_D)I_F$ and $\beta_{FD}I_F$, respectively. Here, β_{FD} describes the rate of transmission from infected fish to dogs, while ϕ_D ($0 \leq \phi_D < 1$) adjusts for the decreased infection risk in owned dogs that are fed by humans, in contrast to stray dogs that scavenge. Exposed dogs transition to an infectious state at a rate γ_{Dj}. Recovery without immunity occurs at a rate η_{Dj}, and natural mortality decreases the population at a rate $\mu_{D\iota}$. Additionally, the populations of owned and stray dogs grow due to birth rates Λ_{D1} and Λ_{D2}, respectively. In conclusion, the dynamics of GWD involving copepods, fish, and dogs are mathematically described by the following equations:

$$\begin{aligned}
{}^{ABC}\mathbf{D}^{l}_{\upsilon}L(\upsilon) &= \theta D(1-\phi_D)I_{D1}(\upsilon)+\theta_D I_{D2}(\upsilon)-\mu_L L(\upsilon),\\
{}^{ABC}\mathbf{D}^{l}_{\upsilon}S_C(\upsilon) &= \Lambda_C-\beta_{LC}L(\upsilon)S_C(\upsilon)-\mu_C S_C(\upsilon),\\
{}^{ABC}\mathbf{D}^{l}_{\upsilon}E_C(\upsilon) &= \beta_{LC}L(\upsilon)S_C(\upsilon)-(\gamma_C+\mu_C)E_C(\upsilon),\\
{}^{ABC}\mathbf{D}^{l}_{\upsilon}S_{D1}(\upsilon) &= \Lambda_{D1}-\beta_{FD}(1-\phi_D)I_F(\upsilon)S_{D1}(\upsilon)+\eta_{D1}I_{D1}(\upsilon),\\
{}^{ABC}\mathbf{D}^{l}_{\upsilon}E_{D1}(\upsilon) &= \beta_{FD}(1-\phi_D)I_F(\upsilon)S_{D1}(\upsilon)-(\mu_{D1}+\eta_{D1})E_{D1}(\upsilon),\\
{}^{ABC}\mathbf{D}^{l}_{\upsilon}I_{D1}(\upsilon) &= \gamma_{D1}E_{D1}(\upsilon)-(\mu_{D1}+\eta_{D1})I_{D1}(\upsilon),\\
{}^{ABC}\mathbf{D}^{l}_{\upsilon}S_{D2}(\upsilon) &= \Lambda_{D2}-\beta_{FD}I_F(\upsilon)S_{D2}(\upsilon)-\mu_{D2}S_{D2}(\upsilon)+\eta_{D2}I_{D2}(\upsilon),\\
{}^{ABC}\mathbf{D}^{l}_{\upsilon}E_{D2}(\upsilon) &= \beta_{FD}I_F(\upsilon)S_{D2}(\upsilon)-(\gamma_{D2}+\mu_{D2})E_{D2}(\upsilon),\\
{}^{ABC}\mathbf{D}^{l}_{\upsilon}I_{D2}(\upsilon) &= \gamma_{D2}E_{D2}(\upsilon)-(\eta_{D2}+\mu_{D2})I_{D2}(\upsilon),
\end{aligned}\qquad (1)$$

$$L(0)=L_0,\ S_C(0)=S_C0,\ E_C(0)=E_C0,\ I_C(0)=I_C(0),\ S_F(0)=S_F(0),$$

$$I_F(0)=I_F(0),\ S_{D1}(0)=S_{D1}(0),\ E_{D1}(0)=E_{D1}(0),\ I_{D1}(0)=I_{D1}(0),$$

$$S_{D2}(0)=S_{D2}(0),\ E_{D2}(0)=E_{D2}(0),\ I_{D2}(0)=I_{D2}(0).$$

Figure 2. Flow diagram illustrating the structure of Model 1.

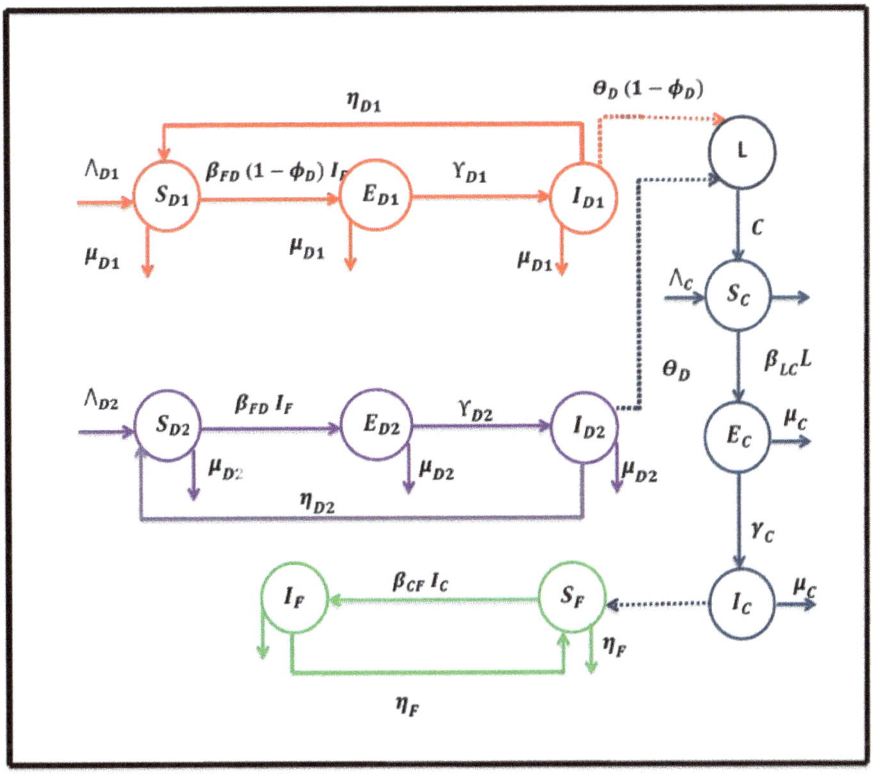

Figure 3.

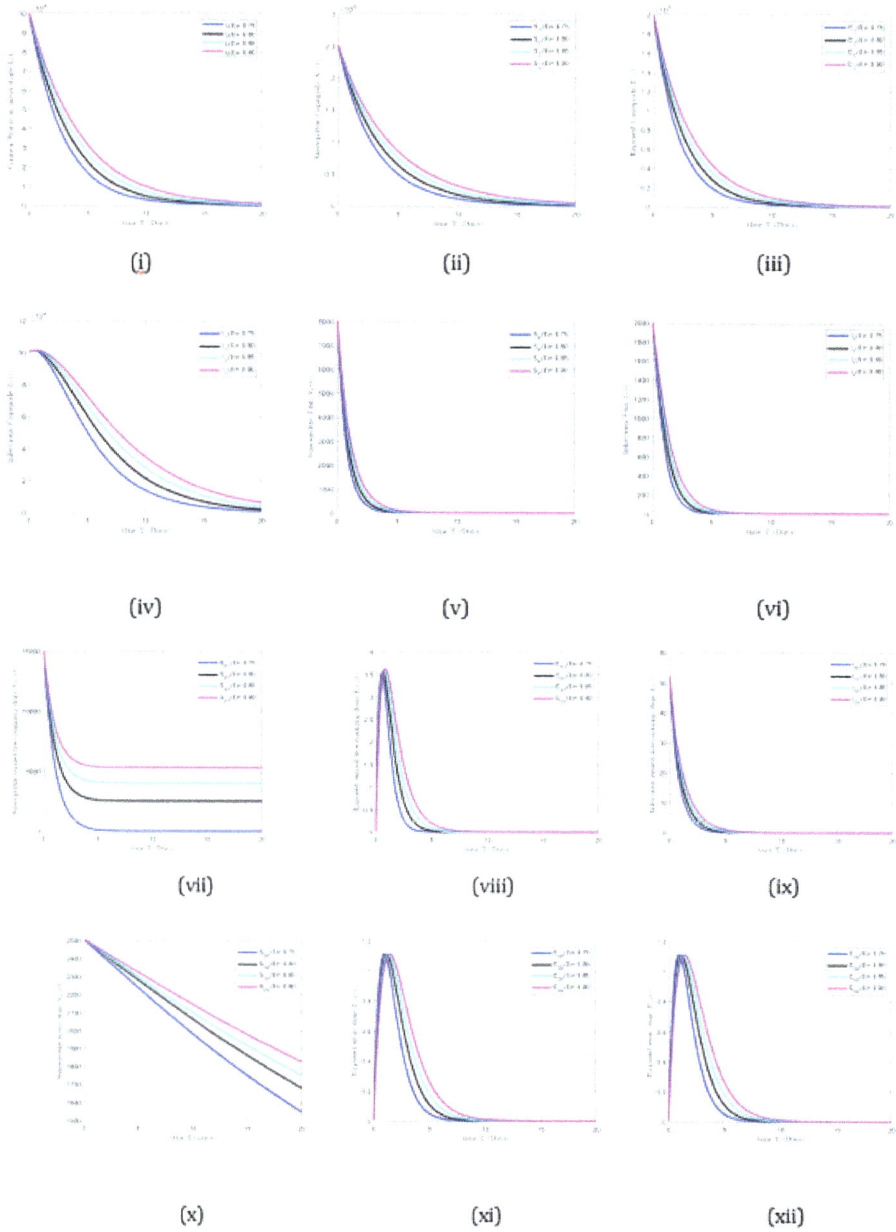

We develop a twelve-compartment fractional model for GWD based on the ABC operator. Within this formulation, we prove existence and uniqueness of the solution to the corresponding fractional initial value problem, and we investigate stability using the Ulam–Hyers criterion. The results show that the model is mathematically sound and stable. To obtain approximate solutions, we use the Newton interpolation method. The fractional parameter in the model adds flexibility to the simulations across the five compartments. To better describe the nonlinear and complex interactions among the different host populations, we also include deep neural networks (DNNs). This complements the fractional framework and improves the accuracy of the predictions. Overall, the method represents population densities on a continuous scale between 0 and 1. The structure of the model is summarized in the flow diagram in Figure 2.

PRELIMINARIES

We first introduce the key notation and definitions used in fractional calculus.

Definition 1. *Let* $\mathbf{U}(\upsilon) \in l$ *with* $l \in [0, 1]$. *The ABC fractional operator is mathematically*

defined as:

$$\mathrm{ABC}\mathbf{D}^{l}_{\upsilon}(\mathbf{U}(\upsilon)) = \frac{M(l)}{1-l}\int_0^{\upsilon} E_l\left(\frac{-l(\upsilon-u)}{1-l}\right)\frac{d}{du}U(u)du. \tag{2}$$

The function M (ℓ) serves as a normalization function, fulfilling the conditions M (0) = M (1) = 1, while $E_l(y)$ represents the ML function, expressed as:

$$E_l(y) = \sum_0^{\infty}\frac{y^k}{\Gamma(lk+1)} \tag{3}$$

Definition 2. *For* $\mathbf{U}(\upsilon) \in L^1(0, T)$, the fractional integral associated with the ABC operator is given by

$$\mathrm{ABC}\mathbf{D}^{l}_{\upsilon}(\mathbf{U}(\upsilon)) = \frac{1-l}{M(l)}\mathbf{U}(\upsilon) + \frac{l}{M(l)}\frac{1}{\Gamma(l)}\int_0^{\upsilon}(\upsilon-u)^{l-1}U(u)du,\ \upsilon > 0. \tag{4}$$

Lemma 1. *For any* $l \in (0, 1]$, the solution of the fractional differential equation with the ABC operator is given by:

$$\mathrm{ABC}\mathbf{D}^{l}_{\upsilon}\mathbf{U}(\upsilon) = \mathbf{U}(\upsilon), \mathbf{U}(\upsilon) = \mathbf{U}_0, \tag{5}$$

With the additional constraint

$$\mathbf{U}(\upsilon) = U_0 + \frac{1-l}{M(l)}\mathbf{U}(\upsilon) + \frac{l}{M(l)}\frac{1}{\Gamma(l)}\int_0^{\upsilon}(\upsilon-u)^{l-1}U(u)du. \tag{6}$$

EXISTENCE THEORY

Here we analyze the practical relevance of the model and show that the system is stable and admits a solution. We then reformulate the problem as follows:

$$\begin{aligned}
\text{ABC}\mathbf{D}_{\upsilon}^{l}(\mathrm{L}(\upsilon)) &= \mathbf{G}_{1}(L,\ S_{C},\ E_{C},\ I_{C},\ S_{F},\ I_{F},\ S_{D1},\ E_{D1},\ I_{D1},\ S_{D2},\ E_{D2},\ I_{D2}),\\
\text{ABC}\mathbf{D}_{\upsilon}^{l}(S_{C}(\upsilon)) &= \mathbf{G}_{2}(L,\ S_{C},\ E_{C},\ I_{C},\ S_{F},\ I_{F},\ S_{D1},\ E_{D1},\ I_{D1},\ S_{D2},\ E_{D2},\ I_{D2}),\\
\text{ABC}\mathbf{D}_{\upsilon}^{l}(E_{C}(\upsilon)) &= \mathbf{G}_{3}(L,\ S_{C},\ E_{C},\ I_{C},\ S_{F},\ I_{F},\ S_{D1},\ E_{D1},\ I_{D1},\ S_{D2},\ E_{D2},\ I_{D2}),\\
\text{ABC}\mathbf{D}_{\upsilon}^{l}(I_{C}(\upsilon)) &= \mathbf{G}_{4}(L,\ S_{C},\ E_{C},\ I_{C},\ S_{F},\ I_{F},\ S_{D1},\ E_{D1},\ I_{D1},\ S_{D2},\ E_{D2},\ I_{D2}),\\
\text{ABC}\mathbf{D}_{\upsilon}^{l}(S_{F}(\upsilon)) &= \mathbf{G}_{5}(L,\ S_{C},\ E_{C},\ I_{C},\ S_{F},\ I_{F},\ S_{D1},\ E_{D1},\ I_{D1},\ S_{D2},\ E_{D2},\ I_{D2}),\\
\text{ABC}\mathbf{D}_{\upsilon}^{l}(I_{F}(\upsilon)) &= \mathbf{G}_{6}(L,\ S_{C},\ E_{C},\ I_{C},\ S_{F},\ I_{F},\ S_{D1},\ E_{D1},\ I_{D1},\ S_{D2},\ E_{D2},\ I_{D2}),\\
\text{ABC}\mathbf{D}_{\upsilon}^{l}(S_{D1}(\upsilon)) &= \mathbf{G}_{7}(L,\ S_{C},\ E_{C},\ I_{C},\ S_{F},\ I_{F},\ S_{D1},\ E_{D1},\ I_{D1},\ S_{D2},\ E_{D2},\ I_{D2}),\\
\text{ABC}\mathbf{D}_{\upsilon}^{l}(E_{D1}(\upsilon)) &= \mathbf{G}_{8}(L,\ S_{C},\ E_{C},\ I_{C},\ S_{F},\ I_{F},\ S_{D1},\ E_{D1},\ I_{D1},\ S_{D2},\ E_{D2},\ I_{D2}),\\
\text{ABC}\mathbf{D}_{\upsilon}^{l}(I_{D1}(\upsilon)) &= \mathbf{G}_{9}(L,\ S_{C},\ E_{C},\ I_{C},\ S_{F},\ I_{F},\ S_{D1},\ E_{D1},\ I_{D1},\ S_{D2},\ E_{D2},\ I_{D2}),\\
\text{ABC}\mathbf{D}_{\upsilon}^{l}(S_{D2}(\upsilon)) &= \mathbf{G}_{10}(L,\ S_{C},\ E_{C},\ I_{C},\ S_{F},\ I_{F},\ S_{D1},\ E_{D1},\ I_{D1},\ S_{D2},\ E_{D2},\ I_{D2}),\\
\text{ABC}\mathbf{D}_{\upsilon}^{l}(E_{D2}(\upsilon)) &= \mathbf{G}_{11}(L,\ S_{C},\ E_{C},\ I_{C},\ S_{F},\ I_{F},\ S_{D1},\ E_{D1},\ I_{D1},\ S_{D2},\ E_{D2},\ I_{D2}),\\
\text{ABC}\mathbf{D}_{\upsilon}^{l}(I_{D2}(\upsilon)) &= \mathbf{G}_{12}(L,\ S_{C},\ E_{C},\ I_{C},\ S_{F},\ I_{F},\ S_{D1},\ E_{D1},\ I_{D1},\ S_{D2},\ E_{D2},\ I_{D2}).
\end{aligned} \tag{7}$$

Writing Equation (1) in the form

$$\begin{aligned}
ABCD_{\upsilon}^{l}U(\upsilon) &= \eta(\upsilon, U(\upsilon)),\\
U(0) &= U_{0}(\upsilon)
\end{aligned} \tag{8}$$

where

$$\begin{aligned}
&U(\upsilon) := (L, S_{C}, E_{C}, I_{C}, S_{F}, I_{F}, S_{D1}, E_{D1}, I_{D1}, S_{D2}, E_{D2}, I_{D2})^{\Im},\\
&U(\upsilon) := (L_{0}, S_{C0}, E_{C0}, I_{C0}, S_{F0}, I_{F0}, S_{D10}, E_{D10}, I_{D10}, S_{D20}, E_{D20}, I_{D20})^{\Im},
\end{aligned} \tag{9}$$

$\eta(\upsilon, U(\upsilon)(\upsilon)) := G_i\left(t, L, S_C, E_C, I_C, S_F, I_F, S_{D1}, E_{D1}, I_{D1}, S_{D2}, E_{D2}, I_{D2}\right)^{\mathfrak{I}}$
$j = 1,2,3,4,5,6,7,8,9,10,11,12.$

In this context, $(\cdot)^{\mathfrak{I}}$ indicates the transpose operation applied to the vector. Based on Lemma 3.3.1, the integral representation of the equation derived from system (8) is given as

$$\mathbf{U}(\upsilon) = U_0 + \frac{1-l}{(l)}\mathbf{Z}(\upsilon, U(\upsilon)) + \frac{l}{M(l)}\frac{1}{\Gamma(1)}\int_0^{\upsilon} (\upsilon - u)^{l-1} U(u) du. \quad (10)$$

To proceed, we define the Banach space $\Upsilon = C([0, \mathfrak{I}], \mathbf{R}^k)$, $1 \leq k \leq n$ with the associated

norm $|\mathbf{U}| = \sup \upsilon \in [0, \mathfrak{I}]|\mathbf{U}(\upsilon)|$. We denote another Banach space as $\Phi = (\Upsilon^5, |\mathbf{U}|)$, where:

$$|\mathbf{U}| = \sup(|L| + |S\,C| + |EC| + |IC| + |S\,F| + |IF| + |S\,D1| + |ED1| + |ID1| + |S\,D2| + |ED2| + |ID2|).$$
$$\upsilon \in [0, \mathfrak{I}]$$

In the subsequent theorem, the existence of solutions is demonstrated utilizing Schauder's fixed-point theorem.

Theorem 1 Consider a continuous function $Z \in \Phi$. Assume that there is a constant $V > 0$satisfying

$|Z(\upsilon, U(\upsilon))| \leq V(1 + |U|)$ for all $\upsilon \in [0, \mathfrak{I}]$ and $U \in \Phi$. Then, the parameter

$$\nabla_1 = \frac{(1 - l)\Gamma(l)V + V\mathfrak{I}^l}{\mathrm{M}\,(\mathrm{l})\Gamma(\mathrm{l})} \quad (12)$$

satisfies $\nabla 1 < 1$. Therefore, the solution of Equation (10) is unique and continuous for all $\upsilon \in [0, \mathfrak{I}]$.

Proof. The solution can also be represented in the integral form equivalent to Equation (10). For this purpose, consider the mapping $\mathcal{U}:\Phi \rightarrow \Phi$defined by

$$(\mho\mathbf{U})(\upsilon) = U_0 + \frac{1-l}{M\,(l)}Z(\upsilon, U(\upsilon)) + \frac{l}{M\,(l)\Gamma(l)}\int_0^{\upsilon} (\upsilon - \varphi)^{l-1} Z(\varphi, U(\varphi)) d\varphi. \quad (13)$$

Next, define a bounded, closed, and convex subset of the Banach space $B_\varrho = \{\mathbf{U} \in \Phi : \mathbf{U} \leq \varrho\}, \varrho \geq \frac{\nabla_2}{1 - \nabla_1}$, where $\nabla_2 = |U_0| + \frac{1-l}{M(l)}V + \frac{T^l}{M(l)\Gamma(l)}V$.
To demonstrate that $(\mho\mathrm{B}_\varrho) \subseteq \mathrm{B}_\varrho$ for all $\upsilon \in [0, \mathfrak{I}]$, consider the following:

$$|(\mho\mathbf{U})(\upsilon)| \le \left|U_0\right| + \frac{1-l}{M(l)}|Z(\upsilon, U(\upsilon))| + \frac{l}{M(l)\Gamma(l)}\int_0^{\upsilon}\left(\upsilon-\lambda\right)^{l-1} Z\left|(\lambda, U(\lambda))d\lambda\right.$$

$$\le \left|U_0\right| + \frac{1-l}{M(l)}V(1+|U(\upsilon)|) + \frac{l}{M(l)\Gamma(l)}\int_0^{\upsilon}\left(\upsilon-\lambda\right)^{l-1} V(1+|U(\upsilon)|)d\lambda.$$

and $U \in B_{\varrho}$. We also obtain

$$\|(\mho\mathbf{U})\| \le \left|U_0\right| + \frac{1-l}{M(l)}V(1+\|U(\upsilon)\|) + \frac{\mathfrak{I}^l}{M(l)\Gamma(l)}V(1+\|U(\upsilon)\|) \tag{14}$$

$$\le \left|U_0\right| + \frac{1-l}{M(l)}V + \frac{\mathfrak{I}^l}{M(l)\Gamma(l)}V + \left[\frac{1-l}{M(l)}V + \frac{\mathfrak{I}^l}{M(l)\Gamma(l)}V\right]\varrho \le \nabla_2 + \nabla_1\varrho \le \varrho.$$

It has been established that $\left(\mho B_{\varrho}\right) \subset B_{\varrho}$. To demonstrate the continuity of the operator $\mho$, let us assume that $\{\mathbf{U}_n\}$ is a sequence such that $U_n \rightarrow U$ in B_{ϱ} as $n \rightarrow \infty$. For every $\upsilon \in [0, \mathfrak{I}]$, the following holds:

$$|(\mho \mathrm{U}_n)(\upsilon) - (\mho\mathrm{U})(\upsilon)| \le \frac{1-l}{M(l)}\left|\mathrm{Z}(\upsilon, U_n(\upsilon)) - \mathrm{Z}(\upsilon, U(\upsilon))\right| + \frac{1}{M(l)\Gamma(l)}\int_0^{\upsilon}\left(\upsilon-\lambda\right)^{l-1}|Z(\lambda, U_n(\lambda)) - Z(\lambda, U(\lambda))|d\lambda$$

$$\le \frac{1-l}{M(l)}\|\mathrm{Z}(\upsilon, U_n(\upsilon)) - \mathrm{Z}(\upsilon, U(\upsilon))\| + \frac{\mathfrak{I}^l}{M(l)\Gamma(l)}\|Z(\lambda, U_n(\lambda)) - Z(\lambda, U(\lambda))\|.$$

From the continuity of Z, we have:

$$\|(\mho Un)(\ell) - (\mho U)(\ell)\| \rightarrow 0\, as\, n \rightarrow 0. \rightarrow 0\, as\, n \rightarrow 0. \tag{15}$$

It can be deduced that $\mho$ maintains continuity over B_{ϱ}. Moreover, we establish that since $\left(\mho B_{\varrho}\right)$ constitutes a relatively compact operator. Since $\left(\mho B_{\varrho}\right) \subseteq B_{\varrho}$, since $\left(\mho B_{\varrho}\right)$ is uniformly bounded. In addition, we show that the operator $\mho$ exhibits "equi-continuity" over B_{ϱ}. Assume $U \in B_{\varrho}$ and let $\upsilon_1, \upsilon_2 \in [0, \mathfrak{I}]$ such that $\upsilon_1 < \upsilon_2$. Under these assumptions, we have:

$\|(\mho\mathbf{U})(\upsilon 2) - (\mho\mathbf{U})(\upsilon 1)$

$\le 1 - lM\, l\|Z\upsilon 2, U\upsilon 2 - Z\upsilon 1, U\upsilon 1 + lM\, l\Gamma l\|[\text{subSup}0\upsilon 2(\upsilon 2-\lambda)l - 1 - \text{subSup}0\upsilon 1$ $(\upsilon 1 - \lambda)l - 1]Z\lambda, U\lambda d\lambda|$

$$\leq \frac{1-l}{M(l)}\left|Z(\upsilon_2, U(\upsilon_2)) - Z(\upsilon_1, U(\upsilon_1))\right| + \frac{l}{M(l)}\frac{L(+\|U\|)}{\Gamma(l+1)}(\upsilon_{2-}^l\upsilon_1^l).$$

As $\nu_2 \rightarrow \nu_1$, the quantity $\| \mho U(\nu_2) - \mho U(\nu_1) \|$ goes to zero. By the Arzelà–Ascoli theorem, $(\mathcal{U} B_\varrho)$ is relatively compact. Therefore, the operator $\mathcal{U}$is compact and continuous, which ensures that problem (1) has at least one solution. We now turn to uniqueness for (1), which will depend on the following assumption:

$$0 \leq \left[1 - \frac{1-l}{M(l)}\varrho - \frac{l\mathfrak{I}^l}{M(l)\Gamma(l)}\varrho\right]. \tag{16}$$

Assume there is another solution, which we denote by L, S_C, E_C, I_C, S_F, I_F, S_{D1}, E_{D1}, I_{D1}, S_{D2}, E_{D2}, I_{D2}. Then, the following condition is satisfied:

$$L(\upsilon) - L_1(\upsilon) = \frac{1-l}{M(l)}\left(F_1(\upsilon, L(\upsilon)) - F_1(\upsilon, L_1(\upsilon)) + \frac{l}{M(l)\Gamma(l)}\int_0^\upsilon (F_1(\lambda, L(\upsilon)) - F_1(\lambda, L_1(\upsilon))\right) d\lambda, \tag{17}$$

using norm to Equation (17), we have

$$\left\|L(\upsilon) - L_1(\upsilon)\right\| = \left\|\frac{1-l}{M(l)}\left(F_1(\upsilon, L(\upsilon)) - F_1(\upsilon, L_1(\upsilon)) + \frac{l}{M(l)\Gamma(l)}\int_0^\upsilon (F_1(\lambda, L(\upsilon)) - F_1(\lambda, L_1(\upsilon))\right) d\lambda\right\|$$

$$\leq \frac{1-l}{M(l)}\varrho\left\|L(\upsilon) - L_1(\upsilon)\right\| + \frac{l}{M(l)\Gamma(l)}\varrho\left\|L(\upsilon) - L_1(\upsilon)\right\| \tag{18}$$

Therefore,

$$\left\|L(\upsilon) - L_1(\upsilon)\right\|\left[1 - \frac{1-l}{M(l)}\varrho - \frac{l\mathfrak{I}^l}{M(l)\Gamma(l)}\varrho\right] \leq 0. \tag{19}$$

It follows that $L(\upsilon) = L_1(\upsilon)$, provided the inequality (16) is satisfied. Furthermore, for all other compartments, the following conditions hold: $L(\upsilon) = L_1(\upsilon)$, , $S_C(\upsilon) = S_{C1}(\upsilon)$, $E_C(\upsilon) = E_{C1}(\upsilon)$, $I_C(\upsilon) = I_{C1}(\upsilon)$, $S_F(\upsilon) = S_{F1}(\upsilon)$, $I_F(\upsilon) = I_{F1}(\upsilon)$, $S_{D1}(\upsilon) = S_{D11}(\upsilon)$, $E_{D1}(\upsilon) = E_{D11}(\upsilon)$, $I_{D1}(\upsilon) = I_{D11}(\upsilon)$, $S_{D2}(\upsilon) = S_{D21}(\upsilon)$, $E_{D2}(\upsilon) = E_{D21}(\upsilon)$ and $I_{D2}(\upsilon) = I_{D21}(\upsilon)$. Under these assumptions, the solution is unique. □

We now study the Ulam–Hyers stability of the system.

Theorem 2. Let $Z \in \lambda$ be a continuous function, and suppose there exists a constant

$K > 0$ such that

$$|Z(\upsilon, \wp) - Z(\upsilon, \widetilde{\wp})| \leq K|\wp - \widetilde{\wp}|$$

for *all* $\upsilon \in [0, \mathfrak{I}]$ and $\wp \in \lambda$. Assume that $1 > \frac{(1-l)\Gamma(l)K + K\mathfrak{I}^{l}}{M(l)\Gamma(l)}$. If $\wp$ and $\wp\wp\sim$ are solutions to Equation (8), then:

$$\text{ABC}\mathbf{D}_{\upsilon}^{l}\widetilde{\wp}(\upsilon) = Z(\upsilon, \widetilde{\wp}(\upsilon)), \widetilde{\wp}(0) = \wp_0 + \varepsilon \geq 0,$$

where $\widetilde{\wp} = \left(\tilde{L}, \tilde{S}_C, \tilde{E}_C, \tilde{I}_C, \tilde{S}_F, \tilde{I}_F, \tilde{S}_{D1}, \tilde{E}_{D1}, \tilde{I}_{D1}, \tilde{S}_{D2}, \tilde{E}_{D2}, \tilde{I}_{D2}\right)^{\mathfrak{I}}$, and $\wp_0 + \varepsilon = \left(L_0 + \varepsilon, S_{C0} + \varepsilon, E_{C0} + \varepsilon, \ldots, I_{D20} + \varepsilon\right)^{\mathfrak{I}}$. Then:

$$\|\wp - \widetilde{\wp}\| \leq [1 - \frac{(1-l)\Gamma(l)K + K\mathfrak{I}^{l}}{\text{M(l)}\Gamma(l)}]^{-1} |\varepsilon|.$$

It follows that:

$$\|\wp - \widetilde{\wp}\| \leq \left[1 - \frac{(1-l)\Gamma(l)K + \text{K}\mathfrak{I}^{l}}{\text{M(l)}\Gamma(l)}\right]^{-1} |\varepsilon|. \tag{20}$$

Hence, the theorem is established. □

NUMERICAL APPROACH

We now describe the numerical framework. The model uses a fractional derivative with a generalized ML kernel. We perform numerical experiments using interpolation polynomials. To approximate the fractional-order integral, we apply the Adams–Bashforth (AB) method, which is known to be computationally efficient (Atangana &

Owolabi, 2018). By enforcing the initial conditions through the operator $\text{ABC}\mathbf{I}_{\upsilon}^{l}$ and adapting the AB scheme to this setting, we obtain the following results:

$$L - L_0 = \text{ABC}\mathbf{I}_{\upsilon}^{l}G_1(L,\upsilon),\ S_C - S_{C0} = \text{ABC}\mathbf{I}_{\upsilon}^{l}G_2\left(S_C,\upsilon\right),$$

$$I_C - I_{C0} = \text{ABC}\mathbf{I}_{\upsilon}^{l}G_3\left(I_C,\upsilon\right),\ E_C - E_{C0} = \text{ABC}\mathbf{I}_{\upsilon}^{l}G_4\left(E_C,\upsilon\right),$$

$$S_F - S_{F0} = \text{ABC}\mathbf{I}_{\upsilon}^{l}G_5\left(S_F,\upsilon\right),\ I_F - I_{F0} = \text{ABC}\mathbf{I}_{\upsilon}^{l}G_6\left(I_F,\upsilon\right),$$

$$S_{D1} - S_{D10} = \text{ABC}\mathbf{I}_{\upsilon}^{l}G_7\left(S_{D1},\upsilon\right),\ E_{D1} - E_{D10} = \text{ABC}\mathbf{I}_{\upsilon}^{l}G_8\left(E_{D1},\upsilon\right),$$

$$I_{D1} - I_{D10} = \text{ABC}\mathbf{I}_{\upsilon}^{l}G_9\left(I_{D1},\upsilon\right),\ S_{D2} - S_{D20} = \text{ABC}\mathbf{I}_{\upsilon}^{l}G_{10}\left(S_{D2},\upsilon\right),$$

$$E_{D2} - E_{D20} = \text{ABC}\mathbf{I}_{\upsilon}^{l} G_{11}(E_{D2}, \upsilon), \; I_{D2} - I_{D20} = \text{ABC}\mathbf{I}_{\upsilon}^{l} G_{12}(E_{D2}, \upsilon) \tag{21}$$

which give

$$L(\upsilon) - L_0 = \frac{1-l}{M(l)} G_1(L(\upsilon), \upsilon) + \frac{l}{M(l)\Gamma(l)} \int_0^{\upsilon} (\upsilon - \lambda)^{l-1} G_1(L(\lambda), \lambda) d\lambda$$

$$S_C(\upsilon) - S_{C0} = \frac{1-l}{M(l)} G_2(S_C(\upsilon), \upsilon) + \frac{l}{M(l)\Gamma(l)} \int_0^{\upsilon} (\upsilon - \lambda)^{l-1} G_2(S_C(\lambda), \lambda) d\lambda$$

$$I_C(\upsilon) - I_{C0} = \frac{1-l}{M(l)} G_4(I_C(\upsilon), \upsilon) + \frac{l}{M(l)\Gamma(l)} \int_0^{\upsilon} (\upsilon - \lambda)^{l-1} G_4(I_C(\lambda), \lambda) d\lambda$$

$$E_C(\upsilon) - E_{C0} = \frac{1-l}{M(l)} G_3(E_C(\upsilon), \upsilon) + \frac{l}{M(l)\Gamma(l)} \int_0^{\upsilon} (\upsilon - \lambda)^{l-1} G_3(E_C(\lambda), \lambda) d\lambda$$

$$S_F(\upsilon) - S_{F0} = \frac{1-l}{M(l)} G_5(S_F(\upsilon), \upsilon) + \frac{l}{M(l)\Gamma(l)} \int_0^{\upsilon} (\upsilon - \lambda)^{l-1} G_5(S_F(\lambda), \lambda) d\lambda$$

$$I_F(\upsilon) - I_{F0} = \frac{1-l}{M(l)} G_6(I_F(\upsilon), \upsilon) + \frac{l}{M(l)\Gamma(l)} \int_0^{\upsilon} (\upsilon - \lambda)^{l-1} G_6(I_F(\lambda), \lambda) d\lambda$$

$$S_{D1}(\upsilon) - S_{D10} = \frac{1-l}{M(l)} G_7(S_{D1}(\upsilon), \upsilon) + \frac{l}{M(l)\Gamma(l)} \int_0^{\upsilon} (\upsilon - \lambda)^{l-1} G_7(S_{D1}(\lambda), \lambda) d\lambda$$

$$E_{D1}(\upsilon) - E_{D10} = \frac{1-l}{M(l)} G_8(E_{D1}(\upsilon), \upsilon) + \frac{l}{M(l)\Gamma(l)} \int_0^{\upsilon} (\upsilon - \lambda)^{l-1} G_8(E_{D1}(\lambda), \lambda) d\lambda$$

$$I_{D1}(\upsilon) - I_{D10} = \frac{1-l}{M(l)} G_9(I_{D1}(\upsilon), \upsilon) + \frac{l}{M(l)\Gamma(l)} \int_0^{\upsilon} (\upsilon - \lambda)^{l-1} G_9(I_{D1}(\lambda), \lambda) d\lambda$$

$$S_{D2}(\upsilon) - S_{D20} = \frac{1-l}{M(l)} G_{10}(S_{D2}(\upsilon), \upsilon) + \frac{l}{M(l)\Gamma(l)} \int_0^{\upsilon} (\upsilon - \lambda)^{l-1} G_{10}(S_{D2}(\lambda), \lambda) d\lambda$$

$$E_{D2}(\upsilon) - E_{D20} = \frac{1-l}{M(l)} G_{11}(E_{D2}(\upsilon), \upsilon) + \frac{l}{M(l)\Gamma(l)} \int_0^{\upsilon} (\upsilon - \lambda)^{l-1} G_{11}(E_{D2}(\lambda), \lambda) d\lambda$$

$$I_{D2}(\upsilon) - I_{D20} = \frac{1-l}{M(l)} G_{12}(I_{D2}(\upsilon), \upsilon) + \frac{l}{M(l)\Gamma(l)} \int_0^{\upsilon} (\upsilon - \lambda)^{l-1} G_{12}(I_{D2}(\lambda), \lambda) d\lambda$$

To construct an iterative approach, the substitution $\upsilon = \upsilon_{\iota+1}$ for $\nu = 0, 1, 2, \ldots$ is applied to the system:

$$L(\upsilon_{\nu+1}) - \mathrm{L}(0) = \frac{1-l}{M(l)} G_1(L(\upsilon_\nu), \upsilon_\nu) + \frac{l}{M(l)\Gamma(l)} \sum_{=0} \int_{\nu}^{\upsilon_{\nu+1}} (\upsilon_{\nu+1} - \lambda)^{l-1} G_1(L(\lambda), \lambda) d\lambda$$

$$S_C\left(\upsilon_{\nu+1}\right) - S_C(0) = \frac{1-l}{M(l)} G_2\left(S_C(\upsilon_\nu), \upsilon_\nu\right) + \frac{l}{M(l)\Gamma(l)} \sum_{=0}^{\nu} \int_{\nu}^{\nu+1} \left(\upsilon_{\nu+1} - \lambda\right)^{l-1} G_2\left(S_C(\lambda), \lambda\right) d\lambda$$

$$E_C\left(\upsilon_{\nu+1}\right) - E_C(0) = \frac{1-l}{M(l)} G_3\left(E_C(\upsilon_\nu), \upsilon_\nu\right) + \frac{l}{M(l)\Gamma(l)} \sum_{=0}^{\nu} \int_{\nu}^{\nu+1} \left(\upsilon_{\nu+1} - \lambda\right)^{l-1} G_3\left(E_C(\lambda), \lambda\right) d\lambda$$

$$I_C\left(\upsilon_{\nu+1}\right) - I_C(0) = \frac{1-l}{M(l)} G_4\left(I_C(\upsilon_\nu), \upsilon_\nu\right) + \frac{l}{M(l)\Gamma(l)} \sum_{=0}^{\nu} \int_{\nu}^{\nu+1} \left(\upsilon_{\nu+1} - \lambda\right)^{l-1} G_4\left(I_C(\lambda), \lambda\right) d\lambda$$

$$S_F\left(\upsilon_{\nu+1}\right) - S_F(0) = \frac{1-l}{M(l)} G_5\left(S_F(\upsilon_\nu), \upsilon_\nu\right) + \frac{l}{M(l)\Gamma(l)} \sum_{=0}^{\nu} \int_{\nu}^{\nu+1} \left(\upsilon_{\nu+1} - \lambda\right)^{l-1} G_5\left(S_F(\lambda), \lambda\right) d\lambda$$

$$I_F\left(\upsilon_{\nu+1}\right) - I_F(0) = \frac{1-l}{M(l)} G_6\left(I_F(\upsilon_\nu), \upsilon_\nu\right) + \frac{l}{M(l)\Gamma(l)} \sum_{=0}^{\nu} \int_{\nu}^{\nu+1} \left(\upsilon_{\nu+1} - \lambda\right)^{l-1} G_6\left(I_F(\lambda), \lambda\right) d\lambda$$

$$S_{D1}\left(\upsilon_{\nu+1}\right) - S_{D1}(0) = \frac{1-l}{M(l)} G_7\left(S_{D1}(\upsilon_\nu), \upsilon_\nu\right) + \frac{l}{M(l)\Gamma(l)} \sum_{=0}^{\nu} \int_{\nu}^{\nu+1} \left(\upsilon_{\nu+1} - \lambda\right)^{l-1} G_7\left(S_{D1}(\lambda), \lambda\right) d\lambda$$

$$E_{D1}\left(\upsilon_{\nu+1}\right) - E_{D1}(0) = \frac{1-l}{M(l)} G_8\left(E_{D1}(\upsilon_\nu), \upsilon_\nu\right) + \frac{l}{M(l)\Gamma(l)} \sum_{=0}^{\nu} \int_{\nu}^{\nu+1} \left(\upsilon_{\nu+1} - \lambda\right)^{l-1} G_8\left(E_{D1}(\lambda), \lambda\right) d\lambda$$

$$I_{D1}\left(\upsilon_{\nu+1}\right) - I_{D1}(0) = \frac{1-l}{M(l)} G_9\left(I_{D1}(\upsilon_\nu), \upsilon_\nu\right) + \frac{l}{M(l)\Gamma(l)} \sum_{=0}^{\nu} \int_{\nu}^{\nu+1} \left(\upsilon_{\nu+1} - \lambda\right)^{l-1} G_9\left(I_{D1}(\lambda), \lambda\right) d\lambda$$

$$S_{D2}\left(\upsilon_{\nu+1}\right) - S_{D2}(0) = \frac{1-l}{M(l)} G_{10}\left(S_{D2}(\upsilon_\nu), \upsilon_\nu\right) + \frac{l}{M(l)\Gamma(l)} \sum_{=0}^{\nu} \int_{\nu}^{\nu+1} \left(\upsilon_{\nu+1} - \lambda\right)^{l-1} G_{10}\left(S_{D2}(\lambda), \lambda\right) d\lambda$$

$$E_{D2}\left(\upsilon_{\nu+1}\right) - E_{D2}(0) = \frac{1-l}{M(l)} G_{11}\left(E_{D2}(\upsilon_\nu), \upsilon_\nu\right) + \frac{l}{M(l)\Gamma(l)} \sum_{=0}^{\nu} \int_{\nu}^{\nu+1} \left(\upsilon_{\nu+1} - \lambda\right)^{l-1} G_{11}\left(E_{D2}(\lambda), \lambda\right) d\lambda$$

$$I_{D2}\left(\upsilon_{\nu+1}\right) - I_{D2}(0) = \frac{1-l}{M(l)} G_{12}\left(I_{D2}(\upsilon_\nu), \upsilon_\nu\right) + \frac{l}{M(l)\Gamma(l)} \sum_{=0}^{\nu} \int_{\nu}^{\nu+1} \left(\upsilon_{\nu+1} - \lambda\right)^{l-1} G_{12}\left(I_{D2}(\lambda), \lambda\right) d\lambda.$$

To approximate the functions $\mathbf{G}_1(L(\lambda), \lambda)$, $\mathbf{G}_2(S_C(\lambda), \lambda)$, $\mathbf{G}_3(E_C(\lambda), \lambda)$, $\mathbf{G}_4(I_C(\lambda), \lambda)$, $\mathbf{G}_5(S_F(\lambda), \lambda)$, $\mathbf{G}_6(I_F(\lambda), \lambda)$, $\mathbf{G}_7(S_{D1}(\lambda), \lambda)$, $\mathbf{G}_8(E_{D1}(\lambda), \lambda)$, $\mathbf{G}_9(I_{D1}(\lambda), \lambda)$, $\mathbf{G}_{10}(S_{D2}(\lambda), \lambda)$, $\mathbf{G}_{11}(E_{D2}(\lambda), \lambda)$, and $\mathbf{G}_{12}(I_{D2}(\lambda), \lambda)$, we employ a two-step interpolation polynomial. We then evaluate the integral over the interval $[\upsilon_\varsigma, \upsilon_{\varsigma+1}]$. As a result, we obtain:

$$G_1(L(\lambda),\lambda) \cong \frac{G_1\left(L(\upsilon_\varsigma),\upsilon_\varsigma\right)}{\Delta}\left(\upsilon-\upsilon_{\varsigma-1}\right)+\frac{G_1\left(L(\upsilon_{\varsigma-1}),\upsilon_{\varsigma-1}\right)}{\Delta}\left(\upsilon-\upsilon_\varsigma\right)$$

$$G_2(S_C(\lambda),\lambda) \cong \frac{G_2\left(S_C(\upsilon_\varsigma),\upsilon_\varsigma\right)}{\Delta}\left(\upsilon-\upsilon_{\varsigma-1}\right)+\frac{G_2\left(S_C(\upsilon_{\varsigma-1}),\upsilon_{\varsigma-1}\right)}{\Delta}\left(\upsilon-\upsilon_\varsigma\right)$$

$$G_3(E_C(\lambda),\lambda) \cong \frac{G_3\left(E_C(\upsilon_\varsigma),\upsilon_\varsigma\right)}{\Delta}\left(\upsilon-\upsilon_{\varsigma-1}\right)+\frac{G_3\left(E_C(\upsilon_{\varsigma-1}),\upsilon_{\varsigma-1}\right)}{\Delta}\left(\upsilon-\upsilon_\varsigma\right)$$

$$G_4(I_C(\lambda),\lambda) \cong \frac{G_4\left(I_C(\upsilon_\varsigma),\upsilon_\varsigma\right)}{\Delta}\left(\upsilon-\upsilon_{\varsigma-1}\right)+\frac{G_4\left(I_C(\upsilon_{\varsigma-1}),\upsilon_{\varsigma-1}\right)}{\Delta}\left(\upsilon-\upsilon_\varsigma\right)$$

$$G_5(S_F(\lambda),\lambda) \cong \frac{G_5\left(S_F(\upsilon_\varsigma),\upsilon_\varsigma\right)}{\Delta}\left(\upsilon-\upsilon_{\varsigma-1}\right)+\frac{G_5\left(S_F(\upsilon_{\varsigma-1}),\upsilon_{\varsigma-1}\right)}{\Delta}\left(\upsilon-\upsilon_\varsigma\right)$$

$$G_6(I_F(\lambda),\lambda) \cong \frac{G_6\left(I_F(\upsilon_\varsigma),\upsilon_\varsigma\right)}{\Delta}\left(\upsilon-\upsilon_{\varsigma-1}\right)+\frac{G_6\left(I_F(\upsilon_{\varsigma-1}),\upsilon_{\varsigma-1}\right)}{\Delta}\left(\upsilon-\upsilon_\varsigma\right) \quad (22)$$

$$G_7(S_{D1}(\lambda),\lambda) \cong \frac{G_7\left(S_{D1}(\upsilon_\varsigma),\upsilon_\varsigma\right)}{\Delta}\left(\upsilon-\upsilon_{\varsigma-1}\right)+\frac{G_7\left(S_{D1}(\upsilon_{\varsigma-1}),\upsilon_{\varsigma-1}\right)}{\Delta}\left(\upsilon-\upsilon_\varsigma\right)$$

$$G_8(E_{D1}(\lambda),\lambda) \cong \frac{G_8\left(E_{D1}(\upsilon_\varsigma),\upsilon_\varsigma\right)}{\Delta}\left(\upsilon-\upsilon_{\varsigma-1}\right)+\frac{G_8\left(E_{D1}(\upsilon_{\varsigma-1}),\upsilon_{\varsigma-1}\right)}{\Delta}\left(\upsilon-\upsilon_\varsigma\right)$$

$$G_9(I_{D1}(\lambda),\lambda) \cong \frac{G_9\left(I_{D1}(\upsilon_\varsigma),\upsilon_\varsigma\right)}{\Delta}\left(\upsilon-\upsilon_{\varsigma-1}\right)+\frac{G_9\left(I_{D1}(\upsilon_{\varsigma-1}),\upsilon_{\varsigma-1}\right)}{\Delta}\left(\upsilon-\upsilon_\varsigma\right)$$

$$G_{10}(S_{D2}(\lambda),\lambda) \cong \frac{G_{10}\left(S_{D2}(\upsilon_\varsigma),\upsilon_\varsigma\right)}{\Delta}\left(\upsilon-\upsilon_{\varsigma-1}\right)+\frac{G_{10}\left(S_{D2}(\upsilon_{\varsigma-1}),\upsilon_{\varsigma-1}\right)}{\Delta}\left(\upsilon-\upsilon_\varsigma\right)$$

$$G_{11}(E_{D2}(\lambda),\lambda) \cong \frac{G_{11}\left(E_{D2}(\upsilon_\varsigma),\upsilon_\varsigma\right)}{\Delta}\left(\upsilon-\upsilon_{\varsigma-1}\right)+\frac{G_{11}\left(E_{D2}(\upsilon_{\varsigma-1}),\upsilon_{\varsigma-1}\right)}{\Delta}\left(\upsilon-\upsilon_\varsigma\right)$$

$$G_{12}(I_{D2}(\lambda),\lambda) \cong \frac{G_{12}\left(I_{D2}(\upsilon_\varsigma),\upsilon_\varsigma\right)}{\Delta}\left(\upsilon-\upsilon_{\varsigma-1}\right)+\frac{G_{12}\left(I_{D2}(\upsilon_{\varsigma-1}),\upsilon_{\varsigma-1}\right)}{\Delta}\left(\upsilon-\upsilon_\varsigma\right)$$

which gives

$$L(\upsilon_{\nu+1}) = \mathrm{L}(0) + \frac{1-l}{M(l)} G_1\left(L(\upsilon_\nu), \upsilon_\nu\right) + \frac{l}{M(l)\Gamma(l)} \sum_{j=0}^{\nu} \left(\frac{G_1\left(L(\upsilon_\zeta), \upsilon_\zeta\right)}{\Delta} I_{\zeta-1,l} + \frac{G_1\left(L(\upsilon_{\zeta-1}), \upsilon_{\zeta-1}\right)}{\Delta} I_{\zeta,l} \right)$$

$$S_C(\upsilon_{\nu+1}) = S_C(0) + \frac{1-l}{M(l)} G_2\left(S_C(\upsilon_\nu), \upsilon_\nu\right) + \frac{l}{M(l)\Gamma(l)} \sum_{j=0}^{\nu} \left(\frac{G_2\left(S_C(\upsilon_\zeta), \upsilon_\zeta\right)}{\Delta} I_{\zeta-1,l} + \frac{G_2\left(S_C(\upsilon_{\zeta-1}), \upsilon_{\zeta-1}\right)}{\Delta} I_{\zeta,l} \right)$$

$$E_C(\upsilon_{\nu+1}) = E_C(0) + \frac{1-l}{M(l)} G_3\left(E_C(\upsilon_\nu), \upsilon_\nu\right) + \frac{l}{M(l)\Gamma(l)} \sum_{j=0}^{\nu} \left(\frac{G_3\left(E_C(\upsilon_\zeta), \upsilon_\zeta\right)}{\Delta} I_{\zeta-1,l} + \frac{G_3\left(E_C(\upsilon_{\zeta-1}), \upsilon_{\zeta-1}\right)}{\Delta} I_{\zeta,l} \right)$$

$$I_C(\upsilon_{\nu+1}) = I_C(0) + \frac{1-l}{M(l)} G_4\left(I_C(\upsilon_\nu), \upsilon_\nu\right) + \frac{l}{M(l)\Gamma(l)} \sum_{j=0}^{\nu} \left(\frac{G_4\left(I_C(\upsilon_\zeta), \upsilon_\zeta\right)}{\Delta} I_{\zeta-1,l} + \frac{G_4\left(I_C(\upsilon_{\zeta-1}), \upsilon_{\zeta-1}\right)}{\Delta} I_{\zeta,l} \right)$$

$$S_F(\upsilon_{\nu+1}) = S_F(0) + \frac{1-l}{M(l)} G_5\left(S_F(\upsilon_\nu), \upsilon_\nu\right) + \frac{l}{M(l)\Gamma(l)} \sum_{j=0}^{\nu} \left(\frac{G_5\left(S_F(\upsilon_\zeta), \upsilon_\zeta\right)}{\Delta} I_{\zeta-1,l} + \frac{G_5\left(S_F(\upsilon_{\zeta-1}), \upsilon_{\zeta-1}\right)}{\Delta} I_{\zeta,l} \right)$$

$$I_F(\upsilon_{\nu+1}) = I_F(0) + \frac{1-l}{M(l)} G_6\left(I_F(\upsilon_\nu), \upsilon_\nu\right) + \frac{l}{M(l)\Gamma(l)} \sum_{j=0}^{\nu} \left(\frac{G_6\left(I_F(\upsilon_\zeta), \upsilon_\zeta\right)}{\Delta} I_{\zeta-1,l} + \frac{G_6\left(I_F(\upsilon_{\zeta-1}), \upsilon_{\zeta-1}\right)}{\Delta} I_{\zeta,l} \right)$$

$$S_{D1}(\upsilon_{\nu+1}) = S_{D1}(0) + \frac{1-l}{M(l)} G_7\left(S_{D1}(\upsilon_\nu), \upsilon_\nu\right) + \frac{l}{M(l)\Gamma(l)} \sum_{j=0}^{\nu} \left(\frac{G_7\left(S_{D1}(\upsilon_\zeta), \upsilon_\zeta\right)}{\Delta} I_{\zeta-1,l} + \frac{G_7\left(S_{D1}(\upsilon_{\zeta-1}), \upsilon_{\zeta-1}\right)}{\Delta} I_{\zeta,l} \right)$$

$$E_{D1}(\upsilon_{\nu+1}) = E_{D1}(0) + \frac{1-l}{M(l)} G_8\left(E_{D1}(\upsilon_\nu), \upsilon_\nu\right) + \frac{l}{M(l)\Gamma(l)} \sum_{j=0}^{\nu} \left(\frac{G_8\left(E_{D1}(\upsilon_\zeta), \upsilon_\zeta\right)}{\Delta} I_{\zeta-1,l} + \frac{G_8\left(E_{D1}(\upsilon_{\zeta-1}), \upsilon_{\zeta-1}\right)}{\Delta} I_{\zeta,l} \right)$$

$$I_{D1}(\upsilon_{\nu+1}) = I_{D1}(0) + \frac{1-l}{M(l)} G_9\left(I_{D1}(\upsilon_\nu), \upsilon_\nu\right) + \frac{l}{M(l)\Gamma(l)} \sum_{j=0}^{\nu} \left(\frac{G_9\left(I_{D1}(\upsilon_\zeta), \upsilon_\zeta\right)}{\Delta} I_{\zeta-1,l} + \frac{G_9\left(I_{D1}(\upsilon_{\zeta-1}), \upsilon_{\zeta-1}\right)}{\Delta} I_{\zeta,l} \right) \tag{23}$$

$$S_{D2}(\upsilon_{\nu+1}) = S_{D2}(0) + \frac{1-l}{M(l)} G_{10}\left(S_{D2}(\upsilon_\nu), \upsilon_\nu\right) + \frac{l}{M(l)\Gamma(l)} \sum_{j=0}^{\nu} \left(\frac{G_{10}\left(S_{D2}(\upsilon_\zeta), \upsilon_\zeta\right)}{\Delta} I_{\zeta-1,l} + \frac{G_{10}\left(S_{D2}(\upsilon_{\zeta-1}), \upsilon_{\zeta-1}\right)}{\Delta} I_{\zeta,l} \right)$$

$$E_{D2}(\upsilon_{\nu+1}) = E_{D2}(0) + \frac{1-l}{M(l)} G_{11}\left(E_{D2}(\upsilon_\nu), \upsilon_\nu\right) + \frac{l}{M(l)\Gamma(l)} \sum_{j=0}^{\nu} \left(\frac{G_{11}\left(E_{D2}(\upsilon_\zeta), \upsilon_\zeta\right)}{\Delta} I_{\zeta-1,l} + \frac{G_{11}\left(E_{D2}(\upsilon_{\zeta-1}), \upsilon_{\zeta-1}\right)}{\Delta} I_{\zeta,l} \right)$$

where

$$I_{\zeta-1,l} = \int_{v_\zeta}^{v_{\zeta+1}} \left(v - v_{\zeta-1}\right)(v_{\iota+1} - v)^{l-1}\, dv,$$

$$I_{\zeta,l} = \int_{v_\zeta}^{v_{\zeta+1}} \left(v - v_j\right)(v_{\iota+1} - v)^{l-1}\, dv.$$

In this step, we compute the integrals $I_{\zeta-1,l}$ and $I_{\zeta l}$ as follows:

$$I_{\zeta-1,l} = -\frac{1}{l}\left[(v_{\zeta+1} - v_{\zeta-1})(v_{\iota+1} - v_{\zeta+1})^{l} - (v_{\iota+1} - v_{\zeta-1})(v_{\iota+1} - v_{\zeta})^{l}\right] - \frac{1}{l(l-1)}\left[\left(v_{\iota+1} - v_{\zeta+1}\right) - \left(v_{\iota+1} - v_{\zeta}\right)\right]$$

and

$$I_{\zeta,l} = -\frac{1}{l}\left[(v_{\zeta+1} - v_j)(v_{\iota+1} - v_{\zeta+1})^{l}\right] - \frac{1}{l(l-1)}\left[(v_{\iota+1} - v_{\zeta+1})^{l+1} - (v_{\iota+1} - v_{\zeta})^{l+1}\right].$$

Assuming that $v_\zeta = j\Delta$, it follows that

$$I_{\zeta-1,l} = -\frac{\Delta^{l+1}}{l(l+1)}[(\iota + 1 - \zeta)^{l}(\iota - \zeta + 2 + l) + (\iota - \zeta + 2 + l) - (\iota - \zeta)^{l}(\iota - \zeta + 2 + 2l)], \tag{24}$$

$$I_{\zeta,l} = \frac{\Delta^{l+1}}{l(l+1)}[(\iota + 1 - \zeta)^{l+1}(\iota - \zeta)^{l}(\iota - \zeta + 1 + l)]. \tag{25}$$

By replacing Equations (24) and (25) into Equation (23), the resulting expression is:

$$L(v_{\iota+1}) = L(v_0) + \frac{(1-l)}{M(l)}[G_1(L(v_1), v_\iota)] + \frac{l}{M(l)}\sum_{j=0}^{\nu}\Big(\frac{G_1\left(L(v_1), v_\iota\right)}{\Gamma(\ell + 2)}$$

$$\times \Delta^{l}[\,(\iota + 1 - \zeta)^{l}(\iota - \zeta + 2 + \ell) - (\iota - \zeta)^{l}(\iota - \zeta + 2 + 2\ell)]$$

$$- \frac{G_1\left(L(v_{\nu-1}), v_{\nu-1}\right)}{\Gamma(\ell + 2)}\Delta^{l}[(\iota + 1 - \zeta)^{l+1} - (\iota - \zeta)^{l}(\iota - \zeta + 1 + l)]\Big), \tag{26}$$

$$= S_C(v_0) + \frac{(1-l)}{M(l)}[G_2(S_C(v_1), v_\iota)] + \frac{l}{M(l)}\sum_{j=0}^{\nu}\Big(\frac{G_2\left(S_C(v_1), v_\iota\right)}{\Gamma(\ell + 2)}$$

$$\times \Delta^{l}[\,(\iota + 1 - \zeta)^{l}(\iota - \zeta + 2 + \ell) - (\iota - \zeta)^{l}(\iota - \zeta + 2 + 2\ell)]$$

$$- \frac{G_2\left(S_C(v_{\nu-1}), v_{\nu-1}\right)}{\Gamma(\ell + 2)}\Delta^{l}[(\iota + 1 - \zeta)^{l+1} - (\iota - \zeta)^{l}(\iota - \zeta + 1 + l)]\Big) \tag{27}$$

$$E_C(\upsilon_{\iota+1}) = E_C(\upsilon_0) + \frac{(1-l)}{M(l)}\left[G_3(E_C(\upsilon_1),\upsilon_\iota)\right] + \frac{l}{M(l)}\sum_{j=0}^{\nu}(\frac{G_3(E_C(\upsilon_1),\upsilon_\iota)}{\Gamma(\ell+2)}$$

$$\times \Delta^l[\ (\iota+1-\zeta)^l(\iota-\zeta+2+\ell)-(\iota-\zeta)^l(\iota-\zeta+2+2\ell)]$$

$$-\frac{G_3(E_C(\upsilon_{\nu-1}),\upsilon_{\nu-1})}{\Gamma(\ell+2)}\Delta^l[(\iota+1-\zeta)^{l+1}-(\iota-\zeta)^l(\iota-\zeta+1+l)]) \quad (28)$$

$$I_C(\upsilon_{\iota+1}) = I_C(\upsilon_0) + \frac{(1-l)}{M(l)}\left[G_4(I_C(\upsilon_1),\upsilon_\iota)\right] + \frac{l}{M(l)}\sum_{j=0}^{\nu}(\frac{G_4(I_C(\upsilon_1),\upsilon_\iota)}{\Gamma(\ell+2)}$$

$$\times \Delta^l[\ (\iota+1-\zeta)^l(\iota-\zeta+2+\ell)-(\iota-\zeta)^l(\iota-\zeta+2+2\ell)]$$

$$-\frac{G_4(I_C(\upsilon_{\nu-1}),\upsilon_{\nu-1})}{\Gamma(\ell+2)}\Delta^l[(\iota+1-\zeta)^{l+1}-(\iota-\zeta)^l(\iota-\zeta+1+l)]) \quad (29)$$

$$S_F(\upsilon_{\iota+1}) = S_F(\upsilon_0) + \frac{(1-l)}{M(l)}\left[G_5(S_F(\upsilon_1),\upsilon_\iota)\right] + \frac{l}{M(l)}\sum_{j=0}^{\nu}(\frac{G_5(S_F(\upsilon_1),\upsilon_\iota)}{\Gamma(\ell+2)}$$

$$\times \Delta^l[\ (\iota+1-\zeta)^l(\iota-\zeta+2+\ell)-(\iota-\zeta)^l(\iota-\zeta+2+2\ell)]$$

$$-\frac{G_5(S_F(\upsilon_{\nu-1}),\upsilon_{\nu-1})}{\Gamma(\ell+2)}\Delta^l[(\iota+1-\zeta)^{l+1}-(\iota-\zeta)^l(\iota-\zeta+1+l)] \quad (30)$$

$$I_F(\upsilon_{\iota+1}) = I_F(\upsilon_0) + \frac{(1-l)}{M(l)}\left[G_6(I_F(\upsilon_1),\upsilon_\iota)\right] + \frac{l}{M(l)}\sum_{j=0}^{\nu}(\frac{G_6(I_F(\upsilon_1),\upsilon_\iota)}{\Gamma(\ell+2)}$$

$$\times \Delta^l[\ (\iota+1-\zeta)^l(\iota-\zeta+2+\ell)-(\iota-\zeta)^l(\iota-\zeta+2+2\ell)]$$

$$-\frac{G_6(I_F(\upsilon_{\nu-1}),\upsilon_{\nu-1})}{\Gamma(\ell+2)}\Delta^l[(\iota+1-\zeta)^{l+1}-(\iota-\zeta)^l(\iota-\zeta+1+l) \quad (31)$$

$$S_{D1}(\upsilon_{\iota+1}) = S_{D1}(\upsilon_0) + \frac{(1-l)}{M(l)}\left[G_7(S_{D1}(\upsilon_1),\upsilon_\iota)\right] + \frac{l}{M(l)}\sum_{j=0}^{\nu}(\frac{G_7(S_{D1}(\upsilon_1),\upsilon_\iota)}{\Gamma(\ell+2)}$$

$$\times \Delta^l[\ (\iota+1-\zeta)^l(\iota-\zeta+2+\ell)-(\iota-\zeta)^l(\iota-\zeta+2+2\ell)]$$

$$-\frac{G_7(S_{D1}(\upsilon_{\nu-1}),\upsilon_{\nu-1})}{\Gamma(\ell+2)}\Delta^l[(\iota+1-\zeta)^{l+1}-(\iota-\zeta)^l(\iota-\zeta+1+l) \quad (32)$$

$$E_{D1}(\upsilon_{\iota+1}) = E_{D1}(\upsilon_0) + \frac{(1-l)}{M(l)}\left[G_8(E_{D1}(\upsilon_1),\upsilon_\iota)\right] + \frac{l}{M(l)}\sum_{j=0}^{\nu}(\frac{G_8(E_{D1}(\upsilon_1),\upsilon_\iota)}{\Gamma(\ell+2)}$$

$$\times \Delta^l[\ (\iota+1-\zeta)^l(\iota-\zeta+2+\ell)-(\iota-\zeta)^l(\iota-\zeta+2+2\ell)]$$

$$-\frac{G_8(E_{D1}(\upsilon_{\nu-1}),\upsilon_{\nu-1})}{\Gamma(\ell+2)}\Delta^l[(\iota+1-\zeta)^{l+1}-(\iota-\zeta)^l(\iota-\zeta+1+l)\ (33 \tag{33}$$

$$I_{D1}(\upsilon_{\iota+1}) = I_{D1}(\upsilon_0)+\frac{(1-l)}{M(l)}[G_9(I_{D1}(\upsilon_1),\upsilon_\iota)]+\frac{l}{M(l)}\sum_{j=0}^{\nu}(\frac{G_9(I_{D1}(\upsilon_1),\upsilon_\iota)}{\Gamma(\ell+2)}$$

$$\times\Delta^l[(\iota+1-\zeta)^l(\iota-\zeta+2+\ell)-(\iota-\zeta)^l(\iota-\zeta+2+2\ell)]$$

$$-\frac{G_9(I_{D1}(\upsilon_{\nu-1}),\upsilon_{\nu-1})}{\Gamma(\ell+2)}\Delta^l[(\iota+1-\zeta)^{l+1}-(\iota-\zeta)^l(\iota-\zeta+1+l) \tag{34}$$

$$S_{D2}(\upsilon_{\iota+1}) = S_{D2}(\upsilon_0)+\frac{(1-l)}{M(l)}[G_{10}(S_{D2}(\upsilon_1),\upsilon_\iota)]+\frac{l}{M(l)}\sum_{j=0}^{\nu}(\frac{G_{10}(S_{D2}(\upsilon_1),\upsilon_\iota)}{\Gamma(\ell+2)}$$

$$\times\Delta^l[(\iota+1-\zeta)^l(\iota-\zeta+2+\ell)-(\iota-\zeta)^l(\iota-\zeta+2+2\ell)]$$

$$-\frac{G_{10}(S_{D2}(\upsilon_{\nu-1}),\upsilon_{\nu-1})}{\Gamma(\ell+2)}\Delta^l[(\iota+1-\zeta)^{l+1}-(\iota-\zeta)^l(\iota-\zeta+1+l] \tag{35}$$

$$E_{D2}(\upsilon_{\iota+1}) = E_{D2}(\upsilon_0)+\frac{(1-l)}{M(l)}[G_{11}(E_{D2}(\upsilon_1),\upsilon_\iota)]+\frac{l}{M(l)}\sum_{j=0}^{\nu}(\frac{G_{11}(E_{D2}(\upsilon_1),\upsilon_\iota)}{\Gamma(\ell+2)}$$

$$\times\Delta^l[(\iota+1-\zeta)^l(\iota-\zeta+2+\ell)-(\iota-\zeta)^l(\iota-\zeta+2+2\ell)]$$

$$-\frac{G_{11}(E_{D2}(\upsilon_{\nu-1}),\upsilon_{\nu-1})}{\Gamma(\ell+2)}\Delta^l[(\iota+1-\zeta)^{l+1}-(\iota-\zeta)^l(\iota-\zeta+1+l)] \tag{36}$$

$$I_{D2}(\upsilon_{\iota+1}) = I_{D2}(\upsilon_0)+\frac{(1-l)}{M(l)}[G_{12}(I_{D2}(\upsilon_1),\upsilon_\iota)]+\frac{l}{M(l)}\sum_{j=0}^{\nu}(\frac{G_{12}(I_{D2}(\upsilon_1),\upsilon_\iota)}{\Gamma(\ell+2)}$$

$$\times\Delta^l[(\iota+1-\zeta)^l(\iota-\zeta+2+\ell)-(\iota-\zeta)^l(\iota-\zeta+2+2\ell)]$$

$$-\frac{G(I_{D2}(\upsilon_{\nu-1}),\upsilon_{\nu-1})}{\Gamma(\ell+2)}\Delta^l[(\iota+1-\zeta)^{l+1}-(\iota-\zeta)^l(\iota-\zeta+1+l) \tag{37}$$

NUMERICAL SIMULATION ANALYSIS AND OBSERVATIONS

We plot the numerical simulation results for several fractional orders and compare them with the data in Table 1, using the initial conditions from Sulayman et al. (2021).

Table 1. Parameters in Model 1 and their corresponding numerical values

Notation	Value	Source	Notation	Value	Source	Notation	Value	Source
γ_D	0.083333	[10]	γ_C	2.14286	[10]	η_D	4.28571	[10]
η_F	2.14286	[10]	μ_L	4.28571	[10]	μ_C	1.93548	[10]
μ_F	0.0151515	[10]	μ_D	0.00833	[10]	β_{LC}	6.6×10^{-6}	Fitting
β_{CF}	4.23×10^{-6}	Fitting	β_{FD}	2.06×10^{-6}	Fitting	ϕ_D	0.9	Fitting
θ_D	9×10^4	Fitting	N_D	2.51×10^4	Fitting	N_C	8×10^6	Fitting

To study the behavior of the model with the ABC operator, we trained a deep neural network with three hidden layers of 10, 100, and 10 neurons. The network was trained for 1,000 epochs using the Levenberg–Marquardt algorithm, which updates the weights to reduce the remaining error. We also used the fractional AB method to process the DNN output and generate approximate solutions based on the training data. Including the DNN in this framework improves both analysis and prediction. By adjusting the weights and reducing residual error, the network supports efficient training, validation, and testing, and helps capture the dynamic behavior of the water supply system.

The fractional Adams–Bashforth method complements this by handling the fractional-order differential equations, so that the numerical simulations agree with the DNN predictions. Together, the DNN and the fractional formulation give insight into the system's stability and convergence, which we confirm using regression analysis and error measures.

Figure 4a shows the DNN performance for $L(\nu)$ using the full dataset. The regression line has a slope very close to 1, which indicates strong agreement between the predictions and the true targets. The model achieves 0.02744 (MSE) and 0.16565 (RMSE). The corresponding EH reports mean/variance error (MVE) values of −0.0025377and 0.16565, which supports the validity of the approach. Figure 4b shows the results for the training subset of $L(\nu)$. The regression coefficient (RC) is still close to 1, and the errors are low: 0.0002926 (MSE) and 0.16657 (RMSE). The residual histogram (RH) gives MSE values of 0.0002926 and 0.1666, indicating consistent behavior on the training data. Figure 4c shows the test subset. The regression slope is again close to 1, with 0.026503 (MSE) and 0.1628 (RMSE). The associated histogram gives MVE values of −0.00016368and 0.16293, showing that the model keeps good predictive accuracy on unseen data. Figure 4d reports the validation subset for $L(\nu)$. Here, the regression coefficient is essentially 1, and the error levels are 0.02696 (MSE) and 0.1642 (RMSE). The histogram gives MVE values of 0.01572 and 0.16358, which supports the reliability of the method. Finally, Figure 4e directly compares the DNN output with the target values for $L(\nu)$, and Figure 4f shows the absolute prediction error.

Figure 4. Predicted dynamics for class L(ν) using the DNN. Subplots show: (i) the complete dataset, (ii) training samples, (iii) testing samples, (iv) the selected validation point, (v) a comparison between predictions and reference, and (vi) the corresponding autoencoder (AE) result.

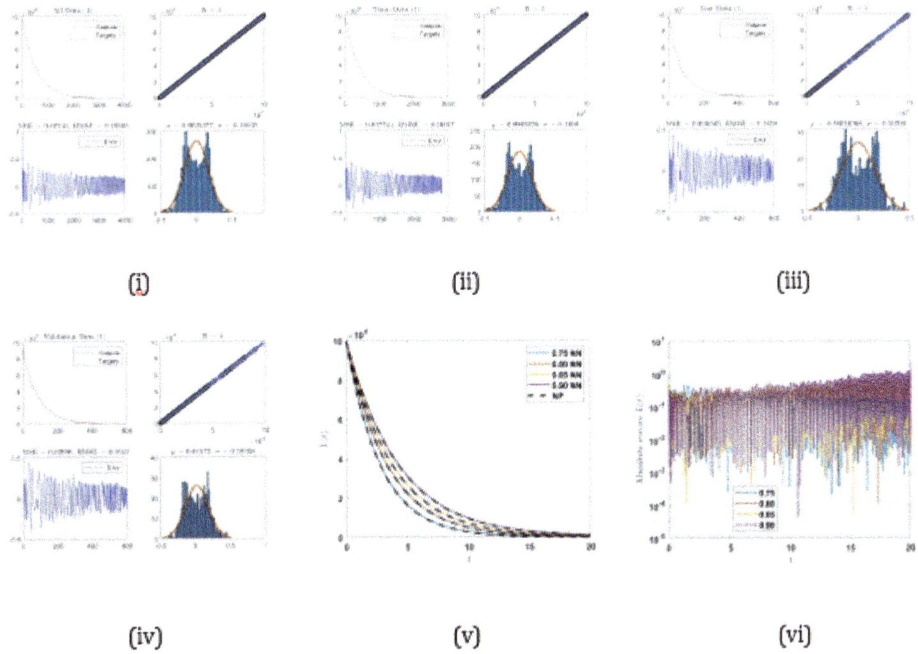

Figure 5. Predicted dynamics for class $S_C(\nu)$ using the DNN. Subplots show: (i) the complete dataset, (ii) training samples, (iii) testing samples, (iv) the selected validation point, (v) a comparison between predictions and reference, and (vi) the corresponding autoencoder (AE) result.

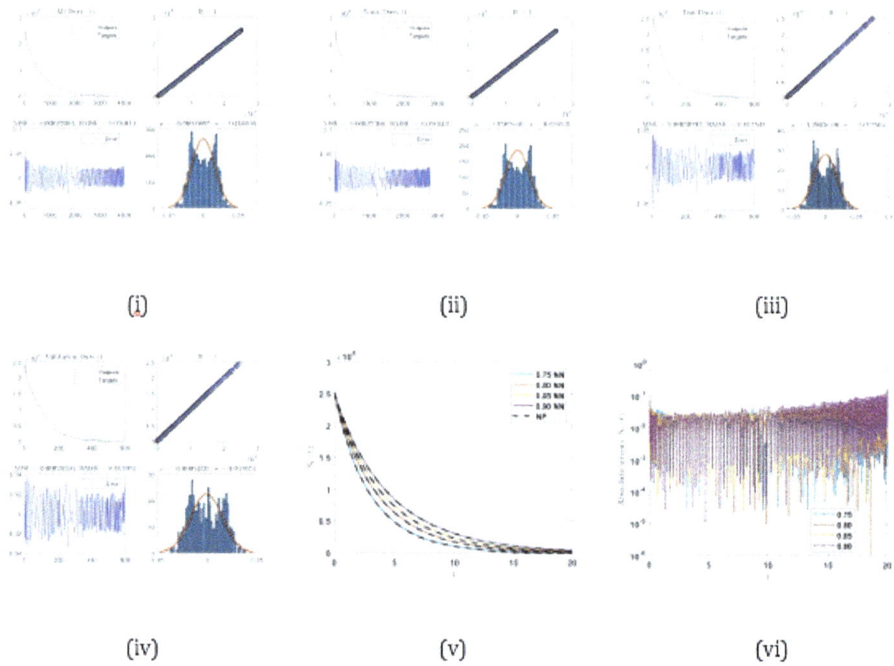

For the $E_C(\nu)$class in Figure 6a, the RC is equal to 1, with 0.13089 (MSE) and 0.36179 (RMSE). The corresponding EH reports MVE values of 0.0070981 and 0.36177, indicating close agreement between the predicted and target responses and supporting the accuracy of the method. Figure 6b shows the training subset for $E_C(\nu)$. In this case, the RC is 1. The DNN gives 0.12724 (MSE) and 0.35671 (RMSE). The RH reports MVE values of 0.0082833 and 0.35667, which indicates that the model behaves consistently on the training data. Figure 6c shows the test set. The regression slope is still essentially 1, with 0.14742 (MSE) and 0.38395 (RMSE). The corresponding histogram gives MVE values of 0.0034076 and 0.38426, showing that the model keeps good predictive accuracy on unseen data. Figure 6d presents the validation subset for $E_C(\nu)$. Here, the regression coefficient is again 1, and the errors are 0.13143 (MSE) and 0.36253 (RMSE). The EH gives MVE values of 0.0052556 and 0.3628, which supports the reliability of the method. Finally, Figure 6e compares the DNN predictions with the targets for $E_C(\nu)$, and Figure 6f shows the absolute prediction error.

Figure 6. Predicted dynamics for class $E_C(\nu)$ using the DNN. Subplots show: (i) the complete dataset, (ii) training samples, (iii) testing samples, (iv) the selected validation point, (v) a comparison between predictions and reference, and (vi) the corresponding autoencoder (AE) result.

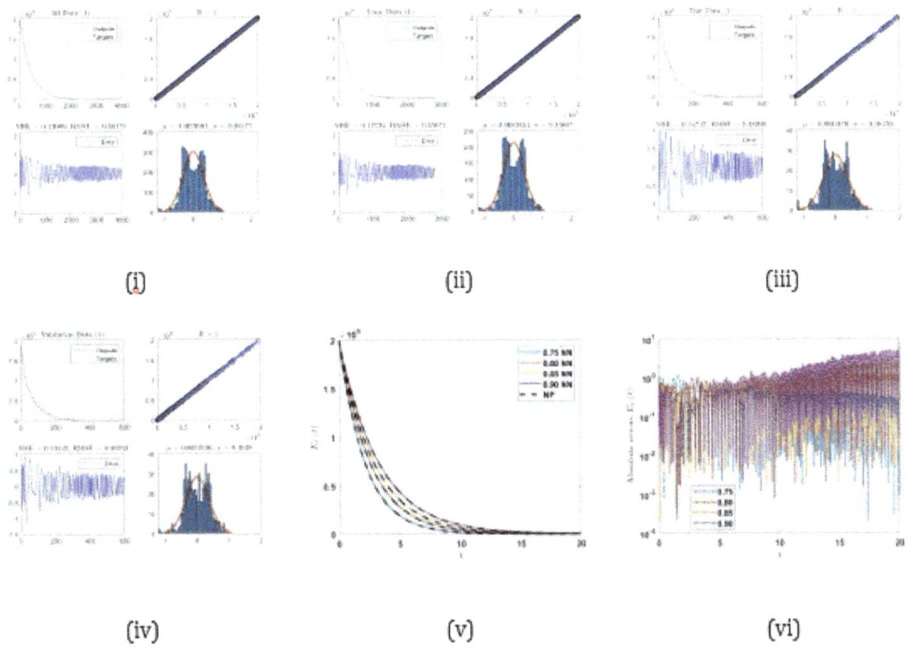

Figure 7a shows the DNN performance for $I_C(\nu)$ on the full dataset. The RC has a slope close to 1, which indicates very good agreement between the predicted and reference values. The model reaches 0.0037331 (MSE) and 0.061099 (RMSE). The corresponding EH reports MVE values of $8.3054 \times 10^{-4}$and 0.061101, supporting the validity of the method. Figure 7b shows the training subset for $I_C(\nu)$. Here, the RC is still close to 1, with 0.003636 (MSE) and 0.060299 (RMSE). The RH gives MVE values of $8.0252 \times 10^{-5}$and 0.06031, which suggests that the model behaves consistently on the training data. Figure 7c shows the test subset. The regression slope is again close to 1. The model yields 0.003961 (MSE) and 0.062937 (RMSE) . The associated histogram gives MVE values of 0.005644 and 0.062735, showing that the model keeps good predictive accuracy on unseen data. Figure 7d reports the validation subset for $I_C(\nu)$. In this case, the RC is effectively 1, and the error levels are 0.0039585 (MSE) and 0.062916 (RMSE). The EH shows MVE values of $-4.8034 \times 10^{-4}$and 0.062967, which supports the reliability of the approach. Finally, Figure 7e compares the DNN predictions with the target values for $I_C(\nu)$, and Figure 7f plots the absolute prediction error.

Figure 7. Predicted dynamics for class $I_C(\nu)$ using the DNN. Subplots show: (i) the complete dataset, (ii) training samples, (iii) testing samples, (iv) the selected validation point, (v) a comparison between predictions and reference, and (vi) the corresponding autoencoder (AE) result.

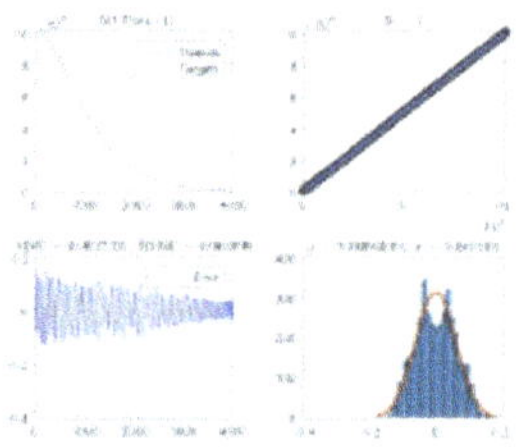

(i)

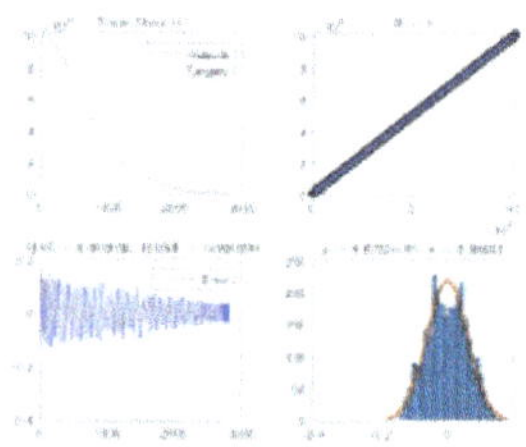

(ii)

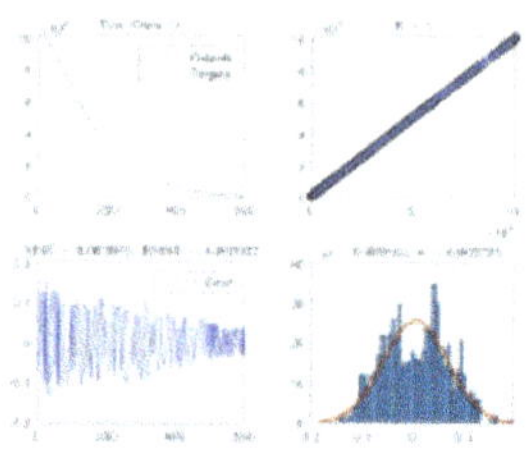

(iii)

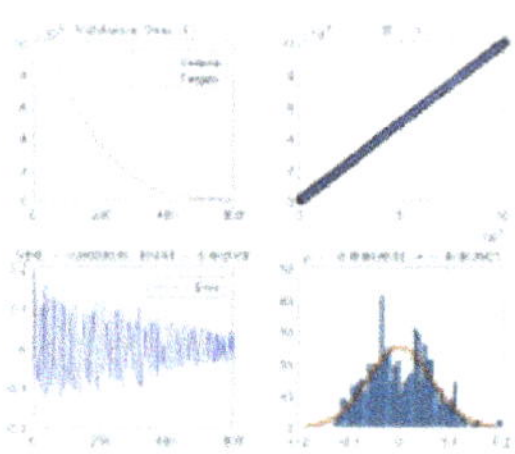

(iv)

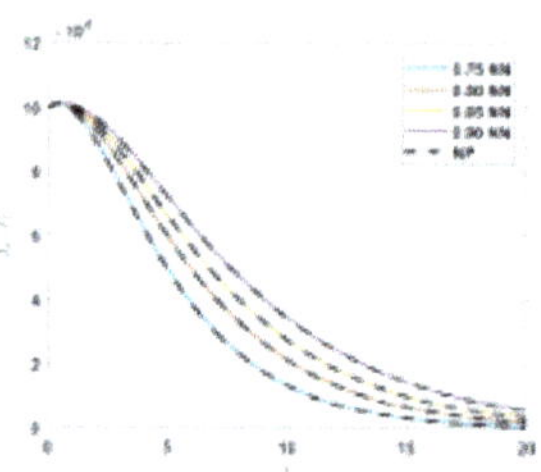

(v)

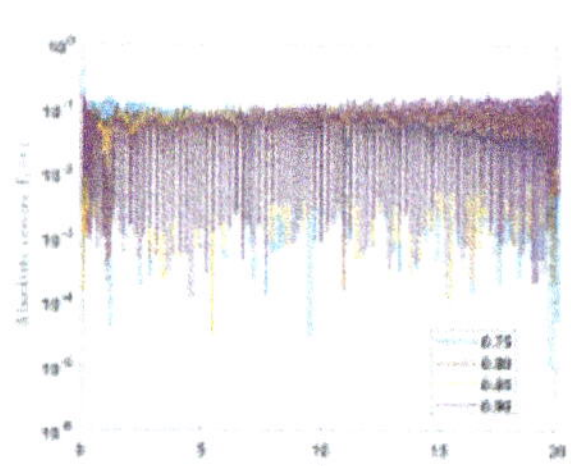

(vi)

Figure 8a shows the DNN performance for $S_F(\nu)$ using the full dataset. The regression line has a slope very close to 1, which indicates strong agreement between the predictions and the reference values. The model reports 0.0012918 (MSE) and 0.035942 (RMSE). The corresponding EH gives MVE values of $-2.2022 \times 10^{-4}$and 0.035946, supporting the accuracy of the method. Figure 8b focuses on the training subset for $S_F(\nu)$. Here, the RC is still close to 1, with 0.0012386 (MSE) and 0.035194 (RMSE). The RH shows MVE values of $3.3548 \times 10^{-6}$and 0.0352, which suggests that the model is consistent on the training data. Figure 8c shows the test subset. The RC remains close to 1, with 0.0015139 (RMSE) and 0.038909 (RMSE). The associated histogram reports MVE values of $-0.001334$and 0.038919, confirming that the model preserves good predictive accuracy on unseen data. Figure 8d presents the validation subset for $S_F(\nu)$. In this case, the RC is effectively 1. The error values are 0.0013181 (MSE) and 0.036305 (RMSE). The EH gives MVE values of $-1.5023 \times 10^{-4}$and 0.036335, further supporting the reliability of the approach. Finally, Figure 8e compares the network output with the target response for $S_F(\nu)$, and Figure 8f shows the absolute prediction error.

Figure 8. Predicted dynamics for class $S_F(\nu)$ using the DNN. Subplots show: (i) the complete dataset, (ii) training samples, (iii) testing samples, (iv) the selected validation point, (v) a comparison between predictions and reference, and (vi) the corresponding autoencoder (AE) result.

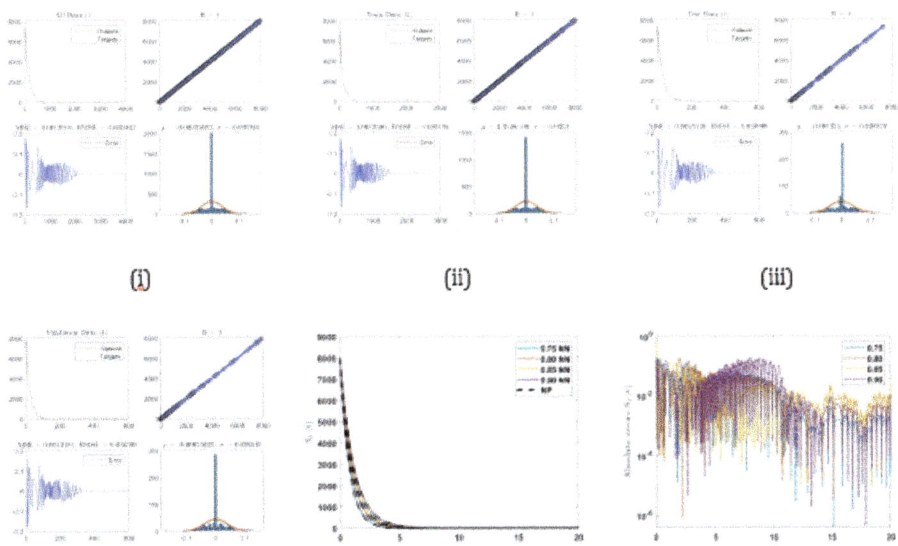

(i) (ii) (iii)

(iv) (v) (vi)

Figure 9a shows the DNN performance for $I_F(\nu)$ using all available data. The RC is 1, which means the model output matches the target values very closely. The model reports 3.8182×10^{-5} (MSE) and 6.1791×10^{-3} (RMSE). The associated EH gives MVE values of $4.2842 \times 10^{-4}$and 6.165×10^{-3}, supporting the accuracy of the method. Figure 9b shows the training subset for $I_F(\nu)$. Here again, the RC is 1. The DNN gives 3.8573×10^{-5}(MSE) and of 6.2107×10^{-3} (RMSE). The RH reports MVE values of $4.1513 \times 10^{-4}$and 6.198×10^{-3}, which indicates that the model behaves consistently on the training data. Figure 9c presents the test set. The regression slope remains essentially 1, with 3.6257×10^{-5}(MSE) and 6.0214×10^{-3} (RMSE). The associated histogram produces MVE values of $2.699 \times 10^{-4}$and 6.0204×10^{-3}, further demonstrating the predictive accuracy of the model on unseen data. Figure 9d reports the validation subset for $I_F(\nu)$. In this case, the RC is again 1, with 3.8277×10^{-5} (MSE) and 6.1868×10^{-3} (RMSE). The EH shows MVE values of $6.49 \times 10^{-4}$and 6.1578×10^{-3}, reinforcing the reliability of the proposed method.

Figure 9. Predicted dynamics for class $I_F(\nu)$ using the DNN. Subplots show: (i) the complete dataset, (ii) training samples, (iii) testing samples, (iv) the selected validation point, (v) a comparison between predictions and reference, and (vi) the corresponding autoencoder (AE) result.

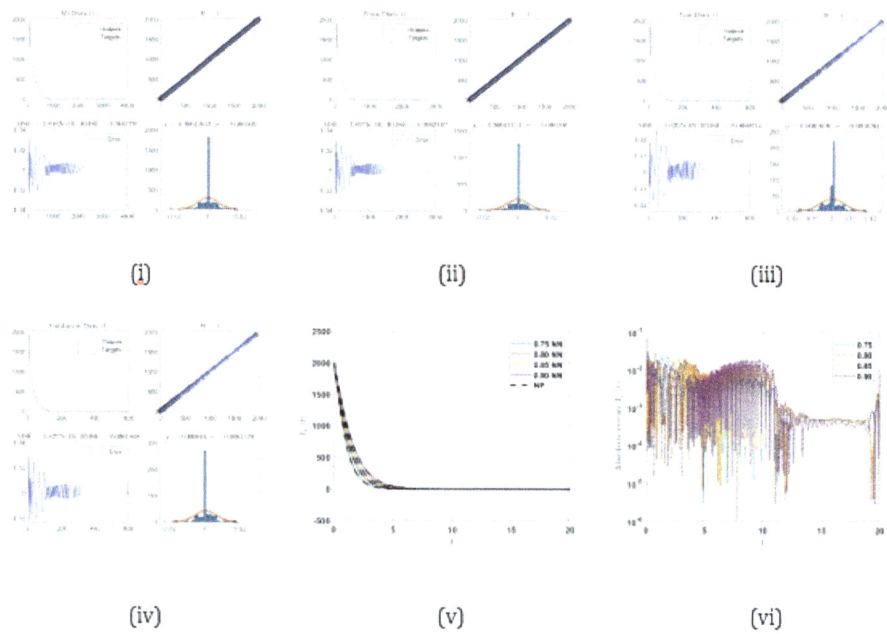

In Figure 10a, the entire $S_{D1}(\nu)$ dataset is modeled using the DNN. The fitted RC has slope 1, showing that the model output follows the target behavior very closely, 0.060625 (MSE) and 0.24622 (RMSE), respectively. The EH reports MVEs of −0.0016656and 0.24625, which supports the accuracy of the approach. Figure 10b then examines only the training data. For this subset, the RC remains equal to 1, with 0.059697 (MSE) and 0.24433 (RMSE). The histogram gives MVEs of −0.0031413and 0.24435, indicating that the technique performs reliably on the learned data. The test results are shown in Figure 10c. Here, the RC is still essentially 1. On the test set, the model achieves 0.059094 (MSE) and 0.24309 (RMSE). The EH reports MVE values of 0.002979 and 0.24328, which shows that the model keeps good accuracy on unseen samples. Figure 10d summarizes the validation results. In this case, the RC is again equal to 1, and the errors are 0.066484 (MSE) and 0.25785 (RMSE). The histogram gives MVE values of 0.00057857 and 0.25806, which further supports the reliability of the method. Figure 10e provides a direct comparison of the DNN prediction and the reference data for $S_{D1}(\nu)$, and Figure 10f shows the absolute error distribution.

Figure 11a summarizes the DNN evaluation for the $E_{D1}(\nu)$ class using the complete dataset. The fitted regression line has a slope essentially equal to 1, indicating excellent agreement between predicted and reference values. The model attains 5.2932×10^{-9} (MSE) and 7.2754×10^{-5} (RMSE). The EH reports MVE values of $-1.0113 \times 10^{-6}$and 7.2756×10^{-5}, which supports the validity of the method. Figure 11b shows the training subset for $E_{D1}(\nu)$. In this case, the RC remains close to 1. The model gives 3.3761×10^{-9} (MSE) and 5.8104×10^{-5}(RMSE). The corresponding histogram reports MVE values of $4.4528 \times 10^{-7}$and 5.8113×10^{-5}, indicating stable behavior on the training data. Figure 11c reports the test results. The RC is again close to 1. The network yields 1.7643×10^{-8} (MSE) and 1.3283×10^{-4} (RMSE). The EH gives MVE values of $-7.4753 \times 10^{-6}$and 1.3273×10^{-4}, which shows that the model maintains good predictive accuracy on unseen data. Figure 11d presents the validation results for $E_{D1}(\nu)$. Here, the RC is effectively 1, with errors of 1.8932×10^{-9}(MSE) and 4.3511×10^{-5}(RMSE). The EH reports MVE values of $-1.3469 \times 10^{-6}$and 4.3527×10^{-5}, reinforcing the robustness of the proposed approach. Finally, Figure 11e directly compares the DNN predictions with the reference response for $E_{D1}(\nu)$, and Figure 11f presents the absolute prediction error.

Figure 10. Predicted dynamics for class $S_{D1}(\nu)$ using the DNN. Subplots show: (i) the complete dataset, (ii) training samples, (iii) testing samples, (iv) the selected validation point, (v) a comparison between predictions and reference, and (vi) the corresponding autoencoder (AE) result.

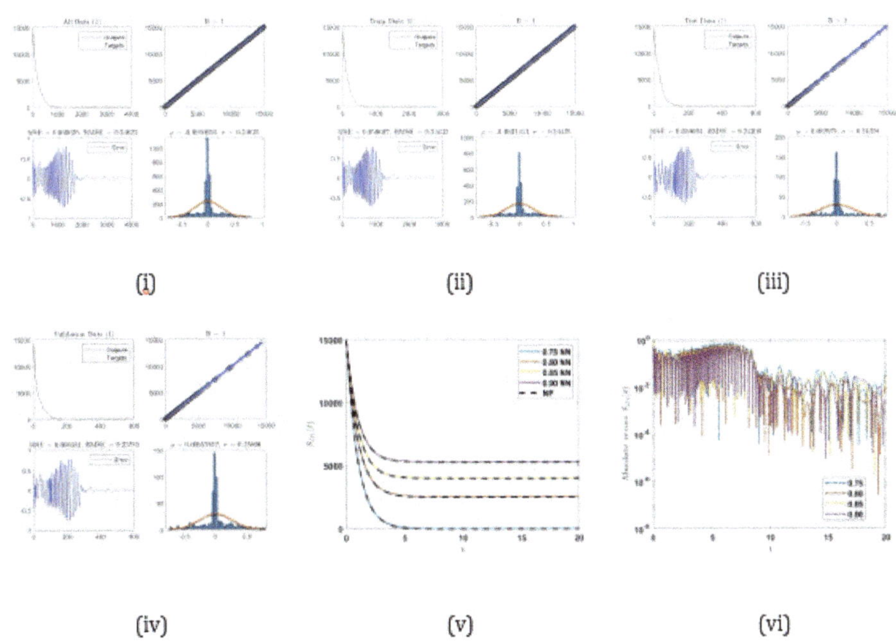

In Figure 12a, the entire $I_{D1}(\nu)$ dataset is evaluated with the DNN. The RC is essentially one, which means the model output closely follows the target response. The network achieves 1.8764×10^{-7} (MSE) and 4.3318×10^{-4} (RMSE). The EH reports MVEs of -4.2244×10^{-6} and 4.3321×10^{-4}, indicating good accuracy. Figure 12b shows the training subset. For these data, the DNN again gives a RC close to unity, with 1.8265×10^{-7} (MSE) and 4.2737×10^{-4} (RMSE). The EH indicates MVEs of -2.9458×10^{-6} and 4.2744×10^{-4}, suggesting stable behavior on the training data. The test set, shown in Figure 12c, also maintains a near-unity regression slope. The model produces 2.0366×10^{-7} (MSE) and 4.5129×10^{-4} (RMSE). The EH gives MVEs of -1.4828×10^{-5} and 4.5142×10^{-4}, supporting the conclusion that the method generalizes. Figure 12d reports performance on the validation data. Here, the RC is effectively one, 1.9495×10^{-7} (MSE) and 4.4154×10^{-4} (RMSE). The histogram returns MVEs of 4.1056×10^{-7} and 4.419×10^{-4}, giving further evidence of method reliability. Finally, Figure 12e plots target vs. predicted response for I_{D1} (ν), and Figure 12f visualizes the

Figure 11. Predicted dynamics for class $E_{DI}(\nu)$ using the DNN. Subplots show: (i) the complete dataset, (ii) training samples, (iii) testing samples, (iv) the selected validation point, (v) a comparison between predictions and reference, and (vi) the corresponding autoencoder (AE) result.

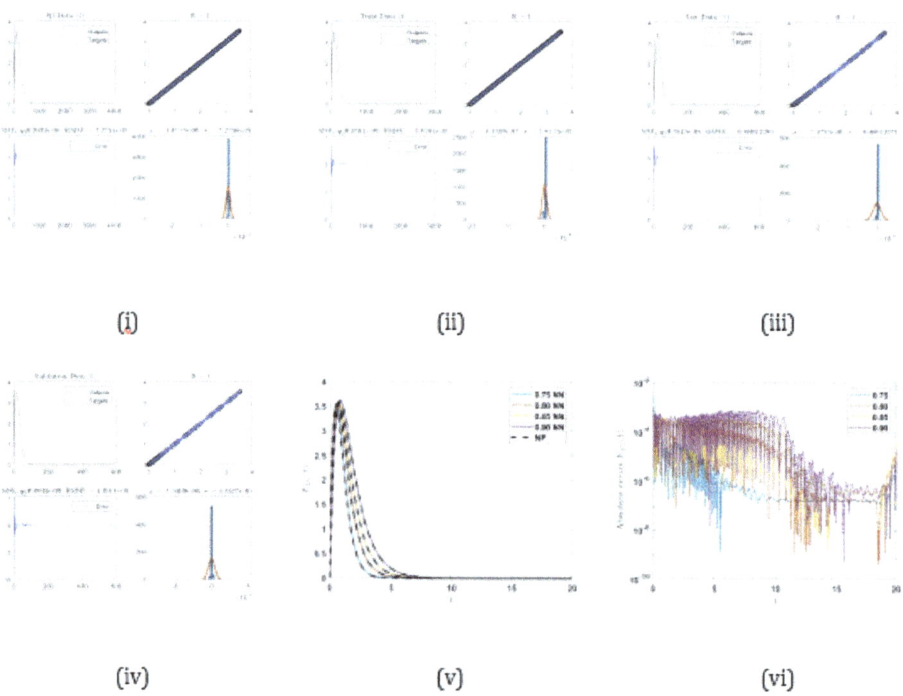

Figure 12. Predicted dynamics for class $I_{D1}(\nu)$ using the DNN. Subplots show: (i) the complete dataset, (ii) training samples, (iii) testing samples, (iv) the selected validation point, (v) a comparison between predictions and reference, and (vi) the corresponding autoencoder (AE) result.

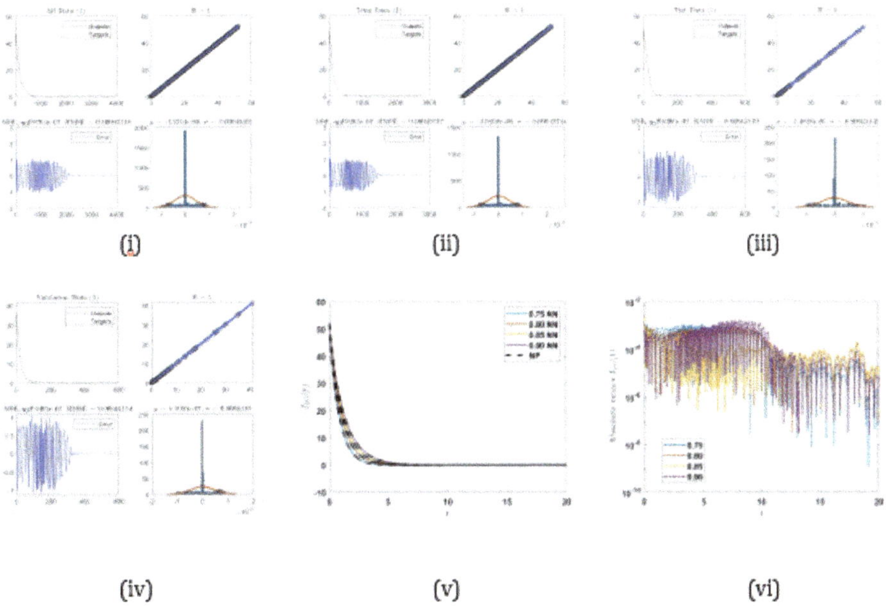

In Figure 13a, the full $S_{D2}(\nu)$set is evaluated with the DNN. The fitted regression line has slope 1, which shows that predicted values closely match the reference data. The model reports 3.3592×10^{-7} (MSE) and of 5.7959×10^{-4} (RMSE). The EH gives MVE values of $-8.9831 \times 10^{-6}$and 5.7959×10^{-4}, which indicates high accuracy. Figure 13b shows the training data only. In this case, the RC is again 1. The DNN achieves 3.2994×10^{-7}(MSE) and 5.744×10^{-4} (RMSE). The EH reports MVE values of $2.2615 \times 10^{-7}$and 5.745×10^{-4}, showing that the method performs consistently on the training set. Figure 13c presents the test results. The RC is still essentially 1. The network produces 3.4257×10^{-7} (MSE) and 5.8529×10^{-4} (RMSE). The corresponding histogram shows MVE values of $1.2636 \times 10^{-6}$and 5.8578×10^{-4}, supporting the model's accuracy on unseen data. For the validation subset (Figure 13d), the RC is again 1. The errors are 3.5721×10^{-7}(MSE) and 5.9767×10^{-4}(RMSE). The EH gives MVE values of $-6.2222 \times 10^{-5}$and 5.9492×10^{-4}, providing further evidence that the approach is reliable. Finally, Figure 13e compares the network output with the target response for $S_{D2}(\nu)$, and Figure 13f shows the absolute error distribution.

Figure 14a shows the full $E_{D2}(\nu)$ dataset evaluated with the DNN. The regression slope is essentially 1, which means the predicted output closely matches the target response. The network reports 6.746×10^{-10}(MSE) and 2.5973×10^{-5} (RMSE). The EH gives MVE values of $-4.3116 \times 10^{-7}$and 2.5973×10^{-5}, supporting the fidelity of the model. Figure 14b shows the training subset. Here, the regression fit is still almost ideal, 6.5076×10^{-10} (MSE) and 2.551×10^{-5}(RMSE). The histogram reports MVE values of $2.9632 \times 10^{-7}$and 2.5513×10^{-5}, which suggests that the approach is stable on the training data. The test set behavior is shown in Figure 14c. The RC again stays close to one, with 7.2951×10^{-10} (MSE) and 2.7009×10^{-5} (RMSE). The corresponding histogram reports MVEs of $-2.309 \times 10^{-6}$and 2.6933×10^{-5}, providing additional evidence that the model predictions remain accurate on unseen data. Validation results are summarized in Figure 14d. In this case, the slope of the regression is effectively unity, and the errors are 7.3099×10^{-10}(MSE) and 2.7037×10^{-5}(RMSE). The EH shows MVEs of $-1.9495 \times 10^{-6}$and 2.6989×10^{-5}, which supports the reliability of the technique. Finally, Figure 14e overlays the network output and the reference values for $E_{D2}(\nu)$, and Figure 14f plots the absolute deviation.

Figure 13. Predicted dynamics for class $S_{D2}(\nu)$ using the DNN. Subplots show: (i) the complete dataset, (ii) training samples, (iii) testing samples, (iv) the selected validation point, (v) a comparison between predictions and reference, and (vi) the corresponding autoencoder (AE) result.

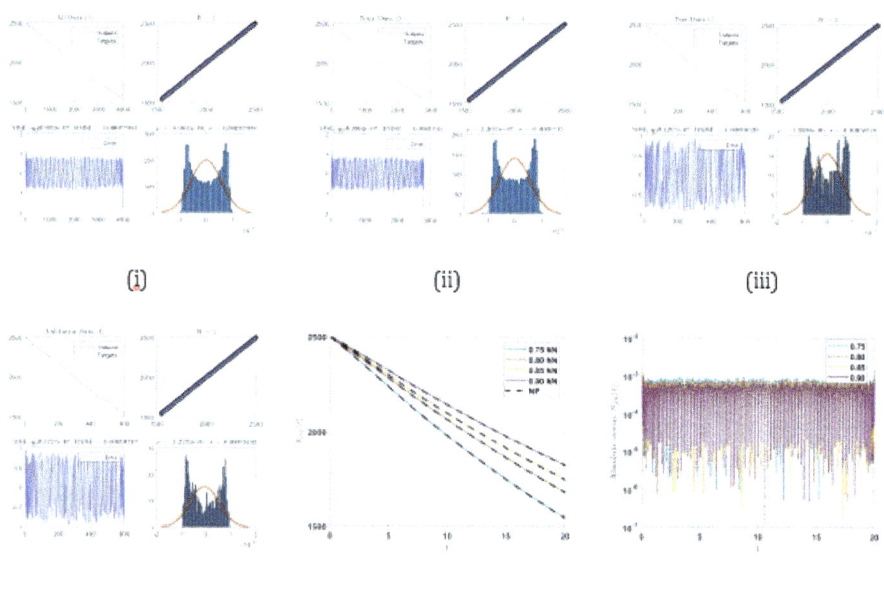

In Figure 15a, the full $I_{D2}(\nu)$ dataset is evaluated with the DNN. The predicted values align closely with the reference values: the RC has slope ≈ 1, 4.558×10^{-8} (MSE), and 2.1349×10^{-4} (RMSE). The HR yields MVE values of $-5.8712 \times 10^{-8}$and 2.1352×10^{-4}, showing that the error is very small. Figure 15b shows only the training data passed through the same network. The RC again stays near unity, with 4.3826×10^{-8}(MSE) and 2.0935×10^{-4}(RMSE). The RH gives $-3.4718 \times 10^{-7}$and $2.0938 \times 10^{-4}$for the MVE, indicating that the method is consistent on the data it was trained on. For the test set (Figure 15c), the regression slope remains close to 1. The network attains 5.0936×10^{-8} (MSE) and 2.2569×10^{-4} (RMSE). The corresponding histogram reports MVE values of $4.9936 \times 10^{-6}$and 2.2582×10^{-4}, demonstrating good generalization. Figure 15d reports the validation set, for which the RC is essentially 1, 4.8412×10^{-8} (MSE), and 2.2003×10^{-4} (RMSE). The histogram MVE is $-3.7643 \times 10^{-6}$and 2.2018×10^{-4}, which further supports the reliability of the approach. Finally, Figure 15e compares the DNN output and the reference response for $I_{D2}(\nu)$, and Figure 15f visualizes the absolute error.

Figure 14. Predicted dynamics for class $E_{D2}(\nu)$ using the DNN. Subplots show: (i) the complete dataset, (ii) training samples, (iii) testing samples, (iv) the selected validation point, (v) a comparison between predictions and reference, and (vi) the corresponding autoencoder (AE) result.

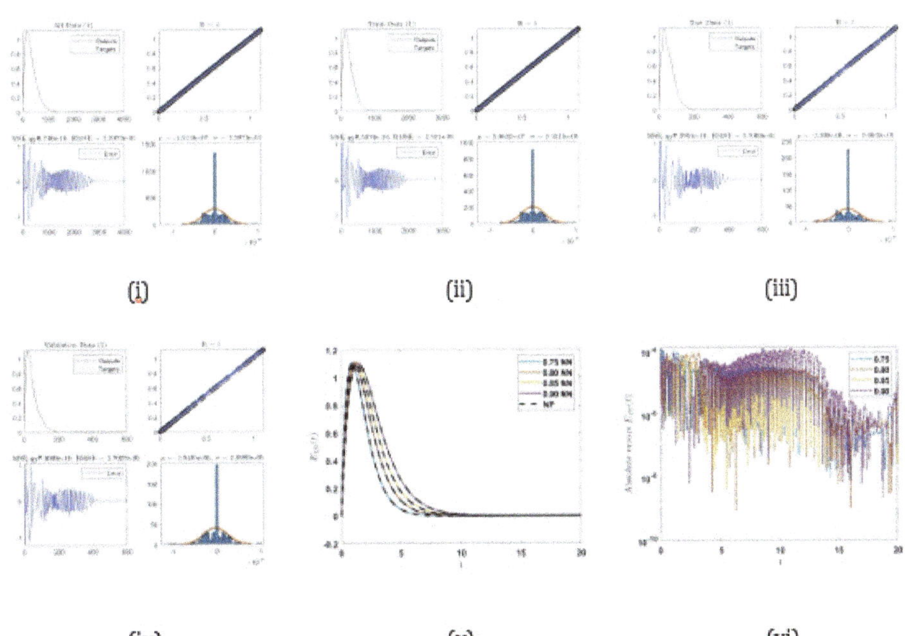

CONCLUSION

This study develops a twelve-compartment Guinea worm model under a generalized ABC fractional operator, proving existence and uniqueness via fixed-point theory, establishing Ulam–Hyers stability, and computing approximate solutions with an Adams–Bashforth scheme cross checked against the Laplace–Adomian approach. Comparative analyses with integer-order dynamics indicate a disproportionate burden among adults; lower fractional orders yield more precise, stable trajectories, whereas higher orders amplify transmission and generate more complex behavior. A DNN pipeline partitions data for training/validation/testing to probe signal structure and generalization. Importantly, these results translate into practice: prioritize adult-focused risk reduction at worksites and water-collection points (reliable safe water access, routine pipe/cloth filter distribution and replacement, and targeted education during peak labor periods); calibrate intervention intensity to local "memory" in transmission standard case containment and filtration in lower-order (stable) settings versus surge strategies with short-interval active surveillance, rapid response, and intensified vector control in higher-order (amplified) settings; and use the model's time-step sensitivity for calendar-based planning to pre-position resources before anticipated spikes, supported by DNN-enabled hotspot detection and adherence monitoring. Collectively, the framework offers an analytically grounded policy sandbox for ministries and partners to compare mixes of safe water provision, filtration campaigns, case containment, and vector control under uncertainty, thereby guiding where to focus effort, how hard to push, and when to act.

Figure 15. Predicted dynamics for class $I_{D2}(\upsilon)$ using the DNN. Subplots show: (a) the complete dataset, (b) training samples, (c) testing samples, (d) the selected validation point, (e) a comparison between predictions and reference, and (f) the corresponding autoencoder (AE) result.

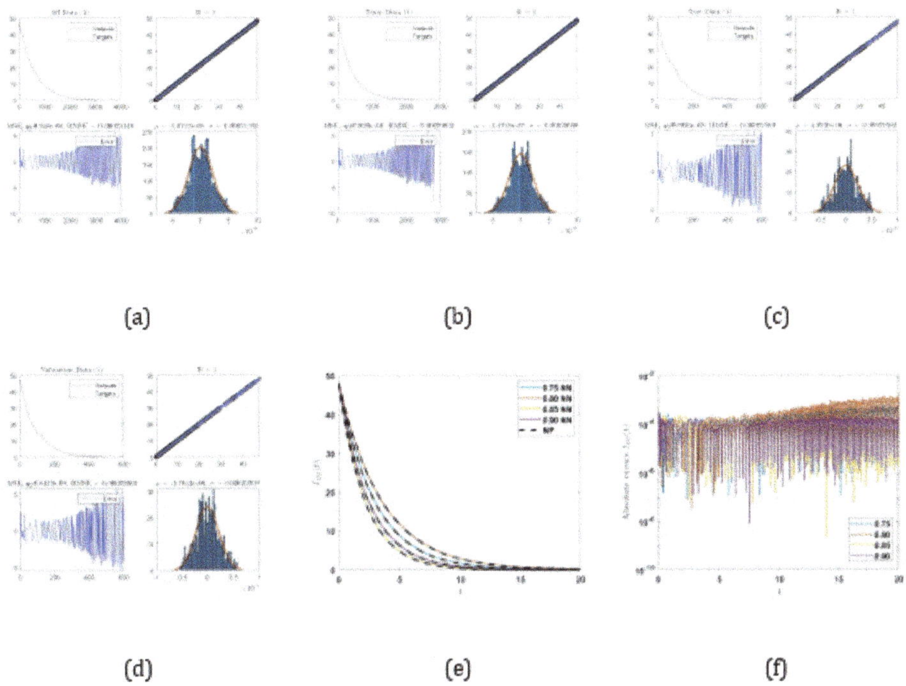

FUTURE DIRECTIONS

Extend the framework to more generalized fractional operators and heterogeneous contact structures (e.g., age/occupation stratification and spatial coupling of villages and water sources); integrate operational constraints such as logistics, adherence, and cost to produce implementation-ready decision tools; link real-time surveillance feeds to the DNN module for automated anomaly detection and micro-targeting; evaluate optimal control policies

that jointly schedule filtration, water-source protection, larvicide (where appropriate), and case-containment resources under budget limits; and validate the model prospectively with field data to refine parameter estimates, calibrate fractional-order selection to local transmission memory, and quantify the thresholds that should trigger escalation from baseline to surge interventions.

REFERENCES

Abuasbeh, K., Shafqat, R., Alsinai, A., & Awadalla, M. (2023). Analysis of the mathematical modelling of COVID-19 by using mild solution with delay Caputo operator. *Symmetry*, *15*(2), 286.

Al-Quran, A., Shafqat, R., Alsaadi, A., & Djaouti, A. M. (2025). Poliomyelitis dynamics with fractional order derivatives and deep neural networks. *Scientific Reports*, *15*(1), 32023.

Belsare, A., & Vanak, A. T. (2020). Modelling the challenges of managing free-ranging dog populations. *Scientific Reports*, *10*(1), 18874.

Boyce, M. R., Carlin, E. P., Schermerhorn, J., & Standley, C. J. (2020). A one health approach for guinea worm disease control: Scope and opportunities. *Tropical Medicine and Infectious Disease*, *5*(4), 159.

Engelhard, C. A. G., Hodgkins, A. P., Pearl, E. E., & Spears, P. K., Rychtáˇr, J., and Taylor, D. (2021). A mathematical model of Guinea worm disease in Chad with fish as intermediate transport hosts. *Journal of Theoretical Biology*, *521*, 110683.

Ghosh, I., Tiwari, P. K., Mandal, S., Martcheva, M., & Chattopadhyay, J. (2018). A mathematical study to control Guinea worm disease: A case study on Chad. *Journal of Biological Dynamics*, *12*(1), 846–871.

Goodwin, C. E., Léchenne, M., Wilson-Aggarwal, J. K., Koumetio, S. M., Swan, G. J., Moundai, T., & McDonald, R. A. (2022). Seasonal fishery facilitates a novel transmission pathway in an emerging animal reservoir of Guinea worm. *Current Biology*, *32*(4), 775–782.

Guagliardo, S. A. J., Roy, S. L., Ruiz-Tiben, E., Zirimwabagabo, H., Romero, M., Chop, E., & Weiss, A. J. (2020). Guinea worm in domestic dogs in Chad: A description and analysis of surveillance data. *PLoS Neglected Tropical Diseases*, *14*(5), e0008207.

Helikumi, M., & Mushayabasa, S. (2023). Dog screening as a novel complementary guinea worm disease control tool to mitigate persistence in Chad: A modeling study. *Parasite Epidemiology and Control*, *23*, e00328.

Pellegrino, C., Patti, G., Camporeale, M., Belati, A., Novara, R., Papagni, R., & Di Gennaro, F. (2022). Guinea worm disease: A neglected diseases on the verge of eradication. *Tropical Medicine and Infectious Disease*, *7*(11), 366.

Reese, J. F. (2005). Dogs and dog control in developing countries.

Roberts, L. (2019). Exclusive: Battle to wipe out debilitating Guinea worm parasite hits 10 year delay. *Nature*, *574*(7777), 157–159.

Shafqat, R., & Alsaadi, A. (2024). Artificial neural networks for stability analysis and simulation of delayed rabies spread models. *AIMS Mathematics*, *9*(12), 33495–33531.

Shafqat, R., & Alsaadi, A. (2025). Mathematical and numerical analysis of a fractional SIQR epidemic model with normalized Caputo–Fabrizio operator and machine learning approaches. *AIMS Mathematics*, *10*(9), 20235–20261.

Shafqat, R., Alsaadi, A., & Alubaidi, A. (2025). A Fractional-Order Alcoholism Model Incorporating Hypothetical Social Influence: A Theoretical and Numerical Study. *Journal of Mathematics*, *2025*(1), 6773909.

Turab, A., Montoyo, A., & Nescolarde-Selva, J. A. (2024). Computational and analytical analysis of integral-differential equations for modeling avoidance learning behavior. *Journal of Applied Mathematics & Computing*, *70*(5), 4423–4439.

Turab, A., Nescolarde-Selva, J. A., Ullah, F., Montoyo, A., Alfiniyah, C., Sintunavarat, W., & Zaidi, S. A. (2025). Deep neural networks and stochastic methods for cognitive modeling of rat behavioral dynamics in T-mazes. *Cognitive Neurodynamics*, *19*(1), 1–28.

Turab, A., Rosli, N., Ali, W., & Nieto, J. J. (2023). The existence and uniqueness of solutions to a functional equation arising in psychological learning theory. *Demonstratio Mathematica*, *56*(1), 20220231.

Turab, A., Shafqat, R., Muhammad, S., Shuaib, M., Khan, M. F., & Kamal, M. (2024). Predictive modeling of hepatitis B viral dynamics: A caputo derivative-based approach using artificial neural networks. *Scientific Reports*, *14*(1), 21853.

Vinson, J. E., Park, A. W., Cleveland, C. A., Yabsley, M. J., Ezenwa, V. O., & Hall, R. J. (2021). Alternative transmission pathways for guinea worm in dogs: Implications for outbreak risk and control. *International Journal for Parasitology*, *51*(12), 1027–1034.

Chapter 8
Detecting Deceptive Behavior in Online Chess: A Machine Learning Approach

Yanyu Chen
Xi'an Jiaotong-Liverpool University, China

Yijian Che
Xi'an Jiaotong-Liverpool University, China

Md Maruf Hasan
Xi'an Jiaotong-Liverpool University, China

Affan Yasin
https://orcid.org/0000-0002-0166-2239
Xi'an Jiaotong-Liverpool University, Suzhou, China

ABSTRACT

Online chess tournaments face persistent threats from engine-assisted cheating, undermining fair competition. This study evaluates six machine learning models - Support Vector Machine (SVM), Random Forest, Decision Tree, Logistic Regression, Naive Bayes, and Long Short-Term Memory (LSTM) - to detect suspicious behaviors such as abnormal move timing, high accuracy, and sudden rating changes. Using the Chess Cheating Dataset under simulated tournament conditions, the Random Forest model achieved the highest accuracy (76.15%), followed by SVM (74.90%) and LSTM (75.78%). While ensemble methods provided strong overall performance, interpretable models like Decision Trees and temporal models like LSTM offered distinct advantages. The findings suggest that combining multiple approaches may enhance detection reliability in online chess.

DOI: 10.4018/979-8-3373-5062-2.ch008

INTRODUCTION

Fair play is the essence of chess; the outcome of games is dependent on the skills, tactics, and behaviour of the players (Laarhoven & Ponukumati, 2022). The advent of the on-line medium has, however created new opportunities for fixing of games. To-day, due to various technological improvements, certain players can use assistance from outside sources, notably strong engines, to gain an illegal advantage (Barnes & Hernandez-Castro, 2015). Such practices not only impede fairness in competition, but sap confidence in the game, whether it is practised on the board, or on-line (Laurens et al., 2007). Recent scandals of considerable prominence have disclosed the inadequacy of existing safeguards (Barnes & Hernandez-Castro, 2015). Tactics such as discreetly advising with engines, or by means of secure communications often elude routine detection (Zaksaitė, 2022). In the electronic arena, however, the situation becomes more acute because physical absence and anonymity on the net precludes the application of tests which are normally effective against tampering. It becomes imperative, therefore, to develop future methods of detection of a more sophisticated nature. It becomes necessary to bridge these gaps if we are to preserve fairness in the game. Effective detection measures, together with effective deterrents should tend to preserve confidence of players and supply a healthy competitive environment (Zaksaitė, 2022). It is absolutely essential to understand all forms of complex behaviour (Turab et al. 2022), whether in the animal kingdom or the human species, it is necessary to have the combination of the rigid precision of the computer and the adaptive qualities of man (Turab & Maliki et al., 2024). The various improvements in deep learning and analytic type of modelling in recent years, has enabled men of research to break down the more complex types of behaviour, and the processes of thinking and imaginary in the decisional processes with greater trepidation (Turab & Montoyo et al. 2024). Provided one can at the same time incorporate the deterministic nature of mathematical models with the data driven approaches of algorithmic functions (Turab et al. 2025), it becomes possible to conduct an examination of the complexity to conduct actual physical analysis, prediction, and interpret the success of dynamic behaviour occurring in experimental or natural situations.

This research proposal warrants an investigation into the potential of machine learning functions to detect, interalia cheating in chess tournaments, through the detection of irregularities in data. This is quire apart from the fact that the kaggle chess cheating database will not necessarily embrace all forms of cheating. By effectively making use of this openly published data base, which gives instances of labelled cheating, and extensive requirements of procedures followed in detail, it will be possible to construct models that can detect irregularities in forms of patterns on the basis of certain criteria such as move accuracy, time differentiations, and behaviour patterns away from the expected norms of a player. It is be made relevant to the study becuase it will restrict the study in question to Examination texts of chess tournament data-set. It is the hope of the writers that other researchers may subsequently pursue the idea of the potential of extending this study to embrace other types of games or platforms, provided usable data can be procured.

- **Research Goals**
  - Compare the performance of 6 different algorithms including support vector machines, random forests, decision trees, logistic regression, long short term memory and naive bayes for the detection of anomalous behaviours of players in chess tournaments.
  - Identify the features which best identify when possible cheating has occurred. For example movement time, accuracy biases
  - Evaluate strategy effectiveness based on standard performance metrics in order to ascertain which detection strategy is the most efficacious.
  - Provide a foundation for future work including possible use of this method in other gaming environments or with a different data set.

LITERATURE REVIEW

The rapid advancement of digital gaming has spawned new forms of misconduct that impair competitive fairness, lower player satisfaction and threaten the financial viability of the games (Saarinen, 2017). To address these problems, researchers are increasingly employing machine learning tools, which have better accuracy and scalability than human supervision and plainly rules-driven approaches. The following survey will describe the present state of research in in-game fraud, noting the prevalent cheating methods, long-standing countermeasures and the latest solutions driven by machine learning.

1. Types of Cheating Behaviours

Online gaming exposes system vulnerabilities that can be exploited by illegal players to gain an unfair advantage. Yan & Randell, 2005 and Flynn et al., 2024 identified four main cheating strategies:

a. Modifying the client infrastructure

This approach can change the game client's environment, such as device drivers, without touching the core program or its settings. For example, an attacker might tweak a graphics driver to make walls transparent, thus revealing hidden opponents (Yan & Randell, 2005). This method known as a "wall hack," is commonly used to gain visual advantages in certain online games.

b. Timing Cheating

Timing manipulation is another strategy used by cheaters in real- time games. By delaying their own moves until they can observe opponents' actions, cheaters can make decisions with full knowledge of opponents' moves, which grants them an unfair advantage. This looks ahead cheat disrupts game fairness by skewing reactions in favor of the cheater (Yan & Randell, 2005). Another form of timing manipulation, the "suppress correct" cheat, allows players to gain an edge by strategically dropping update messages to control outcomes (Yan & Randell, 2005; Yeung & Lui, 2008).

c. Aim-bot/Trigger Bot

Aim-bots and trigger bots are cheats that automate the aiming process, ensuring near perfect accuracy by automatically targeting enemies or firing when the cross-hairs are over an opponent. This type of cheat negates the skill required for precision aiming, making combat unbalanced and removing the challenge and satisfaction associated with landing difficult shots. Since aiming is a core mechanic in many games, this cheat can severely diminish the experience for other players (Flynn et al., 2024).

d. Extra Sensory Perception (ESP)

ESP cheats reveal information that would normally require effort or strategic insight to obtain, such as an opponent's life value, location, or equipment. By eliminating the need for reconnaissance and planning, these cheats grant players an unfair advantage and dramatically increase their chances of winning. Targets of ESP violations are often extremely frustrated because such exploits undermine the fundamentals of fair play and disrupt the immersive experience of the game (Flynn et al., 2024).

These cheats are among the most pervasive and destructive forms of misconduct in online games. Each of these cheating behaviors alters the core mechanics of the game, enabling the offender to circumvent the challenges deliberately set in the game. As a result, competitive balance is weakened and the fun and integrity of the game environment is further compromised.

2. Application of Techniques in Chess Cheating Detection

Cheating, both on the board (OTB) and online, has become a major challenge for modern chess. A number of high-profile cheating incidents have forced organizers to tighten regulations, banning the use of cell phones, installing metal detectors, and conducting full- body searches in extreme cases, yet some resourceful players still find covert ways to avoid detection (Barnes & Hernandez-Castro, 2015).

a. Predictive Analytics Methods

Regan's research demonstrates how predictive analytics can identify suspicious chess games (Regan & Haworth, 2011). His system evaluates a player's moves based on historical data from players whose engine recommendations are comparable to the Elo rating. In tournaments, large deviations can trigger alerts. Nonetheless, Barnes et al. observe that pure engine comparisons sometimes miss subtle, contextually relevant decisions, leaving some undetected misbehavior (Barnes & Hernandez-Castro, 2015).

b. Legal and Ethical Dimensions

FIDE's Code of Ethics (CoE) provides a formal basis for penalizing dishonest behavior (Zaksaitė, 2020). However, Zaksaitė argues that sanctions remain uneven due to differences in the interpretation and application of these rules across federations. Therefore, the development of a coherent cross-coalition policy is crucial (Zaksaitė, 2020).

c. Hardware Assisted Screening

New scanning equipment enhances site security. Linear scanners can locate metallic objects, while nonlinear scanners expose hidden electronic devices, such as miniature headphones, by sensing characteristic materials not visible to the naked eye (Zaksaitė, 2022). While these tools are effective, they require specialized interpretation and may raise privacy or fairness concerns from competitors.

d. Software Driven Detection

Major online platforms are increasingly relying on artificial intelligence models and large-scale data analytics. For example, Chess.com trains probabilistic models over millions of games to estimate how well a player's moves match the engine lines; flagged cases are manually reviewed to minimize false positives (Iliescu, 2020).

Research teams have also begun experimenting with advanced systems such as DeepMind's MuZero to capture complex tactical patterns with near perfect fidelity to further enhance preventative measures (Iliescu, 2020).

e. Future Directions

Cutting-edge hardware and sophisticated software raise the bar for would be cheaters, but there is no single solution that balances accuracy, transparency, and scalability. Next generation frameworks should integrate predictive analytics, legal guidance, and technical screening into a coherent global strategy. Only by harmonizing technical, ethical, and legal perspectives will the chess community be able to maintain competitive fairness at all levels (Zaksaitė, 2022).

3. RESEARCH GAP

Table 3 at the end in the Appendix expands on these gaps. Recent research has shown a decisive shift in cheat detection research for online gaming and chess, from static rule-based heuristics to sophisticated machine learning and deep learning processes. Combining behavioral telemetry with game history metrics and engine evaluation has certainly improved detection accuracy, but four insurmountable obstacles remain open:

a. Accuracy and Reliability

False alarms and omissions still exist, especially when algorithms are based on fragmented records or judge each game individually.

b. Privacy

Many systems sift through sensitive player data, so there is a trade-off between depth of investigation and data protection (privacy).

c. Real-time Detection

Fast-changing, highly interactive arenas require tools that can detect anomalies as soon as they occur, without disrupting the player experience.

d. Data Diversity and Generalizability

Models typically learn from narrow, game- specific datasets, so their cross-platform robustness is largely untested.

To offer a broader perspective, we have included a comparison of relevant research on cheating detection and its application to chess in the appendix (Tables 3 and 4).

Therefore, future research should aim to develop frameworks that protect privacy, scale gracefully to new game types and strategies, and further improve accuracy. Advances in these areas will enhance the technological foundation needed to maintain fairness and security in online gaming.

METHODOLOGY

This research presents an architecture that combines machine-learning inference and behavior analysis in order to find cheating and fraud in online games. By parsing the game logs, the architecture detects statistical outliers that deviate from normal patterns of player behavior who behave in this manner, leading to violations of the rules. This architecture uses a hybrid pipeline, i.e., it uses conventional classifiers along with deep learning architectures, thus maintaining both scalability and transference across games and modes. The ultimate aim is to provide developers and administrators of games with automated real-time guarantees to maintain competition, fairness and to enhance user satisfaction. The research flow of activity is summarized in Figure 1 the following steps are: (1) Acquisition of raw game data. (2) Cleaning and pre-processing of data records. (3) Selection of suitable algorithms and architecture of model. (4) Training of the model and tuning of hyper-parameters. (5) Evaluation of performance with the aid of quantitative metrics. (6) Assessment of results, optimisation of pipeline and iteration until appropriate accuracy is achieved.

Figure 1. Methodology Flowchart

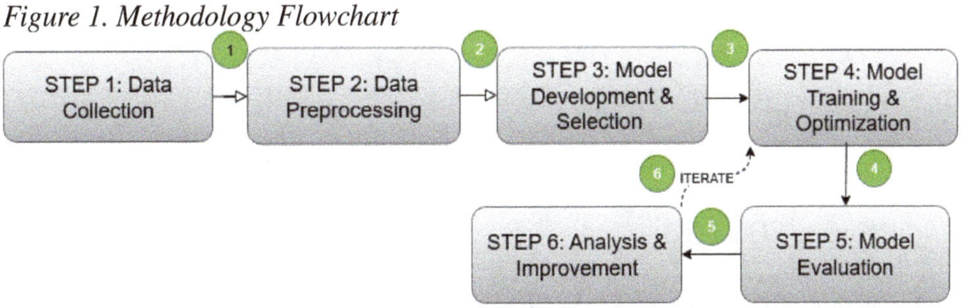

Model Development & Algorithm Selection

1. **Decision Trees**

Decision trees are a core technique for supervised learning because they are both intuitive and transparent. The algorithm recursively divides the data based on predicted values. At each internal node, it selects the attribute that yields the greatest information gain or the lowest impurity which usually measured by the Gini coefficient or entropy. As shown in Figure 2, internal nodes encode conditional tests, branches describe outcome options, and leaves represent final classifications or predictions. The partitioning process stops when a predefined stopping condition is reached, such as maximum tree depth or minimum sample size of leaf nodes (De Ville, 2013).

Figure 2. Decision tree (Olugbenga et al. 2024)

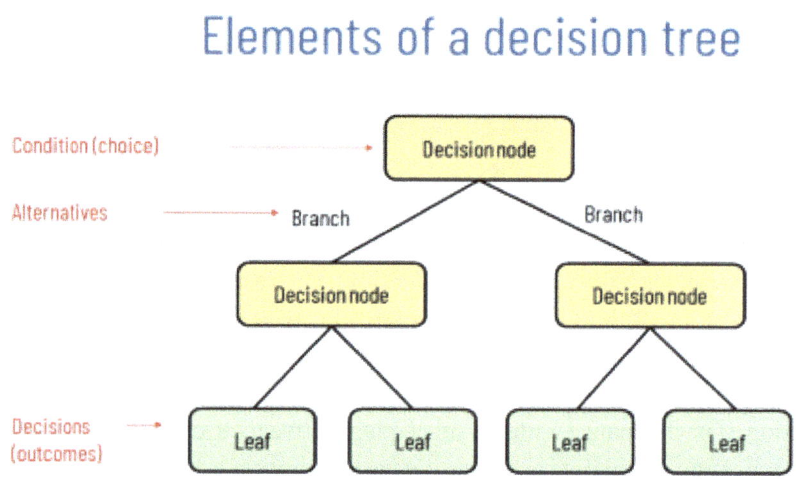

Key Formulas:

a. Information Gain (IG)

Information gain quantifies the reduction in entropy when data is divided by specific attributes.

$$\text{IG (T, A)} = \text{H(T)} - \sum_{v \in values(A)} \frac{|T_v|}{|T|} \mathbf{H}\left(\mathbf{T}_v\right)$$

H(T): *Entropy of the current dataset* T

T_v: *Subset of* T *after splitting by feature* A *on value* v

b. Gini Impurity

Gini impurity measures the uncertainty of a dataset:

$$G(T) = 1 - \sum_{i1} \boldsymbol{pi}^2$$

pi: *Proportion of class* i *in the dataset.*

2. **Support Vector Machines (SVM)**

Support Vector Machines (SVMs) represent a classical supervised learning technique. The algorithm starts by finding an optimal hyperplane that clearly divides the observations into different classes. During training, the boundary between this boundary and the closest samples, i.e., the support vectors, is maximized, as shown in Figure 3. These support vectors play a crucial role in defining the decision boundary, ensuring that the model achieves the best generalization for classification tasks (Suthaharan & Suthaharan, 2016).

Figure 3. Support Vector Machines[1]

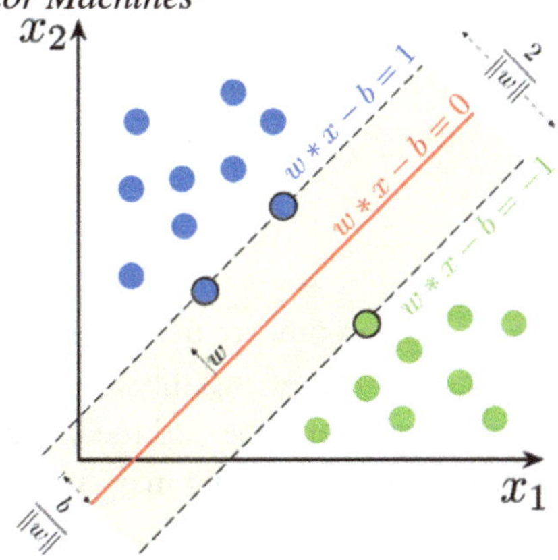

Key Formulas:

a. Hyperplane Equation

$W^T X + b = 0$

W: Weight vector
b: Bias term

The equation $W^T X + b = 0$ defines the decision boundary in an SVM model. In this expression, WTX represents the dot product of the weight vector ω and the input feature vector X, effectively calculating the projection of X onto the direction defined by W. The term b is the bias, which shifts the hyperplane away from the origin. Data points that satisfy $W^T X + b = 0$ lie exactly on the decision boundary. Points for which $W^T X + b$ is greater than zero fall on one side of the boundary, while points for which it is less than zero fall on the opposite side. This hyperplane, therefore, serves to separate the data into distinct classes based on their projections onto W.

b. Optimization Objective

Maximize the margin (distance between support vectors and the hyperplane), while ensuring correct classification:

$$\min \frac{1}{2}\|\mathbf{w}\|^2 \text{ s.t.} \boldsymbol{y}_i(\boldsymbol{w}^T\boldsymbol{x}_i + b) \geq 1$$

y_i: Label of the sample (1 or -1).

This formulation represents the optimization problem for a support vector machine (SVM) with a hard margin. Here's a breakdown:

i. Objective ($\min \frac{1}{2}\|w\|^2$):

The goal is to minimize the squared norm of the weight vector W (divided by 2 for mathematical convenience). Minimizing this term indirectly maximizes the margin- the distance between the hyperplane and the closest data points (support vectors). A smaller $\| W \|$ corresponds to a wider margin, which generally improves the classifier's generalization ability.

ii. **Constraint** ($y_i(w^T x_i + b) \geq 1$):

This constraint ensures that each training example (x_i, y_i) is correctly classified and lies on the correct side of the margin. For a sample with label $y_i = +1$, the condition $(w^T x_i + b) \geq 1$ must hold, and for a sample with $y_i = -1$, the condition ($w^T x_i + b) \leq 1$ must hold. Overall, the formulation ensures that every data point is at least a unit distance away from the decision boundary (when projected along the direction of W), leading to robust separation between classes.

Thus, this optimization problem seeks to find the optimal hyperplane that not only separates the classes but does so by maximizing the margin, which is believed to contribute to better performance on unseen data.

3. **Naive Bayes**

Naive Bayes is a probabilistic classifier based on Bayes' theorem, which assumes that the features used for classification are conditionally independent given the class label (Figure 4). Despite this strong assumption, Naive Bayes often performs well in practice, especially when the dimensionality of the input is high.

In the image, circles, squares, and triangles in different colors represent various features or data points. Naive Bayes applies Bayes' theorem - as shown in the central formula, to compute posterior probabilities for each class label. For instance, if we are trying to determine which category anew shape belongs to, we calculate how likely it is for that shape's features (color, form, etc.) to appear in a specific class based on prior knowledge of all shapes. The classifier then assigns the new shape to the class with the highest posterior probability, illustrating how Naive Bayes balances prior assumptions P(A) with evidence P(BIA) to produce P(AIB).

Figure 4. Naïve Bayes[2]

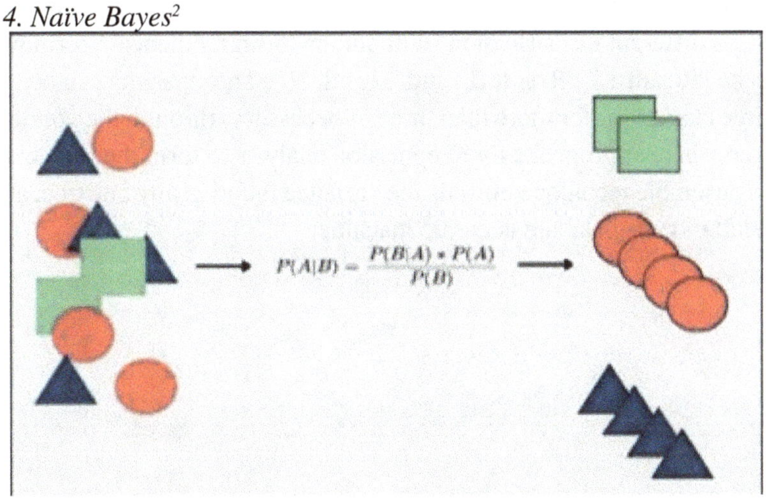

Key Formulas:

a. Bayes' Theorem

$$P(y \mid x_1, x_2, \ldots, x_n) = \frac{P(y)\prod_{i=1}^{n} P(x_i \mid y)}{P(x_1, x_2, \ldots, x_n)}$$

$P(y \mid x_1, x_2, \ldots, x_n)$: Posterior probability of class y given features.
P(y): *Prior probability of class* y.
$P(x_i \mid y)$: Likelihood of feature xi given class y.

4. **Random Forest**

Random forests are a powerful ensemble method of supervised learning, which seeks to enhance the accuracy of classifications by combining the results of various tree models. For this purpose, the method produces a number of trees through the creation of bootstrap samples, which are taken from the training data set. In the case of random forests, this is performed on both the samples of data as well as the predictors themselves, which introduces sufficient variability into the ensembles so that they do not tend to overfit (a common fault of decision trees) and the generalization ability of the models is improved.

In Figure 5, we see a diagram of a random forest in which independent trees are created and their results combined for the final classification. Each tree works on a different bootstrap sample of the training data, as well as a random selection of predictors at each splitting node. When a new sample is classified, it traverses each tree giving a different classification (without any disagreements in terminologies, these can be "Result 1," "Result 2," and "Result 3"). These results can be averaged for the three classes (or for more than three, if necessary) through the voting means, or averaged where appropriate for a regression analysis to form the final classification. This ensemble technique curtails the variance found in any one tree, and leads to an overall more robust and accurate machine.

Figure 5. Random Forest[3]

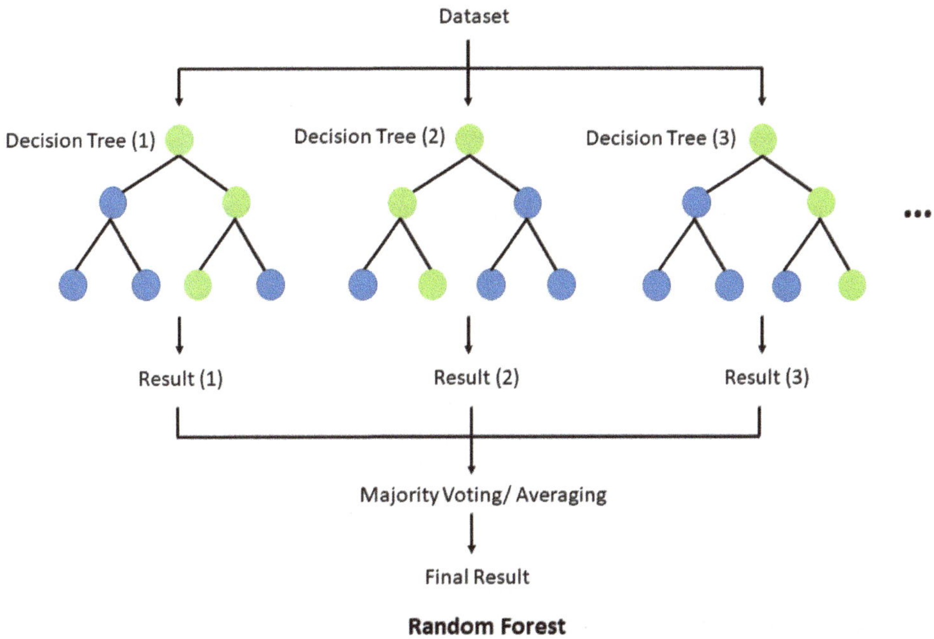

Key Formulas:

a. Decision Rule

$y\ \Lambda = \text{mode}\{\boldsymbol{h}_1(\text{x}), \boldsymbol{h}_2(\text{x}), \ldots, \boldsymbol{h}_n(\text{x})\}$

In a Random Forest, each decision tree independently generates a prediction, denoted as $\boldsymbol{h}_i(\text{x})$ for the ***ith*** tree, and the forest as a whole consists of N such trees. The final predicted class label, y Λ, is obtained by taking the majority vote among these individual predictions, thereby ensuring a robust and accurate overall classification.

b. Gini Impurity

Gini impurity is commonly used to evaluate the quality of splits in each decision tree. For a node with K classes, the impurity is defined as:

$G = \sum_{k=1}^{k} \mathbf{P}_\mathbf{k} \left(1 - \mathbf{P}_\mathbf{k}\right)$

It defines the Gini impurity, a metric used to evaluate the purity of a node in decision trees. In this formula, P_k represents the proportion of samples in the node that belong to class k, and K is the total number of classes. The term $P_k\ (1 - P_k)$ measures the probability of misclassifying a sample from class k if it were randomly labeled according to the class distribution in that node. By summing this over all classes, the Gini impurity provides an overall indication of how mixed the classes are in the node. A lower Gini impurity suggests a purer node, where most samples belong to a single class, whereas a higher impurity indicates a more diverse class distribution.

5. **Logistic Regression**

Logistic Regression is a supervised learning technique widely used for binary classification, modeling the probability that an observation belongs to a particular class (for instance, "Yes" vs. "No" or "1" vs. "0"). Instead of fitting a linear boundary directly, Logistic Regression applies a logistic (sigmoid) function to map the outputs of a linear combination of features into a range between 0 and 1, representing the predicted probability of belonging to the positive class.

Logistic Regression is represented fundamentally in Figure 6. The logistic curve separates the two classes by translating raw scores of features (held along the horizontal axis) into probabilities (for example, values along the vertical axis). The points in the lower left corners will map to small probabilities of being in the positive class, while those in the upper right corners will map to increased probabilities of being in the positive class. The sigmoid (logistic) function thus provides a smooth interface between these two extremes of probabilities of belonging to a given class; hence, providing interpretable, probability-based classifications from the Logistic regression classifiers.

Figure 6. Logistic Regression[4]

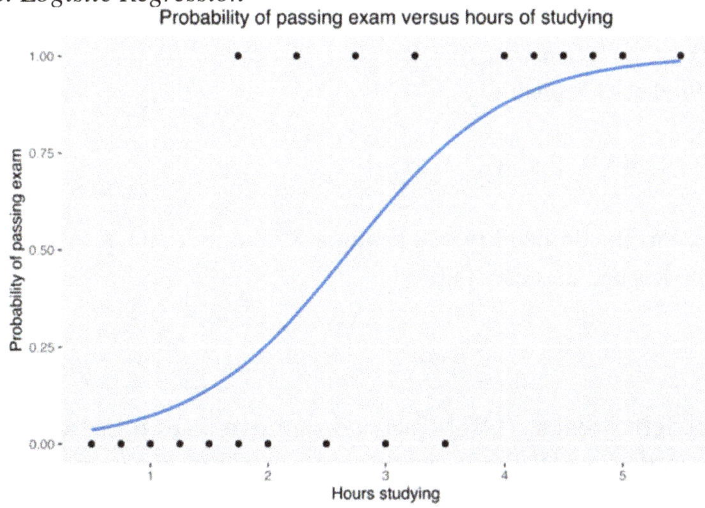

Key Formulas:

a. Logistic (Sigmoid) Function

$$\sigma(z) = \frac{1}{1 + e^{-z}}$$

defines the sigmoid (or logistic) function. This function takes a real-valued input z and maps it to a value between 0 and 1, making it particularly useful for modeling probabilities. Here's a breakdown of its components and behavior:

i. e^{-z}

This term involves the natural exponential function. As z increases, e^{-z} decreases rapidly, and as z decreases (i.e., becomes more negative), e^{-z} increases.

ii. *Denominator* $1 + e^{-z}$

Adding 1 ensures that the denominator is always greater than 1, which bounds the output of the sigmoid function between 0 and 1.

iii. Output Behavior

(1) When z is very large (tending towards $+\infty$), $e^{-z} \to 0$, so $\sigma(z) \to 1$ (2) When z is very small (tending towards $-\infty$), e^{-z} becomes large, so $\sigma(z) \to 0$ (3) At $z = 0$, $e^{-0} = 1$, hence $\sigma(0) = \frac{1}{2}$

b. Predicted Probability

$$P(y \Lambda = 1 \text{ I } X) = \sigma(\beta_0 + \beta_1 x_1 + \ldots + \beta_n x_n)$$

This represents the probability that an input X belongs to the positive class ($y\Lambda = 1$), given the learned parameters β_i.

6. LSTM

Long Short-Term Memory (LSTM) networks are a type of recurrent neural network (RNN). They are designed to model time-dependent relationships among sequential observations. Differing from standard RNNs, LSTM networks deal gracefully with the vanishing gradient problem through their gating mechanisms that control the flow of the information. Thus, LSTM networks are well suited to time-dependent relationships in data used in regression and classification problems.

In LSTM a horizontal line represents the cell state, which acts as a conveyor belt carrying long- term memory across time steps. On the left, the forget gate, using a sigmoid function, determines which information from the previous cell state should be discarded. In the center, the input gate combines a sigmoid function with a tanh activation to generate and regulate new candidate values that will be added to the cell state. Finally, on the right, the output gate, again employing a sigmoid function, decides which parts of the updated cell state are output as the hidden state. This hidden state is then passed on to the next time step. Together, these gating controls allow the LSTM to selectively retain, update, and output information to efficiently capture both short-term and long- term dependencies in sequence data.

Key Formulas:

a. Forget Gate

$$\mathbf{f}_t = \boldsymbol{\sigma}\left(\mathbf{w}_f \bullet \left[\mathbf{h}_{t-1}, \mathbf{x}_t\right] + \mathbf{b}_f\right)$$

The forget gate f_t determines which information from the previous cell state $c_{t\ 1}$ should be discarded based on the previous hidden state h_{t-1} and the current input x_t.

b. Input Gate and Candidate Cell State

$$\mathbf{i_t} = \boldsymbol{\sigma}\left(\mathbf{w_i} \bullet \left[\mathbf{h_{t-1}}, \mathbf{x_t}\right] + \mathbf{b_i}\right)$$

$$c_t^{\sim} = \mathbf{tanh}\left(\mathbf{w_c} \bullet \left[\mathbf{h_{t-1}}, \mathbf{x_t}\right] + \mathbf{b_c}\right)$$

The input gate it controls the extent to which the candidate cell state $c_t^{\sim}$ (which carries new information) is added to the cell state.

c. Cell State Update

$$c_t = f_t \odot c_{t-1} + i_t \odot c_t^{\sim}$$

The cell state c_t is updated by combining the previous state, modulated by the forget gate, and the candidate state, modulated by the input gate.

d. Output Gate and Hidden State

$$o_t = \sigma\left(w_o \bullet \left[h_{t-1}, x_t\right] + b_o\right)$$

$$h_t = o_t \odot \tanh(c_t)$$

The output gate o_t determines which parts of the cell state contribute to the hidden state h_t that is passed to the next time step and used for predictions.

In conclusion, LSTM cells process sequential data by preserving internal state and selectively updating the state through input gates, forget gates, and output gates. These gating paths regulate the information that enters, retains, or leaves the cell at each time step, thus enabling the network to capture long-range dependencies. As a result, LSTMs are widely used in speech recognition, time series prediction, and other tasks that depend on temporal context.

EXPERIMENTAL DESIGN

Dataset

This study utilizes Kaggle's publicly available Chess Cheating dataset[5], which provides a detailed record of games played on the board with clear labels to distinguish between fair play and fraud. The dataset comprises 48,000 games played between bots. To reduce computational overhead, in most games only one side is allowed to use Stockfish (i.e., only one side engages in "cheating"), while the other side has zero probability of using it. Each match provides player ratings, the full move order in PGN format, the final result, and coded markers that indicate suspicious activity, making the dataset ideal for supervised classification.

Key variables of the dataset are summarised below:

Table 1.Overview of the Attributes of the Chess Cheating Dataset

Column	Description
Liste cheat white **Liste cheat black**	Encoded strings (scientific notation) that capture potential infractions by White and Black, respectively. Further decoding is required before modelling.
Game	Full move list in Portable Game Notation, tracing play from the opening through to termination.
Elo white / Elo black	Elo ratings for each competitor; larger values indicate stronger players.
Score	Match outcome (1-0 = White wins, 0-1 = Black wins, ½-½ = draw).
Cheating	Target label: 0 means no irregularity; 1 means cheating confirmed.

Figure 7. Sample Records from the Chess Cheating Dataset

Since this dataset (Figure 7) correlates player strength, move order, and outcome labels, it allows for detailed exploration of the interplay between anomalous performance, the impact of illegal assistance, and the interaction between rank score (Elo) differences and outcomes. Prior to model development, we cleaned the data, addressed category imbalances, and reformatted the features to meet the input requirements of the deep learning classifier while minimizing sampling bias. Detail of the attributes can be seen in the Table 1.

The preprocessing steps are outlined below:

1. Handling missing or anomalous data
   a. Unrealistic Elo ratings

Entries below 1,000 are discarded because official participants are rarely rated below this threshold; retaining such records compromises the analysis of professional,cheating.

b. Null values

When blank fields make up less than 5% of the corpus, the affected rows are removed. Eliminating sparse missing observations avoids the bias and numerical instability that can result from ad hoc filling.

c. Duplicate games

Duplicate records are eliminated to maintain the assumption that each observation is independent; otherwise, redundant samples would exaggerate the weight of certain features and lead to overfitting.

2. Feature Engineering

The transformation of raw variables to domain-specific predictor variables increases the ability of the model to filter out variations of interest and filter out noise. In this paper, the feature construction attempts to balance three objectives: (1) To discover patterns in the data via a mathematical transformation; (2) To incorporate chess-specific knowledge; and, (3) To highlight all aspects that differ between legitimate and illegitimate games. In this way, the final feature set will be able to balance mathematical meaning, domain context, and relevance of tasks.

a. Target Variable: Cheating

Binary label cheating equals 0 in fair games and 1 in games where collusion can be proved. The model learns to predict this on inputs constructed such as each player's coded cheated score, Elo pairs and the results thus locating automatically future abnormalities.

b. Game Characteristics

i. Move Count (*move_count*)

The number of moves played in a game was estimated by counting the number of '.' characters in the game notation.

ii. Elo Rating Difference (*Elo_diff*)

Calculated as Elo White - Elo Black, this measures the strength difference between the two players.

c. Supplementary Features

i. Synthesized based on logical estimations

Some chess-related metrics were not provided in the dataset.

ii. Time per Move

A random value between 1 and 60 seconds was assigned for each move, assuming reasonable move durations.

iii. Game Duration

Estimated as *move_count* × *Time per move* to approximate the total game length.

iv. Accuracy Score

A randomly generated value between 0.5 and 1.0, simulating a performance evaluation metric.

v. Elo Deviation Metrics

(1)Elo_deviation_white: The deviation of the white player's Elo rating from the dataset mean.(2)Elo_deviation_black: The deviation of the black player's Elo rating from the dataset mean.

3. Feature Selection and Transformation

The final set of features entered into the model were: (1)black_cheat_ratio (2) move_count (3) score_numeric (4) Elo White (5)Elo Black (6) Elo_diff (7) Time per move (8) Game Duration (9) Accuracy Score (10) Elo_deviation_white (11) Elo_deviation_black To preserve constancy of the dataset that was finally used, any features in the above which were not present were replaced with a value of 0. It was decided upon after the analysis given below that this was justified.

a. Logical Consistency Preservation

For those features that were ratio based (for example, black_cheat_ratio, Accuracy Score), frequent nulls indicated either technological failures in the measurement of the phenomenon (for example, interruption in the recording of data) or the complete absence of the phenomenon (for example, no cheating indications have been detected). Hence, the allowable response was to assign a zero value, whereby "no phenomenon observed" was operating to maintain the logical scenario, rather than changing to introduce inevitably some sort of unwanted noise. Elo System Parameter Values: The Elo_deviation values were missing for those players who did not have any historical statistics to exhibit. The assignment of zero allowed a certain transparency to the analysis of the players and the team plays in which they were concerned and this prevents any erroneous connection with low deviations presumed to have occurred irrespective of their magnitude.

b. Computational Integrity Assurance

In the various values such as Elo_diff, to have had unilateral nulls (for example Elo Black = null, while Elo White valid) would loose the entire structural advantage of pair comparisons. The substituted value of zero puts a value on the effective measurement (for example Elo_diff = Elo White - 0) of maintaining the entire arithmetic operability and prevents any systemic computation failures. Temporal Characteristics: If for example in Time per move, then Game Duration, statistical nulls had become evident, the calculated derivative values would be made impossible (for example, move velocity). Setting of zero voila! provides flexibility down through the immediate matter of analysis inherent in the produced data but also allows further disqualifications against illogicality of entries post hoc (for example, games giving a total duration of zero).

c. Bias Mitigation & Information Retention
   i. Non-Random Missingness

Certain missing patterns (e.g., absent score_numeric in games terminated by forfeit) represented inherently anomalous events. Deletion would induce survivorship bias, whereas zero-imputation retained sample integrity while allowing the model to learn suppressed weights for these edge cases.

ii. Cross-Feature Alignment

A uniform substitution approach eliminated risks of distributional skews from heterogeneous imputation methods (e.g., mean-based replacement for some features vs. regression-based estimates for others).

d. Interpretability Enhancement

All features underwent standardization to neutralize the distortive impact of zero-encoding on continuous distributions (e.g., Elo White values naturally $\neq 0$). Sensitivity analyses confirmed that models correctly interpreted zeros as missing-value flags rather than literal numerical inputs.

4. Standardization

All selected features were standardized using StandardScaler from Scikit-learn to ensure numerical stability.

5. Data Splitting

The dataset was split into 80% training data and 20% testing data to evaluate the model's generalization performance.

6. Data Balancing Report

In the preparatory phase of this study, we addressed the issue of class imbalance in the training data using the Synthetic Minority Over-sampling Technique (SMOTE). We implemented the imblearn. over_sampling module SMOTE class and defined random_state = 42 for reproducibility. Then we produced a balanced feature matrix (X_train_bal) and labels (y_train_bal) from the standardized training features (X_train_scaled) and labels (y_train). Sampling yielded a balanced training set; the counts of the categories were printed to confirm that a few were sufficiently populated. By equalling the frequencies of the categories the averaged corpus consequently reduced sampling bias and allowed the model to better identify rare situations, in turn improving the accuracy and stability of the predictions in the learning phases that followed. The combination of data cleaning, feature engineering and resampling delivers a well structured dataset designed for deep learning classifiers. The intelligently designed feature set achieves player behaviour, game flow and suspect patterns and renders the system more sensitive to illegal assistance in chess. Post preprocessing, samples were made into training and test sets at 80:20 ratio to ensure the fitting of the models and an unbiased assessment of the material. Input and performance were assessed by accuracy, precision, recall and F1 score. The convergence of this transformed dataset with interpretable machine leaning models provides a trustworthy base for exposing cheating behaviour whilst balancing transparency with predictive prowess.

Evaluation Metrics

Model performance is measured using five widely accepted metrics in machine learning.

1. **Precision** indicates the proportion of true cheating cases among all games labeled as cheating by the classifier.

$$\text{precision} = \frac{\text{True positives}}{\text{True positives} + \text{False positives}}$$

2. **Recall (Rec)** indicates the proportion of correctly detected cheating games.

$$\text{Recall} = \frac{\text{True positives}}{\text{True positives} + \text{False NeJatives}}$$

3. **F1 Score** provides a single and balanced indicator of detection quality.

$$\text{F1} = 2 \bullet \frac{\text{Precision} \bullet \text{Recall}}{\text{Precision} + \text{Recall}}$$

4. **Average Precision (AP)** integrates the precision of different decision thresholds.

$$\text{Ap} = \Sigma\ (\text{precision} \bullet \Delta\text{Recall})$$

5. **Mean Average Precision (mAP)** averages the APs of the normal and cheating categories.

$$\text{mAP} = \frac{\Sigma\text{AP}}{\textit{Number of Classes}}$$

As a result, tests performed in different gaming environments compare accuracy, computational cost, and fitness; the higher the score on these metrics, the more effective the cheat detection.

RESULTS

1. Support Vector Machine (SVM)

The confusion matrix (Figure 8) shows that the SVM correctly classified 3998 legitimate games and 2663 cheating games, but still produced 1021 false positives and, more importantly, 1212 omissions; these raw counts are converted in the Figure 9 report to a precision, recall, F1 of 0.77/0.79/0.78 for the non-cheating category, and 0.72/0.69/ 0.71 for the cheating category, giving an overall accuracy of 74.9%. 20% false positive rate (1021/5019) suggests that one in five honest games would have been flagged as requiring censorship if manual adjudication was cheap, which is tolerable. 0.71, for an overall accuracy of 74.9%. The 20% false positive rate (1021/5019) suggests that one in five honest games will be flagged as needing scrutiny, which is tolerable if manual adjudication is inexpensive, while the 31% false negative rate (1212/3875) is more worrisome, as nearly one-third of cheating attempts evaded detection. The gap between the two categories reflects residual labeling imbalance and feature overlap: a polynomial kernel support vector machine (SVM) with C=0.01 appears to have smoothed the decision boundary enough to prevent overfitting on noisy labels, but at the cost of insufficiently separating highly skilled operations from engine-assisted ones. Improving the recall of the cheating category would therefore require adjusting the operating point by cost-sensitive weights or lowering the decision threshold, while supplementing the feature space with engine-consistency scores or shifting time variance to enhance category separability; these changes should improve the macro-mean recall (currently 0.74) without inflating the false alarm rate beyond the operation tolerance.

Figure 8. SVM Confusion Matrix on the Test Set

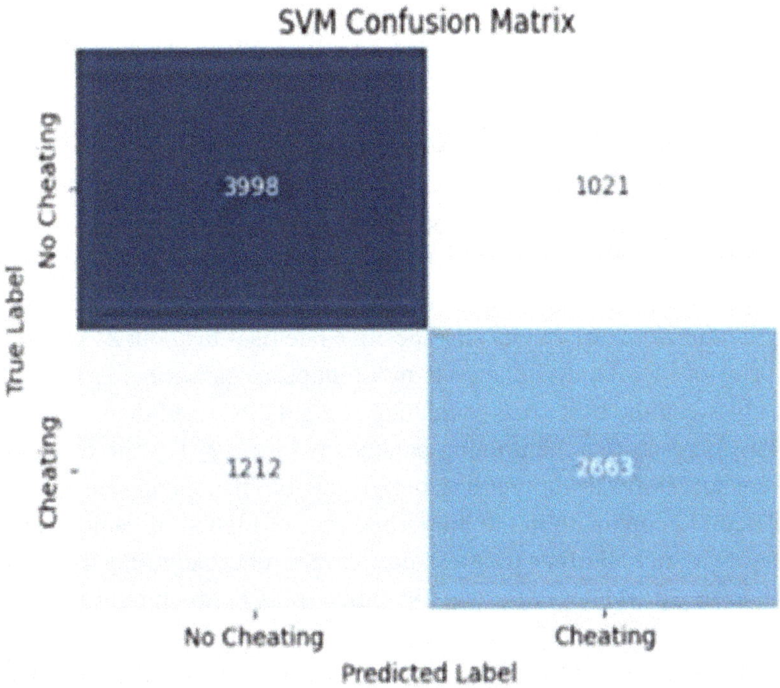

Figure 9. SVM Classification Metrics

```
SVM Model Accuracy: 0.7492691702271194

SVM Model Classification Report:
              precision    recall  f1-score   support

           0       0.77      0.79      0.78      5019
           1       0.72      0.69      0.71      3875

    accuracy                           0.75      8894
   macro avg       0.75      0.74      0.74      8894
weighted avg       0.75      0.75      0.75      8894
```

2. Decision Tree

Figure 10 illustrates the confusion matrix for the adapted decision tree, showing that the model correctly identifies 3,840 legitimate games and 2,787 cheating games, while generating 1,179 false positives and 1,088 misses. These counts support the metrics in Figure 11: the decision tree has an overall accuracy of 75.5%, with precision/recall/F1 of 0.78/0.79/0.78 for the non-cheating category and 0.72/0.72/0.72/ F1 for the cheating category. compared to the previous Support Vector Machines (SVMs), the decision tree reduces the false-negative rate for the cheating category from about 31% to 28% (which is a significant reduction). to 28% (a modest but meaningful improvement), but its false-positive rate rises to about 24%, suggesting that the price of increased vigilance is more innocent games being flagged. The proximity between the best cross-validation score (0.751) and the retention accuracy (0.756) suggests that the pruning parameters (depth ≤ 15, minimum samples ≥ 2/4) were successful in suppressing overfitting, but the single-tree structure remains difficult to cope with in the borderline case of high-skill games mimicking the engine assistance. Further progress may come from integrating variants (e.g., gradient boosting or random forests) to stabilize splits between bootstrap replicas, as well as from richer behavioral features (engine consistency scores, move-time discretization) to further differentiate between true expertise and covert cheating.

Figure 10. Decision Tree Confusion Matrix on the Test Set

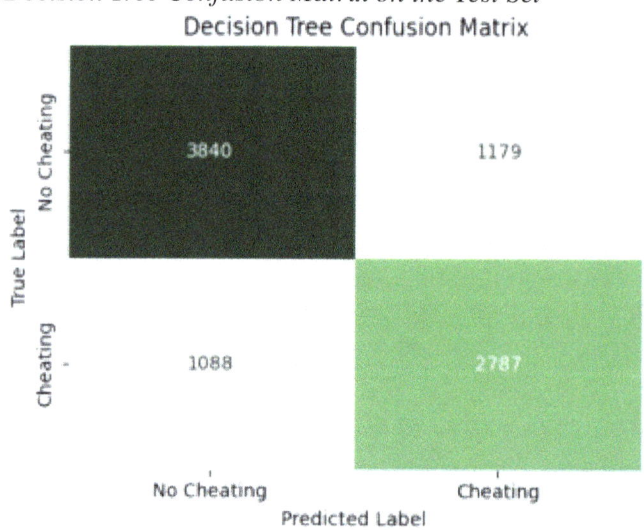

Figure 11. Decision Tree Classification Metrics

```
Best cross-validation score: 0.7514916019052394
Optimized Decision Tree Model Accuracy: 0.755453114459186

Optimized Decision Tree Model Classification Report:
              precision    recall  f1-score   support

           0       0.78      0.79      0.78      5019
           1       0.72      0.72      0.72      3875

    accuracy                           0.76      8894
   macro avg       0.75      0.75      0.75      8894
weighted avg       0.76      0.76      0.76      8894
```

3. Naive Bayes

Figure 12 illustrates the plain Bayesian confusion matrix: the classifier correctly labeled 3964 legitimate games and 2643 cheating games, but it generated 1055 false positives and 1232 false negatives. These counts are summarized in Figure 13, where the overall accuracy of the model is 74.3%, with the categories of non-cheating games classified as 0.76/0.79/0.78 (precision, recall, F1) and the categories of cheating games classified as 0.71/0.68/0.70. While its precision is comparable to that of the baseline of the SVM and the Decision Tree with respect to the illegal games, the plain Bayes sacrifices recall, i.e., misses 32% of cheating attempts, because its conditional independence assumption underestimates subtle feature interactions indicative of engine assistance. The slightly lower false positive rate (21% vs. 24% for the tree) reflects the model's conservative tendencies, but this comes at the cost of the highest false negative rate of the three methods. Correcting this imbalance either requires expanding the feature space with interaction terms (thus lowering the independence constraint) or moving to a semi-parsimonious variant such as tree- augmented parsimonious Bayes; both of these strategies recapture the correlation between the features and boost the recall of the cheating class without significantly increasing the false positive rate.

Figure 12. Naive Bayes Confusion Matrix on the Test Set

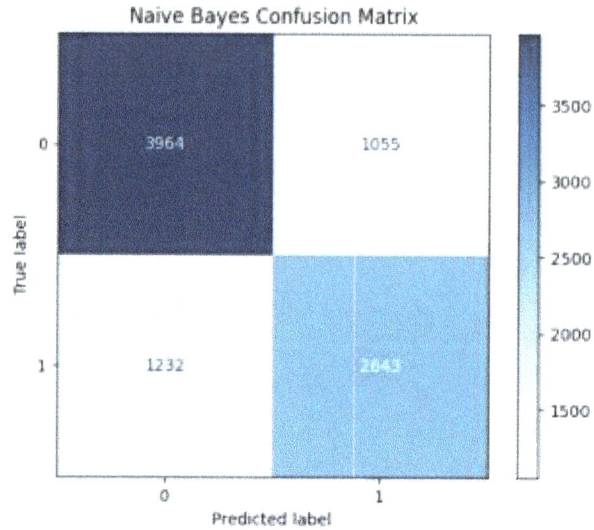

Figure 13. Naive Bayes Classification Metrics

Naive Bayes Model Accuracy: 0.7429

Naive Bayes Model Classification Report:

	precision	recall	f1-score	support
0	0.76	0.79	0.78	5019
1	0.71	0.68	0.70	3875
accuracy			0.74	8894
macro avg	0.74	0.74	0.74	8894
weighted avg	0.74	0.74	0.74	8894

4. Random Forest

Figure 14 illustrates the Random Forest confusion matrix, showing that the integrated model correctly labeled 3924 legitimate games and 2863 cheating games, while generating 1095 false positives and 1012 false negatives. These statistics yield the metrics in Figure 15: an overall accuracy of 76.3%, with precision/recall/F1 of

0.79/0.78/0.79 for the non-cheating category, and 0.72/0.74/0.73 for the cheating category. Relative to the single decision tree, the forest reduces the false-positive rate from 24% to about 22%, and increases the recall of the cheating category by 2 percentage points. The forest reduces the false positive rate from 24% to about 22% and increases the recall of the cheating class by 2 percentage points, demonstrating the variance reduction advantage of bagging. Its recall gap between classes (4pp) is the narrowest of all four baseline models, indicating a more balanced sensitivity, but the absolute number of false negatives (1012) still implies that a quarter of the cheating attempts were able to evade detection. Error analysis showed that many misses occurred in games with small Elo distributions and move-time patterns similar to human games, suggesting that feature interactions captured by individual trees are sometimes averaged out in integrated voting. Future improvements may include (i) increasing the depth of the tree through stronger regularization (maximum feature $\sqrt{d}$, minimum sample leaf ≥ 2) to recover fine-grained divisions; (ii) combining engine consistency and temporal rhythm features to allow the tree to exploit richer signals; and (iii) applying category-balanced bootstrap sampling or focus loss adaption to increase cheat recall above 0.80, without increasing false positives.

Figure 14. Random Forest Confusion Matrix on the Test Set

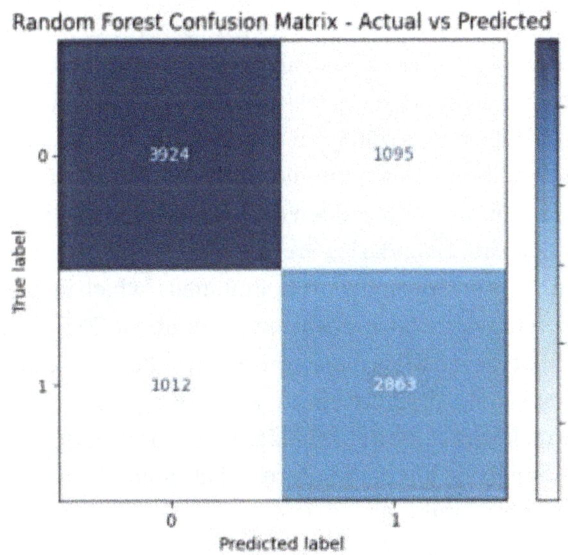

Figure 15. Random Forest Classification Metrics

```
Random Forest Model Evaluation:
Test Set Accuracy: 0.7631

Random Forest Model Classification Report:
              precision    recall  f1-score   support

           0       0.79      0.78      0.79      5019
           1       0.72      0.74      0.73      3875

    accuracy                           0.76      8894
   macro avg       0.76      0.76      0.76      8894
weighted avg       0.76      0.76      0.76      8894
```

5. Logistic Regression

Figure 16 plots the confusion matrix for the logistic regression baseline: the linear model correctly labels 4016 legitimate games and 2608 cheating games, while giving 1003 false positives and 1267 false negatives. After transforming these counts, Figure 17 shows an overall accuracy of 74.5%. The performance is asymmetric: the non- cheating category has an accuracy of 0.76, a recall of 0.80, and an F of 10.78, while the cheating category has an accuracy of 0.72, a recall of 0.67, and an F of 10.70. The cheating category has a leakage rate of 33%, which is the highest of both the tree- based model and the integrated model, and stems from the inability of the linear decision boundaries to capture non-additive interactions (e.g., spikes in engine consistency combined with sudden drops in movement time), and from the fact that the linear decision boundaries are not capable of capturing non-additive interactions. sudden drop-in movement time combined), which indicate the presence of implicit aids. In contrast, its false-positive rate of about 20% is the lowest of all models, suggesting that the model is more conservative but less sensitive. To change this contradiction, one could (i) apply elastic network regularization and adjust the category weights to make the slope of the bias towards the cheating category steeper; (ii) introduce polynomials or interaction terms that model feature synergies while maintaining linear interpretability; or (iii) use calibrated probability thresholds that minimize cost-weighted errors to reduce the number of false positives without unduly increasing false alarm loads by 1267 undetected cheating cases.

Figure 16. Logistic Regression Confusion Matrix on the Test Set

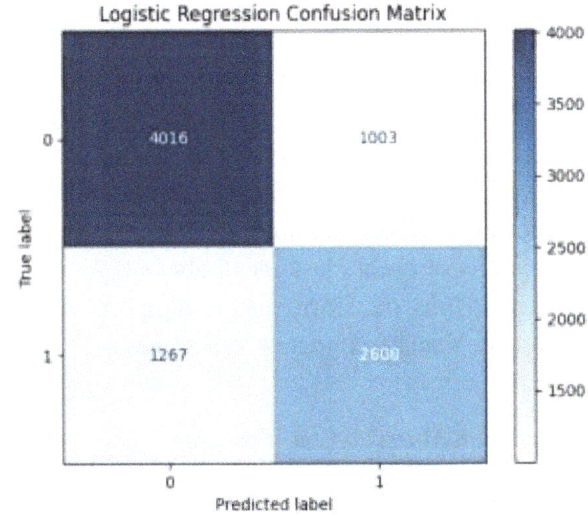

Figure 17. Logistic Regression Classification Metrics

```
Logistic Regression Model Evaluation:
Test Set Accuracy: 0.7448

Logistic Regression Model Classification Report:
              precision    recall  f1-score   support

           0       0.76      0.80      0.78      5019
           1       0.72      0.67      0.70      3875

    accuracy                           0.74      8894
   macro avg       0.74      0.74      0.74      8894
weighted avg       0.74      0.74      0.74      8894
```

6. LSTM

Figure 18 illustrates the LSTM confusion matrix with 3995 true negatives, 2747 true positives, 1024 false negatives, and 1128 false negatives; these data support the metrics in Figure 19, where the overall accuracy of the network is 75.8%, with a category precision/recall/F1 of 0.77/0.81/0.79 for the non-cheating games, and a cheating game with a category precision/recall/F1 of 0.74/0.69/0.71. Thus, the recurrent model has the highest recall among all tested classifiers for legitimate games, but still misses 29% of the cheating attempts, mainly those games where the time-movement patterns mimic human rhythms in spite of the engine-level accuracy, which diminishes the sequence sensitivity ofthe LSTM. Meanwhile, the 20% false positive rate suggests that one in five honest games will be flagged, a workload that many platforms could afford if manual review was inexpensive. To improve cheat detection, the model could benefit from a longer input window (capturing deeper strategy shifts), an attention layer that weights key move sequences, and class-balanced focus loss to bias learning toward rare cheating patterns; such improvements aim to increase cheat class recall above 0.75 without substantially increasing false positives, thus transforming the temporal modeling strength of LSTM translates into more decisive integrity guarantees.

Figure 18. LSTM Confusion Matrix on the Test Set

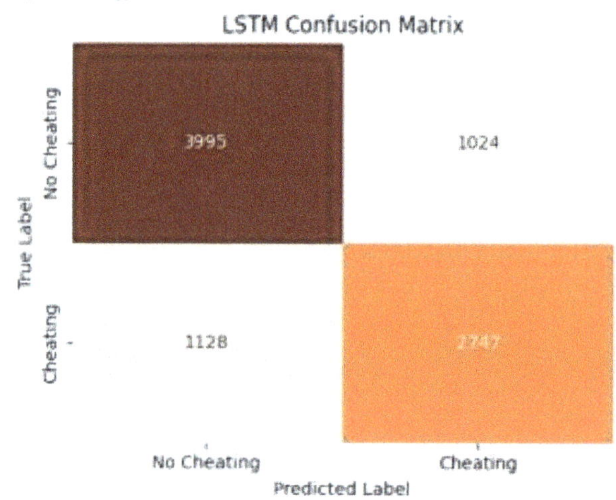

Figure 19. LSTM Classification Metrics

```
Test Loss: 0.5160
Test Accuracy: 0.7578
278/278 ━━━━━━━━━━━━━━━━━━━━ 0s 835us/step

Classification Report:
              precision    recall  f1-score   support

           0       0.77      0.81      0.79      5019
           1       0.74      0.69      0.71      3875

    accuracy                           0.76      8894
   macro avg       0.75      0.75      0.75      8894
weighted avg       0.76      0.76      0.76      8894
```

7. Comparative Analysis

While the accuracy of the six classifiers studied was relatively similar at between 74% and 76%, the difference in performance lay largely in how they balanced missed cheats with unwanted alerts. Random Forest does best in achieving a good compromise; the number of shallow trees, because of the noise added, picks up about three-quarters of cheating games and slightly more than one-fifth of incorrectly labelled games. An SVM fitted with a strongly regularised polynomial kernel is softer on honest users but with the result that about a third of cheats are missed; relaxing the regularisation or reweighting the classes makes it bolder but at the expense of more false positives. Specific decision trees show similar accuracy but appear to be tending to overfit; while their rating for cheats is as high this is because a mis-chosen split can cause a whole branch to misbehave in the wrong way, which meaning that forest, type bagging would help explain why this is. Simple Bayes is the fastest, but suffers from its own simplicity, exploring each feature as acting independently, thus missing to discriminate on the subtle combos of human-powered and engine-powered type behaviours which would otherwise miss most cheating. Logistic regression does much the same but for different reasons; the linear boundaries are nicely transparent, but fail to cope with the curved boundaries differentiating fair play and foul, leading to about one-third of cheating cases escaping their notice. Last of all, Long Short-Term Memory (LSTM) adds temporal cues to the function of fair play, but still leads to about 30% of cheating behaviours generating no alert i.e., a longer sequence of instances or a more attention-grabbing layer might focus on the key moments when behaviours diverge. In short, the richer models tend to detect more cheating behaviours but also generate in some ways more unnecessary false positives, while being easier to interpret and deploy, the thinner models run the risk of more complex cheating behaviours passing undetected. The best solution therefore depends on whether the platform is more concerned with placing innocent players under unwarranted suspicion or trying to treat all cheats below detection, but the probable answer is somewhere in the region of generating layers of quick screening models but correcting any suspicious behaviours found with the help of more heavy-duty models to examine them. Based on the performance criteria in Table 2, there are three separate line plots derived from the method to give a more convenient representation of the way in which different models behave on the two classes of events. Figure 20 gives the precision curves of Class 0 and Class 1 using all six methods, Figure 21 the appropriate remember values, and Figure 22 the appropriate F1 values. These plots show three points clearly. First of all, the highest precision in the non-cheating category was obtained by Random Forest. Secondly, the highest remember in this category was obtained by LSTM and ind. decision trees. Thirdly, the F1 scores in both categories are pretty well the same for all models.

In order to enhance the generalizability of the study, further evaluations needs be conducted using more diverse datasets.

Table 2. Class-wise Evaluation Metrics for Cheating Detection Methods

Method	Class	Precision	Recall	F1-score
SVM	0	0.77	0.79	0.78
	1	0.72	0.69	0.71
Decision Tree	0	0.77	0.81	0.79
	1	0.74	0.68	0.71
Naive Bayes	0	0.76	0.79	0.77
	1	0.71	0.68	0.7
Random Forest	0	0.79	0.78	0.79
	1	0.72	0.74	0.73
Logistic Regression	0	0.76	0.8	0.78
	1	0.72	0.67	0.7
LSTM	0	0.77	0.81	0.79
	1	0.74	0.69	0.71

Figure 20. Precision by Model and Class

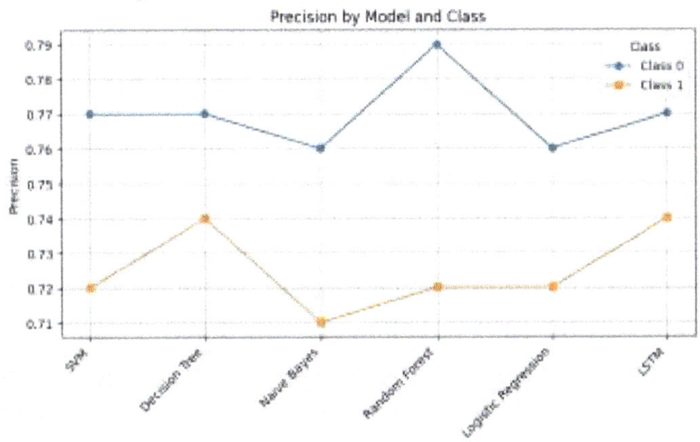

Figure 21. Recall by Model and Class

Figure 22. F1-score by Model and Class

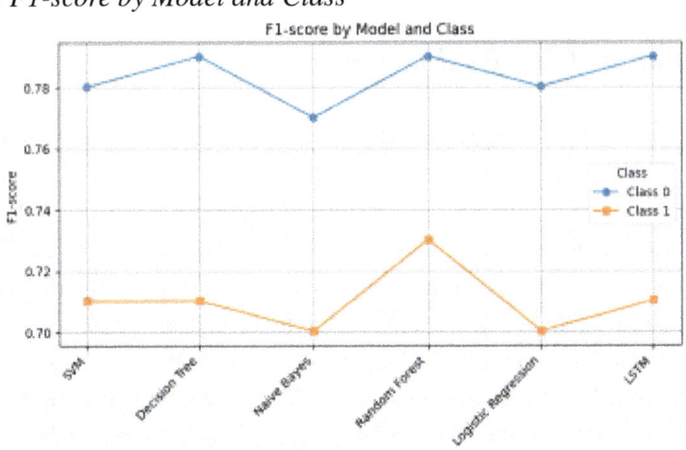

CONCLUSION

In conclusion, this study indicates that machine learning methods can help identify cheating in tournaments of chess. We examined the performance of six algorithms (SVM, Decision Tree, Naïve Bayes, Random Forest, and LSTM) that offered useful trade-offs in terms of interpretability, execution time and accuracy. Decision trees and logistic regression lend themselves easily to interpretation and require a short time to be trained, but their simple format does not capture the complexity of cheating behavior. SVM machines are good at high-dimensional input and code complex structures if their kernel function and parameters are tuned. Naïve Bayes is computationally much lighter and capable of identifying those who play fairly, but its independence assumptions prevent detection of collusion with engines. The integrated structure of Random Forest raises its accuracy and provides the most consistent relative distinction between fair and foul play. LSTM does well and encodes temporally relevant behaviour by characterising sequences of moves over time, but fails slightly in memory recall of cheating behaviour - further tuning of the depth of the network or the learning rate will help. Taken collectively, the results indicate that what is needed is a scalable and credible detection instrument if the credibility of organised chess tournaments is to be preserved. The framework of the authors can be adapted for other competitive environments or enriched by the addition of new behavioural features. Future research may involve examining real-time deployment, improving of model for real-time purposes or tackling ethical issues such as privacy issues and the risk of unfair bias in automated decisions. For tournament organisers Random Forest may be the most suitable model for a good trade-off in detection performance as well as practical applicability. It is hoped that future lines of experimentation will include experimentation with more varied datasets and the use of real-world player behaviour to increase the generalizability, and robustness of the models.

FUTURE RESEARCH DIRECTIONS

These positive results suggest a number of opportunities for future work. First, a real- time implementation of the model in a competitive environment is worth examination. The implementation of on-line detection creates a number of engineering challenges: problems of latency, of load distribution, of fault tolerance must all be solved by careful engineering. Second, a wider range of features may improve detection. Statistics like recent match history, average player action speed, or consistency scores developed by engine calculus may reveal subtler forms of cheating behavior. Experimentation with deeper network layers, or hybrid algorithms combining traditional algorithms with current neural models, would help develop this idea. Third, the models developed here may be implemented in other areas in which it is important to detect anomalies, such as eSports, remote tests, or financial transactions. This would provide information as to which aspects of the software are generally useful, and which must be tailored to other domains. Finally, an automated automated supervisory degree raises considerable ethical concerns. Safeguards of privacy, safeguards against bias, and satisfactory remedial avenues for aggrieved parties must be established. Models consistent with ethical requirements, and guidance from various experts in ethics and legality, are the sine qua non for the establishment and sustenance of trust of the players. In sum, on-line operation, a greater set of features, inter-dominational verification, and rigorous ethical safeguards are the necessary pillars of the more efficient and reliable detection system.

REFERENCES

Agarwal, N., Danielsen, N. F., Gravdal, P. K., & Bours, P. *(2022, October). Contract cheat detection using biometric keystroke dynamics. In 2022 20th International Conference on Emerging eLearning Technologies and Applications (ICETA) (pp. 15-21). IEEE.* DOI: 10.1109/ICETA57911.2022.9974870

Alayed, H. A. (2015). *Behavior-Based Approaches for Detecting Cheating in Online Games* (Doctoral dissertation, University of Southern California).

Anjum, S. H., & Patil, G. (2022, November). Cheat Detection for Credit Cards Using Artificial Intelligence. *In 2022 IEEE North Karnataka Subsection Flagship International Conference (NKCon) (pp.* 1-6*).* IEEE. DOI: 10.1109/NKCon56289.2022.10126820

Barnes, D. J., & Hernandez-Castro, J. (2015). On the limits of engine analysis for cheating detection in chess. *Computers & Security*, *48*, 58–73. DOI: 10.1016/j.cose.2014.10.002

Chess, O. An Application of Human and Computer Decision-Making Preferences. In *International Conference on Computers and Games* (pp. 163-180). Cham: Springer Nature Switzerland.

Dang, T. L., Hoang, N. M. N., Nguyen, T. V., Nguyen, H. V., Dang, Q. M., Tran, Q. H., & Pham, H. H. (2025). Auto-proctoring using computer vision in MOOCs system. *Multimedia Tools and Applications*, *84*(23), 26187–26213. DOI: 10.1007/s11042-024-20099-w

De Ville, B. (2013). Decision trees. *Wiley Interdisciplinary Reviews: Computational Statistics*, *5*(6), 448–455. DOI: 10.1002/wics.1278

Egri-Nagy, A., & Törmänen, A. (2020, November). Derived metrics for the game of Go–intrinsic network strength assessment and cheat-detection. In *2020 Eighth International Symposium on Computing and Networking (CANDAR)* (pp. 9-18). IEEE. DOI: 10.1109/CANDAR51075.2020.00010

Erdem, B., & Karabatak, M. (2025). Cheating detection in online exams using deep learning and machine learning. *Applied Sciences (Basel, Switzerland)*, *15*(1), 400. DOI: 10.3390/app15010400

Flynn, A. J., Tischer, B. D., Mandujano, J. D., & Pisano, M. A. (2024). An Analysis of Methodologies for the Prevention and Mitigation of Cheating in Online Gaming Using Artificial Intelligence and its Ethical Impact. In *Proceedings of the ISCAP Conference ISSN* (Vol. 2473, p. 4901).

Iliescu, D. M. D. (2020). The impact of artificial intelligence on the chess world. *JMIR Serious Games, 8*(4), e24049. DOI: 10.2196/24049 PMID: 33300493

Laarhoven, T., & Ponukumati, A. (2022, November). Towards Transparent Cheat Detection in

Laurens, P., Paige, R. F., Brooke, P. J., & Chivers, H. (2007, July). A novel approach to the detection of cheating in multiplayer online games. In *12th IEEE International Conference on Engineering Complex Computer Systems (ICECCS 2007)* (pp. 97-106). IEEE. DOI: 10.1109/ICECCS.2007.11

Mujagić, A., & Mehanović, D. (2024, June). Predictive Analysis of Chess Player Performance: An Analysis of Factors Influencing Competitive Success Using Machine Learning Techniques. In *International Symposium on Innovative and Interdisciplinary Applications of Advanced Technologies* (pp. 392-408). Cham: Springer Nature Switzerland. DOI: 10.1007/978-3-031-71694-2_29

Olugbenga, A. M., Adenike, A. E., Esther, O. O., Michael, A. A., Samsudeen, B. O., & Ibrahim, A. O. (2024). Development of a Distributed Denial of Service Detection Model Using Ensemble Machine Learning Techniques. *Adeleke University Journal of Science, 3*(1), 205–218.

Patria, R., Favian, S., Caturdewa, A., & Suhartono, D. (2021, December). Cheat detection on online chess games using convolutional and dense neural network. In *2021 4th International Seminar on Research of Information Technology and Intelligent Systems (ISRITI)* (pp. 389-395). IEEE. DOI: 10.1109/ISRITI54043.2021.9702792

Regan, K., & Haworth, G. (2011, August). Intrinsic chess ratings. *Proceedings of the AAAI Conference on Artificial Intelligence, 25*(1), 834–839. DOI: 10.1609/aaai.v25i1.7951

Saarinen, T. (2017). *Toxic behavior in online games* (Master's thesis, T. Saarinen).

Suthaharan, S., & Suthaharan, S. (2016). Support vector machine. *Machine learning models and algorithms for big data classification: thinking with examples for effective learning*, 207-235.

Turab, A., Mlaiki, N., Fatima, N., Mitrović, Z. D., & Ali, W. (2022). Analysis of a class of stochastic animal behavior models under specific choice preferences. *Mathematics, 10*(12), 1975. DOI: 10.3390/math10121975

Turab, A., Montoyo, A., & Nescolarde-Selva, J. A. (2024). Computational and analytical analysis of integral-differential equations for modeling avoidance learning behavior. *Journal of Applied Mathematics & Computing, 70*(5), 4423–4439. DOI: 10.1007/s12190-024-02130-3

Turab, A., Nescolarde-Selva, J. A., Ullah, F., Montoyo, A., Alfiniyah, C., Sintunavarat, W., Rizk, D., & Zaidi, S. A. (2025). Deep neural networks and stochastic methods for cognitive modeling of rat behavioral dynamics in T-mazes. *Cognitive Neurodynamics*, *19*(1), 1–28. DOI: 10.1007/s11571-025-10247-9 PMID: 40290756

Turab, A., Sintunavarat, W., Ullah, F., Zaidi, S. A., Montoyo, A., & Nescolarde-Selva, J. A. (2024). Computational modeling of animal behavior in T-mazes: Insights from machine learning. *Ecological Informatics*, *81*, 102639. DOI: 10.1016/j.ecoinf.2024.102639

Weatherton, A. V. (2025). *Detecting Tool-Assisted Cheating in Competitive Video Gaming Using Machine Learning*. The George Washington University.

Yan, J., & Randell, B. (2005, October). A systematic classification of cheating in online games. In *Proceedings of 4th ACM SIGCOMM workshop on Network and system support for games* (pp. 1-9). DOI: 10.1145/1103599.1103606

Yeung, S. F., & Lui, J. C. (2008). Dynamic Bayesian approach for detecting cheats in multi-player online games. *Multimedia Systems*, *14*(4), 221–236. DOI: 10.1007/s00530-008-0113-5

Zaksaitė, S. (2020). Cheating in chess: a call for an integrated disciplinary regulation. *Kriminologijos studijos, 8*, 57-83.

Zaksaitė, S. (2022). Anti-cheating protection measures in chess: Current state of play. *Crime Prevention and Community Safety*, *24*(3), 255–265. DOI: 10.1057/s41300-022-00149-x

Zaksaitė, S. (2022). Anti-cheating protection measures in chess: Current state of play. *Crime Prevention and Community Safety*, *24*(3), 255–265. DOI: 10.1057/s41300-022-00149-x

ENDNOTES

1 https://commons.wikimedia.org/wiki/File:SVM_margin.png

2 https://databasecamp.de/en/ml/naive-bayes-algorithm

3 https://commons.wikimedia.org/wiki/File:Random_forest_explain.png

4 https://commons.wikimedia.org/wiki/File:Exam_pass_logistic_curve.svg

5 https://www.kaggle.com/datasets/brieucdandoy/chess-cheating-dataset

APPENDIX

Table 3. Overview of Studies in Online Game and Chess Cheat Detection

Sr No	Title of Paper	Objective(s)	Method	Results and Findings	Ref
1	*On the Limits of Engine Analysis for Cheating Detection in Chess*	To examine the challenges and limitations of Detecting cheating in chess by analyzing moves with chess engines and identifying risks of false positives.	Analysis of a large dataset of games where no cheating occurred; evaluation of misclassification risks; examination of chess-engine similarity metrics under different evaluation conditions.	The study suggests that examining the moves of a single game is not credible proof of cheating and emphasizes the large risk of false positives in engine-based analysis. Because of the examination of depth and multi-threading, current Measurements differ.	Barnes, D. J., & Hernandez-Castro, J. (2015). On the limits of engine analysis for cheating detection in chess. *Computers & Security*, 48, 58-73.
2	*A Systematic Classification of Cheating in Online Games*	To provide a comprehensive taxonomy of Cheating methods in online games, categorize them by vulnerabilities, consequences, and the cheating principal.	A three-dimensional taxonomy is developed based on (1) vulnerabilities (e.g., system inadequacies or user behavior), (2) consequences (e.g., fairness violation, data theft), and (3) the identity of the cheating principal.	Identified 15 cheating forms and showed that fairness, beyond traditional security aspects (e.g., confidentiality, integrity), is crucial. The taxonomy helps developers and researchers design and operate fair and secure online games.	Yan, J., & Randell, B. (2005, October). A systematic classification of cheating in online games. In *Proceedings of 4th ACM SIGCOMM workshop on Network and system support for games* (pp. 1-9).

continued on following page

Table 3. Continued

Sr No	Title of Paper	Objective(s)	Method	Results and Findings	Ref
3	*Predictive Analysis of Chess Player Performance: An Analysis of Factors Influencing Competitive Success Using Machine Learning Techniques*	Represent factors influencing chess performance (e.g., experience, skill level, current form, and psychological aspects) as features in a dataset and use machine learning for prediction.	Data collection, cleaning, and feature extraction; model training using various machine learning techniques; Random Forest classifier combined with an award-streak form for evaluation function.	The Random Forest classifier achieved a peak accuracy of 68.67% and an average accuracy of ~60.40%. The most influential factor is the relative difference in playing strength. Larger recent game sets improve prediction accuracy.	Mujagić, A., Mujagić, A., & Mehanović, D. (2024, June). Predictive Analysis of Chess Player Performance: An Analysis of Factors Influencing Competitive Success Using Machine Learning Techniques. In International Symposium on Innovative and Interdisciplinary Applications of Advanced Technologies (pp. 392-408). Cham: Springer Nature Switzerland.

continued on following page

Table 3. Continued

Sr No	Title of Paper	Objective(s)	Method	Results and Findings	Ref
4	*Behavior-Based Approaches for Detecting Cheating in Online Games*	To analyze and propose behavior-based methods for detecting cheating in online games without breaching user privacy.	Examines existing anti-cheating measures in the gaming industry, highlighting their strengths and weaknesses, with a focus on privacy-preserving Behavioral detection techniques.	Many anti-cheating solutions involve privacy breaches. The study emphasizes the importance of behavior-based detection techniques as a more ethical and effective approach to detecting and preventing cheating in online games.	Alayed, H. A. (2015). *Behavior-Based Approaches for Detecting Cheating in Online Games* (Doctoral dissertation, University of Southern California).
5	*Cheat Detection on Online Chess Games Using Convolutional and Dense Neural Network*	To develop and evaluate cheat detection tools for online chess using analyzed and unanalyzed data with CNN and densely connected neural networks.	Comparison of CNN and densely connected neural networks; testing with analyzed and unanalyzed chess game data to evaluate the effectiveness of both algorithms and data types.	CNN outperformed the densely connected neural network for cheat detection. Analyzed data improved the accuracy of both models, though the type of data did not change which neural network performed best.	Patria, R., Favian, S., Caturdewa, A., & Suhartono, D. (2021, December). Cheat detection on online chess games using convolutional and dense neural network. In *2021 4th International Seminar on Research of Information Technology and Intelligent Systems (ISRITI)* (pp. 389-395). IEEE.

Table 4. Overview of Studies focused on Cheating Detection across different domains

Domain	Primary Goal	Key Methods & Techniques	Key Results & Findings	Paper Reference / Citation
Online Exam Proctoring	Ensure academic integrity in remote assessments.	DNN, CNN, SVM, Random Forest	**High Accuracy (81% - 98%)**. Effective but can be computationally heavy and raise privacy concerns.	Erdem, B., & Karabatak, M. (2025).
Competitive Video Games	Maintain fair play by detecting automated cheating tools.	CatBoost, Transformers, Random Forest, LSTM	**Highly Effective (F1 up to 0.96, Acc. up to 99%)**. Server-side behavioral analysis is a robust, non-invasive method.	Weatherton, A. V. (2025).
Strategy Games (GO)	Detect if a player is receiving computer assistance.	AI-based Evaluation Metrics	**Methodologically Sound**. Provides a blueprint for using an AI engine to evaluate human moves, directly applicable to chess.	Egri-Nagy, A., & Törmänen, A. (2020, November)
Financial Fraud Detection	Identify fraudulent transactions in real-time.	Random Forest, XGBoost, LightGBM	**Extremely High Accuracy (98% - 99.9%)**. Success hinges on handling severe class imbalance in the data.	Anjum, S. H., & Patil, G. (2022, November).
AI-Generated Text Detection	Distinguish between human-written and AI-generated text/code.	SVM, AST-based Deep Learning, Contrastive Learning	**Highly Accurate (>90%)**. Can detect stylistic differences, though performance may drop against sophisticated mimicry.	Dang, T. L., Hoang, N. M. N., Nguyen, T. V., Nguyen, H. V., Dang, Q. M., Tran, Q. H., & Pham, H. H. (2025).
Contract Cheating (Keystroke)	Verify the authorship of submitted work.	Traditional ML Classifiers	**Effective with High Specificity**. Reliable for user discrimination under a "zero false accusation" constraint.	Agarwal, N., Danielsen, N. F., Gravdal, P. K., & Bours, P. (2022, October).
Proposed Chess Cheating Detection	Identify instances of computer assistance in chess games.	*Support Vector Machine (SVM), Random Forest, Decision Tree, Logistic Regression, Naive Bayes, and Long Short-Term Memory (LSTM)*	*Random Forest: 76.15%, SVM: 74.90%, The Decision Tree model: 74.53%, Logistic Regression: 74.50%, Naive Bayes: 74.14%, The LSTM model: 75.78%.*	Our Study

Chapter 9

Behavioral Biometric Authentication using Keystroke and Mouse Dynamics on a Non-Touch Virtual Keyboard Using Machine Learning Approaches

D. Shanmugapriya
https://orcid.org/0000-0002-7446-6749
Avinashilingam Institute for Home Science and Higher Education for Women, India

S. Sivasankari
https://orcid.org/0009-0005-4550-8005
Avinashilingam Institute for Home Science and Higher Education for Women, India

S. Asha
https://orcid.org/0000-0001-6302-1528
Avinashilingam Institute for Home Science and Higher Education for Women, India

ABSTRACT

Behavioral biometrics is one of the approaches to mitigate the vulnerabilities of traditional authentication methods. This chapter examines behavioral biometrics,

DOI: 10.4018/979-8-3373-5062-2.ch009

focusing on keystroke and mouse click patterns on a non-touch virtual keyboard. This study proposes a non-touch virtual keyboard system (static and dynamic layouts) for collecting keystroke and mouse dynamics. A total of 144 features were extracted from real-time data collection system with 100 users and preprocessed using IQR clipping, min–max scaling, and low-pass filtering. Data augmentation was performed using a vanilla GAN, followed by RFE-based feature selection. Models including RF, SVM, and XGBoost were evaluated, achieving up to 91% accuracy with very low FAR/FRR and minimal training time. These results demonstrate that behavior-based security provides an effective additional layer of protection, particularly valuable in sensitive domains such as finance, defence, and critical infrastructure.

INTRODUCTION

User authentication is a key process in the world of digital security; It is important for securing confidential information and digital resources from unethical users and unauthorized access. The process of user authentication involves verifying and identifying the authorized individuals who seek access to digital services and their data. It plays as a crucial security mechanism that ensures that only legitimate users are authorized to access secured systems and platforms.

User authentication traditionally includes a series of verification steps to verify the authorization of a person's original identity. This process involves the submission of credentials—such as usernames, passwords, PINs, or even biometric data—which are validated every time, comparing the pre-registered information stored within the database. This process of authentication works as a protective mechanism that allows access only to those users who can prove their identity through the provided credentials.

Recent advancements in understanding complex behaviors in both humans and animals demand the integration of computational precision and adaptive learning. Recent developments in deep learning and analytical modeling have enabled researchers to accurately decode behavioral patterns, cognitive processes, and decision-making mechanisms. The integration of machine learning or deep learning models with data-driven algorithms facilitates a comprehensive analysis, prediction, and interpretation of dynamic behavioral responses in both natural and experimental contexts (Turab et al., 2022; Turab et al., 2024a; Turab et al., 2024b; Turab et al., 2025). These advancements improve computational comprehension and offer methodological frameworks suitable for secure and intelligent authentication systems. Hence, this chapter positions behavioral biometric authentication within the broader framework of computational and deep learning approaches for advanced behavioral analysis, aligning with current research trends in cognitive and security informatics.

Types of Biometric Authentication

Biometric authentication usually relies on remarkable physical or behavioural properties of every individual for verifying the identity. Enormous biometric modalities offer different levels of accuracy, convenience, and security. Various biometric authentication methods, such as those below, employ diverse techniques for verifying and identifying users.

Fingerprint Recognition: It depends on the unique fingertip design for exact accuracy and convenience, usually combined with devices like smartphones and access systems.

Facial Recognition: Detect individuals by analyzing facial features, which is mostly used but faces privacy and bias concerns, especially in surveillance and access control.

Iris Recognition: Provides high security by analyzing iris patterns but requires the most complicated hardware.

Voice Recognition: Authenticates users based on distinctive voice traits, convenient yet susceptible to environmental factors, suitable for phone and dedicated devices.

Behavioral Biometrics: Analyzes behavior patterns like typing speed and then provides an extra layer of security, though continuous monitoring may raise privacy issues.

Keystroke Dynamics

Keystroke dynamics or typing biometrics is an authentication technique that analyzes users' typing patterns. Every keyboard interaction from every user is different; it includes the velocity of key presses, timing of pauses, and even the timing of typographical errors.

Unlike legacy systems, where a user logs in with something they know, either a password or a PIN, keystroke dynamics allows for continuous verification. Instead of confirming the identity of the user only once upon login, it switches to monitoring the user's typing patterns during the whole session in real time.

Nonetheless, there are several issues to address. A person's mood, fatigue, or stress can impact their typing habits, which makes maintaining the profile in question unreliable. Additionally, profiles built from typing patterns require a lot of data before making automated decisions due to their low validation. Regardless, this approach offers powerful solutions for reducing security risks while enhancing user awareness.

Mouse Dynamics

Mouse dynamics analyzes the speed, how fast it changes, the path, and the clicking pattern. By making a unique profile for each user based on these moves, mouse moves give a way to check identities all the time. This gives an extra layer of safety apart from the usual methods.

Mouse moves have various benefits that include boosting security and giving continuous checks. But they also face issues like changes in how people use the mouse due to being tired or distracted. Additionally, enough data is needed to make a true profile, which can be tough if there isn't much user activity. Still, mouse click patterns can be used to secure systems by using the unique behaviors of mouse use.

BACKGROUND

The following tables, Table 1 and Table 2, analyze the literature available along with the dataset used, algorithms applied, and key observations of the work done.

Table 1. Review analysis on recent research work

Study	Dataset Used	Algorithms applied	Observations
Bansal, P., & Ouda, A. (2024). Continuous authentication in the digital age: An analysis of reinforcement learning and behavioral biometrics.	BB- MA DATASET	Double deep Q- network (DDQN)	Accuracy:81.06% EE R:0.0323 FAR:0.0356 FRR:0.0174
Altwaijry, N. (2023). Authentication by keystroke dynamics: The influence of typing language.	Bilingual Keystroke Dynamics Dataset	AdaBoost, decision tree, random forest, and support vector Machine.	Arabic and English, hampers authentication systems as identical letter patterns and consistent finger movements complicate accurate user identification.
Grunova, D., & Tsimperidis, I. (2023). Finding the age and education level of Bulgarian-speaking internet users using keystroke dynamics.	Collected from Bulgarian Users	Naïve Bayes, SVM, Multilayer Perceptron and Random Forest.	It resulted in possibility of creating reliable systems for identifying the age and educational level of the Bulgarian speaking users with accuracy of 93% and 86%

continued on following page

Table 1. Continued

Study	Dataset Used	Algorithms applied	Observations
Tsimperidis, I., Grunova, D., & Papakostas, G. A. (2022). The way we type reveals our native language.	Collected from different native speakers.	SVM, RBFN, TBM, BNC	SVM served as the best and most effective model in detecting the native language of each user based on keystroke events.
Nascimento, T. M. L., Oliveira, et al. (2021). Investigating the use of feature selection techniques for gender prediction systems based on keystroke dynamics.	Gout Database and Hand-Based database	k-NN, SVM and Naive Bayes	SVM performed well without selection, after the feature selection using the PSO, k-NN provides prominent results
Toosi, R., & Akhaee, M. A. (2021). Time-frequency analysis of keystroke dynamics for user authentication.	CMU dataset and GREYC dataset	WD process	Various versions for this proposed method are tested to imply the effectiveness of every part of the model.
Kiyani et al., (2020). Continuous user authentication featuring keystroke dynamics based on robust recurrent confidence model and ensemble learning approach.	The keystroke dataset provided by University of Buffalo has been used	SVM, ANN and XGboost	SVM, ANN, and XGboost were used to increase the accuracy for every action.
Buker, A. A., Roffo, G., & Vinciarelli, A. (2019). Type like a man! Inferring gender from keystroke dynamics in live-chats.	Collected from Live-chats	Recurrent Neural Networks (RNNs) or Long Short-Term Memory (LSTM) ***networks***	Presents the results of the gender inference experiment, including accuracy rates and any challenges or limitations encountered during the analysis.
Salem, A., & Obaidat, M. S. (2019). A novel security scheme for behavioral authentication systems based on keystroke dynamics.	Dataset extracted from several devices such as classical keyboard and built- in software keyboard in touch screen and smart phone devices	Neural network classifiers	keystroke dynamics resulted in best level for measures as the second authentication way.
Hriez, S., Obeid, N., & Awajan, A. (2019). User authentication on smartphones using keystroke dynamics.	Dataset used in this research consists of 71 features for 42 users with 2142 records.	Random Forest machine learning algorithm	Accuracy of 94.26%.
Anusasamornkul, T. (2019). Strengthening password authentication using keystroke dynamics and smartphone sensors.	A mobile application was developed to collect a new dataset using Android Studio with JAVA language and SQLite database.	Naïve Bayes, k Nearest Neighbors (kNN), and Random Forest	Random Forest classifier gives the best performance with the accuracy percentage which is high at 97.90% and EER is 5.1% .

continued on following page

Table 1. Continued

Study	Dataset Used	Algorithms applied	Observations
Cilia, D., & Inguanez, F. (2018). Multi-model authentication using keystroke dynamics for smartphones.	***An Android typing app collected touch data from 24 users***	SVM ***classifier***	SVM classifier with Equal Error Rate values as low as 0.44%.
Krishnamoorthy, S., Rueda, L., & Saad, S. (2018). Identification of user behavioral biometrics for authentication using keystroke dynamics and machine learning.	***Data from 94 users were collected to carry out the research***	Support Vector Machine (SVM) classifier	It implies that pressure on the touch and size of the touch coordinates contribute in detecting every user.
Salmeron-Majadas, S., Baker, R. S., Santos, O. C., & Boticario, J. G. (2018). A machine learning approach to leverage individual keyboard and mouse interaction behavior from multiple users in real-world learning scenarios.	The dataset was collected from participants using MOKEETO ***(Mouse and Keyboard logging Essay writing Tool)***	***Random Forest and SVM***	Random Forest, SVM. found the important issue in identifying the effect of old non-intrusive interaction sources.
Tsimperidis, I., Arampatzis, A., & Karakos, A. (2018). Keystroke dynamics features for gender recognition.	Data was gathered via the "IRecU" free- text keylogger on Windows devices from 117 participants, yielding 75 log file returns	RBFN model	The RBFN model accurately predicts gender in keystroke dynamics with a 95.6% accuracy
Mäntyjärvi, J., Koivumäki, J., & Vuori, P. (2017). Keystroke recognition for virtual keyboard.	***Realtime data***	***K-Nearest Neighbor (k-NN), Multilayer Perceptron (MLP)***	Recognition accuracy: 78%–99% for k-NN, 69%–96% for MLP; experiments and results presented

Table 2. Review analysis on recent research work based on selected features

STUDY	DATASET USED	FEATURES USED	RESULTS AND OBSERVATIONS
Khan, S., Devlen, C., Manno, M., & Hou, D. (2024). Mouse dynamics behavioral biometrics: A survey.	Data collection categories based on user actions and the app/data collection software	Mouse Features: mouse down; mouse up; mouse scroll; mouse click	Highlighting their promising performance in user authentication and identifying research opportunities.
Tsimperidis, I., Grunova, D., Roy, S., & Moussiades, L. (2023). Keystroke dynamics as a language profiling tool: Identifying mother tongue of unknown internet users.	100 of users from 5 different languages were approached to participate in the project	Keyboard features: PR,keystroke duration	82% accuracy was attained in recognizing an unknown user's mother tongue
Hosseinia, P., Abinb, A. A., & Rajc, A. T. (2023). Continuous user authentication using a combination of operation and application-related features.	The dataset was collected internally.	Keystroke Features: Extent of using specific keys, Typing speed per minute Mouse Features: velocity of mouse, mouse movements, Mouse clicks, Duration of holding mouse	Employed a hybrid OCSVM and PSO method for detection
Shi, Y., Wang, X., Zheng, K., & Cao, S. (2022). User authentication method based on keystroke dynamics and mouse dynamics using HDA.	Human–Computer Interaction (HCI)	Keystroke: Press & Release, Dwell Time, Flight Time, Press–Press, Release–Release, Press–Release, Release–Press Mouse: Mouse Move, Point-and-Click, Drag-and-Drop, Silence	Achieved 89.22% user authentication accuracy
Acien, A., Morales, A., & Vera-Rodriguez, R. (2022). Detection of mental fatigue in the general population: Feasibility study of keystroke dynamics as a real-world biomarker.	Aalto, neuroQWE RTY Sleep Inertia, neuroQWE RTY Crowdsource	Keystroke Features: press times, release times,hold times, flight times, interkey latency ,interrelease latency	SVMs achieving 72.2% to 80% Accuracy
Zeid, S. S., ElKamar, R. A., & Hassan, S. I. (2022). Fixed-text vs. free-text keystroke dynamics for user authentication.	The MOBIKEY Keystroke Dynamics Password Database,The Politehnica University Timisoara	Keyboard features: Press and Release, hold time, flight time, down down time and up down time.	Highest accuracy with RF classifier.

continued on following page

Table 2. Continued

STUDY	DATASET USED	FEATURES USED	RESULTS AND OBSERVATIONS
Thomas, P. A., & Mathew, K. P. (2021). A broad review on non-intrusive active user authentication in biometrics.	User Trials	Keystroke Features: Press Time, Release Time, Press-Release ,Pres- Press,Release-Release,Release- Press, Hold Time Mouse Features: Mouse event e Horizontal coordinate , Vertical coordinate , Movement offset, Acceleration	RF strategy
Tsimperidis, I., Yucel, C., & Katos, V. (2021). Age and gender as cyber attribution features in keystroke dynamic-based user classification processes.	387 log files	Keyboard features: Press and Release, down- down diagram latencies; down-up;up-down; up- up	Finding the gender and age of an unknown user, for each different feature set, using SVM
Li, J., Chang, H.-C., & Stamp, M. (2021). Free-text keystroke dynamics for user authentication.	Clarkson II keystroke dataset and the Buffalo keystroke dataset	Keystroke Features: Press Time, Release Time, Press-Release ,Pres- Press,Release-Release,Release- Press, Duration Time	CNN architecture outperforms a combination of CNN and RNN
Tsimperidis, I., & Arampatzis, A. (2020). The keyboard knows about you: Revealing user characteristics via keystroke dynamics.	Collected free- text data from volunteers who agreed to participate	Keyboard features: Press and Release, keystroke duration, down- down digram latencies.	KD features are selected to identify the gender, age, handedness and educational level of an unknown user
Cockell, R., & Halak, B. (2020). On the design and analysis of a biometric authentication system using keystroke dynamics.	Data obtained from 32 users	Keyboard features: Press and Release Time	Cost-efficient solution for biometric user authentication with an average error rate of 4.5%.
Ayotte, B., & Hou, D. (2020). Fast free-text authentication via instance-based keystroke dynamics.	Clarkson II uncontrolle d free-text dataset and the Buffalo partially controlled free- text dataset	Keyboard features: Press and Release, Release—Press, Press—Press, Release—Release, Press— Release	Capable of detecting impostors more than twice as fast as the previous state-of-the-art.

continued on following page

Table 2. Continued

STUDY	DATASET USED	FEATURES USED	RESULTS AND OBSERVATIONS
Wang, X., Zheng, Q., Zheng, K., & Wu, T. (2020). User authentication method based on MKL for keystroke and mouse behavioral feature fusion.	Volunteer data, uncontrolled condition	Keystroke: Hold Time, RP Time, PR Time, PP Time, RR Time Mouse: Mouse Move, Drag Drop, Point-and-Click, Silence	Best time-slice: 5 min; accuracy: 89.6%
Antal, M., & Fejer, N. (2020). Mouse dynamics-based user recognition using deep learning.	The Balabit Mouse Challenge data set] and the DFL data set.	Segment mouse events based on threshold.	The impact of preprocessing on biometric identification using mouse dynamics data.
Li, G., Borj, P. R., Bergeron, L., & Bours, P. (2019). Exploring keystroke dynamics and stylometry features for gender prediction on chat data.	Text data were gathered during Skype chats among participants conversing on preferred topics to facilitate acquaintance.	Keyboard features: duration of first letter, duration of second letter, latency between first key released and the second key pressed, latency between first key pressed and the second key pressed. latency between first key released	A Random Forest with 72% prediction accuracy
Escobar-Grisales et al., (2020). Identity verification in virtual education using biometric analysis based on keystroke dynamics.	Virtual education platform; 5 tasks	Keystroke: Hold Time, Flight Time (133 keystrokes)	Used Gaussian Mixture Models (GMMs); EER: 15.7%, CUA considered both intrusive & non-intrusive modes
Tzafilkou, K., & Protogeros, N. (2018). Mouse behavioral patterns and keystroke dynamics in end-user development: What can they tell us about users' behavioral attributes?.	30 end users interacting with web-based EUD tool for Developing a easy web forms.	Keystroke Features: keydown, keypress, keyup, Dwell Time, Flight Time Mouse Features: mouse clicks; mouse moves; mouse hovers; key press; key release.	Mouse and keyboard monitoring can offer valuable real-time feedback in EUD environments
Salmeron-Majadas, S., Baker, R. S., Santos, O. C., & Boticario, J. G. (2018). A machine learning approach to leverage individual keyboard and mouse interaction behavior.	MOKEETO dataset	Keystroke: Dwell Time, Press Time, Release Time, Digraph, Trigraph, Typing Speed Mouse: Distance-based features, precision, distance covered	Used Random Forest, SVM; addressed affect detection from non-intrusive sources

continued on following page

Table 2. Continued

STUDY	DATASET USED	FEATURES USED	RESULTS AND OBSERVATIONS
Mondal, S., & Bours, P. (2017). Person identification by keystroke dynamics using pairwise user coupling.	Datasets from online exams involving 64 individuals across three typing modes	Keyboard features: Key Press, Key Release	SVM, CPANN and DT in a weighted fusion approach have achieved 9.9% to 19.7% less identification of accuracy
Pentel, A. (2017). Predicting age and gender by keystroke dynamics and mouse patterns.	Avar Pentel Tallinn University , School of Digital Technolog ies Tallinn, Estonia	Mouse features direction, angle, distance and velocity Keyboard features: hold times, seek times,and n-graph latencies	***Nearest Neighbor f-scores over 0.9***

From Tables 1 and 2, it is observed that there are significant advancements in behavioral biometric authentication using keystroke and mouse dynamics, and these authentication methods are used for continuous and non-intrusive user verification. Multiple datasets were used for the study. However, the combined Keystroke and Mouse dynamics dataset is not available. Machine learning algorithms were also used in identifying or authenticating users. All these studies were done on traditional keyboards, and no study was done on non-touch virtual keyboards.

METHODOLOGY AND IMPLEMENTATION

The overall methodology is shown in Figure 1. The methodology consists of seven phases, namely Data Collection, Data Cleaning, Feature Extraction, Pre-processing, Data Augmentation, Feature Selection, and classification. Each phases are explained elaborately in the following subsections.

Figure 1. Methodology overview

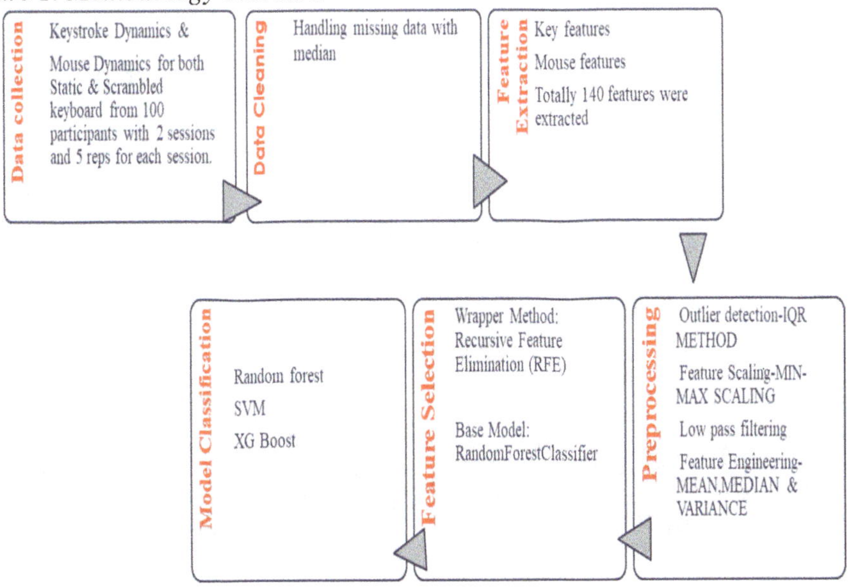

Phase 1: Data Collection

A real-time data collection system was designed to collect data from the users. Data is collected using a non-touch Static virtual keyboard, which is shown in Figure 2, and using a non-touch Dynamic Virtual keyboard, which is shown in Figure 3. The term "Non-Touch Virtual Keyboard" refers to a software-based on-screen keyboard operated with a mouse rather than a physical or touchscreen input.

Figure 2. GUI of Static Keyboard

Figure 3. GUI of Dynamic Keyboard

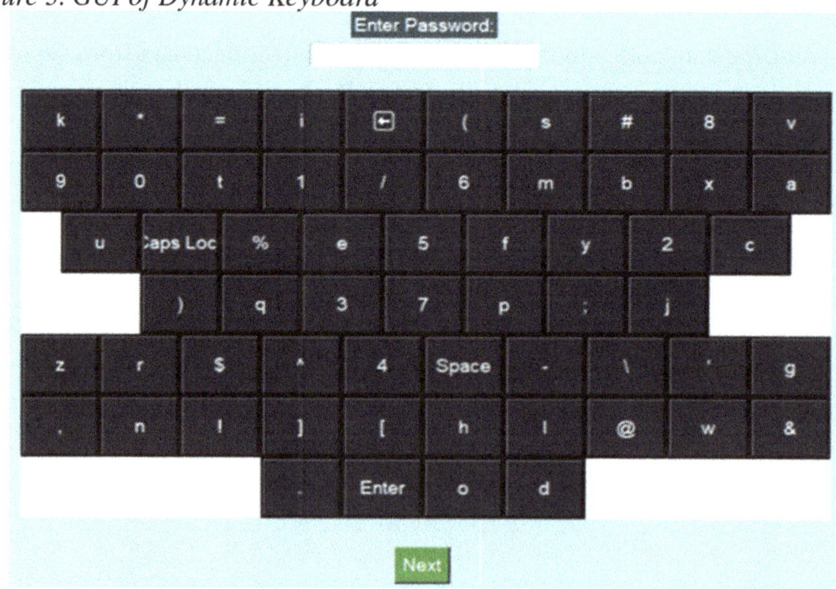

Description of Keyboard Layouts

The Static virtual keyboard is created in the format of a QWERTY layout with numbers 0-9 and symbols. Special keys like Caps Lock, backspace, enter, and space keys are also present. The layout is fixed, so the keys remain in the same position during every session. The key font colour is given as white with a black background. The caps lock key toggles the capitalization of letter keys when clicked. A text box for entering the given password field is placed below the label. Since the GUI should hide the real password, the password field is masked and displayed as * instead of actual characters while typing. The user has to type the predefined password "j2nWdak.ml" and it is designed to capture the keystroke and mouse dynamic events. A button with the label "Next" is created. The font is set to white with a green background. The Next button is responsible for handling repetitions of password entry. This will make sure that the user enters the password multiple times. When this button is clicked, the next_repetition() function is called. It increases the repetition count by 1 and tracks how many times the password has been entered. It records the data to the file and resets the password field. The maximum repetition is set as 5. If the repetition count exceeds the maximum repetition count, the button is disabled. The button turns red to indicate that no further input is required. A message "All repetition completed" is printed. Unlike the static keyboard, which has a static QWERTY layout, the Dynamic keyboard shuffles the key positions for every repetition. After pressing the "Next" button, a new randomized keyboard is generated. This ensures that users rely more on visual recognition rather than muscle memory, making behavioural biometrics more difficult to fake. The remaining functionalities are the same as those of the Static keyboard. Every data that has been entered is stored in the database.

Keystroke and Mouse Dynamics Features Captured:

This section details the features captured by both Keystroke and Mouse dynamics with static and dynamic non-touch virtual keyboards.

Keystroke Dynamics Features Captured:

Both the Static and Dynamic virtual keyboard capture detailed **keystroke dynamics**, which include:

- Press & Release Times (for dwell time)
- Keystroke Transition Timings
- Down-Down (DD)

- Up-Down (UD)
- Press-Release (PR)
- Release-Release (RR)
- Digraph & Trigraph Timing

These features collectively describe the user's typing rhythm, timing consistency, and transition fluency between successive keys.

Mouse Dynamics features captured.

Similarly, both the Static and Dynamic virtual keyboard records comprehensive **mouse dynamics**, which include

- Click Duration
- Mouse Speed
- Direction
- Distance
- Hover Time

These parameters help analyze how users interact with the virtual keyboard through cursor control, click precision, and hand movement behavior.

The Caps Lock key toggles between uppercase and lowercase every time it is pressed. Each participant typed the same password "j2nWdak.ml" five times per session. The entire process was repeated in subsequent sessions.

Password Design

The password "j2nWdak.ml" was carefully designed with a balanced combination of letters, numbers, and symbols, making it suitable for security and keystroke dynamics analysis. The following subsections elaborate on the components, strength analysis, and character diversity of the password used for the study.

A. Components of the password

The password "j2nWdak.ml" consists of the following elements:

- Lowercase Letters: j, n, d, a, k, m, l - 7 characters
- Uppercase Letters: W - 1 character
- Numbers: 2 - 1 character
- Special Characters: "." - 1 character

- Total Length: 10 Characters

B. Strength Analysis

A password's strength is analysed by using many factors like its length, character diversity, and difficulty of prediction. With 10 characters, "j2nWdak.ml", exceeds the traditional length of an 8-character security recommendation, making it resilient to brute-force attacks.

C. Character Diversity

The strength of the password is increased by the inclusion of capital and lowercase letters, digits, and special characters.

- Adding just one capital letter (W) to the password makes it stronger without making it too hard to remember.
- Since many password-cracking algorithms have trouble with non-alphanumeric characters, including a period ('.') as a special character improves security.

D. Unpredictability

The password does not follow any sequence of any common word or phrase, making it resistant to dictionary attacks. Randomized letter-number-symbol combinations reduce the likelihood of an attacker guessing the password.

E. Security

The password used for the study is resilient to Brute-Force attacks, Dictionary attacks, and social engineering attacks, and is detailed below:

Protection Against Brute-Force Attacks.

Brute-force attacks involve systematically guessing passwords. With the password of four-character type (Lowercase, Uppercase, Digits, and Symbols), and a length of 10 characters, the number of possible combinations is:

$(26_{\text{lowercase}}+26_{\text{uppercase}}+10_{\text{digits+}}33_{\text{symbols}})^{10}$ ------- (1)

This results in the combinations of trillions, making brute-force cracking highly impossible.

Defence Against Dictionary Attacks.

The Dictionary attacks use pre-defined word lists to guess the passwords. Since "j2nWdak.ml" is not a common word or phrase, it is resistant to this type of attack. The combination of letters and numbers further increases resistance.

Resistance to Social Engineering Attacks

Users frequently choose a password related to personal details such as birthdays or pet names. But the password "j2nWdak.ml" does not contain such information, making it resistant to social engineering attacks.

F. Relevance to Keystroke and Mouse Dynamics Research

This password is specifically chosen for keystroke and mouse dynamics research for the following reasons:

1. Diverse Typing Patterns, as it has a mix of both left-handed and right-handed keystrokes, which ensures that various typing patterns are available. The password changes between letters, numbers, and symbols, which creates unique digraph and trigraph transitions.
2. Keystroke Timings Analysis as the uppercase 'W' introduces a time delay where the user has to type the caps lock before entering the letter W. The period ('.') requires a different hand motion, adding complexity to the typing pattern.
3. Impact on Biometric Authentication, as the unique typing rhythms and speed help to differentiate between different users. It enables research into press and release timings, dwell time, and transition speeds.

G. Data Capture Process and Ethical Considerations

As the user types the password, the keystroke and mouse event timings are captured and stored in the database, which analyse how the user interacts with the virtual keyboard. Totally, six events are collected from the users. For keystroke, UD (UP-Down), DD (Down_Down), and Hold Time were collected. For Mouse dynamics, ClickDown, ClickUp, and Mouse Position were recorded. The following Figure 4 shows the raw keystroke events captured during password entry.

Figure 4. Raw keystroke events

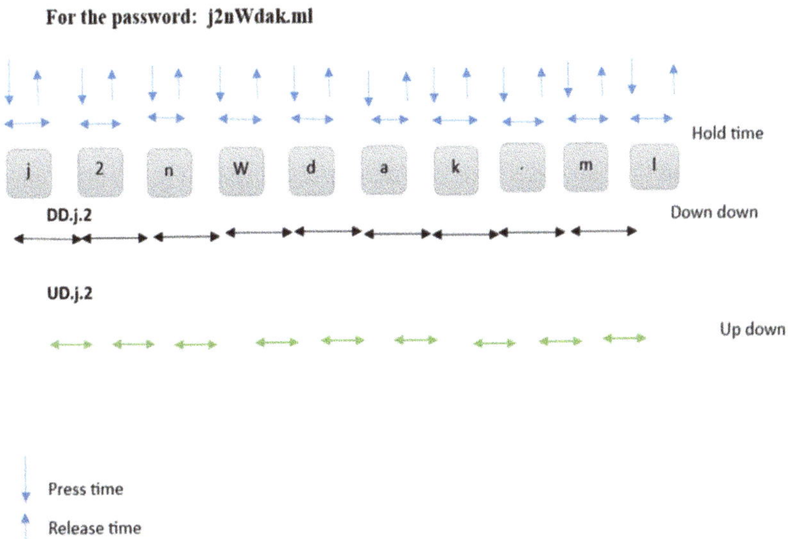

The Up-Down Latency, denoted as UD. key1.key2 measures the time between releasing one key and pressing another, the Down-Down Latency, DD. key1.key2 measures the time that happens between pressing two consecutive keys, and the Hold Time, H.key measures the duration of time that has been taken for a key that is being held before being released. These raw features are used to calculate the typing speed, fluency, and key-pressing patterns. Shorter hold times indicate faster typists, while the longer hold times suggest hesitation. The mouse dynamics, clickDown. key, captures the timings of pressing a key using the mouse button, ClickUp.key captures the timings of releasing a key using the mouse button, and MousePosition. key captures the cursor's x-y coordinates at the time of clicking the mouse button. Mouse dynamics help understand hand movement, reaction time, and screen navigation patterns. Variations in mouse movement will help to differentiate users based on cursor behavior while typing.

All the behavioural data were collected from the participants with informed consent. The data were anonymized, stored securely, and used only for research purposes.

Phase 2: Data Cleaning

Data collected with the virtual keyboard during the data collection phase includes timestamps, key press durations, transition times between keys, and mouse dynamics. However, due to many reasons such as data collection errors, latency issues, or user interruptions, certain values might be missing. If these missing values are not handled properly, they can inversely affect the analysis and classification process.

Steps in the Preprocessing Approach

1. Reading the Raw Keystroke Data. The process starts by loading the collected keystroke data from the database. This raw database consists of many columns, each representing various keystrokes and mouse events. Some values may be missing due to incorrect typing of the password.

2. Identifying and Removing Empty Columns. Within the collected raw dataset, some features may be completely empty, which represents that no valid data was captured for any of the events. Such null columns do not contribute to the next processes, like feature extraction. So, they need to be removed to maintain consistency and reduce the complexity.

3. **Handling missing values using the median.** For any events that are captured with only limited missing values, the median imputation method is applied, instead of removing them completely. The median is calculated by sorting the list of numbers and taking the middle value.

Phase 3: Feature Extraction

After data cleaning, the refined dataset was processed to extract keystroke and mouse dynamics features. Several variables are created to track the previous user actions.

A variable **previous mouse position**, calculate the movement direction, and mouse acceleration. Another variable tracks the last time the cursor was moved. Multiple other variables store previous key press and release times, allowing the calculation of time gaps between successive key actions. A dedicated variable records the timestamp of the last mouse click event for combined keyboard-mouse timing analysis.

Initially, the columns that contain mouse position are represented as text/strings. These are converted into numerical coordinates (x,y) to facilitate the computation. The cursor speed is calculated by dividing the movement distance by the time elapsed. The direction of mouse movement is computed based on the horizontal, vertical, or diagonal movement of the mouse and represented as angular or categorical values.

For columns corresponding to key press and key release, Hold Time (Dwell Time), Press-Press interval, Digraph, Trigraph, Typing Speed, and Sequence timing were extracted. When a key press follows a mouse click, the delay between these two events is also recorded to capture cross-modal response timing. Figure 5 and Figure 6 illustrate the Keystroke events and Mouse Path Deviation for the password used in the study.

Figure 5. Diagrammatic representation of keystroke events for the password "j2n-Wdak.ml"

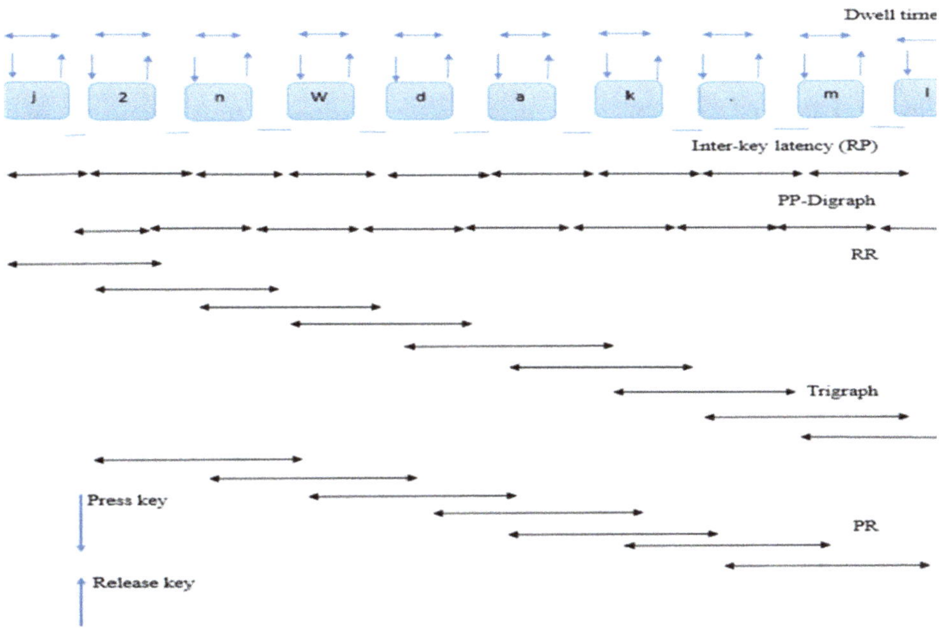

Figure 6. Mouse path deviation

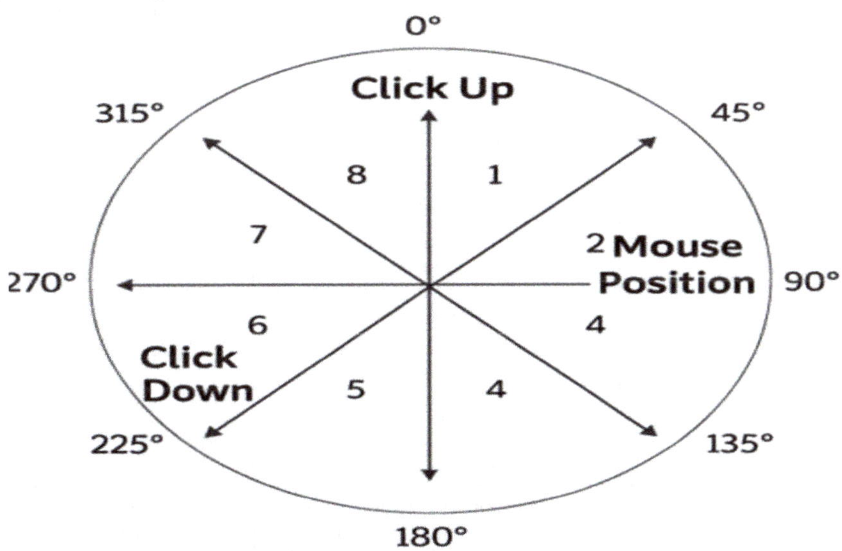

A detailed overview of all extracted features, their definitions, and formulas is presented in **Table 4**, which summarizes the extracted keystroke and mouse dynamics features used in the study.

Table 4. Extracted features

Feature Extracted	Definition	Formula
Dwell Time (Hold Time)	Time a key remains pressed during typing.	D = T_Release(Key) - T_ Press(Key)
Press Time	Moment a key is pressed down, marking the start of a keypress.	-
Release Time	Moment a key is released after being pressed.	-
Release-Release (RR)	Time interval between releasing one key and releasing the next key.	RR = T_Release(Key2) - T_ Release(Key1)
Press-Release (PR)	Time taken between current press and the next key release.	PR = T_Release(Key2) - T_ Press(Key1)
Inter-Key Latency (RP) UD	Time gap between release of one key and press of the next.	RP = T_Press(Key2) - T_ Release(Key1)
Digraph (PP) DD	Time interval between pressing two consecutive keys.	DG = T_Press(Key2) - T_ Press(Key1)
Trigraph	Time taken to press three consecutive keys in sequence.	TG = T_Press(Key3) - T_ Press(Key1)
Typing Speed (TS)	Rate at which keys are pressed, measured in keys per second.	TS = Total Keys Pressed / Total Time Taken
Key Sequence Time (KST)	Total time taken to press and release a sequence of keys.	KST = T_Release(Last Key) - T_Press(First Key)
Variance_TypingSpeed_ PerRep	Measures the variation in typing speed across a repetition.	σ^2(TS)
Mean_PressRelease	Average time taken between press of one key and release of the next.	ΣPR / n
Mean_ReleasePress	Average inter-key latency between releasing one key and pressing the next.	ΣRP / n
Mouse Position (MP)	Records the cursor position at the time of an event.	-
Click Up	Moment when a mouse button is released.	-
Click Down	Moment when a mouse button is pressed.	-
Hover Time	Time duration a cursor hovers over a key before a click.	HoverTime = T_ClickDown - T_HoverStart
Click Duration	Time duration between pressing and releasing a mouse button.	ClickDuration = T_ClickUp - T_ClickDown

continued on following page

Table 4. Continued

Feature Extracted	Definition	Formula
Cursor Speed	Speed of cursor movement between two events.	CursorSpeed = Distance / Time
Cursor Direction	Angle of cursor movement between two points.	CursorDirection = arctan(Δy / Δx)

From the six primary raw data features, twenty new features were extracted for each character of the password. A total of 144 distinct keystroke and mouse dynamics behavioural features were extracted, which form a base database for preprocessing, feature selection, and classification stages.

Phase 4: Data Preprocessing

Data preprocessing ensures that the data is clean, consistent, and suitable for further processing. It involves outlier detection, feature scaling, low-pass filtering, and feature engineering as explained below:

Outlier Detection

Outliers are extreme values that deviate largely from the other data. In keystroke and mouse dynamics, these outliers can arise due to unexpected events like user pauses while typing intentionally or sudden changes in their behaviour. If untreated, these can distort the feature distributions. For numerical columns, outliers are detected using the Interquartile Range (IQR), which involves the following steps:

Step 1: Calculate the IQR

IQR=Q3−Q1
IQR=Q3−Q1\{IQR} = Q3 - Q1
Where, Q1 = 25th percentile and Q3 = 75th percentile.

Step 2: Define the Bounds

Upper Bound $= Q3 + 1.5 \times IQR$

----- (2)

Lower Bound=Q1−1.5×IQR -------- (3)

Step 3: Cut any outliers that lie under the lower bound and set it to the lower bound, and similarly, any values above the upper bound is cut off to the upper bound.

Clipping is used instead of removal as it keeps the sample data size static, especially when the data is set to a limit, and safeguards the user identity traits by preserving the real variations in the behavioural.

Feature Scaling

In behavioural biometrics, features like TypingSpeed may range from 0.3 to 6.0, which is a normalized unit, while PressRelease may range from 50 to 100ms. Many models compute the distances or assign some weights. Features with the larger magnitude will suppress the smaller ones unless scaled properly, which results in model bias. Min-Max Normalization is used for feature scaling as it scales each feature to [0, 1] based on its minimum and maximum values across the dataset. Min-Max normalization is applied to ensure that all features contribute equally during model training. Features Scaled are TypingSpeed, PressRelease, and ReleasePress. Other normalization methods, such as Z-score, will transform the distributions, while the Min-Max keeps the actual behaviour. It stabilizes the optimization during the training period and works well with algorithms that assume data ranges (e.g., Neural Networks, SVM). Min-Max scaling compares values accurately across users and sessions when they lie within [0,1].

Low-Pass Filtering

Mouse features include click position (X, Y), click duration, Hover time, Cursor movement path, speed, and direction. A low-pass filter is applied to the CursorSpeed and HoverTime to smooth the data and reduce noise.

Feature Engineering

Feature engineering involves extracting higher-level behavioral indicators from the extracted features. The following features were engineered to capture user consistency and typing rhythm more effectively.

Mean_TypingSpeed_PerRep represents the median of all typing speeds per repetition. Median is preferred due to its robustness against sudden spikes or pauses, offering a stable measure of the user's typical rhythm.

Variance_TypingSpeed_PerRep measures how consistent a user is within a single repetition. High variance indicates unsteady or distracted typing. Low variance indicates confident and rhythmic typing.

Mean_PressRelease defines the average time a key is held down over the repetition. The Hold time is a unique user characteristic. It may correlate with personality traits or the experience of an individual - experienced typists often have shorter press durations.

Mean_ReleasePress defines the time between the release of one key and the press time of the next. Short interval indicates practiced behavior, while long gaps indicate uncertainty, possibly during password typing or unfamiliar sequences.

Phase 5: Data Augmentation

The purpose of data augmentation is to refine the performance and generalization of a model by creating altered or synthetic samples for a given dataset. Since the keystroke biometric data includes only a limited count of typing behavior records from 100 users, adding timing features such as dwell time, flight time, and latency is helpful. Moreover, creating a large set of keystroke data with data augmentation is important for training the user authentication models. In deep learning, Generative Adversarial Networks (GANs) can be used to create synthetic data to improve the performance of models that aim to identify unique keystroke patterns used for authentication. In this phase, data augmentation with GANs is performed, and the steps explained below are used for both types of keystroke data.

A GAN consists of two neural networks: the Generator and Discriminator. In Generator, the neural network analyses the available keystroke data to produce synthetic keystroke data that closely mimics the sample received. In Discriminator, the created synthetic keystroke data is compared with actual keystroke samples. Both networks undergo competitive training where the generator seeks to make believable samples and the discriminator gets better at spotting the fake versus the real. The training goes on until the generator is able to create extremely realistic keystroke dynamics.

A GAN is made up of two main networks: the generator and the discriminator. These work together in the vanillaGAN model to achieve a set goal. The training objective of the Vanilla GAN model can be expressed as:

$$\min \max V(G, D)$$

$$= \min \max E_{x\sim pr}[\log D(x)] + E_{z\sim pz}[\log (1 - D(G(z)))] \text{ ------}$$

(4)

Here, "z" is random noise. It follows the distribution pz while pr is the input sample distribution and pg is the attack sample distribution in the generator network. E stands for the expected value. The generator (G) and the discriminator (D) train against each other. With each round, they aim to get better. The discriminator wants to be better at telling real from fake samples. The generator wants to make fake samples that trick the discriminator. This goes on until the GAN reaches a high level of performance.

Procedure for Data Augmentation using GAN Architecture:

Step 1: Collect Data: Start with a real keystroke dataset that has been collected.
Step 2: Fix Features: Clean the data and simultaneously change it by normalizing it and turning it into a series sequences.
Step 3: Train the GAN:

- The generator tries to copy real keystroke data.
- The discriminator learns to spot fake data.
- Adversarial loss functions help guide training until it works well.

Step 4: Check Metrics: Study how good the GAN-made keystroke data is with these:

- Frechet Inception Distance (FID): Checks how close it is to real data.
- t-SNE Visualization: Looks at how real and made-up data mix.
- Machine Learning Performance: Tests model accuracy with the added data.

Table 5 shows that before data augmentation, there are 1000 rows. This number is too small for good keystroke checks using both scrambled and static keystroke data. After data boost, rows increase to 10,000 for both types.

Table 5. Data Augmentation

Dataset	Before data augmentation	After data augmentation
Scrambled dataset	Number of Rows: 1000	Number of Rows: 10000
Static dataset	Number of Rows: 1000	Number of Rows: 10000

Phase 6: Feature selection

Feature selection identifies the most informative attributes contributing to user classification and authentication accuracy.

In this study, **Recursive Feature Elimination (RFE)** integrated with a **Random Forest** classifier was employed to select the optimal subset of features from the 144 extracted attributes. This method ensures that only the most relevant keystroke and mouse dynamics features are retained, improving model efficiency and interpretability.

Working Procedure of Recursive Feature Elimination (RFE)

Recursive Feature Elimination (RFE) picks key features for models through a step-by-step process.

1. Train Model: First, a Random Forest model learns from the data.
2. Rank Features: Then, it judges the parts of data, scoring how each helps the model.
3. Remove Least Important: The ones that matter least get taken out, one by one.
4. Repeat: This goes on till the top features remain.

The RFE with random forest works well with many features, judges feature quality by how it splits trees, and makes quick arrangements with many parallel jobs done at once (n_jobs=-1).

Feature selection by RFE

The feature selection process by RFE involves the following steps:

Step 1: Load Data: The cleaned dataset consists of extracted keystroke and mouse data that is loaded for further processing. This dataset includes the target variable Class_ID, representing individual user identities.

All keystroke and mouse features are separated from the **Class_ID** column. The **Class_ID** is encoded numerically to ensure compatibility with machine learning algorithms.

Step 2: Split Features and Target: All keystroke and mouse features are set apart from Class_ID, and Class_ID is encoded to a numeric form to make it compatible with machine learning algorithms.
Step 3: Encoding the Class_ID: A unique numerical representation for Class_ID is assigned using a label encoder for facilitating supervised learning.
Step 4: Data Split for Training and Testing: The dataset is split into training and testing sets with an 80 - 20 ratio, where 80% is for training, 20% for testing.
Step 5: Find Mouse and Keystroke Features: Combine the features that are under mouse and key press based on their names.
Step 6: Apply RFE

The RFE process, using a Random Forest classifier, iteratively evaluates and removes the least significant features. This continues until only the top-performing features remain. Finally, five keystroke features and five mouse features were selected as the most discriminative.

Step 7: Save the selected Features: Selected features, along with the Subject_ID, are stored in a new dataset, which is used for model training.

A new data file is created to add every. This file is saved as a new Excel file. This data will be used for more checks or model training.

The algorithms select the following TEN features from 144 original features, which are also illustrated in Figure 7.

Selected Features for Keystroke Dynamics

1.HoldTime.a - How long key 'a' is pressed before it's released, which represents the user's unique key-hold behavior.

2. HoldTime.l - How long 'l' is pressed before being released.
3. ReleaseGap.l - Time it takes between releasing of 'l' and the next key. This shows how smooth typing is and how fast a user moves between keys.

4.Avg_Speed_PerTry - Mid Median typing speed per repetition. It signifies that typing speed is a strong biometric sign, as some users type fast with little wait, and others type at a slower pace.

5.Speed_Range_Per Rep - Variation in typing speed within a single repetition. Low variation suggests steady, confident typing; high variation may indicate hesitancy or inexperience.

Selected Features for Mouse Dynamics

6. HoverTime.W - It defines the time that the mouse hovers over the ‘W’ before clicking. It shows how fast a user decides and how well they are used to the keyboard.
7. CursorSpeed.a - It defines how fast the mouse moves to or from the key 'a ', signifying user precision and hand control.
8. CursorSpeed.k - Defines how fast the mouse moves near the key 'k', providing additional spatial movement characteristics for comparison.
9. CursorSpeed.m - defines the movement speed of the mouse near the key 'm'. It provides information on the overall movement of the mouse.
10. HoverTime.l - Time duration the cursor hovers over the 'l' key before pressing, which provides information on a user-specific metric that varies based on decision confidence and control.

Figure 7. Selected Features

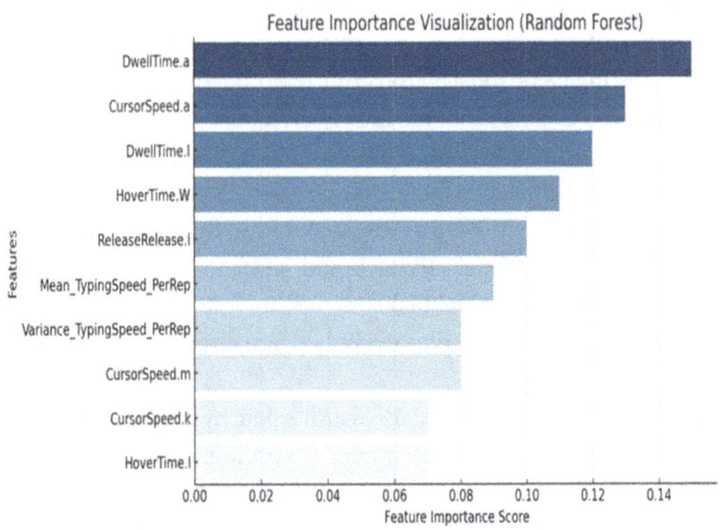

Phase 7: Model Training and Evaluation

Model training and evaluation are important phases in behaviour-based user authentication systems. In this study, machine learning models were trained using behavioral data extracted from keystroke dynamics and mouse movement patterns to accurately identify legitimate users based on their interaction behavior.

The dataset was partitioned into training (80%) and testing (20%) sets such that users were mutually exclusive across splits (i.e., no overlap of user samples between train and test). This ensured genuine user-disjoint evaluation, avoiding data leakage.

The split is done carefully to keep consistent class spreads, especially useful if there are many samples per user. Each sample is a user session, with features from typing (such as dwell time, flight time, digraphs, trigraphs, and typing speed) and mouse use (like click duration, cursor speed, movement direction, and hover time). These events will act as the base for the training model.

Various machine learning models, such as Random Forest (RF), Support Vector Machine (SVM), and Extreme Gradient Boosting (XGBoost), are selected and tested to identify the best one for these keystroke and mouse events. The Random Forest model makes many decision trees during the training period. It guesses by taking an average or by voting from the trees, which helps avoid overfitting and increases accuracy. It deals well with high data dimensions and can capture complex links between features. The SVMs are good with high-dimensional data and find the line or plane that leaves the biggest gap between different classes (users here). This model is more effective when there are few samples but many features. The Extreme Gradient Boosting (XGBoost) builds by step procedure and then refines it using a regularized function. This model is highly efficient, flexible, and accurate, which makes the classification perfect and makes it suitable for tasks like behavioral biometrics. Every model is trained on the training set, with tuning of settings done through grid search or random search with cross-validation to identify the best setup for each algorithm. Tree-based models like RF and XGBoost also allow checking which behavior traits are crucial for the task.

Various performance metrics, as explained below, are used to evaluate the model's performance.

Accuracy. The correct predictions made are divided by the total predictions. Accuracy will provide a final idea of the model's working, but can be deceptive with imbalanced data.

Precision, Recall, and F1-Score. Precision shows how often predicted positives are true positives, indicating correctness in positive guesses.

Recall (sensitivity) shows how many actual positives the model identified.F1-Score blends precision and recall, useful for balanced evaluation, especially with inconsistent class distribution.

False Acceptance Rate (FAR). The share of wrong inclusions of impostors as real users. Lower FAR is crucial for high-security uses.

False Rejection Rate (FRR). The percentage of wrong denials of authenticated users is defined as FRR. Lower FRR is key for ease, which allows only legitimate users to use the system. Both FAR and FRR metrics are important in biometric systems for safety and ease.

RESULTS AND DISCUSSIONS

The static and Dynamic non-touch virtual keyboards were developed with Python. A total of 1,000 samples with the designated password were collected from 100 users over two sessions with five repetitions for each keyboard. The collected data is augmented to 10000 samples for each non-touch virtual keyboard. Following data collection, the Data are cleaned, pre-processed, and New features are extracted from the raw data set. The model is evaluated with various machine learning algorithms. Median values with Inter Quartile Ranges [IQR] were computed for each metric by averaging the results over 10 randomized train–test splits. This was done to maintain the robustness across different models that are used for the study. Statistical significance between model performances was evaluated using the Wilcoxon signed-rank test ($p < 0.05$). The median Inter Quartile Ranges [IQR] accuracy obtained for the machine learning algorithms that were shown in tables 6 and 7 indicates stable and consistent model performance with no statistically significant difference ($p > 0.05$).

Table 6. Evaluation of static virtual keyboard

Algorithms	Accuracy (%)	Precision (%)	Recall (%)	F1Score (%)	FAR (%)	FRR (%)
Random Forest	91	92	92	91	0.00	0.08
Support Vector Machine	85	85	86	85	0.00	0.14
XGBoost	91	90	91	90	0.00	0.08

Table 7. Evaluation of dynamic virtual keyboard

Algorithms	Accuracy (%)	Precision (%)	Recall (%)	F1Score (%)	FAR (%)	FRR (%)
Random Forest	91	91	91	90	0.00	0.08
Support Vector Machine	85	84	85	83	0.00	0.14
XGBoost	91	91	91	90	0.00	0.08

From the above tables 6 and 7, it is observed that the Random Forest classifier outperformed the others, with high accuracy, precision, recall, and F1-score, making it the most reliable for user authentication in this scenario. The false acceptance and rejection rates were also low, which is crucial in a security system for both Static and Dynamic Keyboards. However, while the Random Forest model was the top performer, the SVM and XGBoost models also demonstrated promising results, with SVM showing good recall and precision but with a slightly higher FAR and FRR. The testing time and training time taken by both the algorithms were also promising which is shown in the Table 8.

It is also observed that both static and dynamic virtual keyboards yielded similar accuracy levels (~91%), which indicates that user behavioral signatures are largely invariant to key position changes, implying the robustness of keystroke–mouse fusion features. It also indicates that features such as hover time and cursor speed play a more key role when key positions vary randomly.

Table 8. Training & Testing Time

Classification Model	STATIC KEYBOARD		DYNAMIC KEYBOARD	
	TRAINING TIME (SEC)	TESTING TIME (SEC)	TRAINING TIME (SEC)	TESTING TIME (SEC)
Random Forest	23	0.11	0.00	0.08
Support Vector Machine	21	3	0.00	0.14
XGBoost	17	0.04	0.00	0.08

CONCLUSION AND FUTURE WORK

This study investigated how key presses and mouse moves distinguish individuals based on their typing and mouse behavior. Both static and dynamic virtual keyboards were used to collect the data. The dynamic keyboard shuffled key positions, which made it too difficult for shoulder surfing and other attacks. Initially, the data was collected by analysing the key press times, mouse moves, and clicks while people typed the given common passwords. The collected data were preprocessed, the best features were selected, and different machine learning algorithms, such as Random Forest, SVM, and XGBoost, were trained and tested for better performance. The obtained results proved that the Random Forest was the best by achieving high scores in accuracy, precision, recall, and F1, making it most trustworthy for behavioural user authentication. FAR and FRR rates were also low, key to a safe system. But SVM and XGBoost had good results too. SVM had good recall and precision, but its FAR and FRR were higher. Findings show that the key press and mouse move data can add safe and simple checks to usual methods, making systems safer in real use. The use of deep learning may result in better capture of how people type or move a mouse over time. Models like LSTM, GRU, and CNNs may easily detect the hard-to-detect patterns in typing and clicking events. Smart setups like Siamese Networks, Attention Mechanisms, and Autoencoders may bring better results in checking users, even when the training data is not large. Getting much more data on gadgets like phones and tablets might make the model strong and widely useful. By integrating these ideas, future systems can score higher accuracy, which will adapt well to changes and can cover more usage on varied platforms and user groups. In real-time deployment, the proposed system can be integrated into any secure login portals where traditional keyboards are unavailable. However, its use is limited as the proposed system uses controlled password entry with a small number of participants, which are left for future researchers.

REFERENCES

Abin, A. A., Hosseini, P., & Torabian Raj, A. (2023). Continuous user authentication using a combination of operation and application-related features. [JICSE]. *Journal of Innovations in Computer Science and Engineering*, *1*(1), 10–21. DOI: 10.48308/jicse.2023.103524

Acien, A., Morales, A., Vera-Rodriguez, R., Fierrez, J., Mondesire-Crump, I., & Arroyo-Gallego, T. (2022). Detection of mental fatigue in the general population: Feasibility study of keystroke dynamics as a real-world biomarker. *JMIR Biomedical Engineering*, *7*(2), e41003. DOI: 10.2196/41003 PMID: 38875698

Altwaijry, N. (2023). Authentication by keystroke dynamics: The influence of typing language. *Applied Sciences (Basel, Switzerland)*, *13*(20), 11478. DOI: 10.3390/app132011478

Antal, M., & Fejér, N. (2020). Mouse dynamics based user recognition using deep learning. *Acta Universitatis Sapientiae Informatica*, *12*(1), 39–50. DOI: 10.2478/ausi-2020-0003

Anusas-amornkul, T. (2019). Strengthening password authentication using keystroke dynamics and smartphone sensors. *Proceedings of the 9th International Conference on Information Communication and Management*. New York, NY, USA: ACM. DOI: 10.1145/3357419.3357425

Ayotte, B., Banavar, M., Hou, D., & Schuckers, S. (2020). Fast free-text authentication via instance-based keystroke dynamics. *IEEE Transactions on Biometrics, Behavior, and Identity Science*, *2*(4), 377–387. DOI: 10.1109/TBIOM.2020.3003988

Bansal, P., & Ouda, A. (2024). Continuous authentication in the digital age: An analysis of reinforcement learning and behavioral biometrics. *Computers*, *13*(4), 103. DOI: 10.3390/computers13040103

Buker, A. A. N., Roffo, G., & Vinciarelli, A. (2019). Type like a man! Inferring gender from keystroke dynamics in live-chats. *IEEE Intelligent Systems*, *34*(6), 53–59. DOI: 10.1109/MIS.2019.2948514

Cilia, D., & Inguanez, F. (2018). Multi-Model authentication using keystroke dynamics for Smartphones. *2018 IEEE 8th International Conference on Consumer Electronics - Berlin (ICCE-Berlin)*. IEEE.

Cockell, R., & Halak, B. (2020). On the design and analysis of a biometric authentication system using keystroke dynamics. *Cryptography*, *4*(2), 12. DOI: 10.3390/cryptography4020012

Escobar Grisales, D., Vásquez-Correa, J. C., Vargas-Bonilla, J. F., & Orozco-Arroyave, J. R. (2020). Identity verification in virtual education using biometric analysis based on keystroke dynamics. *TecnoLógicas*, *23*(47), 197–211. DOI: 10.22430/22565337.1475

Grunova, D., & Tsimperidis, I. (2023). Finding the age and education level of Bulgarian-speaking Internet users using keystroke dynamics. *Eng*, *4*(4), 2711–2721. DOI: 10.3390/eng4040154

Hriez, S., Obeid, N., & Awajan, A. (2019). User authentication on smartphones using keystroke dynamics. *Proceedings of the Second International Conference on Data Science, E-Learning and Information Systems*. New York, NY, USA: ACM. DOI: 10.1145/3368691.3368725

Khan, S., Devlen, C., Manno, M., & Hou, D. (2024). Mouse dynamics behavioral biometrics: A survey. *ACM Computing Surveys*, *56*(6), 1–33. DOI: 10.1145/3640311

Kiyani, A. T., Lasebae, A., Ali, K., Rehman, M. U., & Haq, B. (2020). Continuous user authentication featuring keystroke dynamics based on robust recurrent confidence model and ensemble learning approach. *IEEE Access : Practical Innovations, Open Solutions*, *8*, 156177–156189. DOI: 10.1109/ACCESS.2020.3019467

Krishnamoorthy, S., Rueda, L., Saad, S., & Elmiligi, H. (2018). Identification of user behavioral biometrics for authentication using keystroke dynamics and machine learning. *Proceedings of the 2018 2nd International Conference on Biometric Engineering and Applications*, 50–57. New York, NY, USA: ACM. DOI: 10.1145/3230820.3230829

Li, G., Borj, P. R., Bergeron, L., & Bours, P. (2019). Exploring keystroke dynamics and stylometry features for gender prediction on chat data. *2019 42nd International Convention on Information and Communication Technology, Electronics and Microelectronics (MIPRO)*, 1049–1054. IEEE.

Li, J., Chang, H.-C., & Stamp, M. (2021). Free-text keystroke dynamics for user authentication. DOI: 10.31979/etd.ku7u-v7s4

Mondal, S., & Bours, P. (2017). Person identification by keystroke dynamics using pairwise user coupling. *IEEE Transactions on Information Forensics and Security*, *12*(6), 1319–1329. DOI: 10.1109/TIFS.2017.2658539

Nascimento, T. M. L., Oliveira, A. V. M., Santana, L. E. A. S., & Da Costa-Abreu, M. (2021). *Investigating the use of feature selection techniques for gender prediction systems based on keystroke dynamics.* In *Proceedings of the 11th International Conference of Pattern Recognition Systems (ICPRS 2021)* (pp. 1–6). Institution of Engineering and Technology. DOI: 10.1049/icp.2021.1446

Pentel, A. (2017). *Predicting age and gender by keystroke dynamics and mouse patterns.* In *Adjunct Publication of the 25th Conference on User Modeling, Adaptation and Personalization* (pp. 280–285). DOI: 10.1145/3099023.3099105

Salem, A., & Obaidat, M. S. (2019). A novel security scheme for behavioral authentication systems based on keystroke dynamics. *Security and Privacy*, *2*(2), e64. DOI: 10.1002/spy2.64

Salmeron-Majadas, S., Baker, R. S., Santos, O. C., & Boticario, J. G. (2018). A machine learning approach to leverage individual keyboard and mouse interaction behavior from multiple users in real-world learning scenarios. *IEEE Access : Practical Innovations, Open Solutions*, *6*, 39154–39179. DOI: 10.1109/ACCESS.2018.2854966

Thomas, P. A., & Preetha Mathew, K. (2023). A broad review on non-intrusive active user authentication in biometrics. *Journal of Ambient Intelligence and Humanized Computing*, *14*(1), 339–360. DOI: 10.1007/s12652-021-03301-x PMID: 34109006

Toosi, R., & Akhaee, M. A. (2021). Time–frequency analysis of keystroke dynamics for user authentication. *Future Generation Computer Systems*, *115*, 438–447. DOI: 10.1016/j.future.2020.09.027

Tsimperidis, I., & Arampatzis, A. (2020). The keyboard knows about you: Revealing user characteristics via keystroke dynamics. *International Journal of Technoethics*, *11*(2), 34–51. DOI: 10.4018/IJT.2020070103

Tsimperidis, I., Arampatzis, A., & Karakos, A. (2018). Keystroke dynamics features for gender recognition. *Digital Investigation*, *24*, 4–10. DOI: 10.1016/j.diin.2018.01.018

Tsimperidis, I., Grunova, D., & Papakostas, G. A. (2023). The way we type reveals our native language. *IEEE Access : Practical Innovations, Open Solutions*, *11*, 98191–98201. DOI: 10.1109/ACCESS.2023.3313510

Tsimperidis, I., Grunova, D., Roy, S., & Moussiades, L. (2023). Keystroke dynamics as a language profiling tool: Identifying mother tongue of unknown Internet users. *Telecom*, *4*(3), 369–377. DOI: 10.3390/telecom4030021

Tsimperidis, I., Yucel, C., & Katos, V. (2021). Age and gender as cyber attribution features in keystroke dynamic-based user classification processes. *Electronics (Basel)*, *10*(7), 835. DOI: 10.3390/electronics10070835

Turab, A., Mlaiki, N., Fatima, N., Mitrović, Z. D., & Ali, W. (2022). Analysis of a class of stochastic animal behavior models under specific choice preferences. *Mathematics, 10*(12), 1975. DOI: 10.3390/math10121975

Turab, A., Montoyo, A., & Nescolarde-Selva, J.-A. (2024). Computational and analytical analysis of integral-differential equations for modeling avoidance learning behavior. *Journal of Applied Mathematics & Computing, 70*(5), 4423–4439. Advance online publication. DOI: 10.1007/s12190-024-02130-3

Turab, A., Nescolarde-Selva, J.-A., Ullah, F., Montoyo, A., Alfiniyah, C., Sintunavarat, W., Rizk, D., & Zaidi, S. A. (2025). Deep neural networks and stochastic methods for cognitive modeling of rat behavioral dynamics in T -mazes. *Cognitive Neurodynamics, 19*(1), 66. DOI: 10.1007/s11571-025-10247-9 PMID: 40290756

Turab, A., Sintunavarat, W., Ullah, F., Zaidi, S. A., Montoyo, A., & Nescolarde-Selva, J.-A. (2024). Computational modeling of animal behavior in T-mazes: Insights from machine learning. *Ecological Informatics, 81*(102639), 102639. DOI: 10.1016/j.ecoinf.2024.102639

Wang, X., Shi, Y., Zheng, K., Zhang, Y., Hong, W., & Cao, S. (2022). User authentication method based on keystroke dynamics and mouse dynamics with scene-irrelated features in hybrid scenes. *Sensors (Basel), 22*(17), 6627. DOI: 10.3390/s22176627 PMID: 36081085

Wang, X., Zheng, Q., Zheng, K., & Wu, T. (2020). User authentication method based on MKL for keystroke and mouse behavioral feature fusion. *Security and Communication Networks, 2020*, 1–14. DOI: 10.1155/2020/9282380

S. Zeid, S., A. ElKamar, R., & I. Hassan, S. (2022). Fixed-text vs. Free-text keystroke dynamics for user authentication. *Engineering Research Journal - Faculty of Engineering (Shoubra), 51*(1), 95–104. DOI: 10.21608/erjsh.2022.224312

Chapter 10
Behavioral Analysis for Customer Loyalty Prediction Using 360° Customer Insights

Rana Muhammad Amir Latif
https://orcid.org/0000-0001-6007-6275
East China Normal University, China

Jahanzaib Latif
https://orcid.org/0000-0002-0866-5133
Northwestern Polytechnical University, China

Umar Raza
https://orcid.org/0000-0002-9810-1285
Manchester Metropolitan University, UK

Hamad Naeem
King Faisal University, Saudi Arabia

Abdul Ahad
https://orcid.org/0000-0002-3914-2503
Northwestern Polytechnical University, China

Farhan Ullah
https://orcid.org/0000-0002-1030-1275
Prince Mohammad Bin Fahd University, Saudi Arabia

ABSTRACT

Customer retention is vital in a competitive market where regaining lost customers is costly. This study proposes a loyalty prediction framework using behavioral analysis and a 360° customer view. By integrating historical interactions, spending habits, sentiment, and CRM data, potential churn can be identified early. A survey of 110 users who evaluated two websites was analyzed using text preprocessing and sentiment analysis, classifying responses as loyal, neutral, or not loyal. The 360° view enabled deeper insights into loyalty indicators, showing how behavior and feedback influence retention. Results confirm that this integrated approach enhances loyalty prediction accuracy and helps optimize customer experience.

DOI: 10.4018/979-8-3373-5062-2.ch010

1 INTRODUCTION

Clients are the most important component of the business world as they are the consumers of the company's products. When companies ignore the interests of consumers, consumers will be unlikely to consume their products, leading to massive losses to the company. No company can do without customers (Rana M Amir Latif et al., 2019). Inclusion of giant corporate bodies in the retail industry has transformed customer perceptions of the retail operations to an extreme level. Retailers face stiff competition; therefore, they carefully consider factors like quality, prices, value for money, income, personalization, and risk factors because these factors greatly influence how consumers make decisions.

The market has become very competitive and has established more performance standards for organizations. Different companies produce the same products with slight changes, giving consumers a choice. Buyers compare the products or services of multiple companies and change their providers to the ones they consider providing better value in the whole package (Rana Muhammad Amir Latif, Farhan, Khan, & Sujatha, 2024). Customers can select an item depending on the specifications among the available options. The chances of leaving the existing company to serve in another company are higher. The purchaser would favor an organization that provides more attractive services regarding price, quality, and risk considerations. A dynamic relationship with the client is significant in competitive advantages in thriving businesses (Rana Muhammad Amir Latif, Farhan, Ahmad, Mostarda, & Cacciagrano, 2025).

In order to survive in this competitive business environment, a company should make sure that the customers prefer its product over other alternatives. It is only possible when the client trusts the company regarding goods and services and is ready to conduct more transactions (Ahad et al., 2025). The client's interaction with the firm is vital in developing a long-term relationship. The client considers numerous product attributes before purchasing, including the producer's reliability. Many specialists admit that loyalty to clients is one of the essential concepts of the marketing profession (Rana Muhammad Amir Latif, 2025; Wolniak, 2024).

Particular clients have the quality over cost; they are ready to spend more money, but not on quality. On the other hand, some consumers buy a product at a discounted cost, at the cost of the quality. The applicability of various aspects like price, quality, and dependability of usability depends on the clients' preferences. Customers would be happy if they found products that matched their taste. In the past, companies were product-oriented, but recently, companies have shifted their strategies to customer-oriented ones to maintain their clients (Shaffi, 2025).

It is important to attract and retain existing and new consumers to generate revenues. Nevertheless, the feeling of engagement of an individual cannot be ensured solely by following the company's site or app. A corporation's primary issue is converting follower involvement to customer engagement behavior (Watson, 2022). Connection with multiple platforms, such as the company site or app, and feedback on the preferences or needs is a critical factor that increases client purchase intent and leads to a high sales level (Mustak et al., 2024).

Organizations employ several instruments and methodologies to realize strategic goals. Customer information helps companies reduce the cost of their products and use business intelligence to generate more income, maintain client relationships, predict demand, and build long-term relationships with consumers. These aims will be important to create a stable relationship between the consumers and the organization that will turn one-time purchasers into Loyal clients.

The achievement of goals depends on business intelligence, customer intelligence, and customer relationship management (CRM) (Carey, 2022). The 360 customer provides an all-inclusive view of the customer profile record, which combines information across numerous channels and structures. All this information includes what is necessary for the client and is used to develop a customized customer experience to meet the desired objectives.

Customer behavior modeling can use network-based approaches to analytics modeling to visualize patterns of interaction and determine loyalty clusters. Techniques like Force-Atlas and Kamada-Kawai are not directly applied in this research. However, they can theoretically define groups of loyal and at-risk customers using bigger behavioral data. In this case, network analysis depicts the structural perspective of the customer relationship that adds to our 360 ° loyalty model (Ullah et al., 2024). Further, this research incorporates sentiment analysis to categorize the user sentiments and give additional insight. A combination of sentiment analysis is provided in this study, wherein the data are categorized into three different levels, which further adds a level of knowledge, as shown in Figure 1.

Document-level Sentiment Analysis (DSA) categorizes opinion documents according to positive or negative sentiments/sentences. The whole work is seen as a singular entity that conveys either an unfavorable or favorable perspective on a particular topic (Katyayan & Singh, 2025).

Sentence-level Sentiment Analysis (SSA): It must account for the emotions expressed in each paragraph. Initially, we must ascertain if the weather described in a statement is subjective or objective. If the statement is subjective, the SSA determines its positivity or negativity. Researchers have shown no significant differences in the assessments of sentences and papers, as sentences may be considered condensed documents (Pasupulati, Mahendran, & Majumdar, 2024).

Aspect Level Sentiment Analysis (ASA): This sentiment is evaluated based on the other attributes of individuals. The entities and their attributes must be identified. For instance, "the hue of this garment is unappealing, yet the material is exceptional," the user will provide distinct evaluations on several aspects of a single individual (Gadiparthi, 2024).

Figure 1. The sentiment analysis process

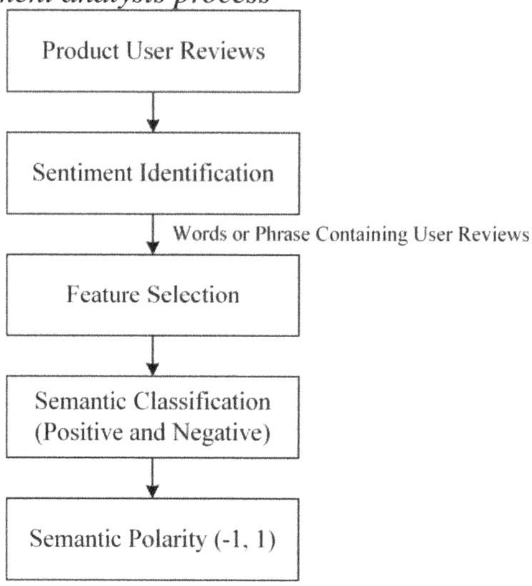

2 BACKGROUND STUDY

2.1 Customer Churn

Customers are central to every business; a company's success depends on its ability to retain them. Customer churn refers to customers' transition from one service provider to another, signifying the company's failure. Consumer loyalty has always been a significant factor in the connection between a consumer and an organization. Customer attrition has become a significant problem, and the factors contributing to it may be identified using customer data. Diverse techniques distinguish between dedicated customers, often classified as churners, and those exhibiting lesser commitment. Most consumer status descriptions concentrate on purchasing behavior and market law principles (More & Unnikrishnan, 2024). When a customer's purchases decline to zero or below, they are called a churner. This legislation often does not apply, and one will monitor the client's actions.

2.1.1 Causes Of Customer Churn

It is essential to delineate the conditions or factors contributing to client disloyalty and churn. This situation may stem from ambiguous information, insufficient comprehension and contact with the consumer, and a dearth of information. This kind of performance shapes the customer's experience and the company's reputation and impacts the consumer. The adverse experiences discourage the consumer and may make him or her never buy the brand. As long as clients face several challenges, they will not withstand, no matter how loyal they are to the brand. The availability of multiple service providers or suppliers who offer favorable deals to attract the consumers is also another cause of client churn (Chibudike et al., 2021). The firm's success depends on the Loyal consumers, as acquiring new customers is more costly than retaining them, thus requiring a firm to invest more resources in client acquisition.

2.1.2 Effect of Customer Churn

Customer attrition results in failure and financial losses for the firm when a significant proportion of its clientele discontinues their usage of goods or services and ceases making new purchases. Companies use many techniques to acquire new customers, enhance the retention duration of current customers, and reduce customer churn to thrive in a competitive market. Customer attrition signifies a deficiency in the existing business plan, indicating the company's inability to understand consumer behavior and forecast future trends. A significant problem is maintaining clients with a high risk of attrition (Subramanian & Prabha, 2022).

2.2 Customer loyalty

Consumer loyalty may be characterized as a commitment to repurchase a preferred product or service in the future. Given the circumstances and marketing strategies that may influence behavioral changes, customer loyalty encourages repeated purchases from the same firm. Consumer loyalty can be demonstrated when a client purchases a product repeatedly and intends to purchase it. Consumer happiness is a key factor that can potentially boost an organization's financial well-being The benefits of consumer loyalty to a product in terms of product profitability are increased production in the market, increased retail space, reduced dependence on competitive trade, reduced price elasticity, and strong customer word-of-mouth promotion (Celestin, Sujatha, Kumar, & Vasuki, 2024; Rana Muhammad Amir Latif, Yoshigoe, et al., 2025). Customer loyalty not only includes the revenue that has been earned in the transaction, but also looks into the retention of the customer in the long run. The number of loyal customers is an indicator of the success of the business. Customers will always be eager to embrace fascinating and favorable offers from a company.

Nevertheless, they can move out to other competitors who make better offers once they exhaust such offers. Active and affordable marketing positively affects client loyalty, and relevant and constantly updated content on various social media platforms. Repeating-buying intentions and positive attitude of the customer indicate the two-sided nature of customer loyalty (Esmeli, Bader-El-Den, & Abdullahi, 2022).

2.2.1 Significance of Customer Loyalty

The customer loyalty benefits both the organization and the consumer. Customers' loyalty toward one brand can indicate their satisfaction with the expectations. One of the success measures of a firm is customer loyalty, as it increases revenue. As a result, a company with a high level of client loyalty can achieve improved profitability. Customer loyalty is positively associated with the profitability of the firm. The customers who remain loyal are the priceless assets of the firm because the organization can save on marketing and transaction costs. Customer loyalty boosts profit and revenue, fortifies the ability to overcome the competition, and provides a wall against competitors. More loyal customers are less sensitive (Rana Muhammad Amir Latif, Ullah, et al., 2025; Lee, Liu, & Tseng, 2022). Implementing the procedures to create a healthy relationship between consumers and the organization is paramount, as such interrelationships result in an instant development of trust, loyalty, and reliance on the firm.

2.2.2 Factors Influencing Customer Loyalty

The connections between the client and the firm are highly delicate. Customer experience in the organization is a major contributor to customer perception. A satisfied customer trusts the company and the products/services it offers, the value of the product/services, and switching costs, all of which influence customer loyalty. These were major predictors of customer loyalty and buying habits (Alrumiah & Hadwan, 2021).

2.2.2.1 Customer Satisfaction

Customer satisfaction is important in building relationships between the customer and the company. It will enhance loyalty to the firm as customers will be more satisfied with its products or services. Performance of the company is viewed as the key determinant of customer satisfaction; therefore, a business needs to determine the particular needs of the customers. The company can offer tailor-made services to offer the best incentives to its customers, thereby increasing their satisfaction.

When the customer perceives that the product or service can meet his or her needs satisfactorily, the customer is satisfied. When clients are satisfied, he must aim for additional transactions with the organization (Islam et al., 2024). It will show the consumer's commitment to the business due to the happiness it brings, and the corporation will definitely favour the new transactional client.

2.2.2.2 Trust

Customer confidence in a firm, its reputation, and the goods or services it provides significantly influences a customer's drive for repeat purchases. If a corporation successfully establishes trust, it has cultivated a lasting connection with its customers. Customer trust may be defined as a customer's belief that a firm will follow their expectations about their connection with that company. Trust in the firm profoundly influences a customer's commitment to the organization. Customer trust may be established by consistent transparency in all corporate interactions (Liu, Lim, Cheah, Ng, & Kamal Basha, 2023). Trust influences client retention and interactions with the organization. The level of trust perceived by a client profoundly influences customer loyalty.

2.2.2.3 Perceived Value

Perceived value is attained when buyers recognize that a product or service may fulfill their desires and requirements. When the consumer realizes the perceived value, it becomes much easier to facilitate future transactions. Currently, firms have transitioned their strategies from a product-centric approach to a customer-centric one. A corporation needs to comprehend client preferences and fulfill orders based on customer demand rather than making items according to their preferences, since the perceived value may directly impact brand loyalty. A company must understand the extent of consumer demand since customer loyalty hinges on the disparity between a customer's expectations for a product and the actual performance of that product. Consumers are likely to be happy when an organization effectively addresses their preferences regarding the presentation of a product or service (Zvarikova, Michalikova, & Rowland, 2022). Companies must tailor products and services to align with client preferences. A consumer's loyalty might affect their decision to continue or discontinue product use.

2.2.2.4 Switching Cost

When consumers encounter challenges and substantial costs in transitioning to an alternative firm or product, they may be inclined to remain Loyal to their existing provider and continue making purchases. Company contributions may mitigate the adverse effects of corporate disappointments and diminish consumer dissatisfaction and intentions to disengage. It does not allow an organization or firm to continue disappointing its client base; instead, it emphasizes that an organization should focus on enhancing customer engagement (Arora, 2024). The benefit of having a client base is their propensity for repeat purchases, which, according to estimates, may render the customer base much more advantageous to an organization than first-time buyers. These clients are the primary source of income for a corporation. Switching costs are fundamental in retaining a customer with his or her firm. The loyalty of customers and the switching costs will show an upward trend, and this will increase the trust of a consumer in a particular firm (Chanpariyavatevong et al., 2021).

2.3 360° View of Customers

The 360° methodology involves supervisors, coworkers, subordinates, internal and external customers, and helps gain insight into the customer perspective regarding the quality of products. Multi-source feedback reviews the products through different interactions, thereby providing a better understanding of how to better the offerings to suit customer preferences, retain customers, and better understand the behaviour of the current customers to develop long-term relationships (Alnofeli, Akter, & Yanamandram, 2023).

Customer centricity strengthens the strategies of companies that are very customer-oriented and are closely tied to customers. Companies need to understand the needs and preferences of consumers so that they make the right decisions that will optimize the customer experience and guarantee retention. The customer data are collected through different sources, records in different forms with different qualities and positions (Hosseini, Abdolvand, & Harandi, 2022).

2.3.1.1 Attributes of a 360° view of customers

Consumers have a holistic perspective based on numerous sources of information through various networks, including their entire interaction with the organization and their cognition and buying behavior. It is the last point of view of the involvement and engagement of the client with the organization and their feelings about their activities. The method is also essential in enabling firms to deliver the best customer experience through all the channels by incorporating the views of different consumer focus areas and customer relations departments. This combined perspective is done by gathering tangible and intangible information from the different networks and sources regarding the organization's customers and associations. Identifying the customer is crucial in creating a rich consumer profile, which gives a picture of the appropriate historical information to give an immediate and holistic perspective (Zhao, Cheng, & Lee, 2023). Among the important information that is usually described in this overview are the identity markers (location, position, gender, age), affiliation (power, connections, partnerships), and the current market state (shipments, defect rates, inventory levels). Additionally, the client's historical information entails details about past dealings, promotions, procedures, and experiences within different industries and connections, as well as the significance of a particular product or service.

2.3.1.2 Significance Of 360° Customer View

A holistic 360° approach informs the customer experience. The holistic view shows the best solution to the consumer, retaining the customer, and providing a personalized, rational, and understanding customer experience. It also requires theoretical projections. There is a 360° graphic that depicts the contact service of every customer. Value is measured on a case-by-case basis. For example, the consequences can be consumer delight and retention, disillusionment and loss of customers concerning a product promotion or customer service experience, and acceptance or refusal of a business offer or advertising (Sann, Lai, Liaw, & Chen, 2022). Depending on specific calculations concerning the client, the system may provide the most relevant and likely actions to be taken in marketing, sales, or support situations.

The 360° view of the consumer is holistic to guarantee continuous interaction. It harmonizes client-related information in the entire organization to enable resource allocation and align operations in the market with customer requirements or other business factors. Customers with low contributions should have personalized customer support and self-service options within an organization. Improving sales significantly impacts market activities, which are clearly defined among customers (Mukherjee, Das, & Chakraborty, 2023). The cross-sectional exchange of data with the customer and a holistic perspective of a customer are beneficial in several ways. The organization helps the agencies cooperate to provide consumers with a smooth and practical experience.

2.3.1.3 Customer Data

A 360° customer view is a comprehensive repository of consumer profiles, including five categories of firm information across numerous channels, integrating data to discern client demands and enhancing business expertise to improve customer service. A 360° perspective constitutes a consumer profile. Client perspective: It also seeks to achieve business success objectives, as seen in Figure 2.

Figure 2. Customer data

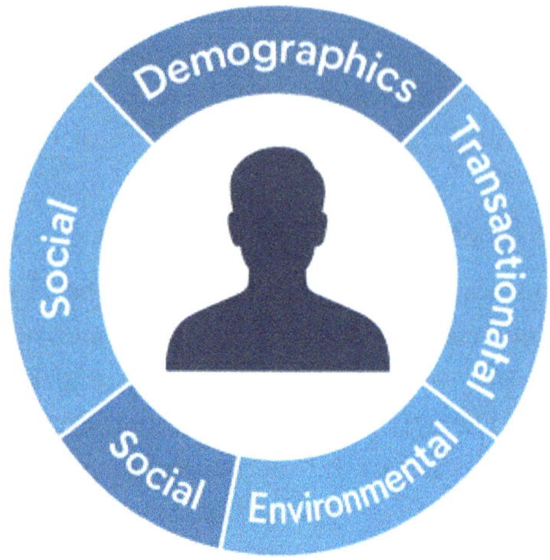

2.3.1.4 Customer Demographic Data

A 360° customer view is a comprehensive repository of consumer profiles encompassing five categories of corporate information across numerous channels, combining data to discern client demands and enhancing business expertise to improve customer service. A 360° perspective constitutes a consumer profile. Client perspective: It also seeks to achieve business success objectives, as seen in Figure 3.

Figure 3. Customer demographic data

2.3.1.5 Customer Transactional Data

To attract customers, firms use their many instruments. Organizations will include customer accounts, including financial activity statistics, to direct commitment and spending toward consumers. Revenue, pricing, comparisons, and returns may provide data about financial transactions. This knowledge can be utilized to design some important metrics and predictors of results. The consumer transaction information is important in developing detailed consumer profiles and attributes that, in turn, assist in recognizing other people with the same attributes. With the help of these insights, the companies can utilize them to steer their clients to greater heights of commitment by manipulating them strategically (Ru & Jantan, 2023). This shift occurs in many ways, as demonstrated by communication exchanges, networking possibilities, reward programs, incentives, specific advertising approaches, and other technologies that facilitate a bond among high-content peer groups, as shown in Figure 4.

Figure 4. Customer transactional data

2.3.1.6 Customer Behavioral Data

Consumer behavior is paramount to the business because it helps the company understand customers' needs, ambitions, goals, and readiness. Businesses gather a large amount of data to enhance consumer knowledge, significantly increasing the profile data to forecast client demands. Moreover, it offers organizations better consumer information and progressively tailored, important, and best offerings (Aljuhmani, Elrehail, Bayram, & Samarah, 2022). The user provides their digital fingerprint when interacting with the application or browsing the business site to establish patterns of valuable products and their corresponding value, and refresh the consumer profile.

Based on multiple visits to the company homepage, the information regarding consumption habits will especially outline customer interest, valuable items, buying intentions, and preferences regarding platforms and contacts. Behavioral data has a weakness in that it is subject to change easily. It measures customer involvement or attrition probability (Alizadeh, Zadeh, Moshiri, & Montazeri, 2023). The real-time integration of client accounts requires an automated control of consumer behavior. Emotional investment and engagement significantly impact customer happiness, as shown in Figure 5.

Figure 5. Customer behavioral data

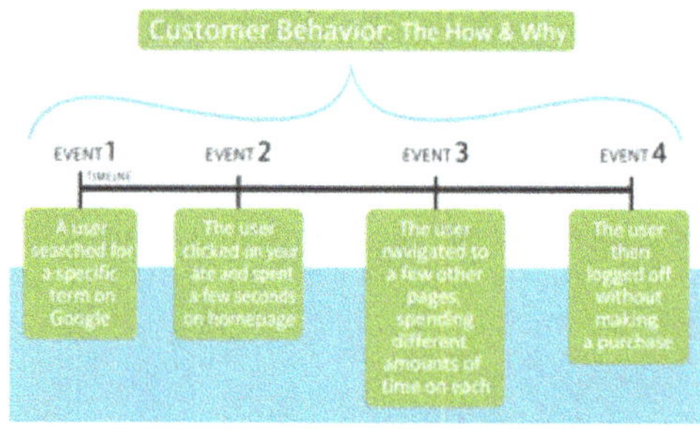

2.3.1.7 Customer Environmental Data

The expansive views in customer data indicate that customers play a significant role in businesses by incorporating environmental issues into their profiles. It is an environmental information based on numerous personal and financial data, including education, family size, household income, home value, occupation, personal income, net worth, disposable income, total assets, travel spending, and retail spending (Popescu, Valaskova, & Horak, 2022). Such insights give a more in-depth insight into the customer. Thus, a business can offer services and interactions to suit a broader perspective of the customer's life and financial situation.

This data can form a more detailed consumer profile, strengthen buyer relationships, form householding, and improve the company's product-client fit. Another best practice in environmental data lies in enriching prospect and lead records with external data (e.g., consumer discretionary income, demographics, retail purchase histories, household income, etc.) to provide better segmentation, targeting, and sales plans (Rane, Choudhary, & Rane, 2023). More detailed record profiles can also be applied to calculate deals to more effectively decide what prospects and leads should be pursued and what ones should not. The outcome is increased client acquisition strategies and decreased sales and marketing efforts, as observed in Figure 6.

Figure 6. Customer Environmental Data

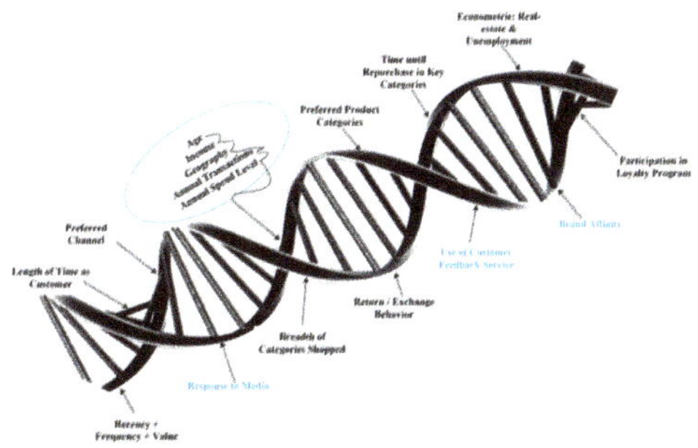

2.3.1.8 Customer Social Data

With the increase in the number of customers using social networks, companies can begin to monitor and use them to engage and build relationships. Viewing the customers' preferences, retweets, or comments builds an evident client social profile. The use of social media promotes the growth of the regional market and gains new consumers at minimal cost (Nica, Poliak, Popescu, & Pârvu, 2022).

By including social credits in the profile of the customers, the organizations will have a better opportunity to segment customers and tailor their offerings to them in a more personalized way, providing the organizations with a chance to offer products, messages, and services that customers will feel more about, eventually increasing loyalty. Market research is also an effective tool of social media, where reviews and comments can be mined to develop new ideas and improve products and services to suit the market's preferences (Matosas-López, 2025). Social media is more effective than traditional communication channels because it provides a chance to engage and interact directly with the person in real-time and at a fraction of the cost, as shown in Figure 7.

Figure 7. Customer Social Data

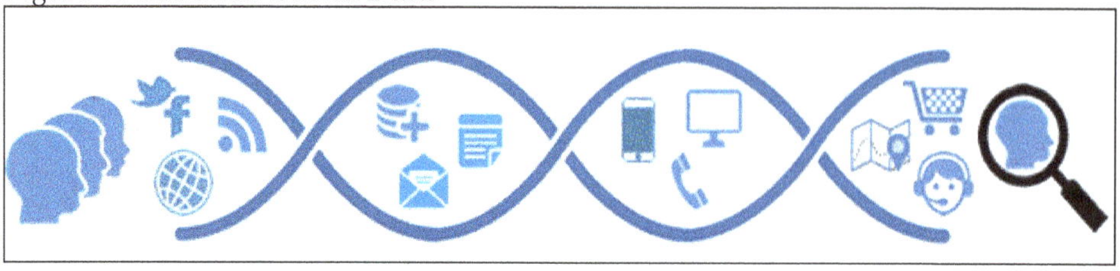

2.4 360° Customer View Effects on Customer Satisfaction

Customer satisfaction is one of the most important indicators of consumer satisfaction with the goods or services received. It is the general evaluation of the customer on a product or a service based on the expectations and experiences of the customer. A customer-centric approach allows businesses to focus on their customers to fulfill their wishes, needs, goals, wants, and expectations. In this case, marketing and manufacturing services collaborate to provide value to their customers, as illustrated in Figure 8. Customer satisfaction may be understood in a variety of ways:

- A critical reflection of the customer's perception of a product or service during its period of effectiveness.
- An interactive recognition insight or an emotional reaction arises from using the product or service.
- The experience of service use and consumption, or a response to the attention given to production expectations.
- A psychological summary where the customer's feelings about past experiences are integrated, forming their overall sentiment towards the product or service.

As rivalry among organizations intensifies, customer retention has become more critical than acquiring new clients. The pivotal success element for a corporation is not an individual transaction but the establishment of a long-term connection.

Figure 8. Dimensions of customer satisfaction

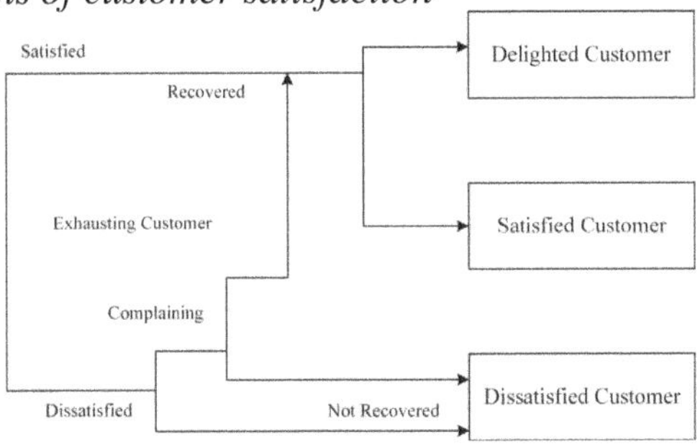

2.5 360° Customer View Effects on Customer Loyalty

Loyalty to customers is a commitment to get products and services only from a particular enterprise. The consumer's allegiance to the brand, amenities, and long-term relationship with the enterprise is crucial. Client loyalty is contingent upon the company's capacity to sustain client connections. Customer loyalty is assessed using six indicators: continued purchasing, acquisition of extra goods or services, experimentation with new offerings, information sharing, favorable verbal endorsements, and recommendations to others, as shown in Figure 9.

Figure 9. Dimensions of customer loyalty

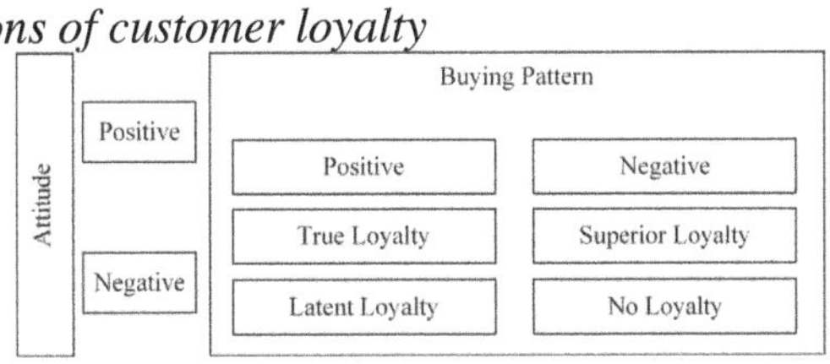

Loyalty denotes the maintenance, repurchase, and enduring commitment in its most fundamental sense. Consumer loyalty refers to the extent of a customer's overall satisfaction with a product or service. The aforementioned elements of customer happiness are influenced mainly by a business's treatment of its consumers and integrity. While delivering acceptable service is crucial for customer retention, fostering an emotional connection with clients is critical to mitigating the risk of attrition. Emotional relationship and a high degree of customer loyalty create an endearing bond between the company and the client, and thus, a dedicated relationship based on love, competence, and value.

3 METHODOLOGY AND DATA COLLECTION

3.1 Overview

The 360° procedure is packed with every source/type of feedback: supervisors, colleagues, subordinates, internal clients, and outsiders. The feedback received from many people gives a good review of the product and how it can be improved as per the customers' requirements. Businesses can use this considerable input to strengthen retention and identify behavioral patterns to develop long-term customer relationships. The main goal of early identification of customer loyalty is to identify the key features and review the past customer interactions, which influence customer behaviour and purchases, as well as customer retention. If companies know which customers are likely to churn and what affects them the most, they can be proactive. Businesses can develop a more devoted community by listening to customers' requirements and making the necessary changes. Customers will stay interested in the company. Engaging customers with customized offers matching their preferences will be essential for the business. We can use open communication to sustain customer information, receive feedback, and continuously improve products and services. Customers always want to feel valued and heard, so having a conversation with them helps create a Loyal customer base.

To further assess the representativeness of our collected data, we compared our dataset with the publicly available e-commerce review datasets, e.g., the Amazon Product Review dataset, to check for similarities in the data patterns. This validation checked if the sentiment and loyalty patterns observed in our sample of 110 participants generally conform to consumer trends. The distribution of public sentiment polarity and loyalty ratios was similar to our study results, suggesting the framework is externally valid. Despite the low number of participants, the agreement of the two datasets makes it reasonable to assume our conclusions are valid. This study will lay the groundwork for future research to employ larger and more diverse datasets in other sectors.

3.2 Methodology of Early Detection of Customer Loyalty

We developed a prototype site with this customer view to determine how the 360 customer view can improve customer experience. A total of 100 students were recruited to test the site and give suggestions, and they were students of the COMSAT University of Sahiwal. A random selection of participants was divided into two groups, where they were requested to analyze their experience of being a customer of the site using the 360° view of the site. The participants were requested to do various tasks on the two sites: freely surfing the site, purchasing a product with only the product details, purchasing a product with still images and product details, and purchasing a product with the 360° product view. It is necessary to mention that the experimental scheme was represented by functional and well-optimized e-commerce websites created to offer users a better user experience. Therefore, the positive sentiment may have been inherently biased by the feedback on the part of the participants, as it may have been related to the satisfaction with the interface quality and usability instead of intentional bias in the data selection. The dataset was not artificially balanced on the sentiment categories; instead, it depicts an actual, real-life perception of a given environment of the experimentation.

The project uses Visual Studio Code (IDE), Google Chrome to develop the website, and Google Analytics for the website metric tracking. We collected feedback from surveys filled out using Google Forms. The Google Colab platform was used to analyze Python, and its IDE was Colab. In order to assess loyalty, feedback from users who had experienced the websites and had 3,600 views was analysed. The collected data were further validated by performing a comparative analysis with publicly available e-commerce review datasets. It included the Amazon Product Review dataset. This confirmation guarantees that the trends we see in a dataset of 110 participants for sentiment and loyalty are consistent with greater behaviour by consumers. The findings of the public dataset on their sentiment polarity segmentation and loyalty ratios were somewhat similar to the experimental results, giving more external validity to the framework. Although we have a small sample group of participants, the close correlation between both datasets compensates for this and proves our findings are valid. In the future, it will focus on expanding this data to different sectors for better generalization.

3.3 Dataset Description

Data for the study were collected through the survey, which participants filled out (n=110). The survey was conducted on Google Forms, and the information received helped determine the users' experience with the site. An example of the dataset is presented in Figure 10.

Figure 10. Here is a sample of the data collected via Google Forms using user feedback entries for sentiment analysis. With Table 1, this dataset provides a clear view of the respondents' demographics and the distribution of sentiments (Loyal, Neutral, Loyal, Not Loyal) to reproduce the loyalty-prediction process.

1	Name	Age	Gender	City	Email	Phone Number	Activity Date	Activity Type	Transaction amount	Comment	Preferences/Interests
2	M.Awais Aslam	21	Male	Sahiwal	hanansal09@gmail.com	3077344610	08-03-19	Product review	0	good collection	monotone shirts
3	Hassan Raza	21	Male	Sahiwal	hanansal09@gmail.com	3017344610	08-05-19	Order	1200	good collection	monotone shirts
4	AQ	21	Male	Sahiwal	hanansal09@gmail.com	3017344610	08-09-19	Delivery	1200	good collection	monotone shirts
5	M.Danial Awais	21	Male	Sahiwal	hanansal09@gmail.com	3017344610	01-11-20	Return/Exchange	0	good collection	jeans
6	M.Danial Awais	21	Male	Sahiwal	hanansal09@gmail.com	3017344610	8/30/2019	Product review	0	nice collection	jeans
7	Qudsia Noreen	21	Male	Sahiwal	hanansal09@gmail.com	3017344610	09-02-19	Product review	0	ıs collection is not eno	jeans
8	Abdul Qadir Saifee	21	Male	Sahiwal	hanansal09@gmail.com	3017344610	8/31/2019	Product review	0	ıs collection is not eno	jeans
9	mubashar	21	Male	Sahiwal	hanansal09@gmail.com	3017344610	09-02-19	Product review	0	ou have less options ir	jeans
10	syed Hammid shah	21	Male	Sahiwal	hanansal09@gmail.com	3017344610	08-06-19	Product review	0	shirt	monotone shirts
11	Asia Rehman	21	Male	Sahiwal	hanansal09@gmail.com	3017344610	8/14/2019	Delivery	1000	good shirts	shirt
12	Adnan Muhammad	21	Male	Sahiwal	hanansal09@gmail.com	3017344610	11/13/2019	Product review	0	good collection	shirts
13	Amna Amin	21	Male	Sahiwal	hanansal09@gmail.com	3017344610	11/15/2019	Order	1800	good collection	shirts
14	Raja M Hassan Tariq	21	Male	Sahiwal	hanansal09@gmail.com	3017344610	11/17/2019	Delivery	1800	good collection	jeans
15	Rimsha	21	Male	Shiwal	hanansal09@gmail.com	3017433610	1/18/2020	Order	2000	nice jeans	jeans
16	Usama din	27	Female	cci	fizaahmad14@gmail.com	3237418648	08-07-19	Product review	0	dresses are nice	dresses
17	Fatima	27	Female	cci	fizaahmad14@gmail.com	3237418648	8/22/2019	Product review	0	dresses are good	dress
18	Mahnoor	27	Female	cci	fizaahmad14@gmail.com	3237418648	8/22/2019	Order	3000	e you will take to deliv	Dress
19	Aimen	27	Female	cci	fizaahmad14@gmail.com	3237418648	09-01-19	Delivery	3000	arcel. Dress is beautifu	dress
20	amna riaz	27	Female	cci	fizaahmad14@gmail.com	3237418648	10-12-19	Product review	0	ut plain articles are fev	plain single shirts

One hundred ten respondents (58 male, 52.7%, 52 females, 47.3%) between 18 and 45 years were taken as a sample of undergraduate and postgraduate students of COMSATS University, Sahiwal. The study was simulated, and the participants were under the same environmental conditions. On average, each user created about 32 comments, amounting to 3,600 reviews.

Sentiment analysis was used to categorize the reviews into three levels according to the thresholds of the polarity: Loyal (polarity is positive and good crossing 0), Neutral Loyal (polarity = 0), and Not Loyal (polarity is harmful across 0). The mean distribution among all the classes slightly leaned towards positive sentiment, which indicated true satisfaction with the experimental websites. The demographic and sentiment statistics are summarized in Table 1.

Table 1. Participant Demographics and Sentiment Category Distribution

Attribute	Category	Count	Percentage (%)
Gender	Male	58	52.7%
	Female	52	47.3%
Age Range (years)	18 – 24	68	61.8%
	25 – 34	31	28.2%
	35 – 45	11	10.0%
Education Level	Undergraduate	76	69.1%
	Postgraduate	34	30.9%
Sentiment Category	Loyal	2,560	71.1%
	Neutral Loyal	740	20.6%
	Not Loyal	300	8.3%

3.4 Pre-processing of Data

Pre-processing of the data is an important process in improving the quality of the findings. It is a process that consists of several steps, such as data cleaning, stop-word removal, and other important processes of optimizing data performance. Sentiment analysis was done by examining user reviews of Amazon. The reviews were handled one by one to obtain useful features. Pre-processing was done in the following steps.

The NLTK library automatically eliminates our stop words. Taking steps to improve sentiment analysis by eliminating the most common words that add very little value to the analysis is incredibly important. This measure helps filter meaningful content.

Spelling correction was made using the TextBlob library. We make this move to ensure the words are correctly detected and ready for additional processing. Further, the move standardizes the text while reducing word variations.

User evaluations term frequency is run on the user reviews to convert them into numbers. Reviews were assessed with the TextBlob library, which translates reviews into a stream of words, making it easier for analysis and processing.

We used the Porter Stemmer of the NLTK library to stem the words to their root form. It removes the suffixes like ing, ly, s, etc. It makes the different forms of a word into a straightforward word. The sentiment classification technique may be placed on a solid baseline due to the polarity analysis that we presented. It makes use of TextBlobs. However, we believe that better-performing NLP systems currently exist. It is because they offer better contextual insight and accuracy. Further explorations will also explore analyzing transformer-based approaches like BERT (Bidirectional Encoder Representations of Transformer), RoBERTa, and VADER sentiment analyzers to learn more significant semantic relationships and nuanced emotional responses. Using these models, the factors of linguistic variations, sarcasm, and domain-specific lexicon can be efficiently dealt with, which polarity-based techniques do not represent well.

3.5 360° Loyalty Prediction Framework

A quantitative model was developed to translate qualitative customer data into a numerical loyalty score. Customers who accumulate data from different touchpoints require a more efficient way to integrate various data streams simultaneously. All five core dimensions- demographic, transactional, behavioral, social, and environmental- were represented as unique customer feature vectors.

Feature Encoding: Normalization of each dataset to a standard scale (0-1), and numerical encoding was performed. The z-score normalization process normalizes numerical variables like age, income, and purchase frequency. Categorical variables, including gender or social activity level, were encoded with the help of one-hot encoding.

- Feature Weighting: A correlation-based weighting scheme was applied to determine each dimension's contribution to loyalty prediction. Behavioral and transactional data received higher weights due to their stronger observed correlation with sentiment-derived loyalty outcomes.
- Composite Loyalty Index (CLI): The normalized feature vectors were combined into a unified loyalty score using a weighted sum formula:

$$CLI = \sum_{i=1}^{n} w_i \times F_i \ldots\ldots\ldots\ldots \quad (1)$$

- where w_i represents the normalized weight of each feature group, and F_i denotes the feature value.
- Sentiment Fusion: The sentiment polarity score derived from user reviews (via TextBlob analysis) was integrated as a modifying factor, amplifying or attenuating the composite loyalty score based on user emotion.
- Loyalty Classification: Finally, the resulting CLI was categorized into three tiers: Not Loyal (CLI < 0), Neutral Loyal ($0 \leq$ CLI ≤ 0.3), and Confirm Loyal (CLI > 0.3), aligning with the thresholds established in the sentiment analysis phase.

This integration offers a multi-dimensional measure of loyalty that combines objective behavioural measures with emotional subjective measures, giving us a 360° view of the customer and can predict loyalty. The integration pipeline shown in Figure 11 combines the five core data categories, such as demographic, transactional, and so on. A dataset places normalized feature vectors in a fusion layer, calculating a CLI. The assessment of sentiment polarity helps to adjust the CLI to the level of loyalty. This model visualizes how other data types are fused to form a single loyalty prediction model.

Figure 11. Proposed 360° Customer Loyalty Prediction Framework

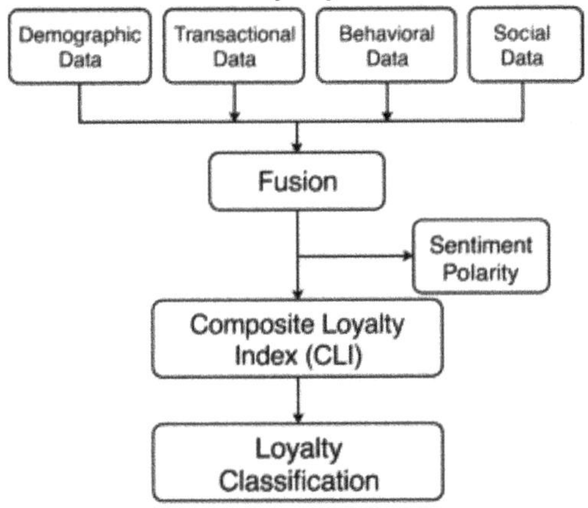

4 RESULTS AND DISCUSSION

4.1 Overview

A comprehensive yet 360° view of the customer brings in behavior, spending patterns, feedback, and relationship management data. It helps assess the firm's performance and increase revenue. Businesses can strengthen customer retention by taking specific steps if they identify customer loyalty early based on this holistic perspective. Over the years, firms have transitioned from being product-oriented to customer-oriented. To stay successful over time, businesses must attract new customers, increase the lifetime value of existing customers, and reduce churn. The loyal customer percentage is an important measure of the business's health. Customers always compare products. So when there is a gap in the promotions, they may switch to another offering a better deal. The moneymaking streams are ripped apart due to high churn rates, and the long-term viability is jeopardized. Central support to growth is the early identification of loyalty.

4.2 Loyalty Ratio Analysis of Users

The 900-website sentiment review, as shown in Figure 12, provides the ratio of loyalty based on sentiment. In case of each review, the loyalty ratio of less than zero represents a negative sentiment (Not Loyal), a loyalty ratio of zero is a Neutral Loyal sentiment (possibly), and a loyalty ratio of more than zero is positive sentiment (loyal). Most of the bars in this visualization are above the zero line, indicating that most users gave positive comments. This positive skewness indicates that such customers will revisit the sites. This sentiment measurement will provide an early warning of who will likely stick around and thus enable businesses to focus on activities that will enhance pleasant experiences and improve retention. The distribution of the loyalty ratio also shows the effects of the underlying churn of the customer base. Customers with a high positive ratio are loyalists with a low rate of churn who use products or services regularly. Neutral scores are associated with potential switchers, the further loyalty of which is determined by the availability of competing proposals or the quality of the services. Negative ratios are used to single out the at-risk customers who are most likely to cease interaction. This segmentation will help the firms focus the retention campaigns and personalized interventions on vulnerable groups before churn.

Figure 12. Loyalty ratio analysis of 110 user comments collected across 3,600 website views. Bars above zero indicate positive sentiment (Loyal customers), values near zero represent neutral sentiment (Neutral Loyal), and negative values correspond to Not Loyal users. These ratios are early indicators of loyalty strength, enabling businesses to identify at-risk customers based on declining polarity trends and implement timely retention measures.

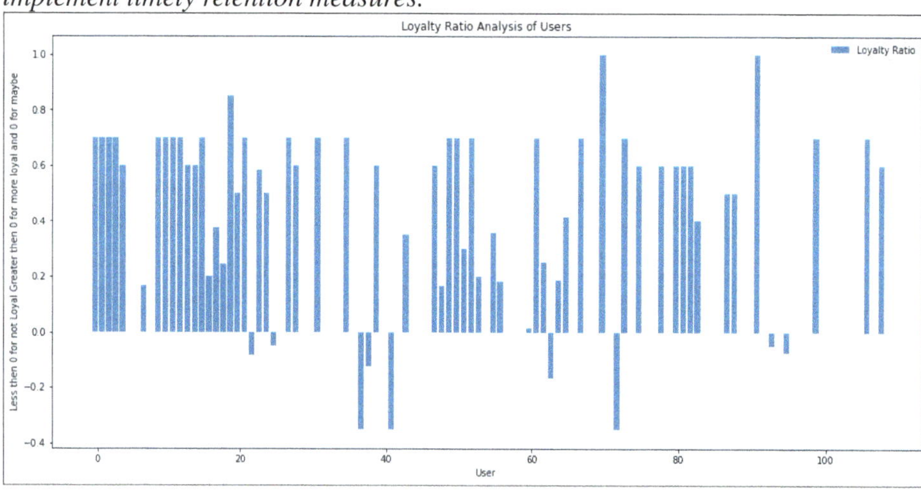

4.3 Users' Comment Sentiment Analysis

Figure 13 shows a scatter plot of the polarities of user reviews regarding 110 reviewers of 3,600 websites. Each red dot shows the score of the polarity of one review, and the numbers above the line indicate positive (loyal) sentiment. Below the line, the numbers reflect negative sentiment. All points being visualized would be above the zero line. The strong and positive reaction always reminds us that the integrated 360° customer view is a powerful tool: merging sentiment intelligence with behavioural and transactional data, the e-stores can serve more relevant product information, higher customer expectation, and ultimately long-term loyalty. Sentiment polarity distribution allows for a finer-grained separation of user sentiments. When the sentiment polarity score of a customer is consistently positive, it means he is delighted. However, even a slight negative deviation may indicate a churn tendency. For instance, those around the neutral threshold (0.0 0.3) may show early disengagement. By monitoring and associating with this group, the business can use predictive churn modeling to initiate retention efforts proactively. These initiatives can include a targeted offer and/or feedback loops. The prevalence of positive mood (Figure 13) means that the dataset is high and skewed, with more favorable reviews than neutral or negative reviews. This asymmetry is created because the study is experimental, since the participants tested operational and user-friendly websites. Even though this arrangement guaranteed the quality of the interaction data, it reduced the range of sentiment expression. This sampling bias may have a slight overinflation effect on loyalty prediction values. To overcome this drawback, future research will involve purposeful gathering of a balanced sample of positive, neutral, and negative responses, stratified sampling, and artificial data enhancement to increase fairness and representativeness in sentiment modeling.

Figure 13. Scatter plot illustrating sentiment polarity of user comments. Each red dot represents a single review's polarity score, where values above zero denote loyalty and below zero indicate potential churn. The clustering of points above the zero line demonstrates the overall positive sentiment distribution, signifying high retention probability and intense customer satisfaction.

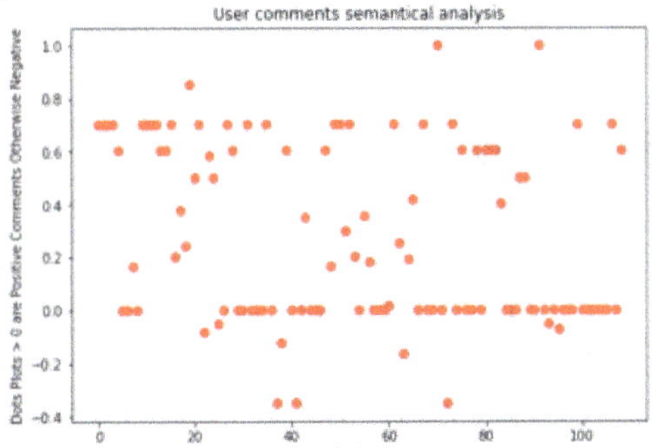

4.4 Customer Activity

Figure 14 breaks down the customer interactions of 3,600 websites by demonstrating the proportionality of four main activities. The pie chart explains the dominant actions throughout the customer journey by counting the number of hits of every type of activity in our dataset and turning the number into a percentage. For example, the most significant slice would tap on the most frequent engagement, ordering, or leaving a review. The smallest slice, however, would be less common, although it is present, such as returning or exchanging. This graph shows each e-commerce department's emphasis on the usual customer interface and where to invest in process improvements or outreach.

Figure 14. A chart shows the percentages of customer activities, product reviews, orders, delivery confirmations, and return requests from 3,600 sites. A strong pattern of purchase and review behaviours indicates hands-on engagement, which is linked to high loyalty and lower churn risk.

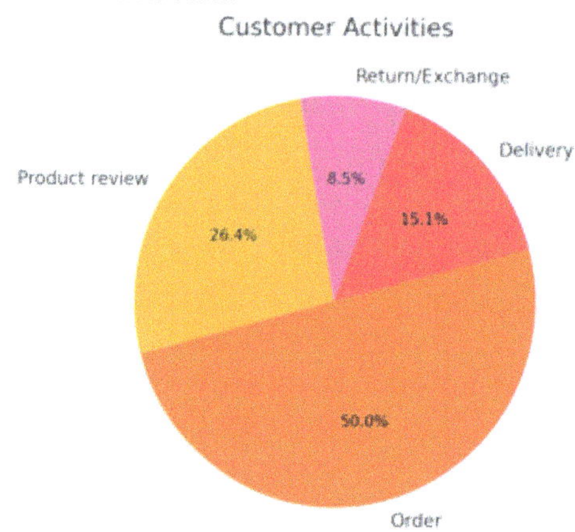

4.5 Customer Categories

The gender breakup of our customer base (3,600 sites) is categorised as Males and Females, as seen in Figure 15. We can easily find the largest group by viewing the pie chart, which counts the users and converts them into percentages. This demographic profile not only makes us aware of whether there are differences in the loyalty trend by gender but also makes our 360° view analysis tailor-made as per the needs of both male and female customers.

Figure 15. Gender distribution of surveyed customers. This demographic segmentation can help us understand loyalty variations among genders and determine which demographic segments are stronger or weaker in retaining customers.

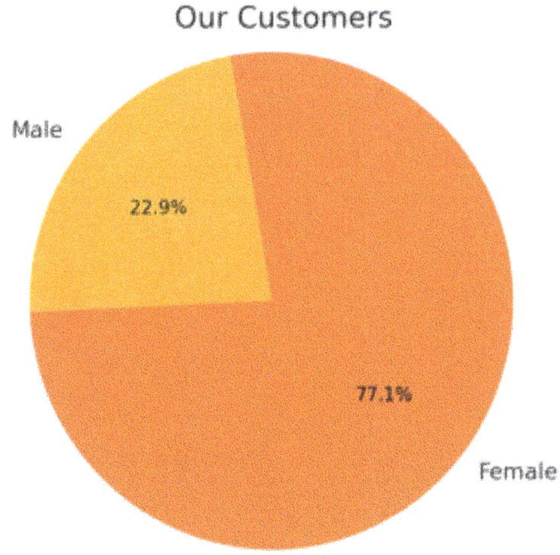

4.6 Customer Who Visited

Figure 16 shows how many of the 3,600 sites we analysed fall into one of three loyalty categories based on sentiment score. Confirm Loyal (score above 0.3), Neutral Loyal (score between 0 and 0.3), Not Loyal (score below zero). Over half of those surveyed respond positively, while an impressive 64% are already devoted customers, indicating high loyalty. The Neutral Loyal slice is less than 25%, so there is a chunk of customers whose sentiment is neutral or slightly positive, and the Not Loyal part is negligible, which means that very few users have negative sentiment. This distribution indicates that most visitors appear loyal, while only a few are indecisive or inattentive.

Figure 16. Distribution of customers across three loyalty tiers, Loyal, Neutral, and Not Loyal, based on sentiment polarity thresholds. The large share of loyal customers indicates a stable core segment, while smaller neutral loyal and Non-loyal groups help identify potential switchers and churn-prone customers for proactive targeting.

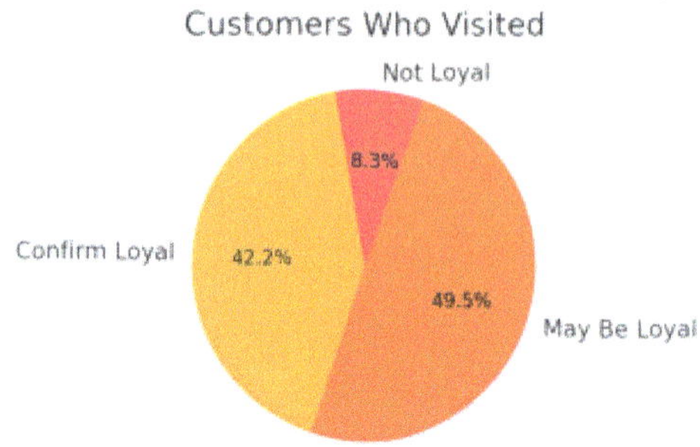

4.7 Testing The Loyalty of the New Comment

Figure 17 shows the analysis of loyalty ratios of a new test group of 110 user comments obtained from 3,600 websites. Each bar is the polarity score of a single comment, with scores below zero referring to non-loyalty, a score of zero to a neutral position, and scores above zero to loyalty. To ensure consistency among all analyses and visualizations, the loyalty sentiment will be classified into three tiers (which are the same as the polarity level): Not Loyal (polarity of less than 0), Neutral Loyal (polarity = 0), and Loyal (polarity of greater than 0). Standard labels are consistently applied in Figures 11-16 and in this report to ensure interpretative clarity. Most bars in this chart go into positive territory, proving most new customers were leaving positive comments about the website they visited. It indicates that these customers will return to us again in the future, which supports the idea that our 360 0 view can pick up early loyalty. The information in Figures 12 to 17, taken together, will show that we can use the sentiment-based loyalty classification as an early warning system to predict churn. Organizations can categorize their customers into risk groups using transactional and behavioral data and overlaying the polarity trend data so that they can take differentiated action, like proactively engaging with at-risk customers or rewarding core loyalists. It will turn the comprehensive perspective of the customers into a simple retention pattern that can lower churn and generate long-term loyalty.

Figure 17. Loyalty ratio analysis of a new test set of user comments. The predominance of positive ratios validates the predictive reliability of the proposed 360° loyalty detection framework and confirms its ability to detect early loyalty signals in previously unseen customer data.

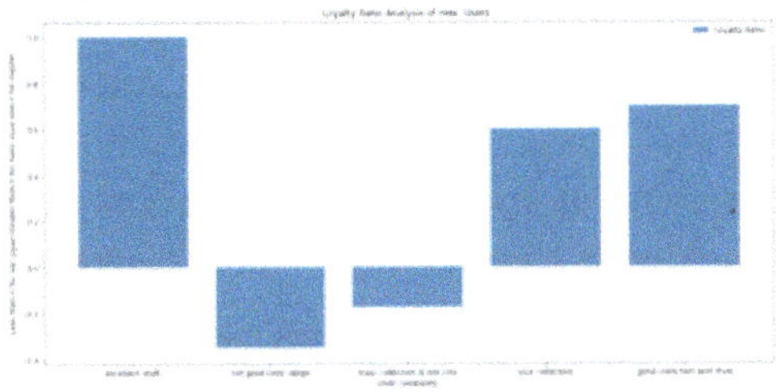

5 CONCLUSION AND FUTURE WORK

The retention of customers is probably one of the most serious problems for organizations in the contemporary digital market, where consumers can easily cross over to rival brands. It is expensive to win back lost customers, and it is important to identify loyalty indicators as early as possible to ensure long-term sustainability. This paper suggested a superior 360 ° customer loyalty model incorporating behavioral, transactional, demographic, social, and environmental information to create a CLI. With multi-dimensional insights and sentiment polarity analysis, the model can predict customer loyalty signs and churn early.

A 110-participant dataset that yielded over 3,600 interactions on the website tested the framework. We removed stop-words and spelling errors and did tokenization, stemming, and sentiment scoring using TextBlob. Positive ratings were labeled Loyal, neutral scores received Neutral Loyal, and negative scores went to Not Loyal. The result showed that the Loyal feedback type was achieved mainly, which proved that behavior and emotional consistency are highly correlated with reducing churn likelihood. The study's outcome was compared to publicly available e-commerce datasets, such as the Amazon Product Review corpus, to examine whether its sentiment trends are externally valid. It showed that these distributions were consistently polar.

The new definition of Figures 1217 connects our sentiment ratios and loyalty segments to churn risk and retention directives, separating our loyalist core from potential switchers and at-risk customers. The lessons show how the framework can identify early-stage behavioural drift and help the implementation of specific interventions that keep customers inside the fold.

Although this yields positive findings, the research paper recognizes shortcomings in sample size and differences in data. The experimental design had been oriented on useful, easy-to-use e-commerce websites; the feedback was naturally biased towards positive sentiment. In later research, the dataset will be extended to industry and geography, with a more balanced positive, negative, and neutral representation with stratified sampling and data augmentation to enhance representativeness and minimize bias.

The present model was an interpretable sentiment analyzer based on Text Blob; further iterations will use other advanced NLP models like BERT, RoBERTa, and Vader to increase the contextual sensitivity of the text, detect sarcasm, and precisely represent polarity. Combining these transformer-based models and the 360° framework will facilitate more profound and scalable sentiment-based loyalty prediction.

In the future, AI-based personalization and multimodal analytics will be incorporated into the 360 customer view in the future work.

- Recommendation Engines will tailor the offer and retention tactics depending on the purchase and sentiment history.
- Conversational Agents (AI Chatbots) will track the real-time customer emotional state, allowing for intervention before customer dissatisfaction leads to churn.
- Multimodal Analytics will combine the textual sentiment, behavioral data, clickstream, and visual engagement metrics of social media to deliver a holistic picture of loyalty behavior.

To make the model quantitative, future experiments will be evaluated based on standard performance measures such as Precision, Recall, F1-Score, ROC-AUC, and Churn Prediction Accuracy. By measuring AI-augmented systems with a baseline TextBlob model, we can have an objective baseline for a better one.

Ultimately, the current research can be used to show that a fusion of a quantitative 360° customer perspective and sentiment-based analytics can provide early-warning signals of customer churn. As deep learning and multimodal integration developments continue, the framework may make a brilliant and scalable loyalty prediction solution, which can be used in marketing, customer engagement, and customer retention strategies based on data in a business environment.

REFERENCES

Ahad, A., Puspitasari, I., Zheng, J., Ullah, S., Ullah, F., Bakhsh, S. T., & Pires, I. M. (2025). Machine Learning Stroke Prediction in Smart Healthcare: Integrating Fuzzy K-Nearest Neighbor and Artificial Neural Networks with Feature Selection Techniques. *Computers, Materials & Continua*, *82*(3), 5115–5134. DOI: 10.32604/cmc.2025.062605

Alizadeh, M., Zadeh, D. S., Moshiri, B., & Montazeri, A. (2023). Development of a customer churn model for banking industry based on hard and soft data fusion. *IEEE Access : Practical Innovations, Open Solutions*, *11*, 29759–29768. DOI: 10.1109/ACCESS.2023.3257352

Aljuhmani, H. Y., Elrehail, H., Bayram, P., & Samarah, T. (2022). Linking social media marketing efforts with customer brand engagement in driving brand loyalty. *Asia Pacific Journal of Marketing and Logistics*, *35*(7), 1719–1738. DOI: 10.1108/APJML-08-2021-0627

Alnofeli, K., Akter, S., & Yanamandram, V. (2023). Understanding the Future trends and innovations of AI-based CRM systems. In *Handbook of Big Data Research Methods* (pp. 279–294). Edward Elgar Publishing. DOI: 10.4337/9781800888555.00021

Alrumiah, S. S., & Hadwan, M. (2021). Implementing big data analytics in e-commerce: Vendor and customer view. *IEEE Access : Practical Innovations, Open Solutions*, *9*, 37281–37286. DOI: 10.1109/ACCESS.2021.3063615

Arora, M. (2024). What Lies in Big Data for Customer Retention? Analyzing the Past, Present, and Future. In *Augmenting Customer Retention Through Big Data Analytics* (pp. 311-326): Apple Academic Press.

Carey, B. (2022). Metaverse technologies, behavioral predictive analytics, and customer location tracking tools in blockchain-based virtual worlds. *Review of Contemporary Philosophy*, (21), 188–204.

Celestin, M., Sujatha, S., Kumar, A. D., & Vasuki, M. (2024). Investigating the role of big data and predictive analytics in enhancing decision-making and competitive advantage: A case study approach. *International Journal of Advanced Trends in Engineering Technology*, *9*(2), 25–32.

Chanpariyavatevong, K., Wipulanusat, W., Champahom, T., Jomnonkwao, S., Chonsalasin, D., & Ratanavaraha, V. (2021). Predicting airline customer loyalty by integrating structural equation modeling and Bayesian networks. *Sustainability (Basel)*, *13*(13), 7046. DOI: 10.3390/su13137046

Chibudike, C. E., Abdu, H., Chibudike, H. O., Ngige, O., Adeyoju, O. A., & Obi, N. (2021). Machine learning-a new trend in web user behavior analysis. *International Journal of Computer Applications*, *975*(5), 8887. DOI: 10.5120/ijca2021921247

Esmeli, R., Bader-El-Den, M., & Abdullahi, H. (2022). An analyses of the effect of using contextual and loyalty features on early purchase prediction of shoppers in e-commerce domain. *Journal of Business Research*, *147*, 420–434. DOI: 10.1016/j.jbusres.2022.04.012

Gadiparthi, S. (2024). Enhancing customer experience with business intelligence: Strategies, tools, and case studies. *International Journal of Management*, *15*(2), 108–116.

Hosseini, M., Abdolvand, N., & Harandi, S. R. (2022). Two-dimensional analysis of customer behavior in traditional and electronic banking. *Digital Business*, *2*(2), 100030. DOI: 10.1016/j.digbus.2022.100030

Islam, M. A., Fakir, S. I., Masud, S. B., Hossen, M. D., Islam, M. T., & Siddiky, M. R. (2024). Artificial intelligence in digital marketing automation: Enhancing personalization, predictive analytics, and ethical integration. *Edelweiss Applied Science Technology*, *8*(6), 6498–6516. DOI: 10.55214/25768484.v8i6.3404

Katyayan, S. S., & Singh, S. (2025). Optimizing Consumer Retention Strategies Through Data-Driven Insights in Digital Marketplaces. *International Journal of Research in All Subjects in Multi Languages*, *13*(1), 153.

Latif, R. M. A. (2025). Enhancing sustainable urban mobility in Pakistan through renewable hydrogen integration and policy interventions. *Discover Cities*, *2*(1), 1–24. DOI: 10.1007/s44327-025-00089-9

Latif, R. M. A., Farhan, M., Ahmad, J., Mostarda, L., & Cacciagrano, D. (2025). Blockchain-Based Medicine Supply Chain for Transparent Healthcare Tracking. In *AI and Blockchain Applications for Privacy and Security in Smart Medical Systems* (pp. 81–106). IGI Global Scientific Publishing. DOI: 10.4018/979-8-3373-0593-6.ch004

Latif, R. M. A., Farhan, M., Khan, N. A., & Sujatha, R. (2024). Sustainable Computing-Based Simulation of Intelligent Border Surveillance Using Mobile WSN. In *Navigating Cyber Threats and Cybersecurity in the Logistics Industry* (pp. 90–122). IGI Global. DOI: 10.4018/979-8-3693-3816-2.ch003

Latif, R. M. A., Ullah, F., Jamal, N., Zhao, Y., Jabbar, S., & Khan, M. A. (2025). *Explainable AI for Big Data Analytics in Urban Mobility Forecasting*. Paper presented at the 2025 IEEE International Conference on Pattern Recognition, Machine Vision and Artificial Intelligence (PRMVAI). DOI: 10.1109/PRMVAI65741.2025.11108680

Latif, R. M. A., Umer, M., Tariq, T., Farhan, M., Rizwan, O., & Ali, G. (2019). *A smart methodology for analyzing secure e-banking and e-commerce websites.* Paper presented at the 2019 16th International Bhurban Conference on Applied Sciences and Technology (IBCAST).

Latif, R. M. A., Yoshigoe, K., Jamal, N., Zhao, Y., Ullah, F., & Ahmad, J. (2025). *Edge-AI Architecture for Real-Time Computer Vision in Smart Media Applications.* Paper presented at the 2025 IEEE International Conference on Pattern Recognition, Machine Vision and Artificial Intelligence (PRMVAI). DOI: 10.1109/PRMVAI65741.2025.11108373

Lee, W.-L., Liu, C.-H., & Tseng, T.-W. (2022). The multiple effects of service innovation and quality on transitional and electronic word-of-mouth in predicting customer behaviour. *Journal of Retailing and Consumer Services, 64*, 102791. DOI: 10.1016/j.jretconser.2021.102791

Liu, X., Lim, X.-J., Cheah, J.-H., Ng, S. I., & Kamal Basha, N. (2023). Food at your doorstep? Examining customer loyalty towards online food delivery applications. *British Food Journal.* Advance online publication. DOI: 10.1108/BFJ-02-2023-0116

Matosas-López, L. (2025). The influence of brand credibility and brand loyalty on customer satisfaction and continued use intention in new voice assistance services based on AI. *Journal of Marketing Analytics, 13*(1), 180–201. DOI: 10.1057/s41270-023-00278-8

More, A., & Unnikrishnan, R. (2024). AI-Powered Analytics in Product Marketing Optimizing Customer Experience and Market Segmentation. *Journal Of Multidisciplinary, 4*(11), 12–19.

Mukherjee, S., Das, M. K., & Chakraborty, T. K. (2023). Viral marketing in increasing brand awareness and predicting purchase intention: Exploring mediating role of brand loyalty in FMCG sector. *Scholars Journal of Economics, Business and Management, 4*(4), 61–77. DOI: 10.36347/sjebm.2023.v10i04.001

Mustak, M., Hallikainen, H., Laukkanen, T., Plé, L., Hollebeek, L. D., & Aleem, M. (2024). Using machine learning to develop customer insights from user-generated content. *Journal of Retailing and Consumer Services, 81*, 104034. DOI: 10.1016/j.jretconser.2024.104034

Nica, E., Poliak, M., Popescu, G. H., & Pârvu, I.-A. (2022). Decision intelligence and modeling, multisensory customer experiences, and socially interconnected virtual services across the metaverse ecosystem. *Linguistic Philosophical Investigations, 21*(0), 137–153. DOI: 10.22381/lpi2120229

Pasupulati, R., Mahendran, J., & Majumdar, A. (2024). Predictive Analysis of Digital Consumer Behaviour: Key to Understanding Success and Failure of a Brand. In *Enhancing and Predicting Digital Consumer Behavior with AI* (pp. 238-267): IGI Global.

Popescu, G. H., Valaskova, K., & Horak, J. (2022). Augmented reality shopping experiences, retail business analytics, and machine vision algorithms in the virtual economy of the metaverse. *Journal of Self-Governance Management Economics*, *10*(2), 67–81.

Rane, N., Choudhary, S., & Rane, J. (2023). *Metaverse marketing strategies: enhancing customer experience and analysing consumer behaviour through leading-edge Metaverse technologies, platforms, and models. Platforms.* Models.

Ru, D., & Jantan, A. H. B. (2023). Relationship between Customer Value, Customer Trust, Customer Commitment and Customer Loyalty in Hospitality Industry of China. *Journal of International Business Management, 6*(9), 01-15.

Sann, R., Lai, P.-C., Liaw, S.-Y., & Chen, C.-T. (2022). Predicting online complaining behavior in the hospitality industry: Application of big data analytics to online reviews. *Sustainability (Basel)*, *14*(3), 1800. DOI: 10.3390/su14031800

Shaffi, S. M. (2025). Enhancing Customer Journey Intelligence: A Unified Framework for 360-Degree Analytics Using Generative AI. *Growth*, *7*, 8.

Subramanian, R. S., & Prabha, D. (2022). Ensemble variable selection for Naive Bayes to improve customer behaviour analysis. *Computer Systems Science and Engineering*, *41*(1), 339–355. DOI: 10.32604/csse.2022.020043

Ullah, F., Mostarda, L., Cacciagrano, D., Alenazi, M. J., Chen, C.-M., & Kumari, S. (2024). Federated Edge Intelligence for Enhanced Security in Consumer Intermittent Healthcare Devices Using Adversarial Examples. *IEEE Transactions on Consumer Electronics*.

Watson, R. (2022). The virtual economy of the metaverse: Computer vision and deep learning algorithms, customer engagement tools, and behavioral predictive analytics. *Linguistic Philosophical Investigations*, (21), 41–56.

Wolniak, R. (2024). *Analyzing customer behavior–employing business analytics within Industry 4.0 ecosystems*. Zeszyty Naukowe. Organizacja i Zarządzanie/ Politechnika Śląska.

Zhao, W., Cheng, Y., & Lee, Y.-I. (2023). Exploring 360-degree virtual reality videos for CSR communication: An integrated model of perceived control, telepresence, and consumer behavioral intentions. *Computers in Human Behavior*, *144*, 107736. DOI: 10.1016/j.chb.2023.107736

Zvarikova, K., Michalikova, K. F., & Rowland, M. (2022). Retail data measurement tools, cognitive artificial intelligence algorithms, and metaverse live shopping analytics in immersive hyper-connected virtual spaces. *Linguistic Philosophical Investigations*, *21*(0), 9–24. DOI: 10.22381/lpi2120221

Chapter 11
Computational Modeling and Analysis of Behavioral Patterns for Infectious Disease Networks Dismantling

Muhammad Usman Akhtar
https://orcid.org/0000-0002-5389-1156
Northwestern Polytechnical University, China

Ahsan Wajahat
https://orcid.org/0000-0003-4848-5281
Northwestern Polytechnical University, China

Abdul Razzaq
https://orcid.org/0000-0002-4465-6365
Northwestern Polytechnical University, China

Iftikhar Ahmed
https://orcid.org/0000-0001-7863-3746
University of Europe for Applied Sciences, Germany

Haleem Farman
https://orcid.org/0000-0003-2344-1522
Prince Sultan University, Riyadh, Saudi Arabia

Khalid Khan
University of Hull, UK

Dilawar Khan
University of Engineering and Technology, Peshawar, Pakistan

ABSTRACT

Infectious disease network dismantling is crucial for controlling disease spread in social and biological systems. One effective strategy is dismantling the network of disease transmission by identifying and targeting key individuals or behavioral hubs. Existing approaches often assume complete and accurate network data. This

DOI: 10.4018/979-8-3373-5062-2.ch011

data is rarely available in real-world scenarios. This lack of data poses challenges in mitigating infectious disease spread. In, addition, these approaches overlook the effects of missing or hidden links, and consequently, many non-essential individuals are unnecessarily targeted, leading to suboptimal control of the epidemic spread. In this chapter, we introduce the Infectious Disease Network Dismantling Algorithm (IDND), which leverages missing link prediction and node centrality context to identify minimal critical nodes for efficient dismantling. Specifically, this work explores how to mitigate the spread of a pandemic by focusing interventions on a small subset of individuals, despite having partial knowledge of the network.

1. INTRODUCTION

Daily life interaction facilitates the wide spread of infectious diseases. Human interactions in public gatherings such as handshakes, stair case, and shared taxi rides is a latent medium of infectious person contact. Every latent interaction facilitates the wide spread of infection spread network (Akhtar et al., 2023; Gündüç & Eryiğit, 2021). An infectious disease spread network, consists of entities (individuals) and relations (interactions). In ideal scenario every interaction between individuals to be recorded to control wide spread of disease. However, in real world scenario the recorded data is fragmented and includes many hidden transmission paths. (Akhtar & Khalil, 2018).

Several network-based control strategies often depend on centrality measures computed from available network information, such as degree centrality, betweenness centrality, closeness centrality, or eigenvector centrality to pin point and target super spreader in the network. These conventional control strategies are fragile in practice for real world scenarios. It requires a more nuanced and resilient approach. This approach must address limitations in the structure of the observed infectious network. However, this logic presumes complete and accurate network data. In real-world situations, particularly in biological or social interaction networks, missing or hidden links is scattered which distort these centrality techniques (Jiang et al., 2019). Therefore, control strategies solely based on observed centrality can inadvertently miscalculation of non-essential critical entities, resulting in suboptimal control of epidemic spread.

In literature computational modeling analysis of infectious disease networks is performed using mathematical and computer simulations to get insights to predict hidden patterns, predict potential interventions, and identify central entities that influence information/ disease spread. Existing disease spread prevention processes including structure-based entity targeting strategies such as, degree centrality, betweenness centrality, or eigenvector centrality are proposed to control processes disease spread (Chumachenko et al., 2022). By utilizing a hybrid modeling technique that combines structure-based approaches, it is feasible to estimate network dynamics and apply targeted control actions with minimal cost and resources, improving the effectiveness of interventions even in situations when complete network data is not available (Akhtar et al., 2023).

This drives the development of a hybrid infectious disease modeling approach, which integrates predicted structural information along with contextual centrality analysis to compute minimal yet highly influential entities for pandemic spread control in social interaction networks (Turab et al., 2023; Zhao et al., 2020). Leveraging link prediction to fill network gaps and recomputing centrality within the enriched context enables effective infectious network dismantling under partial information. The major contributions of this chapter are:

1. Discuss the traditional structure based theoretical foundations of infectious disease network dismantling.
2. Propose Infectious Disease Network Dismantling (IDND) algorithm, including its mathematical basis and computational steps.
3. Explore and discuss future research directions for epidemic control in infectious disease networks.

The rest of the chapter is structured as follows: we present motivation of the study in **Section 2**. We discuss related work on network dismantling and epidemic modeling in **Section 3**. We discuss theoretical research foundations in **Section 4**. We present the proposed IDND algorithm in **Section 5**. We describe experimental setup in **Section 6**. We discuss different behavioral, societal, and ethical considerations **in Section 7**. We discuss about integration of blockchain with infectious disease network analysis **in Section 8**. Finally, conclude and discuss future research directions in **Section 9**.

2. MOTIVATION

Global epidemic spreads like SARS, COVID-19, and Ebola underscore the need of network-based approaches to control pandemic situations. Human interactions create intricate networks in which spatial proximity, social behavior, geographic closeness, and temporal dynamics all have an impact on the patterns of disease transmission. In such networks, a small set of highly connected individuals or immunization hubs often plays a disproportionately large role in disease spread. Identifying and neutralizing these hubs through network dismantling can significantly reduce the risk of large-scale outbreaks (Fan et al., 2020b).

Figure.1. illustrates the infectious disease network dismantling performance by targeting the highest degree centrality entities and measuring the size of largest connected component (LCC) in infectious network. We adopt a node attack strategy in which all edges connected to a removed high-degree node are also eliminated. It is evident from the predicted network structure information that the size of LCC's decreases more significantly in to smaller parts when focusing on high-degree influential entities.

Figure 1. Dismantling performance of the infectious disease network on different observed and predicted network information.

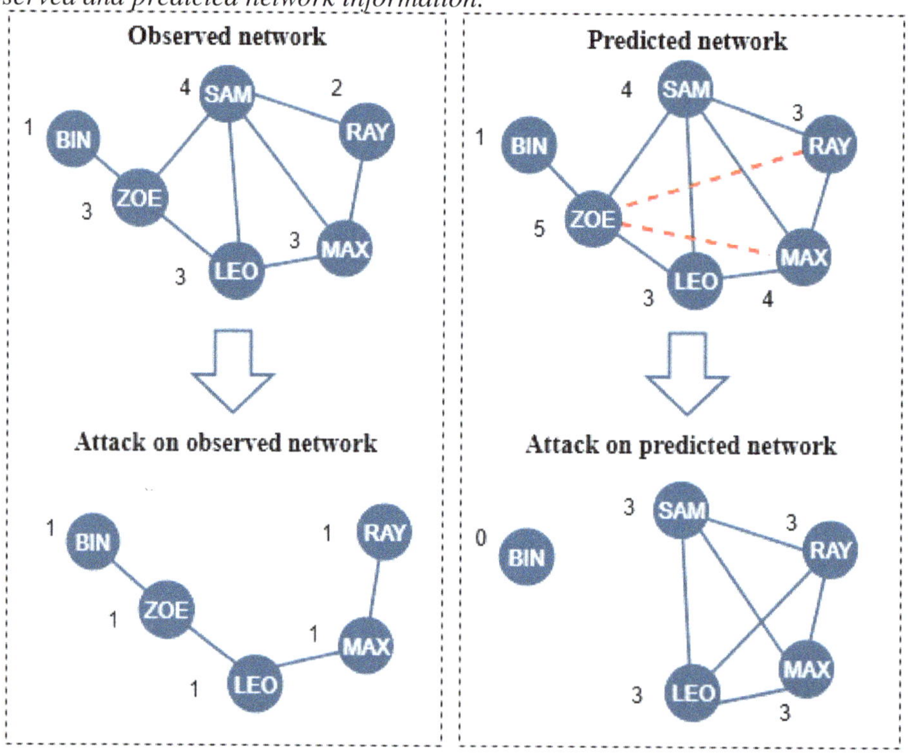

3. RELATED WORK

Previously several approaches have been proposed for infectious disease network dismantling problem, such as game theory (Saxena et al., 2018), machine learning

(Chumachenko et al., 2022; Fan et al., 2020b), graph theory (Gündüç & Eryiğit, 2021; Jiang et al., 2019), and optimization techniques (Song et al., 2019; Zhang et al., 2018). Jahanpour and Chen (2013) uses centrality measures including degree centrality, betweenness centrality, reciprocal closeness centrality, complement-derived closeness, and eigenvector centrality, (Jahanpour & Chen, 2013) proposed different heuristic-based entity removal algorithms. They evaluated performance of their algorithms on September 11 hijackers' network, with random removal and locally optimal solutions. Moreover, compared the effectiveness across six performance metrics. In order to enhance the evaluation of infection probabilities among entities in an infectious network, Gündüç and Eryiğit (2021) introduced the time-dependent centrality metrics for graphs. They also contended that the network's evolving structural characteristics had an impact on a entities risk of infection. The early stage of contamination usually starts with isolated entities with little connectedness, leading to a slow rate of transmission, the authors noted based on simulations on two real networks. However, there is a noticeable and quick transmission of the disease's transmission if it infects highly connected (central) entities. Jiang et al. (2019) tackled the issue of controlling virus spread by redefining it as an issue of identifying influential spreaders. Given that these clusters are crucial to the spreading process, the method concentrated on finding highly connected clusters in networks. The spread of the infection can be effectively stopped by locating and eliminating the most powerful entities in the closely clustered groups. This study proposed an algorithm to identify central entities with highly connected clusters for infection spread control. The experimental testing results from six real-world networks suggests that the proposed method outperformed bench mark algorithms.

Saxena et al. (2018) presented vaccination method for infectious network based on concept of graph theory and game theory. They select highly influential entities for immunization in network by computing Shapley value as centrality measure. Shapley value systematically ranks the influential entities in their descending order of degree distribution. Gündüç (2019) investigated how people respond to epidemic situations by fusing the SIR (Susceptible-Infected-Recovered) model with an information spreading technique. Instead, they would prefer to wait until they realize the benefit of precautions measures. The study presented that the preventative measures can greatly slow the spread of pandemic by demonstrating the efficacy of behavioral responses and public awareness in reducing the spread of infectious disease. Ren et al. (2019) proposes a solution that accounts for arbitrary non-negative actual costs related to targeting an entity. The model formulates the problem as a weighted vertex cover optimization and takes advantages of the spectral properties of a node-weighted Laplacian operator. In contrast to traditional methods, their solution is independent of a preset order of targeting entities. Experimental results demonstrates that the proposed method outperforms the current state-of-the-art methods. Additionally,

Qin et al. (2019) addressed the network dismantling problem by concentrating on the node removal sequence along with computational efficiency. They introduced belief-propagation-guided decimation technique with a node explosive percolation strategy to systematically determine the ideal node removal sequence. The experiments results showed that this sequential dismantling methodology significantly improves network dismantling performance over traditional methods. The results demonstrate how carefully planning entity removal strategy may result to improved overall network dismantling performance.

Fan e`t al. (2020a) proposed FINDER, a deep reinforcement learning framework aimed to enhance reliability of the network. However, FINDER was trained on small synthetic networks produced by basic models, its scalability to real networks is doubted. Although FINDER shows potential in revealing the principles of network organization, its performance on large real networks is poor, and because of implementation constraints, its use is only limited to networks consisting of maximum 50–60 entities. Its limitation indicated that examining different approaches to implementation may yield additional insights for real-world scenarios. Despite its practical limitations the study embodies a substantial advancement in the use of machine learning in network dismantling research.

The issue of maximizing the secondary distribution of HIV self-testing kits in environments with limited resources was addressed by Jing et al. (2022). To maximize economic gains in terms of both expanded testing coverage and identification of positive/newly-tested persons, the authors developed two new data-driven integer linear programming models based on implementation data from the men who have sex with men (MSM) community. They used greedy algorithms built on top of optimization solver solutions strategy. Their findings shows that data-driven optimization approach potentially improve the cost-effectiveness and individuals' health results of HIV self-testing kits distribution schemes, compared to traditional approaches.

Zhao et al. (2020) addresses large network scalability problem by introducing evolutionary divide-and-conquer technique. The proposed Network-Community-based Decomposition Co-Evolutionary Algorithm (NCD-CEA). The algorithm is based on two-step approach: Initially, it lowers the problem's dimensionality by clustering densely connected entities using a community detection technique. Then, using a collaborative coevolution technique, specialized sub-swarms develop solutions for each community using local fitness functions, while a global swarm integrates those partial solutions through a global fitness evaluation technique. Comprehensive benchmarking across different network topologies validates the effectiveness of this iterative optimization technique, which switches between global synthesis and local refinement, in resolving challenging network dismantling issues. NCD-CEA's collaborative evolutionary process and community-aware cluster decomposition make it especially effective for resource allocation problems (RAPs) in real world large-scale networks.

Huang et al. (2022) proposes a mathematical optimization-based model for pandemic risk prevention based on observed networks information, which especially considers individual social traits as the main factors influencing the widespread spread of infectious disease. The model systematically combines prevention and control strategies to mitigate the various latent transmission paths present in different clusters. Considering the effectiveness of its characteristic-driven approach to epidemic management. However, the model has a flaw as it is specifically designed for statis infectious network mitigation problems rather than real-world evolving outbreak problem. This limitation presents the possibility of future extensions to address changing pandemic scenarios. By highlighting the critical role that individual heterogeneity plays in transmission networks, the study presents insightful information on pandemic control and prevention.

Song et al. (2019) proposed to solve the target controllability problem in two-layer multiplex networks by controlling the allocation of scarce sources when external inputs only impact one network layer. The authors claim that propose method addresses the limited path cover optimization, which includes preventing paths from being started by second-layer entities and determining the least directed paths and cycles that cover target subsets. Their main theoretical contribution, is the Maximum Flow-based Target Path-cover (MFTP) technique, is the formal establishment of a similarity between the path cover problem and a maximum network flow problem in networks. In addition, through rigorous analysis they showed MFTP performance to identify the absolute minimum of control sources needed for full target controllability. This study provides basic theoretical computation foundation for managing intricate multilayer networks, and has significant implications for real-world situations while managing layered network interactions for prevention and control.

In order to address the issue of multi-path HIV transmission, Zhang et al. (2018) proposed a novel multiplex social network model that reveals latent relationships among influential entities in different clusters. As part of this approach, they created a novel partition-based random search technique with network and memory prioritization (PRS-NMP) to improve prevention strategies. This improved critical entity identification technique efficiently selects high-impact individuals for prevention interventions by leveraging network structure and past search history. Experimental results and simulations results illustrates that the PRS-NMP-based HIV treatments significantly outperform traditional methods such as the nested partitions approach and standard network metrics in lowering HIV transmission rates. The study shows how thorough network analysis and astute search algorithms can enhance the accuracy and efficacy of public health programs in real world social systems.

Different from existing methods this study addresses the limitations of insufficient infectious disease network information problem and provides a novel framework to enhance infectious disease network dismantling performance. The performance of previous methods is limited by missing or biased information, our model combines missing link prediction with targeted entity removal techniques. When we encounter partially observed networks with a large number of missing connections, we first use novel link prediction techniques to infer missing relations from observable network properties. This predicted network information is then used to for targeted node removal strategy that is more accurate and based on degree centrality context. Experimental results demonstrate that compared to traditional algorithms that operate with limited observed data our hybrid network dismantling strategy, which combines optimal entity targeting strategy with network completion through link prediction, offers significantly better performance. The idea is particularly helpful for infectious disease networks, where thorough connectivity data is often lacking but crucial for creating effective control strategies. Recent studies have investigated a variety of techniques, from machine learning frameworks to graph-theoretic methods, to maximize network teardown and epidemic containment. This analysis summarizes the main methods, together with their benefits and drawbacks, as seen in Table 1.

By using predicted connection information to identify key entities, the proposed IDND model improves on current methods and makes network dismantling more efficient. Even with limited network information, IDND can more effectively reduce the size of the largest connected component than conventional techniques that just use observed structure information.

Table 1. Techniques for Network-Based Disease Spread Intervention: Performance Trade-offs and Implementation Challenges

Study year	Technique Name/Method	Pros	Cons
Jahanpour & Chen (2013)	Heuristics-based centrality measures (Degree, Betweenness, etc.)	- Outperforms random removal strategies - Simple and computationally efficient	- Static centrality may not capture dynamic spread - Less effective in evolving networks
Gündüç & Eryiğit (2021)	Time-dependent centrality measures	- Captures dynamic infection spread - Better reflects real-world transmission	- Computationally intensive - Requires temporal network data
Jiang et al. (2019)	Dense group detection & influential node removal	- Effective in disrupting tightly connected clusters - Validated on real-world networks	- May overlook sparse but critical bridges - Relies on complete network data

continued on following page

Table 1. Continued

Study year	Technique Name/Method	Pros	Cons
Saxena et al. (2018)	Shapley value-based centrality (Game Theory)	- Optimizes node selection for immunization - Balances cost and impact	- High computational complexity - May not scale well for large networks
Gündüç (2019)	SIR + Information diffusion model	- Accounts for human behavior in epidemics - Highlights preventive measures' impact	- Limited to static behavioral assumptions - Ignores cost constraints
Ren et al. (2019)	Node-weighted Laplacian spectral method	- Incorporates removal costs - No predefined node order needed	- Assumes known node weights - Less effective for unweighted networks
Qin et al. (2019)	Belief-propagation-guided node removal	- Optimizes removal sequence - Improves computational efficiency	- Requires iterative updates - May struggle with highly modular networks
Fan et al. (2020a)	FINDER (Deep Reinforcement Learning)	- Learns from synthetic networks - Potential for adaptive robustness	- Poor scalability (>60 entities) - Weak real-world performance
Jing et al. (2022)	Data-driven integer linear programming (HIVST kits)	- Maximizes health/ economic benefits - Greedy algorithms enhance solvability	- Limited to specific resource allocation problems - Requires granular data
Zhao et al. (2020)	NCD-CEA (Community-based co-evolution)	- Scalable for large networks - Balances local and global optimization	- Dependent on community detection accuracy - Complex implementation
Huang et al. (2022)	Individual-characteristic-based optimization	- Accounts for heterogeneity in spread - Combines treatment and prevention	- Only applicable to static scenarios - Ignores temporal dynamics
Song et al. (2019)	MFTP (Max Flow-based Target Path-cover)	- Provably minimal control sources - Efficient for multilayer networks	- Restricted to two-layer systems - Control limited to one layer
Zhang et al. (2018)	PRS-NMP (Multiplex network + Random Search)	- Outperforms benchmarks in HIV prevention - Leverages network topology	- May require high computational resources - Dependent on network completeness

4. THEORETICAL FOUNDATIONS OF INFECTIOUS DISEASE NETWORK DISMANTLING

In Network science, epidemiology, and behavioral modeling are the foundations of network dismantling in the context of infectious disease spread control. Reducing or eliminating extensive connectivity within a network is the main goal in order to break the chains of disease transmission (Rossi & Ahmed, 2015). This idea acknowledges that disease spread is really a process over a complicated network of contacts, combining the analytical rigor of graph theory with epidemiological concepts (Zhang et al., 2018).

4.1 Conceptual Basis in Network Science

A network (or graph) is made up of entities (which stand in for people, groups, or entities) and relations (which stand for interactions or contact events that have the potential to spread disease) according to network science (Akhtar & Khalil, 2018). The network's density indicates how fast and widely an infectious disease can spread.

Entities and relations must be carefully targeted and removed to efficiently divide a network into smaller, fragmented pieces. In epidemiology, this is similar to removing high-risk individuals and groups, keeping infected people safe, or preventing interactions between subgroups (Rossi & Ahmed, 2015). The basic theoretical understanding is very effective to eliminate a small percentage of influential entities. This could lead to a significant decrease in the largest connected component (LCC) (Razzaq et al., 2025).

4.2 Epidemiological Relevance

Most of the literature infectious disease control models including, SIR (Susceptible–Infectious–Recovered) and SEIR (Susceptible–Exposed–Infectious–Recovered), usually provide an aggregated view of disease dynamics. However, they do not specifically account for the underlying social interaction network. Infectious disease network dismantling (IDND) integrates the epidemiological process into the network architecture to address this issue.

For example, removing an entity with high betweenness centrality disrupts multiple infection pathways, decreasing the risk of the epidemic to spread across the network. This aligns with realistic strategies such as targeted vaccination campaigns, which prioritize individuals who pose the greatest risk of disease transmission in the community.

4.3 Graph-Theoretical Principles

Graph-theory provides the fundamental base for various dismantling strategies, including:

1. Percolation theory looks how overall network is affected by targeting entities or relations. It studies the threshold point at which LCC breaks down into smaller parts.
2. Centrality measures such as degree, closeness, betweenness, and eigenvector are quantitative metrics that identify the crucial entities the bridges the network clusters.
3. Community structure represents the densely connected clusters in networks. Attacking individuals within cluster may not be as effective as targeting the influential one that serve as connections within and between different clusters.
4. Networks robustness is the ability to withstand random attacks as opposed to targeted attacks (in our case infectious disease immunization).

4.4 Role of Missing Links

In real-world social biological and infectious disease settings, complete interaction information between individual is rarely available. Due to privacy restrictions, or insufficient data collection can all result in missing or incomplete information. Moreover, ignoring this latent information while model designing can result in ineffective dismantling strategies because they may act as silent pathways for the spread of infectious disease (Akhtar & Khalil, 2018). Predictive modeling of missing information linkages is crucial in real world scenarios. Methods like link prediction algorithms are used to approximate the real network topology. This makes dismantling more effective. This stage is particularly important in epidemic situations where time and data are scarce (Akhtar et al., 2023).

4.5 Behavioral Patterns and Social Dynamics

Network disintegration is linked to human behavior and is more than just a structural phenomenon. Individuals' social interactions, preferences, and intervention all influence the network topology over time in real world scenario. Mathematical models of choice behavior based on fixed point theory provide rigorous frameworks for understanding how people weigh their options and make decisions during epidemics (Turab & Sintunavarat, 2019, 2020). These theoretical foundations ensure the presence and uniqueness of solutions in behavioral dynamics, which are necessary for predicting latent intervention and risk perception dynamics. For instance:

- Social distancing reduces the effective degree of entities.
- Community gatherings increase clustering coefficients.
- Travel restrictions alter network modularity and edge weights.

Incorporating behavioral insights into dismantling strategies ensures interventions are not only theoretically optimal but also practically feasible.

5. METHODOLOGY AND FRAMEWORK FOR INFECTIOUS DISEASE NETWORK DISMANTLING

A systematic technique that provides balance between theoretical background and real-world application is needed to dismantle infectious disease networks. Our proposed method, which is based on the Infectious Disease Network Dismantling (IDND) algorithm, logically combines state-of-the-art missing link prediction techniques, traditional network science metrics, and targeted network dismantling strategies. The proposed method is designed to work in partially available network information, where noisy or missing data exists the result of unreported infection cases, poor contact tracing, or limitations in epidemic control.

There are two main objectives of the proposed Infectious Disease Network Dismantling Algorithm (IDND):

1. Firstly, to minimize the number of target entity set responsible for infectious disease transmission.
2. Secondly, predict latent or missing relationship information for real world networks.

This chapter presents IDND's theatrical basis, fundamental algorithmic stages, and illustrates data integration strategies within infectious networks.

5.1 Overview of the IDND Framework

To increase dismantle efficiency, the IDND model combines behavioral modeling, link prediction, and network science ideas. The IDND is made up of three essential parts:

1. **Network Preprocessing and Representation**

First, a graph representation G=(V,E) is created from the original infectious disease network (obtained from observed epidemiology records, proximity sensors, or human contact data), where V stands for individual entities and E for interactions or relation that are significant to the disease. To provide a solid foundation, data cleaning removes duplicate linkages, inconsistencies, and temporal aggregation of contacts.

2. **Missing Link Prediction Module**

Unreported or hidden interactions are estimated via a supervised link prediction model. Since data on infectious diseases in the actual world is typically limited, this stage is crucial. Asymptomatic carriers, privacy constraints, and data collecting limitations are some of the causes.

3. **Centrality-Enhanced Node Targeting**

To rank entities according to their impact on network connection and the potential for disease spread, the augmented network, which is made up of original plus anticipated links is subjected to centrality analysis. Unlike classical methods that use a single centrality measure, IDND incorporates a weighted multi-centrality score integrating degree, betweenness, and eigenvector centrality in a context-aware fashion.

5.2 Missing Link Prediction: Enhancing Structural Awareness

Traditional dismantling methods assume the network is complete, but in infectious disease scenarios, **contact tracing data is almost always partial**. For example, wearable sensor networks may fail to detect all interactions, and self-reported contact diaries may omit transient encounters.

The IDND addresses this by applying a link prediction phase before dismantling. Key features of the missing link prediction module:

- **Feature Engineering:** Each potential edge (u,v) is described by a vector of features, including:
  - Number of shared neighbors.
  - Average clustering coefficient of common neighbors.
  - Shortest path length between u and v in the observed network.
  - Node attribute similarity (if demographic or behavioral data are available).
- **Learning Approach:**
  - **Heuristic methods** for small datasets (e.g., common neighbor, adamic adar, resource allocation index).
  - **Machine learning classifiers** (e.g., Random Forest, XGBoost) for larger datasets.

- o **Deep graph models** (e.g., GraphSAGE, GCN) for large-scale, high-dimensional networks.

The predicted links are then merged with the observed network to form an enriched structure G′, which better approximates the true interaction patterns.

5.3 Centrality-Based Critical Node Identification

Centrality measures capture different aspects of a node's influence:

- A measure of the number of direct connections, or degree centrality (DC), is helpful in locating super-spreaders.
- The frequency with which a node appears on shortest paths is known as Betweenness Centrality (BC), and it is used to identify structural bridges.
- Eigenvector Centrality (EC), which emphasizes entities in dense, powerful clusters, is a measure of influence based on neighbor connection.

Instead of relying on a single measure, IDND uses a **hybrid score**:
$\text{Hybrid Centrality}(v)=\alpha\cdot DC(v)+\beta\cdot BC(v)+\gamma\cdot EC(v)$
where α,β,γ are tunable parameters determined through cross-validation or domain knowledge.

5.4 Iterative Node Removal Process

The disassembly procedure employs an incremental, high-impact removal approach:

1. Use hybrid centrality to rank entities in network.
2. Eliminate the network's top highest degree entities.
3. Update network metrics, such as infection reachability and biggest connected component size (LCC).
4. Using the modified network, recalculate hybrid centrality.
5. Continue until the LCC size falls below a predetermined level, such as 20% of the initial network size.

This adaptive re-ranking makes sure that during execution, the dismantling technique adapts to structural changes.

5.5 Computational Complexity and Scalability

- **Link Prediction Phase:**
  - o For dense networks, the heuristic measures such as common neighbors and adamic-adar scale as $O(|V|)^2$. However, with proper sampling, embedding-based techniques can achieve near-linear scalability.
- **Centrality Computation:**
  - o Degree: O(|V|+|E|)
  - o Betweenness: O(|V||E|)
  - o Eigenvector: O(k|E|), where k is the number of iterations until convergence.
- **Iterative Removal:**
  - o A maximum of O(|V|) iterations, where each step involves recalculating centrality.

    Approximate centrality measures and parallel processing are advised for big networks.

5.6 Advantages of the IDND Methodology

- **Robustness to Missing Data:** Predictive augmentation mitigates the loss of dismantling efficiency from incomplete contact tracing.
- **Behavioral Sensitivity:** By integrating centrality context, the algorithm accounts for entities whose influence derives from network position rather than raw degree.
- **Adaptive Targeting:** modifies priorities as the network breaks up through iterative re-ranking.
- **Generalizability:** The paradigm is generalizable to various areas, such as disinformation diffusion networks, cybersecurity intrusion networks, and financial fraud networks.

5.7 Data Preprocessing and Network Representation

Real-world epidemiology datasets, including Infection-Dublin and Infection-Hyper, are made up of proximity sensor-collected high-resolution temporal contact records. The pipeline for preprocessing consists of:

- **Temporal Aggregation**: Static snapshots or weighted networks are created by aggregating contact events over predetermined time intervals (e.g., 5–10 minutes).

- **Edge Weight Assignment:** Individuals' cumulative exposure time or contact intensity is represented by weights.
- **Threshold Filtering:** Low-weight edges that indicate very little contact are eliminated in order to prevent overestimating the transmission channels.

Assuming bidirectional contact, the resulting graph, G=(V,E,W), is weighted to capture different levels of infection risk and is undirected.

5.8 Summary of Methodology Advantages:

The proposed model aims to predict vital partially missing link information used for infectious disease spread control. In addition, it uses centrality context of entities in observed and predicted graph to prevent bias while computing minimal set of entities for immunization. The model is generalizable for different kinds of networks such as financial and disinformation contagion.

6. EXPERIMENTAL SETUP

Experiments are performed to assess the effectiveness, and robustness of the suggested Infectious Disease Network Dismantling Algorithm (IDND) in real-world situations. The datasets, baseline methodologies, assessment measures, and simulation environment utilized to thoroughly analyze IDND's performance are described in this section. Because real-world interaction data is incomplete and infectious disease networks are complicated, our experimental approach is developed to replicate real-world settings as nearly as feasible while allowing for thorough comparison analysis.

6.1 Datasets

We chose two real-world datasets that have been widely utilized in epidemic modeling research in order to guarantee empirical validity:

1. **Infection-Dublin**

This dataset, which is derived from proximity-sensing wearables placed in a school setting, records high-resolution temporal contact events between people over several days. Every interaction is a chance for the spread of an infection. Entities serve as people's representatives within the school and edges show instances of recorded in-person proximity. In addition, realistic everyday contact cycles are reflected by the high temporal granularity.

2. **Infection-Hyper**

Fathered from wearable sensors that monitored patterns of human contact at a scientific meeting. A dynamic, diverse population's short- and long-duration contacts are captured in the dataset. Where entities stand in for attendees of the conference and edges represents interactions during meetings, coffee breaks, and casual get-togethers, represent measured proximity. Features include severe clustering periods and sparse, highly dynamic connections.

Due to their capacity to capture both heterogeneous, open-population dynamics and localized, closed-population interactions, these datasets were selected. This variability guarantees the applicability of the deconstruction algorithm in many social circumstances.

6.2 Baseline Methods

In order to demonstrate IDND's benefits, we contrasted it with well-known network dismantling and node-targeting techniques:

1. Degree Centrality (DC): Targets those with the most direct contacts, DC chooses entities with the highest degree for removal.
2. Closeness Centrality (CC): Gives top priority to entities with the shortest travel distances to all other entities.
3. Betweenness Centrality (BC): Focuses on organizations that serve as vital conduits for network communications.
4. Eigenvector Centrality (EC): It computer the important clusters by identifying entities that are related to other highly connected entities in a network.

These methods are common standards in social network research and epidemic control. They do not, however, take into consideration hidden or absent links and function under the assumption of full network knowledge.

6.3 Missing Link Prediction Integration

One of the primary features of the proposed model is missing link prediction module. It uses link prediction techniques and topological similarity metrics to predict likely latent or missing relations (Alkhalil et al., 2025; Razzaq et al., 2022, 2025). IDND enriches missing relations information by adding predicted relations to the network before targeting entities in observed network, which is a typical practice in real world pandemic control.

6.4 Evaluation Metrics

Different performance measures are used to measure network dismantling performance:

1. **Size of the Largest Connected Component (LCC):** represents the size of the cluster in infectious network that is still connected after induvial entity removal.
2. **Relative Efficiency of Dismantling (RED):** It computes the speed at which crucial network components are removed.
3. **Node Removal Fraction:** Is the measure of smallest set of entities needed to dismantle the LCC, such as 10% to 20% of its initial size.

7. BEHAVIORAL IMPLICATIONS AND THEORETICAL PERSPECTIVES

This section examines the behavioral implications of infectious network topology as well as the broader theoretical implications of dismantling interventions in real-world infectious disease networks. Graph theory is useful for gaining a quantitative understanding of network dismantling. However, the true effectiveness of these strategies is closely related to human behavioral dynamics in infectious networks (Turab & Sintunavarat, 2020).

7.1 Behavioral Drivers of Network Structure

Infectious disease transmission is mainly related to the interaction of social factors, environmental situations, and individual characteristics. The following are the crucial behavioral elements that influence network architecture are:

- **Social mixing patterns:** Individual preferences, work environments, and cultural conventions all affect how frequently and how long interaction events occur.
- **Compliance with health interventions:** Mask wearing, quarantine, and voluntary or required social separation all directly alter contact structures.
- **Mobility and migration:** Creating temporary hubs and bridges, daily commutes, travel, and migration dynamically rewire network connections.

This results in networks that are not only intricate but also dynamic, necessitating methods that deal with behavioral realities and transcend static structural study.

7.2 Impact of Behavioral Adaptations on Dismantling

The individual and groups behavioral responses may change the infectious network's topology when dismantling techniques, such as targeted vaccination or isolating important individuals, are used:

- **Compensatory behaviors:** when one individual is targeted in a network, others might take over to carry out the same social tasks, which could lead to the re-establishment of disease spread pathways.
- **Risk compensation:** Increased interactions among non-targeted individuals may result from perceptions of decreased risk after disease control measures.
- **Behavioral heterogeneity:** Differences in social norms may positively or negatively affect the effectiveness of dismantling performance.

7.3 Ethical and Societal Considerations

Targeting certain individual or groups presents moral dilemmas, particularly when those actions entail monitoring issues in public health contexts (Turab et al., 2022), including: Privacy control for contact tracing and predictive modeling need to protect personal information. Equity for vulnerable populations shouldn't be disproportionately burdened by interventions. Trust and compliance to guarantee public acceptance and efficacy, open communication and community involvement are essential.

7.7 Summary

In conclusion, breaking down networks of infectious disease transmission is essentially a socio-behavioral problem rather than just a structural or computational one. In order to effectively control epidemics, network analysis and behavioral insights must be combined to create strong, moral treatments that can change with the times.

8. INTEGRATING BLOCKCHAIN WITH DISEASE NETWORK ANALYSIS

The modern research tools include network theory, agent-based modeling with machine learning, to study the human behaviors such as abidance to social distancing rules, intention to get vaccinated and resistance toward false information. Computational models that incorporate such features enable researchers to identify the most vulnerable sites in a network. This can be useful in developing policies like focused vaccination of some groups, taking aside individuals who spread infection quickly or by changing the mobility patterns to control disease. (Turab et al., 2023).

Modern research methods combine network theory, agent-based modeling, and machine learning to study human behaviors for example following the social distancing rules, readiness to get vaccinated, and resistance to false information. By including these factors in computational models, researchers can determine the high-risk points within a network. It helps to make the plan for effective strategies such as vaccination for specific groups, and for those who spread infection rapidly; these patterns help to control disease transmission.

The Blockchain technology plays a very important role in this field by supporting trustworthy behavioral data collection and accurate disease modeling (Alkhalil et al., 2025; Razzaq et al., 2022). Health data has often faced reliability issues due to delayed reporting, disconnected healthcare traditional databases, and limited trust between the organizations (Turab et al., 2022). Blockchain helps to reduce and overcome these challenges by using a decentralized system of agreement, that allows secure and real-time sharing of updates on infection, vaccination data, and other behavioral information among different stakeholders. As an example, the patient information stored on a blockchain can enhance computational models by offering reliable and verifiable data inputs to predict possible outbreak patterns.

As a structural point of view to ensure that blockchain-based systems used for interventions remain transparent and accountable. The computer model that finds about the top 10–12% of the most influential points in a disease-spreading network. Blockchain-based health systems allow stakeholders to ensure that vaccination and isolation measures are carried out securely while the spread of false information reduced. Blockchain does not act as a data ledger but as a tool that builds decentralized trust in computational epidemiology which helps to ensure that control strategies are carried out effectively (Jahanpour & Chen, 2013). Figure 2 describes a multi-layered framework that integrates blockchain technology with computational models of system for analyzing infectious disease networks. The system incorporates a wide range of data sources including standard epidemiological metrics like infection, and fatality rates, as well as behavioral data such as mobility patterns, vaccination, and adherence to preventive measures. It accounts for outer signals from social media including the spread of misinformation. These vast inputs are processed by a computational modeling engine that employs machine learning algorithms, and graph-theoretical techniques. The goal is to identify individuals or groups at heightened risk, prediction potential outbreak trajectories, and evaluate the likely impact of various intervention strategies. A distinctive feature of this framework is the integration of a blockchain layer. This layer gives secure, tamper-evident storage of data, utilizes consensus mechanisms to validate information, and deploys smart contracts to automate essential public health responses such as issuing timely alerts or enforcing compliance thresholds.

Figure 2. Blockchain-enabled framework for computational modeling of infectious disease networks.

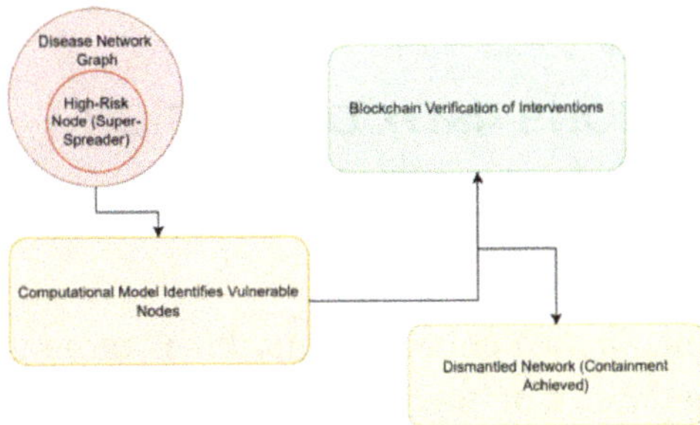

Figure 3. Blockchain-assisted dismantling of infectious disease networks.

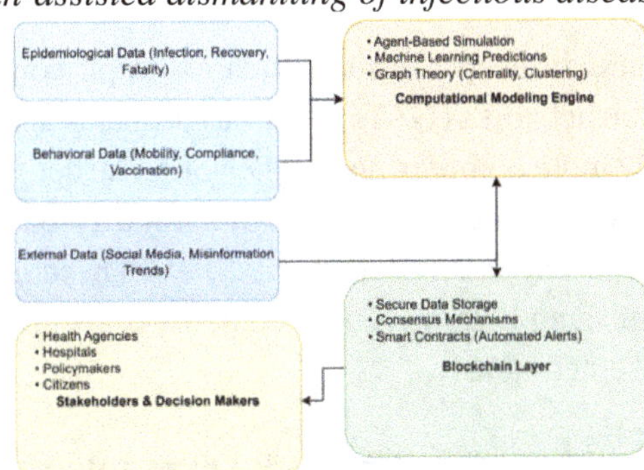

Figure 3 discusses a system based on blockchain technology that is designed to disrupt infectious disease networks. In this model, individuals are described as nodes in a social graph, and their interactions as edges. Main supper nodes those with disproportionate influence on transmission are identified. The system applies computational dismantling strategies, such as targeted removal or separation of super-spreaders, prioritized vaccination of central actors, and interventions to interrupt transmission pathways. These measures are reinforced by a blockchain verification layer, which ensures tamper-proof intervention execution, enforces compliance through smart contracts, testing, and quarantine processes. The result is a fragmented network, divided into smaller, less linked clusters, thus limiting the potential for widespread outbreaks. This figure also describes the computational modeling integration and blockchain technology, that can be implemented in a transparent, secure, and ethically responsible manner. The smart contracts could automate and transparently execute public health interventions such as prioritizing individuals for vaccination based on their verified centrality in the network ensuring that the dismantling strategy is applied fairly and as intended, without manipulation.

9. FUTURE DIRECTIONS AND CONCLUSION

9.1 Future Directions

Rapid advancements in data collection, machine learning, and computational techniques are driving the area of infectious disease network disassembly. Building on the ideas presented in this chapter, the following useful applications and research avenues merit more investigation:

9.1.1 Integration of Deep Learning for Link Prediction

Recent developments in deep learning, such as graph convolutional networks (GCNs), graph attention networks (GATs), and variational graph autoencoders, offer the capacity to identify more complex and higher-order structural pattern networks, while classical machine learning and traditional similarity-based approaches offer a basis for predicting missing links (Ren et al., 2019). These methods have a lot of potential to increase missing link inference accuracy, especially in dynamic, large-scale infectious disease networks.

9.1.2 Temporal and Multilayer Network Dismantling

Human social networks encompass social, digital, and physical domains and are dynamic and multimodal. Multilayer network analysis and temporal graph models must be included in future teardown algorithms to take this complexity into consideration (Huang et al., 2022). These methods facilitate accurate identification of clusters and individual in infectious networks in real time.

9.1.3 Behavioral Feedback and Adaptive Intervention

The integration of real-time feedback system is essential for effective epidemic control in response to behavioral shifts (Jing et al., 2022). Combining dynamic network deconstruction methods with agent-based simulations offers a viable way to achieve flexibility for real time pandemic control.

9.1.4 Ethical AI and Privacy-Preserving Mechanisms

Ethical guidelines for individual and community privacy must be followed when using prediction algorithms in public health. To protect individual anonymity while keeping the effectiveness of interventions, future research should give top priority to the creation of privacy-preserving algorithms, such as those based on federated learning or differential privacy (Jiang et al., 2019).

9.2 Conclusion

This chapter has provided an overview of computational and theoretical techniques for dismantling infectious networks. Using the Infectious Disease Network Dismantling Algorithm (IDND), which combines missing link prediction and centrality-based targeting strategy, we demonstrated improved efficiency in partially observed networks. Implementing IDND requires careful consideration of both computational and ethical factors for real world infectious networks. In addition, large infectious networks will require memory and processing power to compute projected links and update centrality metric. In conclusion, to properly break down infectious disease it is important to ensure privacy, storage, and data retrieval compliance. Future development in this area will depend on handling the temporal dynamics of human social interaction along with technical advancements to make it morally sound.

ACKNOWLEDGMENT

This work was supported in part by the National Natural Science Foundation of China under Grant No. 52335001. The authors also acknowledge the use of Gen AI tools for language improvement in some parts of the manuscript.

REFERENCES

Akhtar, M. U., & Khalil, M. I. K. (2018). Link prediction techniques in complex networks. *International Review of Basic and Applied Sciences*, *6*(8), 60–69.

Akhtar, M. U., Liu, J., Liu, X., Ahmed, S., & Cui, X. (2023). NRAND: An efficient and robust dismantling approach for infectious disease network. *Information Processing & Management*, *60*(2), 103221. Advance online publication. DOI: 10.1016/j.ipm.2022.103221

Alkhalil, A., Razzaq, A., Ahmad, A., Abdelrhman, M., Altameemi, Y., Altamimi, M., & Tao, Z. (2025). A framework for blockchain-based secure management of mobile healthcare (mHealth) systems. *Journal of Web Engineering*, *24*(3), 317–354. DOI: 10.13052/jwe1540-9589.2431

Chumachenko, D., Piletskiy, I., Sukhorukova, M., & Chumachenko, T. (2022). Predictive model of Lyme disease epidemic process using machine learning approach. *Applied Sciences (Basel, Switzerland)*, *12*(9), 4282. Advance online publication. DOI: 10.3390/app12094282

Fan, C., Zeng, L., Sun, Y., & Liu, Y. (2020a). Finding key players in complex networks through deep reinforcement learning. *Nature Machine Intelligence*, *2*(6), 317–324. DOI: 10.1038/s42256-020-0177-2 PMID: 34124581

Fan, C., Zeng, L., Sun, Y., & Liu, Y. (2020b). A novel learning-based approach for efficient dismantling of networks. *International Journal of Machine Learning and Cybernetics*, *11*(9), 2101–2111. DOI: 10.1007/s13042-020-01104-8

Gündüç, S. (2019). A study on the effects of diffusion of information on epidemic spread. *International Journal of Modeling, Simulation and Scientific Computing*, *10*(3), 1950015. Advance online publication. DOI: 10.1142/S1793962319500156

Gündüç, S., & Eryiğit, R. (2021). Time dependent correlations between the probability of a node being infected and its centrality measures. *Physica A*, *563*, 125483. Advance online publication. DOI: 10.1016/j.physa.2020.125483 PMID: 33106728

Huang, C. D., Behara, R. S., & Goo, J. (2022). Optimal investment in prevention and recovery for mitigating epidemic risks. *Risk Analysis*, *42*(1), 206–220. DOI: 10.1111/risa.13707 PMID: 33580512

Jahanpour, E., & Chen, X. (2013). Analysis of complex network performance and heuristic node removal strategies. *Communications in Nonlinear Science and Numerical Simulation*, *18*(12), 3458–3468. DOI: 10.1016/j.cnsns.2013.04.030

Jiang, L., Zhao, X., Ge, B., Xiao, W., & Ruan, Y. (2019). An efficient algorithm for mining a set of influential spreaders in complex networks. *Physica A*, *516*, 58–65. DOI: 10.1016/j.physa.2018.10.011

Jing, F., Wang, Z., Hu, Z., Xu, S., Holme, P., & Weiss, S. H. (2022). Optimal resource allocation in HIV self-testing secondary distribution among Chinese MSM: Data-driven integer programming models. *Philosophical Transactions. Series A, Mathematical, Physical, and Engineering Sciences*, *380*(2214), 20210128. Advance online publication. DOI: 10.1098/rsta.2021.0128 PMID: 34802269

Qin, S., Ren, X., & Lü, L. (2019). Efficient network dismantling via node explosive percolation. *Communications in Theoretical Physics*, *71*(6), 764. DOI: 10.1088/0253-6102/71/6/764

Razzaq, A., Gill, H. K., Qureshi, N. M. F., Ullah, S., Masud, F., & Alyami, S. A. (2022). Blockchain in healthcare: A decentralized platform for digital health passport of COVID-19 based on vaccination and immunity certificates. *Health Care*, *10*(12), 2453. Advance online publication. DOI: 10.3390/healthcare10122453 PMID: 36553977

Razzaq, A., Wajahat, A., Akhtar, M. U., & Tao, Z. (2025). Redefining healthcare data storage and access with decentralized technologies. In *AI and Blockchain Applications for Privacy and Security in Smart Medical Systems* (pp. 371–398). IGI Global Scientific Publishing., DOI: 10.4018/979-8-3373-0593-6.ch014

Ren, X., Ren, N., & Lü, L. (2019). Generalized network dismantling. *Proceedings of the National Academy of Sciences of the United States of America*, *116*(14), 6554–6559. DOI: 10.1073/pnas.1806108116 PMID: 30877241

Rossi, R., & Ahmed, N. (2015). The network data repository with interactive graph analytics and visualization. In *Proceedings of the AAAI Conference on Artificial Intelligence* (Vol. 29, No. 1, pp. 4292-4293). DOI: 10.1609/aaai.v29i1.9277

Saxena, C., Doja, M. N., & Ahmad, T. (2018). Group based centrality for immunization of complex networks. *Physica A*, *508*, 35–47. DOI: 10.1016/j.physa.2018.05.107

Song, K., Li, J., & Li, L. (2019). Target controllability of two-layer multiplex networks based on network flow theory. *IEEE Transactions on Cybernetics*, *51*(5), 2699–2711. DOI: 10.1109/TCYB.2019.2906700 PMID: 30990210

Turab, A., Mlaiki, N., Fatima, N., Mitrović, Z. D., & Ali, W. (2022). Analysis of a class of stochastic animal behavior models under specific choice preferences. *Mathematics*, *10*(12), 1975. Advance online publication. DOI: 10.3390/math10121975

Turab, A., Rosli, N., Ali, W., & Nieto, J. J. (2023). The existence and uniqueness of solutions to a functional equation arising in psychological learning theory. *Demonstratio Mathematica*, *56*(1), 20220231. Advance online publication. DOI: 10.1515/dema-2022-0231

Turab, A., & Sintunavarat, W. (2019). On analytic model for two-choice behavior of the paradise fish based on fixed point method. *Journal of Fixed Point Theory and Its Applications*, *21*(2), 56. Advance online publication. DOI: 10.1007/s11784-019-0694-y

Turab, A., & Sintunavarat, W. (2020). On the solution of the traumatic avoidance learning model approached by the Banach fixed point theorem. *Journal of Fixed Point Theory and Its Applications*, *22*(2), 50. Advance online publication. DOI: 10.1007/s11784-020-00788-3

Zhang, Q., Zhong, D., Gao, J., & Li, Y. (2018). Optimizing HIV interventions for multiplex social networks via partition-based random search. *IEEE Transactions on Cybernetics*, *48*(12), 3411–3419. DOI: 10.1109/TCYB.2018.2853611 PMID: 30010610

Zhao, T., Cao, Z., & Duan, W. (2020). Evolutionary divide-and-conquer algorithm for virus spreading control over networks. *IEEE Transactions on Cybernetics*, *51*(7), 3752–3766. DOI: 10.1109/TCYB.2020.2975530 PMID: 32175884

Chapter 12 Drift Diffusion Models as an Interpretable Framework for Modeling Decision-Making Behavior

Alberto Carpio
https://orcid.org/0000-0002-1616-315X
Universidad Rey Juan Carlos, Spain

Roberto Fernandes-Magalhaes
https://orcid.org/0000-0002-4541-7016
Universidad Rey Juan Carlos, Spain

David Ferrera
https://orcid.org/0000-0002-2367-3051
Universidad Rey Juan Carlos, Spain

María Eugenia de Lahoz
https://orcid.org/0000-0003-2561-1222
Universidad Rey Juan Carlos, Spain

ABSTRACT

The Drift Diffusion Model (DDM) provides a principled, interpretable framework for modeling binary choices and response-time distributions. In this chapter, we synthesize DDM theory and applied practice, and we contribute a ready-to-use workflow that combines (i) concise exposition of core assumptions and parameters, (ii) recommended estimation strategies and diagnostics (including hierarchical

DOI: 10.4018/979-8-3373-5062-2.ch012

Bayesian inference), and (iii) a synthetic-data parameter-recovery example that illustrates best practices for ensuring identifiability and robustness. We review empirical applications in perception, cognitive control, and clinical research, and critically evaluate recent extensions such as collapsing boundaries and hybrid machine–cognitive integrations. We close with concrete recommendations for study design, model comparison, and ethical deployment in clinical and AI settings. This chapter aims to bridge theory and practice, equipping researchers with both conceptual clarity and actionable tools for diffusion-model analyses.

1. INTRODUCTION

To examine human decision making, we require models bridging behavior to cognitive processes. Evidence-accumulation models like the Drift Diffusion Model (DDM) are preferred as they yield psychologically interpretable parameters rather than black-box outputs. By dissociating choice accuracy and reaction time into hidden factors like evidence quality (drift rate) and decision caution (threshold), DDM accounts for slow or fast responses (Forstmann & Wagenmakers, 2016; Ratcliff & McKoon, 2008). DDM is a member of the post-1960s generation of serial sampling models (Stone, 1960; Townsend & Ashby, 1983; Smith & Ratcliff, 2004).

These have been based on the premise that noisy evidence builds up to a threshold. Currently, the DDM is being suggested as an ideal measure of two choice tests. This model provides balance between speed and accuracy within one goal measure. The parameters have a direct relation to cognitive processes; for instance, more difficulty in responding to a stimulus implies a reduction in the drift rate, the speed-accuracy trade-off causes the threshold to shift, and previous experience influences the starting point. This chapter presents an overview of a broad range of the DDM: its mathematics and methodology foundations and parameter meaning; it also offers an applied guide for validation and fitting, along with applications to cognitive processes like perception, cognitive control, and clinical and applied research. Bayesian, hierarchical, and hybrid models will also be introduced, bridging the DDM to AI. Ethical issues and possibilities for the future will be addressed, such as how DDM can be a complement to classical analyses. The chapter brings theory, methodology, and applications together in an attempt to discuss new models.

2. DRIFT DIFFUSION MODEL FUNDAMENTALS

The Drift Diffusion Model offers a straightforward but potent mathematical account of two-option choice (Wagenmakers et al., 2007). When the subjects are given two options, as time advances, they start to build up internal evidence for either of the options. This can be noisy, i.e., contain internal random fluctuations, until there is a decision boundary for the correct option. By mathematically modeling this process, the DDM can account both the resulting choice of the subject and the time taken to make the decision, enabling examination of the speed-accuracy trade-off and possible attentional biases. The DDM rests on three core assumptions that define much evidence-accumulation models:

1. **Evidence is integrated over time:** Decisions are not based on a single instantaneous snapshot, but rather on accumulating information gradually.
2. **Accumulation is stochastic:** The process is subject to noise or variability in perception and cognition, meaning accumulation varies randomly from moment to moment.
3. **Threshold crossing triggers a decision:** A choice is made once the accumulated evidence for one alternative reaches a threshold amount.

These assumptions align with the intuition that difficult decisions require gathering more evidence and that random fluctuations can sometimes lead to errors or variability in timing. Notably, DDM is the continuous counterpart of a random-walk or stepwise accumulation model, and under certain conditions it implements an optimal decision policy in two-choice tasks. In fact, Bogacz et al. (2006) proved that if one aims to maximize accuracy for a given decision speed (or vice versa), a drift–diffusion mechanism is statistically optimal – which helps explain why this strategy might be used by human and animal decision-makers (Bogacz et al., 2006). In its classic form, the DDM has four primary parameters, each linked to a distinct psychological aspect of decision-making (see Figure 1 for a representation) (Ratcliff, 1978; Ratcliff & McKoon, 2008):

- **Drift rate (v):** The drift rate reflects the average speed of evidence accumulation, indexing the quality or strength of information driving a decision. A high drift rate means evidence builds quickly toward one option, producing faster and more accurate choices. A drift rate near zero indicates weak or noisy evidence, leading to slower responses and chance-level accuracy. In the psychological construct, it reflects the informative capacity of the stimulus: perceptually obvious stimuli exhibit high drift rates, whereas more ambiguous ones show reduced rates. Experiments in this regard have shown that reducing obviousness or the signal-to-noise ratio reliably decreases the drift rate (Ratcliff and McKoon, 2008). In summary, the drift rate allows for the analysis of processing efficiency, in other words, it measures the speed at which practical information is extracted from the world. **Decision thresh-**

old (a): The threshold (or boundary separation) is the amount of evidence required to make a decision. A higher threshold decreases response speed but increases accuracy; conversely, a lower threshold increases speed but decreases accuracy. This parameter itself reflects the speed-accuracy construct. Instructions emphasizing speed lower the threshold, while accuracy instructions raise it. Neurophysiologically, threshold adjustments are linked to activity in the pre-supplementary motor area and basal ganglia, which regulate how much evidence is needed to act. In short, threshold indexes response caution: higher thresholds signal carefulness, lower thresholds signal a bias for speed.

- **Starting point (z):** The starting point indicates prior bias at trial onset. If unbiased, it lies midway between boundaries (e.g., 0.5 if boundaries are 0 and 1). A shift toward one boundary reflects a predisposition or expectation favoring that choice, effectively giving it a head start. This model biases due to prior probability, payoff, or attentional cues. For instance, when one alternative is more likely, participants show a bias captured as a shifted starting point (or altered drift criterion) (Ratcliff & McKoon, 2008). Conceptually, z represents the decision-maker's initial belief before evidence accumulation.
- **Non-decision time (Ter):** Not all reaction time reflects decision-making. Ter (or t_0) captures sensory encoding at the start and motor execution at the end, excluding evidence accumulation. Typically, ~200–400 ms, Ter shifts the RT distribution without affecting accuracy. Tasks with greater perceptual demands or individuals with slower motor responses show longer Ter. By modeling Ter, the DDM separates decision-related timing from peripheral processes, clarifying whether RT differences arise from decision policies (e.g., drift, threshold) or non-decision delays (see Table 1).

In the standard DDM, a decision variable $X(t)$evolves over time starting from an initial point $z$according to the stochastic differential equation

$$dX = v\,dt + \sigma dW(t),$$

where v is the drift rate (representing evidence strength), σ is the noise scale, and $dW(t)$ is a Wiener process increment. Two boundaries at $\pm a$ define the decision thresholds: hitting the upper boundary corresponds to one choice and hitting the lower boundary corresponds to the alternative. The drift rate v determines the average rate of evidence accumulation; higher values reflect clearer or stronger evidence. The threshold a reflects the amount of evidence required to make a decision and is related to speed–accuracy trade-offs: larger thresholds produce slower but more accurate decisions. The starting point z represents an initial bias toward one alternative. The model also includes a non-decision time parameter T_0, which accounts for processes that occur outside the decision process itself. Importantly, T_0 encompasses both sensory encoding before evidence accumulation begins and motor execution after the decision has been made. Observed reaction times are therefore modeled as the sum of decision time and T_0. By fitting the model jointly to reaction time distributions and choice proportions, researchers can infer how experimental manipulations affect different components of cognition. For example, in a perceptual discrimination task, increasing stimulus clarity typically increases drift rate, whereas instructions emphasizing accuracy increase threshold settings. Each parameter has a clear psychological interpretation, which makes the DDM highly interpretable compared to purely descriptive behavioral measures.

Figure 1. Diagrammatic representation of the key parameters in the Drift Diffusion Model (DDM). Drift rate (v), decision boundary (a), starting point (z), and non-decision time (Ter) are indicated. Adapted from Ratcliff and McKoon (2008).

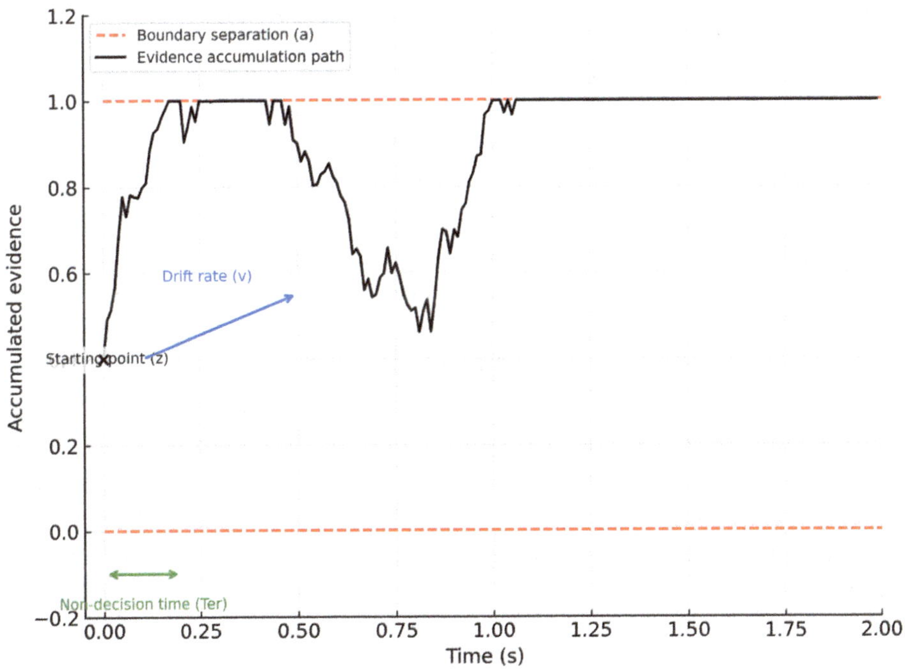

Table 1. Core parameters of the Drift Diffusion Model (DDM) and concise interpretations. (See main text for formal definitions.)

Parameter	Cognitive role (interpretation)	Higher values imply… (and are influenced by…)
Drift rate (v)	Speed of evidence accumulation; quality of information.	Faster information uptake, leading to quicker and more accurate decisions for the favored option. *Higher v in easier tasks (strong stimuli); v approx 0 yields chance performance.*
Decision threshold (a)	Amount of evidence required to decide; decision caution.	More cautious decision policy – slower responses with fewer errors. *Increases under accuracy emphasis or high stakes; decreases under speed emphasis.*
Starting point (z)	Initial bias toward one option before evidence begins.	Preferential initial leaning toward one choice. *Shifted by prior probability, payoffs, or cues (e.g., if one option is expected or rewarded more).*
Non-decision time (T_{er}, T_0)	Time for processes outside the decision (sensory encoding, motor response).	A uniform delay is added to all responses. *Longer for more complex stimuli or slower responders (e.g., older adults), as these factors prolong perception or action execution.*

DDM dynamics and predictions. The interplay of these parameters gives the DDM its characteristic predictions for behavior. A higher drift rate v will lead to faster and more likely correct responses for the favored alternative (since evidence accumulates quickly toward the correct boundary). A higher threshold a will generally increase reaction times for both correct and error responses (because more evidence is needed) and usually increase accuracy (fewer errors, as "flukes" of noise are less likely to prematurely trigger a decision). A biased starting point z will skew the proportion of choices (favoring one side) and produce faster responses for choices in the biased direction (since the distance to that boundary is smaller) while slowing responses for the opposite direction. Non-decision time T_{er} simply adds a constant to all reaction times. Importantly, the DDM makes nuanced predictions about entire RT distributions, not just their means. For instance, it predicts the typical finding that error responses can be either slower or faster than correct ones depending on task conditions; in many two-choice tasks with neutral instructions, errors are often slightly slower on average than corrects. The DDM can capture this pattern through a combination of drift variability and starting biases affecting slow errors (Ratcliff & McKoon, 2008) (Figure 2).

Figure 2. Simulated evidence accumulation trajectories in a DDM. Single-trial stochastic traces (thin lines) and the average accumulation (thick line) are shown, with threshold crossings marked for decision times.

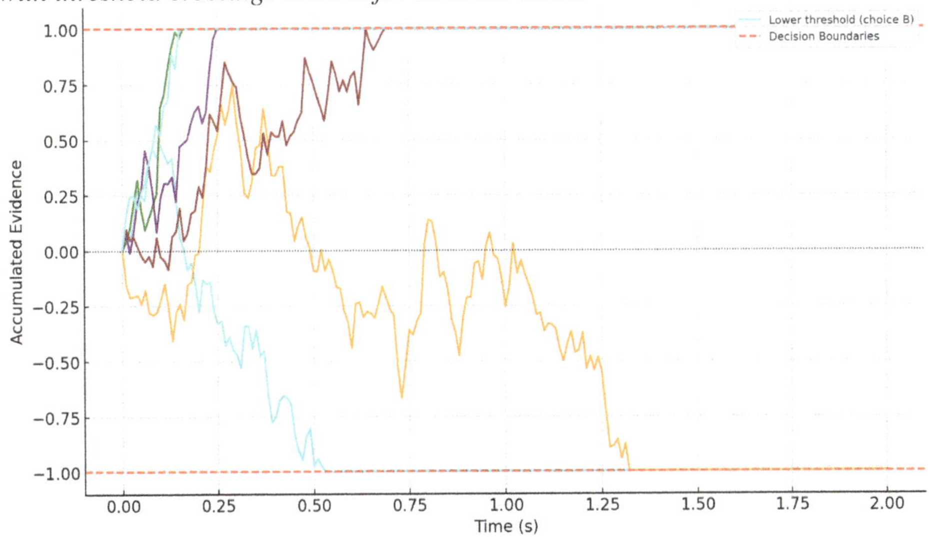

Six example sample paths of a decision variable are shown (each a different color), starting at 0 and undergoing noisy accumulation with a positive average drift. The dotted red lines indicate the upper and lower decision thresholds. When a path hits the upper boundary, it triggers one choice; hitting the lower boundary corresponds to the alternative. In this simulation, most trajectories reached the upper threshold (choice "A") quickly, but one trajectory (cyan) eventually hit the lower threshold (choice "B") after a longer time. The slope of the trajectories is influenced by the drift rate (here v>0, favoring the upper choice on average), while their variability comes from diffusion noise. The distance between the boundaries represents the threshold setting: narrower bounds would lead to faster but more error-prone decisions, whereas wider bounds (as shown) require more evidence and yield slower, more accurate decisions. The simulated trajectories in the example show that the DDM is capable of linking human decision-making with the distribution of response times. This model allows the decomposition of decision-making into objective and measurable parameters, being able to capture the balance between signal (drift rate) and noise (diffusion rate). As a simple model, easy to interpret and with a solid experimental foundation, the DDM has become a highly useful tool in cognitive psychology and neuroscience (Ratcliff and Smith, 2004; Ratcliff and McKoon, 2008; Myers et al., 2022). In the next section, practical issues will be analyzed regarding how research has demonstrated the usefulness of this type of model, which provides a validated and alternative explanation of human behavior.

2.1. Limitations of the DDM

While DDM is now applied to a broad set of situations, this model rests on methodological assumptions that are occasionally extremely simplistic and can restrict the use of this model for certain sciences. To begin with, the DDM assumes that the drift rate and noise are fixed variables during decision-making. However, in real-life situations, this is often not the situation as response the rates are updated dynamically with time. For instance, the drift rate in a moving-dot task varies with time, and this results in errors in predictions from the DDM (Evans & Hawkins, 2019). Second, the DDM is a two-choice model, which is intended to study how the subjects make two-alternative decisions. Applying it in situations where there are several alternatives demands expanding the model's parameters to accommodate multidimensional decision-making (Tsetsos et al., 2011). These modifications interfere with the simplicity of the analysis and may result in conclusions drawn by the experimenters. Third, the model does not work well with difficult tasks, including speeded sequential decisions, mixed cognitive and motor processes, or decisions in fluctuating contexts over time. For example, some tasks involve time-pressure or variable reward decision making, where collapsing decision boundaries must be included (Heathcote et al., 2024). However, one can extend and widen the DDM parameters through adding, but in the process, data interpreting and estimation complexity are directly enhanced. Fourth, the DDM is inclined to commit score distributions to be Gaussian, assuming that processing stages like feature coding, information summation, and resultant motor response are separate. Those assumptions are too unrealistic to hold true in experimental settings. Scientific evidence demonstrates that these kinds of variation and potential parameter differences have the capability to generate behavioral patterns that are hard to account for with the DDM (Schumacher et al., 2025). Lastly, the model itself and the compensatory manual adjustments between parameters have some implementational limitations. Drift rate, threshold, and non-decision time trade with each other in model fitting, particularly in cases of noisy measurements or sparse data. This could lead to unreliable parameter estimates lower interpretability, a feature commonly mentioned as being among DDM's major strengths (Liesefeld & Janczyk, 2019).

2.2. Alternative Evidence-Accumulation Models

While DDM is the most applied model, a number of alternatives have been formulated to overcome some of its weaknesses, enhancing computational manipulation and facilitation of more flexible modeling of decision-making. These new models suggest various assumptions regarding how evidence is built up and how individual variability is indicated, offering a substitute and complementary perspective of the decision-making cognitive processes.

Linear Ballistic Accumulator (LBA)

Linear Ballistic Accumulator (LBA) model (Brown & Heathcote, 2008) is arguably the simplest and computationally less demanding option relative to the DDM. In the LBA, it's assumed evidence on every trial is free of noise and linearly accumulates to a decision boundary with a constant drift rate for each trial. Drift rates and starting positions' variability gives rise to behavioral variability. Closed-form likelihood functions are supplied by its deterministic trial dynamics under the LBA model. Under such conditions, parameter estimation is easily and rapidly obtained. The LBA was recently applied to dynamic decision-making paradigms, hierarchical inference, and multi-alternative decisions (Trueblood et al., 2014). Moreover, even though structurally more primitive, the LBA inclined in comparison to the DDM for goodness of fit and less subject to noisy or sparse data. Its utility in tasks involving within-trial theoretical variability, however, could be compromised by the rich temporal dynamics provided by stochastic diffusion processes.

Leaky Competing Accumulators (LCA)

In order to implement more realistic decision-making processes, Leaky Competing Accumulator (LCA) models are vested with competition (mutual inhibition of the accumulators) and leak (loss of accumulated evidence with time). Ornstein–Uhlenbeck processes are typically employed to make these models mathematically tractable. In contrast to DDMs, the latter allow for evidence to accumulate and spread, leading to more complex temporal dynamics. Three of these areas in which LCAs can be useful are in illuminating indicators of urgency, limits of temporal integration, and impacts of memory decay. LCAs are useful for realistic decision-making tasks like multi-attribute decisions, working memory performance, and dynamic scenarios (Lo & Ip, 2021). Some recent studies have added LCA mechanisms to reinforcement learning to show that value learning changes over time, providing a strong hybrid model that bridges the gap between cognitive and neural theories (Bogacz & Larsen, 2011). The drawback with LCAs is that they are likely more difficult to fit than LBAs or DDMs because they contain more parameters and nonlinear dynamics. Computational methods over recent years and hierarchical Bayesian inference, however, have enabled one to estimate these models for large and complex data sets.

Race Models

Race models (Tillman et al., 2020) take it that different independent accumulators race towards reaching their personal limits, and the accumulator that reaches its threshold first decides the selection. Race models are easier to implement and visualize compared to DDMs because race models do not assume that accumulators stop each other. Race models are especially inviting for multialternative decisions because race models naturally extend to the case of multiple options without invoking intricate adjustments. Advancements have made race models capture dynamic evidence accumulation, temporally varying drift rates, and urgency of decision (Radillo et al., 2017). They have also been used for cognitive control, perceptual decision, and value-based choice, and they give us some tools to use in understanding how change in evidence happens between decision channels. But race models are not able to correctly represent how competitive competition is when deciding within neural networks as they treat accumulators separately. In certain contexts, hybrid models that integrate race dynamics with lateral inhibition or urgency signals yield a superior alignment with empirical data. Recent comparative studies indicate that no single model consistently outperforms the others across all tasks; instead, model selection should be driven by task structure, data availability, and the specific cognitive mechanisms under investigation (Forstmann et al., 2016). For an explicit comparison of these trade-offs, see Table 2, which summarizes each model's core assumptions, key parameters, typical estimation procedures, and principal strengths and limitations. Consult this table alongside formal model-comparison metrics (e.g., cross-validation, Bayes factors, AIC/BIC) when selecting a modeling framework.

Table 2. Comparative summary of the Drift Diffusion Model (DDM), Linear Ballistic Accumulator (LBA), Leaky Competing Accumulator (LCA) and Race models.

Feature	Drift Diffusion Model (DDM)	Linear Ballistic Accumulator (LBA)	Leaky Competing Accumulator (LCA)	Race models
Core idea	Continuous stochastic accumulation (drift + noise) to a boundary.	Deterministic linear accumulation per trial; between-trial variability gives RT spread.	Accumulators with leak and lateral inhibition (dynamic competition).	Multiple accumulators race; first to threshold wins.
Key params	drift rate, threshold, start bias, non-decision time (Ter), noise.	slope (drift) per accumulator, threshold, start-point variability, Ter.	drift, leak, inhibition strength, threshold, Ter, noise.	drift/slope per accumulator, threshold, Ter; sometimes interactions.
Best for	Binary decisions, detailed RT/ accuracy modelling; rich psychological interpretation.	Fast, stable fitting; practical multi-choice fits when simplicity preferred.	When explicit competition/inhibition dynamics are theoretically important.	Natural multi-alternative tasks; intuitive "winner-takes-all" interpretation.
Assumptions / limits	Stationary drift within trial; identifiability trade-offs (drift vs threshold vs Ter).	No within-trial noise (simpler but less realistic intra-trial variability).	More realistic dynamics but greater complexity & identifiability issues.	If independent, ignores interactions; adding interaction increases complexity.
Estimation	MLE, quantile methods, hierarchical Bayesian (e.g., HDDM).	MLE/Bayesian; typically fast.	MLE/Bayesian; computationally heavier.	MLE/Bayesian; simple when independent, heavier with interaction.
When to choose	If you need psychologically interpretable parameters and to model RT distributions.	If you want fast, robust fits with fewer computational costs.	If inhibition/leak mechanisms are central to your hypothesis.	If modelling many choices intuitively or simulating simple race behaviour.

3. PRACTICAL GUIDE TO FITTING AND VALIDATING DDMS

3.1. Data requirements and preprocessing

DDM analysis uses data from two-alternative forced-choice tasks, considering both the chosen option and reaction time (RT). It requires many trials per condition and careful preprocessing: removing anticipatory responses (< 200 ms) and slow outliers without biasing the distribution. Examining RT histograms or cumulative plots helps confirm the expected right-skewed shape. Model validation compares empirical and predicted RT distributions (Figure 3). When properly parameterized, the DDM reproduces characteristic shapes for correct and error RTs, providing a more stringent test than mean RT comparisons (Ratcliff & McKoon, 2008).

Figure 3. Example of a DDM fit to empirical reaction-time (RT) distributions. Observed RT histograms and empirical quantiles (points) are plotted alongside model-predicted densities/quantiles (solid lines) for correct and error responses.

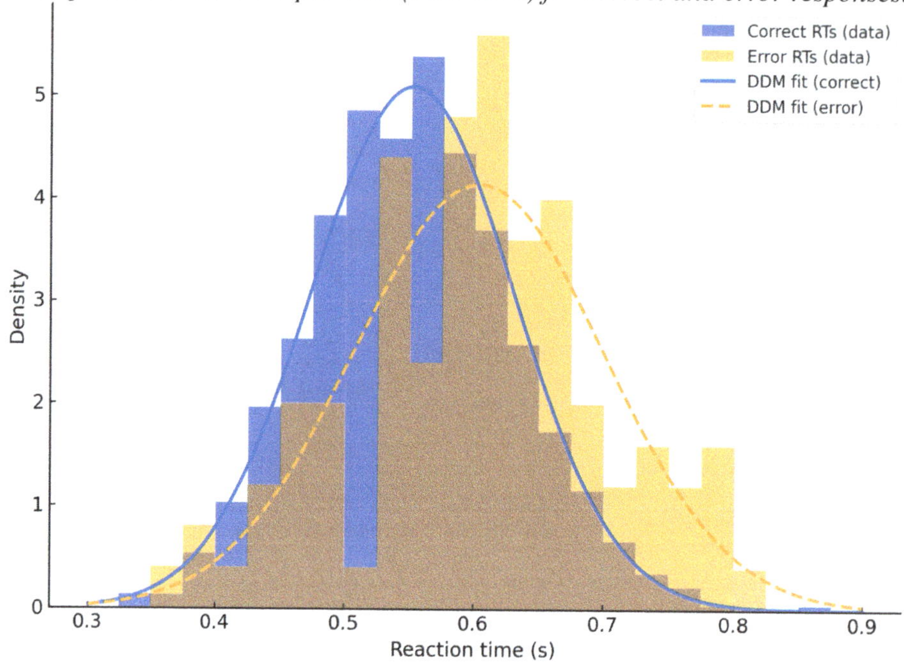

Another key step is to separate trials by experimental condition if factors might influence DDM parameters. For example, easy vs. hard stimuli or speed vs. accuracy instructions should be modeled with distinct parameters or parameter relationships (e.g., drift rate may vary by difficulty, threshold by instruction set). Properly labeling conditions and deciding which parameters vary is essential before fitting. Special cases (e.g., catch or post-error trials) may be treated separately, but typically the DDM is fit to all response data simultaneously (both correct and error trials). After data preparation, DDM parameters are estimated to best explain observed choices and RT distributions (see Table 3). Common methods include:

- **Maximum Likelihood Estimation (MLE):** This classical approach finds parameter values that maximize data likelihood. Because the DDM's first-passage time likelihood has analytic solutions, numerical algorithms iteratively adjust parameters to fit observed RT distributions. MLE provides efficient point estimates and was historically standard (Ratcliff & Tuerlinckx, 2002), but it requires good initial guesses and may face local maxima or slow convergence.
- **Distribution fitting (chi-square or KS minimization):** This older approach matches observed and predicted RT summary statistics (e.g., quantiles) to minimize discrepancies, often using quantile-probability plots. Tools like fast-dm (Voss & Voss, 2007) fit parameters using analytic cumulative distribution functions and KS or chi-square distances. It is fast and robust but less informative, since it compresses data into few quantiles, and is now mostly replaced by full likelihood methods.
- **Bayesian estimation (MCMC or variational):** Bayesian methods estimate posterior parameter distributions instead of single values, using techniques like MCMC or variational inference (Wiecki et al., 2013). They provide uncertainty estimates, incorporate priors, and support hierarchical models pooling data across subjects or conditions (Vandekerckhove et al., 2011). Hierarchical Bayesian DDMs (e.g., HDDM; Wiecki et al., 2013) improve parameter recovery and power, especially with few trials per subject. The trade-off is higher computational cost, though modern tools (e.g., Stan, JAGS, PyMC) have made them increasingly practical.

Table 3. Common methods for estimating DDM parameters

Method	Approach	Strengths & Limitations
Maximum Likelihood (MLE)	Maximizes likelihood of RT and choice data under DDM via numerical optimization.	+ Statistically efficient, uses full data. – Sensitive to local optima, needs good starting values and enough data.
Distribution fitting (Chi^2, KS)	Fits parameters to match RT distribution summaries (quantiles, CDF).	+ Fast, robust to outliers. – Ignores fine details, less precise, mostly replaced by MLE/Bayesian.
Bayesian (MCMC/Hierarchical)	Bayesian inference for posterior distributions allows priors and hierarchical models.	+ Provides uncertainty estimates, partial pooling, flexible. – Computationally heavy, convergence/prior-sensitive, complex to implement.

(adapted from Ratcliff & Tuerlinckx, 2002; Voss & Voss, 2007; Wiecki et al., 2013).

DDM parameters can be estimated by fitting the model to observed data using likelihood-based or Bayesian approaches. For a dataset of N trials with choices $c_i \in \{+,-\}$ and reaction times t_i, the likelihood of parameters $\theta = (v, a, z, T_0)$ is

$$L(\theta) = \prod_{i=1}^{N} f_{c_i}(t_i \mid \theta),$$

where is the first-passage time density for the chosen boundary. These densities are available in closed form, making maximum likelihood estimation feasible.

In a Bayesian framework, priors are placed over parameters and the posterior distribution is computed as

Markov chain Monte Carlo or variational inference methods are used to approximate the posterior, often implemented in hierarchical Bayesian models that pool information across participants. Modern tools such as HDDM facilitate efficient hierarchical Bayesian estimation, providing parameter estimates and credible intervals even for complex datasets. When fitting DDMs, several practical guidelines can improve reliability:

- **Adequate data:** As DDMs can fit full RT distributions, they require large numbers of trials per condition and subject. Hierarchical modeling is helpful in the case of sparse data as it enables subjects to share information.
- **Inspect parameter plausibility:** in-plausible parameters (e.g., negative drift on easy conditions or very long non-decision times) might reflect fitting or data issues, typically stemming from insufficient error trials or parameter confounds. Prevent overfitting and maintain interpretability by imposing reasonable constraints.
- **Collinearity of effects:** Multiple effects can be represented by unique parameters (e.g., drift vs. threshold). Make the relevant interpretation choice by employing theory and experimental design (e.g., speed–accuracy manipulations). To resolve ambiguities, take into account the application of constraints or neural data.
- **Model assumptions:** From trial to trial, the DDM assumes stationary boundaries and fixed drift. Misfits can occur due to violations (e.g., shifting strategies or time-varying data). Residual analyses may indicate additions like urgency signals or time-varying drift.
- **Transparency and reporting:** Transparently report model fitting strategies, goodness-of-fit, and free vs. fixed parameters and variability terms.

3.2. Worked Example: Synthetic Data and Parameter Recovery

We created a synthetic dataset using known parameter values and then tried to recover those parameters using conventional fitting techniques to demonstrate how Drift Diffusion Models can be fitted to behavioral data. This method makes the previously introduced abstract ideas more tangible by transparently demonstrating how model parameters affect reaction time (RT) distributions and how well they can be estimated from data. In particular, we used the following parameter values to simulate 3,000 trials from a standard DDM: non-decision time $T0 = 0.30$ seconds, decision threshold $a = 1.50$, and drift rate $v = 0.30$ (Figure 4). The threshold establishes the quantity of evidence needed before making a decision, the drift rate regulates the average speed at which evidence accumulates, and the non-decision time takes into consideration the processes of motor execution and sensory encoding. For each trial, a decision time was drawn from the theoretical first-passage time distribution defined by these parameters, and non-decision time was added to produce the final simulated RT. Choices were generated according to whether the accumulation process crossed the upper or lower decision boundary first. The resulting dataset was then refitted using standard DDM parameter estimation procedures based on maximum likelihood, in which the model likelihood function is maximized to find the parameter values that best explain the observed RT distributions and choice proportions. In this synthetic example, the recovered parameter estimates closely matched the true generating values, demonstrating that the DDM can reliably capture the underlying cognitive processes when its assumptions are met and data are sufficiently informative.

Figure 4. Synthetic RT distribution and DDM fit used for parameter-recovery validation. Histogram of synthetic response times with overlaid model predictions and quantile markers.

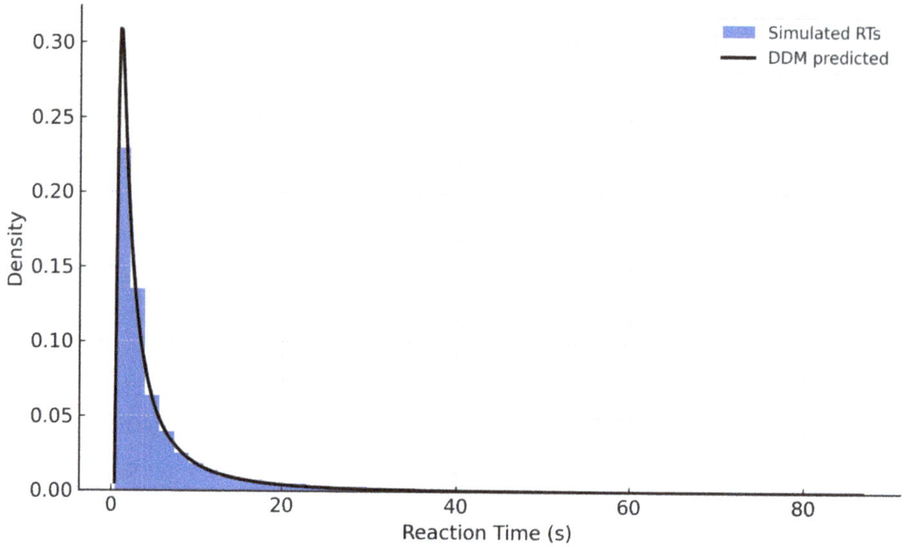

Figure 4 displays the simulated RT distribution as a blue histogram and overlays the predicted distribution from the fitted DDM as a black curve. The close alignment between simulated and predicted distributions provides a visual demonstration of good model fit and successful parameter recovery.

This worked example illustrates the real-world procedures of model-based cognitive analysis, from parameter estimation and data generation to model evaluation it shows how the DDM analyzes behavioral data into psychologically meaningful elements.

4. APPLICATIONS THAT SHOWCASE INTERPRETABILITY

4.1. Perceptual decision-making

DDM remains a basic tool originally developed for this type of two alternative questions (Ratcliff & Smith, 2004; Ratcliff & McKoon, 2008). Sensory evidence integrity is measured by the accuracy with which one can modulate stimulus difficulty (e.g., modulating intensity), and DDM analyses also consistently show that such manipulations affect drift rate.

Random-dot motion task. A classic example is motion direction determination in a random-dot kinetogram, whose task difficulty is controlled by motion coherence. Low coherence causes slow, near-chance response, while larger coherence causes fast, accurate responding. Drift and coherence have nearly linear ratios, as per DDM fits: high coherence yields high drift, and low coherence yields near-zero drift (Palmer, Huk, & Shadlen, 2005; Ratcliff & McKoon, 2008). Non-decision time is quite poorly varied for invariant stimuli; threshold is generally invariant across amounts of coherence. This gives a clear reading: quicker buildup is the consequence of more robust evidence provided by more coherent stimuli. Therefore, drift rate can be associated with neural accounts of predicting evidence strength and is a direct measure of sensory evidence.

Speed–accuracy trade-offs. DDM also describes the relationship between strategy and stimulus difficulty. According to Ratcliff and Rouder (1998), participants lower their decision thresholds when given speed instructions, which results in faster but less accurate responses; however, performance is still predicted by stimulus-driven drift differences. It is possible to attribute performance differences to different mechanisms by distinguishing between strategic effects (threshold) and stimulus effects (drift).

Neural correlates. Neural decision mechanisms have been clarified by DDM applications to perceptual decisions. During motion discrimination, classical primate studies discovered that neurons in LIP exhibit ramping activity, with ramp rates varying according to coherence, mirroring drift rate effects (Gold & Shadlen, 2007) (Figure 5). This implies that a diffusion-like accumulation process might be used by the brain. Neural signatures of evidence accumulation and threshold setting have been found in humans using EEG and fMRI. The centroparietal positivity (CPP) in EEG builds up over time and predicts choices and RTs, consistent with diffusion-to-bound dynamics (Balci & Simen, 2014; O'Connell et al., 2018). Correlating fitted DDM parameters with neural measures further validates interpretations: for example, higher drift rates are linked to stronger sensory cortical responses, and higher thresholds to increased frontal activation related to caution (Mulder et al., 2014; Hanks & Summerfield, 2017).

Figure 5. Effect of stimulus strength (motion coherence) on decision performance. Accuracy and mean RT plotted as a function of coherence; data are qualitatively similar to those reported by Roitman & Shadlen (2002).

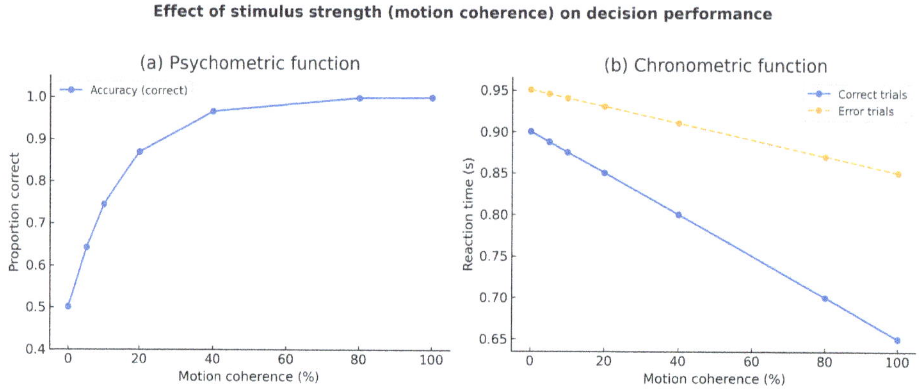

4.2. Applications in Economics, Human–AI Interaction, and Driving Behavior

Recent applications of Drift Diffusion Models to an expanding array of real-world and interdisciplinary domains have shown their adaptability and interpretability as cognitive modeling tools, going beyond perceptual and clinical research. DDMs have been applied in economics to reveal the mental processes that underlie value-based choices.

Berlinghieri et al. (2023) used hierarchical diffusion models in order to fit binary choice tasks upon which subjects made decisions between monetary bets. They were able to fit individual utility functions directly from reaction time and choice data by scaling drift rates to subjective difference between alternatives in utility. Their results supported that threshold parameters accounted for individual variation in decision caution but drift rate always represented subjective value contrasts. Through deriving mechanistic accounts of response times and decision probabilities, the method provides a robust alternative to traditional econometric models and allows for researchers to isolate decision strategy and valuation. Lalvani & Katsaggelos (2024) employed a DDM-based model to estimate the reliability of crowd annotators for mass-scale labeling tasks in human-AI interaction. They could estimate the reliability of each annotator in real time by converting threshold as a placeholder for caution or ambivalence and drift rate as a placeholder for the quality of evidence accumulation at labeling. When compared to standard majority-vote approaches, collective annotation accuracy and speed were dramatically improved by feeding these DDM-derived values as inputs to label aggregation algorithms. This example illustrates how DDMs can be applied to improve the quality and structure of AI systems that are grounded in human feedback in beyond single cognition modeling. Huang et al. (2025) applied DDMs to explore how drivers make decisions between steering and braking responses in virtual emergency situations with urgency. The results showed that task difficulty and speed always affected DDM parameters. Increased urgency reduced decision thresholds, leading to faster but more risky responses, and increasing difficulty lowered drift rates, which pulled out weaker or noisier evidence. The DDM provided a theoretically grounded account of behavioral adaptation to environmental demands by decomposing reaction times and decisions into latent components. This knowledge is relevant to driver assistance system engineering and traffic safety interventions. DDM parameters retain their psychological interpretability without imparting a strict quantitative foundation for modeling complicated behavior, such as high-risk sensorimotor tasks such as driving or value-based decision-making, or cooperative human-AI systems.

4.3. Cognitive control and speed–accuracy trade-offs

Cognitive control tasks tend to involve the suppression of prepotent responses, on-line adjustment of decision policy, or conflict resolution among competing demands (e.g., speed vs. accuracy). Drift diffusion theory has been used in goal-directed strategic modulation (e.g., to bias for speed or accuracy) and the Stroop, flanker, go/no-go, and task-switching tasks. Although drift rates could represent the degree of automatic over controlled processing or quality of evidence, the threshold parameter of the DDM will likely be determinative in these cases since it defines the degree of caution or control used.

Speed–accuracy trade-off (SAT) adjustments. The DDM provides a simple way of quantifying how people change their strategy of decision-making in response to instructions of comparison of speed and accuracy. The sole difference between the DDMs fitted to "accuracy emphasis" and "speed emphasis" conditions is invariably that of boundary separation (threshold): thresholds are higher for accuracy instructions and lower for speed instructions (Bogacz et al., 2010; Ratcliff & McKoon, 2008). The amount of evidence required prior to responding differ, but drift rates generally do not change due to changes in task difficulty and sensory information.

Neural evidence. Forstmann et al. (2008) in an fMRI perceptual choice task found that while attention to accuracy had definite patterns, preparation to respond quickly enhanced activation within the striatum and pre-SMA, which are areas associated with fast responding. Relevantly, threshold reduction size correlated with neural activation within the areas, showing they modulate decision thresholds. Fitted DDM supported threshold differences. This illustrates the model interpretability:

the threshold parameter quantitatively connects changes in behavior, internal control mechanisms, and brain mechanisms, showing how the brain adapts its decision standards (Forstmann et al., 2008) (Figure 6).

Figure 6. Neural correlates of threshold modulation under speed–accuracy instructions. Example neural activity (single-unit or population average) aligned to decision events, illustrating how threshold adjustments map onto neural dynamics.

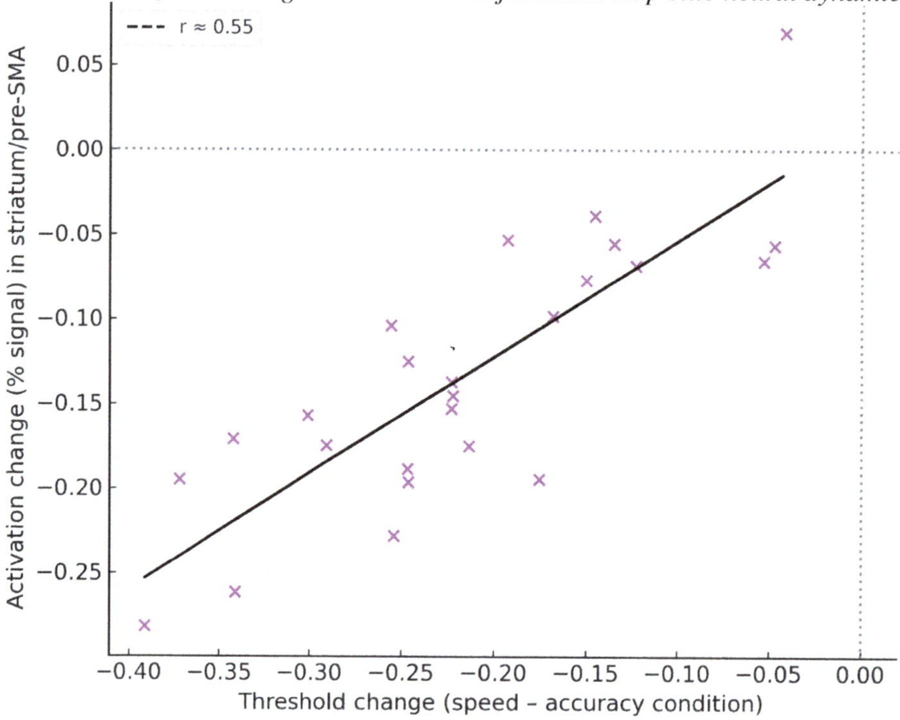

Each point in this illustrative scatter plot represents an individual participant in a study (Forstmann et al., 2008). The x-axis shows how much the participant lowered their decision threshold in a speed-emphasis condition compared to an accuracy-emphasis condition, and the y-axis shows the corresponding increase in activation (percent signal change) in striatal and pre-SMA brain regions (associated with quick responding). There is a positive correlation (here, r \approx 0.55), indicating that individuals who reduced their thresholds more (i.e. became much less cautious to respond quickly) also showed greater activation in these brain areas under speed pressure. This suggests a neural mechanism for adjusting decision thresholds: increased activation in striatum/pre-SMA "pushes" the decision policy toward faster (lower-threshold) decisions.

Inhibitory control (go/no-go and related tasks): Diffusion models have been applied to tasks requiring response withholding, such as go/no-go or stop-signal paradigms. A go/no-go task can be modeled as a two-alternative decision, where on no-go trials the process ideally evolves without crossing the go threshold (Carpio et al., 2024). Some variants, like drift diffusion models for conflict tasks, introduce competing "stop" processes or dynamic thresholds, but even standard DDMs can capture key dynamics on go trials. In go/no-go tasks with frequent go and rare no-go signals, participants often develop a starting point bias toward the go response, reflecting expectations, and may adopt a lower threshold to respond quickly. When evidence surpasses the go boundary before inhibition is successful, this bias raises the number of false alarms. These parameters are impacted by manipulating the no-go probability; generally speaking, a higher no-go likelihood leads to more cautious strategies (e.g., higher thresholds or reduced go bias). Therefore, diffusion modeling shows how proactive control works by modifying the decision policy (starting point, threshold) as opposed to altering processing speed. Participants that are extremely cautious, for instance, might set very high thresholds, which would result in slower but more accurate performance with fewer false alarms.

4.4. Clinical and individual differences

The study of individual and group differences, such as contrasting clinical populations with healthy controls or looking at the relationship between particular traits and decision parameters, is another important area where the interpretability of DDM parameters excels. A patient group may be slower or less accurate on a task according to traditional measures; the DDM can explain why, whether it's because of bias, lapses in attention, slower information processing, or a difference in caution. Theories of cognitive impairments benefit from this degree of explanation, which can also direct interventions (e.g., should training focus on improving evidence accumulation or on adjusting decision thresholds?).

Neurodegenerative and neurological disorders: In conditions like Parkinson's disease (PD) and Huntington's disease that impact the basal ganglia and cortical circuits, the DDM provides a helpful framework for connecting cognitive alterations to deficits in decision-making. Patients with Parkinson's disease (PD), especially those who are not taking medication, frequently exhibit higher decision thresholds, which can result in bradykinesia, or delayed decision initiation, which goes beyond motor slowing. This probably illustrates how dopamine helps people cross thresholds. According to studies, dopaminergic drugs can restore a more normal speed–accuracy balance by normalizing thresholds (Moustafa et al., 2008). Slower cognitive processing, which may be related to cortical pathology, may also be indicated by reduced drift rates. Different DDM parameter patterns across disorders are highlighted in a review by Gupta et al. (2021). Numerous studies show reduced drift rates on attention-demanding tasks in ADHD, which is consistent with ineffective evidence accumulation brought on by attentional lapses. In DDM, elevated drift variability or distinct lapse processes are indicative of ADHD's high RT variability. This differentiates inattention (low drift or variable) from impulsivity (low threshold). As with some investigations, major depressive disorder is responsible for heightened non-decision times (psychomotor slowing) and relatively lower reward-based choice drift rates (reflective of anhedonia), but thresholds typically being similar to controls (Huang et al., 2017). Hence, they have a similar "parameter profile," with an emphasis on hidden neurological or cognitive dysfunctioning. Such profiles have mechanistic interpretations because DDM parameters correspond to neural circuits. As an example, thresholds are controlled by the subthalamic nucleus (STN) of the basal ganglia; deep brain stimulation of STN in Parkinson's disease (PD) is able to reduce thresholds, leading to faster but more impulsive decisions (Frank et al., 2007; Cavanagh et al., 2011). The STN maintains the threshold high until there is sufficient evidence accumulates, and serves as a check on the diffusion model. That is a perspective provided by computational models. Balance-wise, DDMs permit greater understanding of neurological and psychiatric illness by inserting itself between patterns of behavior and brain mechanisms.

5. RECENT EXTENSIONS & LINKS TO EXPLAINABLE AI

5.1. Hierarchical and Bayesian diffusion models

Hierarchical Bayesian approach is a significant improvement over diffusion modeling. Standard DDM estimates parameters following sole inspection by subject. Hierarchical models are able to assume group distributions whose parameters themselves are estimated to be the source of individual parameters (e.g., drift rate). In sparse data distribution, this partial pooling recovers individual variations while preventing individual estimates from being too variable by leveraging group trends. Thus, group differences can be accurately ascertained at the latent parameter level, and parameter estimates are more likely to be on the mark (Gelman et al., 2013; Wiecki et al., 2013). For instance, although two individuals are never identical, a hierarchical model might suggest that the drift rate mean of a patient group is 20% below controls with credible intervals. Probabilistic claims, such as "95% probability that this patient's drift rate is at least X below normative mean," are supported by posterior distributions at group and individual levels. This synthesizes heightened statistical inference with explainability without compromising on DDM parameter interpretability. In model-based cognitive neuroscience, where sample sizes are frequently small (e.g., 20–30 imaging participants), hierarchical models are particularly useful. They make it easier to relate parameter variations to neural or genetic measurements and permit simultaneous fitting across subjects. For example, Wiecki et al. (2013) demonstrated, using hierarchical modeling, that trial-by-trial EEG fluctuations had a higher statistical power than non-hierarchical approaches in predicting drift rate variations.From an XAI perspective, hierarchical Bayesian DDMs provide multi-level explainability: they capture variability at individual and group levels and generate interpretable explanations for each (e.g., "Subject A's slow responses stem from a high threshold and moderately low drift, while Subject B's are due to an extremely low drift rate"). This makes them powerful tools for transparent, generalizable cognitive modeling.

5.2. Time-varying and non-standard evidence accumulation

The classic DDM assumes a constant drift rate within a trial and a fixed decision boundary until a decision is made. However, in some situations, these assumptions might not hold. For example, if the decision-maker expects that taking too long is problematic (say, a prey animal making a decision under threat, where delay is costly), they might effectively use a collapsing decision boundary that lowers over time, forcing a decision by a certain deadline. Researchers have introduced models with time-varying boundaries (sometimes called *urgency-gating models* or *collapsing-bound diffusion models*) to account for situations where people seem to "give up" or make a guess as time goes on. These models add one more function to specify: how the threshold changes with time. If the threshold decays (collapses) as time passes, the model encourages faster decisions with more errors as time progresses. Collapsing boundaries have been proposed to be optimal in certain contexts where longer decision times carry external penalties (Drugowitsch et al., 2012). They provide a normative explanation for why one would decide faster toward the end of a trial or before a deadline. Empirically, some datasets (especially in time-critical tasks) fit better with a collapsing-boundary model than a fixed-boundary DDM (Hawkins et al., 2015). The interpretability of the threshold parameter remains – the difference is that the threshold is now a dynamic policy rather than static. One can interpret the *collapse rate* as an "urgency signal" that pushes the decision to a conclusion as time runs out. For example, when people are under a deadline, the model might find a steep collapsing boundary, reflecting an increasing urgency to respond as the deadline nears. This extension preserves interpretability (we still have drift = evidence quality, threshold schedule = strategic policy) but allows explaining more complex patterns, like an increase in error rate for long responses that a fixed-bound DDM might not capture (Figure 7).

Figure 7. Illustration of collapsing decision boundaries. Comparison of fixed versus collapsing boundary trajectories and their influence on predicted RT distributions and error rates.

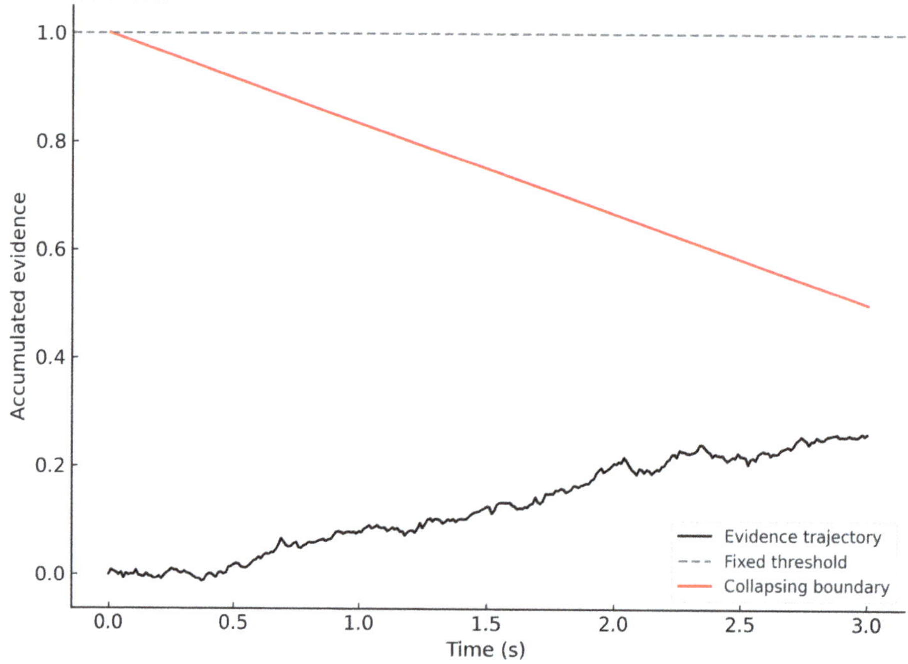

The black trace shows a single simulated evidence accumulation trajectory over time that, under a fixed threshold (horizontal grey dashed line), would not have reached a decision within 3 seconds. The red line represents a collapsing decision boundary that starts at the same height but decreases linearly over time. In this scenario, the decision process "hits" the collapsing boundary at around 3 s (red circle), triggering a decision that would not have occurred yet under a fixed boundary. Collapsing or time-decaying thresholds effectively impose an urgency to decide as time goes on, less evidence is required to make a choice. This mechanism can account for increasing error rates on very slow trials and is thought to be used when prolonged deliberation is costly (Drugowitsch et al., 2012; Hawkins et al., 2015).

The difficulty lies in making sure that models are testable and not merely curve-fitting instruments as they get more intricate. Promising approaches are the generalized drift diffusion model (GDDM) framework of Donkin et al. (2009), which provides a software framework to successfully fit such generalizations (time-varying drifts, urgency signals, etc.) by solving the corresponding Fokker–Planck equation. Significantly, these models are constructed to be interpretable in mechanistic terms (they tend to map onto hypothesized cognitive or neural processes). An adapting drift, for instance, can be employed in dynamic environments in which the credibility of the evidence changes over time. Through drift trajectory analysis, one can thus determine how the decision-maker was weighing recent compared to older information. This relates to XAI because, instead of fitting the data with a generic black box, we are introducing domain knowledge into the model, such as "decisions might have urgency" or "evidence might fluctuate."

5.3. Hybrid models combining DDM with machine learning

A promising frontier is combining cognitive models like the DDM with machine learning, seeking ML's predictive power plus cognitive interpretability. Two main directions stand out:

Reinforcement Learning–DDM hybrids (RL-DDM):

Pedersen et al. (2017) substituted a drift diffusion step for the softmax rule in RL, connecting drift rate to value differences and threshold to exploration–exploitation. Both choices (RL) and RT distributions (DDM) are explained by this hybrid, and each part is interpretable: diffusion controls choice timing and accuracy, while learning updates values. Pedersen et al. discovered that stimulant medication primarily impacted drift scaling rather than learning rates in ADHD, a subtle dissociation that was only apparent in such a hybrid. RL-DDM provides a step-by-step explanation in terms of XAI: value learning through prediction errors comes first, followed by evidence accumulation and threshold crossing.

Neural-network-assisted DDM:

Neural networks handle complex inputs, i.e., images, and output DDM parameters, i.e., drift rate. Although the diffusion phase is still understandable, the network handles feature extraction, which allows one to examine drifts and thresholds for error detection purposes (e.g., low threshold = haste, deceptive drift = fallacious evidence). Learned models are compelled to explicitly convey evidence strength and speed–accuracy trade-offs because of this "white-box" structure. Though still in its early stages, it can ultimately give rise to AI that doesn't simply make choices but provides human-like reasons for caution, timing, and confidence levels.

While promising, hybrid methods bring new challenges that must be taken seriously. One major challenge is computational cost: hybrid RL–DDM and neural–DDM model estimation can be computationally expensive, particularly in hierarchical Bayesian models, because they often involve the extensive application of large parameter nested estimation loops (i.e., diffusion plus learning dynamics). This can be partially avoided by sound inference methods such as variational Bayes or amortized inference, but there remain trade-offs between accuracy and scalability (Evans & Wagenmakers, 2020). Interpretability trade-offs are also an issue. The neural network learned feature mappings tend to be interpretable, and representations of boundaries or drift rates as a function of these mappings obfuscate the psychological rationale behind the learned parameters, although the DDM layer does offer interpretable parameters.

For example, it is challenging to distinguish demonstrated effects due to nonlinear mappings of complex nature in learned representations and cognitive processes where a neural network maps inputs to latent features that detect drift rates (Kumar, 2025). Finally, hybrid architectures render model identifiability and verification harder. Though learning dynamics or neural parts may induce parameter degeneracy, overfitting, or make cognitive signal separation harder, statistical artifacts, outdated DDMs have an appreciable there exists identifiability properties and diagnostic tool benefit. To ensure hybrid models actually possess stronger explanatory power than raw flexibility, this involves strenuous cross-validation, conservative prior specification, and interpretability auditing.

Among the most auspicious ways to the development of explainable AI systems integrating the scalability of modern machine learning with transparency of cognitive models is that of hybrid DDM methods, despite such challenges. Appropriately deployed, they could provide mechanistically valid explanations of AI decisions, fostering more confidence, enlightening diagnosis, and rationality compatibility with human reason. Nonetheless, for such promise to be realized, the compromises that such unifications require in the arena of interpretability and computation needs to be detected and addressed.

6. CONCLUSION

DDM has been discussed in this chapter as a way of modeling decision-making behavior with its interpretability and strong links to cognitive theory and data. This chapter presents a novel integration of conceptual, methodological, and ethical perspectives on the DDM as well as an overarching overview. Specifically, we have integrated controversies surrounding technical estimation procedures, uses across many different fields, parameter interpretability, and new work on hybrid cognitive-AI models. This synoptic overview is widely dispersed in literature, and its articulation into a readable form is intended to promote theoretical reflection and practical application. DDM is a fine example of a mathematically precise but cognitively insightful model whose parameters map onto notionally intuitive variables such as evidence quality, decision caution, and bias.

This enables researchers to translate rich patterns of behavior into lucid, translucent explanations. From the refined impact of stimulus difficulty on perceptual tasks, to strategic compensation for cognitive control tasks and normal decision dynamics in clinical populations, we saw how the model can be made to fit phenomena from a broad range of domains. At the process level, the estimation of a DDM enables one not just to explain what is different between conditions or groups, but how and why (e.g., "errors increased as the evidence accumulation became noisier, not because the person became less cautious"). The key message is demonstrated by the long-standing success of drift diffusion models in psychology and neuroscience: commutability through interpretability. Outcomes of many studies can be combined and contrasted easily because parameters of DDM have clear meanings. Outcomes that "older adults have lower drift rates in task X" and "sleep deprivation decreases drift rate" can be reasonably compared collectively, which suggests a possible mechanism (neural noise or fatigue on evidence accumulation) that can be common to quite different situations. If those studies had only reported changes in mean RT or had used opaque machine learning models, it would be much harder to build such connections. Interpretability also facilitates communication: scientists can discuss decision-making in a common language of drift and threshold and even lay descriptions (like "needing more evidence to be sure before deciding") resonate with these concepts (Yarkoni, & Westfall (2017).

Looking forward, there are several promising avenues and challenges for the drift diffusion modelling approach:

- **Integration with neural data:** Advances in recording technologies (e.g., large-scale neuronal recordings, real-time imaging) allow linking DDM parameters to neural signals in real time. Pupil dilation or EEG, for instance, can monitor the accumulation of latent evidence on individual trials, which may allow for closed-loop systems in which the model makes decisions prior to behavioral response. DDM connects the neural and behavioral levels; for example, Gold and Shadlen (2007) state that "parietal neurons represent the accumulating decision variable, and reaching a firing threshold signals the decision."
- **Beyond binary choices:** Several choices or sequential dependencies are present in many decisions. Interpretable modeling of complex choices is made possible by extensions such as value-based DDMs and multi-hypothesis sequential probability ratio tests, in which each accumulator represents the evidence for an option. For example, these models can explain why choices with highly competing accumulators are slower or more prone to errors.

- **Decision-making in context:** DDM can be incorporated into sequential or hierarchical frameworks, such as planning or resource allocation models, where each choice affects the one before it. Higher-level strategies optimize overall decision policies, like when to stop gathering information, while drift and thresholds are still interpretable at the micro level.
- **Ethical considerations:** Differences in parameters can help with diagnosis in clinical settings, but they also run the risk of being misinterpreted (e.g., non-decision time may reflect motor factors). Equity in AI cannot be assured by DDM-based transparency; biases should be accurately considered, and parameters must be connected to system features. If results are exaggerated, transparent models can still be manipulated.

In short, drift diffusion theory has been a useful and informative model for describing decision-making. It is strong in balancing conceptual clarity and quantitative accuracy. From the lab to potential applications in artificial intelligence, we have traced its origins, its application in the real world, and its diverse applications. Interpretability has been with us along the way: it allows the model to function as a shared language across phenomena, it assists in identifying explanations of why models fail or succeed, and it leaves space for human-centric AI design. Models such as the DDM demonstrate how we can strive to have systems that not only work but can be comprehended, a goal that is never more desirable in science and society as the scientific and technological environment evolves.

REFERENCES

Balci, F., & Simen, P. (2014). A decision model of timing. *Current Opinion in Behavioral Sciences, 5*, 193–199. DOI: 10.1016/j.cobeha.2016.02.002

Berlinghieri, R., Krajbich, I., Maccheroni, F., Marinacci, M., & Pirazzini, M. (2023). Measuring utility with diffusion models. *Science Advances, 9*(34). Advance online publication. DOI: 10.1126/sciadv.adf1665

Bogacz, R., Brown, E., Moehlis, J., Holmes, P., & Cohen, J. D. (2006). The physics of optimal decision making: A formal analysis of models of performance in two-alternative forced-choice tasks. *Psychological Review, 113*(4), 700–765. DOI: 10.1037/0033-295X.113.4.700

Bogacz, R., & Larsen, T. (2011). Integration of reinforcement learning and optimal decision-making theories of the basal ganglia. *Neural Computation, 23*(4), 817–851. DOI: 10.1162/NECO_a_00103

Brown, S. D., & Heathcote, A. (2008). The simplest complete model of choice response time: Linear ballistic accumulation. *Cognitive Psychology, 57*(3), 153–178. DOI: 10.1016/j.cogpsych.2007.12.002

Carpio, A., Drehr, J.C., Ferrera, D., Galán, D., Mercado, F. & Obeso I. (2024). Causal computations of supplementary motor area on spatial impulsivity. *Sci Rep.* 24;14(1):17040. DOI: 10.1038/s41598-024-67673-8

Cavanagh, J. F., Wiecki, T. V., Cohen, M. X., Figueroa, C. M., Samanta, J., Sherman, S. J., & Frank, M. J. (2011). Subthalamic nucleus stimulation reverses mediofrontal influence over decision threshold. *Nature Neuroscience, 14*(11), 1462–1467. DOI: 10.1038/nn.2925

Donkin, C., Averell, L., Brown, S., & Heathcote, A. (2009). Getting more from accuracy and response time data: Methods for fitting the linear ballistic accumulator. *Behavior Research Methods*. Advance online publication. DOI: 10.3758/BRM.41.4.1095

Drugowitsch, J., DeAngelis, G. C., Angelaki, D. E., & Pouget, A. (2012). Optimal decision-making with time-varying evidence reliability. In *Advances in Neural Information Processing Systems 25* (NIPS 2012).

Evans, N. J., & Hawkins, G. E. (2019). When humans behave like monkeys: Feedback delays and extensive practice increase the efficiency of speeded decisions. *Cognition, 184*, 11–18. DOI: 10.1016/j.cognition.2018.11.014

Evans, N. J., & Wagenmakers, E. J. (2020). Evidence accumulation models: Current limitations and future directions. *The Quantitative Methods for Psychology, 16*(2), 73–90. DOI: 10.31234/osf.io/74df9

Forstmann, B. U., Dutilh, G., Brown, S., Neumann, J., von Cramon, D. Y., Ridderinkhof, K. R., & Wagenmakers, E.-J. (2008). Striatum and pre-SMA facilitate decision-making under time pressure. *Proceedings of the National Academy of Sciences of the United States of America, 105*(45), 17538–17542. DOI: 10.1073/pnas.0805903105

Forstmann, B. U., Ratcliff, R., & Wagenmakers, E.-J. (2016). Sequential sampling models in cognitive neuroscience: Advantages, applications, and extensions. *Annual Review of Psychology, 67*, 641–666. DOI: 10.1146/annurev-psych-122414-033645

Frank, M. J., Scheres, A., & Sherman, S. J. (2007). Understanding decision-making deficits in neurological conditions: Insights from models of natural action selection. *Philosophical Transactions of the Royal Society of London. Series B, Biological Sciences, 362*(1485), 1641–1654. DOI: 10.1098/rstb.2007.2058

Gelman, A., Carlin, J., Stern, H., Dunson, D., Vehtari, A., & Rubin, D. (2013). *Bayesian data analysis* (3rd ed.). CRC Press., DOI: 10.1201/b16018

Gold, J. I., & Shadlen, M. N. (2007). The neural basis of decision making. *Annual Review of Neuroscience, 30*, 535–574. DOI: 10.1146/annurev.neuro.29.051605.113038

Gupta, A., Bansal, R., Alashwal, H., Kacar, A. S., Balci, F., & Moustafa, A. A. (2021). Neural substrates of the drift-diffusion model in brain disorders. *Frontiers in Computational Neuroscience, 15*, 678232. DOI: 10.3389/fncom.2021.678232

Hanks, T., & Summerfield, C. (2017). Perceptual decision making in rodents, monkeys, and humans. *Neuron, 93*(1), 15–31. DOI: 10.1016/j.neuron.2016.12.003

Hawkins, G. E., Forstmann, B. U., Wagenmakers, E.-J., Ratcliff, R., & Brown, S. D. (2015). Revisiting the evidence for collapsing boundaries and urgency signals in perceptual decision-making. *The Journal of Neuroscience : The Official Journal of the Society for Neuroscience, 35*(6), 2476–2484. DOI: 10.1523/JNEUROSCI.2410-14.2015

Heathcote, A., Verbruggen, F., Boehler, C. N., & Matzke, D. (2024). Cognitive Control of Choices and Actions. In *An Introduction to Model-Based Cognitive Neuroscience* (pp. 361–385). Springer International Publishing.

Huang, H., Li, Z., Cheng, H., Wang, H., Jiang, J., Li, X., & Zgonnikov, A. (2025). Understanding driver cognition and decision-making behaviors in high-risk scenarios: A drift diffusion perspective. *Accident; Analysis and Prevention*, *220*, 108123. DOI: 10.1016/j.aap.2025.108123

Huang, S., Lin, P.-H., & Strickland, L. (2017). *DDM in depression: Task complexity and reward processing* (Conference presentation).

Kumar, P. (2025). Diffusion Models and Generative Artificial Intelligence: Frameworks, Applications and Challenges. *Archives of Computational Methods in Engineering*, •••, 1–44. DOI: 10.1007/s11831-025-10266-z

Lalvani, S., & Katsaggelos, A. (2024). Crowdsourcing with the drift diffusion model of decision making. *Scientific Reports*, *14*(1), 11311. DOI: 10.1038/s41598-024-61687-y

Liesefeld, H. R., & Janczyk, M. (2019). Combining speed and accuracy to control for speed-accuracy trade-offs. *Behavior Research Methods*, *51*(1), 40–60. DOI: 10.3758/s13428-018-1076-x

Lo, C. F., & Ip, H. Y. (2021). Modified leaky competing accumulator model of decision making with multiple alternatives: The Lie-algebraic approach. *Scientific Reports*, *11*(1), 10923. DOI: 10.1038/s41598-021-90356-7

Moustafa, A. A., Sherman, S. J., Frank, M. J., & Chopra, M. (2008). A role for dopamine in temporal decision making and reward maximization in Parkinsonism. *The Journal of Neuroscience : The Official Journal of the Society for Neuroscience*, *28*(47), 12294–12304. DOI: 10.1523/JNEUROSCI.3116-08.2008

Mulder, M. J., van Maanen, L., & Forstmann, B. U. (2014). Perceptual decision neurosciences – a model-based review. *Neuroscience*, *277*, 872–884. DOI: 10.1016/j.neuroscience.2014.07.031

Myers, C. E., Interian, A., & Moustafa, A. A. (2022). A practical introduction to using the drift diffusion model of decision-making in cognitive psychology, neuroscience, and health sciences. *Frontiers in Psychology*, *13*, 1039172. DOI: 10.3389/fpsyg.2022.1039172

O'Connell, R. G., Shadlen, M. N., Wong-Lin, K., & Kelly, S. P. (2018). Bridging neural and computational viewpoints on perceptual decision-making. *Trends in Neurosciences*, *41*(11), 838–852. DOI: 10.1016/j.tins.2018.06.005

Palmer, J., Huk, A. C., & Shadlen, M. N. (2005). The effect of stimulus strength on the speed and accuracy of a perceptual decision. *Journal of Vision (Charlottesville, Va.)*, *5*(5), 376–404. DOI: 10.1167/5.5.1

Pedersen, M. L., Frank, M. J., & Biele, G. (2017). The drift diffusion model as the choice rule in reinforcement learning. *Psychonomic Bulletin & Review, 24*(4), 1234–1251. DOI: 10.3758/s13423-016-1199-y

Radillo, A. E., Veliz-Cuba, A., Josić, K., & Kilpatrick, Z. P. (2017). Evidence accumulation and change rate inference in dynamic environments. *Neural Computation, 29*(6), 1561–1610. DOI: 10.1162/NECO_a_00957

Ratcliff, R. (1978). A theory of memory retrieval. *Psychological Review, 85*(2), 59–108. 10.1037/0033-295X.85.2.59

Ratcliff, R., & McKoon, G. (2008). The diffusion decision model: Theory and data for two-choice decision tasks. *Neural Computation, 20*(4), 873–922. DOI: 10.1162/neco.2008.12-06-420

Ratcliff, R., & Smith, P. L. (2004). A comparison of sequential sampling models for two-choice reaction time. *Psychological Review, 111*(2), 333–367. DOI: 10.1037/0033-295X.111.2.333

Ratcliff, R., & Tuerlinckx, F. (2002). Estimating parameters of the diffusion model: Approaches to dealing with contaminant reaction times and parameter variability. *Psychonomic Bulletin & Review, 9*(3), 438–481. DOI: 10.3758/bf03196302

Roitman, J. D., & Shadlen, M. N. (2002). Response of neurons in the lateral intraparietal area during a combined reaction-time and discrete trial motion discrimination task. *The Journal of Neuroscience : The Official Journal of the Society for Neuroscience, 22*(21), 9475–9489. DOI: 10.1523/JNEUROSCI.22-21-09475.2002

Schumacher, L., Schnuerch, M., Voss, A., & Radev, S. T. (2025). Validation and comparison of non-stationary cognitive models: A diffusion model application. *Computational Brain & Behavior, 8*(2), 191–210. DOI: 10.1007/s42113-024-00218-4

Smith, P. L., & Ratcliff, R. (2004). Psychology and neurobiology of simple decisions. *Trends in Neurosciences, 27*(3), 161–168. DOI: 10.1016/j.tins.2004.01.006

Stone, M. (1960). Models for choice-reaction time. *Psychometrika, 25*(3), 251–260. DOI: 10.1007/BF02289729

Tillman, G., Van Zandt, T., & Logan, G. D. (2020). Sequential sampling models without random between-trial variability: The racing diffusion model of speeded decision making. *Psychonomic Bulletin & Review, 27*(5), 911–936. 10.3758/s13423-020-01719-6

Townsend, J. T., & Ashby, F. G. (1983). *Stochastic modeling of elementary psychological processes*. Cambridge University Press.

Trueblood, J. S., Brown, S. D., & Heathcote, A. (2014). The multiattribute linear ballistic accumulator model of context effects in multialternative choice. *Psychological Review, 121*(2), 179. 10.1037/a0036137

Tsetsos, K., Usher, M., & McClelland, J. L. (2011). Testing multi-alternative decision models with non-stationary evidence. *Frontiers in Neuroscience, 5*, 63. DOI: 10.3389/fnins.2011.00063

Vandekerckhove, J., Tuerlinckx, F., & Lee, M. D. (2011). Hierarchical diffusion models for two-choice response times. *Psychological Methods, 16*(1), 44–62. DOI: 10.1037/a0021765

Voss, A., & Voss, J. (2007). Fast-dm: A free program for efficient diffusion model analysis. *Behavior Research Methods, 39*(4), 767–775. DOI: 10.3758/bf03192967

Wagenmakers, E.-J., van der Maas, H. L., & Grasman, R. (2007). An EZ-diffusion model for response time and accuracy. *Psychonomic Bulletin & Review, 14*(1), 3–22. DOI: 10.3758/bf03194023

Wiecki, T. V., Sofer, I., & Frank, M. J. (2013). HDDM: Hierarchical Bayesian estimation of the drift–diffusion model in Python. *Frontiers in Neuroinformatics, 7*, 14. DOI: 10.3389/fninf.2013.00014

Yarkoni, T., & Westfall, J. (2017). Choosing prediction over explanation in psychology: Lessons from machine learning. *Perspectives on Psychological Science, 12*(6), 1100–1122. DOI: 10.1177/1745691617693393

Chapter 13

Computational Approaches to Predator–Prey Models With Behavioral Adaptations:

Refuge, Harvesting, and Fear Dynamics in Deterministic and Stochastic Frameworks

Israar Ali
https://orcid.org/0009-0003-9873-946X
Northwestern Polytechnical University, China

Abdulwasea Alkhazzan
https://orcid.org/0000-0002-6504-8705
Xi'an Fanyi University, China

Hui Zhang
https://orcid.org/0000-0003-0046-1483
Northwestern Polytechnical University, China

Yassine Sabbar
Moulay Ismail University of Meknes, Morocco

ABSTRACT

This chapter examines the combined use of computational modeling and behavioral analysis in the study of predator–prey dynamics, which form a cornerstone of ecological theory. The objective is to connect theoretical developments with ecological

DOI: 10.4018/979-8-3373-5062-2.ch013

applications, offering a coherent reference for researchers working in computational ecology and behavioral dynamics. The discussion begins with a critical review of the classical Lotka–Volterra and Rosenzweig–MacArthur frameworks, followed by an analysis of their limitations and subsequent extensions. Attention is directed to the computational methods employed to simulate complex predator–prey interactions, with particular focus on mechanisms such as prey refuge, fear effects, harvesting, Crowley–Martin functional response, and environmental variability. Numerical simulations are used to investigate how computational tools enhance predictive capability and uncover previously unrecognized patterns, including transitions between oscillatory and chaotic behavior.

1. INTRODUCTION

1.1 Background and Motivation

Classical predator–prey theory (rooted in the Lotka–Volterra equations and refined by Rosenzweig–MacArthur to include prey self-limitation and handling time) explains how trophic interactions generate equilibria and cycles. Yet decades of field and experimental work show that demographic rates alone cannot reproduce the organization of real food webs. Encounter processes, energy allocation, and mortality are reshaped by behavior and management: prey retreat to refuges, individuals reduce foraging and reproduction under perceived risk, and human harvesting alters predator demography. To place these factors on firm footing, this chapter develops a mathematically rigorous and computationally tractable framework that augments the classical models with explicit behavioral and policy levers (prey refuge, fear-mediated modulation of foraging and fecundity, regulated predator harvest) and a predator-dependent Crowley–Martin functional response capturing interference and saturation. Environmental variability is represented as stochastic forcing, allowing us to study how noise shifts thresholds for stability, persistence, and oscillation in ecologically realistic regimes.

Behavioral mechanisms act as nonlinear feedbacks that reshape predator–prey dynamics beyond what demographic rates predict. Refuge use lowers encounter rates and stabilizes prey at low to moderate levels, but excessive refuge can starve predators and precipitate their loss. Risk-induced "fear" alters prey movement and allocation to reproduction, reducing effective growth; when intense, it suppresses both trophic levels. Predator harvest displays a tipping behavior: modest effort may damp oscillations, whereas overexploitation collapses the predator while releasing prey to high densities. These effects are captured more faithfully by predator-dependent functional responses (such as the Crowley–Martin form with interference and saturation) than by classical Holling types, refining how attack, handling, and crowding shape per-capita predation.

From a management perspective, understanding these feedbacks is essential: they determine how populations respond to stressors, exploitation, and habitat change, and thus where sustainable operating points lie. Environmental variability further tightens the coexistence window by elevating extinction risk and shifting critical thresholds, so policies that balance refuge provision, harvest intensity, and risk exposure must account for noise as well as mean conditions.

1.2 Related Works

The interaction between prey and predator is foundational relationships in ecology and shapes population balance, regime shifts, and biodiversity outcomes across many systems. It helps us understand population dynamics, species survival, and biodiversity conservation (Abrams, 2000; Berryman, 1992). Mathematical modeling provides a disciplined way to investigate these processes by translating mechanisms into equations that can be analyzed and simulated. Continuous time systems of differential equations have become standard for predator prey dynamics, beginning with the classical formulations of (Lotka, 1925) and (Volterra, 1926) in the early 20th century and evolving through later work that exposed structural complexity beyond the earliest models (Beroual & Sari, 2020; Hoppensteadt, 2006; Liu & Li, 2021; Rosenzweig & MacArthur, 1963; Sáez & González-Olivares, 1999).

Subsequent research introduced ecological mechanisms that are essential for realism. In natural populations, behavioral responses such as prey refuge (Wei & Chen, 2023), environmental stochasticity, switching predators (Saha & Samanta, 2021) or reductions in prey reproduction due to fear are of profound effect on population dynamics (Sahoo & Samanta, 2024). Each one of them introduces complex dynamics to the system in terms of bi-stability, oscillations, chaos, and extinction thresholds (Freedman, 1980; Holling, 1959; Kar & Matsuda, 2008; Murdoch & Oaten, 1975). Over-simplification by excluding these behavioral refinements can generate outcomes that are incompatible with empirical fact. Functional responses link consumption to prey density and encode behavioral adaptation by predators. The three canonical forms are widely used: Type I (Robertson et al., 2022), Type II (Liu et al., 2021) and Type III (Debnath et al., 2022). These shapes encompass a range of ecological contexts, ranging from passive feeding to complex foraging behavior. Scientists have developed extended forms like the (Beddington, 1975; DeAngelis et al., 1975) and (Crowley & Martin, 1989) functional responses to describe the biological realistic interaction. Ratio-dependent responses (Arditi & Ginzburg, 1989) and Hassell-Varley models (Hassell & Varley, 1969) framework address group-foraging and crowding. Stochastic and spatial analogues include environmental noise and habitat heterogeneity (Cantrell & Cosner, 2004). They are mechanistic descriptions of foraging that must be calibrated with careful experiments in order to predict stability boundaries and long term outcomes with credibility (Uiterwaal & DeLong, 2020).

Behavioral processes also play a central role. Prey refuge reduces encounter rates and can stabilize dynamics, but density dependent refuge can generate bistability and Hopf bifurcations. (Sasmal & Takeuchi, 2020) experiments illustrate the possibility of refuge stabilizing predator-prey dynamics through decreased encounter rates, and (Huang et al., 2006) established that density-dependent refuge produces bi-stability or Hopf bifurcations. The fear effect, whereby prey reproduction is suppressed or mortality enhanced through perceived predation risk, has emerged as a key non-consumptive driver. (Wang et al., 2016) illustrated that fear can generate Turing patterns in spatial systems, and (Pal et al., 2019) illustrated its dual role in stabilizing as well as destabilizing populations depending upon the parameter value. Similarly, harvesting pressure is among the most significant anthropogenic forces and has been well-studied in such systems. (Zhang et al., 2019) recently derived threshold conditions for sustainable harvesting in fear-mediated systems, and it was found that harvest effort above threshold induces overexploitation causing predator extinction due to food limitation. Stochastically extended forms of these models (Mandal & Tiwari, 2024) have further suggested that environmental noise may enhance or suppress the impact of behavior, particularly in small populations. Beside this, many researchers have studied the effect of different behavioral phenomenon in the dynamic of predator prey system (Ali et al., 2025; Cai et al., 2025; Liang & Meng, 2023; Mandal & Tiwari, 2024; Thirthar et al., 2022; Tiwari et al., 2021).

Advances in computation and learning further enrich this agenda. Physics informed neural networks, neural ordinary differential equations, and universal differential equations fuse data with mechanistic structure to recover dynamics from sparse or noisy observations and to extrapolate beyond the training range. Modern systems for behavioral analysis provide segmentation, pose estimation, and unsupervised feature extraction that support high resolution inference on movement rules. Multi agent reinforcement learning platforms generate emergent predator prey tactics that can be probed under controlled conditions. These advanced methods present robust frameworks in the modeling of predator–prey relations that surpass mathematical models by incorporating learning-based predictions, pattern detection, and nonlinear inference of behavior. The integration of such methods leads to a new frontier for behavioral ecology, particularly for the research of functional responses, prey refuge, and harvesting effects on predator populations. Notably, fixed point theory and machine learning procedures have been applied effectively in modeling decision-making behaviors of animals, avoidance learning, and cognitive responses in maze problems (Turab et al., 2022; Turab & Sintunavarat, 2019, 2020). These approaches provide the basis for the further exploration of behavioral strategies in ecological dynamics. As, (Panchal et al., 2025) studied a predator prey model using Holling Type III functional response in the physics-informed neural network framework. Neural ODEs and Universal Differential Equations are used by (Devgupta et al., 2024) for extrapolating and predicting Lotka–Volterra systems from sparse noisy observations—highlighting the robustness of UDEs for ecological prediction. (Fazzari et al., 2025) larger survey collates the state of deep learning in the analysis of animal behavior, including unsupervised segmentation and pose estimation methods required for behavioral phenotype measurement. Moreover, the Aquarium platform (Kölle et al., 2024) uses multi-agent reinforcement learning to simulate emergent predator–prey tactics and is a useful resource to investigate behavioral ecology. Similarly, (Park et al., 2021) demonstrate how co-evolution of deep RL agents in predator–prey models can lead to sustainable and adaptive population dynamics. A Behavioral Approach" strictly analyzes traditional predator–prey models and brings together computational models, bifurcation analyses, and machine learning insights to describe population behavior, both deterministic and stochastic. Recent research has also introduced deep neural networks and hybrid computational models for simulating learning behavior in cognitive environments such as T-mazes, further attesting to the relevance of AI-based methods in behavioral ecology (Turab, Montoyo, et al., 2024; Turab et al., 2025; Turab et al., 2023; Turab, Sintunavarat, et al., 2024).

As environmental variability grows in intensity and frequency, stochastic modeling has become indispensable. Formulating ecological dynamics with stochastic differential equations enables quantitative study of persistence, extinction risk, and noise induced transitions. Moment bounds, first passage calculations, and sample path simulations together provide a coherent view of how variability shifts thresholds and compresses the parameter regions that permit coexistence (Gray et al., 2011; Mao, 2007).

1.3 Novelty and Contribution

Despite steady advances, most formal treatments still examine behavioral mechanisms one at a time or at most in pairs. Consequently, the joint effects of refuge, fear, harvesting policy, and predator-dependent functional responses remain poorly resolved when they operate simultaneously. This chapter closes that gap. We begin with a concise survey of classical and extended predator–prey models, then develop an integrated system that couples fear effects, refuge, regulated predator harvest, and a Crowley–Martin response. The deterministic core is established for positivity and boundedness, its equilibria characterized, and its stability analyzed with attention to bifurcations that reorganize the phase portrait. A stochastic counterpart introduces environmental noise to quantify shifts in coexistence domains and the likelihood of extinction events. Comparative simulations link theory to management by charting sustainable-harvest regions, identifying refuge levels that sustain predators, and showing how variability displaces these boundaries. The outcome is a unified framework that ties mechanism to prediction and informs conservation and resource policy under realistic, fluctuating conditions.

1.4 Work Structure

The remainder of the chapter is organized as follows. Section 2 revisits the classical Lotka-Volterra predator prey model and its principal extensions, with emphasis on alternative functional responses. It also reports selected numerical analyses and simulations that substantiate the main points. Section 3 studies the influence of individual behavior, including prey refuge, harvesting, and fear effects, and presents their theoretical implications together with supporting simulations. Section 4 introduces an integrated predator prey model that combines these behavioral mechanisms with the Crowley Martin functional response, and provides proofs of positivity, boundedness, and equilibrium stability, accompanied by extensive computational experiments. Section 5 extends the integrated model to a stochastic setting in order to represent environmental variability, and offers both theoretical results and simulation evidence. Section 6 outlines directions for future research and methodological development. Section 8 concludes with the key findings and their implications for ecological applications.

2. DYNAMICS OF PREDATOR PREY SYSTEM

Classical predator–prey models provide the mathematical machinery to describe interactions between two biological species, one predator and the other its prey. The models try to describe population growth dynamics, predation, and mortality using systems of ordinary differential equations.

3.1 Lotka-Volterra Model

The Lotka–Volterra model, independently discovered by both Alfred Lotka and Vito Volterra is the oldest and most renowned mathematical model for predator–prey systems. The system is given by:

$$\begin{aligned} \frac{dx}{dt} &= x(\alpha - \beta y) = f_1, \\ \frac{dy}{dt} &= -y(\gamma - \eta x) = f_2, \end{aligned} \tag{1}$$

Here, x and y represent the prey and predator population, respectively. α denotes the growth rate in the absence of prey, while β represents the predator attack rate. Similarly, γ is the predator death rate and η denote growth rate of predator from consuming preys.

Figure 1. Dynamics of Lotka-Volterra Model (1) and its corresponding Phase Portrait. The parameter values are α = 1.1, β = 0.4, γ = 0.4, η = 0.1

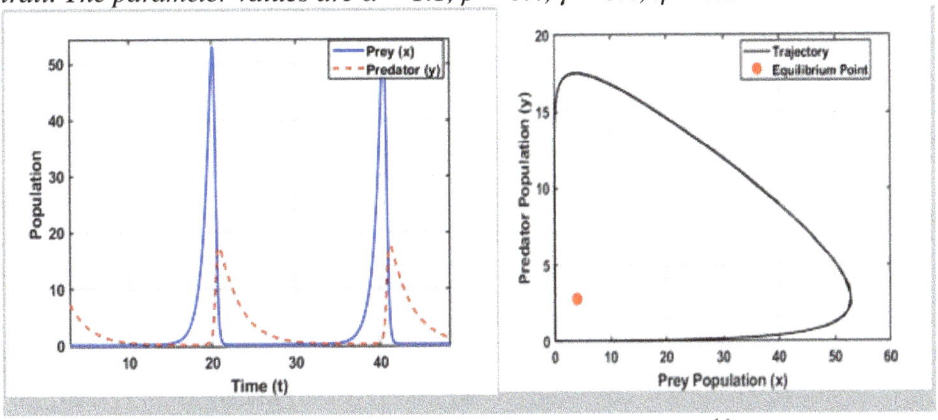

a) b)

The equilibrium points through the numerical analysis of model (1) are $(x = 0, y = 0)$ and $(x = \frac{\gamma}{\eta}, y = \frac{\alpha}{\beta})$. To study the local stability of the model (1), we find the Jacobian matrix and check the sign of eigenvalues. i-e.

$$J(x,y) = \begin{pmatrix} \frac{\delta f_1}{\delta x} & \frac{\delta f_1}{\delta y} \\ \frac{\delta f_2}{\delta x} & \frac{\delta f_2}{\delta y} \end{pmatrix} = \begin{pmatrix} \alpha - \beta y & -\beta x \\ \beta y & \gamma - \eta x \end{pmatrix}$$

Since we have $E^*(\frac{\gamma}{\eta}, \frac{\alpha}{\beta})$. Therefore, $J(E^*) = \begin{pmatrix} 0 & -\gamma \\ \alpha & 0 \end{pmatrix}$.

Hence the characteristic equation will be $\lambda^2 + \alpha\gamma = 0$. So $\lambda = \pm i\sqrt{\alpha\gamma}$. The eigenvalues are purely imaginary, so the trajectories are neutrally stable. This can be clearly observed in Figure 1(a) and 1(b).

3.2 Limitation of Lotka-Volterra and Advance Models

The historical Lotka–Volterra predator–prey model, while foundational to theoretical ecology, is underpinned by highly abstracted assumptions that bar direct application to ecosystem processes. The addition of functional responses, i.e., predators' per capita rate of prey consumption, yields a more realistic representation of interaction and has led to several influential generalizations of the Lotka–Volterra model.

3.2.1 Holling Type II Functional Response

(Holling, 1959) classified three functional responses, among which Type II and Type III are of greatest biological interest to most systems. Unlike the Lotka-Volterra model (where the predation rate was assumed to be linear and unlimited), these models incorporate handling time saturation and predator effectiveness effects.

The Holling Type II functional response can be expressed as

$$g(x) = \frac{\beta x}{1 + \beta h x}.$$

where, β denotes the attacking rate of predator, h is the handling time, and $x$represents the population of prey. We can see the denominator will always be bigger than numerator because of term "1+" and this term ensures the model handles low prey densities realistically. The longer it takes the process prey, the smaller the value of overall consumption rate.

Therefore, replacing the linear term $\beta xy$with $g(x)$, the model (1) becomes

$$\begin{aligned} \frac{dx}{dt} &= x(\alpha - \frac{\beta y}{1 + \beta h x}), \\ \frac{dy}{dt} &= -y(\gamma - \frac{c\beta x}{1 + \beta h x}), \end{aligned} \tag{2}$$

In model (2), c represents the conversion rate of prey into predator. Similarly, just like as in model (1), we can perform the local stability analysis of model (2) through Jacobian matrix and eigenvalues. So we have the equilibrium points $E^*(x,y) = \left(\frac{\gamma}{\beta(c - h\gamma)}, \frac{\alpha}{\beta}\left(1 + \frac{h\gamma}{\beta - h\gamma}\right)\right)$. We have shown the dynamics of model (2) and its corresponding phase portrait in Figure 2(a) and 2(b).

In the Holling type II functional response, the predation rate increases linearly at low prey density and it often lead to unstable oscillation. This lead to the derivation of Holling type III functional response.

Figure 2. Dynamics of Modified Lotka Volterra Model (2) with Holling Type II Functional Response and its corresponding Phase Portrait. The parameter values are $\alpha = 1$, $\beta = 0.2$, $\gamma = 0.5$, and $h = 0.1$

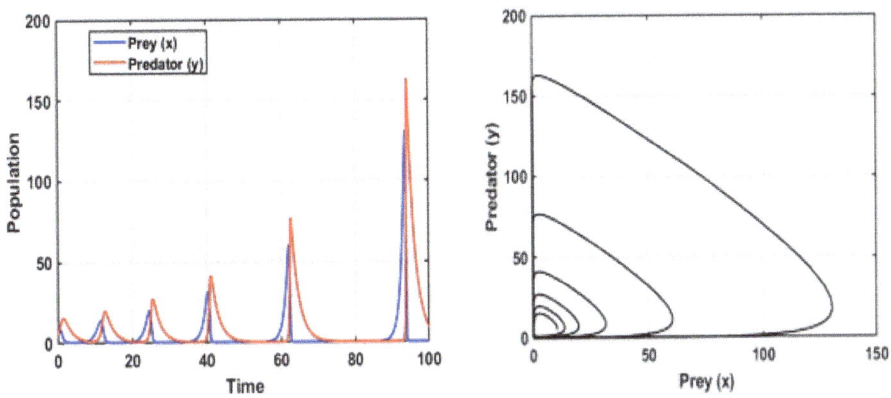

a) b)

3.2.2 Holling Type III Functional Response

The Holling Type III functional response assumes that:

i. At low prey density, predator consume fewer prey due to prey hiding or switching behavior.
ii. As prey density increase, the consumption rate increases.
iii. At high prey density, it saturates just similar to Holling Type II due to predator handling limitations.

The Holling Type III functional response is given as

$$g(x) = \frac{\beta x^2}{1 + \beta h x^2}.$$

When prey densities are low then the attack rate becomes low too but when increases prey densities, predators encounter more preys resulting the sigmoid shape. The denominator $(1 + \beta h x^2)$ grows more quickly at low prey density, which cause in reduction of predation rate.

Similarly, using Holling Type III functional response the model (1) becomes

$$
\begin{aligned}
\frac{dx}{dt} &= x(\alpha - \frac{\beta xy}{1+\beta h x^2}), \\
\frac{dy}{dt} &= -y(\gamma - \frac{c\beta x^2}{1+\beta h x^2}),
\end{aligned} \tag{3}
$$

In the same way as for the local stability analysis of model (1), we have the equilibrium points for model (3),

$$E^*(x,y) = \left(\sqrt{\frac{\gamma}{\beta-\gamma h}}, \frac{\alpha}{\beta}\left(\sqrt{\frac{\beta-\gamma h}{\gamma}} + \beta h\sqrt{\frac{\gamma}{\beta-\gamma h}}\right)\right)$$

We have shown the graphical representation of model (3) in Figure 3(a) and 3(b). As we can see for the same parameter values, it shows stabilization which is due to impact of Holling type III functional response.

The Holling functional response did not captured the competition or conflicts between predators.

Figure 3. Dynamics of Model (3) with Holling Type III Functional Response and its corresponding Phase Portrait. The parameter values are $\alpha = 1$, $\beta = 0.2$, $\gamma = 0.5$, and $h = 0.1$

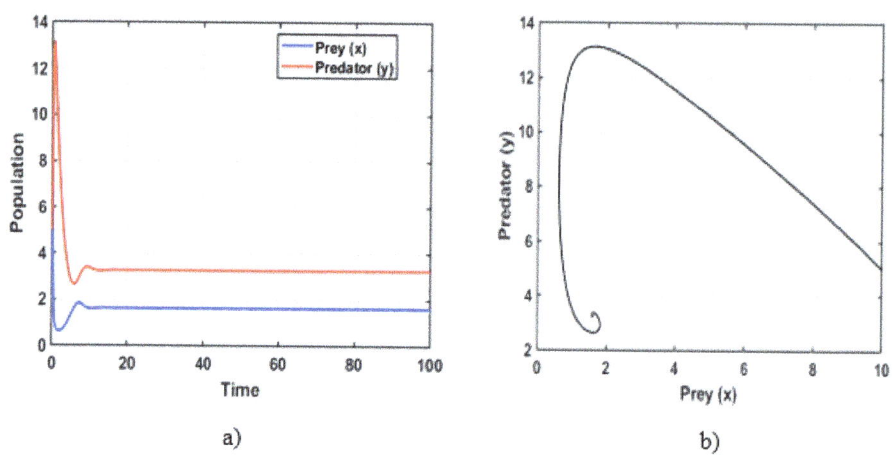

3.2.3 Beddington-DeAngles Functional Response

(Beddington & DeAngles, 1975), extended the Holling Type II functional response by adding interference term (*by*) in the denominator. It also saturates with prey density just like Holling type II and decrease with predator density due to interference. Mathematically it is shown as

$$g(x) = \frac{\beta x}{1 + \beta hx + by}$$

Where, β denotes the attacking rate of predator, h is the handling time, and x,y represents the population of prey and predator respectively. The parameter $p$denotes mutual interference if predators. It also explains the paradox of enrichment—unlike Type II, which predicts destabilization under high prey resources, Beddington-DeAngles is able to stabilize systems via oscillation damping through interference. Applications extend from ecological conservation to epidemiology (modeling disease transmission with host competition).

Using Beddington-DeAngles functional response and logistic growth rate $rx(1 - \frac{x}{k})$ model (1) can be express as

$$\begin{aligned} \frac{dx}{dt} &= rx(1 - \frac{x}{k}) - \frac{\beta xy}{1 + \beta hx + by}, \\ \frac{dy}{dt} &= \frac{c\beta xy}{1 + \beta hx + by} - mx, \end{aligned} \tag{4}$$

where r represents logistic growth rate and k is carrying capacity. Hence, the Beddington-DeAngles functional response captures the lost time during predators fighting or competition but he also assumes interference occur only during searching time not prey handling. Therefore, Crowly-Martin proposed another functional response by taking into account this problem. The simulation results are shown in Figure 4(a) and 4(b).

Figure 4. Dynamics of Model (4) with Deddington-DeAngles Functional Response and Phase Portrait. The parameter values are r = 1.5, k = 100, β = 0.8, h = 0.1, b = 0.05, c = 0.6, m = 0.3

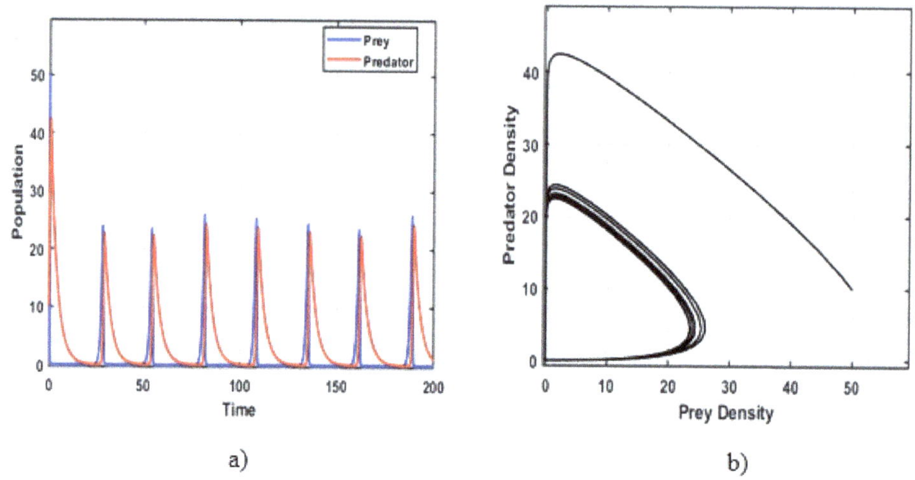

3.2.4 Crowley-Martin Functional Response

Crowly & Martin functional response also generalizes predator interference by making the assumption that the handling of prey and avoidance of competitors occur simultaneously but independently. Predators waste time during both searching and predation on prey and Interference effects are more powerful at high densities of predators, which results in faster reduction in predation rates. The response is applicable in systems where intraspecific competition is high, such as cannibalistic species (e.g., dragonfly larvae) or fish cohorts. The Crowly-Martin functional response can express as

$$g(x) = \frac{\beta x}{(1 + \beta hx)(1 + by)}.$$

Unlike Beddington-DeAngles functional response, the denominator factors handling $(1 + \beta hx)$ and interference $(1 + by)$ are in multiplicative form, which implies that predators are wasting time both searching and consuming prey.

Using Crowly-Martin functional response and logistic growth rate $rx(1 - \frac{x}{k})$ model (1) can be express as

$$\frac{dx}{dt} = rx(1-\frac{x}{k}) - \frac{\beta xy}{(1+\beta hx)(1+by)},$$
$$\frac{dy}{dt} = \frac{c\beta xy}{(1+\beta hx)(1+by)} - mx, \tag{5}$$

We have shown the graphical representation of model (5) in Figure 5(a) and 5(b). In addition, we have constructed the comparison table for different functional responses in Table 1.

Figure 5. Dynamics of Model (5) with Crowly-Martin Functional Response and Phase Portrait. The parameter values are r = 1.5, k = 100, β = 0.8, h = 0.1, b = 0.05, c = 0.6, m = 0.3

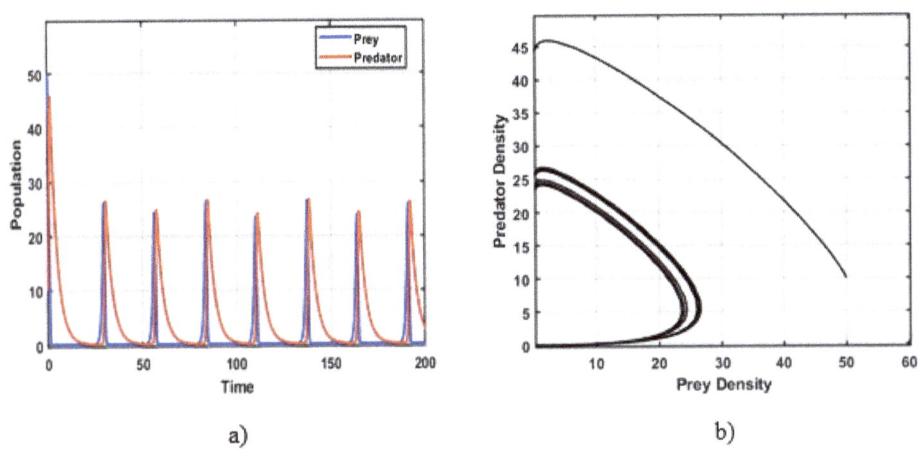

An Advanced Predator Prey Model

Now, we study a predator prey model that incorporates key ecological mechanisms like the Crowley-Martin functional response that captures predator interference during search and handling, fear effects whereby the reproduction of the prey is inhibited by the threat of predation, prey refuge that provides partial protection from predation, and linear harvesting to represent human exploitation. We will explore how these interacting influence dynamics of the system such as stability and coexistence. We will perform an extensive mathematical analysis and numerical simulation to show the effect of behavioral adaptations and quantifying their synergistic effects on equilibrium states and oscillatory dynamics. Outcomes will be illustrated through detailed phase portraits, and time-series simulations depicting transitions among stable coexistence, limit cycles, and potential population collapse throughout parameter regimes.

Recently (Liang & Meng, 2023) have studied a delayed predator prey model incorporating prey refuge, fear effect, harvesting and Martin functional response. Although Liang and Meng did enough efforts in the analysis of model but they did not analyze it clearly. Therefore, there is need to further explore it perfectly. In addition, (Liang & Meng, 2023) did not study the model in stochastic environment because without taking into account the noise or randomness of the real world, the model cannot describe real scenario. Therefore, first we thoroughly study the model in deterministic environment and then in next section we will study the noise effect in the dynamics of the system.

The deterministic model is expressed as

$$\begin{aligned} \frac{dx}{dt} &= \frac{rx}{1+ky} - (1+ny)ax - cx^2 - \frac{\beta(1-\phi)xy}{(1+h(1-\phi)x)(1+by)} - h_1M_1x \\ \frac{dy}{dt} &= \frac{\lambda\beta(1-\phi)xy}{(1+h(1-\phi)x)(1+by)} - ey - my^2 - h_2M_2y \end{aligned} \tag{6}$$

a denotes natural death rate and c represents death due to intra-specific competition. β is conversion rate, λ is efficiency of predators consuming prey and $(1-\phi)$ represents prey refuge, which is controlled by parameter ϕ. h is handling time, $(1+by)$ denotes interference, e is natural death rate of predator and m represents death due to intra-specific competition. In addition, $\frac{1}{1+ky}$ represents the fear effect, h_1, h_2 denote prey and predator harvesting respectively. The parameter n denotes level of fear. Similarly, M_1, M_2 denote the harvesting efforts of prey and predator.

Table 1. Comparison table for different functional responses

Type	*Mathematical Formula*	*Key Features*
Holling Type I	$g(x)=\beta x$	*Simple, no handling time, unrealistic for many cases.*
Holling Type II	$g(x)=\dfrac{\beta x}{1+\beta hx}$	*Common in many species, Ignores predator learning.*
Holling Type III	$g(x)=\dfrac{\beta xy}{1+\beta hx^2}$	*More realistic in some system, Captures predator learning.*
Beddington & DeAngles	$g(x)=\dfrac{\beta x}{1+\beta hx+by}$	*Significant for predator prey Interaction, Suitable for systems.*
Crowly & Martin	$g(x)=\dfrac{\beta x}{(1+\beta hx)(1+by)}$	*More flexible than Beddington & DeAngles.*
Ratio – Dependent	$g(x)=\dfrac{\beta \frac{x}{y}}{1+\beta h\frac{x}{y}}$	*Useful when predator interference is strong.*

In the next subsections, we perform an exhaustive qualitative analysis of the predator-prey model (6) to ascertain its ecological consistency and dynamical behavior. We initially establish positivity and boundedness of solutions for biologically realistic trajectories for all time. We then perform equilibrium analysis to obtain all feasible steady states (extinction, predator-free, coexistence) and examine their local stability via Jacobian linearization. Global stability of coexistence equilibria will be analyzed using Lyapunov functions, and bifurcation analysis will reveal critical thresholds in harvesting pressure and fear parameters that trigger stability shifts. The systematic approach links theoretical ecology with conservation practice, measuring sustainable harvesting bounds under behavioral constraints.

3.3 Boundedness and Positivity of Model

Lemma 4.1.1: For any initial condition $(x(0), y(0)) \in R_+^2$ where $x(0) > 0, y(0) > 0$. The solution $(x(t), y(t))$ of system remain positive for all $t > 0$.

Proof: The system can be written as

$$\frac{dx}{dt} = x\psi_1(x,y),\quad \frac{dy}{dt} = y\psi_2(x,y), \tag{i}$$

We can solve the system (i) by separation of variable method.

For example, from first equation of system (i), we have

$$\frac{1}{x}dx = \psi_1(x,y)\,dt$$

By integrating from both side of equations we have

$$\int_0^t \left(\frac{1}{x}(l)\,dx\right)\left(\frac{dx}{dl}\right)dl = \int_0^t \psi_1(x(l),y(l))\,dl$$

Therefore, by simple calculations we have

$$x(t) = x(0)\,e^{\int_0^t \psi_1(x(l),y(l))dl} \geq 0$$

Similarly, by the same way we can find

$$y(t) = y(0)\,e^{\int_0^t \psi 2(x(l),y(l))dl} \geq 0$$

where

$$\psi_1(x,y) = \frac{r}{1+ky} - (1+ny)a - cx - \frac{\beta(1-\phi)y}{(1+h(1-\phi)x)(1+by)} - h_1M_1$$

$$\psi_2(x,y) = \frac{\lambda\beta(1-\phi)x}{(1+h(1-\phi)x)(1+by)} - e - my - h_2M_2$$

Therefore, this proved that the solution remains positive for all time.

Next, we show the boundedness through the following lemma.

Lemma 4.1.2: All solutions $(x(t), y(t))$of the system in positive quadrant R_+^2 are ultimately bounded and converge to the invariant region.

$$\chi = \left\{(x,y)\middle|\, 0 \leq x \leq \frac{r}{c}, 0 \leq qx + y \leq \frac{qx\eta^*}{2c}\right\}$$

where $\eta^* = \min(a,e)$.

Proof: From first equation of system (6), we have

$$\frac{dx}{dt} = \frac{rx}{1+ky} - (1+ny)ax - cx^2 - \frac{\beta(1-\phi)xy}{(1+h(1-\phi)x)(1+by)} - h_1M_1x$$

As we can see only first term is positive and all other are negative terms, so can bound like this

$$\frac{dx}{dt} \leq rx - ax - cx^2$$

This implies that

$$\frac{dx}{dt} \leq rx - ax - cx^2 = x(r - a - cx)$$

$$\frac{dx}{dt} \leq x(a - cx).$$

We can see this is logistic growth inequality. Therefore, we can solve it through separation of variable, so we multiply both side by x^{-2}, we get $x^{-2}\frac{dx}{dt} \leq rx^{-1} - a$. Suppose, $\omega = x^{-1}$then we have $\frac{d\omega}{dt} \leq a - r\omega$. This implies that

$$\frac{d\omega}{dt} + r\omega \geq a$$

Multiply both side by integrating factor e^{rt}, we have

$$e^{rt}\frac{d\omega}{dt} + e^{rt}r\omega \geq a\,e^{rt}$$

Now through simple mathematical calculations, we got

$$\omega \geq \frac{c}{r} + (\frac{1}{x(0)} - \frac{c}{r})e^{-rt}$$

This implies that

$$\omega \geq \omega^{-1} \leq \frac{1}{\frac{c}{r} + (\frac{1}{x(0)} - \frac{c}{r})e^{-rt}}$$

As we can see when $t \to \infty$, the exponential term vanish and we got

$$\lim_{x\to\infty} \sup x(t) \leq \frac{r}{c}.$$

Now consider, $N(t) = qx(t) + y(t)$,then we have

$$\frac{dN}{dt} = q\left[\frac{rx}{1+ky} - (1+ny)ax - cx^2 - \frac{\beta(1-\phi)xy}{(1+h(1-\phi)x)(1+by)} - h_1M_1x\right] + \left[\frac{\lambda\beta(1-\phi)xy}{(1+h(1-\phi)x)(1+by)} - ey - my^2 - h_2M_2y\right]$$

Though simple calculations and drop negative terms, we are left with

$$\dot{N} = \frac{qrx}{1+ky} - q(1+ny)ax - qcx^2 - qh_1M_1x - ey - my^2 - h_2M_2yx$$

$$\dot{N} \leq qrx - qax - e$$

$$\leq \frac{qr^2}{c} - \eta^* N,$$

where $\eta^* = \min(a, e)$.Now through combination of initial condition and constant, we have

$$N \leq \frac{qr^2}{\eta^* c} + (qx(0)+y(0) - \frac{qr^2}{\eta^* c})e^{-r^*t},$$

Hence $\lim_{x\to\infty} \sup N(t) \leq \frac{qr^2}{\eta^* c}$.

Now, we can show if the solution start in χ, then it should remain in$\chi$for all time.

If $x = 0$, then we can see $\frac{dx}{dt} = 0$.Similarly, if $y = 0$, then $\frac{dy}{dt} = 0$.

Here, we can observe that $x > \frac{r}{c}$ $and N > \frac{qr^2}{\eta^* c}$then we have

$$\frac{dx}{dt} \leq x(r - cx) < x(r - c.\frac{r}{c}),$$

$$\frac{dM}{dt} \leq \frac{qr^2}{c} - \eta^* N < \frac{qr^2}{c} - \eta^* \frac{qr^2}{\eta^* c}) = 0.$$

This completes the proof; hence the solution of system is bounded.

3.4 Local Stability Analysis

We analyze Jacobian matrix to determine the local stability of equilibrium points. For each equilibrium we compute the Jacobian at examine its eigenvalues. If all eigenvalues possess negative real parts, the equilibrium is locally asymptotically stable; if there is any eigenvalue with a positive real part, the equilibrium is unstable. Purely imaginary eigenvalues, special cases, identify Hopf bifurcations, where stable limit cycles can be present. The system has following equilibrium points.

$$E_1(0,0), E_2(\tilde{x},0), E^*(x^*,y^*).$$

Theorem 4.2.1: The zero equilibrium point $E_1(0, 0)$will be locally asymptotically stable if $r - a \leq h_1 M_1$and is unstable if $r - a > h_1 M_1$.

Proof: Let the Jacobian matrix is defined as

$$\begin{bmatrix} a_{11} & a_{12} \\ a_{21} & a_{22} \end{bmatrix}$$

Where

$$a_{11} = \frac{r}{1+ky} - (1+ny)a - cx - \frac{\beta(1-\phi)y}{(1+h(1-\phi)x)(1+by)} - h_1 M_1$$
$$a_{12} = \frac{rkx}{(1+ky)^2} - anx - \frac{\beta(1-\phi)x}{(1+h(1-\phi)x)(1+by)^2}$$
$$a_{21} = \frac{\lambda\beta(1-\phi)y}{(1+h(1-\phi)x)^2(1+by)}$$
$$a_{22} = \frac{\lambda\beta(1-\phi)x}{(1+h(1-\phi)x)(1+by)^2} - e - 2my - h_2 M_2$$

Characteristic equation at

$E_1(0,0)$

will be

$$(\Omega - (-e - h_2 M_2))(\Omega - (r - a - h_1 M_1)) = 0.$$

Since $\Omega_1 = -e - h_2 M_2 < 0$ and if $\Omega_2 = r - a_2 < h_1 M_1$, then both eigenvalues have negative sign. Therefore, the $E_1(0,0)$ will be locally asymptotically stable but if $r - a_2 > h_1 M_1$, then $E_1(0,0)$ will be unstable.

Theorem 4.2.2: The equilibrium point $E_2(\tilde{x},0)$ will be locally asymptotically stable if $\lambda\beta(1-\phi)(r-a-h_1M_1) < e + h_2M_2(c + h(1-\phi)(r-a-h_1M_1))$ and is unstable if it is inverse of this inequality.

Proof: Since the first equation of model (6) is

$$\frac{dx}{dt} = \frac{rx}{1+ky} - (1+ny)ax - cx^2 - \frac{\beta(1-\phi)xy}{(1+h(1-\phi)x)(1+by)} - h_1 M_1 x$$

When $y = 0$, the above equation becomes

$$\frac{dx}{dt} \le rx - ax - cx^2 - -h_1 M_1 x = 0$$

This implies that

$$\frac{dx}{dt} \le r - a - h_1 M_1 - cx = 0.$$

Therefore, $\tilde{x} = \frac{r - a - h_1 M_1}{c}$. This shows that the equilibrium point exist only if $r - a - h_1 M_1 > 0$.

The Jacobian matric at $E_2(\tilde{x},0)$ will be

$$\begin{bmatrix} -(r-a-h_1M_1) & 0 \\ 0 & \frac{\lambda\beta(1-\phi)\tilde{x}}{1+h(1-\phi)\tilde{x}} - e - h_2M_2 \end{bmatrix}.$$

Figure 6. Extinction of the predator of Model (6) with Crowly-Martin Functional Response The parameter values are r = 3, a = 0.6, c = 1.5, ϕ = 0.3, h = 0.3, b = 0.01, β – 2, λ = 0.4, e = 0.8, k = 10, h_1 = 0.01, n = 0.5, h_2 = 0.01, M_2 = 1.5, M_1 = 1

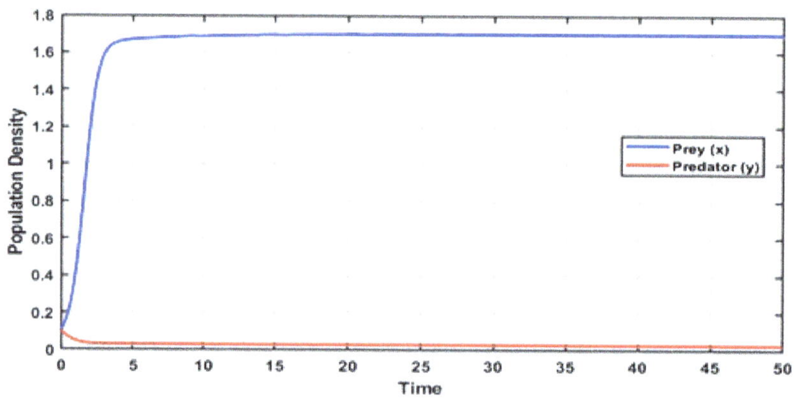

Similarly, the characteristic equation at $E_2(\tilde{x},0)$ will be

$$(\Omega - (r-a-h_1M_1-2c\tilde{x}))\left(\Omega - (\frac{\lambda\beta(1-\phi)\tilde{x}}{(1+h(1-\phi)\tilde{x})} - e - h_2M_2)\right) = 0,$$

So the eigenvalues are $\Omega_1 = -(r-a_2-h_1M_1)$, and $\Omega_2 = \frac{\lambda\beta(1-\phi)\tilde{x}}{(1+h(1-\phi)\tilde{x})} - e - h_2M_2),$

This implies that

$$\Omega_2 = \frac{\lambda\beta(1-\phi)(r-a_2-h_1M_1)}{(1+h(1-\phi)(r-a_2-h_1M_1))} - e - h_2M_2).$$

Since $\Omega_1 = -(r-a_2-h_1M_1) < 0$ and if $\lambda\beta(1-\phi)(r-a-h_1M_1) < e + h_2M_2 (c+h(1-\phi)(r-a-h_1M_1))$ then $E_2(\tilde{x},0)$ will be locally asymptotically stable, otherwise it is unstable.

Therefore, we have the following threshold for the stability of $E_2(\tilde{x},0)$

$$R = \frac{\lambda\beta(1-\phi)(r-a_2-h_1M_1)}{(e+h_2M_2)(1+h(1-\phi)(r-a_2-h_1M_1))}.$$

When $R < 1$, then the it will be locally asymptotically stable, this means the predator will not invade or persist. This scenario can be clearly see in Figure 6, where the prey is in a stable position but the predator is in the verge of extinction. Using the parameter values used in Figure 6, we have $R = 0.820 < 1$. Similarly using parameter values from Figure 7, we have $R = 24.54 > 1$. Therefore, the prey and predator will coexist, which can be clearly observes in Figure 7(a) and (7b).

Figure 7. Coexistence of Model (6) with Crowly-Martin Functional Response and corresponding phase portrait with different initial conditions. The parameter values are $r = 3$, $a = 0.6$, $c = 1.5$, $\phi = 0.3$, $h = 0.3$, $b = 0.01$, $\beta = 5$, $\lambda = 0.9$, $e = 0.8$, $k = 10$, $h_1 = 0.01$, $n = 0.5$, $h_2 = 0.01$, $M_2 = 1.5$, $M_1 = 1$

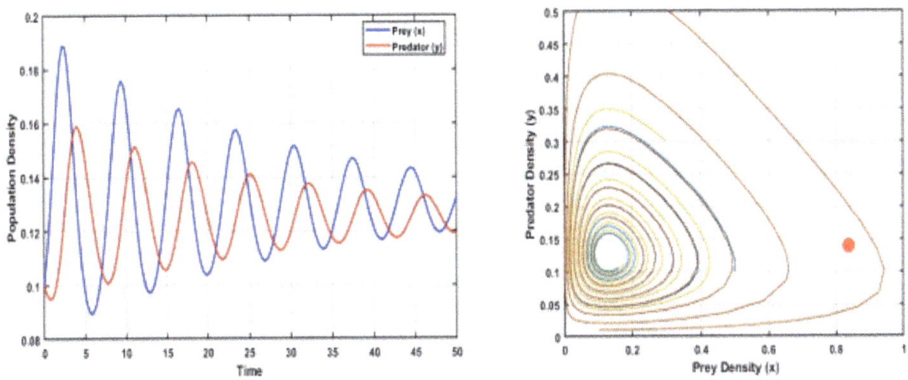

a) b)

Theorem 4.2.3: The equilibrium point $E^*(x^*, y^*)$ will be locally asymptotically stable if $cb^*(h^*)^2 > \beta h(1-\phi)y^*$, where $h^* = 1 + h(1-\phi)x^*$, $b^* = 1 + by^*$. the characteristic equation at $E^*(x^*, y^*)$ will be

$$\Omega + B_1\Omega + B_2 = 0, \tag{a}$$

Where $B_1 = cx^* - \dfrac{\beta h(1-\phi)^2 x^* y^*}{(h^*)^2 b^*} + \dfrac{\lambda\beta b(1-\phi)x^* y^*}{h^*(b^*)^2} + my^*$ and

$$B_2 = \left[cx^* - \frac{\beta h(1-\phi)^2 x^* y^*}{(h^*)^2 b^*)}\right]\left[\frac{\lambda\beta b(1-\phi)x^* y^*}{h^*(b^*)^2} + my^*\right] + \frac{\lambda\beta(1-\phi)y^*}{(h^*)^2 b^*)}\left[\frac{rkx^*}{(1+ky)^2} + anx^* + \frac{\beta(1-\phi)x^*}{h^*(b^*)^2}\right],$$

Also $h^* = 1 + h(1-\phi)x^* > 0$, and $b^* = 1 + by^* > 0$.

The Routh-Hurwitz criteria state that the roots of equation (a) will be negative if $B_1 > 0$ and $B_2 > 0$. This condition can be fulfilled only if $c > \dfrac{\beta h(1-\phi)^2 y^*}{(h^*)^2 b^*)}$.

Therefore, under the condition $c > \frac{\beta h(1-\phi)^2 y^*}{(h^*)^2 b^*)}$, $B_1 > 0$ and $B_2 > 0$. Hence the roots of characteristic equation will be negative according to Routh-Hurwitz criteria, so $E^*(x^*, y^*)$is locally asymptotically stable.

Using the parameter values $\beta = 2, h = 0.02, c = 0.5, b = 0.01, \phi = 0.3$, we have $h^* = 1.0112, b^* = 1.0014$ and thus the condition satisfied $c > 0.5 > 0.0026$. Which can be clearly seen in Figure 8(a) and 8(b).

Figure 8. Stability of interior equilibrium point of Model (6) with Crowly-Martin Functional Response and corresponding phase portrait with different initial conditions. The parameter values are $r = 3$, $a = 0.6$, $c = 0.5$, $\phi = 0.3$, $h = 0.02$, $b = 0.01$, $\beta = 2$, $\lambda = 0.9$, $e = 0.8$, $k = 10$, $h_1 = 0.01$, $n = 0.5$, $h_2 = 0.01$, $M_2 = 1.5$, $M_1 = 1$

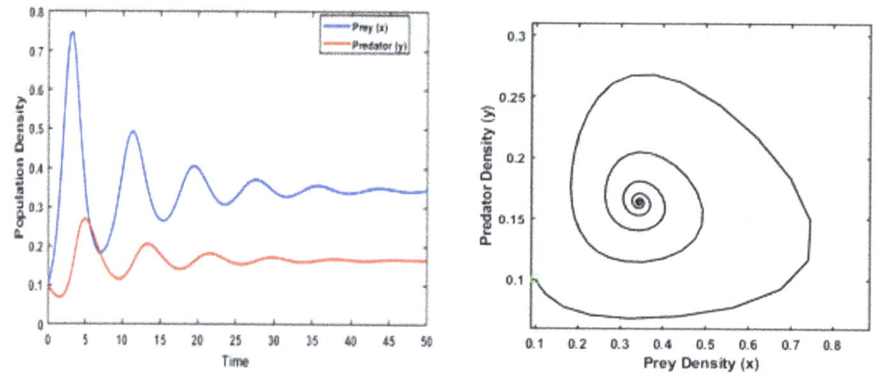

a) b)

4 BEHAVIORAL EFFECTS IN SYSTEM

The mechanism of Behavior in predator prey model play a vital role incorporating non-consumptive effects that influence population stability, coexistence, and ecosystem structure. The classical models that simply focus on consumption rates but behavioral models also describe the adaptive decision-making, risk perception, and many more. We describe key behavioral mechanisms and their mathematical formulations below.

4.1 Prey Refuge

Any method that reduces the predation rate is called refuge. It reduces the mortality rate of the prey by lessening the predation pressure and hence enables the growth of the prey populations. Refuge allows an improved growth and reproductive success of prey species due to its safe environment, thus benefiting the overall population stability. A growing number of researchers have concentrated on adding various functional responses along the prey refuge to make the prey-predator model more realistic.

The study examines the influence of prey refuge (ϕ) on predator-prey dynamics by holding ϕ constant at different levels in a systematic variation while other parameters remain constant. The results exhibit an unequivocal pattern: as the refuge parameter ϕ increases, prey population density rises consistently due to heightened protection from predators as shown in Figure 9 (a) and 9(b). The protection reduces predation pressure, which allow to survive more individuals of the prey. When θ exceeds a critical value, the prey population reach to a maximum density and the predator population drops to zero, leading to a predator-free equilibrium state E_2 $(\tilde{x}, 0)$This is because once this threshold value is exceeded, the refuge provides all but complete protection, leading to too few prey being left to support the predator population.

Figure 9. Effect of prey refuge in the dynamics of Model (2) with Crowly-Martin Functional Response. The parameter values are are $r = 3$, $a = 0.6$, $c = 0.5$, $k = 10$, $h = 0.02$, $b = 0.01$, $\beta = 2$, $\lambda = 0.5$, $e = 0.5$, $m = 0.025$, $n = 0.5$, $h_1 = 0.01$, $M_1 = 1$, $h_2 = 0.05$, $M_2 = 1.5$

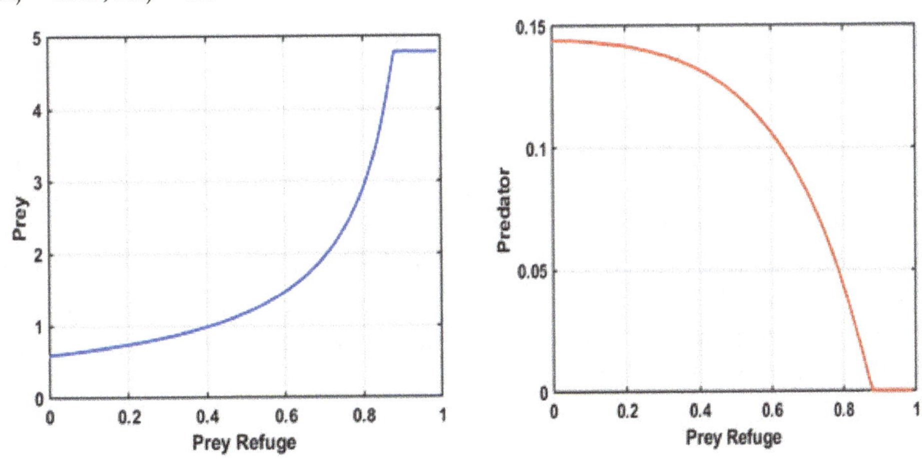

a) b)

The level of ϕ below which the refuges bring about their stabilizing effect is revealed to be sensitive to predator's effectiveness of hunting and metabolic expenses, revealing that prey refuge effects will need to be carefully managed in conservation efforts. The ϕ threshold at which refuges have their stabilizing effect is found to be sensitive to predator hunting efficiency and metabolic costs, suggesting that refuge effects will need to be precisely calibrated in conservation practice. These results agree with theoretical expectations of bi-stable systems, where moderate variation in refuge availability leads to large regime changes in population dynamics. Three regimes of the system response to increasing refuge availability are revealed by the analysis. Firstly, prey populations benefit directly from improved protection, while predator populations decline gradually. The system becomes stable at intermediate levels of refuge, when more protection results in decreasing benefits for the prey but disastrous effects on the predators. Finally, beyond the critical level, the ecosystem enters another stable regime where predators are unsustainable. This nonlinear response underscores the importance of understanding how protective processes like refuges can have propagating effects across ecological communities. The research offers useful lessons in wildlife management that optimal refuge design is a matter of compromise between the protection of prey and keeping viable predator populations to maintain ecosystem integrity.

4.2 Anti-Predator Behavior and Fear Effects

The general biological hypotheses assume that prey reproductive rates remain the same when predators or anti-predator behavior is absent. However, when prey undergo highly developed defense mechanisms or are exposed to the presence of high predator densities, their reproductive capacity declines drastically and, under extreme circumstances, even to zero. This decline in reproduction follows directly from the intensity of anti-predator behavior or predator density—i.e., with intensifying fear-based behavior or predator density, prey fertility declines. Experimental research supports the phenomenon, demonstrating that the mere threat of predation causes an increase in prey death. For instance, in a seminal experiment, researchers contrasted grasshopper nymph survival when predators were absent and when spiders had disabled mouthparts. Predators present actually caused a 20% rise in nymph death merely because they were present, confirming that threat of predation alone—separate from actual consumption—can significantly alter prey demographics by increasing stress-provoked mortality.

Figure 10. Fear effect in the dynamics of Model (6) with Crowly-Martin Functional Response The parameter values are are $r = 3$, $a = 0.6$, $c = 0.5$, $\phi = 0.3$, $h = 0.02$, $b = 0.01$, $\beta = 2$, $\lambda = 0.5$, $e = 0.5$, $m = 0.025$, $n = 0.5$, $h_1 = 0.01$, $M_1 = 1$, $h_2 = 0.05$, $M_2 = 1.5$

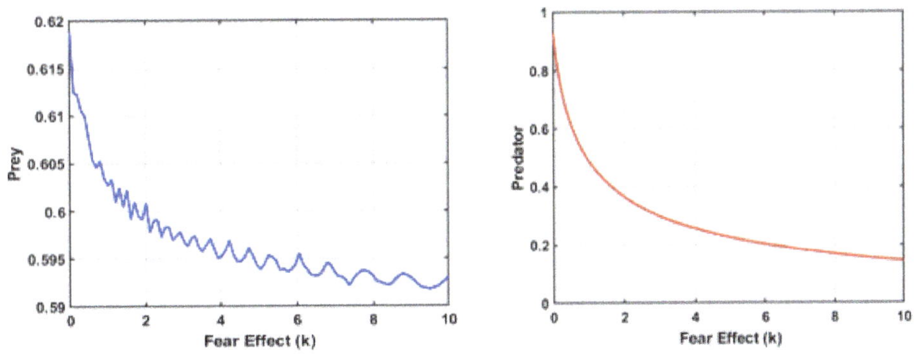

a) b)

The study investigates the effect of fear on predator-prey dynamics by examining the effect of two most critical parameters: *k*, representing fear-induced reduction in prey birth rate, and *n*, representing fear-induced prey death rate. The value of the fear parameter *k* was raised to reduce both prey and predator population densities (Figure 10(a) and 10(b)). This is because higher levels of fear make the prey engage in anti-predator acts that compromise their reproductive success, leading to a reduction in the prey population. Therefore, predator populations also decrease due to food deficiency.

Figure 11. Death rate due to fear in the dynamics of Model (6) with Crowly-Martin Functional Response The parameter values are $r = 3$, $a = 0.6$, $c = 0.5$, $\phi = 0.3$, $h = 0.02$, $b = 0.01$, $\beta = 2$, $\lambda = 0.5$, $e = 0.5$, $m = 0.025$, $k = 10$, $h_1 = 0.01$, $M_1 = 1$, $h_2 = 0.05$, $M_2 = 1.5$

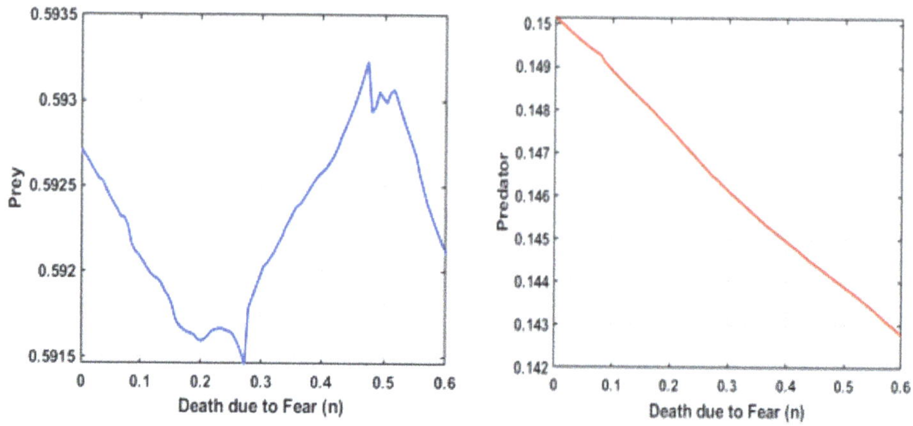

a) b)

In other cases, however, a pattern that seems counterintuitive emerges—when k is increased, there is moderate growth in the prey population. This occurs because a decrease in predator number (through fear-induced scarcity of prey) can, under some conditions, lower predation pressure to the level of offsetting the negative reproductive effect of fear. Thus, when the positive effect of lowered predators outweighs the decline in prey reproduction due to fear, a temporary build-up of prey density occurs.

Similarly, for fear parameter n, fear-induced mortality (e.g., stress deaths) simulated, higher values tend to suppress both prey and predator population (Figure 11(a) and 11(b)). Higher n leads to higher prey mortality, in turn depriving predators of food. However, within certain ranges, prey density experiences an abrupt spike. This rebound takes place when the population of predators has declined so drastically that the following release from predation pressure allows for the prey population to rebound strongly, despite the heavy death caused by fear.

4.3 Harvesting

The addition of harvesting in predator-prey models is necessary in order to account for human impact on populations, e.g., fishing, hunting, or farming. Linear harvesting—where rates of removal are proportional to population sizes—provides a tractable way of replicating sustainable yield or overexploitation. This type of model reveals critical thresholds: moderate rates of harvesting will stabilize populations by damping oscillations, but high levels of harvesting lead to extinction or trophic cascades. Fisheries models, for instance, illustrate how predators' overharvesting creates prey outbreaks, destabilizing a whole ecosystem. Thus, the measurement of harvesting impacts reconciles ecological preservation and resource removal.

Figure 12. Effect of prey harvesting in the dynamics of Model (6) with Crowly-Martin Functional Response The parameter values are $r = 3$, $a = 0.6$, $c = 0.5$, $\phi = 0.3$, $h = 0.02$, $b = 0.01$, $\beta = 2$, $\lambda = 0.5$, $e = 0.5$, $m = 0.025$, $k = 10$, $h_1 = 0.01$, $n = 0.5$, $h_2 = 0.05$, $M_2 = 1.5$

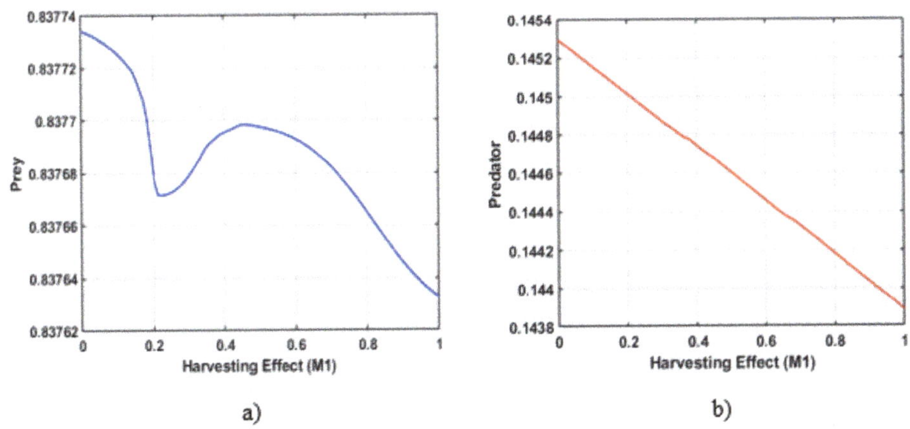

Figure 13. Effect of predator harvesting in the dynamics of Model (6) with Crowly-Martin Functional Response The parameter values are $r = 3$, $a = 0.6$, $c = 0.5$, $\phi = 0.3$, $h = 0.02$, $b = 0.01$, $\beta = 2$, $\lambda = 0.5$, $e = 0.5$, $m = 0.025$, $k = 10$, $h_1 = 0.01$, $n = 0.5$, $h_2 = 0.05$, $M_1 = 1$

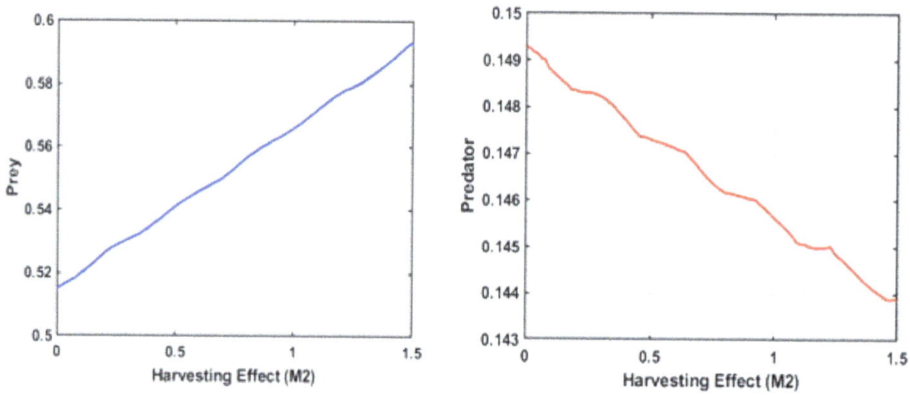

a) b)

The study reveals that complete system collapse (extinction of the predator and prey) occurs at even greater harvesting intensities, demonstrating how groups of predators are a measure of ecosystem stress at an early point (Figure 12(a) and 12(b)). The results have important implications for wildlife management and fishery regulation, forecasting that monitoring of predator populations would enable detection of the thresholds of impending collapse before they are actually reached.

The non-linear dynamics displayed serve to underscore the fact that ecosystems have the ability to present themselves in stable conditions up until sudden, irreversible alterations occur once thresholds are passed. Our findings agree with ecological theory that top-down regulation (e.g., predation) and bottom-up regulation (e.g., resource availability) intersect subtly under the influence of anthropogenic drivers. This work presents a quantitative method for identifying sustainable harvest levels with regard to consideration of the complex interdependencies found in predator-prey systems. On the other hand, the reduction on the population of predator cause increases in the population of prey as shown in Figure 13(a) and 13(b).

6. STOCHASTIC EXTENSION OF MODEL (6)

In natural ecosystems, population dynamics are rarely governed by deterministic interactions alone. Environmental fluctuations resulting from seasonal changes, climatic variability, habitat disturbances, and unpredictable predator–prey encounters inevitably introduce stochasticity into the system. Such random disturbances can substantially affect species persistence, extinction probabilities, and oscillatory behavior, and in some cases, even reverse the stability predicted by deterministic models. To better capture these ecological realities, it is essential to include noise terms in the governing equations, leading to stochastic differential equation formulations of predator–prey models.

Motivated by these considerations, we will construct an advanced predator–prey model that extends the deterministic framework to a stochastic one by incorporating environmental noise into key population growth rates. This formulation enhances ecological realism and provides valuable insight into how environmental variability—represented by independent random processes—shapes collective behaviors such as fear effects, prey refuge use, harvesting intensity, and functional responses. As a result, the stochastic model offers a more accurate and ecologically meaningful representation of population dynamics under natural environmental variability. Therefore, the stochastic version of model (6) can be expressed as

$$\begin{aligned} \frac{dx}{dt} &= \frac{rx}{1+ky} - (1+ny)ax - cx^2 - \frac{\beta(1-\phi)xy}{(1+h(1-\phi)x)(1+by)} - h_1M_1x + \sigma_1 xW_1(_t \\ \frac{dy}{dt} &= \frac{\lambda\beta(1-\phi)xy}{(1+h(1-\phi)x)(1+by)} - ey - my^2 - h_2M_2y + \sigma_2 yW_2(_t \end{aligned} \tag{7}$$

6.1 Preliminaries

In this subsection, we introduce the foundational concepts and tools necessary for the subsequent theoretical developments. We begin by establishing the probabilistic framework that underpins the stochastic modeling approach adopted in this work. Specifically, let $(\Omega, f, \{f_t \geq 0, p\}$ denote a complete filtered probability space, where the filtration $\{f_t \geq 0\}$ is assumed to satisfy the standard conditions (namely, right-continuity and completeness with respect to p -null sets in f_0. We consider a stochastic process $z(t) \in \mathfrak{R}^n$evolving according to a general stochastic integral equation influenced by continuous disturbances:

$$dz(t) = F_1(z(t),t)\,dt + F_2(z(t),t)\,dW(t) \tag{8}$$

where the time variable t lies within a finite interval $[0, T]$, and the system dynamics are defined by the following components:

$F_1 : \mathfrak{R}^n \times \mathfrak{R}_+ \rightarrow \mathfrak{R}^n$ denotes the deterministic drift term;

$F_2 : \mathfrak{R}^n \times \mathfrak{R}_+ \rightarrow \mathfrak{R}^{n \times d}$ represents the diffusion coefficient governing the continuous noise.

The functions $F_1(z(t),t)$ and $F_2(z(t),t)$ are assumed to be jointly measurable in their respective domains. The process $W(t)$ denotes a n-dimensional standard Brownian motion, which captures the effect of continuous stochastic perturbations.

To analyze such systems, we define the infinitesimal generator$L$corresponding to the stochastic process governed by equation (8). For any test function G in $C^{1,2}($ $\mathfrak{R}^n \times \mathfrak{R}_+;\mathfrak{R}_+)$,, the generator is given by:

$$LG(z,t)= G_t(z(t),t)+G_z(z(t),t)F_1(z(t),t)+\frac{1}{2}Tr\left[F_1{}'(z(t),t)G_{ss}(z(t),t)F_2(z(t),t)\right].$$

Here,

$G_t = \frac{\partial G}{\partial t}$ is the partial derivative with respect to time;

$G_t = \left(\frac{\partial G}{\partial s_i}, \ldots\ldots, \frac{\partial G}{\partial s_t}\right)$ denotes the gradient with respect to the state variables;

$G_{ss} = \left(\frac{\partial^2 G}{\partial s_i \partial s_j}\right)$ is the Hessian matrix of second-order derivatives.

Using the generator L, the stochastic Itô formula can be written as:

$$dG(z(t),t)= LG(z(t),t)dt + G_z(z(t),t)F_2(z(t),t)dW(t) \tag{9}$$

Lemma 6.1.1. Let $Q \in C(\Gamma 0,+\infty) \times \Omega,(0,+\infty)$ be strictly positive and continuous stochastic process. Suppose there exist constant $A_1 > 0$ and $A_2 > 0$ such that for all $t \geq 0$,

$$\ln Q(t)\geq A_1 t - A_2\int_0^t Q(s)ds + T(t),$$

where $T \in C(\Gamma 0,+\infty) \times \Omega, \mathfrak{R})$ is a continuous process satisfying

$$\lim_{t\to\infty}\frac{T(t)}{t} = 0,$$

then

$$\lim_{t\to\infty}(Q(t))\geq \frac{A_1}{A_2},$$

a.s.

6.2 The Existence of Solution

Theorem 6.2.1. For any initial condition $(x(0),y(0)) \in R_+^2$ where $x(0) > 0, y(0) > 0$. The solution $(x(t),y(t))$ of system (7) will remain in R_+^2 with probability one for all time $t \geq 1$ almost surely.

Proof: It is enough to demonstrate that $\Psi_e = \infty$, is almost certainly true in order to demonstrate that the solution is global. Let n_0 be a nonnegative integer so that (x_0, y_0) is contained within interval $\left[\frac{1}{n_0}, n_0\right]$. Therefore, for every integer $n \geq n_0$ the stopping time will be

$$\Psi_n = \inf\left\{t \in [0, \Psi_e): \min\left\{(x(t),y(t)\right\} \leq \tfrac{1}{n}, or \max\left\{(x(t),y(t)\right\} \geq n\right\},$$

where Ψ_n is increasing when $n \rightarrow \infty$. Let $\Psi_\infty = \lim_{x\rightarrow\infty} \Psi_n$, then we have $\Psi_\infty \leq \Psi_e$, Therefore for proof, we just need to prove that $\Psi_\infty = \infty$. So we can do it through contradiction, suppose $\Psi_\infty \leq \Psi_e$, then there should be pair of constants $\varsigma \in (0,1)$ and $T > 0$. Which implies that

$$Q(\Psi_\infty < T) > \varsigma.$$

Hence, there exist $n_1 \geq n_0$ such that $n \geq n_1$.

$$Q(\varpi_\infty < T) > \varsigma.$$

Where $\varpi_n = \left\{\Psi_n \leq T\right\}$. Now we define C^2 -function $V: R_+^2 \rightarrow R$ as

$$V = x - \frac{e}{2\lambda\beta(1-\phi)} - \frac{e}{2\lambda\beta(1-\phi)} \ln \frac{2\lambda\beta(1-\phi)x}{e} + \tfrac{1}{\lambda}(y - 1 - \ln y).$$

For simplicity we let $C = \frac{e}{2\lambda\beta(1-\phi)}$, $V_1(x,y) = x - C - C\ln\frac{2\lambda\beta(1-\phi)x}{e}$ and $dV_2 = \frac{1}{\lambda}(y - 1 - \ln y)$.

Using Ito's formula, we have

$$dV(x,y) = LV(x,y)dt + (\sigma_1 x - C\sigma_1)dW_1(t) + \left(\tfrac{\sigma_2 y}{\lambda} - \tfrac{\sigma_2}{y}\right)dW_2(t), \tag{i}$$

Let's explain each term for more understanding. For this purpose, now we first take

$$V_1(x,y) = x - C - C\ln\frac{2\lambda\beta(1-\phi)x}{e}$$

We compute first and 2nd derivatives

$$\frac{\partial V_1}{\partial x} = 1 - \frac{C}{x}, \ \frac{\partial^2 V_1}{\partial x^2} = \frac{C}{x^2}$$

Now using Ito's formula, we have

$$dx = f_1(x,y)\,dt + \sigma_1 x W_1(t)$$

$$dV_1 = \left(\frac{\partial V_1}{\partial x} f_1(x,y) + \frac{1}{2}\frac{\partial^2 V_1}{\partial x^2}\sigma_1{}^2 x^2\right)dt + \left(\frac{\partial V_1}{\partial x}\sigma_1 x\right)dW_1(t).$$

$$dV_1 = \left(\left(1 - \frac{C}{x}\right)f_1(x,y) + \frac{1}{2}\frac{C}{x^2}\sigma_1{}^2 x^2\right)dt + \left(1 - \frac{C}{x}\right)\sigma_1 x dW_1(t).$$

$$dV_1 = \left(f_1(x,y) - \frac{C}{x} f_1(x,y) + \frac{C}{2}\sigma_1{}^2\right)dt + (\sigma_1 x - C\sigma_1)dW_1(t).$$

(a)

Similarly for $dV_2 = \frac{1}{\lambda}(y - 1 - \ln y)$.
We compute first and 2nd derivatives

$$\frac{\partial V_1}{\partial x} = \frac{1}{\lambda}\left(1 - \frac{1}{y}\right), \ \frac{\partial^2 V_1}{\partial x^2} = \frac{1}{\lambda y^2}$$

Now using Ito's formula, we have

$$dy = f_1(x,y)\,dt + \sigma_2 y W_2(t)$$

$$dV_2 = \left(\frac{\partial V_2}{\partial y} f_2(x,y) + \frac{1}{2}\frac{\partial^2 V_2}{\partial y^2}\sigma_2{}^2 y^2\right)dt + \left(\frac{\partial V_2}{\partial y}\sigma_2 y\right)dW_2(t).$$

$$dV_2 = \left(\frac{1}{\lambda}\left(1 - \frac{1}{y}\right)f_2(x,y) + \frac{1}{2}\cdot\frac{1}{\lambda y^2}\sigma_2{}^2 y^2\right)dt + \frac{1}{\lambda}\left(1 - \frac{1}{y}\right)\sigma_2 y dW_2(t).$$

$$dV_2 = \left(\frac{f_2(x,y)}{\lambda} - \frac{f_2(x,y)}{\lambda y} + \frac{1}{2\lambda}\sigma_2{}^2\right)dt + \left(\frac{\sigma_2 y}{\lambda} - \frac{\sigma_2}{y}\right)dW_2(t).$$

(b)

No we combine (a) and (b), $dV = dV_1 + dV_2$. This implies that

$$dV = f_1(x,y) - \frac{C}{x} f_1(x,y) + \frac{C}{2}\sigma_1{}^2 + \frac{f_2(x,y)}{\lambda} - \frac{f_2(x,y)}{\lambda y} + \frac{1}{2\lambda}\sigma_2{}^2.$$

Now we substitute the values of $f_1(x,y)$ and $f_2(x,y)$, we have

$$LV(x,y)=\left[\frac{rx}{1+ky}-(1+ny)ax-cx^2-\frac{\beta(1-\phi)xy}{(1+h(1-\phi)x)(1+by)}-h_1M_1x\right]$$
$$-\frac{C}{x}\left[\frac{rx}{1+ky}-(1+ny)ax-cx^2-\frac{\beta(1-\phi)xy}{(1+h(1-\phi)x)(1+by)}-h_1M_1x\right]$$
$$+\frac{C}{2}\sigma_1{}^2+\frac{1}{\lambda}\left[\frac{\lambda\beta(1-\phi)xy}{(1+h(1-\phi)x)(1+by)}-ey-my^2-h_2M_2y\right]$$
$$-\frac{1}{\lambda y}\left[\frac{\lambda\beta(1-\phi)xy}{(1+h(1-\phi)x)(1+by)}-ey-my^2-h_2M_2y\right]+\frac{1}{2\lambda}\sigma_2{}^2. \quad \text{I}$$

Let's simplify each term one by one

$$-\frac{C}{x}f_1(x,y)=-C\left[\frac{r}{1+ky}-(1+ny)a-cx-\frac{\beta(1-\phi)y}{(1+h(1-\phi)x)(1+by)}-h_1M_1\right]$$
$$=-\frac{rC}{1+ky}+(1+ny)aC-cxC+\frac{\beta(1-\phi)Cy}{(1+h(1-\phi)x)(1+by)}+Ch_1M_1$$

Similarly, $-\frac{f_2(x,y)}{\lambda y}=-\frac{\beta(1-\phi)x}{(1+h(1-\phi)x)(1+by)}+\frac{e}{\lambda}+\frac{my}{\lambda}+\frac{h_2M_2}{\lambda}$.
Substitute all values of terms in equation I, we have

$$dV=\frac{rx}{1+ky}-(1+ny)ax-cx^2-\frac{\beta(1-\phi)xy}{(1+h(1-\phi)x)(1+by)}-h_1M_1x$$
$$-\frac{rC}{1+ky}+(1+ny)aC-cxC+\frac{\beta(1-\phi)Cy}{(1+h(1-\phi)x)(1+by)}+Ch_1M_1$$
$$+\frac{\beta(1-\phi)xy}{(1+h(1-\phi)x)(1+by)}-\frac{ey}{\lambda}-\frac{my^2}{\lambda}-\frac{h_2M_2y}{\lambda}$$
$$-\frac{\beta(1-\phi)x}{(1+h(1-\phi)x)(1+by)}+\frac{e}{\lambda}+\frac{my}{\lambda}+\frac{h_2M_2}{\lambda}.$$
$$\leq -cx^2+\left[\frac{r}{1+ky}\right]x+\left[naC+\frac{\beta(1-\phi)C}{(1+h(1-\phi)}\right]y+aC+Ch_1M_1++\frac{e}{\lambda}+\frac{my}{\lambda}+\frac{h_2M_2}{\lambda}.$$

$$\leq aC+Ch_1M_1+\frac{e}{\lambda}+\frac{my}{\lambda}+\frac{h_2M_2}{\lambda}+\widetilde{D}=D.$$
Here

$$\widetilde{D}=\sup_{(x,y)\in(0,\infty)}\left\{-cx^2+\left[\frac{r}{1+ky}\right]x+\left[naC+\frac{\beta(1-\phi)C}{(1+h(1-\phi)}\right]y\right\}.$$

Integrate and take expectation of (i) for $T>0$, we have

$$EV(x(\Psi_n\wedge T),y(\Psi_n\wedge T)\leq V(x(0),y(0))+DE(\Psi_n\wedge T)\leq V(x(0),y(0))+DT.$$
Therefore, we can see for every $\theta\in\varpi_n$, $x(\Psi_n,\theta)$or $y(\Psi_n,\theta)$is equal to n or $\frac{1}{n}$.

$$V(x(\Psi_n),y(\Psi_n)) \geq \left[n - \frac{e}{2\lambda\beta(1-\phi)} - \frac{e}{2\lambda\beta(1-\phi)}\ln\frac{2\lambda\beta(1-\phi)n}{e}\right]$$
$$\wedge\left[\frac{1}{n} - \frac{e}{2\lambda\beta(1-\phi)} - \frac{e}{2\lambda\beta(1-\phi)}\ln\frac{2\lambda\beta(1-\phi)}{ne}\right]$$
$$\wedge\left[\frac{1}{\lambda}(n-1-\ln n)\right]\wedge\left[\frac{1}{\lambda}(\frac{1}{n}-1-\ln n)\right].$$

This contradict the bounded expectation when $n \to \infty$,

$$\infty > V(x(0),y(0)) + DT = \infty .$$

Therefore, this implies that $\Psi_\infty = \infty$.

This completes the proof.

6.3 The Extinction of both prey and predator populations

Theorem 6.3.1. Let $(x(t),y(t))$ denotes the solution of model (7) with any strictly positive initial condition $(x(0),y(0)) \in \mathfrak{R}^2_+$. Then:

- If $2(r - h_1M_1) < \sigma_1{}^2$, the prey population will be extinct a.s., that is

$$\lim_{x\to\infty} x(t) = 0.$$

- If $\left(e + h_2M_2 + \frac{\sigma_2{}^2}{2}\right) > 0$, the predator population will be extinct a.s., that is

$$\lim_{x\to\infty} y(t) = 0.$$

Proof: In the beginning of this proof, we define a function $G_1(x,t) = \ln(x(t)) \in C^{1,2}(\mathfrak{R}^n \times \mathfrak{R}_+;\mathfrak{R}_+)$.Applying Ito formula on$G_1$, we obtain

$$dG_1(x(t),t) = LG_1(x(t),t)dt + \sigma_1 dW_1(t) \tag{10}$$

where

$$LG_1(x(t),t)$$

$$= \frac{r}{1+ky} - (1+ny)a - cx - \frac{\beta(1-\phi)y}{(1+h(1-\phi)x)(1+by)} - h_1M_1 - \frac{\sigma_1{}^2}{2} \tag{11}$$

This implies

$$LG_1(x(t),t) \leq r - h_1M_1 - \frac{\sigma_1{}^2}{2} \tag{12}$$

Substituting (12) into (10), integrating both sides on the interval $[0, t]$ and then dividing by t we get

$$\frac{\ln(x(t))}{t} \leq r - h_1 M_1 - \frac{\sigma_1^{\ 2}}{2} + \frac{\sigma_1 W_1}{t} + \frac{\ln(x(0))}{t} \tag{13}$$

Given that $2(r - h_1 M_1) < \sigma_1^{\ 2}$ and observing that $\frac{\sigma_1 W_1}{t} + \frac{\ln(x(0))}{t}$ as $t \to \infty$, it follows that

$$\lim_{x\to\infty}\sup\frac{\ln(x(t))}{t} \leq r - h_1 M_1 - \frac{\sigma_1^{\ 2}}{2} < 0,$$

which implies $\lim_{x\to\infty} x(t) = 0$, a.s.

Next, we define another function $G_2(y,t) = \ln(y(t))$ which belongs to $C^{1,2}(\mathfrak{R}^n \times \mathfrak{R}_+; \mathfrak{R}_+)$.

By applying Ito formula to G_2, we obtain

$$dG_2(y(t),t) = LG_2(y(t),t)dt + \sigma_2 dW_2(t) \tag{14}$$

where

$$dG_2(y(t),t) = \frac{\lambda\beta(1-\phi)x}{(1+h(1-\phi)x)(1+by)} - e - my - h_2 M_2 - \frac{\sigma_2^{\ 2}}{2}$$

$$\leq \lambda\beta(1-\phi)x - e - h_2 M_2 - \frac{\sigma_2^{\ 2}}{2} \tag{15}$$

By substituting (15) into (14), integrating both sides over the interval $[0, t]$ and subsequently dividing through by t we get

$$\frac{\ln(y(t))}{t} \leq \frac{1}{t}\left[\lambda\beta(1-\phi)\int_0^t x(s)\,ds + \ln(y(0)) + \sigma_2 W_2\right] - e - h_2 M_2 - \frac{\sigma_2^{\ 2}}{2} \tag{16}$$

Given that $(e + h_2 M_2 + \frac{\sigma_2^{\ 2}}{2}) > 0$, and noting that $\frac{1}{t}\left[\lambda\beta(1-\phi)\int_0^t x(s)\,ds + \ln(y(0)) + \sigma_2 W_2\right]$ as $t \to \infty$, it follows that

$$\lim_{x\to\infty}\sup\frac{\ln(y(t))}{t} \leq -(e + h_2 M_2 + \frac{\sigma_2^{\ 2}}{2}) < 0$$

which implies $\lim_{x\to\infty} y(t) = 0$,a.s.

6.3 Long-Term Survival of Prey

Theorem 6.4.1. Let $(x(t),y(t))$ be the unique global positive solution of model (7) corresponding to any strictly positive initial condition $(x(0),y(0)) \in \Re_+^2$. If $\left(r - a - h_1 - M_1 - \frac{\sigma_1^2}{2}\right) > 0$, then the prey population persists in the time-average sense. More precisely, almost surely

$$\liminf_{x \to \infty} \langle x(t) \rangle \geq \frac{r - a - h_1 - M_1 - \frac{\sigma_1^2}{2}}{c}.$$

Proof: From the proof of Theorem 6.3.1, we have

$$LG_1(x(t),t) = \frac{r}{1+ky} - (1+ny)a - cx - \frac{\beta(1-\phi)y}{(1+h(1-\phi)x)(1+by)} - h_1 M_1 - \frac{\sigma_1^2}{2}$$

$$\geq r - rky - (1+ny)a - cx - \beta(1-\phi)y - h_1 M_1 - \frac{\sigma_1^2}{2},$$

which leads

$$LG_1(x(t),t) \geq r - h_1 M_1 - \frac{\sigma_1^2}{2} - cx - (r + na + \beta(1-\phi)y) \tag{17}$$

Inserting (17) in (10), then integrating both sides over the interval $[0,t]$ and subsequently dividing through by t we get

$$\frac{\ln(x(t))}{t} \geq r - a - h_1 M_1 - \frac{\sigma_1^2}{2} - \frac{c}{t}\int_0^t x(s)\,ds + M_1(t) \tag{18}$$

where,

$$M_1(t) = \frac{1}{t}\left[\sigma_1 W_1 + \ln(x(0)) - (r + na + \beta(1-\phi))\int_0^t y(s)\,ds\right].$$

Inequality (18) can be written as follows:

$$\ln(x(t)) \geq \left(r - a - h_1 M_1 - \frac{\sigma_1^2}{2}\right)t - c\int_0^t x(s)\,ds + tM_1(t) \tag{19}$$

Since the condition $r - a - h_1 M_1 - \frac{\sigma_1^2}{2} > 0$, we apply Lemma 6.1.1 to inequality (19) to conclude that:

$$\liminf_{x\to\infty} \langle x(t)\rangle \geq \frac{r - a - h_1 - M_1 - \frac{\sigma_1^2}{2}}{c} > 0.$$

6.4 Numerical Analysis of the Model

To conduct reliable and meaningful numerical experiments with the stochastic model (7), we employ a Milstein numerical scheme specifically designed to account for the presence of Brownian perturbations in the system. This scheme has been widely recognized as a powerful and accurate tool for solving stochastic differential equations, particularly in cases where the noise term enters the model in a multiplicative form. Unlike the simpler Euler–Maruyama method, which is often limited in accuracy due to its neglect of certain higher-order stochastic components, the Milstein approach incorporates additional correction terms that capture higher-order effects of the stochastic integrals. As a result, it offers improved convergence properties and a more faithful representation of the system's underlying stochastic dynamics. This enhanced level of precision is critical when investigating ecological systems such as prey–predator interactions, where small variations introduced by noise can have significant long-term impacts on the population trajectories and stability characteristics of the model.

We partition the time interval $[0, T]$ into $N^* \in N$ equal subintervals, each of length $\Delta t = \frac{T}{N^*}$. At every discrete time step $i \in \{0, 1, 2, ...N - 1\}$, the state variables x_i, y_i are updated according to the numerical scheme.

The increments of the Brownian motions are expressed as

$$\Delta W_{j,i} = W_j(t_{i+1}) - W_j(t_i) = \sqrt{\Delta t \zeta_{ji}},$$

where $\sqrt{\Delta t \zeta_{ji}} \sim N(0,1)$ for $j \in \{1,2\}$.

Thus, the Milstein numerical scheme takes the form:

$$x_{i+1} = x_i + \Delta t\left(\frac{rx_i}{1 + ky} - (1 + ny)ax_i - cx_i^2 - \frac{\beta(1 - \phi)x_iy_i}{(1 + h(1 - \phi)x_i)(1 + by)} - h_1M_1x_i\right)$$

$$+\sigma_1 x_i \Delta W_{1,i} + \frac{\sigma_1^2}{2} x_i(\Delta W^2_{1,i} - \Delta t),$$

$$y_{i+1} = y_i + \Delta t\left(\frac{\lambda\beta(1 - \phi)x_iy_i}{(1 + h(1 - \phi)x_i)(1 + by)} - ey_i - my_i^2 - h_2M_2y_i\right)$$

$$+\sigma_2 y_i \Delta W_{2,i} + \frac{\sigma_2^2}{2} y_i(\Delta W^2_{2,i} - \Delta t),$$

Example 6.4.1 To validate the results stated in Theorem 6.3.1, we use the following parameter values for the model:

$$\beta = 2, \phi = 0.3, \lambda = 0.9, r = 0.6, h = 0.02, e = 0.8, k = 10, h_1 = 0.3$$
$$h_2 = 0.1, M_1 = 2, M_2 = 1.5, n = 0.5, b = 0.6, c = 0.5, a = 0.6, m = 0.1$$
$$\sigma_1 = \sigma_2 = 0.5.$$

We also set the initial conditions as $x(0) = 0.4, y(0) = 0.3$ and choose a time step of $\Delta t = 0.1$

Using these values, we compute

$$\left(r - h_1 M_1 - \frac{\sigma_1^{\ 2}}{2}\right) = -0.125 < 0,$$
and

$$\left(e - h_2 M_2 - \frac{\sigma_2^{\ 2}}{2}\right) = 1.075 > 0.$$

As we can clearly see, according to the theoretical results, this implies that both the prey and predator populations will become extinct almost surely. The simulation results presented in Figure 14 corroborate these conclusions.

When both of the noise levels are high enough ($\sigma_1 = \sigma_2 = 0.5.$), the impact of harvesting and environmental stochasticity together force the prey population to extinction because their net growth rate becomes negative. While the predator's threshold may remain positive—i.e., they would mathematically survive in isolation—their eventual demise comes after that of the prey due to starvation. This domino effect, where extinction of prey results in extinction of predator, shows how overexploitation and environmental noise can destabilize an ecosystem into irreversible loss of both species. From simulation results, we can see that high noise and intensive harvesting cause extinction of prey and predators, lending credence to the necessity for sustainable management measures to shield against such losses.

Figure 14. Simulation outcomes of the stochastic model (7) compared with its deterministic version using the parameter values specified in Example 6.4.1

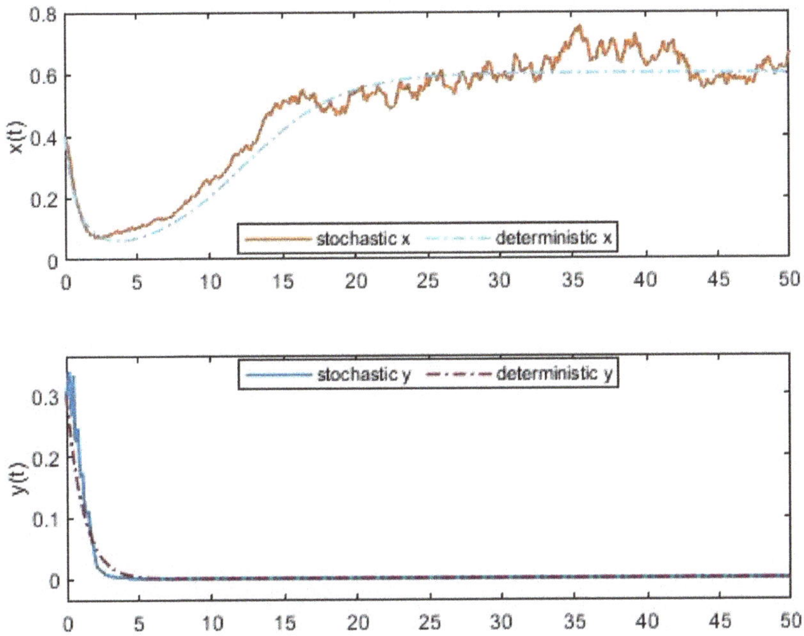

Example 6.4.2. Theorem 6.4.1. represents one of the central results of this chapter. To verify its validity, we adopt the same parameter set as in Example 6.4.1, with the exception of three parameters, which are modified to $r = 1, h = 0.05, \sigma_1 = 0.09$. With these adjustments, we obtain

$$\left(r - a - h_1 M_1 - \frac{\sigma_1^{\ 2}}{2}\right) = 0.2960 > 0.$$

Moreover, the long-term lower bound of the prey population is estimated as:

$$\liminf_{x\to\infty} \langle x(t)\rangle \geq \frac{r - a - h_1 - M_1 - \frac{\sigma_1^{\ 2}}{2}}{c} = 0.5919 > 0.$$

According to Theorem 6.4.1, meeting this inequality ensures the long-term persistence of the prey population. The numerical results displayed in Figure 15 corroborate this theoretical prediction, clearly illustrating the sustained presence of the prey species over time.

When the net prey growth rate the prey population thrives with strong intrinsic growth and reduced environmental fluctuation. Nevertheless, even when prey is abundant, the predator will become extinct if its mortality rate and competition coefficient are too large.

Figure 15. Simulation outcomes of the stochastic model (7) compared with its deterministic version, using the parameter values specified in Example 6.4.2

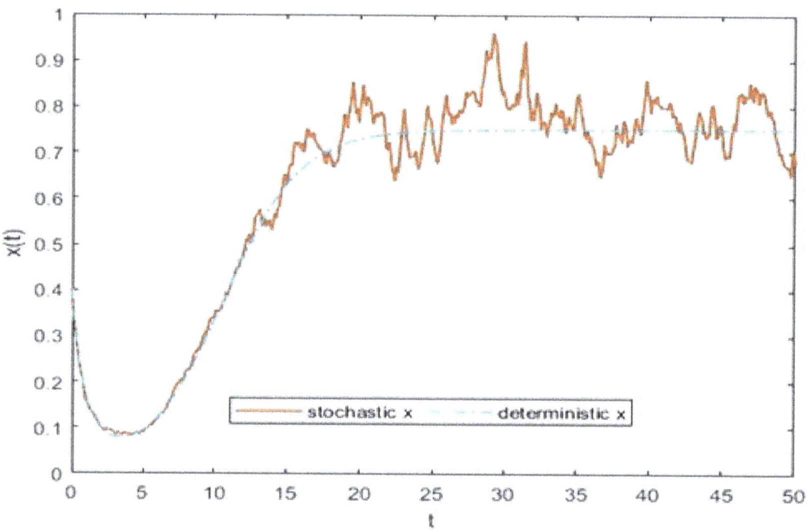

Increasing up intra-species competition among predators, while a small stabilizes prey populations, preventing the boom-bust cycles that would otherwise transiently sustain predators. As such, despite the existence of prey persistence, rampant predator death and competition—coupled with an insufficient degree of predation efficiency—have the ability to crash the predator population. This example illustrates that prey survival alone will not guarantee predator persistence if other ecological pressures overwhelm them.

Example 6.4.3. In this example, we investigate the influence of white noise on the dynamics of the prey population to validate the realism of the stochastic model. Using the same parameter values listed in Example 6.4.2 and only changing the value of σ_1 to be large enough, as $\sigma_1 = 0.8$.According to these values, we observe that in the stochastic model, the prey population dies out, whereas in the deterministic model, it persists, as illustrated in Figure 16.

In the present example, we conduct a detailed examination of the effect that white noise exerts on the overall dynamics and long-term behavior of the prey population, with the primary aim of assessing and validating the realism and applicability of the proposed stochastic model. For this investigation, we employ exactly the same set of parameter values as those specified in Example 6.4.2, with the single modification that the value of σ_1 is increased to a sufficiently large magnitude in order to highlight the impact of random fluctuations. Based on these adjusted values, our observations reveal a clear distinction between the outcomes predicted by the stochastic and deterministic frameworks. Specifically, in the stochastic model, the prey population eventually dies out as a direct consequence of the intensified noise effect, whereas in the deterministic model, the prey population can persist over time. This contrast in behavior between the two modeling approaches is visually presented in Figure 16, which provides an intuitive graphical representation of the results.

Figure 16. Simulation outcomes of the stochastic model (7) compared with its deterministic version, using the parameter values specified in Example 6.4.3

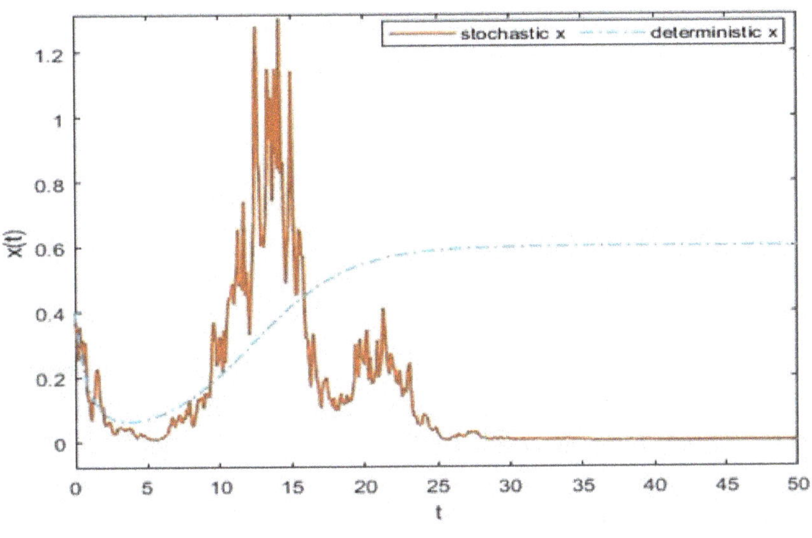

Example 6.4.4. One of the most significant parameters that exerts a negative influence on the overall dynamics and long-term behavior of the prey population is M_1. In particular, a decrease in the value of this parameter tends to promote an increase in the size of the prey population over time. To clearly illustrate this relationship, we present an example in which the same set of parameter values as those used in Example 6.4.2 are employed, with the sole exception that the value of M_1 is intentionally reduced to 0.5 in order to observe the resulting changes. Under these modified conditions, the size of the prey population rises noticeably, increasing from an initial equilibrium value of 0.5919 to a higher value of 0.7419. This notable change can be more intuitively appreciated through the graphical depiction

provided in Figure 17, which offers a visual representation of how the reduction in the parameter directly contributes to the observed growth in the prey population.

Figure 17. Simulation outcomes of the stochastic model (7) compared with its deterministic version, using the parameter values specified in Example 6.4.4

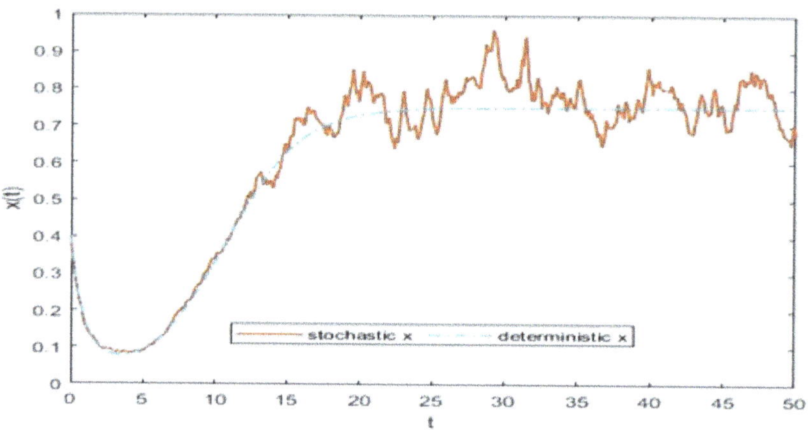

7. FUTURE RESEARCH DIRECTION

The presented modeling framework highlights the prominence of behavioral processes—i.e., predator refuge for the prey, fear effects, and harvesting—in predetermining predator-prey dynamics, setting a strong platform for forthcoming ecological and computational research. While our deterministic and stochastic models provide a rich understanding of population stability and risk of extinction, integration of deep learning with AI-enriched behavioral modeling can change the paradigm of predicting and managing intricate ecosystems. Advanced neural networks and reinforcement learning mechanisms can replicate adaptive predator-prey dynamics in dynamic systems, such as instantaneous behavioral outputs unobtainable through traditional differential equations. For instance, deep reinforcement learning can forecast how prey evolve best refuge-use strategies with respect to varying levels of predation pressure, or predators modify foraging strategies to accommodate fear-driven prey reactions. Additionally, hybrid models that integrate mechanistic equations with machine learning can enhance predictive performance by parameterizing parameters from empirical observations to offer more valid conservation planning.

Through the integration of ecological theory and computational technology, future studies would be able to open up new avenues in behavioral ecology, ranging from conservation of wildlife to invasive species control, and open a window into AI-facilitated ecological decision-making. In addition, the thresholds for extinction of species in a stochastic environment can be useful for using stochastic deep learning methods to analyze the dynamics of ecosystem.

8. CONCLUSION

In this chapter, we systematically investigated the dynamics of predator–prey systems, beginning with the classical Lotka–Volterra model and progressing through its major extensions, such as Holling's functional responses that represent varying predation efficiencies. Through theoretical analysis and numerical simulations, we demonstrated how stability, oscillation, and coexistence in predator–prey interactions are influenced by different functional responses.

Building on these foundations, we developed a comprehensive predator–prey model that integrates key behavioral and anthropogenic factors, including prey refuge, fear effects, harvesting, and the Crowley–Martin functional response. Mathematical analysis established the model's positivity, boundedness, and local stability at equilibrium points, confirming that behavioral interactions significantly reshape system dynamics. To incorporate environmental variability, we extended the deterministic model to a stochastic framework and analyzed how random perturbations influence long-term persistence and extinction. We rigorously derived extinction thresholds, showing that high noise intensities can drive prey populations to collapse, whereas predator extinction may occur when mortality and competition dominate despite prey persistence.

Compared with earlier works such as (Liang & Meng, 2023) and related studies, which typically examined subsets of these mechanisms in isolation, the present study offers a novel unified framework that simultaneously integrates refuge behavior, fear responses, harvesting pressure, and the Crowley–Martin functional response within both deterministic and stochastic settings. This integration advances the field by capturing the combined and often interacting effects of behavioral and environmental processes on ecosystem stability. Our comparative simulations bridge theoretical findings with management implications by identifying sustainable harvesting regions, quantifying refuge thresholds that ensure predator survival, and demonstrating how environmental variability shifts coexistence boundaries.

Collectively, these findings highlight that behavioral processes (refuge and fear) and human pressures (harvesting) are intricately coupled with environmental stochasticity in shaping ecological stability. By linking mechanism to prediction, the developed framework provides new theoretical and practical insights that strengthen population dynamics theory under changing environments and support evidence-based strategies for biodiversity conservation and sustainable ecosystem management.

REFERENCES

Abrams, P. A. (2000). The evolution of predator-prey interactions: Theory and evidence. *Annual Review of Ecology and Systematics*, *31*(1), 79–105. DOI: 10.1146/annurev.ecolsys.31.1.79

Ali, I., Zhang, H., Shah, S. M. A., Alkhazzan, A., & Sabbar, Y. (2025). An epidemiological stochastic predator prey model with prey refuge and harvesting. *Chinese Physics B*. Advance online publication. DOI: 10.1088/1674-1056/adf17f

Arditi, R., & Ginzburg, L. R. (1989). Coupling in predator-prey dynamics: Ratio-dependence. *Journal of Theoretical Biology*, *139*(3), 311–326. DOI: 10.1016/S0022-5193(89)80211-5

Beddington, J. R. (1975). Mutual interference between parasites or predators and its effect on searching efficiency. *Journal of Animal Ecology*, *44*(1), 331–340. DOI: 10.2307/3866

Beroual, N., & Sari, T. (2020). A predator-prey system with Holling-type functional response. *Proceedings of the American Mathematical Society*, *148*(12), 5127–5140. DOI: 10.1090/proc/15166

Berryman, A. A. (1992). The orgins and evolution of predator-prey theory. *Ecology*, *73*(5), 1530–1535. DOI: 10.2307/1940005

Cai, Y., Chen, Q., Teng, Z., Zhang, G., & Rifhat, R. (2025). Bifurcations in a discrete-time Beddington–DeAngelis prey–predator model with fear effect, prey refuge and harvesting. *Nonlinear Dynamics*, *113*(1), 931–969. DOI: 10.1007/s11071-024-10232-7

Cantrell, R. S., & Cosner, C. (2004). *Spatial ecology via reaction-diffusion equations*. John Wiley & Sons. DOI: 10.1002/0470871296

Crowley, P. H., & Martin, E. K. (1989). Functional responses and interference within and between year classes of a dragonfly population. *Journal of the North American Benthological Society*, *8*(3), 211–221. DOI: 10.2307/1467324

DeAngelis, D. L., Goldstein, R., & O'Neill, R. V. (1975). A model for tropic interaction. *Ecology*, *56*(4), 881–892. DOI: 10.2307/1936298

Debnath, S., Majumdar, P., Sarkar, S., & Ghosh, U. (2022). Global dynamics of a prey–predator model with Holling type III functional response in the presence of harvesting. *Journal of Biological System*, *30*(01), 225–260. DOI: 10.1142/S0218339022500073

Devgupta, R., Dandekar, R. A., Dandekar, R., & Panat, S. (2024). Scientific machine learning in ecological systems: A study on the predator-prey dynamics. *arXiv preprint arXiv:2411.06858.*

Fazzari, E., Romano, D., Falchi, F., & Stefanini, C. (2025). Animal behavior analysis methods using deep learning: A survey. *Expert Systems with Applications, 289*, 128330. DOI: 10.1016/j.eswa.2025.128330

Freedman, H. I. (1980). *Deterministic mathematical models in population ecology.* No Title.

Gray, A., Greenhalgh, D., Hu, L., Mao, X., & Pan, J. (2011). A stochastic differential equation SIS epidemic model. *SIAM Journal on Applied Mathematics, 71*(3), 876–902. DOI: 10.1137/10081856X

Hassell, M., & Varley, G. (1969). New inductive population model for insect parasites and its bearing on biological control.

Holling, C. S. (1959). Some characteristics of simple types of predation and parasitism1. *Canadian Entomologist, 91*(7), 385–398. DOI: 10.4039/Ent91385-7

Hoppensteadt, F. (2006). Predator-prey model. *Scholarpedia Journal, 1*(10), 1563. DOI: 10.4249/scholarpedia.1563

Huang, Y., Chen, F., & Zhong, L. (2006). Stability analysis of a prey–predator model with Holling type III response function incorporating a prey refuge. *Applied Mathematics and Computation, 182*(1), 672–683. DOI: 10.1016/j.amc.2006.04.030

Kar, T., & Matsuda, H. (2008). A bioeconomic model of a single-species fishery with a marine reserve. *Journal of Environmental Management, 86*(1), 171–180. DOI: 10.1016/j.jenvman.2006.12.001 PMID: 17240520

Kölle, M., Erpelding, Y., Ritz, F., Phan, T., Illium, S., & Linnhoff-Popien, C. (2024). Aquarium: A Comprehensive Framework for Exploring Predator-Prey Dynamics through Multi-Agent Reinforcement Learning Algorithms. *arXiv preprint arXiv:2401.07056*. DOI: 10.5220/0012382300003636

Liang, Z., & Meng, X. (2023). Stability and Hopf bifurcation of a multiple delayed predator–prey system with fear effect, prey refuge and Crowley–Martin function. *Chaos, Solitons, and Fractals, 175*, 113955. DOI: 10.1016/j.chaos.2023.113955

Liu, J., Lv, P., Liu, B., & Zhang, T. (2021). Dynamics of a Predator-Prey Model with Fear Effect and Time Delay. *Complexity, 2021*(1), 9184193. DOI: 10.1155/2021/9184193

Liu, Y., & Li, X. (2021). Dynamics of a discrete predator-prey model with Holling-II functional response. *International Journal of Biomathematics, 14*(08), 2150068. DOI: 10.1142/S1793524521500686

Lotka, A. J. (1925). *Elements of physical biology*. Williams & Wilkins.

Mandal, S., & Tiwari, P. K. (2024). Schooling behavior in a generalist predator–prey system: Exploring fear, refuge and cooperative strategies in a stochastic environment. *The European Physical Journal Plus, 139*(1), 29. DOI: 10.1140/epjp/s13360-023-04787-4

Mao, X. (2007). *Stochastic differential equations and applications*. Elsevier.

Murdoch, W. W., & Oaten, A. (1975). Predation and population stability. [). Elsevier.]. *Advances in Ecological Research, 9*, 1–131. DOI: 10.1016/S0065-2504(08)60288-3

Pal, S., Pal, N., Samanta, S., & Chattopadhyay, J. (2019). Fear effect in prey and hunting cooperation among predators in a Leslie-Gower model. *Mathematical Biosciences and Engineering, 16*(5), 5146–5179. DOI: 10.3934/mbe.2019258 PMID: 31499707

Panchal, A., Beniwal, K., & Kumar, V. (2025). Predator Prey Scavenger Model using Holling's Functional Response of Type III and Physics-Informed Deep Neural Networks. *International Journal of Applied and Computational Mathematics, 11*(2), 44. DOI: 10.1007/s40819-025-01862-5

Park, J., Lee, J., Kim, T., Ahn, I., & Park, J. (2021). Co-evolution of predator-prey ecosystems by reinforcement learning agents. *Entropy (Basel, Switzerland), 23*(4), 461. DOI: 10.3390/e23040461 PMID: 33924723

Robertson, M. D., Koen-Alonso, M., Regular, P. M., Cadigan, N., & Zhang, F. (2022). Accounting for a nonlinear functional response when estimating prey dynamics using predator diet data. *Methods in Ecology and Evolution, 13*(4), 880–893. DOI: 10.1111/2041-210X.13795

Rosenzweig, M. L., & MacArthur, R. H. (1963). Graphical representation and stability conditions of predator-prey interactions. *American Naturalist, 97*(895), 209–223. DOI: 10.1086/282272

Sáez, E., & González-Olivares, E. (1999). Dynamics of a predator-prey model. *SIAM Journal on Applied Mathematics, 59*(5), 1867–1878. DOI: 10.1137/S0036139997318457

Saha, S., & Samanta, G. (2021). Modelling of a two prey and one predator system with switching effect. *Computational and Mathematical Biophysics*, *9*(1), 90–113. DOI: 10.1515/cmb-2020-0120

Sahoo, D., & Samanta, G. (2024). Impact of fear effect in a two prey-one predator system with switching behaviour in predation. *differential equations and dynamical systems, 32*(2), 377-399.

Sasmal, S. K., & Takeuchi, Y. (2020). Dynamics of a predator-prey system with fear and group defense. *Journal of Mathematical Analysis and Applications*, *481*(1), 123471. DOI: 10.1016/j.jmaa.2019.123471

Thirthar, A. A., Majeed, S. J., Alqudah, M. A., Panja, P., & Abdeljawad, T. (2022). Fear effect in a predator-prey model with additional food, prey refuge and harvesting on super predator. *Chaos, Solitons, and Fractals*, *159*, 112091. DOI: 10.1016/j.chaos.2022.112091

Tiwari, P. K., Verma, M., Pal, S., Kang, Y., & Misra, A. K. (2021). A delay nonautonomous predator–prey model for the effects of fear, refuge and hunting cooperation. *Journal of Biological System*, *29*(04), 927–969. DOI: 10.1142/S0218339021500236

Turab, A., Mlaiki, N., Fatima, N., Mitrović, Z. D., & Ali, W. (2022). Analysis of a class of stochastic animal behavior models under specific choice preferences. *Mathematics*, *10*(12), 1975. DOI: 10.3390/math10121975

Turab, A., Montoyo, A., & Nescolarde-Selva, J.-A. (2024). Computational and analytical analysis of integral-differential equations for modeling avoidance learning behavior. *Journal of Applied Mathematics & Computing*, *70*(5), 4423–4439. DOI: 10.1007/s12190-024-02130-3

Turab, A., Nescolarde-Selva, J.-A., Ullah, F., Montoyo, A., Alfiniyah, C., Sintunavarat, W., Rizk, D., & Zaidi, S. A. (2025). Deep neural networks and stochastic methods for cognitive modeling of rat behavioral dynamics in $$\mathbb {T} $$-mazes. *Cognitive Neurodynamics*, *19*(1), 1–28. DOI: 10.1007/s11571-025-10247-9 PMID: 39749104

Turab, A., Rosli, N., Ali, W., & Nieto, J. J. (2023). The existence and uniqueness of solutions to a functional equation arising in psychological learning theory. *Demonstratio Mathematica*, *56*(1), 20220231. DOI: 10.1515/dema-2022-0231

Turab, A., & Sintunavarat, W. (2019). On analytic model for two-choice behavior of the paradise fish based on the fixed point method. *Journal of Fixed Point Theory and Its Applications*, *21*(2), 56. DOI: 10.1007/s11784-019-0694-y

Turab, A., & Sintunavarat, W. (2020). On the solution of the traumatic avoidance learning model approached by the Banach fixed point theorem. *Journal of Fixed Point Theory and Its Applications*, *22*(2), 50. DOI: 10.1007/s11784-020-00788-3

Turab, A., Sintunavarat, W., Ullah, F., Zaidi, S. A., Montoyo, A., & Nescolarde-Selva, J.-A. (2024). Computational modeling of animal behavior in T-mazes: Insights from machine learning. *Ecological Informatics*, *81*, 102639. DOI: 10.1016/j.ecoinf.2024.102639

Uiterwaal, S. F., & DeLong, J. P. (2020). Functional responses are maximized at intermediate temperatures. *Ecology*, *101*(4), e02975. DOI: 10.1002/ecy.2975 PMID: 31944271

Volterra, V. (1926). Fluctuations in the abundance of a species considered mathematically. *Nature*, *118*(2972), 558–560. DOI: 10.1038/118558a0

Wang, X., Zanette, L., & Zou, X. (2016). Modelling the fear effect in predator–prey interactions. *Journal of Mathematical Biology*, *73*(5), 1179–1204. DOI: 10.1007/s00285-016-0989-1 PMID: 27002514

Wei, Z., & Chen, F. (2023). Dynamics of a delayed predator–prey model with prey refuge, Allee effect and fear effect. *International Journal of Bifurcation and Chaos in Applied Sciences and Engineering*, *33*(03), 2350036. DOI: 10.1142/S0218127423500360

Zhang, H., Cai, Y., Fu, S., & Wang, W. (2019). Impact of the fear effect in a prey-predator model incorporating a prey refuge. *Applied Mathematics and Computation*, *356*, 328–337. DOI: 10.1016/j.amc.2019.03.034

Compilation of References

Abgrall, G., Holder, A. L., Chelly Dagdia, Z., Zeitouni, K., & Monnet, X. (2024). Should AI models be explainable to clinicians? *Critical Care*, *28*(1), 301. DOI: 10.1186/s13054-024-05005-y PMID: 39267172

Abin, A. A., Hosseini, P., & Torabian Raj, A. (2023). Continuous user authentication using a combination of operation and application-related features. [JICSE]. *Journal of Innovations in Computer Science and Engineering*, *1*(1), 10–21. DOI: 10.48308/jicse.2023.103524

Abou Elassad, Z. E., Mousannif, H., Al Moatassime, H., & Karkouch, A. (2020). The application of machine learning techniques for driving behavior analysis: A conceptual framework and a systematic literature review. *Engineering Applications of Artificial Intelligence*, *87*, 103312. DOI: 10.1016/j.engappai.2019.103312

Abrams, P. A. (2000). The evolution of predator-prey interactions: Theory and evidence. *Annual Review of Ecology and Systematics*, *31*(1), 79–105. DOI: 10.1146/annurev.ecolsys.31.1.79

Abuasbeh, K., Shafqat, R., Alsinai, A., & Awadalla, M. (2023). Analysis of the mathematical modelling of COVID-19 by using mild solution with delay Caputo operator. *Symmetry*, *15*(2), 286.

Acien, A., Morales, A., Vera-Rodriguez, R., Fierrez, J., Mondesire-Crump, I., & Arroyo-Gallego, T. (2022). Detection of mental fatigue in the general population: Feasibility study of keystroke dynamics as a real-world biomarker. *JMIR Biomedical Engineering*, *7*(2), e41003. DOI: 10.2196/41003 PMID: 38875698

Agarwal, N., Danielsen, N. F., Gravdal, P. K., & Bours, P. *(2022, October). Contract cheat detection using biometric keystroke dynamics. In 2022 20th International Conference on Emerging eLearning Technologies and Applications (ICETA) (pp. 15-21). IEEE.* DOI: 10.1109/ICETA57911.2022.9974870

Aggarwal, J. K., & Ryoo, M. S. (2011). Human activity analysis: A review. *ACM Computing Surveys*, *43*(3), 1–43.

Agrawal, R., & Sharma, K. (2024). An Extensive Review on Significance of Explainable Artificial Intelligence Models in Discrete Domains for Informed Decisions Making. *Revue d'Intelligence Artificielle*, *38*(3), 957–968. Advance online publication. DOI: 10.18280/ria.380321

Ahad, A., Puspitasari, I., Zheng, J., Ullah, S., Ullah, F., Bakhsh, S. T., & Pires, I. M. (2025). Machine Learning Stroke Prediction in Smart Healthcare: Integrating Fuzzy K-Nearest Neighbor and Artificial Neural Networks with Feature Selection Techniques. *Computers, Materials & Continua*, *82*(3), 5115–5134. DOI: 10.32604/cmc.2025.062605

Ahmad, Z., Shahid Khan, A., Wai Shiang, C., Abdullah, J., & Ahmad, F. (2021). Network intrusion detection system: A systematic study of machine learning and deep learning approaches. *Transactions on Emerging Telecommunications Technologies*, *32*(1), e4150. DOI: 10.1002/ett.4150

Ahmed, M. W., & Jalal, A. (2024, February). Dynamic adoptive Gaussian mixture model for multi-object detection over natural scenes. In 2024 5th International Conference on Advancements in Computational Sciences (ICACS) (pp. 1-8). IEEE.

Ahmed, M. R., Shatabda, S., Islam, A. M., & Robin, M. T. I. (2021). Intrusion Detection System in Software-Defined Networks Using Machine Learning and Deep Learning Techniques—A Comprehensive Survey. *Authorea Preprints*. DOI: 10.36227/techrxiv.17153213.v1

Akhtar, M. U., & Khalil, M. I. K. (2018). Link prediction techniques in complex networks. *International Review of Basic and Applied Sciences*, *6*(8), 60–69.

Akhtar, M. U., Liu, J., Liu, X., Ahmed, S., & Cui, X. (2023). NRAND: An efficient and robust dismantling approach for infectious disease network. *Information Processing & Management*, *60*(2), 103221. Advance online publication. DOI: 10.1016/j.ipm.2022.103221

Al Jallad, K., Aljnidi, M., & Desouki, M. S. (2019). Big data analysis and distributed deep learning for next-generation intrusion detection system optimization. *Journal of Big Data*, *6*(1), 88. DOI: 10.1186/s40537-019-0248-6

Al-Adaileh, A., Al-Kfairy, M., Tubishat, M., & Alfandi, O. (2024). A sentiment analysis approach for understanding users' perception of metaverse marketplace. *Intelligent Systems with Applications*, *22*, 200362. DOI: 10.1016/j.iswa.2024.200362

Alang, K. S., & Kumar, D. M.Karan Singh AlangDr Munish Kumar. (2025). Explainable AI in Cyber Security: Enhancing Model Transparency. *Universal Research Reports, 12*(1), 85–96. DOI: 10.36676/urr.v12.i1.1463

Alayed, H. A. (2015). *Behavior-Based Approaches for Detecting Cheating in Online Games* (Doctoral dissertation, University of Southern California).

Alharbi, Y., & Khan, S. S. (2025). Classifying multi-lingual reviews sentiment analysis in Arabic and English languages using the stochastic gradient descent model. *Computers, Materials & Continua, 83*(1), 1275–1290. DOI: 10.32604/cmc.2025.061490

Ali, I., Zhang, H., Shah, S. M. A., Alkhazzan, A., & Sabbar, Y. (2025). An epidemiological stochastic predator prey model with prey refuge and harvesting. *Chinese Physics B*. Advance online publication. DOI: 10.1088/1674-1056/adf17f

Alizadeh, M., Zadeh, D. S., Moshiri, B., & Montazeri, A. (2023). Development of a customer churn model for banking industry based on hard and soft data fusion. *IEEE Access : Practical Innovations, Open Solutions, 11*, 29759–29768. DOI: 10.1109/ACCESS.2023.3257352

Aljuhmani, H. Y., Elrehail, H., Bayram, P., & Samarah, T. (2022). Linking social media marketing efforts with customer brand engagement in driving brand loyalty. *Asia Pacific Journal of Marketing and Logistics, 35*(7), 1719–1738. DOI: 10.1108/APJML-08-2021-0627

Alkhalil, A., Razzaq, A., Ahmad, A., Abdelrhman, M., Altameemi, Y., Altamimi, M., & Tao, Z. (2025). A framework for blockchain-based secure management of mobile healthcare (mHealth) systems. *Journal of Web Engineering, 24*(3), 317–354. DOI: 10.13052/jwe1540-9589.2431

Almolhis, N. A., & Alsubhi, M. A. (2025). *Detecting Advanced Persistent Threats Using Machine Learning and Behavioral Analysis.* Paper presented at the International Conference on Information Technology-New Generations. DOI: 10.1007/978-3-031-89063-5_9

Alnofeli, K., Akter, S., & Yanamandram, V. (2023). Understanding the Future trends and innovations of AI-based CRM systems. In *Handbook of Big Data Research Methods* (pp. 279–294). Edward Elgar Publishing. DOI: 10.4337/9781800888555.00021

al-Qallawi, S., & Raghavan, M. (2022). A review of online reactions to game-based assessment mobile applications. *International Journal of Selection and Assessment, 30*(1), 14–26. DOI: 10.1111/ijsa.12346

Al-Quayed, F., Ahmad, Z., & Humayun, M. (2024). A situation based predictive approach for cybersecurity intrusion detection and prevention using machine learning and deep learning algorithms in wireless sensor networks of industry 4.0. *IEEE Access : Practical Innovations, Open Solutions, 12*, 34800–34819. DOI: 10.1109/ACCESS.2024.3372187

Al-Quran, A., Shafqat, R., Alsaadi, A., & Djaouti, A. M. (2025). Poliomyelitis dynamics with fractional order derivatives and deep neural networks. *Scientific Reports, 15*(1), 32023.

Alrumiah, S. S., & Hadwan, M. (2021). Implementing big data analytics in e-commerce: Vendor and customer view. *IEEE Access : Practical Innovations, Open Solutions, 9*, 37281–37286. DOI: 10.1109/ACCESS.2021.3063615

Alsaeedi, A., & Al-Sarem, M. (2020). Detecting rumors on social media based on a CNN deep learning technique. *Arabian Journal for Science and Engineering, 45*(12), 10813–10844. DOI: 10.1007/s13369-020-04839-2

Alturaief, N., Aljamaan, H., & Baslyman, M. (2021). *Aware: Aspect-based sentiment analysis dataset of apps reviews for requirements elicitation.* Paper presented at the 2021 36th IEEE/ACM International Conference on Automated Software Engineering Workshops (ASEW). DOI: 10.1109/ASEW52652.2021.00049

Al-Tuwairqi, S., Al-Sheikh, S., & Al-Amoudi, R. (2015). Qualitative analysis of a rumor transmission model with incubation mechanism. *OAlib, 2*(1), 1–12. DOI: 10.4236/oalib.1102040

Altwaijry, N. (2023). Authentication by keystroke dynamics: The influence of typing language. *Applied Sciences (Basel, Switzerland), 13*(20), 11478. DOI: 10.3390/app132011478

Alzhrani, A., Alatawi, A., Alsharari, B., Albalawi, U., & Mustafa, M. (2022). Towards Security Awareness of Mobile Applications using Semantic-based Sentiment Analysis. *International Journal of Advanced Computer Science and Applications, 13*(4). Advance online publication. DOI: 10.14569/IJACSA.2022.0130493

Anjum, S. H., & Patil, G. (2022, November). Cheat Detection for Credit Cards Using Artificial Intelligence. *In 2022 IEEE North Karnataka Subsection Flagship International Conference (NKCon) (pp.* 1-6*)*. IEEE. DOI: 10.1109/NKCon56289.2022.10126820

Antal, M., & Fejér, N. (2020). Mouse dynamics based user recognition using deep learning. *Acta Universitatis Sapientiae Informatica, 12*(1), 39–50. DOI: 10.2478/ausi-2020-0003

Anusas-amornkul, T. (2019). Strengthening password authentication using keystroke dynamics and smartphone sensors. *Proceedings of the 9th International Conference on Information Communication and Management*. New York, NY, USA: ACM. DOI: 10.1145/3357419.3357425

Arditi, R., & Ginzburg, L. R. (1989). Coupling in predator-prey dynamics: Ratio-dependence. *Journal of Theoretical Biology, 139*(3), 311–326. DOI: 10.1016/S0022-5193(89)80211-5

Arora, M. (2024). What Lies in Big Data for Customer Retention? Analyzing the Past, Present, and Future. In *Augmenting Customer Retention Through Big Data Analytics* (pp. 311-326): Apple Academic Press.

Ashbaugh, L., & Zhang, Y. (2024). A comparative study of sentiment analysis on customer reviews using machine learning and deep learning. *Computers, 13*(12), 340. DOI: 10.3390/computers13120340

Ashker, S. E. (2011). Technical and tactical aspects that differentiate winning and losing performances in boxing. *International Journal of Performance Analysis in Sport, 11*(2), 356–364.

Asudani, D. S., Nagwani, N. K., & Singh, P. (2023). Impact of word embedding models on text analytics in deep learning environment: A review. *Artificial Intelligence Review, 56*(9), 10345–10425. DOI: 10.1007/s10462-023-10419-1

Athey, S., & Imbens, G. W. (2015). Machine learning methods for estimating heterogeneous causal effects. stat, 1050(5), 1-26.

Ayotte, B., Banavar, M., Hou, D., & Schuckers, S. (2020). Fast free-text authentication via instance-based keystroke dynamics. *IEEE Transactions on Biometrics, Behavior, and Identity Science, 2*(4), 377–387. DOI: 10.1109/TBIOM.2020.3003988

Ba, J. L., Kiros, J. R., & Hinton, G. E. (2016). Layer normalization. arXiv preprint arXiv:1607.06450.

Baccouche, M., Mamalet, F., Wolf, C., Garcia, C., & Baskurt, A. (2011, November). Sequential deep learning for human action recognition. In International workshop on human behavior understanding (pp. 29-39). Berlin, Heidelberg: Springer Berlin Heidelberg.

Baj-Rogowska, A., & Sikorski, M. (2023). Exploring the usability and user experience of social media apps through a text mining approach. *Engineering Management in Production Services, 15*(1), 86–105. DOI: 10.2478/emj-2023-0007

Balci, F., & Simen, P. (2014). A decision model of timing. *Current Opinion in Behavioral Sciences*, *5*, 193–199. DOI: 10.1016/j.cobeha.2016.02.002

Bansal, M., Kumar, M., Sachdeva, M., & Mittal, A. (2023). Transfer learning for image classification using VGG19: Caltech-101 image data set. *Journal of Ambient Intelligence and Humanized Computing*, *14*(4), 3609–3620. PMID: 34548886

Bansal, P., & Ouda, A. (2024). Continuous authentication in the digital age: An analysis of reinforcement learning and behavioral biometrics. *Computers*, *13*(4), 103. DOI: 10.3390/computers13040103

Barbosa, B., Saura, J. R., Zekan, S. B., & Ribeiro-Soriano, D. (2024). RETRACTED ARTICLE: Defining content marketing and its influence on online user behavior: a data-driven prescriptive analytics method. *Annals of Operations Research*, *337*(S1, Suppl 1), 17–17. DOI: 10.1007/s10479-023-05261-1

Bareinboim, E., & Pearl, J. (2016). Causal inference and the data-fusion problem. *Proceedings of the National Academy of Sciences of the United States of America*, *113*(27), 7345–7352. DOI: 10.1073/pnas.1510507113 PMID: 27382148

Barnes, D. J., & Hernandez-Castro, J. (2015). On the limits of engine analysis for cheating detection in chess. *Computers & Security*, *48*, 58–73. DOI: 10.1016/j.cose.2014.10.002

Bastias, P. G., & Brand, J. E. (2020). *Causal Inference*. Oxford University Press., DOI: 10.1093/obo/9780199756384-0240

Bazi, Y., Bashmal, L., Rahhal, M. M. A., Dayil, R. A., & Ajlan, N. A. (2021). Vision transformers for remote sensing image classification. *Remote Sensing*, *13*(3), 516.

Beddington, J. R. (1975). Mutual interference between parasites or predators and its effect on searching efficiency. *Journal of Animal Ecology*, *44*(1), 331–340. DOI: 10.2307/3866

Bellary, S., Bala, P. K., & Chakraborty, S. (2024). Exploring cognitive-behavioral drivers impacting consumer continuance intention of fitness apps using a hybrid approach of text mining, SEM, and ANN. *Journal of Retailing and Consumer Services*, *81*, 104045. DOI: 10.1016/j.jretconser.2024.104045

Belsare, A., & Vanak, A. T. (2020). Modelling the challenges of managing free-ranging dog populations. *Scientific Reports*, *10*(1), 18874.

Berlinghieri, R., Krajbich, I., Maccheroni, F., Marinacci, M., & Pirazzini, M. (2023). Measuring utility with diffusion models. *Science Advances*, *9*(34). Advance online publication. DOI: 10.1126/sciadv.adf1665

Beroual, N., & Sari, T. (2020). A predator-prey system with Holling-type functional response. *Proceedings of the American Mathematical Society*, *148*(12), 5127–5140. DOI: 10.1090/proc/15166

Berryman, A. A. (1992). The orgins and evolution of predator-prey theory. *Ecology*, *73*(5), 1530–1535. DOI: 10.2307/1940005

Birjali, M., Kasri, M., & Beni-Hssane, A. (2021). A comprehensive survey on sentiment analysis: Approaches, challenges and trends. *Knowledge-Based Systems*, *226*, 107134. DOI: 10.1016/j.knosys.2021.107134

Bogacz, R., Brown, E., Moehlis, J., Holmes, P., & Cohen, J. D. (2006). The physics of optimal decision making: A formal analysis of models of performance in two-alternative forced-choice tasks. *Psychological Review*, *113*(4), 700–765. DOI: 10.1037/0033-295X.113.4.700

Bogacz, R., & Larsen, T. (2011). Integration of reinforcement learning and optimal decision-making theories of the basal ganglia. *Neural Computation*, *23*(4), 817–851. DOI: 10.1162/NECO_a_00103

Bonidia, R. P., Rodrigues, L. A., Avila-Santos, A. P., Sanches, D. S., & Brancher, J. D. (2018). Computational intelligence in sports: A systematic literature review. *Advances in Human-Computer Interaction*, *2018*(1), 3426178.

Boyce, M. R., Carlin, E. P., Schermerhorn, J., & Standley, C. J. (2020). A one health approach for guinea worm disease control: Scope and opportunities. *Tropical Medicine and Infectious Disease*, *5*(4), 159.

Brouillard, P., Taslakian, P., Lacoste, A., Lachapelle, S., & Drouin, A. (2022). Typing assumptions improve identification in causal discovery. Conference on Causal Learning and Reasoning.

Brown, S. D., & Heathcote, A. (2008). The simplest complete model of choice response time: Linear ballistic accumulation. *Cognitive Psychology*, *57*(3), 153–178. DOI: 10.1016/j.cogpsych.2007.12.002

Buker, A. A. N., Roffo, G., & Vinciarelli, A. (2019). Type like a man! Inferring gender from keystroke dynamics in live-chats. *IEEE Intelligent Systems*, *34*(6), 53–59. DOI: 10.1109/MIS.2019.2948514

Cai, Y., Chen, Q., Teng, Z., Zhang, G., & Rifhat, R. (2025). Bifurcations in a discrete-time Beddington–DeAngelis prey–predator model with fear effect, prey refuge and harvesting. *Nonlinear Dynamics*, *113*(1), 931–969. DOI: 10.1007/s11071-024-10232-7

Çallı, L. (2023). Exploring mobile banking adoption and service quality features through user-generated content: The application of a topic modeling approach to Google Play Store reviews. *International Journal of Bank Marketing*, *41*(2), 428–454. DOI: 10.1108/IJBM-08-2022-0351

Cantrell, R. S., & Cosner, C. (2004). *Spatial ecology via reaction-diffusion equations*. John Wiley & Sons. DOI: 10.1002/0470871296

Cardino, P. C. C., Chua, J. L. T., & Llaga, J. R. R. R. (2022). Advance scorecard for boxing: Combat sport analysis with deep learning.

Carey, B. (2022). Metaverse technologies, behavioral predictive analytics, and customer location tracking tools in blockchain-based virtual worlds. *Review of Contemporary Philosophy*, (21), 188–204.

Carloni, G., Berti, A., & Colantonio, S. (2025). The role of causality in explainable artificial intelligence. Wiley Interdisciplinary Reviews. Data Mining and Knowledge Discovery, 15(2), e70015. doi:10.1002/widm.70015

Carpio, A., Drehr, J.C., Ferrera, D., Galán, D., Mercado, F. & Obeso I. (2024). Causal computations of supplementary motor area on spatial impulsivity. *Sci Rep*. 24;14(1):17040. DOI: 10.1038/s41598-024-67673-8

Cavanagh, J. F., Wiecki, T. V., Cohen, M. X., Figueroa, C. M., Samanta, J., Sherman, S. J., & Frank, M. J. (2011). Subthalamic nucleus stimulation reverses mediofrontal influence over decision threshold. *Nature Neuroscience*, *14*(11), 1462–1467. DOI: 10.1038/nn.2925

Celestin, M., Sujatha, S., Kumar, A. D., & Vasuki, M. (2024). Investigating the role of big data and predictive analytics in enhancing decision-making and competitive advantage: A case study approach. *International Journal of Advanced Trends in Engineering Technology*, *9*(2), 25–32.

Chan, G. C., Lim, C., Sun, T., Stjepanovic, D., Connor, J., Hall, W., & Leung, J. (2022). Causal inference with observational data in addiction research. *Addiction (Abingdon, England)*, *117*(10), 2736–2744. DOI: 10.1111/add.15972 PMID: 35661462

Chankuna, D. (2006). Video Analysis for the Causes of Head and Face Injuries in Amateur Muaythai Boxers (Doctoral dissertation, Chulalongkorn University).

Chanpariyavatevong, K., Wipulanusat, W., Champahom, T., Jomnonkwao, S., Chonsalasin, D., & Ratanavaraha, V. (2021). Predicting airline customer loyalty by integrating structural equation modeling and Bayesian networks. *Sustainability (Basel)*, *13*(13), 7046. DOI: 10.3390/su13137046

Chantaprasert, B., Chumchuen, P., & Wangsiripitak, S. (2019, July). Comparison of gesture in Thai boxing framework using angular dynamic time warping. In 2019 16th International Conference on Electrical Engineering/Electronics, Computer, Telecommunications and Information Technology (ECTI-CON) (pp. 601-604). IEEE.

Chen, X., & Li, Q. (2024). Causality-driven user modeling for sequential recommendations over time. Companion Proceedings of the ACM Web Conference 2024.

Cheng, D., Xu, Z., Li, J., Liu, L., Liu, J., Gao, W., & Le, T. D. (2024). Instrumental variable estimation for causal inference in longitudinal data with time-dependent latent confounders. Proceedings of the AAAI Conference on Artificial Intelligence.

Cheng, L., Guo, R., Moraffah, R., Sheth, P., Candan, K. S., & Liu, H. (2022). Evaluation methods and measures for causal learning algorithms. *IEEE Transactions on Artificial Intelligence*, *3*(6), 924–943. DOI: 10.1109/TAI.2022.3150264

Chen, W., Zhang, Y., Yeo, C. K., Lau, C. T., & Lee, B. S. (2018). Unsupervised rumor detection based on users' behaviors using neural networks. *Pattern Recognition Letters*, *105*, 226–233. DOI: 10.1016/j.patrec.2017.10.014

Chen, X., & Wang, N. (2020). Rumor spreading model considering rumor credibility, correlation and crowd classification based on personality. *Scientific Reports*, *10*(1), 5887. DOI: 10.1038/s41598-020-62585-9 PMID: 32246112

Chen, Y., Xie, Z., & Chiu, D. K. (2024). Analytics of motivational factors of educational video games: LDA topic modeling and the 6 C's learning motivation model. *Education and Information Technologies*, *29*(16), 1–34. DOI: 10.1007/s10639-024-12726-8

Che, S., Nan, D., Kamphuis, P., Zhang, S., & Kim, J. H. (2022). Examining crisis communication using semantic network and sentiment analysis: A case study on NetEase Games. *Frontiers in Psychology*, *13*, 823415. DOI: 10.3389/fpsyg.2022.823415

Chess, O. An Application of Human and Computer Decision-Making Preferences. In *International Conference on Computers and Games* (pp. 163-180). Cham: Springer Nature Switzerland.

Chia, H. L. B. (2023). The emergence and need for explainable AI. *Advances in Engineering Innovation*, *3*(1), 1–4. DOI: 10.54254/2977-3903/3/2023023

Chibudike, C. E., Abdu, H., Chibudike, H. O., Ngige, O., Adeyoju, O. A., & Obi, N. (2021). Machine learning-a new trend in web user behavior analysis. *International Journal of Computer Applications*, *975*(5), 8887. DOI: 10.5120/ijca2021921247

Choi, D., Oh, H., Chun, S., Kwon, T., & Han, J. (2022). Preventing rumor spread with deep learning. *Expert Systems with Applications, 197*, 116688. DOI: 10.1016/j.eswa.2022.116688

Chumachenko, D., Piletskiy, I., Sukhorukova, M., & Chumachenko, T. (2022). Predictive model of Lyme disease epidemic process using machine learning approach. *Applied Sciences (Basel, Switzerland), 12*(9), 4282. Advance online publication. DOI: 10.3390/app12094282

Cilia, D., & Inguanez, F. (2018). Multi-Model authentication using keystroke dynamics for Smartphones. *2018 IEEE 8th International Conference on Consumer Electronics - Berlin (ICCE-Berlin)*. IEEE.

Cockell, R., & Halak, B. (2020). On the design and analysis of a biometric authentication system using keystroke dynamics. *Cryptography*, *4*(2), 12. DOI: 10.3390/cryptography4020012

Crowley, P. H., & Martin, E. K. (1989). Functional responses and interference within and between year classes of a dragonfly population. *Journal of the North American Benthological Society*, *8*(3), 211–221. DOI: 10.2307/1467324

Cust, E. E., Sweeting, A. J., Ball, K., & Robertson, S. (2019). Machine and deep learning for sport-specific movement recognition: A systematic review of model development and performance. *Journal of Sports Sciences*, *37*(5), 568–600. PMID: 30307362

D'Orazio, T., & Leo, M. (2010). A review of vision-based systems for soccer video analysis. *Pattern Recognition*, *43*(8), 2911–2926.

Da Costa, K. A., Papa, J. P., Lisboa, C. O., Munoz, R., & de Albuquerque, V. H. C. (2019). Internet of Things: A survey on machine learning-based intrusion detection approaches. *Computer Networks*, *151*, 147–157.

Dablander, F., & van Bork, R. (2022). Causal inference. In *Network Psychometrics with R* (pp. 213–232). Routledge. DOI: 10.4324/9781003111238-16

Dai, C., Liu, X., & Lai, J. (2020). Human action recognition using two-stream attention based LSTM networks. *Applied Soft Computing*, *86*, 105820.

Dai, C., Liu, X., Lai, J., Li, P., & Chao, H. C. (2019). Human behavior deep recognition architecture for smart city applications in the 5G environment. *IEEE Network*, *33*(5), 206–211.

Daley, D., & Kendall, D. (1964). Epidemics and rumors. *Nature*, *204*(4963), 1118. DOI: 10.1038/2041118a0 PMID: 14243408

Dang, T. L., Hoang, N. M. N., Nguyen, T. V., Nguyen, H. V., Dang, Q. M., Tran, Q. H., & Pham, H. H. (2025). Auto-proctoring using computer vision in MOOCs system. *Multimedia Tools and Applications*, *84*(23), 26187–26213. DOI: 10.1007/s11042-024-20099-w

Danyal, M. M., Haseeb, M., Khan, S. S., Khan, B., & Ullah, S. (2024). Opinion mining on movie reviews based on deep learning models. *Journal of Artificial Intelligence (2579-0021), 6.*

Danyal, M. M., Khan, S. S., Khan, M., Ullah, S., Ghaffar, M. B., & Khan, W. (2024). Sentiment analysis of movie reviews based on NB approaches using TF–IDF and count vectorizer. *Social Network Analysis and Mining*, *14*(1), 87. DOI: 10.1007/s13278-024-01250-9

Danyal, M. M., Khan, S. S., Khan, M., Ullah, S., Mehmood, F., & Ali, I. (2024). Proposing sentiment analysis model based on BERT and XLNet for movie reviews. *Multimedia Tools and Applications*, *83*(24), 64315–64339. DOI: 10.1007/s11042-024-18156-5

Danyal, M., Khan, S., Khan, M., Ghaffar, M., Khan, B., & Arshad, M. (2023). Sentiment analysis based on performance of linear support vector machine and multinomial naïve Bayes using movie reviews with baseline techniques. *Journal of Big Data*, *5*, 1–18. DOI: 10.32604/jbd.2023.041319

Dashtipour, K., Gogate, M., Adeel, A., Larijani, H., & Hussain, A. (2021). Sentiment analysis of Persian movie reviews using deep learning. *Entropy (Basel, Switzerland)*, *23*(5), 596. DOI: 10.3390/e23050596

De Ville, B. (2013). Decision trees. *Wiley Interdisciplinary Reviews: Computational Statistics*, *5*(6), 448–455. DOI: 10.1002/wics.1278

DeAngelis, D. L., Goldstein, R., & O'Neill, R. V. (1975). A model for tropic interaction. *Ecology*, *56*(4), 881–892. DOI: 10.2307/1936298

Debnath, S., Majumdar, P., Sarkar, S., & Ghosh, U. (2022). Global dynamics of a prey–predator model with Holling type III functional response in the presence of harvesting. *Journal of Biological System*, *30*(01), 225–260. DOI: 10.1142/S0218339022500073

Delp, C. (2005). Muay Thai Basics: Introductory Thai Boxing Techniques. blue snake books.

Delp, C. (2013). *Muay Thai Counter Techniques: Competitive Skills and Tactics for Success*. North Atlantic Books.

Deng, Z., Zheng, X., Tian, H., & Zeng, D. D. (2022). Deep causal learning: representation, discovery and inference. arXiv preprint arXiv:2211.03374. https://doi.org/DOI: 10.1145/3762179

Devgupta, R., Dandekar, R. A., Dandekar, R., & Panat, S. (2024). Scientific machine learning in ecological systems: A study on the predator-prey dynamics. *arXiv preprint arXiv:2411.06858.*

Dijk, S. W., Korf, M., Labrecque, J. A., Pandya, A., Ferket, B. S., Hallsson, L. R., Wong, J. B., Siebert, U., & Hunink, M. M. (2025). Directed Acyclic Graphs in Decision-Analytic Modeling: Bridging Causal Inference and Effective Model Design in Medical Decision Making. Medical Decision Making, 0272989X241310898. DOI: 10.1177/0272989X241310898

Dong, X., Huang, B., Ng, I., Song, X., Zheng, Y., Jin, S., Legaspi, R., Spirtes, P., & Zhang, K. (2023). A versatile causal discovery framework to allow causally-related hidden variables. arXiv preprint arXiv:2312.11001./arXiv.2312.11001DOI: 10.48550

Donkin, C., Averell, L., Brown, S., & Heathcote, A. (2009). Getting more from accuracy and response time data: Methods for fitting the linear ballistic accumulator. *Behavior Research Methods*. Advance online publication. DOI: 10.3758/BRM.41.4.1095

Dornala, S. K., & Senthilkumar, P. (2025). Real-Time threat identification and categorization in network traffic using deep learning behavioral analysis. *International Journal on Smart Sensing and Intelligent Systems*, *18*(1), 20250017. DOI: 10.2478/ijssis-2025-0017

dos S Silva, F. H., Bezerra, G. M., Holanda, G. B., de Souza, J. W. M., Rego, P. A., Neto, A. V. L., ... & Rebouças Filho, P. P. (2021). A novel feature extractor for human action recognition in visual question answering. Pattern Recognition Letters, 147, 41-47.

Doshi, R., & Hiran, K. K. (2024). Explainable artificial intelligence as a cybersecurity aid. In *Advances in Explainable AI Applications for Smart Cities* (pp. 98–113). IGI Global., DOI: 10.4018/978-1-6684-6361-1.ch003

Drugowitsch, J., DeAngelis, G. C., Angelaki, D. E., & Pouget, A. (2012). Optimal decision-making with time-varying evidence reliability. In *Advances in Neural Information Processing Systems 25* (NIPS 2012).

Durairaj, A. K., & Chinnalagu, A. (2021). Transformer based contextual model for sentiment analysis of customer reviews: A fine-tuned BERT. *International Journal of Advanced Computer Science and Applications, 12*(11). Advance online publication. DOI: 10.14569/IJACSA.2021.0121153

Durvasula, S. (2024). Unlocking Decision-Making Potential with Causal AI-Driven What-If Simulations. *International Journal for Research in Applied Science and Engineering Technology, 12*(4), 4912–4922. DOI: 10.22214/ijraset.2024.60819

Egri-Nagy, A., & Törmänen, A. (2020, November). Derived metrics for the game of Go–intrinsic network strength assessment and cheat-detection. In *2020 Eighth International Symposium on Computing and Networking (CANDAR)* (pp. 9-18). IEEE. DOI: 10.1109/CANDAR51075.2020.00010

El Azzouzy, O., Chanyour, T., & Andaloussi, S. J. (2025). Transformer-based models for sentiment analysis of YouTube comments. *Scientific African, 29*, e02836. Advance online publication. DOI: 10.1016/j.sciaf.2025.e02836

Elsayed, S., Mohamed, K., & Madkour, M. A. (2024). A comparative study of using deep learning algorithms in network intrusion detection. *IEEE Access : Practical Innovations, Open Solutions, 12*, 58851–58870. DOI: 10.1109/ACCESS.2024.3389096

Elwert, F. (2013). Graphical causal models. In *Handbook of causal analysis for social research* (pp. 245–273). Springer., DOI: 10.1007/978-94-007-6094-3_13

Engelhard, C. A. G., Hodgkins, A. P., Pearl, E. E., & Spears, P. K., Rychtář, J., and Taylor, D. (2021). A mathematical model of Guinea worm disease in Chad with fish as intermediate transport hosts. *Journal of Theoretical Biology, 521*, 110683.

Erdem, B., & Karabatak, M. (2025). Cheating detection in online exams using deep learning and machine learning. *Applied Sciences (Basel, Switzerland), 15*(1), 400. DOI: 10.3390/app15010400

Erkan, A., & Güngör, T. (2023). Analysis of deep learning model combinations and tokenization approaches in sentiment classification. *IEEE Access : Practical Innovations, Open Solutions, 11*, 134951–134968. DOI: 10.1109/ACCESS.2023.3337354

Escobar Grisales, D., Vásquez-Correa, J. C., Vargas-Bonilla, J. F., & Orozco-Arroyave, J. R. (2020). Identity verification in virtual education using biometric analysis based on keystroke dynamics. *TecnoLógicas, 23*(47), 197–211. DOI: 10.22430/22565337.1475

Esmeli, R., Bader-El-Den, M., & Abdullahi, H. (2022). An analyses of the effect of using contextual and loyalty features on early purchase prediction of shoppers in e-commerce domain. *Journal of Business Research, 147*, 420–434. DOI: 10.1016/j.jbusres.2022.04.012

Evans, N. J., & Hawkins, G. E. (2019). When humans behave like monkeys: Feedback delays and extensive practice increase the efficiency of speeded decisions. *Cognition, 184*, 11–18. DOI: 10.1016/j.cognition.2018.11.014

Evans, N. J., & Wagenmakers, E. J. (2020). Evidence accumulation models: Current limitations and future directions. *The Quantitative Methods for Psychology, 16*(2), 73–90. DOI: 10.31234/osf.io/74df9

Faker, O., & Dogdu, E. (2019). *Intrusion detection using big data and deep learning techniques.* Paper presented at the Proceedings of the 2019 ACM Southeast conference. DOI: 10.1145/3299815.3314439

Fan, C., Zeng, L., Sun, Y., & Liu, Y. (2020a). Finding key players in complex networks through deep reinforcement learning. *Nature Machine Intelligence, 2*(6), 317–324. DOI: 10.1038/s42256-020-0177-2 PMID: 34124581

Fan, C., Zeng, L., Sun, Y., & Liu, Y. (2020b). A novel learning-based approach for efficient dismantling of networks. *International Journal of Machine Learning and Cybernetics, 11*(9), 2101–2111. DOI: 10.1007/s13042-020-01104-8

Fatani, A., Dahou, A., Al-Qaness, M. A., Lu, S., & Elaziz, M. A. (2021). Advanced feature extraction and selection approach using deep learning and Aquila optimizer for IoT intrusion detection system. *Sensors (Basel), 22*(1), 140. DOI: 10.3390/s22010140 PMID: 35009682

Faye, C. (2007). Governing the grapevine: The study of rumor during World War II. *History of Psychology, 10*(1), 1–21. DOI: 10.1037/1093-4510.10.1.1 PMID: 17575811

Fazzari, E., Romano, D., Falchi, F., & Stefanini, C. (2025). Animal behavior analysis methods using deep learning: A survey. *Expert Systems with Applications, 289*, 128330. DOI: 10.1016/j.eswa.2025.128330

Filieri, R., Galati, F., & Raguseo, E. (2021). The impact of service attributes and category on eWOM helpfulness: An investigation of extremely negative and positive ratings using latent semantic analytics and regression analysis. *Computers in Human Behavior, 114*, 106527. DOI: 10.1016/j.chb.2020.106527

Fimoza, D., Amalia, A., & Harumy, T. H. F. (2021, November). Sentiment analysis for movie review in Bahasa Indonesia using BERT. In *2021 International Conference on Data Science, Artificial Intelligence, and Business Analytics (DATABIA)* (pp. 27–34). IEEE. DOI: 10.1109/DATABIA53375.2021.9650096

Flynn, A. J., Tischer, B. D., Mandujano, J. D., & Pisano, M. A. (2024). An Analysis of Methodologies for the Prevention and Mitigation of Cheating in Online Gaming Using Artificial Intelligence and its Ethical Impact. In *Proceedings of the ISCAP Conference ISSN* (Vol. 2473, p. 4901).

Fong, S. S. (2014). Martial arts for health: translating research into practice.

Forstmann, B. U., Dutilh, G., Brown, S., Neumann, J., von Cramon, D. Y., Ridderinkhof, K. R., & Wagenmakers, E.-J. (2008). Striatum and pre-SMA facilitate decision-making under time pressure. *Proceedings of the National Academy of Sciences of the United States of America, 105*(45), 17538–17542. DOI: 10.1073/pnas.0805903105

Forstmann, B. U., Ratcliff, R., & Wagenmakers, E.-J. (2016). Sequential sampling models in cognitive neuroscience: Advantages, applications, and extensions. *Annual Review of Psychology, 67*, 641–666. DOI: 10.1146/annurev-psych-122414-033645

Fosker, N., Anderson, A., Morton, L., & Pisa, A. (2022). Can Behavioural Science Be the Key to Unlocking Patient Adherence? Evidence-Led Development of an Engaging Digital Health Solution. Proceedings of the International Symposium on Human Factors and Ergonomics in Health Care.

Frank, M. J., Scheres, A., & Sherman, S. J. (2007). Understanding decision-making deficits in neurological conditions: Insights from models of natural action selection. *Philosophical Transactions of the Royal Society of London. Series B, Biological Sciences, 362*(1485), 1641–1654. DOI: 10.1098/rstb.2007.2058

Freedman, H. I. (1980). *Deterministic mathematical models in population ecology.* No Title.

Fuchs, A., Passarella, A., & Conti, M. (2023). Modeling, replicating, and predicting human behavior: A survey. *ACM Transactions on Autonomous and Adaptive Systems, 18*(2), 1–47. DOI: 10.1145/3580492

Gadiparthi, S. (2024). Enhancing customer experience with business intelligence: Strategies, tools, and case studies. *International Journal of Management, 15*(2), 108–116.

Gandhi, U. D., Kumar, P. M., Babu, G. C., & Karthick, G. (2021). Sentiment analysis on Twitter data by using convolutional neural network (CNN) and long short-term memory (LSTM). *Wireless Personal Communications*, 1–10. DOI: 10.1007/s11277-021-08580-3

Gartland, S., Malik, M. H. A., & Lovell, M. E. (2001). Injury and injury rates in Muay Thai kick boxing. *British Journal of Sports Medicine*, *35*(5), 308–313. PMID: 11579062

Gaul, W., & Homburg, C. (1989). Exploratory Approaches for the Analysis of Causal Models: Marketing Applications and Theory. Operations Research Proceedings 1988: DGOR Papers of the 17th Annual Meeting/Vorträge der 17.

Gelman, A., Carlin, J., Stern, H., Dunson, D., Vehtari, A., & Rubin, D. (2013). *Bayesian data analysis* (3rd ed.). CRC Press., DOI: 10.1201/b16018

Gentzel, A., Garant, D., & Jensen, D. (2019). The case for evaluating causal models using interventional measures and empirical data. *Advances in Neural Information Processing Systems*, 32.

Ghosh, I., Tiwari, P. K., Mandal, S., Martcheva, M., & Chattopadhyay, J. (2018). A mathematical study to control Guinea worm disease: A case study on Chad. *Journal of Biological Dynamics*, *12*(1), 846–871.

Ghosh, M., & Das, P. (2025). Analysis of online misinformation spread model incorporating external noise and time delay and control of media effort. *Differential Equations and Dynamical Systems*, *33*(1), 261–301. DOI: 10.1007/s12591-023-00657-8

Ghosh, S. S., Dwivedi, A., Tajer, A., Yeo, K., & Gifford, W. M. (2024). Cascading Failure Prediction via Causal Inference. *IEEE Transactions on Power Systems.* Advance online publication. DOI: 10.1109/TPWRS.2024.3516477

Glymour, C., Zhang, K., & Spirtes, P. (2019). Review of causal discovery methods based on graphical models. *Frontiers in Genetics*, *10*, 524. DOI: 10.3389/fgene.2019.00524 PMID: 31214249

Gold, J. I., & Shadlen, M. N. (2007). The neural basis of decision making. *Annual Review of Neuroscience*, *30*, 535–574. DOI: 10.1146/annurev.neuro.29.051605.113038

Goodwin, C. E., Léchenne, M., Wilson-Aggarwal, J. K., Koumetio, S. M., Swan, G. J., Moundai, T., & McDonald, R. A. (2022). Seasonal fishery facilitates a novel transmission pathway in an emerging animal reservoir of Guinea worm. *Current Biology*, *32*(4), 775–782.

Gray, A., Greenhalgh, D., Hu, L., Mao, X., & Pan, J. (2011). A stochastic differential equation SIS epidemic model. *SIAM Journal on Applied Mathematics, 71*(3), 876–902. DOI: 10.1137/10081856X

Greenland, S., & Pearl, J. (2011). Causal Diagrams. In International Encyclopedia of Statistical Science (pp. 411-421). DOI: 10.1007/978-3-642-04898-2_162

Grunova, D., & Tsimperidis, I. (2023). Finding the age and education level of Bulgarian-speaking Internet users using keystroke dynamics. *Eng, 4*(4), 2711–2721. DOI: 10.3390/eng4040154

Guagliardo, S. A. J., Roy, S. L., Ruiz-Tiben, E., Zirimwabagabo, H., Romero, M., Chop, E., & Weiss, A. J. (2020). Guinea worm in domestic dogs in Chad: A description and analysis of surveillance data. *PLoS Neglected Tropical Diseases, 14*(5), e0008207.

Gündüç, S. (2019). A study on the effects of diffusion of information on epidemic spread. *International Journal of Modeling, Simulation and Scientific Computing, 10*(3), 1950015. Advance online publication. DOI: 10.1142/S1793962319500156

Gündüç, S., & Eryiğit, R. (2021). Time dependent correlations between the probability of a node being infected and its centrality measures. *Physica A, 563*, 125483. Advance online publication. DOI: 10.1016/j.physa.2020.125483 PMID: 33106728

Guo, X. (2022). Research on multiplayer posture estimation technology of sports competition video based on graph neural network algorithm. *Computational Intelligence and Neuroscience, 2022*(1), 4727375. PMID: 35401733

Gupta, A., Bansal, R., Alashwal, H., Kacar, A. S., Balci, F., & Moustafa, A. A. (2021). Neural substrates of the drift-diffusion model in brain disorders. *Frontiers in Computational Neuroscience, 15*, 678232. DOI: 10.3389/fncom.2021.678232

Gutierrez, E., Karwowski, W., Fiok, K., Davahli, M. R., Liciaga, T., & Ahram, T. (2021). Analysis of human behavior by mining textual data: Current research topics and analytical techniques. *Symmetry, 13*(7), 1276. DOI: 10.3390/sym13071276

Halpern, J. Y., & Pearl, J. (2005). Causes and explanations: A structural-model approach. Part I: Causes. *The British Journal for the Philosophy of Science, 56*(4), 843–887. DOI: 10.1093/bjps/axi147

Hanks, T., & Summerfield, C. (2017). Perceptual decision making in rodents, monkeys, and humans. *Neuron, 93*(1), 15–31. DOI: 10.1016/j.neuron.2016.12.003

Harbich, S., & Hassenzahl, M. (2011). Using behavioral patterns to assess the interaction of users and product. *International Journal of Human-Computer Studies, 69*(7-8), 496–508. DOI: 10.1016/j.ijhcs.2011.03.003

Harini, B., Gouri, M., Balaji, V., Sangeetha, K., & Harshini, A. (2024). *Advanced Sound Detection and Behavior Examination for Real-Time Intruder Detection using Deep Learning: A Comprehensive Security Framework.* Paper presented at the 2024 2nd International Conference on Artificial Intelligence and Machine Learning Applications Theme: Healthcare and Internet of Things (AIMLA).

Hassell, M., & Varley, G. (1969). New inductive population model for insect parasites and its bearing on biological control.

Haugh, M. B., & Singal, R. (2023). Counterfactual analysis in dynamic latent state models. International Conference on Machine Learning.

Hawkins, G. E., Forstmann, B. U., Wagenmakers, E.-J., Ratcliff, R., & Brown, S. D. (2015). Revisiting the evidence for collapsing boundaries and urgency signals in perceptual decision-making. *The Journal of Neuroscience : The Official Journal of the Society for Neuroscience, 35*(6), 2476–2484. DOI: 10.1523/JNEUROSCI.2410-14.2015

Heathcote, A., Verbruggen, F., Boehler, C. N., & Matzke, D. (2024). Cognitive Control of Choices and Actions. In *An Introduction to Model-Based Cognitive Neuroscience* (pp. 361–385). Springer International Publishing.

Helikumi, M., & Mushayabasa, S. (2023). Dog screening as a novel complementary guinea worm disease control tool to mitigate persistence in Chad: A modeling study. *Parasite Epidemiology and Control, 23*, e00328.

Heyn, H.-M., & Knauss, E. (2022). Structural causal models as boundary objects in AI system development. Proceedings of the 1st International Conference on AI Engineering: Software Engineering for AI.

Holling, C. S. (1959). Some characteristics of simple types of predation and parasitism1. *Canadian Entomologist, 91*(7), 385–398. DOI: 10.4039/Ent91385-7

Hoppensteadt, F. (2006). Predator-prey model. *Scholarpedia Journal, 1*(10), 1563. DOI: 10.4249/scholarpedia.1563

Hosseini, M., Abdolvand, N., & Harandi, S. R. (2022). Two-dimensional analysis of customer behavior in traditional and electronic banking. *Digital Business, 2*(2), 100030. DOI: 10.1016/j.digbus.2022.100030

Host, K., & Ivašić-Kos, M. (2022). An overview of Human Action Recognition in sports based on Computer Vision. *Heliyon, 8*(6). PMID: 35706961

Hriez, S., Obeid, N., & Awajan, A. (2019). User authentication on smartphones using keystroke dynamics. *Proceedings of the Second International Conference on Data Science, E-Learning and Information Systems.* New York, NY, USA: ACM. DOI: 10.1145/3368691.3368725

Huang, S., Lin, P.-H., & Strickland, L. (2017). *DDM in depression: Task complexity and reward processing* (Conference presentation).

Huang, C. D., Behara, R. S., & Goo, J. (2022). Optimal investment in prevention and recovery for mitigating epidemic risks. *Risk Analysis, 42*(1), 206–220. DOI: 10.1111/risa.13707 PMID: 33580512

Huang, H., Li, Z., Cheng, H., Wang, H., Jiang, J., Li, X., & Zgonnikov, A. (2025). Understanding driver cognition and decision-making behaviors in high-risk scenarios: A drift diffusion perspective. *Accident; Analysis and Prevention, 220*, 108123. DOI: 10.1016/j.aap.2025.108123

Huang, Y., Chen, F., & Zhong, L. (2006). Stability analysis of a prey–predator model with Holling type III response function incorporating a prey refuge. *Applied Mathematics and Computation, 182*(1), 672–683. DOI: 10.1016/j.amc.2006.04.030

Hussain, K., & Ihsan, I. (2023). Sentiment analysis in movie reviews using knowledge graph embeddings with deep learning. *Journal of Computing and Biomedical Informatics, 6*(1), 222–229.

Iliescu, D. M. D. (2020). The impact of artificial intelligence on the chess world. *JMIR Serious Games, 8*(4), e24049. DOI: 10.2196/24049 PMID: 33300493

Imbens, G. W., & Rubin, D. B. (2015). Causal inference in statistics, social, and biomedical sciences. Cambridge university press.

Imran, L. B., Latif, R. M. A., Farhan, M., Tariq, T. J. I. J. o. S.-B., & Computing, S. (2019). Real-time simulation of smart lighting system in smart city. *9*(2), 90-98.

Imran, M., Haider, N., Shoaib, M., & Razzak, I. (2022). An intelligent and efficient network intrusion detection system using deep learning. *Computers & Electrical Engineering, 99*, 107764. DOI: 10.1016/j.compeleceng.2022.107764

Irfan, M., Venkatesam, A. S., Shanmugasundaram, H., Gourisaria, M. K., Chowdhury, S., & Patra, S. S. (2025, February). Sentiment analysis of movie reviews: Optimizing predictions through TF-IDF vectorization. In *2025 3rd International Conference on Intelligent Data Communication Technologies and Internet of Things (IDCIoT)* (pp. 102–107). IEEE.

Islam, M. A., Fakir, S. I., Masud, S. B., Hossen, M. D., Islam, M. T., & Siddiky, M. R. (2024). Artificial intelligence in digital marketing automation: Enhancing personalization, predictive analytics, and ethical integration. *Edelweiss Applied Science Technology*, *8*(6), 6498–6516. DOI: 10.55214/25768484.v8i6.3404

Iyer, K. I. (2021). From Signatures to Behavior: Evolving Strategies for Next-Generation Intrusion Detection. *European Journal of Advances in Engineering Technology*, *8*(6), 165–171.

Jackson, M. (2000). *Problem Frames: Analyzing and structuring software development problems.* Addison-Wesley Longman Publishing Co., Inc.

Jahanpour, E., & Chen, X. (2013). Analysis of complex network performance and heuristic node removal strategies. *Communications in Nonlinear Science and Numerical Simulation*, *18*(12), 3458–3468. DOI: 10.1016/j.cnsns.2013.04.030

Jahrestagung, Gendron, G., Witbrock, M., & Dobbie, G. (2023). A survey of methods, challenges and perspectives in causality. arXiv preprint arXiv:2302.00293. DOI: 10.1177/2327857922111007

Jaimini, U., & Sheth, A. (2022). Causalkg: Causal knowledge graph explainability using interventional and counterfactual reasoning. *IEEE Internet Computing*, *26*(1), 43–50. DOI: 10.1109/MIC.2021.3133551

Jiang, L., Zhao, X., Ge, B., Xiao, W., & Ruan, Y. (2019). An efficient algorithm for mining a set of influential spreaders in complex networks. *Physica A*, *516*, 58–65. DOI: 10.1016/j.physa.2018.10.011

Jiang, Y., Choo, K.-K. R., & Ko, H. (2021). A special section on deep & advanced machine learning approaches for human behavior analysis. *Journal of Information Processing Systems*, *17*(2), 334–336.

Jing, F., Wang, Z., Hu, Z., Xu, S., Holme, P., & Weiss, S. H. (2022). Optimal resource allocation in HIV self-testing secondary distribution among Chinese MSM: Data-driven integer programming models. *Philosophical Transactions. Series A, Mathematical, Physical, and Engineering Sciences*, *380*(2214), 20210128. Advance online publication. DOI: 10.1098/rsta.2021.0128 PMID: 34802269

Jogo, F. S. (2025). Statistical Prediction and Machine Learning: John Tuhao Chen, Clement Lee, Lincy Y. Chen, CRC Press, 2024, 314 pp., $74.99, ISBN 9780429318689. In: Taylor & Francis.

Kaewplee, K., Khamsemanan, N., & Nattee, C. (2015). An Instructional Support System for Muay Thai (Doctoral dissertation, Thammasat University).

Kalake, L., Dong, Y., Wan, W., & Hou, L. (2022). Enhancing detection quality rate with a combined hog and cnn for real-time multiple object tracking across non-overlapping multiple cameras. *Sensors (Basel)*, *22*(6), 2123. PMID: 35336294

Karabila, I., Darraz, N., El-Ansari, A., Alami, N., & El Mallahi, M. (2025). A hybrid approach combining sentiment analysis and deep learning to mitigate data sparsity in recommender systems. *Neurocomputing*, *636*, 129886. DOI: 10.1016/j.neucom.2025.129886

Kar, T., & Matsuda, H. (2008). A bioeconomic model of a single-species fishery with a marine reserve. *Journal of Environmental Management*, *86*(1), 171–180. DOI: 10.1016/j.jenvman.2006.12.001 PMID: 17240520

Kasiri-Bidhendi, S., Fookes, C., Morgan, S., Martin, D. T., & Sridharan, S. (2015, September). Combat sports analytics: Boxing punch classification using overhead depthimagery. In 2015 IEEE international conference on image processing (ICIP) (pp. 4545-4549). IEEE.

Katyayan, S. S., & Singh, S. (2025). Optimizing Consumer Retention Strategies Through Data-Driven Insights in Digital Marketplaces. *International Journal of Research in All Subjects in Multi Languages*, *13*(1), 153.

Kaur, K., & Batth, J. S. (2024). *Implementation of Deep Learning and Machine Learning for Designing and Analyzing IDS (Intrusion Detection System) Through Novel Framework.* Paper presented at the International Conference on Innovation and Emerging Trends in Computing and Information Technologies.

Keshavarzian, A., Sharifian, S., & Seyedin, S. (2019). Modified deep residual network architecture deployed on serverless framework of IoT platform based on human activity recognition application. *Future Generation Computer Systems*, *101*, 14–28.

Khamparia, A., & Gupta, D. (2024). *Explainable Artificial Intelligence for Biomedical and Healthcare Applications.* CRC Press. DOI: 10.1201/9781003220107

Khan, S. S., Mondal, P. K., Shaqib, S., Ahmed, N., Prova, N. N. I., & Sattar, A. (2024, June). Performance analysis of LSTM and Bi-LSTM model with different optimizers in Bangla sentiment analysis. In *2024 15th International Conference on Computing Communication and Networking Technologies (ICCCNT)* (pp. 1–7). IEEE. DOI: 10.1109/ICCCNT61001.2024.10726142

Khan, A. N., Salar Khan, A. A., Mansoor, M. A. J., Jameel, A., Rustam, R., Aslam, R., & Shah, J. (2025). Artificial Intelligence in Computer Science: Evolution, Techniques, Challenges, and Multidisciplinary Applications. *Sch J Eng Tech*, *4*(4), 246–263. DOI: 10.36347/sjet.2025.v13i04.006

Khan, A. R., Kashif, M., Jhaveri, R. H., Raut, R., Saba, T., & Bahaj, S. A. (2022). Deep learning for intrusion detection and security of Internet of things (IoT): Current analysis, challenges, and possible solutions. *Security and Communication Networks*, *2022*(1), 4016073. DOI: 10.1155/2022/4016073

Khan, M., Khan, M. S., & Alharbi, Y. (2020). Text mining challenges and applications, a comprehensive review. *IJCSNS*, *20*(12), 138.

Khan, S. S., & Alharbi, Y. (2024). Sentiment analysis of movie review classifications using deep learning approaches. *International Journal of Advanced Applied Science*, *11*(8), 146–157. DOI: 10.21833/ijaas.2024.08.016

Khan, S. S., Khan, M., Ran, Q., & Naseem, R. (2018). Challenges in opinion mining, comprehensive. [Ciencia e Tecnica Vitivinicola]. *Sci Technol J*, *33*(11), 123–135.

Khan, S., Devlen, C., Manno, M., & Hou, D. (2024). Mouse dynamics behavioral biometrics: A survey. *ACM Computing Surveys*, *56*(6), 1–33. DOI: 10.1145/3640311

Khyani, D., Siddhartha, B. S., Niveditha, N. M., & Divya, B. M. (2021). An interpretation of lemmatization and stemming in natural language processing. *Shanghai Ligong Daxue Xuebao*, *22*(10), 350–357.

Kiyani, A. T., Lasebae, A., Ali, K., Rehman, M. U., & Haq, B. (2020). Continuous user authentication featuring keystroke dynamics based on robust recurrent confidence model and ensemble learning approach. *IEEE Access : Practical Innovations, Open Solutions*, *8*, 156177–156189. DOI: 10.1109/ACCESS.2020.3019467

Klonoff, D. C. (2019). Behavioral theory: The missing ingredient for digital health tools to change behavior and increase adherence. *Journal of Diabetes Science and Technology*, *13*(2), 276–281. DOI: 10.1177/1932296818820303 PMID: 30678472

Kocher, G., & Kumar, G. (2021). Machine learning and deep learning methods for intrusion detection systems: Recent developments and challenges. *Soft Computing*, *25*(15), 9731–9763. DOI: 10.1007/s00500-021-05893-0

Kölle, M., Erpelding, Y., Ritz, F., Phan, T., Illium, S., & Linnhoff-Popien, C. (2024). Aquarium: A Comprehensive Framework for Exploring Predator-Prey Dynamics through Multi-Agent Reinforcement Learning Algorithms. *arXiv preprint arXiv:2401.07056*. DOI: 10.5220/0012382300003636

Krauss, E. (2006). *Muay Thai Unleashed: Learn Technique and Strategy from Thailand's Warrior Elite*. McGraw Hill Professional.

Krishnamoorthy, S., Rueda, L., Saad, S., & Elmiligi, H. (2018). Identification of user behavioral biometrics for authentication using keystroke dynamics and machine learning. *Proceedings of the 2018 2nd International Conference on Biometric Engineering and Applications*, 50–57. New York, NY, USA: ACM. DOI: 10.1145/3230820.3230829

Kubanek, M., & Szymoniak, S. (2024). Ethical challenges in AI integration: a comprehensive review of bias, privacy, and accountability issues. The Leading Role of Smart Ethics in the Digital World, 75-85.

Kumari, V., Bala, P. K., & Chakraborty, S. (2024). A text mining approach to explore factors influencing consumer intention to use metaverse platform services: Insights from online customer reviews. *Journal of Retailing and Consumer Services, 81*, 103967. DOI: 10.1016/j.jretconser.2024.103967

Kumar, P. (2025). Diffusion Models and Generative Artificial Intelligence: Frameworks, Applications and Challenges. *Archives of Computational Methods in Engineering*, •••, 1–44. DOI: 10.1007/s11831-025-10266-z

Kunicki, Z. J., Smith, M. L., & Murray, E. J. (2023). A primer on structural equation model diagrams and directed acyclic graphs: When and how to use each in psychological and epidemiological research. *Advances in Methods and Practices in Psychological Science, 6*(2), 25152459231156085. DOI: 10.1177/25152459231156085

Kwon, H., Kim, Y., Lee, J. S., & Cho, M. (2018). First person action recognition via two-stream convnet with long-term fusion pooling. *Pattern Recognition Letters, 112*, 161–167.

La Mastra, C., Barchitta, M., Maugeri, A., & Agodi, A. (2024). Application of artificial intelligence to study the causality in public health: a systematic review. European Journal of Public Health, 34(Supplement_3), ckae144. 1198. DOI: 10.1093/eurpub/ckae144.1198

Laarhoven, T., & Ponukumati, A. (2022, November). Towards Transparent Cheat Detection in

Lalvani, S., & Katsaggelos, A. (2024). Crowdsourcing with the drift diffusion model of decision making. *Scientific Reports, 14*(1), 11311. DOI: 10.1038/s41598-024-61687-y

Latif, R. M. A., Imran, L.-B., Farhan, M., Bah, M. J., Ali, G., & Abid, Y. A. (2019). *Real-time simulation of iot based smart home live mirror using wsn.* Paper presented at the 2019 International conference on frontiers of information Technology (FIT). DOI: 10.1109/FIT47737.2019.00019

Latif, R. M. A., Ullah, F., Jamal, N., Zhao, Y., Jabbar, S., & Khan, M. A. (2025). *Explainable AI for Big Data Analytics in Urban Mobility Forecasting.* Paper presented at the 2025 IEEE International Conference on Pattern Recognition, Machine Vision and Artificial Intelligence (PRMVAI). DOI: 10.1109/PRMVAI65741.2025.11108680

Latif, R. M. A., Umer, M., Tariq, T., Farhan, M., Rizwan, O., & Ali, G. (2019). *A smart methodology for analyzing secure e-banking and e-commerce websites.* Paper presented at the 2019 16th International Bhurban Conference on Applied Sciences and Technology (IBCAST).

Latif, R. M. A., Yoshigoe, K., Jamal, N., Zhao, Y., Ullah, F., & Ahmad, J. (2025). *Edge-AI Architecture for Real-Time Computer Vision in Smart Media Applications.* Paper presented at the 2025 IEEE International Conference on Pattern Recognition, Machine Vision and Artificial Intelligence (PRMVAI). DOI: 10.1109/PRMVAI65741.2025.11108373

Latif, R. M. A. (2025). Enhancing sustainable urban mobility in Pakistan through renewable hydrogen integration and policy interventions. *Discover Cities, 2*(1), 1–24. DOI: 10.1007/s44327-025-00089-9

Latif, R. M. A., Farhan, M., Ahmad, J., Mostarda, L., & Cacciagrano, D. (2025). Blockchain-Based Medicine Supply Chain for Transparent Healthcare Tracking. In *AI and Blockchain Applications for Privacy and Security in Smart Medical Systems* (pp. 81–106). IGI Global Scientific Publishing. DOI: 10.4018/979-8-3373-0593-6.ch004

Latif, R. M. A., Farhan, M., Khan, N. A., & Sujatha, R. (2024). Sustainable Computing-Based Simulation of Intelligent Border Surveillance Using Mobile WSN. In *Navigating Cyber Threats and Cybersecurity in the Logistics Industry* (pp. 90–122). IGI Global Scientific Publishing. DOI: 10.4018/979-8-3693-3816-2.ch003

Latif, R. M. A., Obaidat, M. S., Ullah, F., & Mahmood, K. (2025). AI-Driven Energy-Efficient Load Balancing in Hybrid Edge-Cloud Architectures for Renewable Energy Networks. *IEEE Networking Letters*, 1. DOI: 10.1109/LNET.2025.3596126

Laurens, P., Paige, R. F., Brooke, P. J., & Chivers, H. (2007, July). A novel approach to the detection of cheating in multiplayer online games. In *12th IEEE International Conference on Engineering Complex Computer Systems (ICECCS 2007)* (pp. 97-106). IEEE. DOI: 10.1109/ICECCS.2007.11

Lee, A. G. (2025, Mar 7, 2025). Causal AI: Current State-of-the-Art & Future Directions. https://medium.com/@alexglee/causal-ai-current-state-of-the-art-future-directions-c17ad57ff879

Lee, S.-W., Mohammadi, M., Rashidi, S., Rahmani, A. M., Masdari, M., & Hosseinzadeh, M. (2021). Towards secure intrusion detection systems using deep learning techniques: Comprehensive analysis and review. *Journal of Network and Computer Applications, 187*, 103111. DOI: 10.1016/j.jnca.2021.103111

Lee, W.-L., Liu, C.-H., & Tseng, T.-W. (2022). The multiple effects of service innovation and quality on transitional and electronic word-of-mouth in predicting customer behaviour. *Journal of Retailing and Consumer Services, 64*, 102791. DOI: 10.1016/j.jretconser.2021.102791

Lestari, V. B., & Utami, E. (2024). Combining Bi-LSTM and Word2vec embedding for sentiment analysis models of application user reviews. *The Indonesian Journal of Computer Science, 13*(1).

Li, G., Borj, P. R., Bergeron, L., & Bours, P. (2019). Exploring keystroke dynamics and stylometry features for gender prediction on chat data. *2019 42nd International Convention on Information and Communication Technology, Electronics and Microelectronics (MIPRO)*, 1049–1054. IEEE.

Liang, Z., & Meng, X. (2023). Stability and Hopf bifurcation of a multiple delayed predator–prey system with fear effect, prey refuge and Crowley–Martin function. *Chaos, Solitons, and Fractals, 175*, 113955. DOI: 10.1016/j.chaos.2023.113955

Li, D., & Ma, J. (2017). How the government's punishment and individual's sensitivity affect the rumor spreading in online social networks. *Physica A, 469*, 284–292. DOI: 10.1016/j.physa.2016.11.033

Liesefeld, H. R., & Janczyk, M. (2019). Combining speed and accuracy to control for speed-accuracy trade-offs. *Behavior Research Methods, 51*(1), 40–60. DOI: 10.3758/s13428-018-1076-x

Li, H., Choi, J., Lee, S., & Ahn, J. H. (2020, January). Comparing BERT and XL-Net from the perspective of computational characteristics. In *2020 International Conference on Electronics, Information, and Communication (ICEIC)* (pp. 1–4). IEEE. DOI: 10.1109/ICEIC49074.2020.9051081

Li, J., Chang, H.-C., & Stamp, M. (2021). Free-text keystroke dynamics for user authentication. DOI: 10.31979/etd.ku7u-v7s4

Li, J., & Xue, E. (2023). Dynamic interaction between student learning behaviour and learning environment: Meta-analysis of student engagement and its influencing factors. *Behavioral Sciences (Basel, Switzerland)*, *13*(1), 59. DOI: 10.3390/bs13010059 PMID: 36661631

Li, M., Zhang, H., Georgescu, P., & Li, T. (2021). The stochastic evolution of a rumor spreading model with two distinct spread inhibiting and attitude adjusting mechanisms in a homogeneous social network. *Physica A*, *562*, 125321. DOI: 10.1016/j.physa.2020.125321 PMID: 33012966

Lin, M. P.-C., Liu, A. L., Poitras, E., Chang, M., & Chang, D. H. (2024). An exploratory study on the efficacy and inclusivity of AI technologies in diverse learning environments. *Sustainability (Basel)*, *16*(20), 8992. DOI: 10.3390/su16208992

Lipsky, A. M., & Greenland, S. (2022). Causal directed acyclic graphs. *Journal of the American Medical Association*, *327*(11), 1083–1084. DOI: 10.1001/jama.2022.1816 PMID: 35226050

Li, S., & Chen, J. (2024). Virtual human on social media: Text mining and sentiment analysis. *Technology in Society*, *78*, 102666. DOI: 10.1016/j.techsoc.2024.102666

Li, S., Liu, F., Zhang, Y., Zhu, B., Zhu, H., & Yu, Z. (2022). Text mining of user-generated content (UGC) for business applications in e-commerce: A systematic review. *Mathematics*, *10*(19), 3554. DOI: 10.3390/math10193554

Liu, H., & Lang, B. (2019). Machine learning and deep learning methods for intrusion detection systems: A survey. *Applied Sciences (Basel, Switzerland)*, *9*(20), 4396. DOI: 10.3390/app9204396

Liu, J., Lv, P., Liu, B., & Zhang, T. (2021). Dynamics of a Predator-Prey Model with Fear Effect and Time Delay. *Complexity*, *2021*(1), 9184193. DOI: 10.1155/2021/9184193

Liu, S., & Liu, Y. (2021). Application of human movement and movement scoring technology in computer vision feature in sports training. *Journal of the Institution of Electronics and Telecommunication Engineers*, 1–7.

Liu, X., Lim, X.-J., Cheah, J.-H., Ng, S. I., & Kamal Basha, N. (2023). Food at your doorstep? Examining customer loyalty towards online food delivery applications. *British Food Journal*. Advance online publication. DOI: 10.1108/BFJ-02-2023-0116

Liu, Y., & Li, X. (2021). Dynamics of a discrete predator-prey model with Holling-II functional response. *International Journal of Biomathematics, 14*(08), 2150068. DOI: 10.1142/S1793524521500686

Li, Y., Li, Q., Huang, Q., Xia, R., & Li, X. (2019). Spatiotemporal interest point detector exploiting appearance and motion-variation information. *Journal of Electronic Imaging*, *28*(3), 033002–033002.

Lo, C. F., & Ip, H. Y. (2021). Modified leaky competing accumulator model of decision making with multiple alternatives: The Lie-algebraic approach. *Scientific Reports*, *11*(1), 10923. DOI: 10.1038/s41598-021-90356-7

Lopez-Martin, M., Carro, B., & Sanchez-Esguevillas, A. (2020). Application of deep reinforcement learning to intrusion detection for supervised problems. *Expert Systems with Applications*, *141*, 112963. DOI: 10.1016/j.eswa.2019.112963

Lorbeer, B., & Mohsen, M. (2023). Comparative Study of Causal Discovery Methods for Cyclic Models with Hidden Confounders. 2023 IEEE 5th International Conference on Cognitive Machine Intelligence (CogMI).

Lotka, A. J. (1925). *Elements of physical biology*. Williams & Wilkins.

Lv, Q., Zhang, S., & Wang, Y. (2022). Deep learning model of image classification using machine learning. advances in multimedia, 2022(1), 3351256.

Ma, J., Gao, W., Mitra, P., Kwon, S., Jansen, B. J., Wong, K. F., & Cha, M. (2016). Detecting rumors from microblogs with recurrent neural networks.

Maas, A. L., Daly, R. E., Pham, P. T., Huang, D., Ng, A. Y., & Potts, C. (2011, June). Learning word vectors for sentiment analysis. In *Proceedings of the 49th Annual Meeting of the Association for Computational Linguistics: Human Language Technologies* (pp. 142–150). Association for Computational Linguistics. https://www.aclweb.org/anthology/P11-1015

Maeng, Y., Lee, C. C., & Yun, H. (2023). Understanding antecedents that affect customer evaluations of head-mounted display VR devices through text mining and deep neural network. *Journal of Theoretical and Applied Electronic Commerce Research*, *18*(3), 1238–1256. DOI: 10.3390/jtaer18030063

Maki, D., & Thompson, M. (1973). *Mathematical models and application*. Prentice-Hall.

Mandal, S., & Tiwari, P. K. (2024). Schooling behavior in a generalist predator–prey system: Exploring fear, refuge and cooperative strategies in a stochastic environment. *The European Physical Journal Plus*, *139*(1), 29. DOI: 10.1140/epjp/s13360-023-04787-4

Manure, A., Bengani, S., & Saravanan, S. (2023). Introduction to Responsible AI: Implement Ethical AI Using Python. Springer. DOI: 10.1007/978-1-4842-9982-1

Mao, X. (2007). *Stochastic differential equations and applications*. Elsevier.

Martínez-López, F., & Gázquez-Abad, J. (2015). Causal Modeling in Marketing. In Wiley Encyclopedia of Management. DOI: 10.1002/9781118785317.weom090037

Martín, G., A., Fernández-Isabel, A., Martín de Diego, I., & Beltrán, M. (. (2021). A survey for user behavior analysis based on machine learning techniques: Current models and applications. *Applied Intelligence*, *51*(8), 6029–6055. DOI: 10.1007/s10489-020-02160-x

Matosas-López, L. (2025). The influence of brand credibility and brand loyalty on customer satisfaction and continued use intention in new voice assistance services based on AI. *Journal of Marketing Analytics*, *13*(1), 180–201. DOI: 10.1057/s41270-023-00278-8

Mayopu, R. G., Wang, Y.-Y., & Chen, L.-S. (2023). Analyzing Online Fake News Using Latent Semantic Analysis: Case of USA Election Campaign. *Big Data and Cognitive Computing*, *7*(2), 81. DOI: 10.3390/bdcc7020081

Meli, D. (2024). Explainable online unsupervised anomaly detection for cyber-physical systems via causal discovery from time series. 2024 IEEE 20th International Conference on Automation Science and Engineering (CASE).

Mezair, T., Djenouri, Y., Belhadi, A., Srivastava, G., & Lin, J. C.-W. (2022). Towards an advanced deep learning for the internet of behaviors: Application to connected vehicles. *ACM Transactions on Sensor Networks*, *19*(2), 1–18. DOI: 10.1145/3526192

Mirthipati, T. (2024). Enhancing airline customer satisfaction: A machine learning and causal analysis approach. arXiv preprint arXiv:2405.09076. DOI: 10.48550/arXiv.2405.09076

Mishra, P., Varadharajan, V., Tupakula, U., & Pilli, E. S. (2018). A detailed investigation and analysis of using machine learning techniques for intrusion detection. *IEEE Communications Surveys and Tutorials*, *21*(1), 686–728. DOI: 10.1109/COMST.2018.2847722

Mishra, S., Shukla, P., & Agarwal, R. (2022). Analyzing machine learning enabled fake news detection techniques for diversified datasets. *Wireless Communications and Mobile Computing*, *2022*(1), 1575365. DOI: 10.1155/2022/1575365

Mitra, A. (2020). Sentiment analysis using machine learning approaches (Lexicon based on movie review dataset). *Journal of Ubiquitous Computing and Communication Technologies*, *2*(3), 145–152. DOI: 10.36548/jucct.2020.3.004

Mojica, M., Palos-Sanchez, P. R., & Cabanas, E. (2024). Is there innovation management of emotions or just the commodification of happiness? A sentiment analysis of happiness apps. *European Journal of Innovation Management.*

Molabanti, S. C., Kanchi, L. K., Sonathi, V., & Annam, R. (2024). Development of optimised causal AI and its application in retail banking. *Journal of Digital Banking*, *9*(2), 110–117. DOI: 10.69554/QPAE5180

Mondal, S., & Bours, P. (2017). Person identification by keystroke dynamics using pairwise user coupling. *IEEE Transactions on Information Forensics and Security*, *12*(6), 1319–1329. DOI: 10.1109/TIFS.2017.2658539

More, A., & Unnikrishnan, R. (2024). AI-Powered Analytics in Product Marketing Optimizing Customer Experience and Market Segmentation. *Journal Of Multidisciplinary*, *4*(11), 12–19.

Moustafa, A. A., Sherman, S. J., Frank, M. J., & Chopra, M. (2008). A role for dopamine in temporal decision making and reward maximization in Parkinsonism. *The Journal of Neuroscience : The Official Journal of the Society for Neuroscience*, *28*(47), 12294–12304. DOI: 10.1523/JNEUROSCI.3116-08.2008

Muhamada, A. W., & Mohammed, A. A. (2022). Review on recent computer vision methods for human action recognition.

Mujagić, A., & Mehanović, D. (2024, June). Predictive Analysis of Chess Player Performance: An Analysis of Factors Influencing Competitive Success Using Machine Learning Techniques. In *International Symposium on Innovative and Interdisciplinary Applications of Advanced Technologies* (pp. 392-408). Cham: Springer Nature Switzerland. DOI: 10.1007/978-3-031-71694-2_29

Mukherjee, S., Das, M. K., & Chakraborty, T. K. (2023). Viral marketing in increasing brand awareness and predicting purchase intention: Exploring mediating role of brand loyalty in FMCG sector. *Scholars Journal of Economics, Business and Management*, *4*(4), 61–77. DOI: 10.36347/sjebm.2023.v10i04.001

Mulder, M. J., van Maanen, L., & Forstmann, B. U. (2014). Perceptual decision neurosciences – a model-based review. *Neuroscience*, *277*, 872–884. DOI: 10.1016/j.neuroscience.2014.07.031

Muller, D., & Judd, C. M. (2014). Direct and Indirect Effects. In Wiley StatsRef: Statistics Reference Online. DOI: 10.1002/9781118445112.stat06589

Murdoch, W. W., & Oaten, A. (1975). Predation and population stability. [). Elsevier.]. *Advances in Ecological Research*, *9*, 1–131. DOI: 10.1016/S0065-2504(08)60288-3

Murray, E. J., & Kunicki, Z. (2022). As the wheel turns: Causal inference for feedback loops and bidirectional effects. DOI: 10.31219/osf.io/9em5q

Musawa, A. H., Iswanto, I. A., & Hidayat, M. F. (2024). Exploring transformer-based models for sentiment analysis of movie reviews. *International Journal of Advanced Technology and Engineering Research.*

Musawa, A. H., Iswanto, I. A., & Hidayat, M. F. (2024, August). Exploring transformer-based model in sentiment analysis of movie review. In *2024 8th International Conference on Information Technology, Information Systems and Electrical Engineering (ICITISEE)* (pp. 214–219). IEEE. DOI: 10.1109/ICITISEE63424.2024.10730492

Mustak, M., Hallikainen, H., Laukkanen, T., Plé, L., Hollebeek, L. D., & Aleem, M. (2024). Using machine learning to develop customer insights from user-generated content. *Journal of Retailing and Consumer Services*, *81*, 104034. DOI: 10.1016/j.jretconser.2024.104034

Myers, C. E., Interian, A., & Moustafa, A. A. (2022). A practical introduction to using the drift diffusion model of decision-making in cognitive psychology, neuroscience, and health sciences. *Frontiers in Psychology*, *13*, 1039172. DOI: 10.3389/fpsyg.2022.1039172

Naeem, H., Ullah, F., Krejcar, O., Alsirhani, A., & Zhao, Y. (2024). Adversarial Malware Detection on Consumer Devices Using Optimized Image-Based Ensembles. *IEEE Consumer Electronics Magazine*, 1–10. DOI: 10.1109/MCE.2024.3507282

Naeem, H., Ullah, F., & Srivastava, G. (2025). Classification of intrusion cyber-attacks in smart power grids using deep ensemble learning with metaheuristic-based optimization. *Expert Systems: International Journal of Knowledge Engineering and Neural Networks*, *42*(1), e13556. DOI: 10.1111/exsy.13556

Nascimento, T. M. L., Oliveira, A. V. M., Santana, L. E. A. S., & Da Costa-Abreu, M. (2021). *Investigating the use of feature selection techniques for gender prediction systems based on keystroke dynamics.* In *Proceedings of the 11th International Conference of Pattern Recognition Systems (ICPRS 2021)* (pp. 1–6). Institution of Engineering and Technology. DOI: 10.1049/icp.2021.1446

Naser, M. (2024). Causal diagrams for civil and structural engineers. Structures

Naskar, I., & Joseph, N. P. (2024, February). Implementation of movie recommendation system using hybrid filtering methods and sentiment analysis of movie reviews. In *2024 IEEE International Conference for Women in Innovation, Technology & Entrepreneurship (ICWITE)* (pp. 513–518). IEEE. DOI: 10.1109/ICWITE59797.2024.10502695

Nica, E., Poliak, M., Popescu, G. H., & Pârvu, I.-A. (2022). Decision intelligence and modeling, multisensory customer experiences, and socially interconnected virtual services across the metaverse ecosystem. *Linguistic Philosophical Investigations, 21*(0), 137–153. DOI: 10.22381/lpi2120229

Ning, W. (2025). Research on movie rating prediction using BERT-base model. *Journal of Intelligent & Fuzzy Systems.*

Norhayati, R., Ahmad Zuber, M. F., & Turab, A. (2024). Mathematical modelling of a rumor spreading with the attitude of adjusting mechanisms. *Sains Malaysiana, 53*(3), 719–731. DOI: 10.17576/jsm-2024-5303-18

Novalia, V., Tania, K. D., Meiriza, A., & Wedhasmara, A. (2024, September). Knowledge discovery of application review using word embedding's comparison with CNN-LSTM model on sentiment analysis. In *2024 International Conference on Electrical Engineering and Computer Science (ICECOS)* (pp. 234–238). IEEE. DOI: 10.1109/ICECOS63900.2024.10791113

O'Connell, R. G., Shadlen, M. N., Wong-Lin, K., & Kelly, S. P. (2018). Bridging neural and computational viewpoints on perceptual decision-making. *Trends in Neurosciences, 41*(11), 838–852. DOI: 10.1016/j.tins.2018.06.005

Oloyede, J. (2024). Ethical reflections on AI for cybersecurity: building trust. Available at SSRN 4733563. DOI: 10.2139/ssrn.4733563

Olugbenga, A. M., Adenike, A. E., Esther, O. O., Michael, A. A., Samsudeen, B. O., & Ibrahim, A. O. (2024). Development of a Distributed Denial of Service Detection Model Using Ensemble Machine Learning Techniques. *Adeleke University Journal of Science, 3*(1), 205–218.

Palmer, J., Huk, A. C., & Shadlen, M. N. (2005). The effect of stimulus strength on the speed and accuracy of a perceptual decision. *Journal of Vision (Charlottesville, Va.)*, *5*(5), 376–404. DOI: 10.1167/5.5.1

Pal, S., Pal, N., Samanta, S., & Chattopadhyay, J. (2019). Fear effect in prey and hunting cooperation among predators in a Leslie-Gower model. *Mathematical Biosciences and Engineering*, *16*(5), 5146–5179. DOI: 10.3934/mbe.2019258 PMID: 31499707

Panchal, A., Beniwal, K., & Kumar, V. (2025). Predator Prey Scavenger Model using Holling's Functional Response of Type III and Physics-Informed Deep Neural Networks. *International Journal of Applied and Computational Mathematics*, *11*(2), 44. DOI: 10.1007/s40819-025-01862-5

Pandey, A., Yadav, R., Pathak, A., Shivani, N., Garg, B., & Pandey, A. (2024, October). Sentiment analysis of IMDb movie reviews. In *2024 First International Conference on Software, Systems and Information Technology (SSITCON)* (pp. 1–6). IEEE.

Pandya, S. (2025, April). Novel framework for sentiment analysis of movie reviews based on large language models and deep learning methods. In *2025 4th International Conference on Distributed Computing and Electrical Circuits and Electronics (ICDCECE)* (pp. 1–7). IEEE. DOI: 10.1109/ICDCECE65353.2025.11035279

Paneru, B., Thapa, B., & Paneru, B. (2025). Sentiment analysis of movie reviews: A flask application using CNN with RoBERTa embeddings. *Systems and Soft Computing*, *7*, 200192. DOI: 10.1016/j.sasc.2025.200192

Park, J., Lee, J., Kim, T., Ahn, I., & Park, J. (2021). Co-evolution of predator-prey ecosystems by reinforcement learning agents. *Entropy (Basel, Switzerland)*, *23*(4), 461. DOI: 10.3390/e23040461 PMID: 33924723

Parmar, N., Vaswani, A., Uszkoreit, J., Kaiser, L., Shazeer, N., Ku, A., & Tran, D. (2018, July). Image transformer. In *International conference on machine learning* (pp. 4055-4064). PMLR.

Pasupulati, R., Mahendran, J., & Majumdar, A. (2024). Predictive Analysis of Digital Consumer Behaviour: Key to Understanding Success and Failure of a Brand. In *Enhancing and Predicting Digital Consumer Behavior with AI* (pp. 238-267): IGI Global.

Patria, R., Favian, S., Caturdewa, A., & Suhartono, D. (2021, December). Cheat detection on online chess games using convolutional and dense neural network. In *2021 4th International Seminar on Research of Information Technology and Intelligent Systems (ISRITI)* (pp. 389-395). IEEE. DOI: 10.1109/ISRITI54043.2021.9702792

Pavlin, G., Laskey, K. B., Mignet, F., Slijkhuis, F. S., Blasch, E., Dragos, V., de Villiers, J. P., & Jansen, L. (2023). Qualitative models of data generation processes: Facilitating data-intensive ai solutions. 2023 26th International Conference on Information Fusion (FUSION).

Pearl, J. (1996). A causal calculus for statistical research. Learning from Data: Artificial Intelligence and Statistics V, 23-33. DOI: 10.1007/978-1-4612-2404-4_3

Pearl, J. (2009). *Causality*. Cambridge university press. DOI: 10.1017/CBO9780511803161

Pearl, J. (2010). The foundations of causal inference. *Sociological Methodology*, *40*(1), 75–149. DOI: 10.1111/j.1467-9531.2010.01228.x

Pearl, J., & Mackenzie, D. (2018). *The book of why: the new science of cause and effect*. Basic books.

Pedersen, M. L., Frank, M. J., & Biele, G. (2017). The drift diffusion model as the choice rule in reinforcement learning. *Psychonomic Bulletin & Review*, *24*(4), 1234–1251. DOI: 10.3758/s13423-016-1199-y

Pellegrino, C., Patti, G., Camporeale, M., Belati, A., Novara, R., Papagni, R., & Di Gennaro, F. (2022). Guinea worm disease: A neglected diseases on the verge of eradication. *Tropical Medicine and Infectious Disease*, *7*(11), 366.

Pentel, A. (2017). *Predicting age and gender by keystroke dynamics and mouse patterns.* In *Adjunct Publication of the 25th Conference on User Modeling, Adaptation and Personalization* (pp. 280–285). DOI: 10.1145/3099023.3099105

Pereira, L. M., & Saptawijaya, A. (2016). Counterfactuals in critical thinking with application to morality. Model-Based Reasoning in Science and Technology: Logical, Epistemological, and Cognitive Issues.

Peters, J., Janzing, D., & Schölkopf, B. (2017). Elements of causal inference: foundations and learning algorithms. The MIT press.

Polak, E., Kulasa, J., de Brito, A. V., Castro, M. A., & de Jesus Fernandes, O. (2015). Motion analysis systems as optimization training tools in combat sports and martial arts. [RAMA]. *Revista de Artes Marciales Asiáticas*, *10*(2), 105–123.

Popescu, G. H., Valaskova, K., & Horak, J. (2022). Augmented reality shopping experiences, retail business analytics, and machine vision algorithms in the virtual economy of the metaverse. *Journal of Self-Governance Management Economics*, *10*(2), 67–81.

Pramana, R., Subroto, J. J., & Gunawan, A. A. S. (2022, November). Systematic literature review of stemming and lemmatization performance for sentence similarity. In *2022 IEEE 7th International Conference on Information Technology and Digital Applications (ICITDA)* (pp. 1–6). IEEE. DOI: 10.1109/ICITDA55840.2022.9971451

Qin, G., Wei, J., Sun, Y., & Du, W. (2025). Research Advance of Causal Inference in Clinical Medicine: A Bibliometrics Analysis via Citespace. *Journal of Multidisciplinary Healthcare, 18*, 2603–2627. DOI: 10.2147/JMDH.S516826 PMID: 40370682

Qin, S., Ren, X., & Lü, L. (2019). Efficient network dismantling via node explosive percolation. *Communications in Theoretical Physics, 71*(6), 764. DOI: 10.1088/0253-6102/71/6/764

Quinn, E., & Corcoran, N. (2022, November). Automation of computer vision applications for real-time combat sports video analysis. In *European conference on the impact of artificial intelligence and robotics* (Vol. 4, No. 1, pp. 162-171).

Quiñonero-Candela, J., Sugiyama, M., Schwaighofer, A., & Lawrence, N. D. (2022). *Dataset shift in machine learning*. Mit Press.

Radford, A., Metz, L., & Chintala, S. (2015). Unsupervised representation learning with deep convolutional generative adversarial networks. arXiv preprint arXiv:1511.06434.

Radillo, A. E., Veliz-Cuba, A., Josić, K., & Kilpatrick, Z. P. (2017). Evidence accumulation and change rate inference in dynamic environments. *Neural Computation, 29*(6), 1561–1610. DOI: 10.1162/NECO_a_00957

Rahevar, M., Ganatra, A., Saba, T., Rehman, A., & Bahaj, S. A. (2023). Spatial–temporal dynamic graph attention network for skeleton-based action recognition. *IEEE Access : Practical Innovations, Open Solutions, 11*, 21546–21553.

Rajšp, A., & Fister, I.Jr. (2020). A systematic literature review of intelligent data analysis methods for smart sport training. *Applied Sciences (Basel, Switzerland), 10*(9), 3013.

Ramzan, M., Awan, S. M., Aldabbas, H., Abid, A., Farhan, M., Khalid, S., & Latif, R. M. A. (2019). Internet of medical things for smart D3S to enable road safety. *International Journal of Distributed Sensor Networks, 15*(8), 1550147719864883. DOI: 10.1177/1550147719864883

Rane, N., Choudhary, S., & Rane, J. (2023). *Metaverse marketing strategies: enhancing customer experience and analysing consumer behaviour through leading-edge Metaverse technologies, platforms, and models. Platforms.* Models.

Ratcliff, R. (1978). A theory of memory retrieval. *Psychological Review, 85*(2), 59–108. 10.1037/0033-295X.85.2.59

Ratcliff, R., & McKoon, G. (2008). The diffusion decision model: Theory and data for two-choice decision tasks. *Neural Computation, 20*(4), 873–922. DOI: 10.1162/neco.2008.12-06-420

Ratcliff, R., & Smith, P. L. (2004). A comparison of sequential sampling models for two-choice reaction time. *Psychological Review, 111*(2), 333–367. DOI: 10.1037/0033-295X.111.2.333

Ratcliff, R., & Tuerlinckx, F. (2002). Estimating parameters of the diffusion model: Approaches to dealing with contaminant reaction times and parameter variability. *Psychonomic Bulletin & Review, 9*(3), 438–481. DOI: 10.3758/bf03196302

Rawal, A., Raglin, A., Sadler, B. M., & Rawat, D. B. (2023). Explainability and causality for robust, fair, and trustworthy artificial reasoning. Artificial Intelligence and Machine Learning for Multi-Domain Operations Applications.

Razzaq, A., Gill, H. K., Qureshi, N. M. F., Ullah, S., Masud, F., & Alyami, S. A. (2022). Blockchain in healthcare: A decentralized platform for digital health passport of COVID-19 based on vaccination and immunity certificates. *Health Care, 10*(12), 2453. Advance online publication. DOI: 10.3390/healthcare10122453 PMID: 36553977

Reese, J. F. (2005). Dogs and dog control in developing countries.

Regan, K., & Haworth, G. (2011, August). Intrinsic chess ratings. *Proceedings of the AAAI Conference on Artificial Intelligence, 25*(1), 834–839. DOI: 10.1609/aaai.v25i1.7951

Ren, X., Ren, N., & Lü, L. (2019). Generalized network dismantling. *Proceedings of the National Academy of Sciences of the United States of America, 116*(14), 6554–6559. DOI: 10.1073/pnas.1806108116 PMID: 30877241

Rezaul Karim, M., Shajalal, M., Graß, A., Döhmen, T., Adugna Chala, S., Boden, A., Beecks, C., & Decker, S. (2022). Interpreting Black-box Machine Learning Models for High Dimensional Datasets. arXiv e-prints, arXiv: 2208.13405. DOI: 10.1109/DSAA60987.2023.10302562

Roberts, L. (2019). Exclusive: Battle to wipe out debilitating Guinea worm parasite hits 10 year delay. *Nature, 574*(7777), 157–159.

Robertson, M. D., Koen-Alonso, M., Regular, P. M., Cadigan, N., & Zhang, F. (2022). Accounting for a nonlinear functional response when estimating prey dynamics using predator diet data. *Methods in Ecology and Evolution, 13*(4), 880–893. DOI: 10.1111/2041-210X.13795

Roitman, J. D., & Shadlen, M. N. (2002). Response of neurons in the lateral intraparietal area during a combined reaction-time and discrete trial motion discrimination task. *The Journal of Neuroscience : The Official Journal of the Society for Neuroscience, 22*(21), 9475–9489. DOI: 10.1523/JNEUROSCI.22-21-09475.2002

Rosenzweig, M. L., & MacArthur, R. H. (1963). Graphical representation and stability conditions of predator-prey interactions. *American Naturalist, 97*(895), 209–223. DOI: 10.1086/282272

Rossi, R., & Ahmed, N. (2015). The network data repository with interactive graph analytics and visualization. In *Proceedings of the AAAI Conference on Artificial Intelligence* (Vol. 29, No. 1, pp. 4292-4293). DOI: 10.1609/aaai.v29i1.9277

Roy, S., & Salimi, B. (2023). Causal inference in data analysis with applications to fairness and explanations. In Reasoning Web. Causality, Explanations and Declarative Knowledge: 18th International Summer School 2022, Berlin, Germany, September 27–30, 2022, Tutorial Lectures (pp. 105-131). Springer. DOI: 10.1007/978-3-031-31414-8_3

Ru, D., & Jantan, A. H. B. (2023). Relationship between Customer Value, Customer Trust, Customer Commitment and Customer Loyalty in Hospitality Industry of China. *Journal of International Business Management, 6*(9), 01-15.

Rysbekov, S., Aitbanov, A., Abdiakhmetova, Z., & Kartbayev, A. (2025). Advancing network security: A comparative research of machine learning techniques for intrusion detection. *International Journal of Electrical and Computer Engineering, 15*(2), 2271. DOI: 10.11591/ijece.v15i2.pp2271-2281

S. Zeid, S., A. ElKamar, R., & I. Hassan, S. (2022). Fixed-text vs. Free-text keystroke dynamics for user authentication. *Engineering Research Journal - Faculty of Engineering (Shoubra), 51*(1), 95–104. DOI: 10.21608/erjsh.2022.224312

Saad, T. B., Ahmed, M., Ahmed, B., & Sazan, S. A. (2024, May). A novel transformer-based deep learning approach of sentiment analysis for movie reviews. In *2024 6th International Conference on Electrical Engineering and Information & Communication Technology (ICEEICT)* (pp. 1228–1233). IEEE. DOI: 10.1109/ICEEICT62016.2024.10534588

Saarinen, T. (2017). *Toxic behavior in online games* (Master's thesis, T. Saarinen).

Saba, T., Rehman, A., Sadad, T., Kolivand, H., & Bahaj, S. A. (2022). Anomaly-based intrusion detection system for IoT networks through deep learning model. *Computers & Electrical Engineering*, *99*, 107810. DOI: 10.1016/j.compeleceng.2022.107810

Sadia, H., Farhan, S., Haq, Y. U., Sana, R., Mahmood, T., Bahaj, S. A. O., & Khan, A. R. (2024). Intrusion detection system for wireless sensor networks: A machine learning based approach. *IEEE Access : Practical Innovations, Open Solutions*, *12*, 52565–52582. DOI: 10.1109/ACCESS.2024.3380014

Saengsawang, P., Siladech, C., & Laxanaphisuth, P. (2015). The history and development of Muaythai boran. *Journal of Sports Sciences*, *3*(3), 148–154.

Sáez, E., & González-Olivares, E. (1999). Dynamics of a predator-prey model. *SIAM Journal on Applied Mathematics*, *59*(5), 1867–1878. DOI: 10.1137/S0036139997318457

Saha, S., & Samanta, G. (2021). Modelling of a two prey and one predator system with switching effect. *Computational and Mathematical Biophysics*, *9*(1), 90–113. DOI: 10.1515/cmb-2020-0120

Sahoo, D., & Samanta, G. (2024). Impact of fear effect in a two prey-one predator system with switching behaviour in predation. *differential equations and dynamical systems*, *32*(2), 377-399.

Salem, A., & Obaidat, M. S. (2019). A novel security scheme for behavioral authentication systems based on keystroke dynamics. *Security and Privacy*, *2*(2), e64. DOI: 10.1002/spy2.64

Salmeron-Majadas, S., Baker, R. S., Santos, O. C., & Boticario, J. G. (2018). A machine learning approach to leverage individual keyboard and mouse interaction behavior from multiple users in real-world learning scenarios. *IEEE Access : Practical Innovations, Open Solutions*, *6*, 39154–39179. DOI: 10.1109/ACCESS.2018.2854966

Salmon, P. M., Stanton, N. A., Walker, G. H., Hulme, A., Goode, N., Thompson, J., & Read, G. J. (2022). Causal loop diagrams (CLDs). In *Handbook of Systems Thinking Methods* (pp. 157–180). CRC Press. DOI: 10.1201/9780429281624-11

Samek, W., Montavon, G., Vedaldi, A., Hansen, L. K., & Müller, K.-R. (2019). *Explainable AI: interpreting, explaining and visualizing deep learning* (Vol. 11700). Springer Nature. DOI: 10.1007/978-3-030-28954-6

Sandler, M., Howard, A., Zhu, M., Zhmoginov, A., & Chen, L. C. (2018). Mobilenetv2: Inverted residuals and linear bottlenecks. In *Proceedings of the IEEE conference on computer vision and pattern recognition* (pp. 4510-4520).

Sangeetha, T., Kumar, B. K., Kaarthik, A. A., & Sankar, R. A. (2025, February). Exploring sentiments in movie reviews using BERT algorithm. In. AIP Conference Proceedings: Vol. 3204. *No. 1* (p. 050015). AIP Publishing LLC. DOI: 10.1063/5.0248539

Sann, R., Lai, P.-C., Liaw, S.-Y., & Chen, C.-T. (2022). Predicting online complaining behavior in the hospitality industry: Application of big data analytics to online reviews. *Sustainability (Basel)*, *14*(3), 1800. DOI: 10.3390/su14031800

Saranya, T., Sridevi, S., Deisy, C., Chung, T. D., & Khan, M. A. (2020). Performance analysis of machine learning algorithms in intrusion detection system: A review. *Procedia Computer Science*, *171*, 1251–1260. DOI: 10.1016/j.procs.2020.04.133

Sarhan, A. M., Ayman, H., Wagdi, M., & Osama, R.. (2024). Integrating machine learning and sentiment analysis in movie recommendation systems. *Journal of Electrical Systems and Information Technology*, *11*(1), 53. Advance online publication. DOI: 10.1186/s43067-024-00177-7

Sasmal, S. K., & Takeuchi, Y. (2020). Dynamics of a predator-prey system with fear and group defense. *Journal of Mathematical Analysis and Applications*, *481*(1), 123471. DOI: 10.1016/j.jmaa.2019.123471

Saxena, C., Doja, M. N., & Ahmad, T. (2018). Group based centrality for immunization of complex networks. *Physica A*, *508*, 35–47. DOI: 10.1016/j.physa.2018.05.107

Schölkopf, B., Locatello, F., Bauer, S., Ke, N. R., Kalchbrenner, N., Goyal, A., & Bengio, Y. (2021). Toward causal representation learning. *Proceedings of the IEEE*, *109*(5), 612–634. DOI: 10.1109/JPROC.2021.3058954

Schumacher, L., Schnuerch, M., Voss, A., & Radev, S. T. (2025). Validation and comparison of non-stationary cognitive models: A diffusion model application. *Computational Brain & Behavior*, *8*(2), 191–210. DOI: 10.1007/s42113-024-00218-4

Selvakumar, B., & Lakshmanan, B. (2022). Sentimental analysis on user's reviews using BERT. *Materials Today: Proceedings*, *62*, 4931–4935. DOI: 10.1016/j.matpr.2022.03.678

Shaffi, S. M. (2025). Enhancing Customer Journey Intelligence: A Unified Framework for 360-Degree Analytics Using Generative AI. *Growth*, *7*, 8.

Shafqat, R., & Alsaadi, A. (2024). Artificial neural networks for stability analysis and simulation of delayed rabies spread models. *AIMS Mathematics*, *9*(12), 33495–33531.

Shafqat, R., & Alsaadi, A. (2025). Mathematical and numerical analysis of a fractional SIQR epidemic model with normalized Caputo–Fabrizio operator and machine learning approaches. *AIMS Mathematics, 10*(9), 20235–20261.

Shafqat, R., Alsaadi, A., & Alubaidi, A. (2025). A Fractional-Order Alcoholism Model Incorporating Hypothetical Social Influence: A Theoretical and Numerical Study. *Journal of Mathematics, 2025*(1), 6773909.

Shahhosseini, M., Hu, G., & Pham, H. (2022). Optimizing ensemble weights and hyperparameters of machine learning models for regression problems. *Machine Learning with Applications, 7*, 100251. DOI: 10.1016/j.mlwa.2022.100251

Sharma, H., Pangaonkar, S., Gunjan, R., & Rokade, P. (2023). Sentimental analysis of movie reviews using machine learning. In *ITM Web of Conferences* (Vol. 53, p. 02006). EDP Sciences. DOI: 10.1051/itmconf/20235302006

Shen, Y., Wang, H., Ho, E. S., Yang, L., & Shum, H. P. (2017). Posture-based and action-based graphs for boxing skill visualization. *Computers & Graphics, 69*, 104–115.

Shetty, A. M., DH, M., & Aljunid, M. F. (2025). Fine-tuning XLNet for Amazon review sentiment analysis: A comparative evaluation of transformer models. *ETRI Journal.*

Shotton, J., Fitzgibbon, A., Cook, M., Sharp, T., Finocchio, M., Moore, R., & Blake, A. (2011, June). Real-time human pose recognition in parts from single depth images. In *CVPR 2011* (pp. 1297–1304). Ieee.

Silva, F. P., Oliveira, H., & Pereira, T. (2024). Causal representation learning through higher-level information extraction. *ACM Computing Surveys, 57*(2), 1–37. DOI: 10.1145/3696412

Simonyan, K., & Zisserman, A. (2014). Very deep convolutional networks for large-scale image recognition. arXiv preprint arXiv:1409.1556.

Smith, P. L., & Ratcliff, R. (2004). Psychology and neurobiology of simple decisions. *Trends in Neurosciences, 27*(3), 161–168. DOI: 10.1016/j.tins.2004.01.006

Song, K., Li, J., & Li, L. (2019). Target controllability of two-layer multiplex networks based on network flow theory. *IEEE Transactions on Cybernetics, 51*(5), 2699–2711. DOI: 10.1109/TCYB.2019.2906700 PMID: 30990210

Spolaôr, N., Lee, H. D., Takaki, W. S. R., Ensina, L. A., Coy, C. S. R., & Wu, F. C. (2020). A systematic review on content-based video retrieval. *Engineering Applications of Artificial Intelligence, 90*, 103557.

Steyer, R., Mayer, A., & Lossnitzer, C. (2023). Causal inference on total, direct, and indirect effects. In *Encyclopedia of quality of life and well-being research* (pp. 1–26). Springer. DOI: 10.1007/978-3-031-17299-1_295

Stone, M. (1960). Models for choice-reaction time. *Psychometrika, 25*(3), 251–260. DOI: 10.1007/BF02289729

Subramanian, R. S., & Prabha, D. (2022). Ensemble variable selection for Naive Bayes to improve customer behaviour analysis. *Computer Systems Science and Engineering, 41*(1), 339–355. DOI: 10.32604/csse.2022.020043

Suthaharan, S., & Suthaharan, S. (2016). Support vector machine. *Machine learning models and algorithms for big data classification: thinking with examples for effective learning*, 207-235.

Syrgkanis, V., Lewis, G., Oprescu, M., Hei, M., Battocchi, K., Dillon, E., Pan, J., Wu, Y., Lo, P., & Chen, H. (2021). Causal inference and machine learning in practice with econml and causalml: Industrial use cases at microsoft, tripadvisor, uber. Proceedings of the 27th ACM SIGKDD conference on knowledge discovery & data mining.

Tan, K. L., Lee, C. P., & Lim, K. M. (2023). RoBERTa-GRU: A hybrid deep learning model for sentiment analysis. *Applied Sciences (Basel, Switzerland), 13*(6), 3915. DOI: 10.3390/app13063915

Thapa, N., Liu, Z., Kc, D. B., Gokaraju, B., & Roy, K. (2020). Comparison of machine learning and deep learning models for network intrusion detection systems. *Future Internet, 12*(10), 167. DOI: 10.3390/fi12100167

Thet, T. T., Na, J. C., & Khoo, C. S. (2010). Aspect-based sentiment analysis of movie reviews on discussion boards. *Journal of Information Science, 36*(6), 823–848. DOI: 10.1177/0165551510388123

Thirthar, A. A., Majeed, S. J., Alqudah, M. A., Panja, P., & Abdeljawad, T. (2022). Fear effect in a predator-prey model with additional food, prey refuge and harvesting on super predator. *Chaos, Solitons, and Fractals, 159*, 112091. DOI: 10.1016/j.chaos.2022.112091

Thomas, P. A., & Preetha Mathew, K. (2023). A broad review on non-intrusive active user authentication in biometrics. *Journal of Ambient Intelligence and Humanized Computing, 14*(1), 339–360. DOI: 10.1007/s12652-021-03301-x PMID: 34109006

Tillman, G., Van Zandt, T., & Logan, G. D. (2020). Sequential sampling models without random between-trial variability: The racing diffusion model of speeded decision making. *Psychonomic Bulletin & Review*, *27*(5), 911–936. 10.3758/s13423-020-01719-6

Tiwari, P. K., Verma, M., Pal, S., Kang, Y., & Misra, A. K. (2021). A delay nonautonomous predator–prey model for the effects of fear, refuge and hunting cooperation. *Journal of Biological System*, *29*(04), 927–969. DOI: 10.1142/S0218339021500236

Toosi, R., & Akhaee, M. A. (2021). Time–frequency analysis of keystroke dynamics for user authentication. *Future Generation Computer Systems*, *115*, 438–447. DOI: 10.1016/j.future.2020.09.027

Townsend, J. T., & Ashby, F. G. (1983). *Stochastic modeling of elementary psychological processes.* Cambridge University Press.

Trueblood, J. S., Brown, S. D., & Heathcote, A. (2014). The multiattribute linear ballistic accumulator model of context effects in multialternative choice. *Psychological Review*, *121*(2), 179. 10.1037/a0036137

Tsetsos, K., Usher, M., & McClelland, J. L. (2011). Testing multi-alternative decision models with non-stationary evidence. *Frontiers in Neuroscience*, *5*, 63. DOI: 10.3389/fnins.2011.00063

Tsimperidis, I., & Arampatzis, A. (2020). The keyboard knows about you: Revealing user characteristics via keystroke dynamics. *International Journal of Technoethics*, *11*(2), 34–51. DOI: 10.4018/IJT.2020070103

Tsimperidis, I., Arampatzis, A., & Karakos, A. (2018). Keystroke dynamics features for gender recognition. *Digital Investigation*, *24*, 4–10. DOI: 10.1016/j.diin.2018.01.018

Tsimperidis, I., Grunova, D., & Papakostas, G. A. (2023). The way we type reveals our native language. *IEEE Access : Practical Innovations, Open Solutions*, *11*, 98191–98201. DOI: 10.1109/ACCESS.2023.3313510

Tsimperidis, I., Grunova, D., Roy, S., & Moussiades, L. (2023). Keystroke dynamics as a language profiling tool: Identifying mother tongue of unknown Internet users. *Telecom*, *4*(3), 369–377. DOI: 10.3390/telecom4030021

Tsimperidis, I., Yucel, C., & Katos, V. (2021). Age and gender as cyber attribution features in keystroke dynamic-based user classification processes. *Electronics (Basel)*, *10*(7), 835. DOI: 10.3390/electronics10070835

Turab, A., Sintunavarat, W., Ullah, F., Zaidi, S. A., Montoyo, A., & Nescolarde-Selva, J.-A. (2024). Computational modeling of animal behavior in T-mazes: Insights from machine learning. *Ecological Informatics*, *81*, 102639. DOI: 10.1016/j.ecoinf.2024.102639

Turab, A., Mlaiki, N., Fatima, N., Mitrović, Z. D., & Ali, W. (2022). Analysis of a class of stochastic animal behavior models under specific choice preferences. *Mathematics*, *10*(12), 1975. DOI: 10.3390/math10121975

Turab, A., Montoyo, A., & Nescolarde-Selva, J. A. (2024a). Computational and analytical analysis of integral-differential equations for modeling avoidance learning behavior. *Journal of Applied Mathematics & Computing*, *70*(5), 4423–4439. DOI: 10.1007/s12190-024-02130-3

Turab, A., Nescolarde-Selva, J. A., Ullah, F., Montoyo, A., Alfiniyah, C., Sintunavarat, W., & Zaidi, S. A. (2025). Deep neural networks and stochastic methods for cognitive modeling of rat behavioral dynamics in $$\mathbb{T}$$-mazes. *Cognitive Neurodynamics*, *19*(1), 1–28. DOI: 10.1007/s11571-025-10247-9 PMID: 39749104

Turab, A., Nescolarde-Selva, J. A., Ullah, F., Montoyo, A., Alfiniyah, C., Sintunavarat, W., & Zaidi, S. A. (2025). Deep neural networks and stochastic methods for cognitive modeling of rat behavioral dynamics in T-mazes. *Cognitive Neurodynamics*, *19*(1), 1–28.

Turab, A., Rosli, N., Ali, W., & Nieto, J. J. (2023). The existence and uniqueness of solutions to a functional equation arising in psychological learning theory. *Demonstratio Mathematica*, *56*(1), 20220231. DOI: 10.1515/dema-2022-0231

Turab, A., Shafqat, R., Muhammad, S., Shuaib, M., Khan, M. F., & Kamal, M. (2024). Predictive modeling of hepatitis B viral dynamics: A caputo derivative-based approach using artificial neural networks. *Scientific Reports*, *14*(1), 21853.

Turab, A., & Sintunavarat, W. (2019). On analytic model for two-choice behavior of the paradise fish based on the fixed point method. *Journal of Fixed Point Theory and Its Applications*, *21*(2), 56. DOI: 10.1007/s11784-019-0694-y

Turab, A., & Sintunavarat, W. (2020). On the solution of the traumatic avoidance learning model approached by the Banach fixed point theorem. *Journal of Fixed Point Theory and Its Applications*, *22*(2), 50. DOI: 10.1007/s11784-020-00788-3

Uiterwaal, S. F., & DeLong, J. P. (2020). Functional responses are maximized at intermediate temperatures. *Ecology*, *101*(4), e02975. DOI: 10.1002/ecy.2975 PMID: 31944271

Ullah, F., Mostarda, L., Cacciagrano, D., Alenazi, M. J., Chen, C.-M., & Kumari, S. (2024). Federated Edge Intelligence for Enhanced Security in Consumer Intermittent Healthcare Devices Using Adversarial Examples. *IEEE Transactions on Consumer Electronics.*

V, Reichardt, C. S., & Gollob, H. F. (1986). Satisfying the constraints of causal modeling. *New Directions for Program Evaluation, 1986*(31), 91–107. DOI: 10.1002/ev.1436

Vandekerckhove, J., Tuerlinckx, F., & Lee, M. D. (2011). Hierarchical diffusion models for two-choice response times. *Psychological Methods, 16*(1), 44–62. DOI: 10.1037/a0021765

Vinson, J. E., Park, A. W., Cleveland, C. A., Yabsley, M. J., Ezenwa, V. O., & Hall, R. J. (2021). Alternative transmission pathways for guinea worm in dogs: Implications for outbreak risk and control. *International Journal for Parasitology, 51*(12), 1027–1034.

Volterra, V. (1926). Fluctuations in the abundance of a species considered mathematically. *Nature, 118*(2972), 558–560. DOI: 10.1038/118558a0

Voss, A., & Voss, J. (2007). Fast-dm: A free program for efficient diffusion model analysis. *Behavior Research Methods, 39*(4), 767–775. DOI: 10.3758/bf03192967

Wagenmakers, E.-J., van der Maas, H. L., & Grasman, R. (2007). An EZ-diffusion model for response time and accuracy. *Psychonomic Bulletin & Review, 14*(1), 3–22. DOI: 10.3758/bf03194023

Wang, C., & Yan, J. (2023). A comprehensive survey of rgb-based and skeleton-based human action recognition. *IEEE Access : Practical Innovations, Open Solutions, 11*, 53880–53898.

Wang, X., Shi, Y., Zheng, K., Zhang, Y., Hong, W., & Cao, S. (2022). User authentication method based on keystroke dynamics and mouse dynamics with scene-irrelated features in hybrid scenes. *Sensors (Basel), 22*(17), 6627. DOI: 10.3390/s22176627 PMID: 36081085

Wang, X., Zanette, L., & Zou, X. (2016). Modelling the fear effect in predator–prey interactions. *Journal of Mathematical Biology, 73*(5), 1179–1204. DOI: 10.1007/s00285-016-0989-1 PMID: 27002514

Wang, X., Zheng, Q., Zheng, K., & Wu, T. (2020). User authentication method based on MKL for keystroke and mouse behavioral feature fusion. *Security and Communication Networks, 2020*, 1–14. DOI: 10.1155/2020/9282380

Wang, Y., & Blei, D. M. (2019). The blessings of multiple causes. *Journal of the American Statistical Association*, *114*(528), 1574–1596. DOI: 10.1080/01621459.2019.1686987

Wang, Y.-Y., Nalluri, V., & Chen, L.-S. (2023). Using a text mining approach to identify important factors influencing the performance of programmatic advertising. *Engineering Proceedings*, *38*(1), 15.

Wang, Z., Gao, P., & Chu, X. (2022). Sentiment analysis from Customer-generated online videos on product review using topic modeling and Multi-attention BLSTM. *Advanced Engineering Informatics*, *52*, 101588. DOI: 10.1016/j.aei.2022.101588

Wang, Z., & Wu, Y. (2024). XLNet-LSTM-CNN for text sentiment analysis applied to movie review datasets. *International Journal of Advanced Computer Science and Applications*, *15*(4), 112–121. DOI: 10.14569/IJACSA.2024.0150414

Wassan, S., Latif, R. M. A., Liudajun, , Ying, H., Farhan, M., & Akbar, W. (2025). Advancements in Optical Glucose Sensing for Diabetes Diagnostics and Monitoring. *Microwave and Optical Technology Letters*, *67*(4), e70190. DOI: 10.1002/mop.70190

Watson, R. (2022). The virtual economy of the metaverse: Computer vision and deep learning algorithms, customer engagement tools, and behavioral predictive analytics. *Linguistic Philosophical Investigations*, (21), 41–56.

Weatherton, A. V. (2025). *Detecting Tool-Assisted Cheating in Competitive Video Gaming Using Machine Learning*. The George Washington University.

Weidlich, J., Hicks, B., & Drachsler, H. (2024). Causal reasoning with causal graphs in educational technology research. *Educational Technology Research and Development*, *72*(5), 2499–2517. DOI: 10.1007/s11423-023-10241-0

Wei, Z., & Chen, F. (2023). Dynamics of a delayed predator–prey model with prey refuge, Allee effect and fear effect. *International Journal of Bifurcation and Chaos in Applied Sciences and Engineering*, *33*(03), 2350036. DOI: 10.1142/S0218127423500360

Wiecki, T. V., Sofer, I., & Frank, M. J. (2013). HDDM: Hierarchical Bayesian estimation of the drift–diffusion model in Python. *Frontiers in Neuroinformatics*, *7*, 14. DOI: 10.3389/fninf.2013.00014

Wolniak, R. (2024). *Analyzing customer behavior–employing business analytics within Industry 4.0 ecosystems*. Zeszyty Naukowe. Organizacja i Zarządzanie/ Politechnika Śląska.

Worsey, M. T., Espinosa, H. G., Shepherd, J. B., & Thiel, D. V. (2020). An evaluation of wearable inertial sensor configuration and supervised machine learning models for automatic punch classification in boxing. *IoT*, *1*(2), 360–381.

Wu, Z., He, Q., Li, J., Bi, G., & Antwi-Afari, M. F. (2023). Public attitudes and sentiments towards new energy vehicles in China: A text mining approach. *Renewable & Sustainable Energy Reviews*, *178*, 113242. DOI: 10.1016/j.rser.2023.113242

Xia, L. L., Jiang, G. P., Song, B., & Song, Y. R. (2015). Rumor spreading model considering hesitating mechanism in complex social networks. *Physica A*, *437*, 295–303. DOI: 10.1016/j.physa.2015.05.113

Xuan, C. D., Duong, D., & Dau, H. X. (2021). A multi-layer approach for advanced persistent threat detection using machine learning based on network traffic. *Journal of Intelligent & Fuzzy Systems*, *40*(6), 11311–11329. DOI: 10.3233/JIFS-202465

Xue, Z., Li, Q., & Zeng, X. (2023). Social media user behavior analysis applied to the fashion and apparel industry in the big data era. *Journal of Retailing and Consumer Services*, *72*, 103299. DOI: 10.1016/j.jretconser.2023.103299

Yadav, A., Garg, P., & Jain, T. (2025, February). Sentiment analysis of movie reviews using machine learning. In *2025 International Conference on Pervasive Computational Technologies (ICPCT)* (pp. 41–45). IEEE. DOI: 10.1109/ICPCT64145.2025.10940336

Yang, G., Xu, Y., & Tu, L. (2023). An intelligent box office predictor based on aspect-level sentiment analysis of movie review. *Wireless Networks*, *29*(7), 3039–3049. DOI: 10.1007/s11276-023-03378-6

Yang, L. X., Li, P., Yang, X., Wu, Y., & Tang, Y. Y. (2018). On the competition of two conflicting messages. *Nonlinear Dynamics*, *91*(3), 1853–1869. DOI: 10.1007/s11071-017-3986-z

Yang, Z., Dai, Z., Yang, Y., Carbonell, J., Salakhutdinov, R. R., & Le, Q. V. (2019). XLNet: Generalized autoregressive pretraining for language understanding. *Advances in Neural Information Processing Systems*, 32.

Yan, J., & Randell, B. (2005, October). A systematic classification of cheating in online games. In *Proceedings of 4th ACM SIGCOMM workshop on Network and system support for games* (pp. 1-9). DOI: 10.1145/1103599.1103606

Yarkoni, T., & Westfall, J. (2017). Choosing prediction over explanation in psychology: Lessons from machine learning. *Perspectives on Psychological Science*, *12*(6), 1100–1122. DOI: 10.1177/1745691617693393

Yeung, S. F., & Lui, J. C. (2008). Dynamic Bayesian approach for detecting cheats in multi-player online games. *Multimedia Systems, 14*(4), 221–236. DOI: 10.1007/s00530-008-0113-5

Yi, J., Kim, J., & Oh, Y. K. (2024). Uncovering the quality factors driving the success of mobile payment apps. *Journal of Retailing and Consumer Services, 77*, 103641. DOI: 10.1016/j.jretconser.2023.103641

Youb, I., Al-Obeidat, F., Hamlich, M., & Essaadoui, A. (2024, October). Enhancing sentiment analysis of movie reviews with PySpark. In *2024 2nd International Conference on Self Sustainable Artificial Intelligence Systems (ICSSAS)* (pp. 1255–1260). IEEE. DOI: 10.1109/ICSSAS64001.2024.10760815

Yu, Y., Dinh, T., Yu, F., & Huynh, V.-N. (2023). *Understanding Mobile Game Reviews Through Sentiment Analysis: A Case Study of PUBGm.* Paper presented at the International Conference on Model and Data Engineering.

Yu, Y., Dinh, D.-T., Nguyen, B.-H., Yu, F., & Huynh, V.-N. (2023). Mining insights from esports game reviews with an aspect-based sentiment analysis framework. *IEEE Access : Practical Innovations, Open Solutions, 11*, 61161–61172. DOI: 10.1109/ACCESS.2023.3285864

Zaidi, S. A., & Chouvatut, V. (2022, December). Mae Mai Muay Thai Layered Classification Using CNN and LSTM Models. In 2022 26th International Computer Science and Engineering Conference (ICSEC) (pp. 351-356). IEEE.

Zaidi, S. A., & Chouvatut, V. (2023). Mae Mai Muay Thai Style Classification in Movement Appling Long-Term Recurrent Convolution Networks. *Journal of Internet Services and Information Security, 13*(1), 95–112.

Zaidi, S. A., Chouvatut, V., & Phongnarisorn, C. (2025b). Endometriosis Lesion Classification Using Deep Transfer Learning Techniques. *International Journal of Advanced Computer Science and Applications, 16*(6).

Zaidi, S. A., Chouvatut, V., Phongnarisorn, C., & Praserttitipong, D. (2025a). Deep learning based detection of endometriosis lesions in laparoscopic images with 5-fold cross-validation. *Intelligence-Based Medicine, 11*, 100230.

Zaksaitė, S. (2020). Cheating in chess: a call for an integrated disciplinary regulation. *Kriminologijos studijos, 8*, 57-83.

Zaksaitė, S. (2022). Anti-cheating protection measures in chess: Current state of play. *Crime Prevention and Community Safety, 24*(3), 255–265. DOI: 10.1057/s41300-022-00149-x

Zanette, D. (2001). Critical behavior of propagation on small-world networks. *Physical Review. E, 64*(5), 050901. DOI: 10.1103/PhysRevE.64.050901 PMID: 11735891

Zhang, H., Cai, Y., Fu, S., & Wang, W. (2019). Impact of the fear effect in a prey-predator model incorporating a prey refuge. *Applied Mathematics and Computation, 356*, 328–337. DOI: 10.1016/j.amc.2019.03.034

Zhang, Q., Zhong, D., Gao, J., & Li, Y. (2018). Optimizing HIV interventions for multiplex social networks via partition-based random search. *IEEE Transactions on Cybernetics, 48*(12), 3411–3419. DOI: 10.1109/TCYB.2018.2853611 PMID: 30010610

Zhang, Y., & Xu, J. (2015). A rumor spreading model considering the cumulative effects of memory. *Discrete Dynamics in Nature and Society, 2015*, 204395. DOI: 10.1155/2015/204395

Zhan, Y., Qiu, Z., Li, X., Shang, J., Liu, Q., & Zhao, Z. (2023). Uncovering the roots of player dissatisfaction in MOBA mobile games: A text mining and complex network theory approach to negative online reviews. *International Journal of Sensor Networks, 42*(3), 196–204. DOI: 10.1504/IJSNET.2023.132539

Zhan, Y., Qiu, Z., Shang, J., Li, X., Liu, Q., & Zhao, Z. (2023). Analysis of players' experience perceptions of mobile games based on text mining and a complex network. *International Journal of Sensor Networks, 42*(4), 248–258. DOI: 10.1504/IJSNET.2023.133241

Zhao, L., Qiu, X., Wang, X., & Wang, J. (2013). Rumor spreading model considering forgetting and remembering mechanisms in inhomogeneous networks. *Physica A, 392*(4), 987–994. DOI: 10.1016/j.physa.2012.10.031

Zhao, T., Cao, Z., & Duan, W. (2020). Evolutionary divide-and-conquer algorithm for virus spreading control over networks. *IEEE Transactions on Cybernetics, 51*(7), 3752–3766. DOI: 10.1109/TCYB.2020.2975530 PMID: 32175884

Zhao, W., Cheng, Y., & Lee, Y.-I. (2023). Exploring 360-degree virtual reality videos for CSR communication: An integrated model of perceived control, telepresence, and consumer behavioral intentions. *Computers in Human Behavior, 144*, 107736. DOI: 10.1016/j.chb.2023.107736

Zhao, X., & Wang, J. (2014). Dynamical behaviors of rumor spreading model with control measures. *Abstract and Applied Analysis, 2014*, 1–11. DOI: 10.1155/2014/247359

Zheng, H. (2025). Artificial intelligence–driven sentiment analysis and optimization of movie scripts. *Discover Artificial Intelligence, 5*(1), 114. DOI: 10.1007/s44163-025-00361-2

Zhong, W., Yu, N., & Ai, C. (2020). Applying big data based deep learning system to intrusion detection. *Big Data Mining Analytics*, *3*(3), 181–195. DOI: 10.26599/BDMA.2020.9020003

Zhou, F. (2024). Sentiment analysis and implementation in film evaluation utilizing BERT. *Applied and Computational Engineering*, *33*(1), 224–233. DOI: 10.54254/2755-2721/33/20230274

Zhou, Y., Zhang, J., Zhu, C., & Wang, H. (2022). Modelling and analysis of rumor propagation based on stochastic optimal control. *Alexandria Engineering Journal*, *61*(12), 12869–12880. DOI: 10.1016/j.aej.2022.06.057

Zhu, G., Xu, C., Huang, Q., Rui, Y., Jiang, S., Gao, W., & Yao, H. (2008). Event tactic analysis based on broadcast sports video. *IEEE Transactions on Multimedia*, *11*(1), 49–67.

Zodage, P., Harianawala, H., Shaikh, H., & Kharodia, A. (2024). Explainable AI (XAI): History, basic ideas and methods. International Journal of Advanced Research in Science. *Tongxin Jishu*, 3.

Zvarikova, K., Michalikova, K. F., & Rowland, M. (2022). Retail data measurement tools, cognitive artificial intelligence algorithms, and metaverse live shopping analytics in immersive hyper-connected virtual spaces. *Linguistic Philosophical Investigations*, *21*(0), 9–24. DOI: 10.22381/lpi2120221

About the Contributors

Ali Turab (IEEE Member) is an Associate Professor at the School of Software, Northwestern Polytechnical University (NPU), China. He holds a Ph.D. in Applied Mathematics from Thammasat University, Thailand, where he also completed postdoctoral research focused on nonlinear modeling and dynamical systems. He has previously served as a Research Associate at the Centre of Excellence for Artificial Intelligence & Data Science at Universiti Malaysia Pahang Al-Sultan Abdullah (UMPSA), Malaysia. His research interests lie at the intersection of mathematical modeling, artificial intelligence, and behavioral sciences, with a particular emphasis on the computational modeling of natural phenomena and cognitive behavior. He integrates game theory, decision-making analysis, probabilistic machine learning models, and cognitive neurodynamics to study adaptive and goal-directed behavior in animals and intelligent systems. His recent work explores hybrid neural-stochastic models and reinforcement learning methods to analyze behavioral dynamics and decision-making under uncertainty. Dr. Turab is actively involved in interdisciplinary research and academic mentorship, contributing to high-impact publications and collaborative projects across applied mathematics, AI, and behavioral prediction.

Josué Antonio Nescolarde Selva, professor at the Department of Applied Mathematics at the University of Alicante, is the author of more than 100 scientific publications (most of them JCR indexed in the Science Citation Index). He has directed a total of 5 doctoral theses (1 with International Mention, 2 as the only supervisor, one of them Extraordinary Doctorate Award). In 2017, he received recognition as a researcher in his field from the University of Alicante, with the highest number of scientific publications indexed in the Web of Science in 2015. His lines of research are developed, mostly, in the fields of Biomathematics, Cybernetics, Data Science and Philosophy of Science, collaborating in a large part of his publications on a stable basis with members of his research group, as well as with researchers from various institutions from different parts of the world among which we find: Dublin City University, Ireland; Northeast Normal University, China; University of Georgia, USA. Among other examples of leadership, he has also been appointed as Guest Editor-in-Chief to several special issues in various JCR journals, including Kybernetes, Cybernetics, and Systems and Foundations of Science; as well as being appointed to several editorial teams, including the JCR journals: International Journal of General Systems and Applied Artificial Intelligence. He has participated in a total of 7 research projects in competitive calls, 4 of them corresponding to the National Plan. He has been involved in 6 contracts with companies and 2 projects (1 national and 1 regional) in the field of knowledge transfer, dissemination, and exchange. He has carried out a total of 5 postdoctoral research stays at universities that occupy leading positions at an international level in the most recognized rankings: Northeast Normal University, Changchun, China, and Northwestern Polytechnical University, Xian, China. At the teaching level, he has given more than 5000 official teaching hours at the different levels of education, teaching Mathematics at all possible levels: from the previous programs of bachelor's degree plans, technical engineering, and higher engineering to the new bachelor's and master's degrees. He has participated in numerous teaching innovation projects. In all the teaching evaluations carried out, before and after the DOCENTIA program, the results have been very favorable. In the academic years 2012/2013 and 2013/2014, he was selected as the most valued professor at his center by the students of all the degrees in which he teaches. From the 2012/2013 academic year to the 2020/2021 academic year, he led the Tutorial Action Program (PAT) at the Polytechnic School. Since 2013, and on an ongoing basis, he has held various individual university management positions, all of them at the School level, developing his activity in various areas such as postgraduate studies, working on the coordination of the master's degrees that are taught as well as in the launching of new degrees; in the area of communication, in the organization of different activities with the aim of giving greater visibility to the School as well as in relations with the students of the center and the management team of the School. His leadership in this area is supported by his experience as Deputy Director of the School from 2017 to the present.

***

Abdul Ahad earned his PhD in Computer Science from Sunway University Malaysia (2018-2022), an M.S. in Computer Science from the Virtual University of Pakistan (2015-2017), and an M.Sc. in Computer Science from Swat University of Pakistan (2012-2014). Currently, Ahad enriches the scientific community as a Postdoctoral Researcher at Northwestern Polytechnical University in Xi'an, China, engaging in groundbreaking research in the Internet of Medical Things (IoMT) and federated deep learning. His journey before this role includes impactful tenures as an Assistant Professor at the University of Management and Technology in Pakistan, a Scientific Researcher at Istanbul Technical University, and a Data Processing Officer for the Government of Pakistan Revenue Department, among other notable positions. His research interests are vast and visionary, focusing on 5G and 6G technologies, smart healthcare, the Internet of Things (IoT), cyber security, machine learning, and deep learning. His work aims to bridge technological innovation with practical healthcare solutions, contributing to smarter, safer, and more efficient cities and communities. His academic and research excellence has been recognized through numerous awards and achievements, including being listed in the top 2\% of scientists worldwide by Stanford University in 2023. He has received merit awards for his Ph.D. and M.S. studies, grants for his contributions to journals and conferences, and several accolades for his teaching and research roles, illustrating a track record of excellence and dedication to his field. He has also contributed to the academic community through workshops, memberships in conferences such as IEEE, Elsevier, Springer, and EAI, and numerous publications in esteemed journals and conferences on subjects central to his research interests, including 5G, 6G, smart healthcare, cyber security, and the Internet of Things (IoT).

Muhammad Fahmi bin Ahmad Zuber is a Post-Doctorate Research Fellow at the National Defence University of Malaysia (UPNM). He received his PhD in Mathematics from Universiti Malaysia Pahang Al-Sultan Abdullah (UMPSA), where his doctoral thesis focused on the development of epidemic models with multiple infectious severity levels, specifically the SI RD model. His research interests include DRAM-MCMC parameter estimation, stochastic numerical simulation, as well as machine learning and deep learning. More broadly, his work involves the use of simulations, algorithms, and computational tools to address real-life problems in applied mathematics and computational modelling.

Iftikhar Ahmed is a Professor at the University of Europe for Applied Sciences, Germany. He holds a master's degree in Computer Science from the University of Freiburg, Germany, and a Ph.D. from the University of Saarland in Saarbrücken, Germany. His scholarly interests are concentrated in the areas of Responsible AI, Explainable AI (XAI), and LLM Evaluation.

Cicik Alfiniyah, Ph.D. is a senior lecturer at the Department of Mathematics, Faculty of Science and Technology, Universitas Airlangga, Indonesia. She earned her PhD in Mathematical Biology from the University of York, United Kingdom, and an MSc in Mathematics from Institut Teknologi Bandung. Her research focuses on mathematical modeling in biology and epidemiology, with applications to infectious diseases such as dengue, tuberculosis, HIV/AIDS, COVID-19, and alcohol addiction. She has published widely in international journals including Scientific Reports, Cognitive Neurodynamics, Partial Differential Equations in Applied Mathematics, MethodsX, and AIMS Mathematics. She is also actively engaged in collaborative research projects, postgraduate supervision, and community development programs.

Israr Ali is a master's Student, in School of Mathematics and Statistics, Northwestern Polytechnical University Xi'an, China, under the supervision of Dr. Hui Zhang. His research focuses on mathematical modeling in epidemiology, infectious diseases, ecological systems and fuzzy sets, with particular interest in both deterministic and stochastic frameworks.

Abdulwasea Alkhazzan received his B.S. degree in Mathematics from Sana'a University, Yemen, in 2008, and his M.S. degree in Applied Mathematics from Hohai University, China, in 2019. He completed his Ph.D. in Applied Mathematics at Northwestern Polytechnical University, Xi'an, China, in 2025. He is now an Assistant Professor at the School of Information Engineering, Xi'an Fanyi University, China. His research primarily focuses on utilizing stochastic differential equations (SDEs) and fractional differential equations to investigate the dynamics of infectious diseases, malware propagation in networks, and related applications. He has published over 30 research papers in international peer-reviewed journals.

Alberto Carpio holds a PhD in Health Sciences from Universidad Rey Juan Carlos (URJC), where he currently works as an Assistant Professor in the Department of Psychology. His doctoral research focused on the use of non-invasive neuromodulation techniques, specifically transcranial static magnetic stimulation (tSMS), to investigate cognitive and motor inhibition processes. His research interests center on the development of predictive and computational models for the analysis of behavioral data, with the aim of characterizing the cognitive mechanisms underlying human performance. He is particularly interested in the modeling of response times and accuracy to infer latent decision-making and cognitive control processes, using interpretable computational frameworks that link observable behavior to underlying cognitive components. More broadly, his work integrates behavioral modeling and neuroscientific approaches to provide mechanistic and theoretically grounded accounts of performance in experimental paradigms.

Yijian Che is currently pursuing her Bachelor's degree at Xi'an Jiaotong-Liverpool University (XJTLU), China. Her academic and research interests include data analysis, machine learning, artificial intelligence applications, multi-agent systems, and technology-enhanced learning.

Yanyu Chen is currently pursuing a Master's degree in Data Science at Johns Hopkins University. His research interests include machine learning, natural language processing, and pattern recognition, with a particular focus on applying AI techniques to behavioral analysis and fraud detection. He has previously worked on projects involving document classification, clustering analysis, and sentiment analysis, and has recently contributed to studies on cheating and fraud detection in online games and competitive environments.

Varin Chouvatut received the B.E., M.E., and Ph.D. degrees in computer engineering from King Mongkut's University of Technology Thonburi (KMUTT), Thailand. She is currently an Associate Professor of computer science with Chiang Mai University. Her current research interests include Computer Vision, 3D Reconstruction, 2D and 3D Motion Processing, Image Processing, Augmented (Mixed) Reality, Virtual Reality, Computer Graphics, Machine Learning, Artificial Intelligence, Web-based Applications, and Medical Imaging Analysis.

ShanmugapriyaD. is the Head of the Department of Information Technology at Avinashilingam Institute for Home Science and Higher Education for Women (Deemed to be University), Coimbatore, India, a position she has held since 2001. She has over 24 years of teaching experience and 10 years of research experience. Her areas of interest include Cyber Security, Biometric Security, and Image Processing. She has successfully executed projects sponsored by DRDO, DST, UGC and is currently executing project funded by MoSPI. She holds both copyrights and patents to her credit. At present, she is supervising four Ph.D. scholars. She has more than 25 publications in peer-reviewed journals and prestigious conferences and serves as a reviewer for several prestigious international journals and conferences. Additionally, she has contributed as a content writer for the SWAYAM-MOOC course on Cyber Security, specifically in the areas of Virtual Currency, Blockchain Technology, and Basics of Security Auditing.

Mian Muhammad Danyal received his Bachelor's degree in Software Engineering from City University of Science and Technology, Peshawar, Pakistan, in 2023. He is currently pursuing an MS in Computer Science from the Institute of Management Sciences, Peshawar. His research interests include sentiment analysis, image processing, opinion mining, text summarization, machine learning, and deep learning.

María Eugenia de Lahoz's research focuses on the cognitive and neural mechanisms of migraine, particularly childhood migraine. My work combines behavioral testing with electrophysiological EEG recordings using ERPs. Currently, I am interested in studying the processes of attention and pain expectancy in childhood migraine by recording and analyzing CNV with auditory and emotional stimulation.

Yunwei Dong is a distinguished member of China computer federation (CCF), a senior member of IEEE. he is one of Top 10 Software youth Talents in Shaanxi province in 2000, and one candidate of top 10 software youth Talents in China in 2001. He is a professor of School of software, Northwestern Polytechnical University (NPU), He is interested in Program synthesis, intelligent software engineering safety-critical embedded system architecture modeling and analysis, Cyber-physical System, software formal verification, testing for AI algorithms. He has published more than 100 papers, and owns more than 20 Chinese patents. Contacts information E-mail: yunweidong@nwpu.edu.cn Mobile: +86-15991618002

Haleem Farman is a distinguished researcher at Prince Sultan University, Riyadh, where he is actively involved in various R&D activities within the Smart Systems Engineering Research Lab. He is specialized in the Internet of Things, Human-Computer Interaction, Adhoc Networks, Smart Cities, Smart Education, and Artificial Intelligence. He has played key roles in numerous research-funded projects, serving as Principal Investigator (PI), Co-Principal Investigator (Co-PI), and team member. Hi work has been supported by esteemed donor agencies, including the British Council, the Research and Development Initiative Authority of Saudi Arabia, Prince Sultan University, and the Government of Pakistan. Hi projects primarily focus on advancements in the Internet of Things and Artificial Intelligence. His extensive experience in teaching and supervision is a testament to my dedication to education and research. He has mentored numerous undergraduate and postgraduate students, guiding them in their research activities and fostering a passion for academic excellence. His extensive publication record, comprising over 60 articles in high-impact journals, conferences, and book chapters, demonstrates his commitment to knowledge dissemination and contribution to the academic community. His active membership in professional organizations such as IEEE (Senior Member) and IEEE Young Professionals further underscores his dedication to the field and ongoing engagement with the professional community. Additionally, he serves as the Vice-Chair of the IEEE Smart Cities Awards and Recognition Committee, reflecting his leadership and commitment to advancing smart city technologies. Moreover, he serves as the IEEE VTS Young Professional Ambassador for 2025-2026.

Rubia Fatima is currently working as Assistant professor at Emerson University, Multan, Pakistan. She completed her Ph.D. in Software Engineering at Tsinghua University (QS ranked 12th), Beijing, China in June 2023. Prior to this, she received her Master's degree in Information Technology (MSIT) from Bahauddin Zakariya

University (B.Z.U), Multan, Pakistan. Her research interests include empirical research and development within Software Engineering, game-based learning, social engineering, serious games, and requirements engineering. She has published more than 25 research studies in reputable venues on various topics of Software Engineering, including requirements engineering, social engineering, game-based education, and empirical software engineering.

Roberto Fernandes-Magalhaes Assistant professor in the Department of Psychology at Universidad Rey Juan Carlos (URJC), specializing in Psychobiology and Neuropsychology. Holds a degree in Psychology from URJC and two master's degrees — in Cognitive Neuroscience and Neuropsychology — from Universidad Complutense de Madrid, as well as a PhD in Health Sciences with international mention. The research career began at the Cognitive Neuroscience Laboratory at URJC, alongside teaching and clinical work in neurorehabilitation. Teaching focuses on courses in Neuropsychology and Cognitive Neuroscience. Research examines the neural mechanisms involved in the processing of emotional faces in healthy individuals and in patients with fibromyalgia, as well as cognitive deficits associated with Fetal Alcohol Spectrum Disorder. International research stays have been completed at Ghent University (Belgium) and the University of Porto (Portugal). Scientific output includes articles in leading journals on event-related potentials (ERPs), pain-related attention and memory, and the neurophysiological basis of conditions such as fibromyalgia.

Massimiliano Ferrara is a Full Professor of Mathematical Economics, Artificial Intelligence, Machine Learning, and Applied Game Theory at Mediterranea University of Reggio Calabria. He previously served as Chairman of the Department of Law, Economics & Human Sciences and as a member of the Academic Senate. He is a Research Affiliate with the ICRIOS–Invernizzi Center for Research on Innovation, Organization, Strategy and Entrepreneurship at Bocconi University Milan (since 2013) and Scientific Director of the DECISIONS Lab. Over his career, he has held visiting positions at Harvard University, Western Michigan University, Morgan State University, Northeastern University of Boston, and Dresden University of Technology. Prof. Ferrara has authored over 220 peer-reviewed articles published by leading publishers including Nature, IEEE, Elsevier, Springer, and Wiley. He serves as Editor, Co-Editor, or Associate Editor for multiple journals, including Nature Scientific Reports (Editorial Board), Soft Computing, and Dynamic Games and Applications. He currently referees for over 300 international journals indexed in SCOPUS, WoS, and MathSciNet. His achievements include Knight Order of Merit of the Italian Republic (2010), the Hepites Award from the Romanian Academy of Science (2010), and the Silver Medal from Universiti Putra Malaysia for the

Invention, Research and Innovation Exhibition (2016). He was also recognized among the top 2% of scientists by Stanford University and Elsevier (2022 onwards).

David Ferrera holds a PhD in Psychology from Rey Juan Carlos University, awarded in 2022 with the highest distinction cum laude and the Extraordinary Doctorate Award. I earned my Bachelor's Degree in Psychology in 2013 and completed the Master's in General Health Psychology at Rey Juan Carlos University in 2016. I am currently an Assistant Professor in the area of Psychobiology within the Department of Psychology. Since 2018, I have been teaching and conducting research at Rey Juan Carlos University, where I have taught in the Bachelor's Degree in Psychology, and various courses in the Master's in Neuropsychology and Cognitive Neuroscience. Regarding my research experience, I am involved in several national and regional research projects. I am the author of various scientific publications aimed at exploring the relationship between genetic, physiological (ERPs), and cognitive (attention, memory, executive function) factors. I am also a member of the Consolidated Research Group in Cognitive Neuroscience, Pain, and Rehabilitation in Health Sciences at Rey Juan Carlos University.

Maruf Hasan is an Associate Professor at the School of AI and Advanced Computing, XJTLU Entrepreneur College, China. He received his Bachelor's, Master's, and Doctoral degrees from Tsinghua University (China), National University of Singapore and Nara Institute of Science and Technology (Japan), respectively. Upon completion of his Doctor of Engineering in 2001, he joined the Knowledge Media Institute (KMi), Open University, UK as a Research Fellow and worked for the Advanced Knowledge Technologies (AKT) project (2001-2003) pioneering Semantic Web and Knowledge Management research. Subsequently, as a Senior Researcher, he helped the National Institute of ICT (NICT, Japan) expanding its RD networks in Thailand and neighbouring ASEAN countries through academic partnership and industrial collaboration (2003-2004). Dr. Hasan worked as an Assistant Professor, Associate Dean and Program Director at the School of IT, Shinawatra University (SIU), Thailand during 2004 -2012. Before joining Xi'an Jiaotong – Liverpool University (XJLTU), he was an Assistant Professor of Information Systems at the College of Computer Sciences and Information Technology (CCSIT), King Faisal University, Saudi Arabia (2012-2021). He also headed the curriculum development and quality assurance at the college overhauling various existing academic programs and introducing industry-recognized skill-development programs towards employability and entrepreneurship. Dr. Hasan is a Certified Information Systems Security Professional (CISSP). He is a recognized IT Practitioner with decades of consulting experience and credentials (PRINCE2, COBIT and ITIL certified). He supervised several postgraduate theses and undergraduate projects, received numerous research grants, and published his research regularly in Natural Language Processing, Information Retrieval, Digital Library, E-learning, Artificial Intelligence and Semantic Web Technologies. With a first degree in Computer Engineering, decades of experiences in teaching a diverse range of computing courses, and an intensive experience in curriculum development and higher education quality assurance, Dr. Hasan made a life-long commitment to Computer Science Education. He is a member of Association for Computing Machinery (ACM) and International Information System Security Certification Consortium, $(ISC)^2$.

Farzana Hussain is a seasoned educator and academic leader with over 30 years of experience teaching mathematics at both undergraduate and graduate levels. She holds a BS in Mathematics, an MS, and a PhD in Applied Mathematics, and currently serves as Chair of the Mathematics Department at Huston-Tillotson University in Austin, Texas. Dr. Hussain has significantly broadened her expertise into the field of data science, completing advanced training and certifications from leading institutions such as the Georgia Institute of Technology, Stanford University, and others. Her commitment to interdisciplinary learning and innovation has earned her several prestigious fellowships, including the NIH AIM-AHEAD Leadership Fellowship, NIH AIM-AHEAD NCATS Fellowship, Apple Golden Teacher Fellowship, and the Propel HBCU Faculty Fellowship. She leads two international student chapters of the National Student Data Corps—one at Huston-Tillotson University in the U.S. and another at Shahjalal University of Science and Technology in Bangladesh—with a combined membership of over 700 students. These chapters offer free training in career readiness, mentoring in data science, blockchain, and other emerging technologies, empowering students across borders to thrive in the digital age. In addition to her academic and mentoring roles, Dr. Hussain organizes the annual International Conference on Science, Technology, Engineering, Mathematics and Education, a fully free virtual event for students and faculty that fosters collaboration, innovation, and knowledge-sharing across STEM and education disciplines. Her work bridges mathematics, data science, and health equity, and she continues to mentor the next generation of scholars and data-driven problem solvers with passion and purpose.

Muhammad Ibrar earned his M.S. in Computer Science from New Mexico Highlands University, where his research centered on Artificial Intelligence and Cybersecurity. His work explores AI-driven usability evaluation, secure software design, ransomware behavior, and resilience in digital systems. Through publications in international journals and conferences, he has contributed to advancing methods that enhance security, usability, and reliability in modern computing environments.

Waqas Junaid received the Ph.D. degree from the School of Computer Science and Engineering, Guangxi Normal University, Guilin, Guangxi, China, the MS (CS) degree from the University of Agriculture Peshawar in 2018, and the MCS degree from Abdul Wali Khan University Mardan in 2014. He is currently a postdoctoral researcher at school of software, Northwestern Polytechnical Unviersity, Xian, China. His research interests are problem-oriented requirements engineering, organization problems, microservices, modeling, verifying, testing, validating cyber physical systems based on Problem Frames, human computer interaction, and Auto repair codes using LLM.

Afsheen Khalid received the M.Sc. degree in Computer Science from the University of Peshawar, Pakistan, in 1998, and the M.S. degree in Computer Engineering from the Center for Advanced Studies in Engineering (CASE), Islamabad, Pakistan, in 2008. She obtained her Ph.D. degree in 2018 from the Institute of Management Sciences (IMSciences), Peshawar, Pakistan. She is currently serving as an Assistant Professor in the School of Computer Science at IMSciences, Peshawar, Pakistan. Her research interests include text mining, big data analytics, natural language processing (NLP), and deep learning.

Muhammad Khalid is currently working as a Lecturer(Assistant Professor) in the school of computer science, University of Hull. Before this, he worked Post-Doctoral Research Fellow at the University of Lincoln, Lincoln. He was responsible for assuring robot autonomy toward safety aspects in the project called MeSAPro. In this project, he ensured robotic safety through human-robot interaction for the robots used in the strawberry collection. Khalid has completed his PhD from Northumbria University in 2020 on Autonomous parking in intelligent smart cities, where he was awarded a fully funded PhD studentship in 2017 under research development framework.

Sarwar Shah Khan is a Lecturer in the Department of Computer Science at the University of Engineering and Technology. He completed his Ph.D. in December 2024, specializing in the field of medical image processing. With seven years of experience in teaching and research, Dr. Sarwar has published over 42 research articles in reputable journals and conferences. His research interests extend to machine learning applications in image processing, and he has developed frameworks that integrate artificial intelligence and natural language processing for various applications. Currently, he is actively pursuing research in two major areas: Data Science (including text processing, natural language processing, and machine learning) and Digital Image Processing. His contributions have significantly enriched these domains.

Zhi Li is a distinguished member of China Computer Federation (CCF), standing committee member of its Technical Council on Software Engineering (TCSE), and a member of its Technical Council on Systems Software and Formal Methods. He graduated with a BSc degree from Fudan University in 1991, an MSc degree from the University of York in 2004, and a PhD degree from The Open University in 2008. Prof. Li had spent over 10 years doing professional and technical work before he entered academia in 2001, with subsequent 9 years in the UK. His research interests are modeling, verifying, testing and validating Cyber-Physical Systems (CPSs) or Internet of Things (IoT) systems based on Problem Frames, and Human-Computer Interaction. His research has been sponsored by 2 grants from the National Natural Science Foundation of China, and 4 grants from Ministry of Education of China, Guangxi Natural Science Foundation, and Guangxi Scientific Research & Technological Development. He has published over 50 research papers (including 3 CCF-A papers and 3 best papers). He has given over 10 invited talks at academic conferences.

Umar Raza is a Senior Lecturer in Networking, IoT, and Smart Systems at Manchester Metropolitan University, where he coordinates the Cisco Networking Academy. His teaching covers engineering, IoT, robotics, smart systems, and embedded platforms. He leads the Smart Design unit, supervises MSc and PhD projects, and actively integrates research-informed teaching into undergraduate and postgraduate curricula. Dr. Raza received his BSc in Electronics from De Montfort University, an MSc in Electronics and Computer-Based Systems Design from the University of Huddersfield, and a PhD from the University of Bradford on Service-Oriented Architectures for Wireless Sensor Networks (WSNs) in industrial manufacturing. Before moving into academia, he spent over seven years as a Software Engineer working on robotics, automation, and traffic control systems. He later joined Staffordshire University as a Lecturer in Robotics, Networking, and Computing before taking up his current role at Manchester Metropolitan University. His research spans IoT, WSNs, machine learning, robotics, and data-driven systems. Current projects focus on IoT and ML for domiciliary care and cognitive health monitoring, WSN-based early warning systems for natural disasters, and smart farming and sustainable agriculture using robotics and AI. He has contributed to research on blockchain, 5G/6G communications, and AI-driven assistive systems for neurodiverse individuals. Dr. Raza has published widely in IEEE, MDPI, and other peer-reviewed venues, and regularly organises international conferences and workshops, including the ASSET conference series. He also serves as Review Editor for Frontiers in Communication and Sensor Networks, Associate Editor of Frontiers IoT Theory and Fundamental Research, and Guest Editor for MDPI journals. He is a Fellow of the Higher Education Academy, Senior member of IEEE and member of IET and BCS.

Abdul Razzaq is currently working as a postdoctoral in the School of Software at Northwestern Polytechnical University of Xian. He did his MS in Software Engineering in 2018 at the International Islamic University of Islamabad (IIUI), Pakistan. He completed his doctoral degree (PhD) at Zhejiang University of China in March 2024. His research areas of interest are Software Engineering, Software Architecture, Blockchain, IoT, Software Processes, Requirement Engineering, Mobile Computing, and Quantum Computing.

Norhayati Rosli is an Associate Professor at the Centre for Mathematical Sciences, Universiti Malaysia Pahang Al-Sultan Abdullah (UMPSA). She obtained a Doctor of Philosophy (Mathematics) from Universiti Teknologi Malaysia, where her doctoral thesis focused on Stochastic Runge–Kutta Methods for Stochastic Delay Differential Equations. Her research interests lie in the development of numerical methods for solving stochastic differential equations (SDEs) and stochastic delay differential equations (SDDEs), with applications across applied mathematics and computational modelling.

AshaS. She is a doctoral researcher at Avinashilingam Institute for Home Science and Higher Education for Women (Deemed to be University), Coimbatore, India. She was awarded as Vijayalakshmi Purushothaman (Master of Science in Information Technology). Her areas of interest include, Cyber Security and Biometric security. She is doing research under Centre for Cyber Intelligence, DST CURIE AI Phase II Project, Avinashilingam Institute for Home Science and Higher Education for Women. She has successfully completed In-House funded project sponsored by DST. She has 3 publications in prestigious conferences and 2 publication in peer-reviewed Elsevier journals.

Sivasankari S is a postgraduate student in Information Technology at Avinashilingam Institute for Home Science & Higher Education for Women, Coimbatore, India specializing in Artificial Intelligence, Machine Learning and Cybersecurity. She has a strong interest in exploring emerging technologies and their practical applications. She is committed to advancing her knowledge and contributing to research in these fields.

Yassine Sabbar received the Ph.D degree from Sidi Mohamed Ben Abdellah University (USMBA), Fez, Morroco, in 2021. He is currently an associate professor with Mouly Ismail University, Morroco and an associate researcher with the IDMS Team, Faculty of Science and Technology, Errachidia. He has a publication record, with over 50 well-indexed research papers in prestigious journals and international conferences. Additionally, he has edited a scientific book. His research interests include mathematical modeling, biostatistics and stochastic analysis, with a focus on applying advanced mathematical techniques to real-world problems in science and engineering.

Ramsha Shafqat is a Ph.D. candidate in Applied Mathematics at Thammasat University. She works on fractional differential equations, fuzzy dynamical systems, controllability/stability, and optimal control, plus data-driven modeling for epidemiology, fluid mechanics, and engineering. She has 50+ papers and presents internationally. Her service includes collaborations with Saudi institutions and reviewing for journals such as Symmetry and Axioms. Awards include first place (ICMMAAC-24, 2024) and a poster prize (Computational Science Summer School, 2025). She previously lectured in Pakistan and holds M.Phil. and M.Sc. degrees.

Muhammad Tahir Currently working as an Assistant Professor in the Department of Engineering & Computer Science, NUML Faisalabad Campus, Pakistan. Completed my Ph.D. in Information & Communication Engineering from the School of Electronics and Information Engineering, Changchun University of Science and Technology, PR China. Research interests include Information and Signal Processing, Underwater Communication and Networks, IOT, and energy optimization in WSNs.

Farhan Ullah is an Associate Research Professor at the Cybersecurity Center, Prince Mohammad Bin Fahd University, Saudi Arabia. He also worked as an Associate Professor at the School of Software, Northwestern Polytechnical University (NPU), P.R. China. He received Ph.D. Computer Science degree in 2020 from College of Computer Science, Sichuan University Chengdu, P.R. China. He was awarded a fulltime Chinese Government Scholarship (CGS) for his Ph.D. He works as editorial board member in several SCIE journals including KSII Transactions on Internet and Information Systems, Electronics, CMC Computers, Materials & Continua, CSSE Computer Systems Science and Engineering, etc. He received research landmark achievement award (2021) from School of Software, NPU, Xian, China. He also received Research Productivity Award (2016) from COMSATS Institute of Information Technology (CIIT), Sahiwal, Pakistan. He is an active researcher who works with well-known professors and scientists. His research work is published in various renowned journals of IEEE, Springer, Elsevier, Wiley, MDPI, and Hindawi.

Ahsan Wajahat received his B.S. and M.S. degrees in Information Technology from Sindh Agriculture University, Pakistan, in 2012 and 2016, respectively. He completed his Ph.D. degree at the Beijing University of Technology, Beijing, China, and is currently a postdoctoral researcher at Northwest Polytechnic University. His research interests include machine learning, information security, network forensics, and data mining. He has authored over 40 publications in peer-reviewed journals and international conferences. During his Ph.D., he was a recipient of the China Scholarship Council (CSC) award and has since received several science and technology awards in 2023, 2024, and 2025.

Affan Yasin (Member, IEEE) received the Ph.D. degree in software engineering from Tsinghua University, Beijing, China. He is currently an Assistant Professor at the School of AI and Advanced Computing, Xi'an Jiaotong Liverpool University, Suzhou, China. Prior to this, he was a Postdoctoral researcher at Northwestern Polytechnical University, Xi'an, China, and a Postdoctoral Fellow at Tsinghua University. He is particularly interested in how these areas can be integrated to enhance learning outcomes and improve system security and usability. His work contributes to both academic advancements and practical applications in these fields. He has published over 35 research papers in reputable journals and conferences. His work has been well-received in the academic community. His research interests include the intersection of empirical software engineering and cutting-edge technologies, with a focus on game-based learning, serious games, social engineering, AI in education, and requirements engineering.

Jiaqi Yin is an Assistant Professor at Northwestern Polytechnical University. He received his Ph.D. in Software Engineering from East China Normal University in 2022. His research focuses on trustworthy AI and formal methods, with publications in peer-reviewed venues including FAC, JSEP, and DATE. Currently serving on the CCF Formal Methods Technical Committee, he teaches both undergraduate and graduate courses, covering Fundamentals of Programming and Mathematical Logic.

Mudasir Younis is an Assistant Professor in the Department of Mathematics at Sakarya University, Turkey. Before joining Sakarya University, he served as a postdoctoral fellow in the Department of Mathematics and Statistics at the Indian Institute of Technology Kanpur, Uttar Pradesh, India. For the past five years, Dr. Younis has focused on advancing fixed-point theory within the graph structures of metric spaces—a relatively new and dynamic area of research. His work has yielded several groundbreaking results, contributing to the understanding and application of fixed-point theorems. He has also explored the existence of solutions to various real-world problems in engineering, science, and physics, including models such as damped spring-mass systems, deformation of elastic beams, vibrations of heavy hanging cables, the ascending motion of rockets, and tuning circuits, among others.

Dr. Younis has published with over 50 research papers published in Web of Science and Scopus-indexed journals, alongside seven additional manuscripts currently under review in prestigious international publications. His research contributions have earned him various national and international fellowships, including the esteemed "Abel Visiting Scholar Program 2022." He has served on the editorial boards of various peer-reviewed journals and presented his work at several international conferences. He is also the author of the book "Fourier Analysis," published by the University of Kashmir Press, and "Recent Developments in Fixed-Point Theory: Theoretical Foundations and Real-World Applications," published by Springer.

Shujaat Ali Zaidi is pursuing his PhD in Computer Science at Chiang Mai University, where his research focuses on a suite of interconnected fields: Computer Vision, 3D Reconstruction, and 2D/3D Motion Processing. Leveraging advanced methods in Machine Learning and Artificial Intelligence, he specializes in their application to Medical Imaging Analysis. This dedicated research focus over the past five years has yielded significant scholarly output, including the publication of over 8 papers in internationally recognized, Web of Science and Scopus-indexed journals.

Hui Zhang is currently an associate professor from School of Mathematics and Statistics at Northwestern Polytechnical University, China. She received her PhD (2012) degree from Lanzhou University. Her research interest center around evolutionary game theory and mathematical biology.

Index

Symbols

A

B

C

D

E

F

H

I

T

U

V

X

www.ingramcontent.com/pod-product-compliance
Lightning Source LLC
LaVergne TN
LVHW062340300926
849161LV00007B/1772